EXPERIENCE THE PASSION
OF THE WOMEN OF WOR

POLITICAL WRITING
Sarojini Naidu's "The Arms Act"—delivered before the Indian National Congress Sofia Pavlovna Iur'eva's impassioned call-to-arms for Russian women

JOURNALISM
Marcelle Capy's "The Child of Rape" and Colette's "Fashions"

BATTLEFRONT REPORTS
Magdeleine ver Mehr's "The Trentino in Trench Time"
Mary Roberts Rinehart's "No Man's Land"

TESTIMONIALS AND DIARIES
Katherine Hodges North's "A Driver at the Front"

WAR WORK AND ESPIONAGE
Mata Hari's "Letter to Captain Bouchardon"

SHORT FICTION
Edith Wharton's "Writing a War Story"

POETRY
Works by Margit Kaffka, Amy Lowell, Beatrice Mayor, Marianne Moore, Edna St. Vincent Millay, and forty others

ILLUSTRATIONS
Propaganda posters, sculpture, and photographs

MARGARET R. HIGONNET received her doctorate from Yale University. She is currently a professor of English at the University of Connecticut and an affiliate of Harvard's Center for European Studies. She is the author of prizewinning literary criticism on topics ranging from the nineteenth century to children's literature and of several books, including *British Women Poets of the 19th Century* (Meridian).

LINES OF FIRE

WOMEN WRITERS OF WORLD WAR I

Edited by

Margaret R. Higonnet

A PLUME BOOK

PLUME
Published by the Penguin Group
Penguin Putnam Inc., 375 Hudson Street, New York, New York 10014, U.S.A.
Penguin Books Ltd, 27 Wrights Lane, London W8 5TZ, England
Penguin Books Australia Ltd, Ringwood, Victoria, Australia
Penguin Books Canada Ltd, 10 Alcorn Avenue, Toronto, Ontario, Canada M4V 3B2
Penguin Books (N.Z.) Ltd, 182–190 Wairau Road, Auckland 10, New Zealand

Penguin Books Ltd, Registered Offices:
Harmondsworth, Middlesex, England

First published by Plume, a member of Penguin Putnam Inc.

First Printing, November, 1999
10 9 8 7 6 5 4 3 2 1

Frontispiece: Käthe Kollwitz, "Never Again War." 1924, German. Lithograph. William Benton Museum of Art, University of Connecticut.

 REGISTERED TRADEMARK—MARCA REGISTRADA

LIBRARY OF CONGRESS CATALOGING-IN-PUBLICATION DATA:

Lines of fire : women writers of World War I / edited by Margaret R.
  Higonnet.
        p.   cm.
      Includes bibliographical references and index.
      ISBN 0-452-28146-6 (alk. paper)
      1. World War, 1914–1918—Women.   I. Higonnet, Margaret R.
D639.W7L48   1999
940.3'082—dc21   98-19253
                                                                 CIP

Printed in the United States of America
Set in New Baskerville and Packard
Designed by Eve L. Kirch

BOOKS ARE AVAILABLE AT QUANTITY DISCOUNTS WHEN USED TO PROMOTE PRODUCTS OR SERVICES. FOR INFORMATION PLEASE WRITE TO PREMIUM MARKETING DIVISION, PENGUIN PUTNAM INC., 375 HUDSON STREET, NEW YORK, NEW YORK 10014.

CONTENTS

ACKNOWLEDGMENTS

Because of the broad sweep of this project, I have drawn on the generous collaboration of a great many historians and literary critics, colleagues and students. The first seeds were planted at a conference held at the Center for European Studies, Harvard University; the encouragement of the Center's Study Group for Gender, Politics, and Society, especially the support of Jane Jenson and Sonya Michel, has sustained me. Over the years, the friendship and intellectual stimulus of several colleagues working on women and war—Jane Marcus, Claire Tylee, Susan Gubar, and Susan Schweik—have kept me on my toes.

Leads for potential texts to be included came from all corners of my life. Some of the historians who defined the field for me are Stéphane Audoin-Rouzeau, Annette Becker, Belinda Davis, John Horne, Arthur Marwick, Billie Melman, Giovanna Procacci, Bonnie Smith, Richard Stites, Françoise Thébaud, Jay M. Winter, and Judith Wishnia. Anna Bravo, Lionel Lemarchand, Melvin Page, and Shulamit Reinharz opened up their research files for me, passing on unpublished materials. Among critics and historians who shared their expertise and time were Sandi Cooper, Gisela Brinker-Gabler, Hadumod Bussmann, Angela Ingram, Maaike Meijer, Sylvia Notini, Sybil Oldfield, Angela Schmidt, Celia Valiente, Jo Vellacott, and Angela Woollacott.

I am especially indebted to those who enabled me to include materials from languages I do not read: Samar Attar, Miriam Cooke, Charlotte Franklin, Eva Jonas, Rasha al Khalidi, Diana Kuprel, Mihaila Rodica, Cynthia Simmons, Svetlana Slapšak, and Dayana Stetko. For help in locating visual materials, I must thank Richard Cork, Anne Higonnet, Paul-André Jaccard, and Jane Sharp, as well as the staff at the Imperial War Museum.

Libraries are the resource without which this kind of retrieval cannot take place. I started by drawing on the printed catalogue of the Hoover Institution on War, Revolution and Peace, and the card catalogue of Widener Library, at Harvard University. At the University of Connecticut, I have abused the patience of Robert Vrecenak in the interlibrary loan department. Other collections from whose riches I profited are the Imperial War Museum (London), the Bibliothèque Nationale (Paris), the Service Historique de l'Armée de Terre (Vincennes), the Bibliothèque Marguerite Durand (Paris), the library of the Invalides (Paris), Rutgers University, the Schomburg Library, the Sezione Storica of the Pavia Red Cross (Italy), the Staatsbibliothek (Munich), and the Y.W.C.A.

The Center for Historical Analysis at Rutgers University, under the direction of John W. Chambers, offered me the opportunity to participate in a dialogue on war and peace for a month; at the Bunting Institute I relished the exchanges at a cross-disciplinary community for a year. The Radcliffe Research Partnership Program gave me the great pleasure and benefit of working with Alexandra Coppet, Amanda Fortini, Alma Hadar, Alexandra Mandelbaum, Tripler Pell, Jennifer Sessions, Beth Tarini, and Laura Weinrib. Discussion with these partners, my students at the University of Connecticut, and with students at the University of Munich led me to new texts and new ways to think about them. Kristine Byron, Katharine Rodier, and Katharine Capshaw Smith have helped in all the stages of this project, not only with the mechanics but with the process of discovery, selection, and organization.

The names of translators are indicated at the end of each text. In addition to colleagues already cited, the translators Ellen Elias-Bursac, John Henriksen, Trudi Nicholas, Sylvia Notini, and Brita Stendahl gave many days and responded creatively to my queries. Where no name is given for translations of French and German texts, the responsibility is my own. I also want to thank the following for their help with translations: Robert Dombroski, Ralph Freedman, Arthur Goldhammer, Nikola Petkovič, Rochelle Ruthchild, Svetlana Slapšak, and Thomas Winnig.

Large and long, this project depended on support both from my home-grown editors, Patrice Higonnet and Guy Cardwell, and from my editors at Dutton NAL, Rosemary Ahern and Kari Paschall.

NOTE ON THE TEXT

Where I have used previously published translations, printer's errors (e.g. *sight* for *sigh*) and variable spellings have been silently corrected. In the case of the Nowosielska translation, grammatical errors have also been corrected.

A number of the headnotes were generously contributed by my students and colleagues. They are indicated by their initials:

RC	Rachel Carey	SO	Sybil Oldfield
MC	Miriam Cooke	TP	Tripler Pell
AF	Amanda Fortini	JS	Jennifer Sessions
AH	Alma Hadar	KCS	Katharine Capshaw Smith
EJ	Eva Jonas	CS	Christina Svendsen
RK	Rasha al Khalidi	LW	Laura Weinrib
AM	Alexandra Mandelbaum	CW	Celia Whitaker

INTRODUCTION

A book about the war may not, perhaps, be written by a man. A man who goes to war, unless he be a member of the high command, sees only one small corner of the army.

—Mary Lee, *"It's a Great War!"*

World War I began in the summer of 1914 at Sarajevo, with the assassination of Archduke Franz Ferdinand of Austria. A violent introduction to the twentieth century, it eventually involved thirty-eight nations, killed roughly ten million men, wounded twenty million (including six million mutilated), and cost $330 billion in direct and indirect costs. The number of civilian deaths is unknown: one historian cites estimates ranging from two to thirteen million dead. Among Armenians alone, perhaps one million died. The further twenty million victims of the influenza epidemic in 1918–19, the majority of them women and children, attest to the vulnerability of populations weakened by wartime shortages of food and fuel. The costs to women, however, direct and indirect, have never been comprehensively calculated.[1]

The war marked dramatic ruptures: it initiated the breakup of the British, French, German, and Ottoman empires; it disintegrated faith in cohesive social traditions; and it spectacularly altered the world as experienced by women. More than ever before, women were thrust into public arenas such as political activism, journalism, munitions work, and even

---

1. See Bonnie Smith, *Changing Lives: Women in European History Since 1700* (Lexington, MA: D.C. Heath, 1989), 395. Avner Offer estimates the female death rate in 1918 Germany was fifty percent above the pre-war level; excess civilian deaths over the pre-war rate may have reached three quarters of a million; see *The First World War: An Agrarian Interpretation* (Oxford: Clarendon, 1989), 34–37. In Italy, the excess deaths among civilians was roughly the same as the number of those killed at the front, around 600,000; see Luigi Tomassini, "The Home Front in Italy," in *Facing Armageddon: The First World War Experienced* (London: Leo Cooper, 1996), 585.

combat. They suffered catastrophic dislocations and losses. Just as colonies contributed to the war effort in the hope of winning independence, many women also contributed to the war effort in the expectation that they would gain the right to vote when the war was over. Millicent Fawcett made a patriotic appeal to English suffragists, "Let Us Show Ourselves Worthy of Citizenship."[2] The number of nations that eventually granted female suffrage when the war was over (Austria, Czechoslovakia, Germany, Great Britain, Lithuania, Turkey, and the United States, among others) confirmed these women's sense that their contributions had earned them fuller participation in the rights of citizenship. The postwar period did witness a backlash against changed roles and a demobilization of women from jobs to which men returned. Nonetheless, the upheaval of war irrevocably marked the minds and attitudes not only of men but of women also.

Histories of the war have generally focused on *combat* and on the experiences of men. The old idea that "the experience of the War" belongs to men and restores masculinity was summed up by Sam Hynes: "A nation at war *is* a male nation."[3] An emphasis on the firing line, which distinguishes the masculine battlefront from the feminine home front, has diverted attention from the history of women's experience of war. The wartime deaths and courage of men have been opposed to the ostensibly calm lives of women secure at home. Yet in France, by 1916, fifty women had received the Croix de Guerre. In Germany, by one calculation, women's rates of illness and death due to industrial disease and accidents doubled, reaching levels twenty-five percent higher than that of men; their deaths in childbirth, due to malnutrition, disease, and lack of medical care, rose over four years by more than sixty percent. Although several hundred British women working in the munitions industry died in accidents, the casualties were censored to maintain morale.[4] As the journalist Corra Harris wrote for *The Saturday Evening Post,* "What men suffer through war is written in histories . . . but what women suffer is never written."

The texts collected here challenge the normative restriction of the history and literature of war to accounts of the battlefield. The narrow focus of traditional history tends to obscure from view the endemic, even epidemic, effects of war in many countries: disrupted agriculture, forced

2. Fawcett, *The Common Cause,* August 14, 1914. Politicians like Herbert Asquith agreed finally that women had "worked out their own salvation" during the war.

3. Samuel Hynes, *A War Imagined: The First World War and English Culture* (London: Bodley Head, 1990), 88. Hynes argues, "War—any war—is for women an inevitably diminishing experience. There is nothing like a war for demonstrating to women their inferior status, nothing like the war experiences of men for making clear the exclusion of women from life's great excitements, nothing like war casualties for imposing on women the guiltiness of being alive and well" (379).

4. Charlotte Lorenz, *Die Gewerbliche Frauenarbeit während des Krieges* (Stuttgart: Deutsche Verlags-Anstalt, 1928), 385, 388; Angela Woollacott, *On Her Their Lives Depend: Munitions Workers in the Great War* (Berkeley: University of California Press, 1994), 10.

labor, food shortages, inflation up to 120 percent or 200 percent, disease, and the destruction of homes and monuments. The distinguishing feature of "total" war is its engulfment of entire populations and its undiscriminating distribution of death, suffering, and hunger across class lines, from urban women to tribal women. The heroic view of death and of self-sacrifice for the larger community masks the tawdry side of war—what Ellen LaMotte calls the "backwash."

"Combat" is not the sum total of "war." Displacements and blockades may differ from combat but their effects resemble a silent warfare against civilians. As the diary of Isabelle Rimbaud and the memoirs of Armenian women testify, women were particularly vulnerable to the effects of mobile warfare along frontiers and in occupied territories. The most heavily propagandized case was that of the Belgians in the first six weeks of the war; one sixth of the civilian population fled, a million of them into Holland. Far more severe in its impact was the Ottoman deportation of Armenians in the spring of 1915, undertaken with the encouragement of the German government to control an ethnic group seeking alliance with Russian Armenians. Then when Russia occupied part of Turkish Armenia in March 1917, Muslims were slaughtered in turn. On the Eastern Front, the movement of German, Austrian, and Russian troops led to a civilian exodus of between 3.2 and 10 million, substantial numbers of whom died; Jews, suspected of sympathizing with Germany, were deported from the frontline regions by the Czarist government. Deportations in the West also became political causes. Roughly one hundred thousand Belgians were sent to Germany for forced labor. Between sixteen and thirty thousand French women, boys, and older men were deported in cattle cars from the region around Lille in April 1916, a military action heatedly denounced by French feminists and by the French government. In each instance, the forcible disruption of normal community ties and the lawlessness of troops and brigands catalyzed violence against women, such as the rape of Jewish girls in Poland that Berta Lask describes in a poem in this volume.

Until recently, the focus on combat removed to the background any consideration of the broad social and economic mechanisms affected by war. Social historians have now turned their attention to the wartime situations of women of different classes, political alignments, and nationalities.[5] We have come to realize that if we do not examine women's roles in the mobilization for war, resistance to war, and demobilization and recovery, we will understand the processes involved in war itself incompletely. For example, when men who were active in the socialist and pacifist move-

5. See Ursula Gersdorff, *Frauen im Kriegsdienst, 1914–1945* (Stuttgart: Verlagsanstalt, 1969); Arthur Marwick, *Women at War 1914–1918* (London: Fontane, 1977); Gail Braybon, *Women Workers in the First World War* (Totowa, NJ: Barnes & Noble, 1981); Françoise Thébaud, *La Femme dans la première guerre mondiale* (Paris: Stock, 1986); Ute Daniel, *Arbeiterfrauen in der Kriegsgesellschaft: Beruf, Familie und Politik im I. Weltkrieg* (Göttingen: Vandenhoek und Ruprecht, 1989); Billie Melman, ed. *Borderlines: Genders and Identities in War and Peace, 1870–1930* (New York: Routledge, 1998).

ments were called up to serve in the military, women carried those movements forward. Similarly, because men working in war-related industries in France, Italy, and Germany could be sent to the front if they went on strike, it was women who, in 1917 and 1918, spearheaded labor unrest in response to escalating numbers of dead, scarcity of food, and the increasing gap between salaries and the cost of living.[6]

The argument about men's inclusion in war and women's exclusion tacitly relies on a model identifying the battlefront as a place where women and other civilians are not. That women have been omitted from histories of World War I is particularly ironic, since it was a "total" war, in which civilian populations from around the world were caught, one in which terror (*Schreckenskrieg*) was deliberately waged against civilian populations. Airplanes, zeppelins, long-range artillery like the German Big Bertha, submarines, and gunboats carried the "line of fire" into cities far from the front. The tidy division of the landscape into battlefront and home front may be a convenient one for purposes of military and political strategy. But as women's writing reveals, the assumption that female populations stood *outside* the line of fire is false.

Earlier historians' and critics' omission of women's war experiences corresponded to a belief that the record of the Great War was an exclusively masculine, veteran's preserve, and that women therefore did not write about the war. We continue to encounter the thesis that women's domestic condition, their lack of education, and their education in femininity prevented them from recording their experiences or reactions to public events, especially to "war," understood to be a male domain. Until very recently, few women's poems and stories were reprinted; their work was not mentioned in bibliographies devoted to the war; official archives gathered testimony almost exclusively from men. Puzzled by the apparent paucity of Frenchwomen's prose and poetry on the topic, Agnès Cardinal, for example, argues that "women did not take naturally to writing fiction about death on the battlefield."[7] With the exception of Käthe Kollwitz, virtually no women artists are included in histories of the visual representation of the war. The doctrine that men and women occupy

6. See Richard Evans, *The Feminist Movement in Germany, 1894–1933* (London: Sage, 1976); Marilyn Boxer and Jean Quataert, *Socialist Women: European Socialist Feminism* (1978); Gisela Brinker-Gabler, *Frauen gegen den Krieg* (Frankfurt am Main: Fischer Verlag, 1980); Anne Wiltsher, *Most Dangerous Women: Feminist Peace Campaigners of the Great War* (Boston: Pandora, 1985); Steven Hause and Anne Kenney, *Women's Suffrage and Social Politics* (1989); Aude and Charles Sowerwine, eds., *Le Mouvement français contre la guerre, 1914–1918: textes et documents* (Paris: EDHIS, 1985), 7 vols.; Richard Stites, *The Women's Liberation Movement in Russia: Feminism, Nihilism, and Bolshevism 1860–1930* (Princeton: Princeton University Press, 1978); Ute Daniel, *Arbeiterfrauen.*

7. Agnès Cardinal, "Women and the Language of War in France," *Women and World War I: The Written Response,* ed. Dorothy Goldman (New York: St. Martin's, 1993), 152–53. Goldman suggests that "war is not a sphere which women writers can inhabit imaginatively" in " 'Eagles of the West'? American Women Writers and World War I," *Women and World War I,* 195.

separate spheres has contaminated the history of women and war. In fact women did write about this world-historical experience, and they did so with poetic fire.[8]

Women's testimony about the Great War has been obscured for decades because of the critical focus on writing from "the trenches" (shorthand for military service). "Soldier" poets, including some who served in ambulance corps or other offices behind the lines, claimed to have captured the "authentic" voice of "real" violence and suffering. But the typical war poet was a civilian, and one fourth of those poets were women. Newspapers and publishers discovered a special aura and marketability in texts "from" the front lines, whether written during active service, on leave, or a decade after the Armistice. Valor and market value became intertwined.

By contrast, women's writing was understood to be "inauthentic" and unrealistic, since they stood—even if only symbolically—outside the line of fire. Women's writing was censored in all combatant countries. Letters to the front about strikes and shortages of food or coal were confiscated; pages of feminist newspapers such as *Zhenskii vestnik* appeared blank; Marcelle Capy's collection of journalism appeared with asterisks in the table of contents and with blank pages, replacing passages the government would not allow her to reprint.

Whether nationalist or antimilitarist, women's vision of the war was thought to be tainted by the fact they did not do military service. That women volunteered as soldiers on the Eastern Front has been forgotten. That Rupert Brooke, usually thought to be a "war poet," died of disease before he ever saw combat was also forgotten. That women and children were used as human shields in Belgium and eastern France was forgotten or denied as mere propaganda. Inadequate concepts of "real" wartime experience and of its relationship to "realistic" or powerful writing have kept us from publishing or reading women's texts.

In order to revise common misconceptions, this volume makes available a wide range of women's writings about World War I. It expands in three ways the horizon of what we can know about writings by women and thus about women's varied experiences. Its international roster includes figures from around the world like Aletta Jacobs, Anna Akhmatova, and Nellie McClung, as well as familiar ones from England and America like Emmeline Pankhurst, Rebecca West, and Edith Wharton. It juxtaposes canonized writers with relatively unfamiliar ones: Amy Lowell with Margit Kaffka, or Marianne Moore with Edith Södergran. And it is interdisciplinary: it juxtaposes fiction and poetry with political tracts, journalism, and

8. See Catherine Reilly, ed., *Scars Upon My Heart* (London: Virago, 1982); Claire M. Tylee, *The Great War and Women's Consciousness* (London: Macmillan, 1989); Gisela Brinker-Gabler, ed., *Frauen gegen den Krieg;* Sandra Gilbert, "Soldier's Heart: Literary Men, Literary Women, and the Great War," *Signs* 8 (1983): 422–50; Jane Marcus, "Corpus/Corps/Corpse: Writing the Body in/at War," afterword to Helen Zenna Smith, *Not So Quiet . . . Stepdaughters of War* (New York: Feminist Press, 1989).

various forms of autobiography. By bringing together women from many different countries, from different economic situations, and from different political alignments, it makes it possible for us to recognize the myriad local conditions and psychological differences that are recorded in these writings. Just as there was not one "War," there was not one "Woman" who was the agent or victim of war.

Little attention has been paid to women's writings about the war in languages other than English. Here, the situation differs sharply from the history of texts by men. The historical documentation of the war has drawn freely on published and unpublished memoirs and on the creative writing of men as soldiers and political leaders from many countries. The study of women's works has by contrast been impoverished.

To remind us of the worldwide impact of this war, the volume includes texts from Europe, Eastern Europe, the Middle East, Africa, and India. Thus aspects of the African experience are voiced by a colonist (Isak Dinesen), a German nurse in Cameroon, a translator for the British War Office, and women porters from Malawi. Although not every country involved in the war appears here, this diversity points toward the kinds of national and cultural contexts within which women recorded their experiences. It provides evidence for women's political responses to the war, including patriotic enthusiasts as well as pacifists and internationalists from Isolde Kurz and Matilde Serao to Jane Addams and Anna Kuliscioff. The reader will find responses to the war by renowned authors (Dinesen, Ricarda Huch, Marina Tsvetaeva) next to oral interviews with Italian and French peasants.

By drawing on many different kinds of writing to reveal women's attitudes, this volume points to women's variable forms of national involvement. Patriotic support of the war effort has one tone in an occupied country like France or Poland, another in England, and yet a third in a colony like India or in an empire with ethnic groups seeking independence, such as the Ottoman Empire. Antiwar and other political activities led to the arrest of Clara Zetkin, Rosa Luxemburg, and Hélène Brion in Germany and France.

Only one woman in 1914–18 had the power to vote for or against the war: the American representative from Montana, Jeannette Rankin. As citizens without suffrage, women as a rule wrote obliquely about this political moment. For example, the inclusion here of a disturbingly ambiguous poem by the African-American writer Alice Dunbar-Nelson and of an ironically framed story by the feminist nationalist Indian writer Svarnakumari Devi invites readers to consider the ways that a minority identity complicates notions of gender, patriotism, and nation. These texts provoke fresh questions about the way the oppression of disenfranchised peoples may serve military purposes by raising expectations of political rewards in return for military or other wartime service. The irony of ex-slaves and colonials fighting under strange skies for their masters was not lost on women like Addie Hunton. They would be divided even in their mourning. After the war, African-American mothers were excluded from

organized trips to visit European war cemeteries. A salient
writings is the suggestion that the European war and col
are interlocking systems and that these systems mesh with
of gender and race.

A growing number of studies argue that women's motives for
wartime choices were extremely varied. They wanted to "break away" and
they relished the sense "that you really belonged." Some were impelled by
patriotism to volunteer as soldiers, relief workers, or auxiliary workers,
others by financial need, some by a spirit of adventure, and still others by
a sense of their moral responsibilities. Mairi Chisholm, who became celebrated for frontline work rescuing the wounded, recalled finding a sense
of purpose and happiness during the war: "The cause was greater than
ourselves."[9] These motives cut across class lines, although the lack of pay
and cost of uniforms and training excluded working-class women from
most of the volunteer corps in Britain.

The difficulty of access to a broad range of texts has channeled much
literary scholarship on the Great War toward women of the social elites in
Britain and the United States. Critics who concentrate on "high" modernist literature omit much that merits our attention. One way to break
out of the confines of writing by and for the elites is to juxtapose materials that are usually considered by different disciplines: political polemic,
journalism, life-writing (such as letters, diaries and memoirs), fiction,
poetry, and visual works. Esthetic theory in the past has routinely segregated historical records from imaginative representations and adhered to
a hierarchy of literary genres. By constrast, a broadened conception of tex-
tuality enables a fresh understanding of women's writing about the war.
Polemic is an art form, just as poetry is. Autobiographical fiction may not
differ in most of its strategies from direct autobiography; diaries and letters may be no more factually reliable than a realistic work of imagination.
As Gerald Brenan wrote, "You can't get at the truth through history; you
can only get it through novels."[10]

Nonetheless it is important to weigh the truth claims made by different vehicles of expression and to recognize the multiplicity of motives
that may generate a text. Political writing may be indifferent to the kind
of neutral observation we expect from journalism. Yet journalism of this
period is marked by a personal voice and a reliance on anecdote or the
resonant interview that may seem strange to modern readers; it is politicized by the very fact that it is censored. The kinds of writing grouped
here as "testimonial"—diaries, letters, memoirs, and interviews—generally differentiate themselves from political writing and journalism, in

9. See Krisztina Robert, "Gender, Class, and Patriotism: Women's Paramilitary Units in
First World War Britain," *International History Review* 19 (1997), 52–65. Mairi Chisholm
quoted in Malcolm Brown, *The Imperial War Museum Book of the First World War* (London:
Sidgwick & Jackson, 1991), 190.

10. Cited in Hugh Cecil, "British War Novelists," in *Facing Armageddon: The First World
War Experienced*, 805.

.art by the recurrence of a personal voice, in part by a more spontaneous structure. Yet newspaperwomen such as Mary Roberts Rinehart
and Colette gathered their articles and notes in books that took on the
air of memoirs, while some memoirists such as Flora Sandes, who
nursed and fought in Serbia, published their narratives as news from
the front while the war was still ongoing in order to raise money for
relief work.

Although the sections of this book do not coincide with easy distinctions between fact and fiction, readers will recognize continuities of genre.
The visual materials help reinforce distinctions among these forms of
expression. Political posters encouraging war work and didactic images
aimed at children enhance the section on polemic and call attention to
the economic impact of war on the home front. The journalists' reports
on wartime changes, especially in women's occupations, find documentation in photographs by women, including an X ray by Marie Curie. Memoirs lead to pictures by artists who were commissioned at the end of the
war by the Imperial War Museum to aid in recording women's work for the
Red Cross, in munitions, in an ambulance corps, or in the British W.R.N.S.
telephone service. Powerful Futurist images by artists such as Olga
Rozanova and Maria Siniakova—as bold an indictment of war as Picasso's
Guernica—frame eloquent fiction and poetry. These images offer visual
corollaries to the range of texts: they emphasize patriotic resolve, camaraderie, labor under hardship, loss, and devastation.

The volume starts from the political in order to outline women's participation in the public debates over the multilateral declarations of war,
mobilization through conscription, and the means to bring the war to an
end. Readers can follow here a dialogue among maternalist pacifists, such
as Emmeline Pankhurst, Nellie McClung, and Jane Addams; they can
observe the sharing of ideas among socialist internationalists, such as
Clara Zetkin, Marcelle Capy, and Alexandra Kollontai. Pacifism was a
cause that women had embraced in the years before the war. Although the
woman who inspired the Nobel Peace Prize, Bertha von Suttner, died in
1914, the great novelist Selma Lagerlöf sent a strong message to suffragists
around the world: "As long as my tongue can frame a word, as long as
blood flows in my veins, so long will I work for the cause of peace, even
though it may cost my life and happiness."[11] In order to provide the background against which other women formulated their views, the opening
section gathers explicitly political materials.

The political spectrum of wartime polemic and analysis ranges from
propaganda to pacifism. Many texts are internationalist in tone, perhaps
because women were not included in definitions of national identity.
Internationalism was one way to respond to wartime discourse that polar-
ized masculinity and femininity, and that exploited traditional images of

11. *Jus Suffragi*, April 1, 1915, 9.

womanly nurture for militarist purposes.[12] The symbolic identification of women with the hearth, itself symbolic of a peaceful arena preserved within the maelstrom of war, led many women to reflect on the relationship between peace and war, and to recognize the dependence of wartime rhetoric on images of "woman" and of domesticity.

Political statements can be addressed to a mass audience, to a courtroom, or to one's neighbors. In order to suggest the many variants of patriotic feeling, the political strategizing of the famous suffragist Emmeline Pankhurst is set next to the simple battlefront oath of the Romanian soldier Ecaterina Theodoroiu. Although each supports the war effort, the class origins and social conditions that separate these women are apparent in their words. Readers can examine the kinds of eloquence that made them spokeswomen for their people, as they continue to speak to us across the decades.

In the second section, journalistic writings demonstrate the urgency with which women tried to expose particular wartime experiences rooted in the female body. Henriette Celarié reports on the German use of women from the region of Lille for forced labor and prostitution, while Claire Studer Goll denounces the deportation and massacre of Armenian civilians. Journalists explore the complicated politics of citizenship for the children of rape or of cohabitation with the enemy, problems that affected social reconstruction in the postwar period. They address problems of provisioning, relatively low wages for women, and questions of national identity. Although commissioned to report with "heartkick" on "women's topics," they also covered the diversity of new occupations that women had entered in order to replace men who were called away for military service.

The journalism suggests many women's desire to claim the status and authority of an eyewitness. As a Russian woman wrote to the newspaper *Zhenskii vestnik*, "We women don't want to be mere idle spectators of great events." When the Imperial War Museum commissioned works of art, it made "authenticity" the primary criterion, an authenticity guaranteed by supplying men (not women) with cars and guides to the front so that they could "behold" events. Such institutionalized arrangements reinforced a gendered line between those who would have the authority to record the war and those who would not. A number of these selections contest the assumption that women didn't see combat and therefore did not know war. Some, like the photographs by Mairi Chisholm or Florence Farmborough and the journalism by Mary Roberts Rinehart, insist on their presence in the trenches.

Other selections complicate the issue of vision by depicting a woman's gaze—whether it is the investigative gaze of the reporter, the diagnostic

12. See Jo Vellacott, "A Place for Pacifism and Transnationalism in Feminist Theory: The Early Work of the Women's International League for Peace and Freedom," *Women's History Review* 2.1 (1993) 32; see also Janet Mackay and Pat Thane, "The Englishwoman," in Robert Colls and Philip Dodd, eds., *Englishness: Politics and Culture, 1880–1920* (London: Croom Helm, 1986), 220–21.

gaze of the nurse, or the gaze blinded by tears. A handbook for nurses suggested that the woman's view of men's bodies must be controlled and dissembled. The eye of a spy such as Mata Hari or Marthe Richer had even more need to dissemble. Furthermore, Colette's advice to wives reminds them that they must cultivate their feminine image to satisfy men's imaginative gaze in times of war. This insistence on women's observing eye and on their self-observation testifies to the problem of women's assuming authority to represent an event and an experience supposed to have been for men's eyes only.

The personal "life-writing" section richly documents the range of women's experiences. A number of the topics to which women devoted their attention resist the segregation of women's experiences from those of men. Most striking is the eyewitness testimony of female soldiers. Writings about the front include memoirs by the combatants Maria Botchkareva, Sophja Nowosielska, Marina Yurlova, and Flora Sandes, who engaged in battle directly. The record of women in the military demystifies the common notion that women are naturally pacifist; these testimonies about fighting women's motives contribute to our understanding of the wartime mobilization of societies.

A more familiar topic, and one that is very fully documented, is nursing and medical care, which permitted women to draw on their identity as "sisters" or symbolic mothers in strenuous public activity, sometimes so close to the front that they were subject to bombardment. After a heavy military engagement, work for a "flying ambulance" (a mobile field hospital) or on a hospital train could mean twenty-four- hour days for a doctor, nurse, or driver. Whether professionals or volunteers, medical staff from Germany, France, Switzerland, Russia, England, Italy, and the United States tell us about their commitment, exhaustion, and occasional despair. They perceive their struggle against death as a "combat" parallel to the one waged by men. The intense stress of handling mutilated bodies in dehumanizing numbers and of having no relief to offer in response to piercing screams leads some to record their own psychic wounding. We can now recognize the momentary breakdown that women like Katherine Hodges North describe as a form of post-traumatic stress comparable to the "shell shock" to which soldiers fell victim. The sense of triumph at reducing the casualty rate from a predicted seventy percent to forty percent had to be balanced against their dismay at curing men only to return them to the killing fields.

Again and again, we hear of the home front experiences of material hardship and bereavement, showing that loss is a pervasive concomitant of war. In a world where all food has been confiscated to feed troops, survival becomes a form of political resistance.[13] Testimony about war work comes

13. In 1917 and 1918, in Germany the harvest of grain and potatoes fell to between 50 percent and 60 percent of the 1913 harvest. By the spring of 1917, the German army took 70 percent of disposable foodstuffs. Women's bread strikes multiplied. In Russia, women's strikes in St. Petersburg catalyzed the February Revolution. See Alyson Jackson, "Germany, the Home Front (2): Blockade, Government, and Revolution," in *Facing Armageddon*, 571.

from munitionettes, peasants, and women doing forced labor. Wartime changes in the labor market are recorded in memories about the transport of cattle and of prostitutes. Some women set up an underground network to help soldiers escape from occupied territory. Countess Nora Kinsky inspected prisons, while others, such as Louise Thuliez, Mata Hari, Ola Piłsudska, and Manya Shohat, were held in them. The variety of women's wartime activities recorded in texts drawn from the margins of history tests the imperialist and paternalist simplifications of a unified (masculine) model of war experience.

Autobiographical writings about the war offer considerable evidence for a change in women's consciousness. A British chief factory inspector reported in 1916 on "the new self-confidence engendered in women." [14] By translating secret German documents, Muriel Dayrell-Browning felt she was altering history. Certainly, as founder of the Women's Battalion of Death, Maria Botchkareva hoped that she might tip the balance of war, just as Jane Addams and Aletta Jacobs hoped to tip the balance of peace. A rise in illegitimacy rates, a change in vocabulary, a stoic pride in rapid assembly-line achievements are some of the manifestations of this shift in women's self-understanding. It may be that physical labor and meaningful work were of greater psychological importance for women from sheltered, elite backgrounds than for working-class women. One aristocrat who served as a nurse remembered, "Little by little I spread my wings and tested my strength; the walls which for so long had fenced me off from reality were now finally pierced." [15]

The national importance of women's labor became evident, even if it was forgotten after 1918. Certain industries and types of work were dominated by women: munitions, transport, communications, and clerical work. In 1916, the Earl of Derby declared that "women are now part and parcel of our great army. Without them it would be impossible for progress to be made, but with them I believe victory can be assured." [16] By 1917, in most of the countries at war female employment had risen by twenty percent or more. Working-class women gained confidence not only as workers but as strikers. In epigrammatic French style, Maréchal Joffre proclaimed, "If the women working in factories stopped for twenty minutes, the Allies would lose the war." [17] In the first months of the war, however, women actually lost jobs, as industries were disrupted by the departure of men to the front. Governments did not seriously attempt to attract women to wartime employment until 1916. And as the end of the war approached, one motive for collecting records about women's work was the expectation that it would cease. As one of the women working to create the collection at the Imperial War Museum wrote, "Now that the

14. Cited in Brown, *Imperial War Museum Book*, 209.
15. Grand Duchess Mariya Pavlovna, *Education of a Princess*, 229.
16. Quoted by Helen Fraser, in *Women and War Work* (New York: Shaw, 1918), 124.
17. Thébaud, *La Femme*, 182.

hostilities have stopped the tram conductress and bus conductress, window cleaner etc. will I imagine shortly cease to exist?"[18]

The evidence of women's transformation by their assumption of new tasks must not be misjudged. Neither gender nor sexual orientation can be equated with job choices. Since this was a war that produced the Russian Women's Battalion of Death, led by the mannish-looking Maria Botchkareva, some historians have assumed that the opening up of active opportunities to serve in auxiliary forces (or even in the military) was particularly welcome to lesbians, who could now enter occupations traditionally defined as masculine. It is true that Radclyffe Hall in *The Well of Loneliness* and in "Miss Ogilvie Finds Herself" explored the wartime liberation of lesbians. Ellen LaMotte's sexual choices may have contributed to her satiric distance from the contradictory wartime definitions of femininity and women's roles. But Botchkareva, Captain Flora Sandes (who served in the Serbian army), and Marina Yurlova (a Cossack fighter) all left memoirs that make clear the compatibility of combat with female heterosexuality. The instability of women's own self-image is suggested here by Lidiia Zakharova, who when she bought practical boots and a leather soldier's coat wrote in her diary, "With God's help my transformation succeeded—there remained in me less and less of the feminine, and I didn't know whether to be sorry or glad." No simplistic gender theories are to be derived from this material. The most obvious conclusion is that the confusion of war allowed for unusual and taboo behaviors at the same time that official propaganda reinforced conventional ideology about feminine proprieties.

From their many different locations, the perspectives of these women lay out a complicated map of the war. The reader will find exposés of forced labor and prostitution organized by the military; opposition to this particular war; calls for worker solidarity by internationalist socialists; economic critiques of wartime profiteering; and opposition to government repression of minorities. We also find resistance to the transformations women appeared to undergo. Women in uniform were mocked, as we learn from Colette; Botchkareva's soldiers were called "babas in breeches."

If the war marked ruptures in women's roles, it also marked ruptures in the ways they wrote. Of course, some writers continued to mold their new materials in traditional forms, such as the verse prayer or the letter. By this very contrast between a familiar form and unfamiliar events, they achieved the shock of innovation. Thus Bowen shows in her "Demon Lover" how the ghosts of the war haunted women decades after the Armistice.

Some experimented with modern and modernist techniques. Florence Farmborough recast her nursing experience in the emerging genre of photographic narrative. Others turned to abbreviated or fragmentary forms to record their immediate reactions to the war, as if it were impos-

18. Meirion and Susie Harries, *The War Artists: British Official War Art of the 20th Century* (London: Michael George, 1983).

sible to dilate on the horror of the encounter. Mary Borden, a friend of Gertrude Stein, justified her publication in 1917 of "fragments of a great confusion" on the grounds that "any attempt to reduce them to order would require artifice on my part and would falsify them."[19] Radclyffe Hall's story can be read as an essay in lesbian surrealism, while Amy Lowell uses imagist compression to capture through brevity the fragility of peace. European writers like Claire Goll, Berta Lask, and Hortensia Papadat-Bengescu experimented with a "telegraphic" style. Marina Tsvetaeva critiques the wartime frenzy of "censings by iron cases and the rattle of spurs"; cubist ruptures in postwar poems by Gertrud Kolmar and Danica Markovič break apart the nostalgic rhetoric used to frame and sanction war. While the Futurist manifesto with its warmongering language predated the war, many artists felt that the chaotic ferocity of the war had energized and tested their art, filtering the tragic from the insignificant. Olga Rozanova, for example, felt her prints were "not only technically stronger than anything I have done before, but also have more content and are more original."[20]

One of the surprises in these texts lies in the way many writers incorporate subversively the ideological line that divides the battlefront from the home front. A number of these writers were acutely conscious that as women they were instruments of cultural self-representation: as mothers, they became identified with the *mater dolorosa* and the motherland, as nurses they were "sisters," and as wives and lovers they could help secure the masculine strength of men. Aware of their multiple allegorical functions, they played with and against these identifications, as in their writings about the "rape" of Belgium.

In some texts, narrators use their assignment to the protected domain of the hearth in order to test the domestication and banalization of war in daily lives. They wittily apply metaphors drawn from the "feminine" realm to the "masculine" realm of war. Changed structures of work and communal life lend new meaning to the language of motherhood when children are born of rape. Fresh ironies sift through the discourse of domesticity and pastoral when men are reshaped like loaves of bread and gardens are dug up to bury the dead. The image of a child's highchair toppled over in a trench forces us to reconsider the location of the home front. Women in munitions "look as if they were practicing a neat domestic craft rather than a deadly domestic process," according to Rebecca West, while they live in "barracks" organized by the Y.W.C.A.; another reporter finds women do metallurgy like knitting.[21]

Yet women can also lose their identity: to Mme. Dorliat one worker proclaims, "We are not women but the arms of the machine." War, according

19. Mary Borden, *The Forbidden Zone* (New York: Doubleday, Doran, 1930), unpaginated preface.

20. Quoted in Richard Cork, *A Bitter Truth: Avant-Garde Art and the Great War* (New Haven: Yale University Press, 1994), 123.

21. Gaston Rageot, *La Française dans la guerre* (Paris: Attinger, s.d.), 5.

to Colette, "becomes a habit . . . as natural as thunder and rainstorms." The domestic arena, once polluted by war, no longer can serve as the anchor of a specific kind of feminine writing. Disqualified from speaking unpatriotically against the war because she stands "out of the line of fire," a writer may have to step "out of line" to speak.[22]

Paul Fussell once claimed that women did not write "good" war poetry: they were not "the custodians of the subtlest sorts of antiwar irony."[23] Perhaps because they drew on a narrow selection of British women poets, earlier feminist critics have sometimes also condemned the language of women's writings as cliché; thus one feminist anthologist argues: "It was not simply their lack of firsthand military experience that inhibited women's poetry, but the inheritance of worn-out and inappropriate modes and language without the catalyst which the experience of the War provided in forcing more shocking and brutal forms of expression."[24] This anthology demonstrates that women, especially nurses, recorded "brutal," transgressive images depicting injuries to the male body and found shocking ways to express their pain.

Their power may explain why a number were subjected to censorship during the war—yet another factor that has led in countries like France and Germany to the disappearance of women's texts from view. Corra Harris was dismissed from her job as a reporter. Advertising of LaMotte's book was blocked, and Henriette Sauret's poetry was collected in a censored volume. An example of Marcelle Capy's censored journalism appears here for the first time since her book was printed with dozens of blank pages.

An important strategy in many of the texts included here is the effort to grasp war systemically so as to incorporate women into the picture and to locate their suffering. Often indirectly, they trace relationships between the politicized masculine domain of death in the front lines and an obscured domain "behind" the lines, where women were supposed to remain, concealed and silent. That opposition, as a number of the writers represented here point out, carried not only a painful emotional burden but a scandalous political burden as well—that of war as "politics by other means." Many of these texts, both patriotic and pacifist, mine the boundaries between war and peace, public and private, nation and people, men and women.

As Gertrude Stein saw from the vantage point of World War II, "There was in a way war all the time."[25] In part because of women's symbolic roles

---

22. See Margaret Higonnet, "Not So Quiet in No-Woman's-Land," in *Gendering War Talk*, ed. Miriam Cooke and Angela Woollacott (Princeton: Princeton University Press, 1993), 205–26.

23. Paul Fussell, *Thank God for the Atom Bomb and Other Essays* (New York: Ballantine, 1988), 111. Similarly, in an early book Jean Bethke Elshtain claimed, "When women have imagined war itself . . . it has frequently been in abstract, stereotypical tropes that bear little relation to war's realities." *Women and War* (New York: Basic Books, 1987), 214.

24. Goldman, ed., *Women and World War I*, 7.

25. Gertrude Stein, *Wars I Have Seen* (New York: Random House, 1945), 7.

as the mourners for the men lost and as nurses for the injured and ill, women were charged with the tasks of remembering and recovery. For them, the war did not end with the Armistice, as the calendar of events included in this volume might suggest. Just as some of the greatest literature by men appeared a decade or more after 1918, so, too, women continued to reflect on the legacies left by this event. They continued to sing the laments for the young men who died.

The record of women's experiences during the Great War was set down by those who were children, teenagers, mothers, and widows. They were farmers, porters, industrial workers, ambulance drivers, nurses, and soldiers. They were rich and dirt poor. Some were victims, and some changed the course of the war. Some were literate, and some found a voice only decades later when they were interviewed. As varied as their voices are, each of these women had something strongly felt to say about the war and her experience of it. Each finds her own form of expression: it may be a strategy of indirection, the use of imagery that domesticates the war, or irony that demystifies the cult of war and the allegorization of the feminine. In order to represent their own dislocations by the machinery of war, both physical and aesthetic, women had to sidestep the familiar lines about battle.

CALENDAR

1901	Canadian Army Nursing Service founded
	National Council of French Women unites 30 reformist and philanthropic societies
1902	German feminists found Union for Women's Suffrage
	Queen Alexandra's Imperial Military Nursing Service (Q.A.I.M.N.S.) is established in Britain
	Australian white women gain federal franchise
1903	Emmeline Pankhurst establishes Women's Social and Political Union
1904	International Woman Suffrage Alliance holds first congress in Berlin
	St. John Ambulance Association founded in Ireland
	German Society for the Protection of Motherhood and Sexual Reform
1905	All-Russian Union for Women's Equality and Russian Women's Progressive Party formed
	Russian "Bloody Sunday," February 4; several hundred women join workers' revolt
1906	Women in Finland gain suffrage
	Nightshift work for women forbidden internationally
1907	The Hague conventions decree separation of armies from civilian populations and ban poisons that cause "superfluous" deaths
	Jane Addams hosts the Women's National Peace Conference in Boston
	Clara Zetkin convokes First International Conference of Socialist Women
	Mabel St. Clair Stobart creates British Women's Convoy Corps; W.C.C. medical unit staffed by women serves in front lines during Balkan war in 1912–13
	Women in Sweden gain suffrage
1908	Russian Women's Congress in St. Petersburg; 1,000 attend
	Imperial law of association permits German women to join political parties
1909	Voluntary Aid Detachment (V.A.D.) founded in England
	British First Aid Nursing Yeomanry Corps (F.A.N.Y.) founded
	French Union for Women's Suffrage founded

1910	Women in New Zealand gain suffrage
1911	Libyan war triggers peace demonstrations by Italian women
1913	Norwegian women who meet economic qualification gain suffrage
	Austrian War Service Act enables general conscription of civilian population
1914	
January 18	French National League for Women's Vote founded
April 5	Irishwomen's Council founded, holds Irish independence a prerequisite to women's suffrage
June 21	Death of Bertha von Suttner, 1905 winner of Nobel Peace Prize
June 28	Archduke Franz Ferdinand and his wife assassinated at Sarajevo by Serb nationalist Gavrilo Princip
July 5	Condorcet demonstration in Paris of women for suffrage draws 5,000 marchers
July 28	Austria-Hungary declares war on Serbia
July 29	Austrian bombardment of Belgrade begins
July 31	Assassination of Jean Jaurès, antiwar leader of French socialists
	Germany declares state of siege, imposes censorship
August 1	Germany declares war on Russia
	Union of German Women's Associations under Gertrud Bäumer announces a National Women's Service, to do social welfare work
August 2	France suspends decrees limiting overtime work in defense industries
	German troops cross Luxembourg
August 3	Germany declares war on France: German troops invade Belgium
	Frida Perlen and Mathilde Planck of German Women's Suffrage Union send telegram to Kaiser Wilhelm II asking him to avoid war
	Ottoman Empire signs secret treaty with Germany
	Italy declares neutrality
August 4	Great Britain declares war on Germany
	Millicent Fawcett addresses 2,000 women at Women's Peace Meeting in London
	Germany declares emergency, suspends protective labor legislation, sets some maximum prices, and revises separation allowances for wives of soldiers
August 5	Clara Zetkin in *Die Gleichheit* calls on proletarian women to oppose war
	British Women's Emergency Corps created to help unemployed women

August 6   Austria-Hungary declares war on Russia
                    Serbia declares war on Germany
                    U.S. government asks British to clarify position on
                    "contraband" to be blocked from shipment to the
                    Central Powers (Germany, Austria-Hungary)

August 7   French government calls on women to bring in har-
                    vest
                    British Expeditionary Force lands at Le Havre,
                    France

August 8   British Defense of the Realm Act (DORA) estab-
                    lishes censorship, revised August 28 and frequently
                    thereafter
                    Russian *Duma* (legislative council) declares "sacred
                    union" and votes credits to pay for the war, dividing the
                    socialists

August 10   France and Britain declare war on Austria-Hungary
                    Amnesty for imprisoned English suffragists and
                    members of Women's Social and Political Union
                    Queen Mary's Needlework Guild founded for unem-
                    ployed women
                    Austria imposes censorship of press and postal ser-
                    vice

August 11   Austrian invasion of Serbia

August 12   Establishment of All-Russian Union of *Zemstvos*
                    (provincial councils) for the Relief of Sick and
                    Wounded
                    First nursing unit organized in Britain departs for
                    Serbia; Flora Sandes is a volunteer
                    Dr. Elsie Inglis begins fundraising for Scottish
                    Women's Hospitals, which will serve in France and
                    Serbia; she herself will arrive in Serbia in May
                    1915

August 14   French troops enter Lorraine, but are pushed back
                    by Germans within a week

August 20   Royal Commission on Women's Employment and
                    Queen's Work for Women Fund established in Britain
                    Six units of Queen Alexandra's Imperial Military
                    Nursing Service sent to France and Belgium
                    British and French expand list of contraband to be
                    seized on seas

August 23   Battle of Mons (Belgium) between German and
                    British armies
                    German troops cross Franco-Belgian border
                    Japan declares war on Germany and two days later
                    on Austria

August 26   German Togoland capitulates to Anglo-French force

August 26–31   German defeat of Russian army at Battle of Tannen-
                    berg; Russian General Samsonov commits suicide
August 30   German planes bomb Paris
August   Germany establishes War Raw Materials Depart-
                    ment, largest industrial combine in Europe
September 3   *La Fronde,* a French feminist newspaper, disappears
                    under censorship
September 5–12   Battle of the Marne marks end of German troops'
                    rapid advance and beginning of trench warfare
September 7   British capture of Douala, Cameroon; Germans do
                    not quit Cameroon until February 9, 1916
September 9–15   Germans defeat Russians at Masurian Lakes
September 9   American Red Cross hospital unit sails for Serbia
September 14   American Red Cross mercy ship (SS *Red Cross*) sails
                    for Europe with hospital units
September 22   First of three British air raids on German airports at
                    Düsseldorf, Cologne, and Friedrichshafen
September 28   German Government food decree regulates bread
                    consistency and forbids use of "bread-grain" for fodder
September   Women's Hospital Corps formed by Dr. Flora Mur-
                    ray, refused by British government but accepted by
                    French government for work in Paris
                    British Women's Defence Relief Corps established
                    Russian decree that women have a right to serve in
                    any Civil Service capacity with the same pay as men
                    Food shortages in Belgium, unemployment
early October   First British nursing unit in Kragujevac, Serbia
October 20   Germany begins submarine campaign against allied
                    commercial fleets
                    Britain prohibits sale of drink to women before
                    11:30 A.M.
October 21   First V.A.D. unit lands at Boulogne, France
October 28   German Bundesrat mandates production of "K-
                    bread" (fixing percentage of rye and potato flour sub-
                    stitute), sets maximum prices for selected foodstuffs
October 29   Belgians open sluices on Yser to slow German
                    advance
                    Turkish fleet bombards Odessa with German support
                    National Union of Women Workers Police Patrols
                    recognized by British Home Office
October 30   International Women's Peace Movement holds mass
                    meeting at Carnegie Hall, New York, addressed by
                    British pacifist Emmeline Pethick-Lawrence
November 1   Pope Benedict XV issues encyclical "Ad Beatissimi"
                    condemning war
                    Russia declares war on Ottoman Empire
                    Australian convoy carries first nursing unit to Egypt

November 4   Nurse Margaret Macdonald of Canadian Army Med-
                     ical Corps is first woman in British Empire to receive
                     rank of major; first Canadian nurses arrive in France
                     during November
November 5   Western Allies declare war on Ottoman Empire
mid-November   Arrival of Lady Muriel Paget's First Serbian Relief
                     Fund Unit near Skopje in southern Serbia
                     German Bundesrat sets ceiling on wholesale price of
                     potatoes
December 5   32 Scottish women form hospital in Paris
December 16   German naval bombardment of Scarborough, New-
                     castle, and West Hartlepool, England
December 17   British declare Egypt a protectorate
December 21   German air raid on Dover, England

1915
January   Scottish Women's Hospital unit goes to Serbia
                     Australian Women's Peace Party formed
                     Russian feminists present Moscow city *duma* with
                     list of women's accomplishments and demand suf-
                     frage
                     300,000 Serbian civilians die in typhus epidemic
                     over four months
January 7   French newspapers open debate over status of
                     unborn children whose mothers had been raped by
                     German soldiers in occupied territories
January 10   American Women's Peace Congress in Washington,
                     D.C., attended by 3,000 women, founds Woman's
                     Peace Party, presided over by Jane Addams, with the
                     Hungarian Rosika Schwimmer as secretary
January 12   Woman's Suffrage Amendment defeated in U.S.
                     House of Representatives
January 19   First German zeppelin raid on Britain (60 airship
                     raids in 1915–16)
January 25   German Imperial Grain Authority assumes right to
                     confiscate bread grains and issues bread ration
                     coupons
February 1   First all-woman military hospital in Britain founded
                     (Endell Street, London)
February 2   British block neutral shipments of grain and flour to
                     Germany as contraband; in March British ban all
                     goods destined for the enemy
February 4   Germans announce blockade of England within two
                     weeks; German submarine warfare against merchant
                     vessels begins
February 18   Rosa Luxemburg imprisoned one year for encour-
                     aging German soldiers to refuse to bear arms against

	French brothers; reimprisoned July 10, 1916, to November 8, 1918
February 19	Allied bombardment of Dardanelles
February 21	Italian socialists demonstrate for neutrality
February 25	Protest in Trafalgar Square, London, over 25 percent rise in cost of living, following loss of 160,000 women's jobs in industry
mid-February	First German food riots over shortage of potatoes
March	Lloyd George agrees with British unions to "dilute" labor force with women
	French Chamber of Deputies votes to "use the female labor force to replace the military labor force wherever possible."
March 5	Shells and Fuses Agreement permitting employment of women in munitions factories accepted by key British trade unions
March 17	Women's War Service Register opened in Britain
March 18	500 German women demonstrate for peace before Berlin Reichstag (Parliament)
March 22	French League for Women's Rights refuses Dutch invitation to Hague Congress on peace
March 25–27	Bern International Conference of Socialist Women, convoked by Clara Zetkin, is attended by women from Great Britain, Germany, Italy, Netherlands, Poland, Russian Empire, France, and Switzerland; they approve a pacifist resolution.
April 15	German Zeppelin raid on Paris
April 20	French Union for Women's Suffrage and National Council of Frenchwomen send manifesto to women from neutral and allied countries, calling for German withdrawal from occupied territories before peace negotiations
April 22	Germans use chlorine gas at Ypres for first time
April 24	Genocide of Armenians begins in Eastern Turkey; two days later, arrest and execution of intellectuals in Constantinople. Over the next months execution of most men; deportation, robbery, rape, and massacre of women, children, and elderly, in successive waves. Between six hundred thousand and one million dead
April 25	Anglo-Australian force lands at Gallipoli, Turkey, supported by French fleet
	French Committee for Women's Socialist Action, led by Louise Saumoneau, prevented by police from meeting to report on Bern conference
April 28–May 1	International Congress of Women at The Hague (1,136 women attend, but no French or Russians); report circulated to heads of state; German printing

	and distribution of report banned; International Women's Committee for a Permanent Peace founded
April 30	Arrests in Berlin of socialist women, following attempts to distribute the pacifist Bern resolution
May 7	German submarine sinks British ocean liner *Lusitania* (1,198 civilians drowned), provoking international condemnation, although the boat was carrying armaments
May 23	Italy declares war on Austria-Hungary
May 25	In Trieste (under Austrian control), a demonstration of Italian women against forced conscription leads to 47 women killed, 300 wounded
May 28	Berlin police disrupt demonstration before parliament house by 1,500 (mostly women) demanding peace, bread, and the return of their men
May 31	German zeppelins raid London
June 3	American Women's Trade Union calls on U.S. government to embargo export of arms
June 9	Ministry of Munitions Act passed by British Parliament; this ministry will encourage and regulate women's work
June 29	First Battle of Isonzo in Italy
July 3	Exception of French Civil Code allows wives of soldiers to petition for temporary authority over their children
	Russian Central Committee of War Industries established
July 9	Surrender of German South West Africa
July 10	French minimum wage law extended to women home-workers in clothing trade, covering production of uniforms
July 11	(St. Olga's Day) Czar Nicholas II establishes the medal of St. Olga for women's contributions to war effort
July 17	With government subsidy of £2,000, Emmeline Pankhurst of W.S.P.U. leads 30,000 women through London demanding war work. Women's "Right to Serve Act" passed by Parliament.
July 19	French Intersyndical Committee against Exploitation of Women founded: motto is "Equal Pay for Equal Work"
July 29	Clara Zetkin arrested for treason: distributing manifesto from the March Bern Conference
August 1	Women's Peace Committee holds peaceful demonstration in Lyons, France
August 3	British Army Council establishes Women's Legion Cookery section

August 4–6   German zeppelins bomb English towns

August 6   War Women's League formed in Britain

August 15   British Bombing of Karlsruhe

August: German Military Service Law orders registration of all women and men between 15 and 25 for potential war service

September 5–8   International meeting of Socialists in Zimmerwald, Switzerland, split between calls for peace and for class war

September 6   Bulgaria signs treaty with Central Powers (Germany, Austria-Hungary)

October 2   Socialist feminist Louise Saumoneau arrested for pacifist campaign in France

October 2   As Serbian army retreat through Albania begins, Mrs. St. Clair Stobart joins the troops leading a "flying field hospital"; she holds rank of major

October 11   Bulgaria invades Serbia, declares war three days later

October 12   German authorities execute English hospital director Edith Cavell for underground activities in Brussels; widespread international condemnation

October 14   German butter riots start in Berlin; unrest continues through following summer

October 15   Great Britain declares war on Bulgaria; Italy and France follow

October 19   Russia suspends protective legislation on women and juveniles in industry

                    German Patriotic Women's League celebrates Kaiserin's birthday as "Jam Day"

October 23   Demonstration against high prices by 2,000 German women in Dresden

October 28   British government sets women's wages in munitions

November 1–5   Serbia falls to Bulgaria

November 24   Anglo-Russian Hospital staff from Canada and Britain arrive in St. Petersburg

December 4   Ford *Peace Ship* sails from New York for Europe

December 8   British hosiery trade agrees to pay women at men's rates

Women's suffrage granted in 1915: Denmark and Iceland (limited)

1916

January 1   International Communist Party adopts Rosa Luxemburg's theses

January 27   Luxemburg and Karl Liebknecht found German Revolutionary Socialist Party

January 29–31   German Zeppelins bomb Paris and English towns

January	Italian central committee for grain supplies established
February 4	Renewal of German submarine attacks
February 9	British Military Service Act imposes conscription
February 21	German bombardment begins battle of Verdun (315,000 Frenchmen and 281,000 Germans dead); siege lasts ten months
March 6	Munich Suffrage League closed down, its leaders barred from public speech and international correspondence
	Women's National Land Service formed in England
March 8	French Committee for Women's Socialist Action barred from celebrating International Women's Day
April 6	Russian women riot following the suspension of meat sales in St. Petersburg; bread riots in Moscow two days later
April	Moscow congress of women
April 20	Germans announce deportation of about 20,000 civilians from the occupied region of Lille starting at 3 A.M. April 22, to perform forced labor
April 21	French Undersecretary of State creates Committee for Women's Work
April 24–May 1	Easter Uprising in Ireland against British rule; rebel leaders include Countess Constance Markievicz
April 25	German cruiser raids British ports
May 1	Karl Liebknecht arrested at pacifist Labor Day demonstrations in Berlin
May 9	Sykes-Picot agreement between France and Britain to divide Asiatic Turkey
May 11	Execution of Arab nationalists by Ottoman government
May 20	In Berlin 60,000 demonstrate against food shortages
May 22	German War Food Office established to regulate production and distribution of all food
May 23	In Budapest, "Bloody Thursday" strike
May 31	Naval battle of Jutland between German and British fleets ends German hope of breaking blockade
June 4	General Aleksey Brusilov launches Russian offensive against Austrian army at Tarnopol (initial success and capture of 375,000 prisoners, relieving pressures on Western front; over one million Russian casualties, however, demoralize Russian army)
June 5	Arab revolt in the Hijaz
June 17–18	Food riot in Munich on Marienplatz
June 29	First French women's strike at munitions factory in Puteaux (15 days) against productivity demands that effectively lower salaries

July 1	British and French launch Battle of Somme (by mid-November 420,000 British, 200,000 French, and 450,000 German dead); demoralized civilians suffer "war weariness"
July 6	In Nuremberg, Germany, food riot by 2,000 women, with support of 50 to 60 soldiers
July 20	French government circular mandates employment of women in certain munitions tasks
July	London County Council Ambulance Corps staffed entirely by women
	Berlin program of centralized public kitchens set up, model copied in other cities
August 18–19	Mounted police with sabres repress looting of food shops by German women in Hamburg
August 27	Romania enters war on side of Allies, Germany declares war on Romania next day; loss of grain supplies for Germany
August 31	Letter from German supreme military command (Hindenburg and Ludendorff) requests Minister of War draft women for labor in industry and agriculture; German chancellor refuses, September 13
September 1	Bulgaria declares war on Romania
September 15	British introduce tank warfare on Western Front
October 1	Frankfurt peace rally draws 30,000 German workers who demand peace on the basis of the status quo
October 3	Germany begins deportation of Belgians (120,000) for forced labor in Germany from militarized zone; deportations from rest of Belgium begin October 26
October 24	British Ministry of Munitions agrees to pay 75 percent of cost for temporary nurseries
November 2	Dresden demonstration of 7,000 for bread and peace; about 5,000 are women, 1,000 of them on strike
November 5	Polish autonomy proclaimed by Central Powers
November 21	Emperor Franz Joseph of Austria-Hungary dies
November 27	Greek government declares war on Germany
December 1	Women's Army Auxiliary Corps (WAAC) authorized in Britain; first enrollments March 3, 1917; on April 9, 1918, renamed Queen Mary's Army Auxiliary Corps
	Central Office for Women's Activities established by National Council of French Women, to provide services (nurseries, canteens, washrooms) under the Committee for Women's Work of the Secretariat for Munitions
December 5	German Auxiliary Service Law mandates employment of every German man age 17–60, but not of

women; instead, meat rations and factory canteens draw women into factory work; children join "Collection Service" to salvage raw materials

December 6	Fall of Bucharest
December 11	At Paris hand grenade factory explosion kills dozens
December 12	German offer of peace, conditional on annexation of Belgium and Northeastern France
	German Central Office for Women's Work established under War Office for Auxiliary Services, headed by Marie-Elisabeth Lüders. National Ausschuß for women's war work established to work with this Referat

Winter 1916–17, "Turnip Winter"

1917

January	French decree establishes equal piece-work rates for women and men: not enforced
January 8	In Leeds, first major strike by 9,200 munitionettes triggered by dismissal of girl for striking forewoman
	In Paris, two-day strike by *midinettes* (seamstresses)
January 10	Congressional Union for Woman's Suffrage pickets U.S. White House
January 13	Food riot by 1,000 women at Harburg, Germany
January 16	Marguerite Francillard executed by French for assisting her German lover in espionage
January 17	"Women's Service" demonstration in London attended by Minister of War, Minister of Labour, and Queen Mary
	French Minister of Labor, Albert Thomas, imposes arbitration in labor disputes
January 19	Explosion at Silvertown chemical factory in East End of London kills 69, injures 400
January 23	Parisians demonstrate over coal shortages, coal rationing begins
January 29	German women's organizations unite in National Committee for Women's War Work
January 31	Germany announces unrestricted submarine warfare
February 4	50,000 Russian workers strike on anniversary of "Bloody Sunday" (1905) in St. Petersburg
February 8	Explosion in Frankfurt armaments factory kills 58 German women workers; during one year, over 2,700 German women die in accidents in armaments industry
February 27– March 3	Between 8,000 and 10,000 women and men demonstrate in Barmen, Germany, over food shortages

February   French wives of soldiers receive rights of guardian-
                  ship over their children if their husbands agree
March 6   Women's Land Army established in Britain
March 8   In St. Petersburg on International Women's Day, the
                  "February" revolution (by the Orthodox calendar)
                  breaks out: striking women textile workers join
                  women in food riots and precipitate demonstrations
                  by hundreds of thousands of Russians, including sol-
                  diers.
March 14   The Petrograd Soviet calls for committees of soldiers
                  and sailors to take control of armaments; breakdown
                  of military hierarchy begins
March 16   Czar Nicholas II abdicates
March 20   New French cabinet under Ribot is first to include
                  women: Jeanne Tardy (for finances) and Berthe
                  Maillard (for labor)
March   Imperial War Museum founded in Britain
April 1   German rations reduced to one-third normal con-
                  sumption; substitute foods often dangerous to
                  health
                  40,000 feminists in Petrograd demonstrate for the
                  right to vote
April 2   Russian announcement of equal rights for women in
                  work, marriage, and divorce
April 6   United States declares war on Germany; Jeannette
                  Rankin, the only Congresswoman, votes no
April 16   "Nivelle" offensive launched by French along
                  Chemin des Dames; its failure costs 200,000 lives and
                  triggers mutinies in 54 divisions; 100,000 court-
                  martialed
April 16–23   125,000 workers in Berlin and Leipzig protest food
                  rationing; workers in armaments (over 50 percent
                  women) join strike for food and peace; women bring
                  along children to inhibit state violence
May 1   Milan demonstration for peace by agricultural and
                  factory workers led by women
                  Paris meeting of socialists draws 5,000 pacifists
May 5–12   German Socialist women celebrate "Red Week," with
                  3,000 assembled in Berlin
May 10   Socialist Congress in Stockholm; Britain, France,
                  and United States refuse passports to delegates
May 12   Parisian seamstresses (*midinettes*) begin a strike, fol-
                  lowed by women in armaments; by June 100,000
                  strikers in 71 industries in Paris region, led by muni-
                  tionettes, demand a 5½ day "English" week
May 20   Thirteen French corps refuse orders to go to front
May 21   Maria Botchkareva founds Women's Battalion of

	Death in Russia; her troops are reviewed by Kerensky in Petrograd on June 21
June 6	Nineteen deep mines with one million pounds of explosive set off at Messines (Mesen) in Belgium below German salient; explosion heard in London; unexploded mines still remain at end of twentieth century
June 11	French law establishes the "English" week and mandates collective contracts
June 13	German bombers drop 118 high-explosive bombs on London in daytime raid
June 14	Russian women lawyers admitted to the bar
June 25	American Expeditionary Force lands in France
June 29	Aleksandr Kerensky, Minister of War, establishes Commission to organize conscription of Russian women for work in the Ministry of War under the feminist Olga Nechaeva
July 1	Russian Chief of Staff Brusilov orders offensive against Austrians in Galicia. General Lavr Kornilov's advance is halted after 10 days by soldiers' mutinies. The failure triggers a Bolshevik coup attempt.
July 8	Maria Botchkareva's Women's Battalion of Death in action
July 15	Virgin of Fátima promises Lucia dos Santos salvation and peace in a vision
July 31	Battle of Ypres and Passchendaele, "battle of the mud" (5 miles gained, 250,000 casualties in three months)
August 1	Pope Benedict XV urges all warring states to return to previous borders
August 1–5	Russian Army nurse E. M. Malison convokes Women's Military Congress
August 2	Russian Provisional Government grants universal suffrage
	Sailors in German navy strike, incurring several death sentences
August 18	French forbid female slavery in the Cameroons
August 21–26	Italian women and youth riot in Turin, are shot; workers refuse to enter factories
September 14	Canadian War-Times Election Act enfranchises women who are close relatives of servicemen, for duration of war
September 14	International Council of Social-Democratic Women in Stockholm, endorse economic, social, and political equality; protection for women workers; and social welfare measures for mothers and children
September 17	Britain institutes nine-penny loaf
September 20	Canada grants vote to War Service women
October 15	French execution of Mata Hari

October 24	Battle of Caporetto, retreat of Italian troops to Piave River (30,000 Italian casualties, 275,000 Italians surrender)
October	Italy rations bread
October 31	Occupying German forces execute Flore Lefrance and Georgine Davel at Tournai for espionage on behalf of the French
November 2	Balfour Declaration: British government favors "the establishment in Palestine of a national home for the Jewish people"
November 7	"October" Revolution: Bolsheviks storm Winter Palace in Petrograd; of 135 female privates guarding the palace, all are beaten, three are raped. Thousands of armed women participate in Bolshevik seizure of power
November 20	Battle of Cambrai: first use of massed tanks
November 25	First Conference of Working Women in Petrograd, led by Alexandra Kollontai
	Mass demonstrations by women workers in Leipzig and Berlin, where police attack with sabers
November 28	Turks discover all-female robber band in Constantinople
November 29	Establishment of Women's Royal Naval Service, commanded by Katharine Furse; 7,000 recruits
	Bread riots in Italy
December 10	Nobel Peace Prize to the International Committee of the Red Cross
December 15	Armistice of Brest-Litovsk provisionally removes Russia from war

Women's suffrage granted in 1917: Canada (limited), Estonia, Latvia, Lithuania, Netherlands, Russia

Independence claimed in 1917 by Estonia, Finland, Moldavian Republic, and Ukrainian People's Republic

Impact of blockade on Germany and Austria-Hungary: average civilian daily diet reduced to 1,000 calories

1918

January	Viennese women strike for provisions
	Thousands of workers in Budapest strike to protest bread rationing
January 8	American President Woodrow Wilson announces "Fourteen Points" for negotiating peace
January 20	Women munitions workers in Ingolstadt, Bavaria, strike against Sunday work

January 21	German manpower shortages lead to placement of women in rearguard services
	Women's auxiliary telephone service set up in Germany
January 24	In protest against food shortages, 250,000 German workers strike in Berlin (joined by workers in Bremen, Hamburg, Essen, Leipzig); virtual stoppage of munitions industry
January 28	400,000 Berlin workers strike; in succeeding week more than one million armaments workers strike for immediate peace
January 30	Gotha bombardment kills 45 in Paris
February 1	Industrial plants in Berlin put under military control; strikers called up for military service; all public meetings banned
February 6	British "Representation of the People Act" grants suffrage to women over 30 and to most men over 21
February 9	In Turkey, first Woman's Labour Battalion attached to First Army
February 25	British Ministry of Food rations meat and fats
February 28	Women's Ottawa War Conference
March 3	Treaty of Brest-Litovsk between Russia and Germany recognizes independence of Finland and Ukraine; ratifies independence of Estonia, Latvia, Lithuania, Poland; treaty raises expectation of better food supplies for Germany
March 6	U.S. female telephone operators sail to Europe
March 9	Anglo-French force lands at Murmansk, Siberia, to intervene against Bolshevik rule
March 15	Explosion at Courneuve munitions factory; French government conceals number dead.
March 21	Second Battle of the Somme begins with German "Michael" offensive
March 23	"Big Bertha," a long-range German cannon, begins bombardment of Paris; attacks kill 256 and wound 628, hitting a maternity hospital and the church of St. Gervais on Good Friday
March 29	Condemnation of Hélène Brion for treason (i.e., pacifism) by the French Council of War; three years' suspended sentence
April 1	British Women's Royal Air Force founded
April 14	8,000 Irish workers strike at Belfast to protest conscription; strike becomes nationwide April 23
April 29	Arrival of 100 female telephonists to join U.S. Signal Corps in France

May 1	British hospital at Etaples, France, bombed
May 19	Canadian hospital at Etaples bombed, several nurses killed
May 29–30	Hospital at Abbeville, France, bombed, 9 WAACs killed, the following night hospitals at Etaples and Doullens hit, several nurses killed
May	Strikes with pacifist overtones in Paris (105,000) and the Loire region (100,000)
June 27	Hospital ship *Llandovery Castle* torpedoed, life boats shelled, 14 Canadian nurses drown
July 1	Explosion at Chilwell No. 6 National Shell-Filling Factory kills 134 workers
July 15	German attack in Champagne launches Second Battle of the Marne
July 19	Explosion in shell factory at Plauen kills 296 German women
July 27	German Ministry of War establishes Women's Signal Corps under military command
August 3–22	In Berlin, strike by over 2,000 women in munitions for 8-hour shifts and 20 percent pay increases; numerous strikes in Germany in the late summer
August 8	British pass Maternity and Child Welfare Act
August 13	First woman enlists in U.S. Marines
September 29	Bulgaria signs armistice with Allies
October 29	German sailors mutiny at Kiel, refuse order to prepare for new battle in North Sea
October 30	Ottoman government signs armistice with Allies
November 3	German naval mutiny becomes armed insurrection; sailors in Kiel demand female suffrage Austria-Hungary signs armistice with Allies
November 8	Munich workers declare German Republic
November 9	Abdication of Kaiser Wilhelm II; German government turned over to Social Democrats; general strike of German workers in Berlin, amid armed uprising by hundreds of thousands
November 11	Armistice signed by Germany and Allies
November 13	French Undersecretary for War demands reinstatement of demobilized soldiers in former jobs; within one month, half of Frenchwomen working in munitions are dismissed
November 14	German troops in Rhodesia surrender
November 19	6,000 union women march on Westminster, London, under the banner "Shall Peace Bring Us Starvation?"
December 5	French deadline for women to receive severance pay by voluntarily giving up jobs

Women's suffrage granted in 1918: Austria, Canada (women of British and French extraction), Czechoslovakia, Germany, Hungary (limited), Luxembourg, Poland, Portugal, United Kingdom (over age 30)

Independence claimed in 1918: Azerbaijan, Armenia, Czechoslovakia, Georgia, Hungary, Lithuania, Latvia, Poland, and United Kingdom of Serbs, Croats and Slovenes (Yugoslavia); return of Alsace-Lorraine to France

Winter influenza: influenza pandemic claims 20 million lives; women and children, weakened by hunger, are particularly affected

1918–19 famine in Central Europe

1919

January 15	Rosa Luxemburg and Karl Liebknecht murdered
January 18	Peace conference at Versailles opens
February 10	Conference of Allied Women convenes for duration of peace conference at Versailles
February 19–21	Pan-African Congress in Paris
May 12–20	Women's International Peace Conference in Zurich
June 28	Treaty of Versailles signed, providing for League of Nations
July 12	Blockade of Germany ends
July 15	Pope Benedict XV endorses women's suffrage
November 6	U.S. Congress grants citizenship to all Native Americans who served in war without altering tribal rights
November 28	Nancy Astor becomes first British woman Member of Parliament
December 23	Sex Disqualification Removal Act opens civil service, legal profession, jury duty to women in Britain

Women's suffrage granted in 1919: Germany, Netherlands, Rhodesia (limited), Sweden, Turkey; French Chamber votes for universal suffrage, but Senate fails to pass law

1920

November 11	Burial of British unknown soldier in Westminster Abbey; burial of French unknown soldier at Arc de Triomphe

Women's suffrage granted in 1920: Belgium (limited), United States

Peace of Paris: treaties create territorial boundaries of new states (Estonia, Latvia, Lithuania)

✝ I ✝

POLITICAL
WRITING

How vocal were women in the political arena during World War I? When war was initially declared, none of the women in the nations involved had the vote. Nonetheless, many women were politically active, and the outbreak of war catalyzed their commentary. Laws against association that had barred women from public meetings had lapsed in the preceding decade in several countries. The fight for suffrage had served as a training ground in a number of countries. After August 1, 1914, many of the women who had led the suffrage movement applied their attention and skills to other forms of organization and mobilization for or against the war effort. Inspired by writers like Bertha von Suttner, women who had played key roles in the pacifist movement anticipated the outbreak of war with dismay. Even more important, preceding decades had seen the growth of women's participation in the socialist movement, which in principle supported the international union of the working class and therefore condemned nationalist wars. Women constituted almost 17 percent of the German Socialist Party, if only 2.3 percent of the French party. While the assassination on July 31, 1914, of Jean Jaurès, held to be the spokesman of socialist pacifism, and the power of nationalist sentiments combined to sway most socialist men to vote credits for the war, many socialist feminists continued to resist endorsing the war.

When leaders of women's organizations decided to endorse or condemn the war, they could turn to journals that had been founded by women and often addressed women, such as Gertrud Bäumer's *Die Frau*, Maria Ivanovna Pokrovskaia's *Zhenskii vestnik*, or the French *La voix des femmes*. These periodicals made it possible for women to announce their positions swiftly and forcefully. Socialist journals such as Anna Kuliscioff's *La difesa delle lavoratrici* published editorials from other countries, especially articles written by Clara Zetkin. And the suffragist paper *Jus suffragii*, published in more than one country, gathered an international range of articles, letters, and announcements, such as Aletta Jacobs's call to women

to attend the pacifist International Congress of Women at The Hague in
April 1915.

One may ask what qualifies a text as "political." Is an oath taken on the
battlefront or a hymn to peasant women an act of propaganda or a con-
fession of political faith? In effect, almost all texts about the war are in
some sense political. The texts gathered here address a general public,
often but not always a public of women. They declare a position for or
against the war. They assess the relationship between nationalist interests
and the interests of a specific organization, or sometimes a competing
revolutionary interest.

When women do address political issues, they often recognize the ways
in which citizenship and nationality are gendered, and the impact on
women of nationalist politics. They raise questions about the relationship
between maternity and political propaganda. They speak out against government abuses. The political statements gathered here demonstrate the
terms in which women formulated their positions and the swiftness with
which they assumed the public stage to discuss the war.

✝ Clara Zetkin, née Eißner
(1857–1933) *German*

Born into a German family sympathetic to the revolutions of 1848, Clara Eißner became familiar with the misery of the laborers, peasants, and home workers of her Saxon neighborhood. She studied to become a teacher like her father. Her mother and normal school teachers, one of whom was the first president of the Federation of German Women's Associations, introduced her to the women's movement. After she met her partner, the Russian revolutionary Ossip Zetkin, in Leipzig, she became a militant socialist worker on behalf of the working class. She worked for a few years as a governess, then followed Zetkin to Zurich, where she wrote for the clandestine Social Democratic press. She spoke out for equal rights for women, especially women workers. She militated for "class war," however, in opposition to "ladies' rights" or liberal feminism. While they were in exile in Paris in 1889, he died; they had two children. Her later marriage to the much younger Georg Zundel ended in divorce in 1927. She helped organize the Second Socialist International in Paris in 1889, at which she gave a major address on the "woman question."

After returning to Germany, Zetkin continued to be active in socialist congresses and party activities. In 1910 at the International Socialist Women's Conference she proposed the creation of an international Women's Day; the first celebrations were in March 1911. From 1892 she edited the socialist women's organ *Die Gleichheit* (Equality) for twenty-five years.

During the war, Zetkin led the socialist feminist opposition to the war, perhaps representing one-third of socialist women. Her November appeal "to all socialist women of all countries" was distributed in Switzerland, France, and illegally in Germany. The failure of the German socialists in the government to oppose the war shocked her: "I thought I would go mad, or that I would have to commit suicide." In spite of illness, in March 1915 she called an International Conference of Socialist Women at Bern. Printing the Bern Manifesto led to her arrest in Germany in July; she was accused of "treason," that is, pacifism and activism among working women. "To the Socialist Women of all Countries" was censored. Her wartime activities were hampered by illness; she suffered a stroke in 1917. On May 18, 1917, the German Socialist Party dismissed her from the editorship of *Gleichheit* because of her internationalist protests against the war.

A gifted orator and journalist, she published speeches and articles on Lenin and on feminist issues in socialism. She helped her friend Rosa Luxemburg found the German Communist Party; from 1920 to 1933 she was a communist deputy at the Reichstag. Because she attacked Hitler, she was forced to flee to Russia, where she became president of the Women's International.

✝ Proletarian Women, Be Prepared

The horrible specter before which the people of Europe tremble has become reality. The war is ready to crush human bodies, dwelling places and fields. Austria has used the senseless outrage of a twenty-year-old Serbian lad against the Successor to the Throne, as a pretext for a criminal outrage against the sovereignty and independence of the Serbian people and in the final analysis, against the peace of Europe.[1] She wants to use this opportune moment because Serbia can hardly hope to obtain help from Russian Tsarism. France at the present moment can hardly support Russian despotism's bellicose plans of conquest. Sessions in the Senate have revealed grave shortcomings in the army, and the reintroduction of the three-year draft has shaken military morale and created bitter dissatisfaction. England is so preoccupied with the situation in Ulster and other tasks of a similar nature that she does not have any great desire to participate in the horrors and crimes of a world war. Thus Austrian imperialism is calculating that it can violate international law in its dealings with Serbia without being challenged by the Triple Entente.[2] She believes that Serbia's defeat will block Tsarism's push towards the Mediterranean Sea.

The proletarian women know that the expansion of Russian Knout Tsarism would mean the worst type of slavery for all of the people concerned. Yet they also understand that Austro-Hungarian imperialism

1. On June 28, 1914, the student Gavrilo Princip, a Serbian, killed Archduke Francis Ferdinand of Austria and his wife in the Bosnian capital of Sarajevo. Supported by Germany, Austria-Hungary delivered an ultimatum to Serbia, which she accepted but with several reservations. Rejecting the reservations the Hapsburg monarchy declared war on July 28. By the first week of August the war had spread to encompass Germany, France, Russia and other countries, bringing about the first World War. [P.S.F.]

2. The Triple Entente was a military alliance formed by Great Britain, France and Russia. It was preceded by the Triple Alliance, uniting Germany, Austria-Hungary and Italy against France. In 1883 Romania was added to the Triple Alliance. [P.S.F.]

does not protect the rights and the liberties of people. It merely fights for the interests of the reactionary Hapsburg Dynasty and for the gold and power hunger of the insensitive, unscrupulous magnates and capitalists. Within its own realm, the Austro-Hungarian Monarchy has smashed the rights of the different nationalities and even more so the rights of the exploited working-class masses. In spite of the raging crisis, it has for years increased the price of even the barest necessities and it has used brutality and tricks to hinder the fight against exploitation and misery. Now it crowns its work by forcing the sons of workers to murder and to let themselves be murdered. It does not constitute a vanguard for the welfare and liberty of the people. Its war must never become a murder of the people.

In Germany, the profit- and laurel-seeking warmongers try to deceive the people in respect to this simple truth. They claim that Austria's war, in the final analysis, is directed against the threatening barbarism of Russia; that it represents a Germanic crusade against "arrogantly advancing Slavdom." In an unscrupulous manner, they scream about duty and about the preservation of "German Nibelung Loyalty." They want to see to it that Germany, as a member of the Triple Alliance, will adopt Austria's war as her own and that she will waste the blood and wealth of her people.

The sacrilege of such an activity is as great as the crime of Austrian imperialism. It wants to ignite a world conflagration in the course of which the peoples of Europe will slaughter each other while a handful of powerful and prescient people smilingly reap their profits. This must never be allowed to happen. The proletarians of Germany, men and women, must prove by deeds that they have been enlightened and that they are ready to assume a life in freedom. Their will to maintain peace, alongside the desire for peace on the part of the workers of other countries, especially of France, is the only guarantee that the war of the clerical Hapsburgs will not turn into a general European holocaust. It is true that the Government of the German Empire assures us that it has done and is doing everything in its power to keep the war localized. But the people have already found out that the tongues of the government's representatives are forked like the tongues of snakes. It is also familiar with the ineptitude of the diplomatic agents of the German Empire. And it certainly has no illusions about this unique fact: The international situation is so intricately enmeshed and entangled that one coincidence can destroy all of the good intentions of the governments. One coincidence could very well decide whether the thin thread from which the sword of world war is suspended over humankind will break.

The proprietors and rulers, too, swear solemnly that they detest the horrible barbarism of war. Yes, they too tremble before its hellish horrors. And yet it is they who constantly prepare and agitate for war. One has only to listen to the left liberal press which, in the name of all kinds of cultural values, urges Germany to join Austria, thereby challenging Russia and France to join the bloody fray. And yet, the pages of this press are still wet from the maudlin tears which it shed over the psalms of peace heard at the Reconciliation Conference of German-French Parliamentarians at Bern.[3] How shamelessly pious Christian newspapers are calling for horrible bloodshed and mass murder while they are daily reciting the commandment of their Almighty: "Thou shalt not kill!" All masks are dropping from the vampire of capitalism which is nourished by the blood and marrow of the popular masses. How could it be otherwise? The killing among nations will never be condemned as fratricide by those who find it perfectly natural that every year hundreds of thousands of people's comrades are slaughtered for profit upon the altars of capitalism.

Only the proletariat uses its broad chest to stem the approaching disaster of a world war. The horrors of this war would already have been upon us if one of the most unscrupulous murderers of people, Tsarism, had not been prevented from plunging upon the craved-for battlefield by the political mass strikes of the Russian proletariat. It has only been the revolutionary struggle of our Russian brothers and sisters which in these fateful days has, until now, preserved world peace. Let us not be more fainthearted than they are. Their glorious battle, waged without guaranteed political rights and in the face of dungeons, exile and death, shows us by deeds what a determined, bold and unified working class is able to accomplish.

Let us not waste a minute. War is standing before the gate. Let us drive it back into the night before its ferocity will strip the unenlightened masses of their last ounce of nationalism and humanity. Leave your factories and workshops, your huts and attics to join the mass protest! Let the rulers and proprietors have no doubt about our serious determination to fight for peace to our last breath.

The exploited masses are strong enough to carry on their shoulders the entire edifice of the new society. They are used to living in poverty while the wealth that they create is being wasted in riotous living by idlers. Every day, while eking out a living, they face death. And these types of people are supposed to shun deprivations, dangers and death when it comes to fighting for peace and freedom? They are supposed to give way before a military cabal which has just been publicly flogged for the brutal mistreatment of their sons and brothers?[4] The mighty peace force of the working-class masses must silence the jingoist screaming in the streets. And wherever two or three exploited men or women are assembled, they must express their detestation of war and their support for peace.

3. The reference is to the Inter-Parliamentary Conference at Bern, Switzerland, which was held from May 11 to May 12, 1913. The conference was arranged by members of the Swiss National Assembly who invited German and French Parliamentarians. The largest number of German participants consisted of Reichstag deputies of the Social-Democratic Party of Germany, among whom were August Bebel and Karl Liebknecht. The conference was to prepare a program against war propaganda and the unbearable increase in the burden of armament in both France and Germany. [P.S.F.]

4. The reference is to attacks by Rosa Luxemburg on German militarists in numerous articles and at meetings during the first half of 1914. [P.S.F.]

For the working class, the brotherhood among peoples is no utopia, and world peace is more than an empty word. A concrete fact supports it: the firm solidarity of all the exploited and suppressed of all nations. This solidarity must not allow proletarians to fire upon proletarians. It must make the masses determined, during a war, to use all available weapons against the war. The might with which the proletarian masses will oppose the fury of war will constitute a victorious battle in their war of liberation. The revolutionary energy and passion of their struggle will expose them to dangers and demand sacrifices. What of it? There comes a moment in the life of each individual and people when everything can be won if one risks everything. Such a moment has come. Proletarian women, be prepared!

Die Gleichheit, August 5, 1914

"Proletarian Women, Be Prepared," in *Clara Zetkin Selected Writings*, trans. Philip S. Foner (New York: International Publishers, 1984), 110–13. Reprinted by permission of International Publishers.

✠ Dame Millicent Garrett Fawcett
(1847–1929) *British*

Millicent Garrett, the seventh child of a merchant, went at twelve to a school run by an aunt of Robert Browning, but her education was irregular. Her work as a suffragist was inspired by the difficulties encountered by an older sister who sought to become a doctor. Her close friend Sarah Emily Davies also made her conscious of the importance of women's education. At eighteen she met Henry Fawcett, a blind professor of economics at Cambridge, whom she married two years later; they had a daughter, Philippa. She helped Fawcett in his work as a member of Parliament; their circle included John Stuart Mill and Leslie Stephen. Supported by her husband, she engaged in suffragist activities from 1867 and contributed to the passage of the Married Women's Property Act in 1882. She participated in the management of Newnham College. After her husband's death she became active in the fight against government control of prostitution. She rejected Home Rule in Ireland and supported the Boer War, but led an inquiry into concentration camps. President of the National Union of Women's Suffrage Societies, she opposed the violent strategies of the Pankhursts.

When war broke out, she urged the suspension of agitation for suffrage. Millicent Garrett Fawcett and Chrystal Macmillan, as leaders of the International Woman Suffrage Alliance, published a manifesto on August 7, 1914, that they had distributed to the British Foreign Office and to embassies in London. The August 7 issue of *Votes for Women* reported on the international women's meeting on August 4 at Kingsway Hall, at which speakers representing twenty-six countries included Olive Schreiner, Rosika Schwimmer of Hungary, Madame Malmburg of Finland, Emmeline Pethick-Lawrence, Mrs. St. Clair Stobart, and Mrs. Fawcett.

In *Common Cause*, August 14, 1914, she urged, "Women, your country needs you. . . . Let us show ourselves worthy of citizenship . . . whether our claim is recognized or not." When limited suffrage was passed in January 1918, she retired from her position as president of the National Union.

She also worked to open the legal profession and civil service to women. At the end of her life she traveled to Palestine and Ceylon. She wrote biographies of women, histories of the suffrage movement, and a treatise on political economy.

✝ International Manifesto of Women

Drawn up by the International Woman Suffrage Alliance and delivered last week at the Foreign Office and Foreign Embassies in London

We, the women of the world, view with apprehension and dismay the present situation in Europe, which threatens to involve one continent, if not the whole world, in the disasters and horrors of war. In this terrible hour, when the fate of Europe depends on decisions which women have no power to shape, we, realising our responsibilities as the mothers of the race, cannot stand passive by. Powerless though we are politically, we call upon the Governments and Powers of our several countries to avert the threatened unparalleled disaster. In none of the countries immediately concerned in the threatened outbreak have women any direct power to control the political destinies of their own countries. They find themselves on the brink of the almost unbearable position of seeing all that they most reverence and treasure, the home, the family, the race, subjected not merely to risks, but to certain and extensive damage which they are powerless either to avert or assuage. Whatever its result the conflict will leave mankind the poorer, will set back civilisation, and will be a powerful check to the gradual amelioration in the condition of the masses of the people, on which so much of the real welfare of nations depends.

We women of twenty-six countries, having banded ourselves together in the International Women's Suffrage Alliance with the object of obtaining our political means of sharing with men the power which shapes the fate of nations, appeal to you to leave untried no method of conciliation or arbitration for arranging international differences which may help to avert deluging half the civilised world in blood.

Signed on behalf of the International Woman Suffrage Alliance
Millicent Garrett Fawcett, First Vice-President
Chrystal Macmillan, Recording Secretary

Votes for Women, August 7, 1914, 1.

✠ Emmeline Pankhurst, née Goulden (1858–1928) *British*

Taking on family responsibility as the oldest sister in a large family, Emmeline Goulden developed a competitive streak as a young woman. Encouraged by liberal parents, she attended her first militant meeting at fourteen in Manchester. In 1872, following the Franco-Prussian War, her father took her to study in Paris at the École Normale, a pioneer school for the higher education of women. The French ruins impressed upon her a distrust of Germans. On her return to England she worked in the civil service. In 1879 she married a feminist lawyer, Richard Pankhurst, active first in the Liberal, then in the Independent Labour party; they had five children, including three daughters, Christabel, Sylvia, and Adela, all of whom became leaders in the suffrage movement. Widowed in 1898, Pankhurst founded the Women's Social and Political Union (WSPU) in 1903, which published a journal, *Votes for Women* (replaced by the *Suffragette* in 1912 after a split with the editors, the Pethick-Lawrences). At a demonstration in 1905 her daughter Christabel launched the militant phase of the suffragette movement. Pankhurst went on a hunger strike in 1909, demanding to be treated as a political prisoner; she was repeatedly imprisoned between 1911 and 1914 under a "cat and mouse" routine, in which she was jailed, then released after a hunger strike.

War confronted Pankhurst with a choice between her belief that "war is not women's way" and her enthusiasm for France. When the government released all suffragettes from prison on August 10, 1914, it deflated the militant movement. In response, Pankhurst suspended WSPU activities in a letter sent August 13 to her constituency. The call to the International Congress of Women at The Hague in 1915 split the feminist movement: Pankhurst and Millicent Fawcett opposed the peace effort, while Pankhurst's daughters Sylvia and Adela, along with allies such as the Pethick-Lawrences, supported it.

Pankhurst plunged into work for conscription and pressed the government to capitalize on the available labor of women in industry and the service sector. (Ironically, the *Suffragette* was raided by the police for its out-spoken militarism.) She urged women to "enlist" in the war against Germany, which she denounced as a "man-state" that maintained "a low conception of the status of women" (March 23, 1915, *Daily Sketch*). As leader of the WSPU Pankhurst called for the right to serve, arguing that full citizenship depended on the mutuality of rights and responsibilities. The *Suffragette* (rebaptized *Britannia* in 1915) appeared with the slogan, "It is a thousand times more the duty of militant Suffragettes to fight the Kaiser for the duty of liberty than it was to fight anti-Suffrage governments." In May 1915 she called upon the government to support welfare measures on behalf of illegitimate children; she adopted four baby girls herself. With a government subsidy of £2,000, she organized a demonstration of thirty thousand women marching for the "right to serve" in June 1915.

Her daughter Christabel came out of exile to join her in patriotic work in England and abroad, pressing for racial purity in a purge of Germans. Sylvia, however, remained antimilitarist, combating the economic effects of war on workers and their families in the East End of London by establishing clinics and food centers for women workers and the wives and children of soldiers. Adela joined the Women's Peace Army in Australia, where she fought conscription by linking war to the "white slave traffic."

In 1916 Pankhurst traveled to America to raise funds for Serbia, and in 1917 she went to Petrograd to interview Aleksandr Kerensky, the moderate revolutionary leader, who had instituted universal suffrage and equal rights for women, urging him to hold firm in the war. Upon meeting Maria Botchkareva she advocated allied intervention in Russia. In 1918 her efforts on behalf of suffrage were rewarded by the passage of the Reform Bill granting limited suffrage to women over thirty. Her daughter Christabel failed to win a seat in Parliament after the war, and Pankhurst collapsed in 1928 while campaigning as a Conservative for a seat representing the East End.

AM

✝ Votes for Women

THE WOMEN'S SOCIAL AND POLITICAL UNION
OFFICES, LINCOLN'S INN HOUSE
KINGSWAY, W.C.

August 13, 1914

Dear Friend,

Even the outbreak of war could not affect the action of the W.S.P.U. so long as our comrades were in prison and under torture.

Since their release it has been possible to consider what should be the course adopted by the W.S.P.U. in view of the war crisis. It is obvious that even the most vigorous militancy of the W.S.P.U. is for the time being rendered less effective by contrast with the untimely greater violence done in the present war not to mere property and economic prosperity alone, but to human life.

As for work for the vote on the lines of peaceful argument, such work is we know futile even under ordinary conditions to secure votes for women in Great Britain. How much less therefore will it avail at this time of international warfare!

Under the circumstances it has been decided to economise the Union's energies and financial resources by a temporary suspension of activities. The resumption of active work and reappearance of *The Suffragette*, whose next issue will be also temporarily suspended, will be announced at the right time. As a result of the decision announced in this letter, not only shall we save much energy and a very large sum of money but an opportunity will be given to the Union as a whole and above all to those members who have been in the fighting line to recuperate after the tremendous strain and suffering of the past two years.

As regards the war, the view the W.S.P.U. expresses is this: we believe that under the joint rule of enfranchised women and men the nations of the world will, owing to women's influence and authority, find a way of reconciling the claims of peace and honour and of regulating international relations without bloodshed; we nevertheless believe also that matters having come to the present pass it was inevitable that Great Britain should take part in the war and with that patriotism which has nerved women to endure torture in prison cells for the national good, we ardently desire that our country shall be victorious—this because we hold that the existence of all small nationalities is at stake and that the status of France and of Great Britain is involved.

It will be the future task of women, and only they can perform it, to ensure that the present world tragedy and the peril in which it places civilisation shall not be repeated, and therefore the W.S.P.U. will at the first possible moment step forward into the political arena in order to compel the enactment of a measure giving votes to women on the same terms as men.

I want in conclusion to thank with all my heart the generous and devoted women who have supported the W.S.P.U. until now, and to assure them of my confidence that at the present time and later when we resume active work that support will be continued.

Yours sincerely,
E. PANKHURST

✠ Anna Kuliscioff, née Rozenstejn
(1854–1925) *Russian/Italian*

Born in the Crimea, Anna Rozenstejn changed her surname to Kuliscioff when she was a student. She was the first woman accepted in technical sciences at Zurich Polytechnic in 1871, where she was influenced by the anarchist theories of Mikhail Bakunin. She returned to Russia as a political organizer; in 1873 she married a Russian noble from Odessa, Petr Markelovic Makarevic. By 1877 she was forced to emigrate, and she was arrested in France, Italy, and Switzerland for anarchist activities in 1878–79. Between 1877 and 1885 she lived with Andrea Costa, with whom she founded the Italian Socialist Party; they had one daughter. She went to Switzerland during this period to study medicine, then returned to care for working-class patients in Milan. She collaborated on the biweekly *Critica sociale* (Social criticism).

From 1885 on, she lived and worked with the socialist Filippo Turati; together they fought for female suffrage, labor legislation to protect women and children, and socialist internationalism, and against Italian militarism in North Africa and involvement in World War I. In 1912 she founded the Italian women's socialist organization and its fortnightly journal, *La difesa delle lavoratrici* (Defense of women workers). It condemned the Italian conquest of Libya (1911–12) as imperialist.

On August 2, 1914, Kuliscioff opposed the war in an editorial; eventually she came to think intervention was inevitable, fearing that the central powers would stabilize conservative militarist forces. "While Brother Kills Brother," a front-page editorial, was one of several she printed in 1914 against the war. Although socialist internationalism collapsed throughout Europe after the assassination of French leader Jean Jaurès in July 1914, Italian socialists remained neutral, and Italy did not enter the war until May 24, 1915. Diffident toward Bolshevism, Kuliscioff opposed the Russian Revolution in 1917; she was an active socialist until her death. Describing her to Friedrich Engels, the Italian philosopher Arturo Labriola said: "In Milan there is only one man—and she is a woman."

⚜ While Brother Kills Brother

Another fifteen days have gone by; in this life of uncertainty and anxiety our very soul seems suspended. Our struggles in the field of labor are in a lull, weakened by the crisis that hampers us in affirming any rights. Our educational work seems ironic, now that the war has so deeply disillusioned us about our strengths.

Yet we must go on living and waiting; the best we can do is to keep alive in our hearts the ideal flame of faith that seems to blow out under the rush of the storm. Meanwhile let us follow the events of the terrible war: we cannot count the dead, hundreds of thousands if not already a million.

The fate that seemed to smile at German audacity now turns against its very arrogance. Like the soul of the common people, we see here a sanction imposed by the justice inherent in things. The Triple Alliance that forbids any ally to make separate peace means, moreover, that the war will be prolonged to the bitter end. Should we then all be pleased? To what extent should we care about who will emerge vanquished or victor?

We know that in some churches and some boarding schools run by nuns, they are praying for a German victory. They go so far as to believe and persuade others that such a victory would reinforce religion. Republican France, it is said, has done the church so much damage, it must be punished. Those nuns, who continue to educate our youth covertly and without regulation, still judge Garibaldi as a malefactor. In this case the Italian government gets what it deserves, since it has never given serious thought to schooling for the common people. General opinion, however, is favorable to France, understandably so: but this creates a dangerous state of mind, producing a desire for war manifest in demonstrations extolling war. People want Italy to move in favor of France.

It is true that what has pushed public opinion increasingly against the Germans are excesses committed against the rules of international law that had been established as preventive measures to make war (as it were) less barbaric. But why would we want to punish the authors of such horrors by spreading further carnage? Do we not have a similar burden on our consciences? Who does not recall the ears of Arabs brought back from Libya as souvenirs by our soldiers?

The United States has undertaken to decide who is responsible for such excesses, and rightly so. The judgment of the civil world will issue a sentence much more useful in its moral effects than punishment inflicted with weapons at our own risk and danger.

Thus we must oppose these false enthusiasms, in whatever quarter they arise.

We women, who feel most responsible for the broken lives and calamities of war, and who therefore are by nature and by logic the most averse to war and least responsive to the lures of patriotism and combat, we are the most vigilant. If in the modest milieux where we live, our modest word can be of any value, let us employ it to dampen false enthusiasms, to recall to reality those who pursue reckless illusions.

We, first among all, defend our party against the accusation of cowardice leveled against it. Let those who want to show their courage keep it for other, more sacred and fruitful battles!

La difesa delle lavoratrici, September 20, 1914, 1.

Translated by Sylvia Notini

✠ Sofia Pavlovna Iur'eva
Russian

The journalist Ivanova comments on this letter of November 1914 printed in *Zhenskii vestnik* (Women's herald), "a public scientific literary monthly devoted to equal rights and improvement of women's condition," that girls from different social strata have run away from home, dressed as men, and tried to join the army, some helped by a relative or friend in the army. Other articles in the same newspaper provide anecdotes about women fighting next to men in the Serbian and Russian armies: the wife of a captain enlisted for active duty as a translator; a woman surgeon disguised herself as the brother of her husband, then calmly worked as an orderly in the trenches; another cross-dressed volunteer, Vasillia G., won acceptance as a brave fighter, until one day she reacted hysterically to a rat, thereby betraying her sex.

There is no record that Iur'eva succeeded in forming a women's unit, but hundreds of Russian women engaged in active service in the military. Anna Karsilnikova fought in nineteen battles and won the Cross of St. George, and Maria Botchkareva founded the Women's Battalion of Death under Aleksandr Kerensky.

✠ Letter

In the age in which we are living, the age of a great European war, everyone desires to offer up their strength on the altar of the fatherland, everyone strives to give at least something to their homeland. We women likewise do not wish to remain the idle spectators of great events—many of you are joining the ranks of soldiers as nurses to lessen, as best you can, the suffering of wounded heroes. I too burn with the desire to be useful to my dear homeland, but I do not feel called to be a nurse: I want to enlist as a volunteer in the active army. I entreat people of wealth to respond to my appeal and to give me the means necessary to fulfill my cherished dream—to form a detachment of Amazons, of women soldiers.

Do not think that this letter is a hoax, or the whim of an unbalanced mind—no, in this I see my calling, my purpose, my happiness!

I want to shed my blood for the fatherland, to give my life for my homeland!

I will give a more detailed explanation to those persons who respond in writing to me at this address: Sofia Pavlovna Iur'eva, Petrograd, Courses of Higher Education for Women.

Zhenskii vestnik, November 1914, 234–35

Translated by Cynthia Simmons

✝ Emmeline Pethick-Lawrence
(1867–1954) *British*

A vital supporter of the suffragette Women's Social and Political Union (WSPU), Emmeline Pethick had learned from her father to hate injustice. Her mother, however, opposed Emmeline's suffragette activities and sent her to boarding school, then to finishing schools in France and Germany; when she spoke of earning her own living, she was told it would take bread from the mouth of a less fortunate woman. Pethick did social work in a mission house, deciding to "accept the gospel of socialism." Five years later, with her friend Mary Neal, she formed the Esperance Guild Society "to offer regular employment in dressmaking at decent wages."

In 1901 she married Fred Lawrence, a lawyer for the poor. They were arrested three times in their work for women's suffrage; Pethick-Lawrence was treasurer of the WSPU until Emmeline Pankhurst forced the two out on the grounds that their law cases were weakening the union. Pethick-Lawrence and her husband published *Votes for Women,* a paper whose scope extended to social inequalities. She maintained that the world is "man-made . . . in the deepest sense of the word. . . . Its laws are men's laws, its rules of commerce and every-day business are men's laws. Its moral standard, its public opinion, is formed by men," without taking into account women's point of view.

In August 1914 she recognized women's desire to serve Britain in this crisis. She herself joined the Women's Emergency Corps Committee, which immediately undertook to care for Belgian refugees and sent women to work as cooks and nurses. Yet Pethick-Lawrence also dedicated herself to work for peace: she was one of very few women who managed to be present at the International Congress of Women for peace at The Hague in 1915, in spite of the blockade. Later that year, with Helena Swanwick and Irene Cooper, she helped form the Women's International League (WIL) in Great Britain to promote peace and negotiation; she was its president from 1926 to 1935.

After the armistice, she ran as a peace candidate supported by soldiers, but not by women—"a strange experience" for a suffragette, she commented. She opposed the continuing postwar blockade of Germany, the exaction of heavy reparations, and allied intervention against the Bolsheviks. Members of the WIL were prosecuted under the Defence of the Realm Act (DORA) for attributing the East European famine to the allied blockade. With her friend Charlotte Despard she attended the International Conference of Women at Zurich in May 1919, a gathering of those who had met in 1915 at The Hague, and founded the Women's International League for Peace and Freedom; there she argued for Irish independence. She believed that "women can kill the war tradition if they will."
AM

✝ Motherhood and War

From time to time the current of the world's life is quickened by some new stream that is poured into it. The emergence of the middle class into political life wrought a commercial revolution in Great Britain. The emancipation of the working classes changed the national outlook upon many industrial and social questions. Today the new force that is entering into the world's life is that of an awakened and still rapidly awakening womanhood.

At the very moment that this new force has been generated, the whole world is standing aghast at the contemplation of its own disruption. We are witnessing in the present European War something that resembles a "twilight of the gods," the passing away in blood and fire of an epoch. It is from the ruins that a new civilization will have to be built up. [. . .]

For, whether there is decisive victory for one side or the other, or whether there is not, peace must come within a measurable distance of time for the simple reason that war cannot feed itself. War is absolutely destructive. It subsists on the resources which can only be accumulated in time of peace. When the substance of the people is almost eaten up, when our life blood is almost sucked away, then exhaustion and bankruptcy will be allowed to withdraw humanity from the clutches of the glutted vampire of war.

But what kind of peace will it be when it comes? That is the question. Who is going to determine it? Who will arrange its conditions? Everything depends upon that. If the same people who by secret diplomacies brought war upon Europe, without the consent, without even the knowledge of their respective democracies, settle in this same way the conditions of peace, then the new peace will only be once again the prelude of a new war, which will ensue some generations hence and will be vaster and more destructive even than the present colossal conflict.

It has been claimed that the aim of the present war is to end war. But war cannot end war, neither can militarism destroy militarism. [. . .]

There are only two forces that can withstand the force of the war's spirit when it seizes upon the world. The one is the force of an independently thinking, free, and articulate democracy. The other is the force of an instructed and enlightened public opinion.

But the democracies, one and all, are utterly impotent in present conditions to inspire, or to criticise, or to direct the foreign policy of their respective nationalities. This condition of things must be brought to an end and some constitutional machinery must be found for the future exercise of democratic control of foreign policy. International treaties and alliances should not be ratified without the consent of the peoples whose destinies they control. In this, and in many other respects, the new epoch must see the rise of a reinforced democracy.

The new force of the woman's movement should be seized upon to further this end. It is vital to the deepest interests of the human race that the mother half of humanity should now be admitted into the ranks of the articulate democracies of the world, in order to strengthen them and to enable them to combine the more effectively in their own defense against the deadly machinery of organized destruction that threatens in the future to crush the white races and to overwhelm civilization.

The bed-rock of humanity is motherhood. The solidarity of the world's motherhood, potential or otherwise, underlies all cleavages of nationality. Men have conflicting interests and ambitions. Women all the world over, speaking broadly, have one passion and one vocation, and that is the creation and preservation of human life. Deep in the hearts of the women of the peasant and industrial classes of every nation, there lies beneath their readiness to endure their full share of their nations' toll of sacrifice and suffering, a denial of the necessity of war. There is a rooted revolt against the destruction of the blossoming manhood of the race. This revolt is now for the first time finding expression, as the race soul of the womanhood of the world comes in this twentieth century to consciousness. The woman's movement has awakened women to their great responsibilities as the natural custodians of the human race. It is vital to the interests of the human race itself that the mother half of humanity should now be admitted to articulate citizenship. The emancipation of women must be included in the program of those who would lay a broad foundation of constructive peace for the rebuilding of the modern world. [. . .]

Since public opinion cannot be educated solely by words, such a campaign, if started, should be linked with certain definite propositions to be decided upon in conference between the men and women who should initiate it. These propositions should be urged as some of the conditions of constructive peace. I tabulate by way of illustration the following suggestions that civilized peoples should unite in demanding from their respective countries.

First, the broadening and strengthening of the democracies by the admission of the mother-half of the human race into the body politic.

Second, the creation, where none already exists, of some adequate machinery for insuring democratic control of foreign policy.

Third, the assurance that no treaty arrangement or undertaking be entered upon, in the name of the country, without the sanction of the people concerned expressed through their representatives.

Fourth, that the manufacture of armaments and ammunition be taken over by the nation itself, and that the export of armaments to other countries be prohibited.

Fifth, that at the termination of the war, the influence of the nation be used to discourage the transfer of any of the European provinces from one government to another without the consent by plebiscite of the population of such province, and that the plebiscite should include the women who have borne the burden of suffering equally with the men.

Sixth, that there should be some representation of women at the Hague conference.

In addition to such concrete proposals as these, public opinion has to be enlightened and organized towards the ideal of international agreement. "We must labor," as says ex-President [Theodore] Roosevelt, "for an international agreement among the great civilized nations which shall put the full force of all of them, back of anyone of them, and of any well-behaved weak nation which is wronged by any other power."

By the initiation throughout the [United] States of a popular campaign carried out upon lines indicated by these suggestions, led by influential men and women, aided by the President, reinforced by great public meetings, America would give a much needed lead to the democracies of Europe.

The better, happier world that we hope for in the future must be built up by the people themselves, upon the foundations of a constructive, lasting peace. This task cannot be left to the detached and secret agencies of Governments. It should be begun now. There is not a moment to lose.

"Motherhood and War," *Harper's Weekly* 59 (December 5, 1914), 542.

✝ Adelheid Popp
(1869–1939) *Austrian*

One of five surviving children in a family of fifteen headed by an alcoholic Austrian weaver, Adelheid Popp received only three years of formal education before she went to work at age ten. Self-educated, she read novels when she was not working as a domestic or in a factory. After Popp joined the labor movement, she founded an educational union for working women in 1890 and became editor of *The Women Workers' Paper* (1891–1934). As a leader of the Austrian Social Democratic women's movement, Popp demanded the vote in 1911, "because we are womanly and motherly," factors that she believed influenced women's contributions to public relief, housing, and schooling at the local level. In spite of her lack of education she published numerous books, including two volumes of autobiography, *Jugendgeschichte einer Arbeiterin* (Youth of a woman worker, 1909) and *Erinnerungen* (Memories, 1915), both of which fuse personal experience with a call for women's rights as workers. Popp wrote a history of the women's Social Democratic movement, and treatises on women's labor. From 1919 to 1934 she was a member of the Austrian National Assembly.

✝ An Appeal to Women from Austrian Socialist Women

Vienna, January 1915

Dear Comrades:

In our hearts, and I think I have the right to speak in the name of all Socialist working women of Austria, the longing is alive to see the end of this terrible war.

The blood of our relatives, friends, and comrades is being shed on the battlefields, and we do not call only the workers of Austria and Germany our own. The workers of Britain, Belgium, France, Russia and Servia are just as dear to us, and we know they have, just as our slaughtered workers have, mothers, wives and children who weep for them. Nothing can separate us from the working class of other nations but the frontiers. We are conscious, even if we speak in different tongues, that we must take joint action, because the working class of all countries must suffer from the same fate. It appears to us that one of the most terrible consequences of the war is the fact that communications between the working men and women of all countries have been cut off. But nevertheless we cannot despair! We are conscious that the brotherhood of the peoples is a historical need, made even more necessary by the miseries of daily life.

We cannot doubt that the Socialist International will be restored, and we are convinced that those Socialists who defend their country with rifle and sword are longing like us for the time when they will again be able to press the hands of the "enemy"!

We women, although we are not at war, daily witness the terrible consequences of the war, and when we look at our returning soldiers we consider it our duty to work hard in order to prevent estrangement and national hatred hindering the future action of the working class International. The command of Christ, "Thou shalt love," has been taken over by the Socialists. We are proud that feelings of international sympathy and friendship have so strongly taken root, and we consider it the duty of all Socialists to do all in their power to see that these feelings are not extinguished. And, therefore, I am glad to have the opportunity to speak to the comrades of Britain and to tell them that the Socialist women of Austria have not a moment forgotten their ideals.

We are deeply longing for the end of this war! We have no greater wish than to be able to cooperate again in fastening strongly and indestructibly the tie which unites all peoples.

Adelheid Popp
Leader of Socialist Women of Austria

From *A Group of Letters from Women of the Warring Nations* (Chicago: Woman's Peace Party, 1915).

✝ Lida Gustava Heymann
(1868–1943) *German*

L
ida Heymann used the wealth she inherited from her merchant family in 1896 to found a girls' school, a day nursery, and a cafeteria for working women. By 1898 she was working in Hamburg through an association for women's welfare to abolish police regulation (and control) of prostitution; although her meetings were banned by the police and she lost abolitionist suits against the police, she achieved publicity for her cause. A liberal philosophy of individual freedom and rights guided her feminism, manifest in publications on sexual hygiene, female suffrage, and women's relation to the state. She belonged to a major association for women's suffrage (Deutscher Verband für Frauenstimmrecht), founded in 1902, and threatened to refuse to pay her taxes if not allowed to vote. In 1912 she resigned from the movement concerned with liberalizing laws on prostitution in order to devote herself to suffrage. With her lifelong friend Anita Augspurg, leader of a radical suffrage society (Deutscher Frauenstimmrechtsbund), she criticized the socialist party for neglecting the question of women's rights; however, the splintering of the suffrage movement contributed to its defeat. She also supported the "new morality" movement, advocating the legal equality of women within marriage, equal rights for children of unsanctioned unions, and the right to contraception.

In 1899 Heymann and Augspurg led a campaign for German participation in a demonstration for peace. She became an Independent Social Democrat during the war to defend her antiwar position. She held that this was a "men's war" between "men's states." With Augspurg she attended the international women's peace congress at The Hague in 1915. Heymann argued that "women who sincerely fight for pacifism must also work for female suffrage," and she expected female franchise to banish war forever. "It should never be forgotten that the complexity of modern male states makes it impossible that great catastrophic outbreaks like war be prevented by a few people outside leadership positions—in this case

women. It verges on irresponsible ignorance to charge women with having
been able to prevent the world war and with having done nothing." When
her suffrage league took pacifist positions it was censored and its meetings
banned from March 1916 onward; it survived in part through its social
work, using international contacts to help families maintain links with prisoners of war. The police monitored its work in Munich as a threat to public security. In early 1915 she published a pamphlet that was censored after
it was reprinted in *Die Frauenbewegung* on February 15; on November 23,
1915, she was barred from public speech, and on February 11, 1917, she
was expelled officially from Bavaria and forced into hiding.

In 1919 Heymann ran unsuccessfully for the National Assembly. On holiday in Italy when the Nazis seized power, the sixty-five-year-old Heymann
and her friend Augspurg went into exile in Switzerland in 1933. They wrote
a joint memoir, *Erlebtes, erschautes* (What we have lived, seen, 1972).

✝ An Appeal to Women from a German Woman

Munich

Women of Europe, when will your call ring out?

Summer's glory was shattered by the lightning of the most frightful of
all wars, and all Europe was set on fire.

Women of all the belligerent States, with head high and courageous
heart, gave their husbands to protect the Fatherland. Mothers and maidens unfalteringly let their sons and sweethearts go forth to death and
destruction.

At home women labored and strove without pause or rest to provide
against the spiritual, physical, and economic distress resulting from the
crisis. Summer passed, autumn came and went, we are now in mid-winter.

Millions of men have been left on the battlefield. They will never see
home again. Others have returned, broken and sick in body and soul.
Towns of the highest civilization, homes of simple human happiness, are
destroyed; Europe's soil reeks of human blood. The flesh and blood of
men will fertilize the soil of the waving cornfields of the future on German, French, Belgian, and Russian ground.

Millions of women's hearts blaze up in anguish. No human speech is
rich enough to express such depths of suffering.

Shall this war of extermination go on?

Women of Europe, where is your voice?

Are you only great in patience and suffering?

The earth reeking of human blood, the millions of wrecked bodies and
souls of your husbands, sweethearts and sons, the outrages inflicted on
your sex. Can these things not rouse you to blazing protest?

In South Europe men have come together to exchange words of peace. In the North of Europe men have met to work for peace.

Women of Europe, where is your voice, that should be sowing seeds of peace? Do not let yourselves be deterred by those who accuse you of weakness because you wish for peace, who say you cannot hold back the bloody march of history by your protest.

Strive at least to put a spoke in the bloody wheel of Time, with strength, courage, and humanity worthy of your sex.

Come together in the North or South of Europe, protest with all your might against this war, which is murdering the nations, and make preparations for peace; return to your own country and perform your duty as wives and mothers, as protectors of true civilization and humanity.

From *A Group of Letters from Women of the Warring Nations* (Chicago: Woman's Peace Party, 1915).

✟ Nelly Roussel
(1878–1922) *French*

As a child, Nelly Roussel had little formal education but read eagerly. In 1898 she married the feminist Henri Godet; when her activism took her on the lecture circuit, her children were cared for by her mother and sister. Pretty, young, married, and a mother, she was an invincible, exceptionally eloquent lecturer for the radical feminist movement. A freethinker and neo-Malthusian, she wanted economic recognition of household work and maternity, but believed that true liberation from biological determinism would only be achieved through contraception, and, if necessary, abortion. "Woman is the sole mistress of her own body," she argued, and she held free choice of maternity to be the sacred right of the individual. Over two decades she wrote two hundred articles on topics related to feminism, women's control over their bodies, and the needs of the working classes.

During the war she opposed jingoism and natalism, defending socialist pacifist politics and becoming a member of the League of Women Against War. At the trial of feminist pacifist Hélène Brion she stood witness for her friend. Roussel rejected a proposal by the nationalist deputy Maurice Barrès that the widows, fathers, or mothers (in that order) inherit the right to vote from dead soldiers: "We do not want to vote by procuration, as delegates, or supplicants. We want to vote as free citizens." Roussel collaborated on *La voix des femmes* (Women's voice) and *La libre pensée internationale* (International free thought), in which her article on atrocities appeared. While she advocated revolutionary propaganda among women's milieux, she also leveled a feminist critique against the "unconscious masculinism" of revolutionaries. She died at age forty-four of tuberculosis.

JS

✝ On Atrocities

In France, the official publication of "German atrocities" has begun. Many are pleased. Some, among whom I count myself, are disturbed. It seems to me inopportune; and I fear that at present it can only lead to two results: at the least pullback of our lines, to terrify the population in regions near the field of battle; and in case we invade Germany, to incite our soldiers to horrifying reprisals.

On the contrary, if it had been a little delayed, put off until the end of hostilities, such a publication might have been healthy . . . on condition, however, that its true character remain clear. It should be presented in a way that would not overheat international hatreds in opposing the German demon to the French angel but would inspire everywhere a salutary terror of the curse that inevitably gives birth to so much useless suffering and dishonorable crime. For all this, it is war itself, war alone that is responsible; war which, even if it sometimes exalts a few fine sentiments, exacerbates or unleashes all the brutal and gross instincts that are so painfully repressed in peacetime by education . . . and by the police; war which in obscuring the conscience of the best transforms doubtful or bad elements into ferocious beasts, whom our great modern armies are unable to expel.—The German people is neither more barbarous nor more abject than any other people. What its soldiers do in Belgium and in France does not differ from what invaders have always done in an invaded country. And the present war does not differ from others except by the length of the line of fire, the number of combatants, and the perfection of engines of destruction.

Is it not extraordinary that it is necessary to state these elementary truths? Isn't it extraordinary that, faced with the revelation of murders and rapes, pillage and fire, we find Germans who protest and Frenchmen who are astonished? Is it not extraordinary that among these two peoples, there are those capable of believing that a war could be not "atrocious"? . . . Ah! what madmen! madmen! . . . perhaps I should write: criminals!—For we have every reason to suppose that these people were among those who pressed for the great conflict, out of ignorance of its abominable side effects and disastrous consequences, by which conqueror and conquered will long remain, alas, equally battered and torn.

La libre pensée internationale, February 6, 1915

"Atrocités," in *Derniers combats* (Paris: L'Émancipatrice, 1932), 63–64.

✝ Hedwig Dohm, née Schlesinger
(1833–1919) *German*

The eleventh of eighteen children of a tobacco manufacturer, Hedwig Schlesinger left school at fifteen, while her brothers were given further education. The Revolution of 1848 in Berlin, which she experienced as a teenager, radicalized her politically. Her training as a schoolteacher was abandoned when in 1852 she married the journalist Ernst Dohm, who later became editor in chief of the satirical Berlin paper *Kladderadatsch*; they had five children.

Until her husband's death when she was fifty, Dohm's home drew such Berlin intellectuals as the socialist and suffragist Ferdinand Lassalle, the naturalist and statesman August von Humboldt, novelist Fanny Lewald, and writers Theodor Fontane and Friedrich von Varnhagen. In her thirties she began to write comedies, novellas, and five novels marked by her radical feminist ideas—such as the right of older women to sexual self-expression. The novella *Wie Frauen Werden* (How women evolve, 1894) and her other novels explore the social exclusions that govern women's lives at different ages. When forty, she launched a career as a polemicist on women's issues, with boldly titled tracts: *Jesuitism in the Household* (1873), *Women's Nature and Rights* (1876), *The Antifeminists* (1902), and *Woman's Education for the Vote* (1909). She defended the economic, political, and intellectual independence of women; although she did not belong to formal organizations, she knew and worked with leaders in various branches of the women's movement including Helene Lange, Alice Salomon, and Lily Braun.

✝ The Misuse of Death

1915

Dear, old, most faithful Friend! Help me in this moment of spiritual need! I understand nothing of politics. I need your clear objectivity, your unerring logic. With a gloomy shudder I endure this world war. At night I cannot sleep. I cannot escape hallucinations about streams of blood through which I must wade, about frightful screams that burst from white lips, about eyes that never cease weeping. My food is poisoned; the flowers in my room disgust me—how they smell, smell!—senseless, thrust into this great dying. Help me, or I will give way to the psychosis of war.

To you alone will I tell all my thoughts; if I told others, they would stone me. For I cannot go along with the wartime fashion of patriotically parading pathos. The most contradictory feelings consume my heart. You see, this war for me is Janus-faced. One side resembles the Medusa. Whoever sees it is petrified by horror. The other has sublime beauty. At the beginning of the war I saw only the Medusa head, and thought: Christ died in vain, he left his work of salvation incomplete. The power of darkness still reigns, as it did a thousand years ago. In war the laws of humanity are suspended, set back to their starting point. We were caught in an enormous error. We believed in the inner culture of European people. We must relearn. It was only varnish and whitewash. The animal, the beast of prey, remained within. Now it has broken out again and with the same rending savagery as that which raged millennia ago. I perish at this recognition. How shall I grasp the horrible madness of the thought that millions of innocent creatures mutually throttle each other, who have never harmed each other! "The person who does not lose his sanity over certain things has none to lose." The most certain of these things is war. [. . .]

Shall I tear up this letter before your bright eyes darken over it?—Didn't I already say that I am completely uneducated politically? But they always claim that women do not need to know anything, learn anything; they know everything intuitively, by feeling, from within. You see what comes out of this mere feeling: the fever of a war psychosis that sees in war only slaughter, not the spirit that hovers above the streams of blood.—Does it hover? Is that your opinion?

No—no—don't you see them?—the many, many blessedly grimacing corpses? Woe, woe! They rise up from their mass graves. Shadows, yet out of terrible wounds stream rivers of blood. Thirstily, thirstily the earth drinks them and steams as if with a bloody fire, whose sparks spray my heart. I must weep every day, every day and every night I must weep forevermore. [. . .]

And my eyes slip over to the second Janus face.

And I hear and read hymns about the "blessedness of death in battle." "War is a religion, war is life, not death." And I read "that in the protracted peace earth became impoverished, narrow, lacking in charm, and that envy and pain burrow in the souls of those who with a daily rumble and squabble of malice slip into familiar old patterns of work, while others exultingly march off to war, ready for death." War promises a fresh becoming and growth for humanity. "War," or so announces an enthusiast, "must exist to realize the concept of humanity." [. . .]

Perhaps the "enthusiasm" for this war was "deep and true." What does that prove? Deep and true as well was the pious ardor, the holy conviction with which heretics and witches were once burned in honor of God and for the salvation of their souls. One can become as enthusiastic for error and superstition (not excluding stupidity) as for truths that bear the stamp of eternity! [. . .]

Let that be our proclamation to those who come: Death to the misuse of death in war! Life to the living, in peace unto its natural fulfillment.

Die Aktion, August 1917

Der Mißbrauch des Todes (Berlin: Die Aktion, 1917).

✝ Aletta Jacobs
(1854–1929) *Dutch*

Aletta Jacobs grew up in an educated doctor's family; she was the eighth child of ten. Following in the footsteps of her father and oldest brother, Jacobs resolved when still a child to study medicine. Given instead a conventional girl's upbringing, she was taught handicrafts, a bit of French, and "good manners," then (when she insisted on leaving her school for ladies) trained in housework and dressmaking. Eventually her unhappiness forced her family to permit her to prepare an examination for pharmacists' assistants and to attend classes at the University of Groningen. "I thought to myself, 'If a woman can become a pharmacist, then she's also capable of being a doctor.' " She became the first woman in the Netherlands to graduate from a university, becoming a physician in 1879.

Jacobs was a passionate combatant for women's rights, who sought to alleviate women's sufferings. From 1879 to 1904, in her practice in Amsterdam, Jacobs held free clinics for working women, where she prescribed contraception, thereby incurring the wrath of the medical establishment. She translated Charlotte Perkins Gilman's *Women and Economics* (1898) and Olive Schreiner's *Woman and Labour* (1941) and campaigned for female suffrage, as she accompanied her husband, Carel Victor Gerritson, to meetings of the Interparliamentary Union.

Having absorbed pacifist values from her father, Jacobs viewed the "armed forces as an unmitigated evil." When war broke out, as president of the Association for Woman Suffrage she convened an emergency meeting of the board, which decided to shift focus to war relief for the wives of soldiers. When she heard in October 1914 that the International Woman Suffrage Alliance conference planned for June 1915 in Berlin was to be canceled, she began work to unite women on the neutral territory of the Netherlands. In her *Memories* (1924) she recalls, "I wanted to call on women from every nation to protest together against the horrors of war. Perhaps we could even find a way to end the hostilities." With Jane

Addams she organized the International Congress of Women at The Hague, attended by 1,136 women from twelve countries between April 28 and May 1, 1915. Her call to women of warring and neutral nations, distributed around the world, was printed in the monthly of the International Women's Suffrage Association.

Among the resolutions passed at the conference were a call for women's suffrage, self-determination, democratic control of foreign policy, arbitration of international disputes, international "pressure" to isolate any country that resorts to arms, and education in peace. Article 8 specifically protests against the assertion that war means the protection of women, calling attention to the suffering of women, as in rape, which is tacitly underreported by the consent of men.

The report was circulated to heads of state in Europe and America, to both warring and neutral nations (Jacobs saw President Woodrow Wilson). The congress also established an International Committee of Women for Permanent Peace, which at the Zurich conference in 1919 changed its name to the Women's International League for Peace and Freedom. After the armistice, Jacobs worked to facilitate the repatriation of prisoners of war, pressing the International Red Cross to handle the continuing task of repatriation and to relieve the Russian famine. Then her health and stamina gave way under the impact of "the extreme emotions of the war years," and she turned to writing her memoirs and to quiet study.

AF

✝ Call to the Women of All Nations

Holland, 1915

From many countries appeals have come asking us to call together an International Women's Congress to discuss what the women of the world can do and ought to do in the dreadful times in which we are now living.

We women of the Netherlands, living in a neutral country, accessible to the women of all other nations, therefore take upon ourselves the responsibility of calling together such an International Congress of Women. We feel strongly that at a time when there is so much hatred among nations, we women must show that we can retain our solidarity and that we are able to maintain a mutual friendship.

Women are waiting to be called together. The world is looking to them for their contribution towards the solution of the great problems of to-day.

Women, whatever your nationality, whatever your party, your presence will be of great importance.

The greater the number of those who take part in the Congress, the stronger will be the impression its proceedings will make.

Your presence will testify that you, too, wish to record your protest against this horrible war, and that you desire to assist in preventing a recurrence of it in the future.

Let our call to you not be in vain!

Jus suffragii, March 1, 1915, 245–46.

✝ Jane Addams
(1860–1935) *American*

J ane Addams's mother died when she was two; of the nine children in
her Middle Western family, only four survived childhood. Initially
Addams sought a medical degree but withdrew from school in ill
health; she was then uncertain how to apply her energies. In 1889, with
Ellen Starr, she moved into Hull-House, which became a model for settlement work. Wealthy Chicago women gave her significant support for a
wide range of initiatives promoting cultural activities and mobilizing
politicians to eliminate sweatshop operations and unsafe industries. Her
speeches about such urban problems appeared in *Democracy and Social
Ethics* (1902). *Twenty Years at Hull-House,* her autobiography published in
1910, made her a national figure, and she received an honorary degree
from Yale University that same year. For many years her closest friendship
was with her confidante and travel companion, Mary Smith. A member of
the Progressive party, Addams fought for female suffrage, becoming a
leader of the National American Woman Suffrage Association.

In 1907 her *Newer Ideals of Peace* embraced a multicultural internationalism. In response to the European war, she became chair of the U.S.A.
Woman's Peace party in January 1915; moreover, she helped organize and
presided over the International Congress of Women at The Hague hosted
by Aletta Jacobs in April 1915, traveling afterward to urge heads of state to
accept the principle of continuous mediation. Aware that women would
be accused of inaction and failure to resist a tidal wave of patriotic sentiment, she also recognized that the majority of women (and men)
endorsed the war as a "just" war. After the United States entered the conflict, Addams turned to the task of providing food relief for war victims.
She reviews her wartime activities in *Peace and Bread in Time of War* (1922).
Until her death she was president of the Women's International League
for Peace and Freedom. In 1920 she helped found the American Civil Liberties Union; in 1931 she won the Nobel Peace Prize.

✝ Women and Internationalism

The group of women from five of the European nations who, under the leadership of Dr. Aletta Jacobs of Amsterdam, convened the International Congress of Women at The Hague, were confident that although none of the existing international associations had met since the beginning of the war, the women, including those from the belligerent nations, would be able to come together in all sobriety and friendliness to discuss their common aims and the perilous stake they all held in the war. [. . .]

The fifteen hundred women who came to the Congress in the face of such difficulties must have been impelled by some profound and spiritual forces. During a year when the spirit of internationalism had apparently broken down, they came together to declare the validity of the internationalism which surrounds and completes national life, even as national life itself surrounds and completes family life; to insist that internationalism does not conflict with patriotism on one side any more than family devotion conflicts with it upon the other. [. . .]

The delegates to the Congress were not without a sense of complicity in the war, and so aware of the bloodshed and desolation surrounding them that their deliberations at moments took on the solemn tone of those who talk around the bedside of the dying. It was intimated on the floor of the Congress that the time may come when the exhausted survivors of the war may well reproach women for their inaction during this year. It is possible they may then say that when a perfervid devotion to the ideals of patriotism drove thousands of men into international warfare, the women refused to accept the challenge for the things of the spirit and in that moment of terror they too failed to assert the supreme sanctity of human life. We were told that wounded lads, lying in helpless pain and waiting too long for the field ambulance, call out constantly for their mothers, impotently beseeching them for help; of soldiers who say to their hospital nurses: "We can do nothing for ourselves but go back to the trenches so long as we are able. Cannot the women do something about this war? Are you kind to us only when we are wounded?" There is no one else to whom they dare so speak, revealing the heart of the little child which each man carries within his own even when it beats under a uniform.

The belief that a woman is against war simply because she is a woman and not a man cannot of course be substantiated. In every country there are women who believe that war is inevitable and righteous; the majority of women as well as men in the nations at war doubtless hold that conviction. On the other hand, quite as an artist in an artillery corps commanded to fire upon a beautiful building like the *duomo* at Florence would be deterred by a compunction unknown to the man who had never given himself to creating beauty and did not know the intimate cost of it, so women, who have brought men into the world and nurtured them until they reach the age for fighting, must experience a peculiar revulsion when they see them destroyed, irrespective of the country in which these men may have been born. [. . .]

It was also said at the Congress that the appeals for the organization of the world upon peaceful lines may have been made too exclusively to reason and a sense of justice, that reason is only a part of the human endowment; emotion and deep-set racial impulses must be utilized as well—those primitive human urgings to foster life and to protect the helpless, of which women were the earliest custodians, and even the social and gregarious instincts that we share with the animals themselves. These universal desires must be given opportunities to expand and to have a recognized place in the formal organization of international relations which, up to this moment, have rested so exclusively upon purely legal foundations in spite of the fact that international law is comparatively undeveloped. There is an international commerce, a great system of international finance, and many other fields in which relationships are not yet defined in law, quite as many of our most settled national customs have never been embodied in law at all. It would be impossible to adjudicate certain of the underlying economic and social causes of this war according to existing international law and this might therefore make more feasible the proposition urged by the Women's Congress at The Hague, of a conference of neutral nations composed of men who have had international experience so long and so unconsciously that they have come to think not merely in the terms but in the realities of internationalism and would therefore readily deal with the economic and human element involved in the situation. Such a conference would represent not one country or another, but human experience as it has developed during the last decades in Europe. It would stand not for "peace at any price," but would seriously and painstakingly endeavor to discover the price to be paid for peace, which should if possible be permanent as well as immediate. [. . .]

A survey of the situation from the humane and social standpoint would consider for instance the necessity of feeding those people in the southeast portion of Europe who are pitifully underfed when there is a shortage of crops, in relation to the possession of warm-water harbors which would enable Russia to send them her great stores of wheat. Such harbors would be considered not in their political significance, as when the blockade of the Bosphorus during the Tripolis War put a stop to the transport of crops from Odessa to the Mediterranean, not from a point of view of the claims of Russia nor the counterclaims of some other nation, but from the point of view of the needs of Europe. [. . .]

Within the borders of every country at war there is released a vast amount of idealism, without which war could never be carried on; a fund which might still be drawn upon when the time for settlement arrives. If the people knew that through final negotiations Europe would be so remade and internationalized that further wars would be impossible, many of them would feel that the death of thousands of young men had not been in vain, that the youth of our generation had thus contributed to the inauguration of a new era in human existence. It is, therefore, both because of the precedent in 1815 and at other times of peace negotiations when social reforms have been considered, and because idealism runs high in the warring nations, that the women in the Hague Congress considered it feasible to urge a declaration that "the exclusion of women from citizenship is contrary to the principles of civilization and human right," as one of the fundamental measures embodied in their resolutions for permanent peace.

But perhaps our hopes for such action are founded chiefly upon the fact that the settlement at the end of this war may definitely recognize a fundamental change in the functions of government taking place in all civilized nations, a change evoked as the result of concrete, social, and economic conditions, approximating similarity all over the world. The recent entrance of women into citizenship coming on so rapidly not only in the nations of Europe and America, but discernible in certain Asiatic nations as well, is doubtless one manifestation of this change, and the so-called radical or progressive element in each nation, whether they like it or not, recognize it as such. Nevertheless, there are men in each of these countries even among those who would grant the franchise to women in city and state, to whom it is still repugnant that women should evince an interest in international affairs. These men argue that a woman's municipal vote may be cast for the regulation of contagious diseases, her state vote for protection of working children, and that war no longer obtains between cities or even between states; but because war is still legitimate in settling international difficulties, and because international relations are so much a matter of fortified boundaries and standing armies, that it is preposterous for women who cannot fight, to consider them. [. . .] Only in time of war is government thrown back to its primitive and sole function of self-defence, belittling for the moment the many other real interests of which it is the guardian. War moreover has always treated the lives of men and women broadly, as a landscape painter who suppresses all details— "The man bold, combative, conquering; woman sympathetic, healing the wounds that war has made."

But because this primitive conception of the function of government and of the obsolete division between the lives of men and women has obtained during the long months of the European war, there is obviously great need at the end of the war that women should attempt, in an organized capacity, to make their contribution to that governmental internationalism between the nations which shall in some measure approximate the genuine internationalism already developed in so many directions among the peoples. [. . .]

Is it too much to hope that the good will and the consciousness of common aims and responsibilities can be extended to include all the European nations and that devices for international government can be provided, able to deal in the interests of the whole with each difficult situation as it arises? The very experience of this war should demonstrate its feasibility and the analogy inevitably suggests itself that as the states of Germany and Italy came together under the pressure of war, possibly this larger federation may be obtained under the same sense of united effort.

Out of the present situation, which certainly "presents the spectacle of the breakdown of the whole philosophy of nationalism, political, racial, and cultural," may conceivably issue a new birth of internationalism, founded not so much upon arbitration treaties, to be used in time of disturbance, as upon governmental devices designed to protect and enhance the fruitful processes of coöperation in the great experiment of living together in a world become conscious of itself.

"Women and Internationalism," in *Women at the Hague: The International Congress of Women and Its Results* (New York: Macmillan, 1915), 124–41.

✝ Nellie Letitia McClung, née Mooney
(1873–1951) *Canadian*

The youngest of six children in a family that had settled in Manitoba, Nellie Mooney grew up in a progressive Methodist environment, scorning the "dull brown primer of Canadian history" written "from the top down." Trained as a teacher, she was influenced by reform movements on behalf of temperance, social welfare, and female suffrage. In 1896 she married Robert McClung. After her marriage, McClung became a controversial activist, who campaigned for female suffrage first in Manitoba and Alberta, then nationally. She defended her cause by drawing on traditional views of female moral superiority. "All this protective love, this instinctive mother love, must be organized in some way, and made effective."

During the war McClung worked for the Red Cross and the Patriotic Fund, as well as for votes for women. In *In Times Like These* (1915) she eloquently attacked female passivity in the face of mindless warfare as a renunciation of women's duty to save the human race. In recognition of her work, McClung was the only woman named to attend the Canadian War Conference of 1918; in 1938 she was a delegate to the League of Nations.

Elected in 1921 to the Alberta legislature for five years, McClung championed temperance, public health, pensions, women's rights, and birth control. *The Next of Kin* (1917) criticizes land speculation and the soaring wartime cost of living. Over four decades she wrote a two-volume autobiography, *Clearing in the West* (1935) and *The Stream Runs Fast* (1945), a dozen novels, and a collection of short stories.

✝ The War That Ends in Exhaustion Sometimes Mistaken for Peace

Away back in the cave-dwelling days, there was a simple and definite distribution of labor. Men fought and women worked. Men fought because
they liked it; and women worked because it had to be done. Of course the
fighting had to be done too, there was always a warring tribe out looking
for trouble, while their women folk stayed at home and worked. They were
never threatened with a long peace. Somebody was always willing to go 'It.'
The young bloods could always be sure of good fighting somewhere, and
no questions asked. The masculine attitude toward life was: 'I feel good
today; I'll go out and kill something.' Tribes fought for their existence,
and so the work of the warrior was held to be the most glorious of all;
indeed, it was the only work that counted. The woman's part consisted of
tilling the soil, gathering the food, tanning the skins and fashioning garments, brewing the herbs, raising the children, dressing the warrior's
wounds, looking after the herds, and any other light and airy trifle which
might come to her notice. But all this was in the background. Plain useful
work has always been considered dull and drab.

Everything depended on the warrior. When 'the boys' came home
there was much festivity, music, and feasting, and tales of the chase and
fight. The women provided the feast and washed the dishes. The soldier
has always been the hero of our civilization, and yet almost any man makes
a good soldier. Nearly every man makes a good soldier, but not every man,
or nearly every man makes a good citizen: the tests of war are not so
searching as the tests of peace, but still the soldier is the hero.

Very early in the lives of our children we begin to inculcate the love of
battle and sieges and invasions, for we put the miniature weapons of warfare into their little hands. We buy them boxes of tin soldiers at Christmas,
and help them to build forts and blow them up. We have military training
in our schools; and little fellows are taught to shoot at targets, seeing in
each an imaginary foe, who must be destroyed because he is 'not on our
side.' There is a song which runs like this:

> If a lad a maid would marry
> He must learn a gun to carry.

thereby putting love and love-making on a military basis—but it goes! Military music is in our ears, and even in our churches. 'Onward Christian soldiers, marching as to war' is a Sunday-school favorite. We pray to the God
of Battles, never by any chance to the God of Workshops! [. . .]

War is the antithesis of all our teaching. It breaks all the command-
ments; it makes rich men poor, and strong men weak. It makes well men
sick, and by it living men are changed to dead men. Why, then, does war

continue? Why do men go so easily to war—for we may as well admit that they do go easily? There is one explanation. They like it! [. . .]

But although men like to fight, war is not inevitable. War is not of God's making. War is a crime committed by men and, therefore, when enough people say it shall not be, it cannot be. This will not happen until women are allowed to say what they think of war. Up to the present time women have had nothing to say about war, except pay the price of war—this privilege has been theirs always.

History, romance, legend and tradition having been written by men, have shown the masculine aspect of war and have surrounded it with a false glory and have sought to throw the veil of glamour over its hideous face. Our histories have followed the wars. Invasions, conquests, battles, sieges make up the subject-matter of our histories.

Some glorious soul, looking out upon his neighbors, saw some country that he thought he could use and so he levied a heavy tax on the people, and with the money fitted out a splendid army. Men were called from their honest work to go out and fight other honest men who had never done them any harm; harvest fields were trampled by their horses' feet, villages burned, women and children fled in terror, and perished of starvation, streets ran blood and the Glorious Soul came home victorious with captives chained to his chariot wheel. When he drove through the streets of his own home town, all the people cheered, that is, all who had not been killed, of course.

What the people thought of all this, the historians do not say. The people were not asked or expected to think. Thinking was the most unpopular thing they could do. There were dark damp dungeons where hungry rats prowled ceaselessly; there were headsmen's axes and other things prepared for people who were disposed to think and specially designed to allay restlessness among the people. [. . .]

The People were a great abstraction, infinite in number, inarticulate in suffering—the people who fought and paid for their own killing. The man who could get the people to do this on the largest scale was the greatest hero of all and the historian told us much about him, his dogs, his horses, the magnificence of his attire.

Some day, please God, there will be new histories written, and they will tell the story of the years from the standpoint of the people, and the hero will not be any red-handed assassin who goes through peaceful country places leaving behind him dead men looking sightlessly up to the sky. The hero will be the man or woman who knows and loves and serves. In the new histories we will be shown the tragedy, the heartbreaking tragedy of war, which like some dreadful curse has followed the human family, beaten down their plans, their hopes, wasted their savings, destroyed their homes, and in every way turned back the clock of progress. [. . .]

War proves nothing. To kill a man does not prove that he was in the wrong. Bloodletting cannot change men's spirits, neither can the evil of men's thoughts be driven out by blows. If I go to my neighbor's house, and break her furniture, and smash her pictures, and bind her children captive, it does not prove that I am fitter to live than she—yet according to the ethics of nations it does. I have conquered her and she must pay me for my trouble; and her house and all that is left in it belongs to my heirs and successors forever. That is war!

War twists our whole moral fabric. The object of all our teaching has been to inculcate respect for the individual, respect for human life, honor and purity. War sweeps that all aside. The human conscience in these long years of peace, and its resultant opportunities for education, has grown tender to the cry of agony—the pallid face of a hungry child finds a quick response to its mute appeal; but when we know that hundreds are rendered homeless every day, and countless thousands are killed and wounded, men and boys mowed down like a field of grain, and with as little compunction, we grow a little bit numb to human misery. What does it matter if there is a family north of the track living on soda biscuits and turnips? War hardens us to human grief and misery.

War takes the fit and leaves the unfit. The epileptic, the consumptive, the inebriate, are left behind. They are not good enough to go out to fight. So they stay at home, and perpetuate the race! Statistics prove that the war is costing fifty millions a day, which is a prodigious sum, but we would be getting off easy if that were all it costs. The bitterest cost of war is not paid by us at all. It will be paid by the unborn generations, in a lowered vitality, the loss of a strong fatherhood, which they have never known. Napoleon lowered the stature of the French by two inches, it is said. That is one way to set your mark on your generation. [. . .]

There is a curative power in human life just as there is in nature. When the pot boils—it boils over. Evils cure themselves eventually. But it is a long hard way. Yet it is the way humanity has always had to learn. Christ realized that when he looked down at Jerusalem, and wept over it: 'O Jerusalem, Jerusalem, how often I would have gathered you, as a hen gathereth her chickens under her wings, but *you would not.*' That was the trouble then, and it has been the trouble ever since. Humanity has to travel a hard road to wisdom, and it has to travel it with bleeding feet.

But it is getting its lessons now—and paying double first-class rates for its tuition!

"The War That Ends in Exhaustion Sometimes Mistaken for Peace," in *In Times Like These* (1915; reprint, Toronto: University of Toronto Press, 1972), 14–18 (page citations are from reprint edition).

✝ Gertrud Bäumer
(1873–1954) *German*

The daughter of a Protestant school inspector who died when she was ten, Bäumer had a quiet childhood. She studied in Halle and Magdeburg to become an elementary schoolteacher in 1892, and taught for six years in a girls' school. In 1898 she moved to Berlin to study philosophy, earning her doctorate in 1904. Helene Lange drew her into the women's movement. From 1893 Bäumer and Lange published the newspaper *Die Frau,* and between 1901 and 1906 they published *Handbuch der Frauenbewegung* (Handbook of the women's movement). From 1910 to 1919 she led the Bund Deutscher Frauenvereine (Union of German Women's Organizations), which worked for women's employment and welfare and entered debates over prostitution, suffrage, and morality. Her political philosophy was nationalist, interventionist, and essentialist. A woman's importance, she maintained, lay in her "female nature" and the development of her female abilities.

When war broke out, she set up the Nationaler Frauendienst (National Women's Service), a cartel to organize women's welfare work. She published *Der Krieg und die Frau* (War and woman, 1914), *Die Lehren des Weltkriegs für die deutsche Pädagogik* (The lessons of the World War for German pedagogy, 1915), and *Weit hinter den Schützengräben* (Far behind the trenches, 1916), a collection of diary entries. Her wartime essays in *Die Frau* welcomed the war as an opportunity to win recognition for women. As late as October 22, 1918, she issued a declaration rejecting punitive conditions of peace and condemning the proposed League of Nations. Bäumer celebrated women's work but also explored ways to meet lower-class women's dramatically increased wartime needs and recognized the suffering wrought by war. She was a maternalist feminist, but argued against natalist politics in a military context: she rejected the argument that women should produce children to be slaughtered on the battlefield. She worked to improve the conditions of working women within a framework of national identity.

After women were granted the vote, she entered politics; she was a delegate from 1920 to 1933 for the German Democratic Party in the Reichs-tag, where the issues that preoccupied her were education and child wel-fare. A nationalist concerned with women's issues, she continued to publish when other feminist journals disappeared under the Nazis; in 1932 she said that the system of governance does not matter as long as it includes women. However, Hitler's seizure of power excluded her from active politics. She became a novelist, historian, and biographer (writing on Dante, Fichte, Goethe, Rilke, Luise Otto Peters, and Ricarda Huch), publishing dozens of books in her lifetime.

✝ The Woman at the Plow

The song of the threshing machine spreads through the air, rising and falling with the September wind, but as unbroken as the bright melody of these unchanging days. In indescribable transparence the earth rests sweetly exhausted. The young seed's damp smell under spring rain, the anxious ripeness in dark blue summer days, the intoxicating mown hay under heavy storm skies—all that has passed. And now a slack wind, thin clear air, a gentle sun play over her naked breast. The high pale sky, wide yearning horizon, firs and heather are warmed to the heart; spider threads flash like solid rays.

Homeland—homeland!

Suddenly they stand before the festive light blue: the brown field horse, the plow, and the woman. They sprang up where the stubble flows away quietly over the curve of the earth. With firm lines and strong colors, close and telling, heavy reproachful reality in the mild, silvery, late-summer dream.

The horse rhythmically nods his great brown head, his mane gleams in the sun as it spills over the worn harness onto his lowered, tired neck. The stubble crackles under hooves that break the peace of the earth with a hollow ring. The blue apron of the woman flutters in the wind, a white sunbonnet hides her face, the weathered skirt beats against rough stock-ings and dusty formless shoes. She steps with a plowman's broad steps measured by the length of the heavy hooves before her, holds the line taut in brown hands, steps with a labored, strained motion, whose hard-ness always reaches beyond the mass of her woman's body. The ploughshare flashes, rough cords leap and tighten, loose clods fall, a cloud of dust trails her.

And as the three, silent, true, and alone dutifully transform strip after strip of the bright hard field into dark clods, it seems as if something springs from this dreamy earth, shakes itself, opens its eyes wide, as if a wrathful fist takes all this bright gaiety that loosely veils the golden gleam-ing field and satin woods and tears it, crumples it, and flings it aside—trickery and dream, begone!

The distant cruel present breaks through the still circle of this sunny hour, bursts in blustering, fills and floods everything.

Yes. Somewhere outside there grenades burst over the silent blond sons of this land. Somewhere out there is the clumsy, mute man who used to harness the brown horse, now become guard and weapon, shield and wall, storm and death. Homeland—for him that meant this field and the house behind the firs, the simple daily demands of all that was his and needed him: beast and tree, border and field; work and sleep, healing Sunday rest, children's glee and the wife's care. Homeland—today that means a noble, holy power, divinely distant and divinely near, that has exacted his poor destiny for Her higher, greater needs. And Her call struck him like the call of a ripe field and his hungry beasts: the imperative conjuration of his deepest, inmost faith.

Now—as she casts a stone to the field's edge she raises her face. A discreet face, not eloquent but simple. No expression but attention to work. Her soul follows the iron in the brown earth, the heavy step of the horse that she drives and curbs; the approach that must be, to which her worn-out limbs have belonged, as long as she can remember. The dumb demand of the earth and her duty are tightly intertwined. She has no rights of her own next to the clod that must receive her seed. Neither this hitherto unknown sense of abandonment, nor this dull amazement at the incomprehensible foreign powers who reached suddenly into her life, nor the natural limit of her womanly power has anything to say before the simple daily law that she follows when she leads the horse from the stall, because the time has come to plow.

In the distant glittering capital where they know and see everything, it is calculated and recorded that in the war year of 1914 a greater German surface was harvested than in the preceding year of peace. The woman at the plow knows nothing of this. But the homeland, which through her and the man at the front grew out of long, simple familiarity high into hard majesty, raises the mute work of their faith into a deathless history of grandeur and splendor.

Fall 1915

"Die Frau am Pfluge," in *Weit hinter den Schützengräben: Aufsätze aus dem Weltkrieg* (Jena: Eugen Diederichs, 1916), 125–27. Reprinted by permission of Eugen Diederichs Verlag GmbH.

✦ Vieille Ortie
Italian

V ieille Ortie was probably the pseudonym (old Thistle) of a contributor to *La difesa delle lavoratrici,* the socialist fortnightly for women
workers edited by Anna Kuliscioff.

✦ The Falsehood of Maternal Love

One of the things destined to be swept away by war as rhetorical fiction
and baroque convention is the familiar legend of maternal love. Never has
the mother been more inert, more absent, more passive than in this time
of universal pain, of immolated victims, of holocausts, of sacrifices. Just
what virtue lies in the mother-woman's vaunted feeling, which poets and
writers have extolled as an agent of heroism and abnegation? How have
grandeur, will, or strength been manifested by this instinct, which sublime
poets have passed off on us as a prodigious tendency to altruism and self-
sacrifice?

Millions of women, millions of mothers have been separated from their
children, millions of these "heroines" of the most miraculous love have
been parted from the most beautiful, the healthiest, the most able-bodied
creatures; if we believe in legend, then millions of mothers have had their
hearts amputated, their wombs lacerated; and yet, no one has screamed
out. No one has uttered a cry, attempted a gesture, dared a defense,
expressed her desperation, her agony, her rebellion. Have any of you
heard of women in Germany, in Russia, or in France opposing the
recruitment of their children, or invading the barracks, or blocking the
gates to stations? No. No one has breathed a word. [. . .]

Some time ago in England thousands of women dashed into noisy public demonstrations to conquer a political right, aware of the dangers and

risks they were facing: they were women whom intellectual evolution had transformed into citizens, that is, beings capable of feeling the power of a principle, the beauty of an abstraction, the value of progress and of an ideal cause.

But the mother-woman has not as yet undergone this evolution. The mother is still in the primordial state of animality. The love that she bears the creature to which she gave life is neither better nor different than that which any female animal bears its offspring. But worse: no female animal would so easily yield the little ones of her brood to the executioner, and if she knew why they were being taken away from her, she would not remain passive and inert before the prospect of slaughter.

In this tragic aspect of war, maternal love, like so many other literary lies, has been most formidably disproven. The fact that no mother has known how to put her arm courageously between her son and the gendarme come to get him, that none has felt the sublime desperation needed to hopelessly lunge to protect him, for the defense and safekeeping of many others, disproves forever the legend that maternal love is the greatest and most heroic kind of love.

The emotional sensitivity attributed to woman because of her greater impressionability, is probably false. Perhaps the idea of a woman's love, emotion, tenderness, is nothing but rhetoric and fiction, or just weak nerves. At heart, she is mean and vile.

Try to send someone to requisition legally her most inviolable, dearest possessions: her bed, her jewelry, her last possessions. What would happen? An uprising, a mass rebellion. We would see women furiously and desperately grasping these goods, defending them with tooth and nail. There would be a revolt in every home. Each object would give rise to a battle. And there would be a general convulsion, a blazing bonfire of anger, a ferocious outbreak of rage and retaliation. Did anything like this happen at the requisition of their sons? Is a son worth less to a mother than a heap of rags or a handful of silver?

I have often seen women's quarrels: relentless and savage quarrels in which passion made features inhuman, and released unheard violence from frail limbs. And I have thought: a revolution of women would be a fearsome thing! But in what cause will women carry out a revolution? In political agitations, in social uprisings, in strikes—in all those demonstrations where a battle for a conquest or for a right is fought—you may see a woman tremble when she is preoccupied about menaced profits or interests. But when it comes to her sons, her acts display nothing other than cowardice and fear. [. . .]

Among bourgeois intellectuals a woman has many ways to mask her cowardice and to make it even seem like a magnanimous virtue. Her superficial and false instruction *ad usum delphini* has imprinted the little official code of moral values in the conscience of woman so that she may, for example, boast of her inaction in the face of war as an expression of patriotic sentiment, or her hostility to political and economic agitation as a sign of her love of order and her respect for the law. A brilliant market-place of conventionalities, of traditional falsehoods, is available to her to justify her critical insufficiency and her social incapacity.

But among the poor classes, where rhetorical pandering has not corrupted or taken root, where life is a hard experience, and suffering is not just a simple literary expression, feelings should be truer and purer, free to develop outside any coercion of conventional deceit, and more in conformity with nature.

Thus mothers should be more simply and more humanly just that—mothers—and their love, unhindered by insidious prejudices, should burn immense and irresistible against the danger that threatens to sweep away a son!

La difesa delle lavoratrici, January 2, 1916

Translated by Sylvia Notini

✝ Maria Gioia
Italian

Maria Gioia was a regular contributor to *La difesa delle lavoratrici* (Defense of women workers), the Italian feminist socialist fortnightly edited by Anna Kuliscioff. Her views were more traditionalist than those of Kuliscioff; her response here to the preceding pseudonymous essay, for example, is maternalist and somewhat utopian.

✝ The Truth of Maternal Love

I have a rational hatred for all idols; I would not raise my voice, or pick up my pen to defend one, not even if the habit of seeing it exposed to the veneration of men or having loved it myself made me feel as though I should. I believe in the evil idols do, rather than the good they have done.

But an article by Vieille Ortie in *La difesa delle lavoratrici* treated as an idol something that for me is truth, light, one of the rare signs testifying to the nobility of the human soul; and she wished to destroy it with irony and violence. I speak of maternal love. I rise to defend it as best I know how, not because one article or even a hundred volumes could ever demolish it, but because our desire to destroy whatever is unjust or harmful must not lead us to want to overthrow that which has a right to remain; and because the truth we feel within must not be silenced.

Where did Vieille Ortie derive the pessimism to make her say maternal love is a literary lie? to place the female animal above woman, in the degree of affection and will she shows towards her offspring? The actual words of the article do not justify such bitter pessimism. "If it is true," she says, "that a son is like a living part of a woman, then millions of women would have had their hearts amputated in this war."

And they have and they do. Let us recall the old woman at the Bay of

Naples during the Libyan war who died on the spot uttering a single cry when she did not see her son among the wounded, and imagined he was dead; or the woman during the first months of the Austro-Italian war who, after embracing her son, fell dead at his bedside, when she realized what horrible mutilation he had suffered.

Two cases, but we could find a thousand more in the vast world wracked by eighteen months of war. Mortal pain can only be based on love rooted in the whole of one's being, that encloses all the good and all the evil in life. If Vieille Ortie intends to strip maternal love of all the intensity and greatness that no century has denied, that art (very often an expression of truth) has consecrated in pure immortal forms, she may also object that brothers and lovers, too, have died of pain on seeing the dead body, the ruin of their beloved. And it is true. But maternal love differs even from that type of love, not just because it can kill: it differs because of its extent, its duration, its immutability. [. . .]

Maternal love does not suffer the vicissitudes of time and life: it is not transformed by external or intimate causes. A son who moves away from his mother to begin his own family is still a son loved in the same way. At times he will feel his affection for his mother weaken in favor of another woman and their children, but the woman whom he has left, perhaps alone in her house, will not stop loving him. She may have words of sorrow or of rebuke for having been abandoned, but she will attempt to excuse her son; and if a moment of misfortune arrives for him, the first to run to him will be the offended mother, bringing her last penny, her last bit of bread, the words of love from the past, and total oblivion of any wrong suffered.

All affections may be wounded by doubt, destroyed by guilt. Even the affection of a brother for a sister, even, perhaps more so, that of a man for a woman. Tell a brother that his sister has stolen, tell a woman that the man she loves walks the evening streets drunk, that he has committed a sordid crime; they will not want to believe it, but if they are forced to do so, they will want to destroy the love with their own hands, they will want to tear the image from thought, see it as it is with its vice and guilt; or, effortlessly, the image will take shape in all its ugliness.

Tell a mother that her daughter steals, that her son is soiled by guilt. She will weep, find words of painful bitterness, but she will still love those wretched children, possibly even more than before. Perceiving moral deformity like physical deformity, she will find misfortune where others see guilt, and she will cling to her loved ones with desperate courage, the more others abandon or condemn them.

Vieille Ortie might say that it is not love, but irrationality. But perhaps the uncontested sign of love *is* irrationality, and the higher we rise, the more reasoning decreases. But Vieille Ortie says that if maternal love were not a lie, mothers would have stopped their sons from being dragged to war. "Do not female animals stop anyone from taking away their offspring?" As civilization has progressed, woman has learned to reason. Lead the woman of the twentieth century back to the caverns and perhaps she will defend her children like a lioness, like a timid deer, like a voluptuous house cat. Better yet, get someone to attack her child and see whether or not she defends him. But it is the law that takes her son away to war; a law that is formidable, armed, more terrible than ever before, and although she may have lived without truly living in this world, she knows that men have created this force for defence and violence. And remember that when choosing between two evils we always choose the lesser, the more remote. If we were to ask all the mothers of Europe, "Which should go to combat, you or your son?" the mothers of Europe would answer: "Take me!" But there is no choice here, the son is called, and he himself says, "If I don't go they will shoot me!" What is a mother to do? You can come home uninjured from a war, not from an execution. It is not egoism that holds her back, but the concept of a power that cannot be resisted and the terror of aggravating the destiny of a son. [. . .]

Oh, but I do not despair of humanity, I do not despair of the future! This real force of pain and love could acquire power in the world if it is drawn to the light, directed towards a goal, made conscious of itself. There have been some rare moments when women have not only shed tears, but have been capable of splendor. Ask Michelet about the French Revolution: "While men prepared for war, the sun made plans for spring!" And while men make war, in the silence and pain perhaps a new harvest of proposals, ideals, and courage is growing.

La difesa delle lavoratrici, January 16, 1916

Translated by Sylvia Notini

✝ Anna Nikitichna Shabanova
(1848–1932) *Russian*

Born among modest gentry, Anna Shabanova was influenced by the Russian nihilist movement of the 1860s; she spent six months in prison at age seventeen for her membership in a women's dressmaking cooperative that was a front for radical activities. Trained as a doctor, she studied first in Helsinki, then in St. Petersburg, where she graduated from the Women's Medical Academy in 1878, receiving her license as a pediatrician in 1883.

Shabanova was a leader of the women's movement in Russia from the 1890s to the revolution. She helped found the first general women's association, the Russian Women's Mutual Philanthropic Society, in 1895, serving as its president from 1896 to 1917 and recording its history, *Ocherk zhenskago dvizheniya v Rossii* (1912). Barred from political activities until 1905, this society embraced a moderate feminism, especially women's right to the vote. Among its charity projects were nurseries, shelters, and soup kitchens—all places where educational work could also be undertaken. Shabanova lobbied extensively for women's participation in governmental assemblies and other organizations. When the Revolution of 1905 failed to gain the vote for women, Shabanova concluded the Russian woman "was neither recognized as a citizen nor granted human rights, but remained as of old at the washtub while the golden fish concealed herself in the depths of the blue sea."

In 1899 she formed the Women's Committee of the Russian League of Peace, and in 1904 opposed the war with Japan. In 1914, however, Shabanova became a "defensist" patriot, who organized voluntary organizations to care for war victims, refugees, abandoned children and prisoners of war and worked with the governmental War Industries Committee, linking all these wartime contributions to her expectation that women would be enfranchised. Typical of her continuing focus on women's access to full citizenship was her petition to permit women to serve in municipal self-government, which was sent to the *dumas* (councils) of the provinces and capitals and published in early 1916. Shabanova supported the provisional government of Aleksandr Kerensky after it passed legislation granting women the vote. In 1917 she hosted Emmeline Pankhurst and Maria Botchkareva at the Petrograd Astoria Hotel. After 1917 she disappeared from the political arena, but continued her medical practice, which was the subject of another book published in 1926. A pediatric journal in 1928 celebrated her fifty years of medical research, teaching, and service.

✝ Petition

January 1916

The Council of the Russian Women's Mutual Philanthropic Society, the oldest women's society in Russia, considers itself morally obliged to address the following petition to you,[1] in the interest of the homeland.

At present, *in light of the apparent shortage of city workers,* the Ministry of Internal Affairs is deciding whether to expand the circle of individuals who have the right to be selected for the ranks of the city *duma.* Such a wartime shortage, with potentially dire consequences for city management, highlights the need to attract new energy to city government—for which women offer a rich resource. The Russian woman is helping her country in its struggle against the unyielding enemy in all areas of labor, with ever wider scope, and this work, proof not only of selflessness but of civic maturity as well, has been found worthy by the entire country. The loud cry "Everything for the war," an imperious appeal from the throne on high, must destroy those archaic limits which have circumscribed women's work. Russian women pay the same duties and taxes as men, they can meet the qualifications for political rights, they receive professional degrees (doctors, lawyers, engineers, architects, agronomists), and engage independently in commerce and industry. They have proved with their work on municipal boards, in schools, field hospitals, soup kitchens, in the rear and at the front, that they can also be effective workers in any branch of city management. An influx of new energy from the intelligentsia, invested with political rights, doing battle with inflation, the adulteration of provisions, the threat of epidemic illnesses, increasing poverty, and social ills, will undoubtedly mitigate the difficult tasks of city government in these hard times. Considering the demands of contemporary reality, the experience of many European nations where women have long and successfully enjoyed rights in municipal self-government, and the preparedness of the Russian woman, the Council of the Women's Society expresses hope that the representatives of municipal organs of government, in the interest not only of justice but

---

1. This petition was sent to the *dumas,* or councils, of the provinces and capitals. [A.S.]

also of efficacy, will consider it timely to express their opinion in support of reform in this area.

Assuming that you, Sir, will react with the necessary sympathy to the recruitment of women to serve in municipal self-government, the Council of the Russian Women's Society appeals to you with the request that you exercise your influence on the resolution of this question in the appropriate spheres.

With the express hope of receiving a reply to this petition, respectfully yours,

A. Shabanova, Chairwoman of the Board
Council of the Russian Women's Mutual Philanthropic Society

Zhenskii vestnik, January 1916, 11–12

Translated by Cynthia Simmons

✠ Organization of Women Workers, Petrograd Bolshevik Committee

This poster issued in 1916 on International Women's Day, which Clara Zetkin had designated as March 8, was signed by the "Organization of Women Workers." The initial aim of this women's day was to achieve universal suffrage, a vote not limited by sex or property. During the war the majority of Russian women adhered to patriotic goals, but unannounced "flash" meetings to oppose the war and call for suffrage—held on approximately this date—drew several hundred supporters.

✠ International Women's Day Poster

Comrades, Working women! This is the day of our solidarity; the day when the working woman, breaking her ancient bonds of submission, slavery, and humiliation, proudly joins the ranks of the international proletariat for the struggle with the common enemy—capital. Working women! The government has sent our sons to their crucifixion for the sake of capital. So build your own organizations, band together in workshop and factory, office and shop, and let us roar in the face of insatiable capital: "Enough blood! Down with the war. Bring the criminal autocracy to justice!"

Organization of Women Workers
Petrograd Bolshevik Committee
1916

Richard Stites, *The Women's Liberation Movement in Russia: Feminism, Nihilism, and Bolshevism 1860–1930* (Princeton: Princeton University Press, 1978). Copyright © 1978 by Princeton University Press. Used by permission.

✝ Ellen Karolina Sofia Key
(1849–1926) *Swedish*

The oldest of six children in a liberal family of aristocratic lineage, Ellen Key helped raise her younger siblings. She received little formal tutelage, teaching herself to read at the age of five; she was shy and a voracious reader. When her father was elected to the Rikstag in 1869 the family spent part of the year in their southern Swedish village, part in Stockholm, where Ellen attended lectures and wrote articles for political journals. She taught at a workers' institute and an elite women's school, and gradually discovered a gift for public speaking, which she used for women's groups. By fifty she was a full-time public speaker, visiting Finland, Norway, and England on behalf of maternalist-feminist and pacifist causes.

Key's political positions offended both left and right: She fought against women's economic insecurity, especially the wretched conditions of maternity and its dependence on marital status. But she opposed the vote for women. She advocated women's sexual education, equality of economic opportunity, and the rights of labor unions. Her contemporaries admired her charisma and optimism, her "physical and spiritual buoyancy." The Italian poet Ada Negri thought of her "as a liberator of woman's soul." And her friend Anna Whitlock praised "her overestimation of human nature, her bright faith in its swift perfectibility."

TP

✝ The Debit Balance of War

The most highly coloured descriptions of the war give me, at least, a fainter picture of its horrors than the quite spontaneous comparisons, drawn from homely occupations, that one finds in letters written on the battle-fields.

One letter speaks of a river where the dead bodies were floating like timber.

With what sadness have we not often watched the forest's mighty stems carried away in such a stream. Yet one knows that the trees must die so that they may become homes for man. But as the bodies are being carried away in this stream, we know that many homes will fall together for lack of their support.

Another tells how the bullets fell like the grains from a sowing-machine. Only these "grains" did not fall to become bread, but to sow death for many thousands of bread-winners for whom millions of hungry mouths wait in vain.

A third speaks of how the bayonets lifted the bodies of the enemy as the pitchfork the hay. We miss the splendour of the fields when the hay is garnered. But on the battle-fields are garnered the mutilated bodies of the men that, when living, helped to make the people's summer glory.

A fourth says that the ranks were mown down as quickly as one mows a field of clover. How often one lingers with a sigh at the sight of a field of sweet, red clover-heads just felled by the scythe! Yet on the battle-field, the heads that lie as thickly side by side, are the heads of those that should have given us new thoughts, new discoveries, and new creations.

Yet another depicts how they burned the dead in heaps like the withered leaves in autumn. It is with a feeling of regret that we stand at such a pyre of leaves, but we do not resent the destruction, for we know that these withered leaves have lived out a long, glorious summer. On the other hand, the sap was still running in the leaves from the tree of man, and we know that they might have had a long and beautiful summer still before them.

On All Saints' Day the thoughts of millions of men and women went out to the loved ones whom they had lost. And many of these were even deprived of what, especially in Catholic countries, means so much: the comfort of laying flowers and weeping at the graves. Many do not even know where their loved one was lost; no thought can go to the spot where he rests, and no message can come from the place where the light flickered that was the light of life for at least one woman.

No descriptions of the violence of war are more suggestive than those which liken it to an earthquake, a volcanic eruption, and avalanches—natural catastrophes before which man is helpless and which arouse our compassion and generosity for the victims. But the havoc wrought by war, which one compares with the havoc wrought by nature, is not an unavoidable fate before which man stands helpless. The natural forces that are the cause of war are human passions which it lies in our power to change. What are culture and civilization if not the taming of blind forces within us as well as in nature?

One speaks of the outbreak of wars as presenting excellent opportunities for practising compassion and charity. He who does not see that the world is already full of opportunities for practising these virtues without adding to the havoc of volcanoes, earthquakes, storms, and icebergs, must be blind indeed. [. . .]

That war, from the point of view of the individual, is a curse, and not a blessing, goes without saying. Yet there are still many who believe that it is our duty in time of war to put the fate of the individual entirely to one side and consider only the blessing for the nation as a whole.

What are these blessings that fall to the nation as a whole? To discover them one must, to begin with, entirely overlook all the loss and suffering caused by the destruction of material property. Some of these—ancient relics, great works of art, beautiful natural scenery—must remain an irreparable loss for the country as a whole. Likewise, hundreds of thousands of homes have become poorer for all time, through the loss of precious heirlooms such as letters, portraits, furniture, works of art, and buildings with their memories and associations. [. . .]

And, in return for all these material losses and expenses, the victors at least may be able to point to new territory or war indemnities or trade treaties as sources of new wealth.

But for the defeated, the opposite is the case. [. . .] How many things of great value are not already irreparably lost! Everywhere in the world, in neutral countries as well as in warring, people feel themselves robbed. They have lost the ideals that warmed and uplifted them; they are cut off from all international work in the fields of science, literature, and art; they are deprived of the joy they shared with one another in intellectual achievements. The bridges that span the boundary rivers of national prejudices and self-interest will be much more slowly replaced than the physical means of communication.

For in the former case it is a question of a mental state that has been achieved with great difficulty. Innumerable fine-spun cables of mutual response have been destroyed; innumerable lives have been thwarted in their normal trend; innumerable thoughts have been blighted. The billions with which war reduces national capital are as nothing compared with the irretrievable loss of cultural wealth we have sustained. And if we stop to consider what we have in its stead,—the brutalizing of feelings, the coarsening of thoughts, the blunting of our sense of justice in the name of nationalism—then the loss is immeasurable indeed. [. . .]

What if people in the intoxication of war are carried away by the thought of a greater future and greater power for their country; what if they point to all the material benefits such as the billions in war indemnities, and the tremendous increase in mental strength that a safeguarded, perhaps even more powerful, political standing will give them? It is not said that these dreams will come true. A victory that isolates a people in an ever so powerful self-sufficiency may cost them morally more than defeat. No gain in territory will compensate the loss if thus they shut themselves out from the domains of the mind. And no dreams of national greatness will ever be able to give a people the same impetus as the consciousness of a mutual sphere for the give and take of creative ideas.

Even if we consider only the sublime feelings that war has called forth,—not only in those who have actively partaken in it but also in all those who have remained at home, prepared for the news of the loss of all that is dear to them—what is the naked truth?

Let us think of all the years to come when those that are left will have to live with their sorrow and to fight for existence in homes robbed of husbands, sons, fathers, and brothers; the long years that are sure to see the rekindling of the old party hatreds; the long years in which the problems of social contrast will still remain unsolved—what then will be left of the glow of sacrifice, unity, and heroism that the war has called forth? The masses will be cheated now as always in their hopes; they have fulfilled their *duties* as citizens but will not reap the *reward*. And for these, as for the other classes, not even the victory of their country will be able to keep the flames from becoming ashes. The mean souls will again become mean, the wicked ones wicked, and the stupid ones stupid. It is only during a time of national psychosis that they can rise above themselves. But until the last hour of their lives they will have to bear the results of the war. Above all, these results of the war will be shown in the numberless children whose bodies and souls have been branded by the bitterness and horror, race-hatred and brutality of war. And those that are, for instance, the fruits of the "military marriages" that took place before the men left for the front, children who will perhaps never see their fathers, and whose mothers are weighed down by the sorrow and the struggle for existence, will their lot be any better than that of the poor illegitimate waifs we already have in our communities?

What gain in power—whether political or financial—will compensate the unheard-of loss in happiness, peace, and beauty in the realm of childhood?

When humanity in all earnest considers all the losses of war, then it will demand an answer to the question whether a nation's power and honour must for all time depend on armaments and be defended by war.

"The Debit Balance of War," in *War, Peace, and the Future: A Consideration of Nationalism and Internationalism, and of the Relation of Women to War,* trans. Hildegard Norberg (New York: G. P. Putnam's Sons, 1916), 1–10.

✦ Sarojini Naidu, née Chattopadhyay
(1879–1949) *Indian*

Alushly sensual lyric poet and political activist, Sarojini Naidu was widely read and memorized in England as well as in India. Born to a Brahmin family in Hyderabad, she knew Urdu and English but not Bengali. Her mother was a poet and her father an educator who founded the Nizam's College; their home welcomed a circle of intellectual, literary, and radical friends. Rising above sectarian divisions, her parents taught Naidu to believe in the goodness of people of all castes and creeds. Precocious in her studies, she passed the matriculation examination for the University of Madras at twelve; she was sent to England at sixteen to study at King's College (London) and Girton (Cambridge). At nineteen, against her family's will, she entered an intercaste marriage with the much older Dr. Govindaraju Naidu; they had eleven children. She published four collections of poetry—*Songs* (1895), *The Bird of Time* (1912), *The Golden Threshold* (1905), and *The Broken Wing* (1917)—which won her a reputation as "the Nightingale of India." Influenced by both Eastern and Western traditions, her work was introduced to the English by Arthur Symons and Edmund Gosse.

In 1903 Naidu began to travel to speak on behalf of Indian national independence. An effective public speaker and organizer, she was a friend of Mahatma Gandhi, who in 1914 formed an Indian ambulance corps while they were both in London. After her return from London to India later that year she worked for the Ladies' War Relief Association, hoping that independence would be furthered by support of Britain during the war. Gandhi's work inspired her to give increasing time to public lectures on the "inalienable trust and responsibility" of womanhood, on brotherhood across differences, and on the liberation of India. From 1915 on, the Indian National Congress was increasingly focused on self-government. Naidu wrote "The Gift of India" as a tribute not to Britain but to India's wartime sacrifices. At the Lucknow Congress of 1916, Naidu was asked by the president to address the inequities of the Arms Act, which prevented Indians from carrying arms in their homeland, and did so to an enthusiastic audience. She led the All-Indian Women's Deputation to the Secretary of State for India (E. S. Montagu) in 1917, the year in which she began her agitation for full suffrage for Indian women. Presiding at the Madras Provincial Conference in May 1918, she described her aim "to hold together the divided edges of Mother India's cloak of patriotism."

After the war Naidu rallied students to give themselves to the freedom of India, drawing a parallel to the European youth who had poured out their blood for the sake of peace and freedom, but insisting on a critical difference: while European warfare was won by slaying the enemy, the Indian victory would be won by self-purification and by transcendence of "sects and provinces and castes." Like Gandhi, she opposed exploitation of Indian indentured labor, and denounced the kidnapping of women sent with the laborers as de facto prostitutes in South Africa. She presided at the Indian National Congress in 1925, the second woman president after Annie Besant. She also chaired the All India Conference on Educational Reform in 1928. As a follower of Gandhi's *satyagraha* movement, she protested the British tax on salt in 1930, and was imprisoned three times in the thirties and forties. At India's independence in 1947, Naidu became governor of Uttar Pradesh; one of her daughters became governor of West Bengal.

✦ The Arms Act

Mrs. Sarojini Naidu, who was asked by the President to speak on the Resolution on the "Arms Act" at the Lucknow Congress of 1916, said:—

Your Honour, President and unarmed citizens of India—It may seem a kind of paradox that I should be asked to raise my voice on behalf of the disinherited manhood of the country, but it is suitable that I who represent the other sex, that is, the mothers of the men whom we wish to make men and not emasculated machines, should raise a voice on behalf of the future mothers of India to demand that the birthright of their sons should be given back to them, so that tomorrow's India may be once more worthy of its yesterday, that their much-valued birthright be restored to the Hindu and Mussalmans of India, to the disinherited martial Rajput and the Sikh and the Pathan. The refusal of the privilege, that gifted privilege and inalienable right to carry arms, is to insult the very core of their valiant manhood. To prevent to-day millions of brave young men willing to carry arms in the cause of the Empire is to cast a slur on the very ideals of the Empire. (*Hear, hear.*) In your name, O citizens of India, I appeal to the representative of the great Emperor of this great Indian Empire to plead for our rights, to support us in our claims, to grant to the children of to-morrow the right that their forefathers of yesterday possessed. (*Cheers.*) Who but a woman shall raise a voice for you who have not been able in all these years to speak for yourselves with any effect. (*Cries of 'Shame'.*) I come from a city where every man is privileged to carry arms—the African, the Rohilla, and the Sikh do carry arms there—and never has it been said in my city of Hyderabad that all these various armed elements have ever been disloyal to the sovereign power. Shall not the greater portion of India, British India, take a lesson from that one native state that knows how to trust the loyalty of its subjects. (*Hear, hear.*) Have we not, the women of India, sent our sons and brothers to shed their blood on the battlefields of Flanders, France, Gallipoli and Mesopotamia? When the hour comes for thanks, shall we not say to them for whom they fought 'when the terror and tumult of hate shall cease and life is refashioned, and when there is peace, and you offer memorial thanks to the comrades that fought in the dauntless ranks, and you honour the deeds of deathless ones, remember the blood of martyred sons,' and remember the armies of India and restore to India her lost manhood. (*Loud Cheers.*)

1916

Speeches and Writings of Sarojini Naidu (Madras: G. A. Natesan, 1919), 78–79.

✠ Alexandra Mikhailovna Kollontai, née Dormontovitch (1872–1952) *Russian*

Alexandra Kollontai's mother, the beautiful Finnish daughter of an enterprising freed serf, left her first forced marriage to elope with General Mikhail Dormontovitch, inspector of the Czar's cavalry. The family raised her in an atmosphere of liberal politics, sensitivity to the lower classes, and respect for women's independence. In 1881 she was deeply impressed by the public hanging of five terrorists, including Sofia Perovskaya. Alexandra earned a teaching diploma in 1888 and taught workers at night school. In a failed attempt to dissuade her from marrying Vladimir Kollontai, her parents took her to Berlin and Paris, where she attended socialist meetings and read the *Communist Manifesto*. Married in 1892, she had a son in 1894. Her first visit to a large factory in 1896 inspired her to organize textile strikes in St. Petersburg.

Kollontai grew increasingly dissatisfied with domesticity: "motherhood was never the kernel of my existence. . . . I still loved my husband, but the contented life of a housewife and spouse became for me a 'cage.' " In 1898 she left her family to study Marxist economics in Switzerland, where she met international socialists and radicals; in 1903 she published a book on the condition of Finnish workers, drawing on her travels in the intervening years. In 1904 she joined the Menshevik party and in 1905 she participated in "Bloody Sunday," calling for the overthrow of the Czar. Kollontai rejected a woman's movement across class boundaries. "Between the emancipated woman of the intelligentsia and the toiling woman with calloused hands" there was "an unbridgeable gulf," counting herself, of course, as an exception. She organized factory women in Russia, Finland, and Germany, and participated in international congresses of socialist women and the All-Russian Women's Congress. She argued for "free love," divorce, maternity benefits, and public day care.

Kollontai opposed the war. Exiled from Russia and Germany, she traveled in Norway, the United States, and Switzerland, where her rhetorical power and linguistic skills made her a brilliant advocate of Leninism and opposition to the war. Her bitter pamphlet "Who Needs the War?" (1916), with its attack on capitalist greed ("our enemy is in the rear"), was published illegally in Russia. She was not a pacifist: she encouraged military enrollment under the Bolsheviks.

In 1917 she joined the Bolsheviks and was elected to the central committee; she founded the Bolshevik women's paper *Rabotnitsa* and rallied women around the protection of maternity. A brief second marriage (1918–1923) to a Bolshevik sailor, Pavel Dybenko, was not happy. In 1920 she defended the independence of unions. As Minister of Social Welfare she fought for health care for women and children. Her finesse and culture permitted her to serve as a diplomat to Norway, Mexico, and Sweden. Her essays, novellas, and stories embrace the sexual revolution. One of the few leaders of the revolution to criticize the Bolshevik Party, she retained a sense of irony and preserved the grudging respect of Soviet officials and foreign statesmen.

TP

✝ Who Needs the War?

'HEROES'

The war had not yet ended, indeed its end was still not in sight, but the number of cripples was multiplying: the armless, the legless, the blind, the deaf, the mutilated . . . They had set off for the bloody world slaughterhouse young, strong, healthy. Their life still lay ahead of them. Only a few months, weeks, even days later, they were brought back to the infirmaries half dead, crippled . . .

'Heroes', say those who started a European war, who sent one people out against another, the worker from one country out against his fellow worker from another. At least now they have won an award! They will be able to walk around wearing their medals! People will respect them!

However, in real life things are different. The 'hero' comes home to his native village or town, and when he arrives he cannot believe his eyes: in place of 'respect' and joy he finds waiting for him fresh sufferings and disillusionment. His village has been reduced to poverty and starvation. The menfolk were dragged off to war, the livestock requisitioned . . . Taxes must be paid, and there is no one to do the work. The women have been run off their feet. They are haggard and starved, worn out with weeping. Cripple-heroes wander about the village, some with one medal, some with two. And the only 'respect' the hero gets is to hear his own family reproach him as a parasite who eats the bread of others. And the bread is rationed!

The 'hero' who returns to the town fares no better. He is met with 'respect', his mother weeps from both grief and joy: her darling son is still alive, her ageing mother's eyes have beheld him once again. His wife smiles . . . For a day or two they will fuss around him. And then . . .

Since when do working people have the time, the leisure, to look after an invalid? Each has his own affairs, his own worries. Moreover, times are difficult. Not a day passes but the cost of living rises. War! . . . The children are ailing; war is always accompanied by epidemics, infection. The wife is trying to do a thousand things at once. She must work for herself and for the 'bread-winner.'

And the tsar's pension?

How much is that? It would hardly pay for one boot for the one leg remaining!

Officers, wounded generals, will, of course, receive their pensions 'according to rank', but who is interested in the ordinary private, the former worker, peasant or artisan? Who cares about his fate? Power in the state is not in the hands of the people, but in the hands of the landowners and industrialists, the lords and masters. The state finances are controlled not by those 'hero-soldiers' who die in hundreds of thousands and millions in the war, but by those same lords: the landowners, industrialists and state officials—the servants of the tsar.

At first, while the memory is still fresh and the cannon are still sounding at the front, the 'hero-soldiers' will be remembered. Various societies, charitable organisations and the Red Cross will come to their aid with miserly handouts . . . First one year passes, then another. Peace comes, and people take up once more their former daily round. What will then become of our 'heroes'?

Wounded colonels and generals will ride about in their cars; they took care of themselves during the war, hoarded up their cash, stuffed their pockets with the soldiers' rations . . . And the 'hero-soldiers', the maimed with their medals? What will their fate be? [. . .]

WHAT WERE THEY FIGHTING FOR?

Ask any soldier, be he Russian or German, what were they fighting for? For what did they shed the blood of their brothers, the workers and peasants of their neighbouring country? For what did they cripple people? They will not tell you, they will not answer, because they themselves do not really know.

Perhaps they were fighting on behalf of the Serbs, or perhaps it was the Germans who attacked Russia. There was talk of land. At first the Russian peasant-soldiers thought: 'We're going to take the land away from the Germans.'

However, they soon realised that the war was not about land! . . . What was it about, then? There are very few who know, who understand. It is not only the Russians who are fighting 'in the dark' without really understanding for what they are knifing, bayoneting and crippling people. The

German, English and French soldiers also have as little idea of the *real reason* for the war. Ask any one of them—each will cite you a different reason.

The German people were told: 'Russia has attacked us. Russian Cossacks are marching on Berlin. We must defend our fatherland. At the same time we will go and liberate Russia from the toils of bureaucracy, from the arbitrariness and lawlessness of the tsar's officials. We are going to die for the "liberty" of the Russian people! [. . .] In millions of issues the capitalist newspapers spread lies about the war, governments introduced wartime censorship, did not allow one word of the truth to be printed, and threw the best friends of the working class into jail. The people were fooled, as the Russian soldiers were fooled when they were assured that it was for 'land' that they were marching into Galicia . . .

In France, the government, the generals, ministers, bankers and industrialists, found another explanation of the war for their people. It was time to take back from the Germans the territory of Alsace and Lorraine, which they had conquered in 1870. 'Citizens of glorious republican France! . . . You live in a free country, you have won all political rights for yourselves at home . . . But next door, in neighbouring Germany, the people are groaning under the yoke of the Kaiser! . . . Let us save the German people! We will fight until we have chased the Kaiser out of Germany and have established a republic for the Germans!'

And noble France decided to 'liberate' the German people and put an end to the Kaiser.

Not a bad cause! Who needs kaisers and tsars? [. . .]

However, on looking a little closer you see that the kaisers and tsars are still safe and sound, still on their thrones with their power intact. The capitalists waxed rich thanks to the war. They 'earned' about 20–40 kopecks for every rouble's worth of supplies for the army, and these supplies are worth hundreds and thousands of millions of roubles. And hundreds of thousands and millions of those very citizens about which the 'great powers' were suddenly so concerned have strewn their own land and foreign lands with their bones. Is it the 'liberation' of a foreign people that is the cause of war? Is there anyone who still believes in such fairy tales?

Let us take another example: the English apparently only came into the war later on in order, on the one hand, to defend Belgium, and on the other to defeat and destroy the German 'military machine'—militarism. This is how it is presented in words. But how does the English monarchy behave in fact? First of all, England loses no opportunity to seize German colonies, German land. And, of course, she does not enquire or ask the population under whose dominion they wish to remain—under German or under English. [. . .]

The English government decided to 'liberate' a foreign country from the evil of 'militarism', and to impose the very same evil upon its own people! However, this is not all! The example given by Germany was so much to the taste of the English government that it decided to do what other countries had done and introduce a 'military system' in manufacture: to mobilise the workers, subordinate them to the military authorities, remove from them the right to strike and defend their interests, and to bind them to the state . . . And this genuine 'military slavery' of the workers has been introduced not only in England but in all the belligerent countries—in France, in Germany and in Russia. 'Work for a pittance, put up with every kind of restriction and insult—if you don't you'll be sent to the front to face the bullets of the enemy'. [. . .]

THE HOMELAND IN DANGER!

But what should one do? One cannot, after all, refuse to fight when one's country has been attacked, and when one's homeland is in danger.

Let those who were ready to die 'for the homeland' ask themselves honestly and in all conscience: what *homeland* does the worker have, what *homeland* do the dispossessed have? Do they have a homeland? If they did, would there be the yearly flow of emigrants from every country into alien lands, the dispossessed and unemployed leaving their native land, believing, hoping that, perhaps, this 'alien land' will prove a more loving step-mother than their own mother country? Would there be, in Russia itself hundreds of thousands of hungry and penniless 'migrants'?

The general has a homeland, and so does the landowner, the merchant, the manufacturer and all those who carry a fat wallet in their pocket. To these, the wealthy with the bulging purses, the homeland gives rights and privileges and the state authorities concern themselves about their fate.

But what does the 'motherland' give to the worker, be he Russian, German or French? The struggle for his daily bread, the struggle against poverty and lack of rights, oppression at the hands of the master, landowner and landlord, insults, grief, illness and humiliation . . . Not infrequently prison! In Russia penal servitude and exile . . . This is what the modern homeland gives to its children, to those who create its wealth with their own hands, to those who purchase its military honour with their lives . . .

For the poor, the motherland is not a mother but a step-mother . . . Nonetheless there are many who say: perhaps our mother does not indulge us, her loyal children who water her land with the sweat of our brow, but we love our land! We will defend our people from attack by foreign enemies, we will save the faith of our fathers from enemies of another creed! . . .

But is modern warfare, warfare among all the major European powers, a war conducted between enemies of different creeds or races? Look more closely. Who is fighting whom—Orthodox against Catholic or Catholic against Lutheran? Christians against Mohammedans? No! This war has mixed everyone together. The Orthodox Russian shoots at the Orthodox Bulgarian and the Austrian, the French Catholic kills the German Catholic, The Mohammedan helps the Christian to aim at a brother Mohammedan, Jew kills Jew and Pole kills Pole. [. . .]

The 'great powers' who are now warring amongst themselves is each an oppressor of numerous peoples and nations. Russia oppresses Jews,

Ukrainians, Poles, Finns and many others. Germany oppresses Poles, Danes, etc. England and France oppress tens and hundreds of millions in their colonies. War is being waged not in the name of freedom for the people, not in the name of one's right to one's native language, not for the survival of institutions beneficial to the working class. No, war is being waged in the name of the 'right' of the great powers to oppress as many alien peoples and to rob as many colonies as possible. The war is being waged by predators in order to divide the spoils.

A grotesque picture emerges: on the order of the great powers, people of one nation, one language, one faith, kill and cripple each other, trample over the land . . . The Russian Ukrainian peasant aims his gun at the Ukrainian peasant from Austria; the worker from Russian Poland points his machine-gun at Polish workers from Germany . . . Forty-five years ago, Alsatians gave their lives for the glory of 'La Belle France'. Now they are defending their 'homeland' under banners that carry the German eagle . . . And who knows? If victory goes to the 'allies', perhaps the Alsatians will have to die in the next war for a French 'homeland'!

And if one thinks of all the soldiers that England and France have brought from their colonies—Africans, Indians . . . For what 'homeland' are they dying? Their homeland is thousands of miles away. But what is left of that homeland since the Europeans invaded it, since the 'great powers' subdued it with fire and sword? They have no homeland any more, and now they must die for the glory of the bourgeoisie of the nation that oppresses them.

However, it is not only the nations that have been conquered and subdued by the capitalist states who are without a homeland; so also are the 'true sons' of Russia, Germany and England if they are merely the 'offspring of common folk'. What kind of homeland is it if tens of millions are hired slaves working day and night for a handful of capitalists? What kind of homeland is it if these tens of millions of workers have nothing to lose but their chains? [. . .]

WHAT IS TO BE DONE[?]

Once the true cause of war, its purpose, has been understood, another question arises: what is to be done? How can the slaughter be stopped? How can the people be spared new conflicts and disputes among the capitalists, new wars, in the future? [. . .]

Wars will only end when the power of the capitalists has been smashed, when the owner-exploiters are no longer able to harm the people and push them into bloody conflicts. War is generated by the unjust, inequitable capitalist structure of society. *In order to put an end to war, the structure of society must be changed.* In order to put an end to war, all the factories, all the plants, all the industrial enterprises must be removed from the capitalist masters: the land must be taken from the landowners, the mines from private proprietors, the banks from the capitalists, and all this wealth *must become common property.*

In order to put an end to war, a new and juster *socialist world* must be won for the people, for the working class. [. . .]

All that is necessary is that each soldier at the front, each worker in the workshop, should realise: my enemy is not the one who, like myself in my own country, has no rights, who is oppressed by capital, whose life is a struggle for his daily bread.

My enemy is in my own country, and this enemy is the same for all the workers of the world. This enemy is *capitalism,* this enemy is the *rapacious, corrupt class government.* This enemy is *the lack of rights suffered by the working class.* Comrade worker, a private in the enemy army, I know now that it is not you who are my enemy. Give me your hand, comrade! We are both of us the victims of deception and violence. Our main and common enemy is at our rear. Let us turn our rifles and guns against our real, our common enemies . . .

And then all our brave commanders, field marshals and generals will take to their heels! . . .

Let us each go to war in our own country against our oppressors, let us cleanse our homelands from the real enemies of the people, from the tsars, kings and emperors!

And when power is in our hands, we will conclude our own peace over the heads of the defeated capitalists [. . .]

. . . To work, comrades, to work!

There have been enough victims to the glory of capital. Our common enemy lies in our rear! Away with those responsible for the war! Away with capitalists and tsars! Let us fight for the freedom of our homeland, for stable peace!

Long live the approaching, long-awaited social revolution! Long live the victory of the socialist brotherhood of nations!

Publ. by the CC RSDLP,
Switzerland, 1916

"Who Needs the War?" in *Selected Articles and Speeches,* trans. Cynthia Carlile (New York: International Publishers, 1984), 75–91. Reprinted by permission of International Publishers.

✝ Rosa Luxemburg
(1870–1919) *Polish/German*

Rosa Luxemburg was a socialist internationalist and antimilitarist, who turned toward feminist action late in her life. Born to an enlightened, assimilated Polish Jewish family, she joined an illegal socialist group in Warsaw, then left at eighteen to study economics and law in Zurich, where she met Leo Jogiches, who became her lover. A founder of the German Communist Party, she was admired as an economic theorist and orator; she was a critic of trade unionism, since it works within the capitalist system. For six years from 1907, she taught political economy at the Party School of the German Socialist Party. In 1907 at the Stuttgart Congress of the International, she maintained that the working classes were obligated to resist any capitalist-inspired war, but also that they should use such a crisis to "rouse the people and thereby to hasten the abolition of class rule." She identified the interests of capitalism with imperialism and militarism, arguing for a "conscious struggle of the international proletariat against imperialism and its method: war." She summed up this position in the slogan, "War on war!" With Karl Liebknecht and Clara Zetkin she led the Spartacus movement.

During the war Luxemburg continued to oppose militarism. She opposed middle-class feminism on the grounds that it ignored more basic social needs, but agreed to attend the Women's Peace Conference at The Hague in 1915; she was arrested, however, as a Spartacist a few days before her planned departure for Holland. She illegally published her critique of social democracy, the "Junius" Pamphlet, in Zurich after her release from prison on February 18, 1916.

In 1912, she spoke on behalf of "general, equal, direct suffrage for women," to "advance and intensify the proletarian class struggle." An article on women that she published in Clara Zetkin's socialist journal, *Die Gleichheit* (Equality), stated her position on feminism: "For the propertied bourgeois woman, her house is the world. For the proletarian woman, the whole world is her house. . . . Bourgeois women's rights advocates want to acquire political rights in order to participate in political life. The proletarian women can only follow the path of the workers' struggles." Nonetheless, she defended the principle that women should have full political freedom and equality.

When the war ended in November 1918, she was released from prison by socialist soldiers, but rearrested and assassinated with Liebknecht shortly thereafter.

✝ The Crisis in German Social Democracy

(The Junius[1] Pamphlet: Part One)

The scene has fundamentally changed. The six weeks' march to Paris has become world drama. Mass murder has become a boring monotonous daily business, and yet the final solution is not one step nearer. Bourgeois rule is caught in its own trap, and cannot ban the spirits that it has invoked.

Gone is the ecstasy. Gone are the patriotic street demonstrations, the chase after suspicious-looking automobiles, the false telegrams, the cholera-poisoned wells. Gone the mad stories of Russian students who hurl bombs from every bridge of Berlin, or of Frenchmen flying over Nürnberg; gone the excesses of a spy-hunting populace, the singing throngs, the coffee shops with their deafening patriotic songs; gone the violent mobs, ready to denounce, ready to mistreat women, ready to yell "Hurrah" and whip themselves into a delirious frenzy over every wild rumor; gone the atmosphere of ritual murder, the Kishinev air[2] that left the policeman at the corner as the only remaining representative of human dignity.

The show is over. The German sages, the vacillating spirits, have long since taken their leave. No more do trains filled with reservists pull out amid the joyous cries of enthusiastic maidens. We no longer see their laughing faces, smiling cheerily at the people from the train windows. They trot through the streets quietly, with their sacks on their shoulders. And the public, with a disturbed face, goes about its daily tasks.

In the sober atmosphere of pale daylight there rings out a different chorus: the hoarse croak of the vultures and hyenas of the battlefield. Ten thousand tents, guaranteed according to specifications; 100,000 kilos of bacon, cocoa powder, coffee substitute—for immediate delivery, cash only! Grenades, lathes, ammunition pouches, marriage bureaus for war

---

1. *Junius:* the pseudonym alludes to the ancient Roman republican leader Lucius Junius Brutus, as well as to an eighteenth-century pseudonymous German critic of government corruption. [D.H.]

2. *Kishinev air:* the atmosphere of a pogrom like that at Kishinev during Passover in 1905. [D.H.]

widows, leather belts, war orders—only serious propositions considered! And the patriotic cannon fodder that was loaded into the trains in August and September rots on the battlefields of Belgium and the Vosges, while profits are springing like weeds from the fields of the dead. The harvest must be brought quickly into the barns. From across the ocean a thousand greedy hands want to take part in the plunder.

Business is flourishing upon the ruins. Cities are turned to rubble, whole countries into deserts, villages into cemeteries, whole populations into beggars, churches into stables. International law, treaties, alliances, the holiest words and the highest authorities have been torn into scraps. Every sovereign by the grace of God is called a cretin, an unfaithful wretch, by his cousin on the other side[3]; every diplomat calls his colleague in the enemy's country a crafty scoundrel; each government looks upon the other as the evil genius of its people, worthy only of the contempt of the world. Hunger revolts in Venetia, in Lisbon, in Moscow, in Singapore; plague in Russia; misery and desperation everywhere.

Shamed, dishonored, wading in blood and dripping with filth—thus stands bourgeois society. And so it is. Not as we usually see it, pretty and chaste, playing the roles of peace and righteousness, of order, of philosophy, ethics and culture. It shows itself in its true, naked form—as a roaring beast, as an orgy of anarchy, as a pestilential breath, devastating culture and humanity.

And in the midst of this orgy a world-historical tragedy has occurred: the capitulation of Social Democracy.[4] To close one's eyes to this fact, to try to hide it, would be the most foolish, the most dangerous thing that the proletariat could do. [. . .]

The catastrophe of the socialist proletariat in the present World War is an unexampled misfortune for humanity. But socialism is lost only if the international proletariat is unable to measure the depths of the catastrophe and refuses to learn from it.

The last forty-five years in the development of the labor movement are at stake. The present situation is a closing of its accounts, a summing-up of the items of half a century's work. In the grave of the Paris Commune lies buried the first phase of the European labor movement and the First International. A new phase has since begun. Instead of spontaneous revolution, revolts, and barricades, after each of which the proletariat relapsed once again into its passivity, there began the systematic daily struggle, the utilization of bourgeois parliamentarism, mass organization, the wedding of the economic with the political struggle and of socialist ideals with the stubborn defense of immediate interests. For the first time the cause of the proletariat and its emancipation were led by the guiding star of scientific knowledge. Instead of sects and schools, utopian undertakings and

3. *Cousin on the other side:* Six of the reigning royal families in Europe were descendants of Queen Victoria of England. [D.H.]

4. *The capitulation of Social Democracy:* the socialist vote on August 4, 1914, for the war credits, called "unprecedented" and "incredible" below. [D.H.]

experiments in every country, each altogether and absolutely separate from the other, there developed a unified, international, theoretical basis that united the nations. Marxist theory gave to the working class of the whole world a compass by which to fix its tactics from hour to hour in its journey toward the one unchanging goal.

The bearer, the advocate, the protector of this new method was German Social Democracy. The war of 1870 and the downfall of the Paris Commune[5] shifted the center of gravity of the European labor movement to Germany. Just as France was the classic site of the first phase of the proletarian class struggle, as Paris was the torn and bleeding heart of the European working class of that time, so the German working class became the vanguard of the second phase. By innumerable sacrifices in untiring small tasks, it built the strongest, the model organization, created the greatest press, developed the most effective educational and propaganda methods. It collected under its banners the most gigantic masses of voters, and elected the largest number of representatives to Parliament. [. . .]

Particularly in the fight against militarism and war, the position taken by German Social Democracy has always been decisive. [. . .]

And what happened in Germany when the great historical test came? The deepest fall, the mightiest cataclysm. Nowhere was the organization of the proletariat put so completely in the service of imperialism. Nowhere was the state of siege so uncomplainingly borne. Nowhere was the press so thoroughly gagged, public opinion so completely choked. Nowhere was the economic and political class struggle of the working class so entirely abandoned as in Germany. [. . .]

One thing is certain: the World War is a turning point for the world. It is a foolish delusion to believe that we need only live through the war as a rabbit hides under the bush to await the end of a thunderstorm, to trot merrily off at the old accustomed pace when it is all over. The World War has changed the conditions of our struggle, and has changed *us* most of all. Not that the laws of capitalist development have changed, or that the life-and-death conflict between capital and labor has diminished or altered. Even now, in the midst of war, the masks are falling and the old, well-known gang sneers at us. But the tempo of development has received a mighty forward impetus through the eruption of the imperialist volcano. The enormity of the tasks that tower before the socialist proletariat in the immediate future make the past struggles of the labor movement seem but a delightful idyl in comparison.

Historically, the war is ordained to give to the cause of the proletariat a mighty impetus. In *Class Struggles in France*, Marx, whose prophetic eyes foresaw so many historical events as they lay in the womb of the future, wrote the following significant passage:

In France, the petty bourgeoisie does what should normally be done by the industrial bourgeoisie (i.e., fight for parliamentary rights); the

5. *Paris Commune:* socialistic government of Paris, March 18–May 27, 1871. [D.H.]

worker does what should normally be done by the petty bourgeoisie (i.e., fight for the Democratic Republic); but who shall solve the problems of labor? They will not be solved in France; they will be proclaimed in France. They will nowhere be solved within national boundaries. Class war in French society will be transformed into a world war. The solution will begin only when the world war has driven the proletariat into the leadership of that nation which controls the world market, to the leadership of England. The revolution that will here find, not its end, but its organizational beginnings is no short-winded one. The present generation is like the Jews who were led by Moses through the wilderness. Not only must it conquer a new world; it must go under to make way for those who are equal to a new world.

This was written in 1850, at a time when England was the only capitalistically developed nation, when the English proletariat was the best organized and, through the industrial growth of its nation, seemed destined to take the leadership in the international working class. Read Germany instead of England, and the words of Karl Marx become a brilliant prophecy of the present World War. This war is ordained to drive the German proletariat to the leadership of the people, and thus to create "the organizational beginnings" of the great international conflict between labor and capital for the political power of the state.

Have we ever had a different conception of the role to be played by the working class in the world war? Have we forgotten how we used to describe the coming event, only a few short years ago?

Then will come the *catastrophe*. All Europe will be called to arms, and sixteen to eighteen million men, the flower of the different nations, armed with the best instruments of murder, will make war upon each other. But I believe that behind this call to arms there looms the final crash. Not we, but they themselves will bring it. They are driving things to the extreme; they are leading us straight to a catastrophe. They will reap what they have sown. The *Götterdämmerung*[6] of the bourgeois world is at hand. Be sure of that. It is in the wind.

Thus spoke *Bebel*, the speaker of our delegation in the Reichstag in the *Morocco debate*.[7] [. . .]

Only a week before the war broke out, on July 26, 1914, the German Party papers wrote:

6. *Götterdämmerung:* twilight of the gods, the title of the last part of Richard Wagner's *Ring* cycle. [D.H.]

7. *Bebel:* August Bebel (1840–1913), parliamentary leader of the German Social Democrats, refused to vote the war credits in July 1870 for the Franco-Prussian War. Morocco debate: in the second Moroccan crisis, when French troops advanced to Fez, the Germans objected and sent the gunboat *Panther* to Agadir, to reinforce demands for part of the French Congo and Cameroon. [D.H.]

We are no marionettes. We fight with all our might against a system that makes men the powerless tools of blind circumstance, against this capitalism that is preparing to change Europe, thirsty for peace, into a smoking slaughterhouse. If destruction takes its course, if the determined will for peace of the German, of the international proletariat which will be expressed in the next few days in mighty demonstrations should not be able to prevent world war, then at least it must be the last war, it must be the *Götterdämmerung* of capitalism.

Again, on July 30, 1914, the central organ of German Social Democracy cried out:

The socialist proletariat rejects all responsibility for the events that are being precipitated by a ruling class that is blinded to the verge of mad-ness. It knows that, *for it, new life will bloom from the ruins.* All responsibil-ity falls on the rulers *of today.* For them it is a question of *existence!* World history is the world court of judgment![8]

And then came the unprecedented, the incredible 4th of August, 1914. Did it have to come? An event of such importance is certainly not a game of chance. It must have deep, extensive, objective causes. But these causes may also be found in the errors of the leader of the proletariat, Social Democracy itself, in the failure of our readiness to fight, our courage and our convictions. Scientific socialism has taught us to under-stand the objective laws of historical development. Man does not make his-tory of his own volition. But he makes it nonetheless. In its action, the proletariat is dependent upon the given degree of ripeness of social devel-opment. But social development does not take place apart from the pro-letariat. The proletariat is its driving force and its cause as well as its product and its effect. The action of the proletariat is itself a codetermin-ing part of history. And though we can no more skip a period in our his-torical development than a man can jump over his shadow, it lies within our power to accelerate or to retard it. [. . .]

Friedrich Engels once said: "Capitalist society faces a dilemma: either an advance to socialism or a reversion to barbarism." What does a "reversion to barbarism" mean at the present stage of European civilization? We have all read and repeated these words thoughtlessly, without a notion of their terri-ble seriousness. At this moment, one glance around us will show what a rever-sion to barbarism in bourgeois society means. This World War—that is a reversion to barbarism. The triumph of imperialism leads to the destruction of culture, sporadically during a modern war, and forever if the period of world wars which has just begun is allowed to take its course to its logical end.

Thus, we stand today, as Friedrich Engels prophesied more than a gen-eration ago, before the choice: Either the triumph of imperialism and the destruction of all culture and, as in ancient Rome, depopulation, desola-

8. *World history:* Hegel, *Philosophy of Right,* paragraph 340. [D.H.]

tion, degeneration, a vast cemetery. Or, the victory of socialism, that is, the conscious struggle of the international proletariat against imperialism and its method: war. This is the dilemma of world history, an Either/Or whose scales are trembling in the balance, awaiting the decision of the class-conscious proletariat. The future of culture and humanity depends on whether the proletariat throws the sword of revolutionary struggle with manly decisiveness upon the scales. Imperialism has been victorious in this war. Its bloody sword of mass murder has dashed the scales with over-whelming brutality into the abyss of shame and misery. If the proletariat learns from this war to assert itself, to cast off its serfdom to the ruling classes, to become the lord of its own destiny, the shame and misery will not have been in vain.

The modern working class must pay dearly for each development of its consciousness of its historic mission. The Golgotha-road of its class libera-tion is strewn with awful sacrifices. The June combatants [of 1848], the vic-tims of the Commune, the martyrs of the Russian Revolution [of 1905]—an endless line of bloody shadows. But they have fallen on the field of honor, as Marx wrote of the heroes of the Commune, "to be enshrined forever in the great heart of the working class." Now millions of proletarians of all nations are falling on the field of shame, of fratricide, of self-destruction, the slave-song on their lips. And that, too, could not be spared us. We are truly like the Jews whom Moses led through the desert. But we are not lost, and we will be victorious if we have not forgotten how to learn. And if the modern leader of the proletariat, Social Democracy, does not know how to learn, it will go under "to make room for those who grow up in a new world."

Zurich, 1916

✝ Annette Kolb
(1870–1967) *German*

The bilingual daughter of a French pianist and the German land-scape architect of the Bavarian royalty, Annette Kolb grew up in Munich in a cultivated circle of diplomats, court officials, and musicians (including Wagner). She was a friend of poet Rainer Maria Rilke, even though his political indecision created distance between them for a time. Passionately pacifist during World War I, she published a major journal, *Die internationale Rundschau,* to which prominent antiwar writers such as Romain Rolland and G. B. Shaw, as well as Germans, contributed. She emigrated to Switzerland; there she published a series of letters to a dead man, *Briefe einer Deutsch-Französin* (Letters of a German-Frenchwoman, 1916), which first appeared in the journal *Weisse Blätter,* a poignant indictment of militarism. She returned in 1919 to Germany, and lived near René Schickele for a decade. *Westliche Tage* followed in 1922. Her fears of Nazism led her into exile in Paris in 1933, then to Switzerland in 1940 and eventually to New York. In 1945 she returned to Europe.

Her witty and melodic fiction, set in aristocratic circles before World War I, stresses women's psychology. She received numerous literary awards, starting with her first novel, *Das Exemplar* (The paragon, 1913), which won the Fontane prize. Her novels have an autobiographical cast, marked by suffering but also admired for their depictions of Munich. Besides her novels, she also wrote biographies of Mozart, Schubert, and Wagner and published translations, as well as seven volumes of essays between 1906 and 1964.

✝ Letters of a German-Frenchwoman: First Letter

October 1914

It is still too soon, although God knows it is hardly unpatriotic, to speak European words in our sealed-off country. But somebody must be the first. Yet I do not wish to cause inconvenience, nor to be misunderstood. And I do not want discussion. Nowadays there is too much demand for that.

But you and I, we were of one mind, and you are dead. Therefore I direct my words toward you and cling to your shadow. And you, with eyes perhaps only for the invisible, you see how exuberantly I would have let my paltry life expire one hundred times over to avert what is happening in the world today. No doubt we were found to be too insignificant, and too few of us glad to be gathered as hostages and thrown to the Gorgons, to ward off their ferocious steps and banish from their heads the hideous serpents now unleashed, whose poisonous brood nests everywhere. Indeed, where the generous earth once bore seeds and fruits, where the peaceful corn-flower sprouted, they now slither zealously across the ravished fields and strangle the men, while their poison like long-range artillery strikes the women who, unspared though far away in protected cities, learn of their men's agony. Thus is the world today.

Has not each person had moments in life which he ought not to have overcome and yet was able to do just that? Clear proof that there must be something in man which rises and therefore will rise above all earthly events, just so long as he does not surrender himself.

I read this sentence today. Who are we? And yet it is necessary to pre-serve loyalty to oneself, even if it costs all community with others. Oh, do not desert me. You see how people now close their windows. The wind that roars over the earth brings them nothing. Each person knows where he belongs and his door locks firmly and smoothly. Only I am left homeless by this war. Yes—had God, who held back Abraham's arm when he raised it to sacrifice his son, had He put an end to the backward course of the infernal wheel, and shown mercy faced with so much wonderful readiness to die, then naturally I too would rejoice in having experienced the pre-lude of this war. For who would ever forget the sight of those faces?

But from that day when the scorching and burning, the shooting and stabbing, the battering and throttling, the bombing and mine-laying all began, from that day forward, you see, I was an outcast. Like a fool, I am cut off from such a world.

For I do not understand. Like a fool, I am frightened of people and am afraid ever since. Otherwise so urban, I am driven into sleepy villages and untamed woodlands, as though there were still an escape; as though the reality of this war had not long since penetrated pathless regions and did not breed on the most deserted moor. It has ploughed through the clean lines of the mountains. The breath of gruesome knowledge brushes the moon on all sides. No pasture preserves its innocence. What once made the war seem unreal now serves as a reminder. Upon no table, upon no door-handle can we lay our hand without prejudice. Like bitter yeast, the war is baked into our bread and its dull knowledge gnaws at us even in our dreams. How easy must your sleep be! You—so privileged, so ineffably distinguished, who no longer endure this collapse: Europe's undying disgrace.

Translated by Trudi Nicholas

"Erster Brief," in *Briefe einer Deutsch-Französin* (Berlin: Erich Reiss, 1916), 12–15.

✟ Ecatarina (Catalina) Theodoroiu (1894–1917) *Romanian*

Born in the commune of Vàdeni to a large peasant family, Ecatarina Theodoroiu had four brothers and two sisters. She grew up immersed in folktales about the river Jiu and poetry about Transylvania. When the war broke out she became a scout and helped the wounded, bringing medicines to hospitals in Tîrgu-Jiu. In October 1916 an enemy column attacked the town, which was protected by 150 local militia, largely women. When she helped win this unequal fight, she was called the Romanian Jeanne d'Arc or the Virgin of Jiu. (In Balkan families without sons, "virgins" sometimes cross-dressed and wore a wooden phallus, assuming the role of the missing son for the rest of their lives.) In a battle on November 6, she was wounded in both legs; while Theodoroiu was in a hospital she met a lieutenant who secured for her the honorific title of second lieutenant. She was the first woman in the Romanian army. Later, she won a military medal of honor and the rank of scout in the Lupeni regiment; Queen Marie praised the "mystic flame" in her eyes. After her death, her comrades reported they had heard her recite this oath under shellfire. A marble sarcophagus with bas-reliefs depicting her life by a woman artist, Milita Petrascu, was erected in her honor.

✟ Battle Oath

I swear to fight until we no longer hear the footsteps of the invader on the soil of my fatherland!
I swear to fight until the eyes of our children and their parents no longer shed tears.

I swear to fight and to avenge those who have fallen far from the quick
waters of the river Jiu and from the shadow of Mount Parîngului.
I swear to fight and to scatter over the tomb of the hero who fell here clay
taken from the old riverbanks which have been invaded and water from
the heart of the Jiu, water which my merciless fight shall set free.

1917?

From I. M. Stephan and V. Firoiu, *Subsemnul Minerve: femei de seamă din trecutul românesc*
(Bucharest: Editura politica, 1975), 233.

✝ Jeannette Rankin
(1880–1973) *American*

At the age of ninety-two, Jeannette Rankin summed up her life's work: "I worked ten years for suffrage and got it. I have worked fifty-six years for peace and have hardly begun." The advancement of pacifism was Rankin's lifelong project; she believed that the elimination of war could be realized only through the work of women.

The daughter of John and Olive Rankin, Jeannette graduated from the University of Montana in 1902 with a BS in biology. Inspired by the work of Jane Addams, she studied from 1908–1909 at the School of Philanthropy in New York City (now the Columbia School of Social Work). After working briefly with orphaned children in Seattle, she recognized that social work did not address the roots of the problems she was facing and turned to women's suffrage as a solution.

Campaigning on a platform of pacifism and suffrage, Rankin became the first woman elected to the United States House of Representatives in 1916. On April 6, 1917, during a special session called by President Wilson, she cast her first vote as a Congresswoman against entry into World War I. Although hers was one of fifty "no" votes, her opposition was widely perceived as an expression of feminine weakness. Suffragist colleagues feared that her vote, coupled with what seemed like emotional frailty, would strike a major blow to the women's movement. Although suffrage was in fact passed by the House for the first time while Rankin was in office, she did not run for reelection in 1918.

From 1919 until 1940 Rankin lobbied in Congress for pacifism and other humanitarian causes. She was a delegate to the 1919 Women's Peace Meeting in Zurich and in 1925 founded the Georgia Peace society. In 1940 Rankin was reelected to Congress and was the only legislator to vote against World War II on December 8, 1941. Her second "no" vote ended

her career in public office, but she continued to work for pacifism and traveled throughout the world promoting these ideals.
   LW

‡ Roll Call Vote, United States House of Representatives

I want to stand by my country—but I can not vote for war. (I vote NO.)

New York Times, April 7, 1917, p. 1

✝ Claire Studer Goll, née Clarisse Liliane Aischmann (1891–1977) German

Born in Nürnberg into a well-to-do German Jewish merchant family, the young "Klara" Aischmann suffered a painful childhood. She and her older brother were battered by her mother; her brother took his life at sixteen, but her sanity was preserved when she was sent to a reform school for girls. To escape her mother, she married a Swiss publisher, Heinrich Studer, with whom she had a daughter, Dorothea, in 1912. Writing in Berlin, she moved in the circles of the publisher Kurt Wolff and the expressionist Herwarth Walden.

In 1917 Claire Studer left her family, divorced, and went into exile in Switzerland, where she studied philosophy in Geneva and met artists in pacifist and expressionist circles, including the Jewish poet Yvan Goll (Isaac Lang), who became her lifelong partner. She translated for the journal *Die Aktion* and collaborated on pacifist papers in Switzerland, the *National-Zeitung* and *Freie Zeitung*. In her antimilitarist journalism of 1917–1918, she argued that women must mature into their responsibility for spiritual revolution and as the mothers of mankind must become critical of the war. She attacked German passivity toward the genocide of Armenians. Forcefully poetic, with quotations from Dostoyevsky and Antigone, her work was blacklisted in Germany. At the war's end she traveled to Munich, where she had a brief affair with Rainer Maria Rilke, to whom she had sent *Mitwelt* (Our times, 1918), a volume of poetry, until the counterrevolution forced her to leave for Berlin. At the same time she brought out a pacifist collection of stories, *Die Frauen erwachen* (Women awake, 1918), in which "The Wax Hand" appeared. This collection on the war, dedicated "to all sisters," provoked reviewers to contest her reputation as a "female Barbusse," and to condemn her ruptured moods as "untruthful" in their pacifist tone.

Discovering herself to be pregnant, Claire had an abortion, since neither Rilke nor Goll wanted to assume responsibility for a child; she then returned to Goll, whom she married in 1921. Although they exchanged passionate lyrics and were admired as a modern poetic couple like Elizabeth and Robert Browning, her happiness was marred by Goll's long affair with Paula Ludwig, which led (in spite of her own many infidelities) to a suicide attempt in 1938.

The couple emigrated to Paris, where they mingled with such artists as Joyce, Colette, Gide, Braque, Picasso, Malraux, and the surrealists. By contrast, she disliked the formally conservative poetry of Anna de Noailles, whom she attacked in a debate with Rilke. In the same year she published a pair of novellas, *Der gläserne Garten* (The glass garden, 1919). Over the next half century she published another four volumes of surrealist poetry that flirts with references to the machine age, four novels, and five volumes of gossipy memoirs. The Golls fled the Nazis in 1939, came to the United States, and returned to Paris in 1947. Her fictional autobiographies display the masks and rage of a sexually wounded woman; she is particularly bold in her odd optical angles, her play with artistic personae, even choosing the perspective of a cannibal. After her husband's death, she devoted herself to his literary estate. At her death, the German national literature archive at Marbach established an "Ivan und Claire Goll" room.

✝ For Armenia

Who among us, when as schoolchildren we learned about the horrors of the persecution of the Christians, would have believed that one day in the twentieth century we would become the contemporaries of atrocities which surpass them in cruelty by far? The only difference between the barbarism then and today is that then they said, "those are heretics," whereas today they say, "those are Armenians." But while the Christians were hunted by heathens alone, today we have a Christian government which could put a stop to it, but which stands with folded arms and silently observes its brothers in faith fighting to the death.

How this war surpasses the most poisonous imagination of the least talented novelist! The simple descriptions of the Armenian children, the dry reports of German teachers or American consuls, appear to us like a new inferno. The diabolical suffering when unarmed Armenians, including women and children, were murdered by cowards, is worse than the torment of the battlefield, which at least belongs to a somewhat honorable struggle.

Last year one could read documents written by Germans who were eyewitnesses to the horror in Aleppo (see *Friedenswarte*, November 1916). They had sent a letter of protest to the Foreign Office in which they listed the atrocities perpetrated by the Kurds and the Turks while German officers, following orders, stood by passively and watched. The result of this petition, which also appeared as a pamphlet, was its immediate ban by the wartime press office with the comment, "It is precisely the Turks whom we need."

Has so-called culture deprived Europeans so completely of all sense of shame and human compassion that they can stand before such slaughter without batting an eyelid? Here there was no question of taking necessary measures for protection or defense. This was murder for the sheer joy of it, the deliberate extermination of an entire nation. That pamphlet and the various consuls' reports are proof that it was not simply a matter of eliminating mortal enemies as far as the Turkish executioners were concerned, but rather a matter of tormenting ordinary people with the most extreme torture.

The following is an excerpt from the report of the American consul in Harput, dated July 11, 1915: "In the first few days of July, the first convoys from Erzurum and Erzincan arrived in Harput, dressed in rags, dirty, exhausted, and sick. They had been on the road for two months with almost no food, no water. They were given hay like animals; they were so exhausted that they threw themselves on it. But the Kurds drove them back, beating them with sticks and slaughtered some on the spot. The Turks sent their doctors to check the health of the young girls and to pick out the most attractive for their harems. Many on the wretched march had been killed en route by the Kurds who attacked them continuously; many died of hunger and exhaustion."

Also from the pamphlets and reports: "The entire country is covered with corpses. The bodies of women, robbed and raped, line the roads. The poor are driven onward with whips and clubs until, almost naked, they drop from hunger and exhaustion. Distraught mothers with children who could go no further were forced to leave them lying on the ground, whereupon the Kurds smashed their skulls.

"The inhabitants of the village Tel Armen on the Baghdad line were burned alive or else thrown into the wells. Thousands were drowned in the Euphrates. The children were tied together on rafts, but often their mothers, by now insane, threw them into the river beforehand. The women were bound together and thrown from high cliffs into the waters of the Euphrates. For an entire month one could see corpses floating downstream almost every day, the men mutilated, the women disembowelled."

Henry Barby described this desecration in his *Diary from Armenia* (Tiflis, August 1915): "In Ardjich, on the banks of Lake Van, the Turks, having killed the Armenian men, brought back their severed limbs for the women."[1]

I have not recorded even one hundredth of the Turkish butchery reported in the documents I have before me. But one can grasp some idea of its extent when one learns that over 800,000 Armenian men, women,

1. Henry Barby, a correspondent of *Le Journal*, accused the German consul at Erzurum and von Wangenheim, the German ambassador in Constantinople, of having failed to intervene at the request of the American ambassador, Robert Morgenthau. Goll excerpted the report by the American consul from Barby.

and children were murdered in the course of a few months. 200,000 people who fled to the Caucasus are all that remains of the Armenian nation, for some of those living in Constantinople were also murdered, as was reported in Dr. Harry Stürmer's book *Two Years in Constantinople* (1917).[2] Of those in the Syrian steppe or those deported to Mesopotamia, mostly women and children, 150,000 remain; the other 300,000 were massacred on the spot. These 150,000, robbed of their families, ekeing out an existence of hunger and suffering, were provided with food by the Americans, but as this supply has now been cut off, one must ask oneself what will become of the survivors now? Will the Germans, who are at present the only civilized nation with influence, indeed complete power over the Turks, will they really watch silently as poor tortured women and children slowly waste away? Or will they finally step in with a helping hand for these remaining Armenians, as it has long since been their duty? For the sake of the German name, let us hope so!

Die Freie Zeitung, November 3, 1917

Translated by Trudi Nicholas

"Für Armenien," in *Der gläserne Garten, Prosa 1917–1939*, ed. Barbara Glauert–Hesse for Fondation Yvan et Claire Goll, Saint–Dié–des Vosges (Berlin: Argon, 1987), 3: 35–38. Copyright © 1987 Argon Verlag GmbH, Berlin.

2. Stürmer, a journalist for the *Kölnische Zeitung* at Constantinople in 1915–16, held the German government equally responsible with the Turks for the atrocities.

☦ Madame Journiac
French

☦ Letter to the Minister of Public Works

January 19, 1918

Dear Mr. Minister,

In the name of all the wives of those fighting at the front, of war widows, of families in the commune of Bézenet whose children are at the front, I protest with all my energy against the unjust, ignoble, scandalous way in which coal is being distributed in this commune. The draft-dodgers of the coal mine, judged to be the only interested parties, receive 540 kilos of coal a month for their homes, while the wives of those who give their blood for the fatherland, the war widows, receive 150 kilos. Please show the willpower to exercise your authority and put a halt to this sleazy behavior, or tell me if it is in our husbands' absence from home that people make fun of us while, to cap the injustice, our men each day give their lives. You have assumed your responsibilities, Minister—well then! Respond or act!

[signed]
Madame Journiac

From A. M. Michelon, "L'opinion publique dans l'Allier pendant la Première Guerre mondiale," master's thesis *(maîtrise)* directed by Jean-Jacques Becker, and deposited at the University of Clermont-Ferrand.

✛ Hélène Brion
(1882–1962) *French*

Feminist syndicalist, socialist, and pacifist, Hélène Brion was the daughter of an army officer; because of her father's travels she was raised by her grandmother. She began her career as a schoolteacher in the suburbs of Paris, where she joined the union (Syndicat des Instituteurs); during the war she served as its assistant secretary. She became active in feminist movements, befriending the radical suffragist Madeleine Pelletier and writing for *L'Équité* (Equity) and *L'Action féministe* (Feminist action), a university women's organ. As a member of the Groupe des Femmes Socialistes, she quarreled over the relative priority of feminism or socialism with the socialist Louise Saumoneau, an exchange that provoked her to reword Proudhon's notorious phrase and describe the Frenchwoman as "housewife *and* harlot."

Brion's first reaction to the war and to a visiting British pacifist was to justify national self-defense. When the socialist feminists and schoolteachers voted to oppose the war, however, she rallied to their position and went as a delegate to the 1915 meeting of international socialists at Zimmerwald. As a result of these activities she was first arrested in November 1916 on charges of pacifism and defeatism. Released, she continued to publish pacifist and feminist pieces, for which she was again arrested and tried by the Conseil de Guerre in Paris, on March 25–31, 1918; she received a suspended sentence of three years' imprisonment. In her own defense on March 29, she challenged the right of the state to condemn her for opposing a war that had been declared without her assent as a voter. The official report of the trial carried a sketch of her reading this "declaration of feminist principles" in self-defense.

After the war Brion remained active in campaigns for peace and for women's suffrage. In 1920 she joined the Communist Party. Brion never married, but had two children out of wedlock by a Russian émigré.

JS

✠ Transcript of Trial, March 29, 1918

I appear here accused of a political crime: yet I am stripped of all political rights.

Because a woman, I am ranked by the laws of my country *de plano,* far below all men of France and the colonies. In spite of an intelligence that not long ago was recognized officially, in spite of the certificates and diplomas awarded me long ago, before the law I am not the equal of an illiterate Negro from Guadeloupe or the Ivory Coast. For *he* can participate by ballot in directing the affairs of our common country and *I* cannot. I am an outlaw.

The law should be logical and ignore my existence when it is a question of sanctions so long as it ignores me when it is a question of rights. I protest this illogic.

I protest the application to me of laws that I neither wanted nor discussed.

This law that I challenge reproaches me with having made remarks of a kind that would lower the morale of the people. I protest with yet more force and deny it! My discreet and nuanced propaganda has always made a constant appeal to reason, to the power of reflection, to the good sense allotted to every human, even in small amounts.

I recall as well, as a formality, that my propaganda never went against national defense and never called for peace at any price: to the contrary, I have always said that there was only one duty, one alone with two versions:

For those at the front: to hold.

For those at the rear: to reflect.

This educative action I have above all conducted in a feminist sense, because I am above all and before all else a *feminist,* every one who knows me will bear witness to this. And it is by virtue of feminism that I am an enemy of the war.

The accusation claims that under the pretext of feminism I pursue pacifism. This deforms my propaganda for its own needs! I affirm the contrary, and it is easy to prove it. I affirm that for years before the war I was a militant feminist: that I have simply continued since the outbreak of war and that I have never remarked on the evils of the moment without adding that, if women had a say in the matter of social questions, things would proceed differently.

I appeal to the testimony.

You want to see in me, not the dedicated feminist I am, who daily used for her feminist goal lessons drawn from the war as she used for the same purpose the least incidents of peace, but a shameful sort of pacifist who under the vague pretext of a fallacious feminism outwitted innocent souls to poison them with pernicious doctrines. For those who know me this is absolutely ridiculous.

Never before the war did I advocate militant pacifism nor did I belong to any pacifist organization, while for years I have been a militant member of feminist associations: Suffrage des Femmes, Union fraternelle des femmes, Fédération féminine universitaire, Ligue pour le droit des femmes, Union Française pour le Suffrage des femmes, Ligue Nationale du vote, etc. . . .

I am an enemy of the war because I am a feminist, war is the triumph of brutal force, feminism can triumph only by moral force and intellectual valor. There is an absolute antinomy between the two.

I do not think that in primitive society the force and value of woman were inferior to those of man, but certainly in present society, the possibility of war has established a scale of factitious values to the detriment of woman.

She has been denied the imprescriptible and sacred right of any individual to defend himself when attacked. She has been made by definition (and from time to time by education) into a weak, docile, insignificant being whose whole life must be protected and directed.

Far from allowing her like the rest of creation to defend her infants, they deny her the right to defend herself. Materially they refuse her physical education, sports, the exercise of the noble profession of arms. Politically they refuse the right to vote—the keystone, Gambetta said, for all other rights—the right to vote thanks to which she could intervene in her own destiny and at least have the means to attempt to resist these horrifying conflicts into which she finds herself thrown, she and her children, like a poor unconscious and impotent machine. . . .

You men, who govern the world alone. At this moment you want to do too much and to do it too well. You should leave well enough alone.

You wish to shield our children from the horrors of a future war: admirable sentiment! I say that henceforth your goal has been attained, and as soon as the atrocious battle that is taking place less than 100 kilometers from us has ended, you may speak of peace. In 1870 two European nations fought, only two, and for only six months: the result was so shocking that all Europe terrified and exhausted passed more than forty years before daring or being able to recommence. Calculate that we at this moment have fought not six but forty-four months a fantastic, formidable struggle, in which not two nations alone but more than twenty from the elite of the so called civilized world are in conflict, that almost the whole white race is involved, that the yellow and black races have been dragged in subsequently, and admit, I beg you, that henceforth your goal has been attained! For the exhaustion of the world is such that more than one hundred years of peace would be assured henceforth if the war ended tonight!

The future tranquillity of our children and grandchildren is assured. Think of assuring their present happiness and future health! Think of the means to give them as much bread and sugar and chocolate for snacks as they desire! Do you calculate the repercussions that their present privations can have on the happiness that you claim to assure in continuing to fight and to make them live in this atmosphere which from all points of view is unhealthy for them?

You want to restore the liberty of subjected peoples, you wish to call to liberty people who do not seem ripe to understand it as you do, in spite of themselves, and you do not realize that in this struggle for liberty, each one loses more and more of the shreds that remained, from the material freedoms to eat as one wishes and to travel at one's pleasure to the intellectual liberties to write, to meet, even to think and above all the possibility of thinking accurately, all this disappears gradually because it is incompatible with the state of war.

Watch out! The world is descending a slope, and it will be difficult to climb back up.

I have always said, I have everywhere written since the beginning of the war: If you do not call women to assist you, the slope will not be reascended and the new world that you claim to inaugurate will be as unjust and as chaotic as the one before the war. . . .

My propaganda has always been rational, never an appeal to violence! And I appeal here to the testimony of those who know me and those who read me!

I call upon the testimony not of the woman who in her zeal to accuse me made declarations that she has been obliged partly to retract, nor of the woman who was forced to acknowledge that I had spoken to her directly no more than once and whose charge was reduced to a report of statements she overheard behind two doors and to flimsy speculation about my acts. No!

I appeal to those who have known me for 10, 15, 20 years or more and above all since the war, to those who have seen me militate almost every day by their side, who have been able to examine and follow my propaganda, because they either opposed or approved it.

Among those witnesses I do not fear contradictions. They know in their hearts that if I have always been a dedicated adversary, I have been loyal, and that if I have always defended to the end my point of view toward and against all, I can say it and will continue to do so. I have never had the least idea in the world of supporting my right with my fists or even curses.

Violence repels me, I have never engaged in it, nor counseled it. It is to put an end to its reign on earth that I have always and in all circumstances appealed to women and commented 100 times, in writing or orally on this saying of Victor Considérant:

"The day when women will be initiated into social questions, revolutions will no longer be made by rifle fire."

From *Revue des causes célèbres politiques et criminelles*, May 2, 1918, 152–54.

✠ Margit Kaffka
(1880–1918) *Hungarian*

Born in Transylvania (now Romania), Margit Kaffka had a Hungarian mother and Slav father; he died when she was six, and she was sent to a Catholic boarding school. *Hangyaboly* (The Ant Heap, 1917) satirizes a convent school disturbed by modern ideas of female independence and precocious sexual desires. She later described her mother's second marriage in *Szinek és Évek* (Colors and years, 1912), the novel that brought her first success. She trained to become a schoolteacher, first at the convent, then after 1899 in Budapest, a struggle described in the autobiographical novel *Mária Évei* (The years of Maria, 1913), whose heroine finally commits suicide. In 1905 she married Bruno Fröhlich, but was unhappy as a provincial housewife and mother; they separated in 1910. After returning to Budapest, to support her child she taught and wrote poetry, stories, and reviews. She joined the circle of avant-garde writers around the journal *Nyugat* (The West). Some of her work concerned the "new woman," while other fiction and poetry focused on the plight of the worker, especially the working-class woman in a moment of revolutionary change. Her style challenges the reader with neologisms, synesthesia, and complex sentence structures.

In 1914 Kaffka married Ervin Bauer, a Jewish doctor ten years younger than herself, who enlisted as a doctor when the war broke out. Kaffka opposed the war as her poems of 1914 demonstrate. A novella, *Két Nyár* (Two summers, 1916), closes in a birth clinic with a balance sheet of blood: "and so a surplus of tiny bundles of steaming bodies; in order that some lives from the womb might always survive all those destined to be exterminated with most terrible weapons, in an infinite variety of bloody ways after twenty, a hundred, a thousand years to come." She traveled to the hospitals where her husband had been posted and wrote a novel to buy a microscope for him. *Nyugat* published a collection of her poems in 1918. That year she also brought out a children's book, *My Little Friends*, whose introduction is a pacifist manifesto. Just as she was relishing peace and the reunion of her family, she and her son died of influenza in the first days of December 1918. Earlier that year, the poet Endre Ady had praised in her work "the triumph of Hungarian feminism": "she is a strong person, an artist with an assured future." Her friend Anna Lesznai (Amalia Moscowitz), a painter and writer, recalled that "she was the only woman regarded by men as a writer of equal status, a surprising person, combining qualities of beauty and plainness in rare harmony. She bore her extraordinary talent as an unwelcome gift." Kaffka believed that "writing is a ruthless profession demanding blood sacrifice."

✟ Introduction, *My Little Friends*

I believe I shall enjoy writing this book for you about the serious activity called play.

As I start to write, in the adult world times are difficult; sad and terribly ugly, wicked things are happening. There is war; sensible, grown people are living on the plains in holes or wet ditches, cut off from their families. They do no useful work, nothing beautiful or serious; they shoot to kill each other, with guns and other ghastly weapons. Millions are out there: Hungarians, Germans, Russians, Italians, English, French. All suffer terribly from fellow humans they do not know and have never seen before. Thousands have horrible wounds, many are crippled for life, others have only a burial mound beneath which they rest, their names unknown forever. At home a sad family may not even know of the death, but wait with tears and hope for his return. And apart from these sorrows, there is terrible inflation everywhere; families at home struggle, worrying, working twice as hard because the duties of those mobilized cannot be neglected.

What I want to say to you is this: do not let these things wound your hearts, or ruin your love of life. This terrible war is the fault of my generation of adults, but you must change the world when you grow up. Be strong, work for our poor country, to heal wounds and satisfy needs not only for us but for all our fellow humans, because the population of the whole world is suffering and cries out for help. Precious human work is destroyed now, houses and machinery and drains—so many artifacts. You, today's children, will have to rebuild all this! Great work awaits you if you want to create a beautiful, enduring world.

So, children, be ready for life's good tasks, do not let your spirit be destroyed. Prepare for life with play because playing is for you a serious matter; true, it is voluntary, no one forces you, for that would make it worthless, but it is precious, for from play you learn most and know yourself best.

Make us happy with your cheerful eyes; and by acting and imagining, work and rest at the same time—that is the nature of play! In this way prepare your future which should be happier, more sensible than ours now;

those whom we now call enemies you will again be able to feel are friends; learn from them, strive for them.

While I write this book I should like to forget the madness and hatred of this terrible world, in which only your play gives hope and beauty! Perhaps by the time I have finished God's sun will shine again; and then we will be able to rejoice in the hope of a happy future for you.

1918

Translated by Charlotte Franklin

"Preface," in *Kis emberek: barátocskáim* (Budapest: Pallas Irodalmi, 1918).

✦ II ✦

JOURNALISM

The growth in the nineteenth century of women's and "family" magazines and newspapers either wholly addressed to women or partly devoted to "women's issues," like the *Saturday Evening Post* and the French *La Française,* provided an outlet for women to write on a regular basis for pay. Journals rooted in the women's movement and in political associations, such as the British *Votes for Women* and the Russian *Zhenskii vestnik,* continued during the war to serve as a platform for women's various views, but they also turned in a new direction, as women recorded their responses to the war. Socialist feminists edited a number of papers, the most important of which was Clara Zetkin's *Die Gleichheit.* In addition, general newspapers, some of them like Matilde Serao's *Il Giorno* now run by women, sought out women to report on women's experiences, focusing on such matters as civilian refugees, relief organizations, hospitals, orphans, and hunger. Although the vast majority of reporting was still done by men, women were considered to be potential specialists on such issues.

In part because the United States remained neutral until 1917, American women were able to get to Europe, even to the front lines on both sides, and to send back articles about what they had seen. These women were convinced that their presence in war-torn villages, or in the battle zone, where they were escorted by the military and Red Cross, marked a rupture with the past, when only men would have been allowed free passage. Writers like Mary Roberts Rinehart finagled their way past checkpoints by explaining that they were going to inspect hospitals or raise funds for relief; they gloated at securing information that eluded their male colleagues, as they scraped the mud off their boots and huddled in bed under their fur coats. Ironically, they had much less time to actually see the battlefront than did nurses who spent months just behind the lines.

Women's news reports from the territories devastated by the war, such as Belgium, France in the wake of German withdrawals, Serbia, and Russia, often had a second economic motive: to raise money at home or abroad for relief efforts. They focus on descriptions of hospitals, work-shops, or working-class women in order to elicit sympathy for those suf-fering from the miseries caused by war. Women's papers also sought to underscore the broadened range of women's active participation in the wartime economy as a way to justify appeals for women's representation on local councils or municipal governments and access to the vote.

Like writing by men, women's journalism about the war can be highly colored by its political motives. The journalist Corra Harris was recalled from Europe by the *Saturday Evening Post* because her reporting was con-sidered too political—or not the right politics. Female journalists were specifically instructed to obtain stories with "heart kick"—to provide telling, often pathetic or sentimental anecdotes and to paint vivid descrip-tions in a personal voice in order to make their points. Therefore, their reports to some extent resemble the more explicitly political tracts, as well as the personal accounts recorded in letters and memoirs. At their best, these women journalists questioned exaggerated atrocity reports, chal-lenged legislative attempts to decide what women should do with their bodies, and recorded for posterity the diversity of women's activities.

✝ Colette, pseudonym of Sidonie-Gabrielle Colette (1873–1954) *French*

Born in Burgundy, Sidonie-Gabrielle Colette spent her childhood in a provincial town in Burgundy with her beloved mother, Sido, and her father, a disabled Zouave captain. When their fortune was dissipated, the family moved in with relatives and, at sixteen, Colette had to leave school. At age twenty, "Gabri" married her first husband, Henry Gauthier-Villars, called "Willy," a member of café society whose profligacy kept them in constant debt. Willy, who built a publishing career on stories ghost-written by others, encouraged her to record for him her school years in *Claudine at School* (1900), "and that," she later recalled, "is how I became a writer." The marriage floundered when Willy took a mistress: they separated and eventually divorced in 1910. On her own, Colette supported herself on the stage as a mime and erotic actress in music halls. Moving in fashionable lesbian artistic circles, she continued to write, drawing on her own experiences and exploring the question of women's independence in *The Vagabond* (1910) and *Music-Hall Sidelights* (1913). In 1912 she married the newspaper editor Henri de Jouvenel, for whose paper, *Le Matin,* she began to write articles; in 1913 their daughter Bel-Gazou was born.

During World War I, Colette wrote articles and reports for *Le Matin* and other papers. Visiting her husband at Verdun in January 1915, she documented life in a military sector from which women were supposed to be banned. A collection of her wartime journalism, *Les heures longues* (The long hours, 1917), met with popular acclaim, as she used the language of the Parisian people to describe what she saw to her audience. Her editor called it "a new form of lyric journalism rooted in history, as it is encoun-

tered every day by a woman, mother, traveler, and artist." Colette also converted an estate near St-Malo into a hospital, where she served as a nurse.
After reading her wartime novel *Mitsou* (1919), which describes an actress
who falls in love with a soldier, Marcel Proust wrote, "I wept a little this
evening."

In the postwar era Colette wrote some of her greatest fiction, *Chéri*
(1920) and *The Last of Chéri* (1926), focusing on postwar spiritual desolation, on maternal love, and on heterosexual and homosexual eroticism.
André Gide wrote to her in response, "what intelligence, what mastery, what
understanding of the least confessed secrets of the body!" By the mid-1920s
her affair with her teenaged stepson, coupled with her husband's affairs,
brought her marriage to an end. In 1925 she began an affair with Maurice
Goudeket, a Dutch Jew sixteen years her junior, whom she married ten years
later; he was hidden by friends during the occupation of France in World
War II. In 1935, she was elected to the Belgian Royal Academy and in 1945
she joined the Goncourt Academy, of which she became president in 1949.
In 1953 she was named Chevalier of the French Legion of Honor; in 1954
she was the first French woman to be given a state funeral.

JS

✠ Fashions

Madame,

Although an unknown non-commissioned officer, I am writing to ask
you to be the most indiscreet of confidants, since by taking note of my
small private sorrow you will speak in the name of a weighty generality.

I am a sergeant, somewhere near the front. In August I left my beloved
young wife. After six and a half months of separation, I was sent on assignment for eight days to Paris, and I spent them with my wife. Suffice it to
say that the mighty of this world, and more particularly several million soldiers, can with justice envy my fate.

Yet I am not altogether content. Don't rush to murmur vindictively, "So
what do you want then?" because, anticipating your question, I was about
to tell you.

I got off at the Gare de l'Est, and moved, my legs giving way, voiceless,
searching the quai for the woman whose last image had never paled over
the preceding six months: a young blonde, slender in her summer dress,
her neck and a little of her breast visible in the décolletage of her lawn
blouse—a young woman so womanly and so weak, and so courageous at
the moment of separation, so illumined by laughter and tears. . . . I was
looking for her, Madame, when a strangled cry called me and I fell into
the arms . . . of a delicious little second lieutenant, who dissolved in tears
on my shoulder stammering, "Dearest, dearest . . ." and embraced me in
the most scandalous manner. This second lieutenant was my wife. A great-

coat of blue-gray cloth with two rows of buttons equipped her in the latest trench fashion, and her little ears emerged quite bare from a police cap braided with burnished gold. A stiff dolman collar lifted her tender neck: she also had pinned on her chest a Belgian flag and another trinket that she immediately called her "darling 75."[1]

We left the station, arm in arm, as lovers; the sleeves of our greatcoats tightly wed. In the cold wind I watched the blond locks fluttering behind the ear of the second lieut—. . . pardon, of my wife. On the sidewalk we crossed strange passersby: I found myself involuntarily sketching a salute to a solid *capitaine* in police blue, severe and buttoned, then brushing against a young person, thin and belted, whose uniform I thought I recognized as a fantastic variant on the *cadre noir*,[2] or making way for an English *officière* in khaki raincoat.

My beloved second lieutenant followed my gaze. She pulled back from my arm a bit to show off her coat and forage cap, and exclaimed, "So, are you happy? Don't you think women have a sense for the situation? Anything for the soldiers! All now dressed as soldiers!"

And she pulled down her broad belt with such a soldierly gesture that I burst into laughter, in order not to burst into sobs of pleasure, at this unexpected moment.

That night we dined tête à tête, tired, astonished, happy, silent like people who have half a year to tell each other about. From time to time my wife exclaimed, "You remember our friend Marcel? He shows off his relations with the QGA[3] all the time, but that doesn't keep him from going mouldy in the GVC.[4] When I saw him the other day, he told me horrifying things about the RVF."[5]

And I looked at her with reproach, as if the fine arc of her lips had hurled obscenities.

The next day, she told me what she had done since the month of August. I learned, without feeling the same intoxication she felt, that the administration had adopted her model for a balaklava, "the only one that doesn't deafen you," and that she was the heart of a vast conspiracy against the return to long trousers for civilians, to the benefit of short shorts, leggings, boots, or silk stockings. I saw that she had replaced the lamp to heat her curling iron with a soldier's portable stove burning solid alcohol.

I cut my tale short, Madame. Suffice it to know that after a week my wife's military virtues had thrown me into the most intolerant, the most unjust, exasperation. I contained myself—my superior, after all, has so many charms! And I left for the front, as they say, calling out to her in her favorite language, through the lowered window, a final JVA,[6] which she translated perfectly by throwing me her last kiss.

1. *75:* French cannon, which shot 75 mm shells.
2. *Cadre noir:* elite cavalry unit.
3. *QGA: Quartier général de l'armée,* General Headquarters.
4. *GVC: Gardes-voies et communications,* railroad guards and signalmen.
5. *RVF: Ravitaillement et viande fraiche,* or P.X.
6. *JVA: Je vous aime,* I love you.

But now that I am once again all alone and sad, Madame, I want to complain about the militarization of our wives and lovers. What did grouchy critics say: that we lacked uniforms for men working in depots? Not surprising: our wives grab the felted wool, loops, and braid. O women, beloved wives, it's this profiteering patriotism that you must abandon if you want to please us. Tunic, dolman, caps with braid—why not a little bayonet pin and a backpack instead of a handbag? Dearest women, think about our victory parade soon in Paris, our parade of patched, faded, variegated, velvet zouaves, bicycle cavalry, blue, gray, brown infantry, sharpshooters in sweaters and Algerian riflemen in mufflers, all handsome, glorious, broken down, heroic . . . And you will be there, you our wives, with your spiffy uniforms, your new greatcoats and your brushed police caps, your unstained belts, watching us pass? Fear the vengeful *poilu*,[7] who will toss over his shoulder a cry of "Go on, shirker!" Fear the moment when back in our good civilian dress, in our city shoes, we will find on you—what? . . . The war at the hearth, the war at 29 francs a blouse, the war at 99 francs the complete outfit, the war at 10 francs 75 per képi . . . I exclaim already, as if I were there, "Ah no!, I know it . . . I waged it! Peace, for God's sake, peace!"

I have finished, Madame. I've said nearly everything I want to say. While I have been writing to you, one of my men, next to me, is delicately painting postcards in watercolor—it's not water that he lacks. He embellishes with love a subject that is always the same: a fat beauty, reclining on the clouds, draped in gauze, a garland, or sometimes a fan and a necklace. He is painting Woman, mirage, hope, magnificent memory, torment and comfort at every hour. But I assure you that this artless painter would never dream of evoking the Wonder of the world in the guise of a little French soldier, narrow shouldered and short, and marching like a doe with feet that hurt.

Dear Madame, I remain your humble servant,

Sergeant X

Le Matin, February 24, 1915

"Modes," in *Les heures longues* (Paris, Fayard, 1917). Translated by permission of André Schmidt, avocat, literary executor for the estate of Colette.

☦ The Child of the Enemy

Soon he will see the light of day. Still enclosed, scarcely quivering, he is already present. Newspapers have called down on his head at times indulgence, at others a curse. Some call him "the innocent" and paint his trou-

7. *Poilu:* G.I., literally "hairy," nicknamed for General Joffre's moustache.

bling portrait between a forgiven mother and a merciful French soldier. . . . But others treat him as poisoned tares, a living crime, and consign him to secret murder. . . . This is what the two camps have come to. Soon we will have lectures about The Child of the Enemy. This is terribly sad. Why so many words, so much ink spilled about him and his humiliated mother?

"But we must counsel and guide these poor women who . . ."

No. They don't need it. They are no longer in the first hours, the first days of somber madness, when they cried out their shame and pleaded, "What am I going to do? What am I going to do?" Do you imagine that a bitter meditation lasting thirty-six months bears no fruit? Give to these women who lack everything: shelter, food, and what else? . . . work . . . a layette—then trust them. The most rebellious, the most vindictive is no longer capable of a crime regardless of those who would absolve her in advance of such an act.

"But what will she do?"

Leave her alone. Perhaps she doesn't know yet. She will know when the time comes. She suffers, but the optimism passed to a female heavy with the precious weight of a human being combats her suffering, pleads for the trembling child, and endows the mother with a new instinct: that of not thinking too much, of not tracing the future in sharp, dark traits. The most vindictive one, even she who awakens at night cursing the imperious prisoner of her flanks, does not need to be enlightened. Perhaps—angry and horrified—she awaits the intruder, the monster that she must, if not crush at its first cry, at least banish. . . . But let us trust that in the moment when she is exhausted, softened, without defence against her better instinct, she will recognize that the "monster" is simply a newborn with vague eyes, silvery down, wrinkled and silky hands like a poppy blossom newly burst from its calyx. . . .

Let the women go their way. Say nothing. . . . Silence. . . .

Le Matin, March 24, 1915

"L'enfant de l'ennemi," in *Les heures longues* (Paris: Fayard, 1917). Translated by permission of André Schmidt, avocat, literary executor for the estate of Colette.

✝ Ivanova
Russian

"Ivanova" was a regular contributor to *Zhenskii vestnik* (Women's herald), the most enduring of Russian feminist political journals, which appeared from 1904–1917. A "public scientific literary monthly devoted to equal rights and improvement of women's condition," the newspaper embraced a vague socialism. It was founded by Dr. Maria Ivanovna Pokrovskaia, a doctor for the indigent who became committed to the movement opposing state regulation of prostitution. Pokrovskaia also set up the Women's Progressive Party, the first women's party in Russia to call for equal civil rights, liberalization of divorce, acceptance of children out of wedlock, equal rights to land for peasant women, and an end to militarism. While the editor believed that only women could "annihilate . . . the mania for world domination which creates slavery and war," the journal also saw the upheaval engendered by war as "clearing from women's path some of the obstacles which previously blocked their aspirations to engage in every sort of work." Ivanova's article was part of a series on "women and war" describing women's changing roles and social contributions.

✝ Women and War

There has been a strong upsurge of patriotism among Russians—men, women, and even children. Despite the reigning view that women's wartime role should be confined to helping the sick and wounded, Russian women are taking up arms to defend their fatherland. . . . In some cases women are already taking part in battles, weapons in hand. Many girls from different social classes are running away from home, dressing up as men, and trying to get into the army. Some succeed with the help of officers with whom they are acquainted. Thus one seventeen-year-old girl, the relative of an officer, asked his regiment to take her to war with them. They found her a uniform for a lower rank and enlisted her in the regiment. The girl demonstrated extraordinary courage during one skirmish, when a soldier by her side was seriously wounded. The Russians had to retreat, abandoning their wounded on the battlefield. At dusk the girl set off with an officer to search for her wounded comrade. They found him and took him up on the saddle, then set off toward their own forces. The enemy fired at them and gave chase, and when the girl's horse went lame, caught up with them; but the girl did not want to surrender and began to shoot. They were rescued by the arrival of a detachment of Cossacks. The girl received the medal of St. George for bravery; later on during a reconnaissance mission, she was wounded.

Famous for her travel on horseback from Siberia to Russia, Kudasheva has enlisted as a private in one of the cavalry regiments.

The aviatrix Princess E. M. Shakhovskaia attempted to enter active army service as a pilot. They refused on the grounds that the enemy would not recognize her as a legitimate member of our armed forces, and would shoot her as a spy if she fell behind enemy lines. She now works in a forward post as a nurse.

In the effort to help healthy and wounded soldiers and their families, Russian women are carrying an enormous burden. In huge numbers they are enlisting as nurses, eager to work at the front. We should note that A. A. Tolstaia and several well-known women artists have become nurses. No assembly on behalf of the families of reservists, wounded, or healthy soldiers occurs without the active participation of women. Patriotic concerts by Dolina, the singer of the imperial theaters, have earned tens of thousands of rubles to benefit various organizations that aid war victims. Women sew and knit essential articles for the soldiers. . . .

In rural areas, aid to families of reservists is administered by the *volost*[1] board, chosen by assemblies made up of persons of both sexes living in the *volost*. Thus the war has broadened the official sphere of rural women's activities, granting them the same rights as men on the *volost* boards.

Wishing to gather as much information as possible on women's efforts to aid the victims of war and their attempts to take up arms in defense of their fatherland, the editors of *Zhenskii vestnik* urgently appeal to male and female readers to pass on additional reports like these.

Zhenskii vestnik, November 1914

Translated by Cynthia Simmons

---

1. *Volost:* the smallest administrative division in czarist Russia.

✝ Corra Harris
(1869–1935) *American*

The daughter of a former Confederate soldier and a strong, religious mother, Corra Mae White showed promise as a writer from an early age. At sixteen, she decided to earn her living as a teacher, moving to a nearby town in Georgia, where she met Lundy Harris, then a student at Emory College. The two married in 1887, just after Harris had embarked on a career as a Methodist circuit preacher, and their only child, Faith, was born within the year. Corra's marriage to Lundy Harris was difficult: after ten years of teaching at Emory, Lundy Harris disappeared, leaving no money for Corra to pay their debts. On his return two weeks later his mental instability was clear; he would attempt suicide six times in the next few years before dying of an overdose of morphine in 1910.

Corra Harris turned to her pen to support the family. In the following ten years, she wrote 1,200 book reviews, editorials, and short stories, including a series of racist articles and analyses of white Southern men and women published in the New York *Independent.* In 1903 she collaborated with Paul Elmer More on a serialized novel in letters, *The Jessica Letters.* Then in 1910 she anonymously serialized her second novel, the autobiographical *A Circuit Rider's Wife,* in the *Saturday Evening Post,* which cemented her popularity.

Now a regular contributor to the *Post,* she went to Europe in 1911 to write about the progress of women's suffrage there. Harris supported suffrage but disapproved of militancy and of women in political office. In 1914 the *Post* sent her to Europe to write about the women's perspective on the war. In London, she was impressed with the well-organized mobilization of women for the war effort, but surprised that the British were so stoic and self-assured. Witnessing the destitution of women in Paris, she denounced war as an institution which destroyed families economically as well as emotionally. She tried in her war articles to remedy the problem that "what women suffer is never written." The editors of the *Post,* frustrated by her tendency to editorialize, quickly replaced her with Mary Roberts Rinehart, and she returned home in December 1914 without having been near the frontlines.

She serialized two autobiographies, and continued to write for the *Post* and later for the Atlanta *Journal* until her death in 1935.

RC

✠ Women of England and Women of France

All wars are waged against women and children. However victorious an army is, it must purchase victory by defeating them. They are the victims who cannot end their suffering on the field of battle; who will never be decorated with the Victoria Cross for their courage; who will have no monuments raised to praise them, but who must serve life sentences to poverty, and endure the long siege of the years helpless and alone. And most of them will; for it is the private soldier who does the dangerous bloody drudgery of the actual fighting, and the average private soldier is a man of no fortune at all, whose family depends on his labor from day to day for support.

This is the fallacy of patriotism: It places the ambition of war lords, the cupidity of national governments and the love for country above the love of a man for his wife and children. The land on which a nation lives is not sacred. It is the nation that is sacred, and the arts and institutions and virtues which uphold it. These are the very things war destroys in the name of patriotism, and for the restoring of which the broken and impoverished people must be enormously taxed. [. . .]

The one reprehensible feature in this whole situation is the perpetual discussion and agitation of German atrocities, more particularly by the women and the press. The papers can publish no war news of any value. The most direct information comes from the Belgian refugees. It is a wonder the War Office does not censor them before they are permitted to land! Therefore, the papers fill their columns with stories of German outrages; but at the end of each there is usually a note saying that the atrocity has not been officially confirmed. [. . .]

What men suffer through war is written in histories. It is remembered. They earn something which is handed down to the generations that come after them, which praise them; but what women suffer is never written. If it is mentioned at all it is simply set down in the debit columns of economic works, showing the lack of food and the percentage of destitution during that period. It is never illustrated with the weary faces of mothers and the pale faces of hungry children. Nobody knows them, and no one ever will.

When one writes of the women's side of the war one cannot tell of battles won, or of the glories that crown the heads of victorious men. It must be a story of sorrows; of despair; of poverty; of privations patiently endured; of defeat in the tender hearts of all women; of the sufferings of little children, who accept them without question, who have no defense, no indemnity against the destruction of their youth and of their fortunes. [. . .]

There is an old mansion in the Rue de la Chaise, built in the reign of Louis XIV by the Marquis de Vaudreuil, the last French Governor of Canada. Long afterward it became the home of Napoleon's sister, Elisa Bonaparte. Then it was a convent. Fifteen years ago the Dominicans added a chapel. In recent years it has been a private hospital, and since this war began it has been the Canadian hospital supported by the readers of the Montreal newspaper.

It was in this place that I came face to face for the first time with the red crime of war. We entered the chapel, one evening just at nightfall, where fifty men lay in a double row of cots—Frenchmen, Turco-French, Arabs and English, all desperately wounded. Most of them wore the clothes they had fought in. Some had lost a leg, others an arm. Some had terrible wounds in their bodies.

So they lay, watching the white-turbaned nurses moving back and forth. Not a groan, only here and there a livid face drawn with pain. One had lain, with his leg nearly off, five days upon the battlefield without food before he managed to attract the attention of a wandering sheep dog. The dog took in the situation and ran back to his master, who brought the man in. Near the middle of the ward an Arab lay with closed eyes. He was a Mohammedan who must eat the food of Christians. He could not understand a word that was said to him nor convey a single wish except by signs. The point was that he was past wishing. As we bent over his bed he looked at us from an infinite distance, through centuries of pain and silence. What had he had to do with all this? He did not know. Yet he also was about to die for France.

It is incredible that one should stand in such a place, surrounded by mutilated men in the prime of their youth and strength, without realizing that war is a ferocious form of insanity. Nothing can justify it. But such ideas are abhorrent to France in her present mood. I suppose they would be to any nation, even to the women of it. Certainly I did not hear a single woman in that place express regret or pity, but only admiration and praise, as we moved about between the beds distributing gifts. And these soldiers did deserve all praise. But I doubt if the world will ever again approve a system of settlement that lays men low like this.

Saturday Evening Post, November 14–December 12, 1914

✠ Marcelle Marquès Capy
(1891–1962) *French*

Daughter of an officer of peasant stock, Marcelle Capy, the French feminist, pacifist, and socialist journalist was born at Cherbourg and raised by her republican grandfather. While studying at the University of Toulouse, she was inspired by Jean Jaurès to become a socialist and a member of the International League for Peace and Freedom. In August 1913 she began a year-long series of articles for the anarchist-syndicalist paper *La bataille syndicaliste* (The union struggle) that was dedicated to exposing labor abuses in the industries and jobs reserved for women. To gather materials, she traveled extensively and worked among the women whose lives she described: fishmongers, sweatshop seamstresses, workers in a lightbulb factory, or assembly-line workers making airplanes. Under the influence of the feminist journalist Séverine, Capy shaped a concise, vital style that aimed at lively evocation rather than statistical precision; the popularity of her journalism enabled her to earn her living by her pen.

Capy clung to Jaurès's internationalist pacifism and defended the pacifist tract *Au dessus de la mêlée* (Above the conflict) by her friend Romain Rolland, who was forced to emigrate to Switzerland. She contributed to the debate that filled the newspapers for several months starting in January 1915 over whether raped women from the occupied zone should have the right to abort. When "the war knocks at our door," she wrote, the natalist politicians offered only the solution of placing these unwanted children in the "dry hands" of charity. In August 1915, *La bataille syndicaliste* began to censor her pacifist pieces: she resigned. Her war journalism collected in *Une voix de femme dans la mêlée* (A woman's voice in the conflict, 1916) was also heavily censored, including her essay on the cathedral of Rheims that is printed here. Séverine, who praised her revolt against women's exploitation, called her book "a mutilated victim of the homefront." A copy with manuscript corrections survives in the Rolland collection at the French

Bibliothèque Nationale. There Capy notes the censor's removal of lines, such as this quotation from a soldier: "Never say that it is fine to kill men."

In 1916 the Commission for Women's Labor requested from Capy a report on the exploitation of women workers in war factories. Capy, in response, depicted war as a moment that crystallized the grievances of women—both as women and as workers. She contributed to the radical newspaper *La voix des femmes* (Women's voice), founded in 1917. With her partner Pierre Brizon, a minority socialist in the legislature, she founded the pacifist socialist journal *La vague* (Wave). Together they agitated for disarmament and guarantees of future peace, opposing the Versailles Treaty, which they saw as overly militaristic and onerous.

In the postwar period she traveled in Germany, where Lida Gustava Heymann reported her flowing eloquence was so powerful that audiences dispensed with translations. Capy's later publications include *L'Oeuvre* (The task), on the reconstruction of postwar Germany, and *Femme de France* (Woman of France), on women's different roles. In 1931 she won the Séverine Peace Prize for *Les hommes passèrent* (Men passed by), a regional novel about the impact of the war on a rural village, which celebrates the possibility of understanding across racial and national lines. In her work as a journalist, Capy concluded that salaried work had given the female proletariat "an unknown liberty, the precise notion of being an active part of society."

JS

✞ The Child of Rape

Never has there been so much talk about civilization. Before the horror of massacres men have been struck dumb. From the greatest to the least, from the most ignorant to the most cultivated, all have felt the need for something more noble than force. "God!" cry some. "Civilization!" say others.

Admittedly, in our times most people have scarcely thought that civilization was an ideal so far beyond their reach. In France, in Germany, everyone thought they were a polished example of civilization. Weren't we in the century of steam, electricity, and aviation? People smiled with disdain when the prophets of doom cried, "Civilization will be an empty word so long as interest governs, so long as each exploits his brother, so long as men scorn their intelligence. Civilization is the conquest of spirit over beast, of right over might."

Poor social organization confined the great mass of humanity to a purely vegetable existence. Ferocious egotism was manifest in the hearts of the rich; submission in the hearts of the poor. The one dreamt only of base pleasures and to satisfy its insatiable appetites forced the other to remain a beast of burden bound to the iron or the furrow.

How could you be surprised that when the reins were dropped, horror reached such a degree?

Those who were stronger trampled on everything we had thought respectable. Educated German brutes ordered carnage and destruction by fire, roused by the evil instincts of their slaves. And the human beast awoke in these armies of pseudo-civilized people intoxicated by alcohol, gunpowder, and the pride of conquest.

Here iniquity will arise from what is weakest, most innocent, most pitiable: children. The fruits of rape prepare for birth. What should be done? That was the question posed recently by Louis Aumont in the *Bataille syndicaliste.* A flood of letters came in on the topic, some from doctors familiar with the delicate problems of reproduction, others from women who by experience know the heavy, fine task of mothers. Soldiers, journalists, priests wrote us.

For a number of our correspondents, liberty is the supreme good. Woman is free to dispose of herself. She therefore has the right to refuse maternity imposed by force. Society may not complete the barbarian's work by condemning the victim to be resigned. To uproot the seed is a right.

Some believe that maternal love will triumph over all difficulties. Certainly, maternal love is the most sublime of human tenderness, but perhaps it has its limits. If women adore the child of the man they love or thought they loved, will they feel the same affection for the child of rape? I know that by nature they are inclined to cherish particularly the most frail, the disinherited. I know that the life of many women is one sacrifice after another. I know that even for the most downtrodden, pity is the guiding star. What could be more pitiable than this poor being conceived in horror! It would be sublime to accept the child under the same guise as the child of a voluntary union and to forget the brute of a father.

However, even admitting that all the victims achieve the sublime—which is far from the case—there remains another difficulty that breaks down even the most ardent maternal love: the implacable need for bread.

In peacetime—not so long ago—how many women abandoned their young! Public Assistance did not lack recruits. Orphanages, more or less philanthropic or Christian, did a good business. How many legitimate or illegitimate children each year swelled the number of little pariahs! And the mothers were not all wretched. One must live. Society is unjust, work is scorned, women's rights are misunderstood, man's heart is often dry. Impotent, maternal love runs up against formidable barriers.

In the case at hand it will be the same, since we must not forget that the victims of hardened soldiers nine times out of ten are poor. Peasants, working women, they had only a little shack in a village, a few sticks of furniture in a suburban room. They stayed home. They knew that these soldiers whose arrival was announced had been torn from their fields, their machinery—that they had just left their mothers, their wives, their children. They believed they would respect unarmed weakness. They were wrong.

The evil is done. Not all maternal love can repair it. We must think about what to do. And since this tragic problem has had such lively interest for our readers, we will publish some of the letters we have received.

La bataille syndicaliste, February 14, 1915

☩ At the Threshold of the Cathedral

Those who wept when they heard about the bombardment of the cathedral of Rheims may dry their tears. It is mutilated, blackened by flames, but stands. It was not without a lively sense of relief that I read in *Le Gaulois* of October 29, 1914, the article by Mme. Colette Yver, where she details what is left and what has been lost of the noble architecture of the basilica.

I felt divided between indignation and contentment. Indignation, because in scorn of the white flag and the red cross of Geneva flying on the building, Prussian officers ordered cannons aimed at these century-old towers. Contentment because, in spite of the shells, it stands.

Suddenly I trembled. One passage in the article struck me with dismay. I sought in vain a further note denying the facts announced, I sought in vain a blank. Nothing. The censors had not honored the article with their scissors. Though so concerned about our national honor, they had not thought it necessary to intervene. So it was true.

The cathedral was in flames. Inside, bedded down on straw, there were German wounded. At any price these poor beings, whose weakness put them under the protection of the well known generosity of the French people, had to be saved. It was an easy task for all to undertake, seeing that a wounded man or a prisoner is a sacred charge for a civilized people. Alas! No such thing. According to Mme. Yver, here is what happened:

"In its distraction the blinded crowd no longer distinguished between those with their cannons over there and these whose wretchedness confined them to French honor. It wanted these to pay for those. Cries of anger, cries of death rose up. Shots were fired. The first four German wounded who fled the flames fell."

Have you read this carefully? Shots fired, on wounded men. . . . Isn't that rather disgusting, rather cowardly? Among the population of Rheims there were creatures barbarous enough to accomplish such a horror.

I finished reading the piece, hoping to find an explanation. Perhaps those guilty of this quadruple murder were only provocateurs or spies who wanted to prevent France from claiming its glory as a civilizing nation. . . . But no, my hope was fruitless.

Then I searched all the papers to learn what appropriate punishment had been meted to these killers of the wounded. I found nothing.

Was this horror perpetrated with impunity? If so, what a stain! What an insult for all those who fight in the name of the law and what a deplorable encouragement for all the vampires who were waiting for such an opportunity.

We have men on the other side of the Rhine. Bit by bit, after long silences, their letters arrive. Some, wounded on the field of battle, have been cared for in German hospitals. They may suffer, but they live.

And we, when they demand the four prisoners fallen at the doors of the cathedral of Rheims, what will we answer? Can we invoke civilization to mask our crime? Can we at least say to the German women who ask— "What have you done with our sons and husbands?"—"We were unable to prevent isolated acts of cruelty, but we have rejected the guilty. They have been punished."

No, we cannot even say that.

And yet if one of ours falls over there, struck down so odiously, would we not have the right to howl our indignation and to appeal to the whole civilized world?

No, we will not have that right, if we too have hands red with the blood of prisoners.

That is why, if the facts reported by Mme. Yver are true—and they are, because the punctilious censor did not find it possible to contradict them—it is our duty to separate ourselves from those who committed this barbarous massacre.

The cathedral of Rheims seems to prove two crimes: one against stones, one against humanity.

Of the two, which is worse?

Une voix de femme dans la mêlée (Paris: Ollendorf, 1916). "At the Threshold of the Cathedral," from manuscript version of essay inscribed in copy at the Bibliothèque Nationale.

✝ Matilde Serao
(1856–1927) *Italian*

Born in Greece of a Greek mother and Neapolitan father, Matilde Serao was brought up in Naples in poverty by her mother and trained as a teacher. She first worked in a telegraph office, then turned to professional journalism, writing for a Piedmont gazette and then for the *Corriere del Mattino*. In 1885 she married Edoardo Scarfoglio, with whom she tried to start up a newspaper, first *Il Corriere di Roma,* and then *Il Corriere di Napoli.* After separating from her husband, she founded her own paper *Il Giorno,* writing a daily column as gadfly. During World War I, she remained neutral but antifascist; her articles on women and the war were gathered in *Parla una donna* (1916). Her journalism focuses on ordinary people, the *contadina* or country woman, and the plight of civilians. She is noted for her realistic representation of Neapolitan everyday life and poverty in *Il ventre di Napoli* (The belly of Naples, 1884). She wrote forty novels and stories, among the best *La ballerina* (1899), on the miseries of the Neapolitan lower classes, and the carnivalesque *Il paese di cuccagna* (The land of Cockayne, 1890). One of her last works, *Mors tua* (1926; *The Harvest,* 1928) draws on women's experience of war for its antimilitarist message.

✝ Country Women

On the fertile planes of Campania as on the warm ones of Sicily, on the uneven and black mounts of Calabria, as on the snowy and candid ones of Abruzzo, on the round hills of Toscana as on the blue ones, on the oriental shores of Puglia, as on the mountains covered with forests of Piedmont, everywhere, the Italian country women were accustomed to sustained fatigue: of all ages, girls aged ten, adolescents aged fourteen, flowering twenty-year-old brides, strong forty-year-old mothers, infertile women of sixty, all carried out their daily tasks in the constant help of man, father, brother, husband, son. But before the war, their tenacious work was limited to that of the household, in the flower and vegetable gardens, taking care of the animals: it was carried out in the vast kitchens with the large stone fireplaces, spinning wool, knitting, mending the clothing and underwear of men, sewing modest trousseaus for would-be brides, a modest layette for the child that was beginning to move in the maternal womb: in all of the minor tasks, tasks that female arms, that female hands carried out, with untiring constance. And if a little girl led sheep to pasture, it was a man who sheared them: and if a young girl put the pig out to grass, it was a man who, at Christmas, slaughtered it, and salted it: and if a woman went to chop wood in the forest, returning at night, it was a man who made charcoal in the smoking pits; and if the women shaped the bundles of wheat or hay, it was the men who had cut it; and if the women picked grapes and piled them in the tubs, it was the men who made wine after the harvest. At the clear brook, the country women washed clothes, beating them on the stone; in the orchard, they climbed trees to pick fruit, select it, and place it in containers; on the sunny terraces, they laid out the hanks of thread and yarn; on the meadows they would stretch cloth to whiten; every task filled their day, from morn to night, helping a man, their men, fathers and sons, husbands and brothers, and husbands-to-be.

But the country men of Italy have departed for war: aged twenty to thirty, throngs, throngs of country men have left their homes, their fields, their farms, their estates, their property, the threshing-floor for wheat and the mills for olives: all, little by little, have been called, have had to go, have gone and fought, the Italian country men, with an impetus and a tenacity that are so admirable that their commanders still and always praise them. And thus the Italian country women in summer and autumn have doubled, tripled their daily work: the heaviest, the hardest, the most extenuating work of men, they have taken on with tacit courage, with mute firmness, keeping within their large heart—yes, large and simple heart!—the sadness and the despair for those who are absent, far away. There were no men for the reaping, the threshing, the pressing of the olives, and of the grapes: the women have reaped, threshed, made oil and wine. In no Italian region, not even where work is the hardest and vastest, in no farmtown where men and machines once worked, has an inch of land been left unharvested, unsown: the country women have done all of this, from girls aged eight to women of seventy, with dedication, with devotion, touching the arid hearts of the meanest landowners. While the Italian country man, obedient and sober, valorous and modest, fought, everywhere, much more, much better than the skeptical and weary city worker, the Italian country woman worked the land, as if she were a man, at the same time nursing a newborn, or feeding soup to an old grandfather. Who will sing your pure and humble glories, Italian country woman? The Italic poet, the virtuous poet, the simple poet, the Poet, Giosuè Carducci, is dead, dead, and you will have no singer worthy of you!

Translated by Sylvia Notini

"Contadine," from *Parla una donna: Diario feminile di guerra, Maggio 1915–Marzo 1916* (Milan: Fratelli Treves, 1916).

✝ Rebecca West, pseudonym of Cicily Isabel Fairfield (1892–1983) *Irish/British*

One of three girls, Cicily Fairfield was a prolific writer and political radical, who became conservative in her final decades. Her socialist father, a journalist, died when she was ten, leaving her mother with three girls to bring up; Cicily left Edinburgh at sixteen for London, where she studied drama. At the age of nineteen she borrowed the stage name of Rebecca West from the feminist protagonist of Ibsen's *Rosmersholm*. A precocious writer, she began to publish witty journalism in socialist papers advocating free love, divorce, and suffrage. Her early journalism is collected in *The Young Rebecca* (1982). The lover of H. G. Wells, she had a son, Anthony, in 1914. In 1934 West married Henry Andrews, a banker.

Her first book, a study of Henry James, appeared in 1916, shortly after his death. Her war novel, *Return of the Soldier* (1918), describes the shell-shock of a soldier in the context of British class differences that make healing possible only at the cost of the old order and of life itself; it is the hero's mistress, not his wife, who would preserve his life. West found her passive experience of the First World War more terrible than that of the Second, she later commented ironically, "because there you were, not in much danger." A novel about suffrage, *The Judge* (1922), followed; she wrote nine more, three of them published posthumously. West is primarily remembered for *Black Lamb and Grey Falcon* (1941), a study of the Balkan States. She opposed Nazism and as a journalist covered postwar trials of Nazi sympathizers in England, as well as the Nuremberg trials of Nazi collaborators. Critical studies include *St Augustine* (1933) and *D. H. Lawrence* (1930), and several volumes of short stories and of nonfiction round out her oeuvre. West was awarded the Order of the British Empire (1949) and several honorary degrees.
KCS

✝ Hands That War

The Cordite Makers

The world was polished to brightness by an east wind when I visited the cordite factory, and shone with hard colours like a German toy-landscape. The marshes were very green and the scattered waters very blue, and little white clouds roamed one by one across the sky like grazing sheep on a meadow. On the hills around stood elms, and grey churches and red farms and yellow ricks, painted bright by the sharp sunshine. And very distinct on the marshes there lay the village which is always full of people, and yet is the home of nothing except death.

In the glare it showed that like so many institutions of the war it has the disordered and fantastic quality of a dream. It consists of a number of huts, some like the government-built cottages for Irish labourers, and some like the open-air shelters in a sanatorium, scattered over five hundred acres; they are connected by raised wooden gangways and interspersed with green mounds and rush ponds. It is of such vital importance to the State that it is ringed with barbed-wire entanglements and patrolled by sentries, and its products must have sent tens of thousands of our enemies to their death. And it is inhabited chiefly by pretty young girls clad in a Red-Riding-Hood fancy dress of khaki and scarlet.

Every morning at six, when the night mist still hangs over the marshes, 250 of these girls are fetched by a light railway from their barracks on a hill two miles away. When I visited the works they had already been at work for nine hours, and would work for three more. This twelve-hour shift is longer than one would wish, but it is not possible to introduce three shifts, since the girls would find an eight-hour day too light and would complain of being debarred from the opportunity of making more money; and it is not so bad as it sounds, for in these airy and isolated huts there is neither the orchestra of rattling machines nor the sense of a confined area crowded with tired people which make the ordinary factory such a fatiguing place. Indeed, these girls, working in teams of six or seven in those clean and tidy rooms, look as if they were practising a neat domestic craft rather than a deadly domestic process.

When one is made to put on rubber over-shoes before entering a hut it might be the precaution of a pernickety housewife concerned about her floors, although actually it is to prevent the grit on one's outdoor shoes igniting a stray scrap of cordite and sending oneself and the hut up to the skies in a column of flame. And there is something distinctly domestic in the character of almost every process. The girls who stand round the great drums in the hut with walls and floor awash look like millers in their caps and dresses of white waterproof, and the bags containing a white substance that lie in the dry anteroom might be sacks of flour. But, in fact, they are filling the drum with gun-cotton to be dried by hot air. And the next hut, where girls stand round great vats in which steel hands mix the gun-cotton with mineral jelly, might be part of a steam-bakery. The brown cordite paste itself looks as if it might turn into very pleasant honey-cakes, an inviting appearance that has brought gastritis to more than one unwise worker.

But how deceptive this semblance of normal life is; what extraordinary work this is for women and how extraordinarily they are doing it, is made manifest in a certain row of huts where the cordite is being pressed through wire mesh. This, in all the world, must be the place where war and grace are closest linked. Without, a strip of garden runs beside the huts, gay with shrubs and formal with a sundial. Within there is a group of girls that composes into so beautiful a picture that one remembers that the most glorious painting in the world, Velasquez's 'The Weavers', shows women working just like this.

One girl stands high on a platform against the wall, filling the cordite paste into one of the two great iron presses, and when she has finished with that she swings round the other one on a swivel with a fine free gesture. The other girls stand round the table laying out the golden cords in graduated sizes from the thickness of rope to the thinness of macaroni, the clear khaki and scarlet of their dresses shining back from the wet floor in a perpetually changing pattern as they move quickly about their work. They look very young in their pretty, childish dresses, and one thinks them good children for working so diligently. And it occurs to one as something incredible that they are now doing the last three hours of a twelve-hour shift.

If one asks the manager whether this zeal can possibly be normal, whether it is not perhaps the result of his presence, one is confronted by the awful phenomenon, beside which a waterspout or a volcano in eruption would be a little thing, of a manager talking about his employees with reverence. It seems that the girls work all day with a fury which mounts to a climax in the last three hours before the other 250 girls step into their places for the twelve-hour night shift. In these hours spies are sent out to walk along the verandah to see how the teams in the other huts are getting on, and their reports set the girls on to an orgy of competitive industry. Here again it was said that for attention, enthusiasm and discipline, there could not be better workmen than these girls.

There is matter connected with these huts, too, that showed the khaki and scarlet hoods to be no fancy dress, but a military uniform. They are a sign, for they have been dipped in a solution that makes them fireproof, that the girls are ready to face an emergency, which had arisen in those huts only a few days ago. There had been one of those incalculable happenings of which high explosives are so liable, an inflammatory mixture of air with acetone, and the cordite was ignited. Two huts were instantly gutted, and the girls had to walk out through the flame. In spite of the uniform one girl lost a hand. These, of course, are the everyday dangers of the high-explosives factory. There is very little to be feared from our enemies by land, and it is the sentries' grief and despair that their total bag for the eighteen months of their patrol of the marshes consists of one cow.

Surely, never before in modern history can women have lived a life so completely parallel to that of the regular Army. The girls who take up this work sacrifice almost as much as men who enlist, for although they make on an average 30s a week they are working much harder than most of them, particularly the large number who were formerly domestic servants, would ever have dreamed of working in peacetime. And, although their colony of wooden huts has been well planned by their employers, and is pleasantly administered by the Young Women's Christian Association, it is, so far as severance of home-ties goes, barrack life. For although they are allowed to go home for Sunday, travelling is difficult from this remote village, and the girls are so tired that most of them spend the day in bed.

And there are two things about the cordite village which the State ought never to forget, and which ought to be impressed upon the public mind by the bestowal of military rank upon the girls. First of all there is the cold fact that they face more danger every day than any soldier on home defence has seen since the beginning of the war. And secondly, there is the fact—and one wishes it could be expressed in terms of the saving of English and the losing of German life—that it is because of this army of cheerful and disciplined workers that this cordite factory has been able to increase its output since the beginning of the war by something over 1,500 per cent. It was all very well for the Army to demand high explosives, and for Mr Lloyd George to transmit the demand to industry; in the last resort the matter lay in the hands of the girls in the khaki and scarlet hoods, and the State owes them a very great debt for the way in which they have handled it.

Daily Chronicle, 1916

"Hands That War: The Cordite Makers," in *The Young Rebecca,* ed. Jane Marcus (New York: Vintage, 1982), 380–83. Reprinted by permission of the Peters Fraser & Dunlop Group Ltd.

✝ Henriette Celarié
(d. 1952?) *French*

D uring World War I, Henriette Celarié wrote four books about the German occupation of France: *Sous les obus: souvenirs d'une jeune femme de Lorraine: 1914–1915* (Under shellfire—Memories of a young woman from Lorraine: 1914–1915, 1916), *En esclavage: journal de deux déportées* (Enslaved, diary of two deported women, 1917), *Quand ils étaient à Saint Quentin* (When they were at St. Quentin, 1918), and *Le martyre de Lille* (The martyrdom of Lille, 1919). In *Enslaved*, she transcribed reports by two women who had been deported by the Germans from Lille to do forced labor in occupied French territory farther from the battlelines. In "Hickel's Visits," she gives Marie X.'s story of her experiences. Marie ironically calls the hut in which she and her friend Jeanne have taken refuge from a sexually exploitative dormitory the "Lille chalet." Numerous accounts like Celarié's of the deportation that began on Easter in 1916 express patriotic outrage and respond with a feminist defense of women's rights.

After the war, Celarié wrote travel books about North Africa, including *Nos soeurs des harems* (Our harem sisters, 1925), as well as biographies of Mme de Sévigné, Voltaire, and Victor Hugo.

✝ Hickel's Visits

Hickel has put his plan into action. Almost every day, under cover of doing his tour, he comes to the village of V . . . and frequently, he enters the "Lille chalet."

As soon as I hear the hooves of his horse, as soon as I see him, I am terrorised. When Jeanne is with me, I don't get too alarmed; but often I am alone. Hickel knows it. Jeanne has gone to find milk, she is at the stream washing our linens. . . .

Hickel comes in; he sits on the only chair; lolling back in the chair, he stretches out his long thin legs; in great puffs he blows out cigar smoke:

—Hello, my little chérie. Are you well? . . .

I throw open the door and two windows. These are low; it will be easy to straddle them and jump out. If Hickel wanted to rape me, I know that in Jeanne's absence I can count only on myself. I am defenseless, surrendered to the fantasy of the German. A cry, a call? No one would come. Who then would want to attract a quarrel with a leader for me, an "émigrée." Hickel is not unaware of this. The day he chooses. . . . For the moment, he is content to address compliments and teasing reproaches to me:

—My treasure, why are you so mean with me? Will you always be mean?

I don't answer the question. This Hickel horrifies me. I complain that I've been carried off from my parents. I ask if I must stay here much longer; Hickel sneers, shrugs his shoulders. Should I tell him to go away, put him out? Impossible. The Germans enter where they want and stay as long as they want. He gets up. This "well brought up" young man is shameless. He takes a tour of my room; he studies the old engravings from *Illustration* with which we decorated our walls, he stops before the bed and in a tone full of suggestion:

—My treasure, is your bed good? Good to lay, mademoiselle? Good to sleep? My little chérie, to lay all alone! Not good . . .

Some work is lying on the table, he takes it and rummages in my things. His questions a minute ago made me blush with shame, now I'd like to wrest from his hands what he is holding, I'd like to yell at him:

—Will you leave that . . .

Finally he goes:

—Farewell, my treasure . . .

He gets back on his horse. My heart stops throbbing. I am saved, for today. Yes, but tomorrow? when he will come back . . .

Jeanne is harassed by one of the policemen. She doesn't know how to fend him off. He is a heavy blond, not so young, married and father of five. When he knows my friend is alone, he enters the room, he tries to embrace her, to take her on his knees, to caress her:

—Pretty little French woman, he says. . . . Graceful little mademoiselle . . .

One morning, Jeanne is getting dressed. She has only her shirt and a slip on. The policeman comes in without knocking. At the sound of boots on the floor, Jeanne turns around. The policeman is right next to her, he is going to seize her. With a shove she disengages him; she jumps out the window, takes refuge with a neighbor. . . . How can you imagine the torture of such an existence with continuous terror.

The fear of being taken some day by one of these Germans was for us the most appalling threat, said Marie X. . . . To know that we would have something to eat, to know that we would not have to work more, we did not think about such matters except occasionally. One idea only obsessed us, made us tremble at the slightest noise of a step or voice. . . . However, we were not the most unhappy.

At the village of B . . . near our hamlet, one hundred and fifty women are lodged, or rather parked in an attic. They sleep pell-mell in the straw; they are eaten up by vermin. There prostitution is publicly organized. Every evening on the doorstep, the soldiers call the women they want for the night:

—Charlotte Z . . . , three chocolate bars.

—Louise G . . . , one mark and a bar.

The poor women leave the hay where they are lodged, and follow the one who calls.

In excuse, the Germans claim that these prisoners are all prostitutes. They lie. We know that they carried off without distinction honest women and public women.

One of the most painful aspects of my captivity, . . . was to feel weighing on me the scornful gaze of those who not knowing me took me for what I am not, at the word of the Germans; it was to hear little children, even very little ones, who made me weep when they called their mother because they made me think of my own, it was to hear them often soiling me as I passed with abusive words:

—B . . . , slut . . . , whore of the Boches!

Whore of the Boches! It was impossible to make them understand, to explain to them. I could only go back to my room and hide.

From *En esclavage: journal de deux déportées* (Paris: Bloud et Gay, 1917), 127–31.

✠ L. Dorliat
French

O ne of the most symbolic wartime changes in women's labor took place when women moved into the masculine arena of munitions industries. The pool of labor included women who had lost their jobs at the outbreak of war, when industries like textiles collapsed, as well as women who shifted from domestic work in private homes. Labor unions opposed the employment of women since lower rates of pay for female labor threatened wages for men. But slaughter on the battlefield forced governments to encourage the replacement of men in factories by women; in France workers were also imported from the colonies, and in Germany prisoners of war were used in factories and mines, and paid minimal wages. Furthermore, in families whose primary wage earner had been drafted, women were forced to seek work. The introduction of women into heavy industry brought them better wages under harsh and often dangerous conditions, as this woman recounts. It also led to "deskilling" of tasks, which had a long-term impact on male labor. Because men who went on strike could be sent to the front, the labor unrest in the last two years of the war was often led by women. Women were proud that they had significantly raised rates of production; in spite of their contribution, however, they were dismissed immediately after the Armistice, not only from munitions factories but from other industrial jobs.

✠ At the Factory

The dwelling I enter is tidy, sun lights up the main room and makes the household objects shine; everything speaks of an orderly woman who likes her home. A few flowers in a vase on the table near which she is working prove to me that I was right about the woman I've come to see. The factory has not destroyed her feminine sense of delicacy. Without a hat she seems to me younger; she is surprised to see me, she confesses, because she doubted I would come. Convalescent, she hasn't worked for a whole month, which is why I am lucky enough to find her.

"The very day after my arrival, I found work, thanks to the foreman of a factory of shells who knew my husband," she hastens to tell me. "There is no comparison between this extremely hard and much more precise work and the little toy-like petards that I was making. Here it's not sheets of white metal but big 120 shells. You must also pay much more attention, a defect is serious. The factory never stops, day and night shifts of eight alternate. It's intensive production; no mawkishness here, we are not women but the arms of the machine. Scarcely any apprenticeship, one or two days and you're set.

"I am in a workshop for tempering the steel, or rather I was—will they give me back my place and my machine when I return to the workshop? At the moment of my accident, which I'll tell you about, I was doing the shop-trial of the steel for the shell, testing or inspecting the casing, of course. Right after the tempering bath, when the steel is still hot and black, the other workers and I had to tap it with a buffing wheel in order to polish the steel on a small surface of the bottom and the ogive of the shell. Doing this we handle at least a thousand shells a day, and as I told you, they are big, very heavy to manipulate. Other workers take these same pieces and make a light mark on the polished area, which must not etch the steel further than a certain depth, in a kind of test; they are equipped with a graduated sheet of metal that lets them evaluate the etched lines. If the mark is too deep, the steel is too soft; if it's too shallow, it is too hard; in either case it can't be used and goes back to be recast. The inspection requires great attentiveness. A final verification is made by a controller and as we are always required to put our number on the pieces that pass through our hands, the imperfections, the errors can be traced to their authors.

"There too you don't talk, you don't even think of it. The deafening noise of the machines, the enormous heat of the ovens near which you work, the swiftness of the movements make this precision work into painful labor. When we do it at night, the glare together with the temperature of the furnace exhausts your strength and burns your eyes. In the morning when you get home, you throw yourself on your bed without even the strength to eat a bite. There are also the lathe workshops, I've never been there; many workers learn quickly to turn a shell without needing to calibrate it; some turners do piece work; they are always the ones who hurt themselves. At the job you become very imprudent, as I told you.

"However, you see, I hurt myself too. Forgetting that my buffing machine does an incalculable number of turns a second, I brushed against it with my arm. Clothing and flesh were all taken off before I even noticed. They had to scrape the bone, bandage me every day, I was afraid of an amputation, which luckily was avoided. Only in the last few days have I been able to go without a sling and use my arm; next week I go back to the workshop. I don't want them to change my job, I'm used to my machine and a fresh apprenticeship would not please me at all. I assure you, the first day I was in this noise, near these enormous blast furnaces, opposite the huge machine at which I had to work for hours, I was afraid. We are all like that, all the more so that we are not given time to reflect. You have to understand and act quickly. Those who lose their heads don't accomplish anything, but they are rare. In general, one week suffices to turn a novice into a skilled worker.

"The foremen scold now and then, but they mustn't count it against us; doesn't everyone know that a man is an apprentice before he becomes a mechanic? But at present, however simplified, however divided up the tasks may be, you become a qualified mechanic right away.

"Yet among us there are women like myself who had never done anything; others who did not know how to sew or embroider; nothing discouraged us. As for me I don't complain, this strained activity pleases me. I can thus forget my loneliness—and not having any children, what else should I do with all my time?

"When the war is over, I will look for a job that corresponds better to my taste. I have enough education to become a cashier in a store. I will then be able to be neater than now, for you can't imagine what care it takes to stay more or less clean if you work in metallurgy.

"A woman is always a woman; I suffered a lot from remaining for hours with my hands and face dirty with dust and smoke. Everything is a matter of habit; among us there are women who seem fragile and delicate—well! if you saw them at work, you would be stunned: it's a total transformation. As for me, I would never have thought I had so much stamina; when I remember that the least little errand wore me out before, I don't recognize myself. Certainly when the day or the night is over, you go home, the fatigue is great, but we are not more tired than the men are. True, we are more sober because we maintain better hygiene and as a result, our sources of energy are more rational and regular, we don't turn to alcohol for strength.

"Our sense of the present need, of the national peril, of hatred for the enemy, of the courage of our husbands and sons—all this pricks us on, we work with all our heart, with all our strength, with all our soul. It is not necessary to stimulate us, each one is conscious of the task assigned to her and in all simplicity she does it, convinced that she defends her country by forging the arms that will free it. We are very proud of being workers for the national defence."

On that proud phrase, I left this valiant woman, with a warm handshake to thank her and to express my admiration.

"À l'usine," in *Souvenirs de Parisiennes en temps de guerre*, ed. Camille Clément (Paris: Berger, 1918)

BATTLEFRONT REPORTS

✝ Colette
(1873–1954) *French*[1]

✝ Verdun

It's ended, that beautiful terrified journey. Here I am—and I wonder for how long?—hidden in Verdun. A fake name, borrowed identity papers were not enough to protect me, during the thirteen hours of the trip, from the new-style gendarme that the war has made shrewd, jeering, indiscreet, or from the bossy railway superintendent at the Châlons station. En route, I ran into every possible peril. There was the volunteer nurse, appointed to meet the trainloads of wounded, she who happened to know me. "Imagine, you here!" she exclaimed. Then there was the ex-journalist in uniform who inquired: "Is your husband all right? Have you come to be with him?" Besides these, there was the army medical officer who "understood what was up," and gave me winks that would have been enough to alert a track watchman . . . The least troublesome hours were those of the "black train," when we ran with all lights out between Châlons and Verdun, going slowly, slowly, as if the train were groping its way, repressing its asthma and its whistle. Long hours? Yes, perhaps, because of my impatience to arrive, but full and anxious hours, alight with the aurora borealis of an incessant cannonading, a rosy glimmer palpitating on the horizon toward the northeast.

A magnificent thunder accompanied it, continuous, sustained, which did not hurt the ear but sounded throughout one's body, in the limbs, the stomach, the head; and sometimes on the horizon a flare sprayed its floral bouquet and splintered the night.

1. See page 105.

No one slept or talked until the wintry daybreak and our arrival at Verdun. And how I envied, in my disguise, those merchants of Verdun who passed the gendarme with a "How goes it?" and a handshake.

No matter. I have arrived, and I will try to remain here, a voluntary prisoner. The nearby cannonading does not roar alone: a coke fire crackles and flames, and my accomplices—a noncommissioned officer the color of ripe wheat, his young wife brown as a chestnut, who are letting me stay in their house—and their laughter, over our coffee with condensed milk. Provided that I don't go out of doors, that I don't approach the windows— "Beware of the medical officers billeted on the other side of the street!"— all will be well. The windowpanes emit a shrill "ee-eee" when the cannonading becomes more intense and obliges us to raise our voices, and a winter sunshine warns of freezing weather to come.

I am wild to hear about everything, to shudder, and to hope. I put questions.

"What's new?"

The noncommissioned officer, who is in the Quartermaster Department, frowns and pulls at his Vercingetorix mustache.

"New? Well, I can tell you the upholsterer is a swine!"

"The . . ."

"The upholsterer, that's right. The butter the upholsterer sells is margarine!"

"Yes . . . and what else?"

"Well, there's the piano merchant. He's just received a marvelous shipment of sardines. I'm hurrying over to his store on my way to look at our horses. . . ."

"Yes, yes, and what else?"

"Why," exclaims the brown-haired young woman, "there's this shameful thing of making us pay three sous for one leek! But the sub-prefect is outraged, and he's going to get a stock of things put in the sub-prefecture— rice, macaroni, potatoes—and then we'll see if the grocers will still have the nerve to . . ."

"Yes, yes, yes! But please, what about the war?"

"The war?"

Vercingetorix looks at me reflectively, his innocent blue eyes wide open. I lose patience.

"The war, in the name of God, yes! What people are saying, what people are reading, what you are doing!"

The blue eyes narrow with laughter.

"Oh yes, of course, the war! Well, it still goes on, it keeps going, it's going very well, don't worry."

I deserved that reply from a calm and courageous man. It did not take me a week to realize that here in Verdun, chock-a-block full of troops, with the railway its unique supply line, war becomes a habit, the inseparable cataclysm of life, as natural as thunder and rainstorms; but the danger, the real danger, is that one may soon not be able to eat. Food comes first, everything else takes second place: the stationer sells sausages, the sewing woman sells potatoes. The piano merchant stacks a thousand tins of sardines and mackerel on his tired pianos that he used to rent out; but butter is a luxurious rarity, a can of condensed milk a precious object, and vegetables exist only for the fortunate of this world. . . .

Eat, eat, eat. Well, yes, one must eat. The freezing weather nips, the East wind makes those who spend the nights out of doors ravenous. The important thing is to keep the blood hot in our veins, although it may at any time pour out in floods, immeasurable floods. Great courage goes with a great appetite, and the stomachs of the people in Verdun are not stomachs that are shrunken by fear.

Some German prisoners passed down the rue d'Antouard. I saw them, between the blades of my Persian blinds, which are always closed. Some civilians were standing in their doorways watching them go by, with a bored look. Their faces yellowed with fatigue and dirt, the prisoners marched in a slovenly way, many of them showing only unconcern and relief from tension, as though saying, "Good! It's over with, for us!" A German soldier, puny but high-spirited, stuck his tongue out at a woman as he passed.

Between seven and eight in the morning and between two and three in the afternoon, the German planes punctually come to drop bombs. They fall just about everywhere, without causing much damage or casualties. But the bombing and the response of our fighter planes and antiaircraft guns, my, what a din it makes! All the same, the neighbor across the street mourns her garden that was ravaged yesterday and her shed that was smashed. Also, a roof of the administration building quite near here, at the foot of the fortress, now yawns open to the sky. The noncommissioned officer, Vercingetorix, swears like a pagan against those *Aviatik*, as he calls them, "that try to keep us from taking care of our horses!"

His wife sets me an example of complete imprudence and comes home today under a veritable hail of shrapnel that didn't touch her.

"Oh, what a nuisance, what a nuisance!" she exclaims. "Just imagine, I had to take shelter under the porte-cochere of the X. family, and we're not on speaking terms!"

In the evening, toward nine or ten o'clock, I risk taking a furtive walk for my health, my legs trembling in fear of encountering a patrol. Not a street light, not a sound, not a glimmer behind the closed shutters or between the crisscrossed window curtains. But sometimes a muffled cry, the fleeing of slippered little feet, a panting: I have blindly bumped into one of those veiled and cloistered wives, one of the voluntary prisoners Verdun hides, she, too, out for a breath of night air. People know about these wives and mistresses, returned to an Oriental way of life; if you name them in a low voice, it is by no means a betrayal. People mention one of the women, they say she has not crossed the threshold of her jail for seven months or seen a human face except that of the man she loves. They say she is an occasional writer, and that she is the happiest of women. . . .

A rather gloomy level pathway beside the canal. But a warm sun that is melting the frost and the cloudless sky give a rosy hue to the fortress and the archbishop's palace and make the water blue. We risk this walk in broad daylight, despite all marital interdictions and the dangers of what my hostess calls "the half-past-two airplanes."

The towpath is lined at intervals with sentinels and with bare poplars, and on the moored canal boats from Belgium, flaxen-haired children play. The spongy fields steam, and the thaw has swollen the streams. A regular peal of thunder scans our steps; it is one of those days when the people of Verdun say gravely, "They're getting a pounding in the Argonne."

"Do you see those dance halls stuck right in the fields?" asks my companion. "You can't imagine what fun we had in them last summer. . . ."

A sharp detonation, a muffled din which comes down from the upper air, interrupts her.

"That's one of *theirs*," she says. "The .75's are firing at it . . . Look, there's the *Aviatik!*"

While I can still hear nothing but the humming of the engine, my Verdun hostess's sharp eyes have already found on the clear blue of the sky the minuscule pigeon which grows bigger and leaves the horizon; here it is, borne by two convex wings, new, gleaming; it circles the town, rises, seems to meditate, hesitates. . . . Five white bouquets blossom in a wreath around it, five pompons of immaculate smoke which mark, suspended in the windless sky, the point where our antiaircraft shells are exploding— five, then seven, and their concerted blasts reach our ears later still. . . .

"Oh, here come some of ours!" my companion exclaims.

And from a nearby post rise, with the buzzing of a furious wasp, two biplanes, two others rushing up from the town. They climb the sky in spirals, show their light bellies in the sunshine, the tricolor on their tails, their flat surfaces. . . . They are buzzards, male falcons, slender swallows, and at a great distance, merely flies. . . .

"Another German!"

"Yes! And another, and another!"

It took only a few seconds to fill that sky, vast and empty just now, with a flight of enemy wings. How many of them will the east, black with pines and rolling hills, hurl at us? One would say that the vertiginous blue space was barely big enough to hold them; they circle, return as suddenly as a bird striking the windowpane, and our guns fill the azure with white roses. . . .

"Those over there are ours! There's going to be an air battle!"

"They are enemy planes. No. At this distance I can't distinguish . . ."

We shout, for the tumult has increased, necessary to the beauty of the aerial chase. The guns of the town and of the fortress bay like a pack of hounds, deep bass some of them; the others sharp, furious barks. The magnificent pursuit is right over our heads. . . .

"He's hit, he's hit! No, no . . . Oh, he's getting away. . . ."

"Farther ahead, farther ahead!" my companion shouts, as if the gunners could hear her. "Can't you see that all your shells are falling short?"

We run, unconsciously following the planes, screaming, and it took the shouts of a company of fusiliers and their emphatic advice to make us seek shelter under an iron bridge. Shelter . . . but why?

We soon know the reason: a weird hailstorm has begun to pepper the canal at our feet, a hot hail that makes the water hiss. Who is hurling this boiling shrapnel at us? We had not thought of this. Excitedly watching the fighter planes, we had forgotten the sparks, the burning cinders that would fall from a battle of demi-gods contesting the rights to the upper airs.

Under the narrow iron bridge, we tensely wait. We hope for and imagine the finest issue of the combat: the fall, the sudden stripping off of all the curved wings, the planes spiraling down, defeated, to crash on the grassy bank. . . . Nothing falls there but a bomb, and the soaked field drinks it up, covers it over without its exploding. It was one of the last projectiles, a wicked tapered seed, thrown out by the German who is vanishing in the distance. The racing of a storm cloud is less rapid than his magical flight: the white smoke of the shells still floats up there where the enemy planes are now only a dotted line, far off, at the bottom of the sky swept clean. The baying of the guns is now intermittent; the fusiliers rejoice.

Returning toward the town, we find the first traces of the aerial bombardment: the trees along the promenade have undergone a brutal pruning, and in a freshly opened hole in the ground children are looking for shrapnel, babbling and scratching like chickens after a shower. . . .

Le Matin, December 1914–January 1915

"Verdun," in *Earthly Paradise,* trans. Herma Briffault, ed. Robert Phelps, copyright © 1966, 227–33. Reprinted by permission of Martin Secker & Warburg Ltd and Farrar Straus & Giroux, Inc. Copyright renewed © 1994 by Farrar Straus & Giroux, Inc.

✝ Mary Roberts Rinehart
(1876–1958) *American*

A prolific writer of mysteries, short stories, novels, plays, travel literature, and journalism, Mary Roberts Rinehart grew up in Pittsburgh amid financial difficulties. A frustrated inventor, her father worked at a sewing machine factory, while her mother took in boarders in a struggle to keep up appearances. Her autobiography, *My Story* (1931), recounts her training as a nurse at Pittsburgh Homeopathic Hospital; at the time there were only 471 graduate-trained nurses in America. Her experience as a nurse influenced her later novels and journalism, whether in a story of an unwed mother or in scrupulous wartime observation of a Belgian hospital. At twenty, four days after her graduation and just a few months after her father's suicide, she married Dr. Stanley M. Rinehart and in subsequent years focused her life on her children until, bedridden with diphtheria, she began to write and sell poetry. When she turned in earnest to autobiographical fiction, she sold forty-five stories and novelettes in the first year, for an astonishing total of $1,842.50.

In December 1914 the *Saturday Evening Post* asked Rinehart to report on the war; she succeeded in maneuvering past other American correspondents in London to reach Belgium—even though she spoke poor French and halting German. Her aim was to document "the plight of the Belgian army and of the Belgian refugees pushed ahead of the army and still trying to subsist behind enemy lines." She was at Dunkirk when German troops bombed the city to celebrate the Kaiser's birthday, and by February made excursions into the trenches and No Man's Land, where sluices had been opened to flood the flat farmland and slow the German advance. She visited Pervyse, the destroyed town where Mairi Chisholm and Elsie Knocker ran an ambulance station. She interviewed the King of Belgium at La Panne, where she also reported on the modern X-ray equipment and professional discipline "under the guns" in the hospital of Dr. DePage. Published first in the *Post,* her descriptive reports were gathered on her return in *Kings, Queens, and Pawns: An American Woman at the Front* (1915).

Rinehart reflected bitterly on what she had seen: "This then was war, this grim and prolonged suffering, this crying of strong men at night." "The war is a series of incidents with no beginning and no end." When the United States entered the war, her husband and two oldest sons both enlisted but returned unscathed.

AM

✝ No Man's Land

Many people have written about the trenches—the mud, the odors, the inhumanity of compelling men to live under such foul conditions. Nothing that they have said can be too strong. Under the best conditions the life is ghastly, horrible, impossible.

That night, when from a semishielded position I could look across to the German line, the contrast between the condition of the men in the trenches and the beauty of the scenery was appalling. In each direction, as far as one could see, lay a gleaming lagoon of water. The moon made a silver path across it, and here and there on its borders were broken and twisted winter trees.

"It is beautiful," said Captain Fastrez beside me, in a low voice. "But it is full of the dead. They are taken out whenever it is possible: but it is not often possible." [. . .]

As of the trenches, many have written of the stenches of this war. But the odor of that beautiful lagoon was horrible. I do not care to emphasize it. It is one of the things best forgotten. But any lingering belief I may have had in the grandeur and glory of war died that night beside that silver lake—died of an odor, and will never live again. [. . .]

As we proceeded the stench from the beautiful moonlit water grew overpowering. The officer told me the reason.

A little farther along a path of fascines had been built out over the inundation to an outpost halfway to the German trenches. The building of this narrow roadway had cost many lives.

Half a mile along the road we were sharply challenged by a sentry. When he had received the password, he stood back and let us pass. Alone, in that bleak and exposed position, always in full view as he paced back and forward, carbine on shoulder and with not even a tree trunk or a hedge for shelter, the first to go at the whim of some German sniper or at any indication of an attack, he was a pathetic, almost a tragic, figure. He looked very young too. I stopped and asked him in a whisper how old he was.

He said he was nineteen.

He may have been. I know something about boys, and I think he was seventeen at the most. There are plenty of boys of that age doing just what that lad was doing.

Afterward I learned that it was no part of the original plan to take a woman over the fascine path to the outpost; that Captain Fastrez ground his teeth in impotent rage when he saw where I was being taken. But it was not possible to call or even to come up to us. So, blithely and unconsciously the tall Belgian officer and I turned to the right, and I was innocently on my way to the German trenches.

After a little I realized that this was rather more war than I had expected. The fascines were slippery; the path only four or five feet wide. On each side was the water, hideous with many secrets.

I stopped a third of the way out, and looked back. It looked about as dangerous in one direction as another. So we went on. Once I slipped and fell. And now, looming out of the moonlight, I could see the outpost which was the object of our visit.

I have always been grateful to that Belgian lieutenant for his mistake. Just how grateful I might have been had anything untoward happened, I cannot say. But the excursion was worth all the risk, and more.

On a bit of high ground stands what was once the tiny hamlet of Oustyvenskerke—the ruins of two small white houses and the tower of the destroyed church—hardly a tower any more, for only three sides of it are standing and they are riddled with great shell holes.

Six hundred feet beyond this tower were the German trenches. The little island was hardly a hundred feet in its greatest dimension.

I wish I could make those people who think that war is good for a country see that Belgian outpost as I saw it that night under the moonlight. Perhaps we were under suspicion; I do not know. Suddenly, the *fusées*,[1] which had ceased for a time, began again, and with their white light added to that of the moon the desolate picture of that tiny island was a picture of the war. There was nothing lacking. There was the beauty of the moonlit waters, there was the tragedy of the destroyed houses, and the church, and there was the horror of unburied bodies. [. . .]

We went back to the automobile, a long walk over the shell-eaten roads in the teeth of a biting wind. But a glow of exultation kept me warm. I had been to the front. I had been far beyond the front, indeed, and I had seen such a picture of war and its desolation there in the center of No Man's Land as perhaps no one not connected with an army had seen before; such a picture as would live in my mind forever.

I saw other trenches that night as we followed the Belgian lines slowly northward toward Nieuport.

Save the varying conditions of discomfort, they were all similar. Always they were behind the railroad embankment. Always they were dirty and cold. Frequently they were full of mud and water. To reach them one waded through swamps and pools. Just beyond them there was always the moonlit stretch of water, now narrow, now wide, and here and there floating things that had been men.

Saturday Evening Post, May 8, 1915

1. *Fusées:* "starlights," magnesium flares.

✟ Magdeleine ver Mehr
Italian-American

✟ The Trentino in Trench Time

August 21, 1915

Yesterday was the most thrilling day of my life. I passed it right in the very midst of the war zone, having been fortunate enough to be allowed as the only woman correspondent to join the other representatives of the Italian and foreign papers who are up here in the Trentino. Being an Italian by birth, this experience is doubly wonderful to me as it enables me to see at close quarters the splendid work which my countrymen have done and are doing, and also to have had the privilege of being the first Italian woman to cross the new boundary line between Italy and Austria.

It was an unforgettable moment, and as we advanced further into what, till a short three months ago, had been Austrian territory, I felt as if I were treading on sacred ground, consecrated by the blood of my people, who had willingly given up their lives to restore to Italy that which was hers. [. . .]

Two sorts of trenches are seen, those built with cement, and those dug out in the ground, earth filled up on top.

The cement ones are like catacombs, they are more comfortable and probably better than the others, but they are infinitely less picturesque, also they give me the impression that war was becoming an institution, and that in the new order of things, to build a permanent trench as up to date as possible, was to be the ambition of many rising young architects and engineers. In fact, it was a new line of their business in which they were going to specialize.

The old fashioned trench gives the war a less permanent feeling. It is open at the back, the walls are of earth, the rain enters, the wind blows through, and the sun shines on it, but though more primitive, it is more comforting as one feels that it is only a hurried makeshift as quickly abandoned as built.

Choosing between the two, I would probably prefer to live in the cement one; as a spectator I get more comfort in seeing the others. I feel that they are so uncomfortable that they cannot have come to stay.

As we went along a heavy gray motor lorry passed us. It carried the post. We caught it up and saw it stop. Suddenly where we had only seen an encampment of white tents and tethered horses grazing in the sunshine, we beheld a swarm of men rushing up from all sides and surrounding it. Eager hands were held out, the dialects of the North and South mingled, voicing the same question: "Any letters for me?" For an instant all those men were carried back to their old life, the life they forgot in the many duties that filled their days. They were no longer soldiers, they became private citizens. Civilization caught them in its grip again. . . .

Living Age, December 4, 1915, 588–90.

✝ Bessie Beatty
(1886–1947) *American*

The daughter of Irish immigrants who settled in Los Angeles, Bessie Beatty was an active child; When she decided at twelve to become a writer, she published a junior social column through a friend at the Los Angeles *Times*. After study at Occidental College, she became a reporter for the Los Angeles *Herald*, working on women's features and drama, then wrote the column "On the Margin" for the San Francisco *Bulletin*.

With the support of her editor, Beatty went to Russia to cover the Russian Revolution, tracing from a Petrograd base Aleksandr Kerensky's rise to power and his descent. At the front she experienced "the dirt, the flies, the vermin, the monotonous round, the endless soup and *kasha*, the waiting," as she later described the life of soldiers. She observed life in the trenches during the July offensive, living for a week with the famous Women's Battalion of Death, led by Maria Botchkareva; she recorded the propaganda with which they attempted to mobilize women and shame men, whose military units had fallen into disarray in the initial phase of the Communist revolution. Beatty traveled with an expert in peasant art who spoke Russian. Other women journalists in Russia at the same time included Rheta Childe Dorr and Mildred Farwell, staff correspondents for the Chicago *Tribune*; the better known Louise Bryant and her husband John Reed focused primarily on the somewhat later evolution of the Bolshevik revolution. Beatty left in January 1918; the same year, she helped translate the Bolshevik decree of peace for publication and published her own report, *The Red Heart of Russia* (1918).

Beatty subsequently became the editor in chief of *McCall's* for three years; she remained in the public eye through her work for magazines, radio, and charity for war veterans. During World War II her radio appeals raised funds for soldiers and arms.

AM

✝ The Battalion of Death

Here were women—two hundred and fifty of them—on their way to battle, and just a fraction of the women's army soon to be.

Destiny, dawn, and an occasional inquiry led me at six o'clock in the morning to their door. They were housed in two pine-board sheds, sandwiched between a dug-out full of Austrian prisoners and the barracks of a battalion of Cossack cavalry.

I found myself in a building a hundred or more feet long, with steep roofs sloping to the floor, and just enough width to allow for two shelves eight feet deep and an aisle between. The shelves at the moment were covered with brown bundles, and as I followed the sentry a hundred close-cropped heads emerged from them.

Above my head, hanging from the rafters, was a jungle of gas-masks and wet laundry, boots, water-bottles, and kit-bags. Beside each girl lay her rifle. At the far end of the barracks we stopped before one of the brown bundles, and the sentry announced, "Gaspadin Nachalnik." The man's head and man's shoulders of Bachkarova arose from the blanket. Next to her, another bundle stirred, and Marya Skridlova, aide-de-camp, moved over and invited me to come up.

In that spot, between the social poles of Russia, Rheta Childe Dorr and I spent all the nights and most of the days in the week that followed.

Without delay I changed my too feminine dress for "overettes," and established myself as unobtrusively as possible in the life of the barracks. [. . .]

We ate our breakfast sitting on the edge of a bunk, slicing off hunks of black bread, and washing it down with tea from tin cups. Bachkarova sat next to me, eating sardines from a can and wiping her greasy fingers on the front of her blouse. Orlova spent most of her time washing these blouses, in a vain attempt to keep the Commander clean.

The routine of the day began with the reading of the army regulations. The women soldiers had chosen to submit to the stern discipline of the Russian army in the days before the Revolution. The ceaseless rain made drilling in the field impossible, but within the narrow limits of the barracks they marched back and forth, counting "Ras, dva, tri, chetiri; ras, dva, tri, chetiri," for several hours a day.

Very soon one soldier girl after another detached herself from the mass and became to me an individual—a warm, personal human being. Bit by bit I gathered their stories. Little by little I discovered some of the forces that had pushed them out of their individual ruts into the mad maelstrom of war.

There were stenographers and dressmakers among them, servants and factory hands, university students and peasants, and a few who in the days before the war had been merely parasites. Several were Red Cross nurses, and one, the oldest member of the regiment, a woman of forty-eight whose closely cropped hair was turning gray, had exchanged a lucrative medical practice for a soldier's uniform.

Many had joined the regiment because they sincerely believed that the honor and even the existence of Russia were at stake, and nothing but a great human sacrifice could save her. Some, like Bachkarova, in the days of the Siberian village had simply come to the point where anything was better than the dreary drudgery and the drearier waiting of life as they lived it.

Personal sorrow had driven some of them out of their homes and on to the battle-line. One girl, a Japanese, said tragically, when I asked her reason for joining: "My reasons are so many that I would rather not tell them." [. . .]

They had come for many reasons, these women soldiers, but all of them were walking out to meet death with grim confidence that it awaited them there in the dark forests a few miles distant.

If there seemed to be any fear of them forgetting it,—if girlish spirits ran too high in the barracks,—Bachkarova quickly recalled it.

"You may all be dead in three days," she would say. And soon afterward the Volga boat-song or the rollicking peasant tune they were singing would change to a deep, melancholy mass, with all the tragedy of the moment and of millions of other moments packed into it.

In a cord around each girl's neck was a collection of sacred medals, and a tiny cloth pouch whose contents I speculated upon.

"What will you do if you are made prisoner?" I asked Skridlova one day.

"No one of us will ever be taken alive," she answered, and pulled out the little gray pouch. "It is the strongest and surest kind there is," she said. [. . .]

Always there was something lacking. First it was the boots. The army shoemaker was not used to providing for such small feet, and the commissariat was sorely taxed. When the boots arrived, the medical supplies were missing. When the big metal soup kitchen on wheels had come, there were no horses to pull it. A week went by, but gradually the entire camp equipment was collected.

Late one Sunday afternoon Bachkarova and Skridlova were summoned to staff headquarters. When they returned, they brought the news for which every girl in the barracks was longing. The Battalion was ordered to march at three o'clock next morning. [. . .]

All the world knows how they went into battle shouting a challenge to the deserting Russian troops. All the world knows that six of them stayed behind in the forest, with wooden crosses to mark their soldier graves. Ten were decorated for bravery in action with the Order of St. George, and twenty others received medals. Twenty-one were seriously wounded, and many more than that received contusions. Only fifty remained to take their places with the men in the trenches when the battle was over.

The battle lasted for two days. Among the pines and the birches of the dusky forests they fought. With forty loyal men soldiers, they became separated from the main body of the troops, and took four rows of trenches before they were obliged to retreat for lack of reinforcements.

I heard the story from the lips of twenty of the wounded women. No one of them can tell exactly what happened.

"We were carried away in the madness of the moment," one of them said. "It was all so strange and exciting, we had no time to think about being afraid."

"No," said Marya Skridlova; "I was not afraid. None of us were afraid. We expected to die, so we had nothing to fear."

Then the demoiselle came to the surface again. "It was hard, though. I have a cousin—he is Russian in his heart, but his father is a German citizen. He was drafted: he had to go. When I saw the Germans, I thought of him. Suppose I should kill him? Yes, it is hard for a woman to fight."

Marya Skridlova got her Cross of St. George, and she came back to Petrograd walking with a limp as a result of shell shock.

"There were wounded Germans in a hut," she said. "We were ordered to take them prisoners. They refused to be taken. We had to throw hand-grenades in and destroy them. No; war is not easy for a woman."

1917

"The Battalion of Death," in *The Red Heart of Russia* (New York: Century, 1918), 98–110.

✦ III ✦

TESTIMONIAL: DIARIES, MEMOIRS, LETTERS, INTERVIEWS

Perhaps one reason that women's experiences of the war have so often been overlooked or simplified by historians is that their autobiographical writings were long excluded from consideration. Soldiers' diaries and letters were acclaimed as eyewitness accounts. But the assumption that women had "seen" nothing led many to assume that women had written nothing that might matter.

In fact, the astonishing body of women's personal writing about their experiences during the Great War reveals their drive to record what they saw and what they did. Many understood that they stood at a historical crossroads, when women were entering into occupations from which they had previously been barred. This war differed from previous wars in the roles that were publicly accepted for women. That change is reflected in both the content and the style of women's autobiographical writing, which reveals a consciousness that women's roles deviated from the "home front" domesticity to which ideology consigned them.

A few women could make the claim that they, like men, had participated in combat. Service in the military, to be sure, like employment as a battlefront reporter, marked a woman as exceptional. Female soldiers' eyewitness accounts inevitably had a political subtext. At a time of shifting citizenship claims, their accounts of battle and of resistance fighting confirmed their active engagement on behalf of their nations. When hired by the state for espionage, a woman's status depended entirely on her ability to survive betrayal and capture: Mata Hari denied that she was a spy, while Marthe Richer proclaimed proudly that she was a spy and won the Legion of Honor.

Women in medical units laid equal claim to having seen war from up close, above all by telling what happened to male bodies. The intensely detailed observation of the destruction of the body is one of the hallmarks of women's testimony about war. These women themselves were sometimes at risk. Ambulance drivers were gassed; hospitals were shelled; infections were passed on by patients. Nurses deal with the gendering of war—whether through their resistance to the sexualization of their bodies, or through their response to the cries of the wounded for their mothers and to their exposure to violated male bodies. The vividness of their observations helps us today to realize the compressed effort required to survive unceasing demands and challenges.

These letters and memoirs show a remarkable range of activities and relationships to combat. They deal with systemic experience of war as it spread out around the globe to include carriers in Africa and ambulance drivers in the Balkans. As always, women and children were victims of wartime conditions: texts here recount deportations, forced labor, rape, and epidemics. Women also recount their triumphs in working for or against the processes of war. As nurses they struggle to reduce the mortality rate in a ward from 30 percent to 19 percent; as interpreters, they break an enemy code for the War Office; as drivers, they may use a pin to repair a clutch. They develop their skills and powers to defend the nation, to protect their fellow colonials, or to mitigate the costs of war.

The damaged environments of everyday civilians emerge also from these accounts: a domestic landscape one day, the next perhaps a torn confusion of trenches, shell holes, and mud. From the oral accounts of rural women we learn of the disruption of agricultural labor by the conscription of men; from urban women we hear about starvation caused by blockades. That landscape of memory also changes through time. Many of these personal accounts were neither deposited in archives nor published until much later. What could be jotted down in the heat of the moment may differ from what spills out when the writer has more leisure or more distance. We move from blanks imposed by official censors to a frank language permitted in a changed world.

BATTLEFRONT

✟ Mademoiselle G.
(b. c.1902) *French*

According to the headnote provided for this document by the French government, Mademoiselle G—, "aged 12, no profession," was "deported from B—(Somme) November 31, 1914." She made a deposition before Monsieur Maillard, Justice of Peace at Troyes, on December 18, 1915. The French Foreign Ministry compiled sworn testimony together with evidence from diaries found on the bodies of dead German soldiers, in order to lodge a formal complaint against the German government for the violations of international law in occupied France. This complaint was delivered to the representatives of neutral governments.

✟ Testimony, Annexe 171 to Note of the Government of the French Republic

Once, in September 1914, about 7 o'clock in the morning, my aunt and I were taken as hostages, when we were at breakfast; they took us, with four other girls, towards the station. There they placed us in front of them (it was a party of Uhlans) and opened fire on the French, who replied; my uncle, Paul V—, who was with us, received a bullet through the heart and fell dead. We lay down on the ground, pretending to be dead; then some Zouaves arrived and captured the party of Uhlans. Then we were free and went home.

"Annexe 171," in *The Deportation of Women and Girls from Lille* (New York: Doran, 1916), 64.

✝ Flora Sandes
(1876–1956) British

Flora Sandes grew up in a large family; she enjoyed physical sports, learning to ride, shoot, and fence. When her schooling was completed she became a secretary. At the age of thirty-eight, within a week after war broke out, she went to Serbia with a St. John's Ambulance Brigade organized by the American wife of a Serb minister. She worked at Kragujevac, then Valjevo, combating the typhus epidemic and working in an operating room under the Serbian Red Cross. After the Bulgarian invasion of Serbia, as the hospitals were evacuated, she joined the Second Infantry Regiment as a wound dresser in November 1915. Within three weeks she took up arms and became a soldier; she was quickly promoted to sergeant. Wounded in 1916, she was decorated for conspicuous bravery. In September 1916 she published a memoir, part of her fund-raising effort for the Serbs; after the retreat, she managed supplies, negotiating between the Serbs and the Allies. Sandes spent seven years in active service until her demobilization in 1922, when her resumption of female dress cost her the invisibility on which her comradely relationships in the military had depended. Continuing in the reserves, she became a captain in 1926. In 1927 she married a Russian émigré, Yurie Yudenich, and published a second memoir, *Autobiography of a Woman Soldier: A Brief Record of Adventure with the Serbian Army, 1916–1919.* The couple lived in Belgrade and Paris; they were briefly interned during the German occupation of Yugoslavia. After her husband's death in 1941 she returned to Suffolk; life in her cottage in England, she found, was "very safe but not very exciting." Her great-nephew writes, "I well remember seeing the considerable scars of shrapnel wounds on her back and legs when we went swimming with her as children. These scars bore witness to the fact that she was very much *in* the line of fire."

✝ Fighting on Mount Chukus

They asked me if I was going to tackle the mountain on foot with them, or if I would rather stay there with the transport. I went with them, of course. Mount Chukus is 1,790 metres high from where we were then, and it certainly was a stiff climb. We left our horses there—I had been riding a rough mountain pony of Captain S——'s—and the whole battalion started up on foot. There was no path most of the way, and in places it was so steep that we had to scramble along and pull ourselves up by the bushes, over the rocks and boulders, and in spite of the cold and wet we were all dripping with perspiration. We of necessity went very slowly, making frequent halts to recover our breath and let the end men catch up, as we did not want to lose any stragglers. It must be remembered that not one of these men but had at least one old wound received either in this or some previous war, and a great number had five or six, and this climb was calculated to catch anybody in their weak spot.

We arrived at the top about 4 P.M., steady travelling since 3 A.M. that morning, most of which had been uphill and hard-going. One officer with an old wound through his chest, and another bullet still in his side, just dropped on his face when we got to the top, though he had not uttered a word of complaint before.

At the very tip-top we camped amongst some pine trees and put up our tents; it was still raining hard and continued to do so all that night, and everything was soaking—there didn't seem to be a dry spot anywhere. The little bivouac tents are made in four pieces, and each man carries one piece, which he wraps round him like a waterproof when he has to march in the rain; and, if it is not convenient to put up tents, rolls himself up in it at night. We made fires, though we were nearly blinded by the smoke from the wet wood; someone produced some bread and cheese and shared it round, and then we all turned in. It was so cold and wet that I crawled out again about 2 A.M., and finished the night by the fire, as did three or four more uneasy souls who were too cold to sleep. My feet were soaking, so I stuck them near the fire and then went to sleep, pulling my coat over my head to keep off the rain, and it was not until some time afterwards that I discovered that I had burnt the soles nearly off my boots. I felt hearty sympathy for a soldier I heard one day in Durazzo being reprimanded by an officer for having half his overcoat burnt away—"Do you think you were the only one who was cold? Why didn't *that* man and *that* man burn their clothes? they were just as cold," and I thought guiltily of my own burnt boots.

Later on the next day the sun put in an appearance, as did also the Bulgarians. The other side of the mountain was very steep, and our position dominated a flat wooded sort of plateau below, where the enemy were. One of our sentries, who was posted behind a rock, reported the first sight of them, and I went up to see where they were, with two of the officers. I could not see them plainly at first, but they could evidently see our three heads very plainly. The companies were quickly posted in their various positions, and I made my way over to the Fourth, which was in the first line; we did not need any trenches, as there were heaps of rocks for cover, and we lay behind them firing by volley. I had only a revolver and no rifle of my own at that time, but one of my comrades was quite satisfied to lend me his and curl himself up and smoke. We all talked in whispers, as if we were stalking rabbits, though I could not see that it mattered much if the Bulgarians did hear us, as they knew exactly where we were, as the bullets that came singing round one's head directly one stood up proved, but they did not seem awfully good shots. It is a funny thing about rifle fire, that a person's instinct always seems to be to hunch up his shoulders or turn up his coat collar when he is walking about, as if it were rain, though the bullet you hear whistle past your ears is not the one that is going to hit you. I have seen heaps of men do this who have been through dozens of battles and are not afraid of any mortal thing.

We lay there and fired at them all that day, and I took a lot of photographs which I wanted very much to turn out well; but, alas! during the journey through Albania the films, together with nearly all the others that I took, got wet and spoilt. The firing died down at dark, and we left the firing line and made innumerable camp fires and sat round them. Lieut. Jovitch, the Commander, took me into his company, and I was enrolled on its books, and he seemed to think I might be made a corporal pretty soon if I behaved myself. We were 221 in the Fourth, and were the largest, and, we flattered ourselves, the smartest, company of the smartest regiment, the first to be ready in marching order in the mornings, and the quickest to have our tents properly pitched and our camp fires going at night. Our Company Commander was a hustler, very proud of his men, and they were devoted to him and would do anything for him, and well they might. He was a martinet for discipline, but the comfort of his men was always his first consideration; they came to him for everything, and he would have given anyone the coat off his back if they had wanted it. A good commander makes a good company, and he could make a dead man get up and follow him.

That evening was very different to the previous one. Lieut. Jovitch had a roaring fire of pine logs built in a little hollow, just below what had been our firing line, and he and I and the other two officers of the company sat round it and had our supper of bread and beans, and after that we spread our blankets on spruce boughs round the fire and rolled up in them. It was a most glorious moonlight night, with the ground covered with white hoar frost, and it looked perfectly lovely with all the camp fires twinkling every few yards over the hillside among the pine trees. I lay on my back looking up at the stars, and, when one of them asked me what I was thinking about, I told him that when I was old and decrepit and done for, and had to stay in a house and not go about any more, I should remember my first night with the Fourth Company on the top of Mount Chukus.

"Fighting on Mount Chukus," in *An English Woman-Sergeant in the Serbian Army* (London: Hodder & Stoughton, 1916), 134–147. Reprinted by permission of the holders of the copyright.

✠ Mary Gotoubyova
(b. 1899) *Russian*

Reportedly the first woman to kill a German in the Women's Battalion of Death led by Maria Botchkareva, Mary Gotoubyova was wounded on her second day at the front and sent back with ten comrades to a hospital in Petrograd. She and the other members of the battalion carried cyanide of potassium in case of capture. Of over two hundred in this command only fifty remained after their first battle: twenty were killed, eight taken prisoner, and the rest wounded. During their engagement near Smorgon at Novospassky Wood, they said they found among their German prisoners a few women soldiers as well. The puzzle these women presented to American men is suggested by the journalist Arno Dosch Fleurot, who interviewed her; he described Gotoubyova as "tall and graceful, with pretty blue eyes" and cropped blond hair; her "rough hospital nightgown could not conceal her well developed, beautiful figure."

Rheta Childe Dorr, an American suffragist and journalist who, along with Bessie Beatty, spent two weeks at the front with Botchkareva's battalion, reported to the Chicago *Daily Tribune* (July 29, 1917) that the women were heckled and harassed en route to their base near Vilno, but set armed sentinels to protect themselves from sexual attack. Praising the unconventionality of the "Legion of Death," Dorr stated: "The girls in it have forgotten everything they were ever taught as women—and you've no idea how nice women can be when they are absolutely natural and unselfish. The girls did their job in dead earnest."

✝ Interview with Arno Dosch Fleurot

I am wounded they say. I call it mere scratches, but it may keep me from the front several weeks after only two days' fighting. At any rate, I was in the front trenches and I got my German. I am feeling better already, and hope I go right back. I must go; my country needs me. That is why I enlisted.

I saw soldiers in Petrograd demanding not to be sent to the front, and I realized that the country needed every man and woman who was not a coward. Then the woman's battalion was formed and I joined immediately. I have never regretted it. I was never afraid, and I ask only the privilege to bear a gun against the enemy again. I must fill the place of men who will not fight.

Going to war is not too much for a woman. I was always strong. Still, being a woman, I wondered if it would be too fatiguing. Once at the front, I forgot whether I was a man or a woman. I was just a soldier. The only preparation I made against contact with the enemy was to wrap the upper portion of my body firmly. In the burning battle I was never hampered for an instant on account of my sex. The soldiers, the real brave soldiers, treated me like a comrade. Only the cowards jeered.

We went into action a fortnight after our arrival at the front, under heavy German fire. Given the order to advance, we rushed out of our trenches. After the first attack I was attached to a machine gun, carrying ammunition to advanced position under the fire of hidden German machine guns. We were advancing and constantly in danger of capture by the Germans.

On one trip over newly captured ground I saw what I considered a wounded German officer lying on the ground. I went to help him with my gun in my right hand and the machine gun ammunition in my left. Seeing me he jumped to his knees and pulled out his revolver, but before he could shoot I dropped the ammunition and killed him.

How did I feel on taking a human life? I had no sensation, except to rid my country of an enemy. There was no sentimentality. We were trying to kill them and they were trying to kill us—that is all. Any Russian girl or any American girl in the same position would have the same feeling.

No, I do not feel that I did anything exceptional. Any well girl can do the same.

I never knew when I was hit. Shells were breaking everywhere. One got me. The next time one may really get me.

Chicago Daily Tribune, July 31, 1917

✠ Maria Leont'evna Botchkareva, née Frolkova
(1889–1919?) *Russian*

According to Emmeline Pankhurst, Botchkareva was "the greatest woman of the century." The semiliterate daughter of a serf and a victim of parental abuse, she married Afanasi Botchkarev at fifteen, falling into another abusive situation, which ended in separation. To survive, she washed dishes, laid concrete, and worked as a butcher. After entering a relationship with Yakov Bok, she went into exile from 1909 to 1914 for her partner's revolutionary activities; this liaison also broke up when Bok tried to kill her.

She enlisted in the Tomsk Reserve Battalion in 1914 with the permission of Czar Nicholas II. From 1915 to 1917 she served on the southwestern front of the Russian Empire, where she was decorated three times (only in the third and fourth degree, because she was a woman) and was promoted to corporal for rescuing wounded comrades. By her own account, her comrades affectionately accepted the woman they called "Yashka." A fragment of shrapnel in her spine left her nearly paralyzed for several months, but on her recovery she returned to combat.

Exhilarated by the collapse of czarism, Botchkareva nonetheless was dismayed by the subsequent military disarray and defeatism; therefore, under the provisional government of Aleksandr Kerensky, she proposed in May 1917 the formation of a women's "battalion of death," which was supported by President Rodzianko of the *Duma* in Petrograd, General Aleksey Brusilov, and Kerensky. As she proclaimed at a meeting, "Our mother is perishing. . . . I want to help save her. I want women whose hearts are pure crystal." No "little soldiers" would be born at the front, she promised. Two thousand women enlisted, forming two battalions; her strict discipline ultimately limited her force to under three hundred women. Many dropped out as a result of Bolshevik agitation, claiming "We want to be independent. We want to exercise our own rights." Her troops addressed her as "Mister Commander," since (as she explained) "all military terms are masculine and it is much too useless a work to go through the list feminizing the nomenclature of war." Her battalion and the female Perm Battalion went into action at the front lines; other women's battalions with up to one thousand soldiers guarded Moscow and Petrograd. In a July attack Botchkareva's troops took two thousand prisoners, at the cost of seventy casualties, earning the hatred of fellow soldiers, who accused her of provoking counterattacks. She supported General Laurus Kornilov in his attempted military coup d'état; when Kerensky was overthrown, twenty of her women were lynched and others battered by male soldiers; the rest were forced to disperse.

In May 1918 with the help of the British Consulate and Mrs. Borden Harriman, Botchkareva traveled to the United States to petition Woodrow Wilson to intervene in Russia. While in America she dictated her autobiography, *Yashka,* to Isaac Levine. When she returned in August to Archangel with the Allied invasion force, in the hope of serving as a mediator, she was stripped of her uniform by a Soviet general, who declared that "the summoning of women for military duties which are not appropriate for their sex would be a heavy reproach and a disgraceful stain on the whole population of the northern region." In the subsequent upheaval Botchkareva disappeared, but numerous women doctors and fighters volunteered in the civil war; by 1920 twenty thousand women served in the Red army.

✟ Introduced to No Man's Land

Our train was composed of a number of box-cars and one passenger-car. A box-car, having two bunks on each side, in which the soldiers sleep, is called *teplushka.* There are no windows in a *teplushka,* as it is really only a converted freight-car. The passenger-car was occupied by the four officers of our regiment, including our new Company Commander, Grishaninov. He was a short, jolly fellow and soon won his men's love and loyalty.

There was much empty space in the passenger-car, and the officers bethought themselves to invite me to share it with them. When the invitation came the soldiers all shook their heads in disapproval. They suspected the motives of the officers and thought that Yashka could fare as well among them as among their superiors.

"Botchkareva," said Commander Grishaninov, when I entered his car, "would you prefer to be stationed in this carriage? There is plenty of room."

"No, your Excellency," I replied, saluting. "I am a plain soldier, and it is my duty to travel as a soldier."

"Very well," declared the Commander, chagrined. And I returned to my *teplushka.*

"Yashka is back! Good fellow, Yashka!" the boys welcomed me enthusiastically, flinging some strong epithets at the officers. They were immensely pleased at the idea that Yashka preferred their company in a *teplushka* to that of the officers in a spacious passenger coach, and made a comfortable place for me in a corner.

We were assigned to the Second Army, then commanded by General Gurko, with headquarters at Polotsk. It took us two weeks to get there from Tomsk. General Gurko reviewed us at Army Headquarters and complimented the officers upon the regiment's fitness. We were then assigned to the Fifth Corps. Before we started the word went out that there was a woman in our regiment. There was no lack of curiosity-seekers. Knots of soldiers gathered about my *teplushka,* peeped through the door and cracks in the sides to verify with their own eyes the incredible news. Then they would swear, emphasizing by spitting the inexplicable phenomenon of a *baba* going to the trenches. The attention of some officers was attracted by the crowd, and they came up to find out what the excitement was about. They reported me to the commandant of the station, who immediately sent for Colonel Grishaninov, demanding an explanation. But the Colonel could not satisfy the commandant's doubts and was instructed not to send me along with the men to the fighting line.

"You can't go to the trenches, Botchkareva," my commander addressed me upon his return from the commandant. "The General won't allow it. He was much wrought up over you and could not understand how a woman could be a soldier."

For a moment I was shocked. Then the happy thought occurred to me that no General had the authority to overrule an order of the Tsar.

"Your Excellency!" I exclaimed to Colonel Grishaninov, "I was enlisted by the grace of the Tsar as a regular soldier. You can look up His Majesty's telegram in my record."

This settled the matter, and the commandant withdrew his objections. There were about twenty versts to Corps Headquarters to be walked. The road was in a frightful condition, sticky and full of mud-holes. We were so tired at the end of ten versts' walking that a rest was ordered. The soldiers, although fatigued, made a dry seat for me with their overcoats. We then resumed our journey, arriving for supper at Headquarters, and were billeted for the night in a stable. We slept like dead, on straw spread over the floor. [. . .]

On the third day came the order to move to the trench lines. Through mud and under shells we marched forward. It was still light when we arrived at the firing-line. We had two killed and five wounded. As the German positions were on a hill, they were enabled to observe all our movements. We were therefore instructed by field telephone not to occupy the trenches till after dark.

"So this is war," I thought. My pulse quickened, and I caught the spirit of excitement that pervaded the regiment. We were all expectant, as if in the presence of a solemn revelation. We were eager to get into the fray to show the Germans what we, the boys of the Fifth Regiment, could do. Were we nervous? Undoubtedly. But it was not the nervousness of cowardice, rather was it the restlessness of young blood. Our hands were steady, our bayonets fixed. We exulted in our adventure.

Night came. The Germans were releasing a gas wave at us. Perhaps they noticed an unusual movement behind the lines, and wished to annihilate us before we entered the battle. But they failed. Over the wire came the order to put on our masks. Thus were we baptized in this most inhuman of all German war inventions. Our masks were not perfect. The deadly gas penetrated some and made our eyes smart and water. But we were soldiers of Mother-Russia, whose sons are not unaccustomed to half-suffocating air, and so we withstood the irritating fumes.

The midnight hour passed. The Commander went through our ranks to inform us that the hour had come to move into the trenches and that before dawn we would take the offensive. He addressed us with words of encouragement and was heartily cheered. The artillery had been thundering all night, the fire growing more and more intense every hour. In single file we moved along a communication trench to the front line. Some of us were wounded, but we remained dauntless. All our fatigue seemed to have vanished.

The front trench was a plain ditch, and as we lined up along it our shoulders touched. The positions of the enemy were less than one verst away, and the space between was filled with groans and swept by bullets. It was a scene full of horrors. Sometimes an enemy shell would land in the midst of our men, killing several and wounding many. Then we would be sprinkled with the blood of our comrades and spattered by the mud.

At two in the morning the Commander appeared in our midst. He was seemingly nervous. The other officers came with him and took their positions at the head of the men. With drawn sabers they prepared to lead the charge. The Commander had a rifle.

"*Viliezai!*"[1] his voice rang out.

I crossed myself. My heart was filled with pain for the bleeding men around me and stirred by an impulse of savage revenge toward the Germans. My mind was a kaleidoscope of many thoughts and pictures. My mother, death, mutilation, various petty incidents of my life filled it. But there was no time for thinking.

I climbed out with the rest of the boys, to be met by a hail of machine gun bullets. For a moment there was confusion. So many dropped around us, like ripe wheat cut down by a gigantic scythe wielded by the invisible arm of Satan himself. Fresh blood was dripping on the cold corpses that had lain there for hours or days. And the moans, they were so heart-rending, so piercing!

Amid the confusion the voice of our Company Commander was raised: "Forward!"

And forward we went. The enemy had perceived us go over the top, and he let loose Hell. As we ran ahead, we fired. Then the order came to lie

1. *Viliezai:* climb out.

down. The bombardment grew even more concentrated. Alternately running for some distance and then lying down for a while, we reached the enemy's barbed wire entanglements. We had expected to find them demolished by our artillery, but, alas! they were untouched. There were only about seventy of our Company of two hundred and fifty left.

Whose fault was it? This was an offensive on a twenty-verst line, carried out by three army corps. And the barbed wire was uncut! Perhaps our artillery was defective! Perhaps it was the fault of someone higher up! Anyhow, there we were, seventy out of two hundred and fifty. And every fraction of a second was precious. Were we doomed to die here in a heap without even coming to grips with the enemy? Were our bodies to dangle on this wire to-morrow, and the day after, to provide food for the crows and strike terror into the hearts of the fresh soldiers who would take our places in a few hours?

As these thoughts flashed through our minds an order came to retreat. The enemy let a barrage down in front of us. The retreat was even worse than the advance. By the time we got back to our trenches there were only forty-eight of our Company left alive. About a third of the two hundred and fifty were dead. The larger part of the wounded were in No Man's Land, and their cries of pain and prayers for help or death gave us no peace.

The remnant of our Company crouched in the trench, exhausted, dazed, incredulous of their escape from injury. We were hungry and thirsty and would have welcomed a dry and safe place to recover our poise. But there we were, smarting under the defeat by the enemy's barbed wire barrier, with the heart-tearing appeals for succor coming from our comrades. Deeper and deeper they cut into my soul. They were so plaintive, like the voices of hurt children.

In the dark it seemed to me that I saw their faces, the familiar faces of Ivan and Peter and Sergei and Mitia, the good fellows who had taken such tender care of me, making a comfortable place for me in that crowded *teplushka,* or taking off their overcoats in cold weather and spreading them on the muddy road to provide a dry seat for Yashka. They called me. I could see their hands outstretched in my direction, their wide-open eyes straining in the night in expectation of rescue, the deathly pallor of their countenances. Could I remain indifferent to their pleas? Wasn't it my bounden duty as a soldier, as important as that of fighting the enemy, to render aid to stricken comrades?

I climbed out of the trench and crawled under our wire entanglements. There was a comparative calm, interrupted only by occasional rifle shots, when I would lie down and remain motionless, imitating a corpse. Within a few feet of our line there were wounded. I carried them one by one to the edge of our trench where they were picked up and carried to the rear. The saving of one man stimulated me to continue my labors, till I reached into the far side of the field. Here I had several narrow escapes. A sound, made involuntarily, was sufficient to attract several bullets, and only my anticipating that, by flattening myself against the ground, saved me. When dawn broke in the east, putting an end to my expeditions through No Man's Land, I had accounted for about fifty lives.

I had no idea at the time of what I had accomplished. But when the soldiers whom I had picked up were brought to the relief-station and asked who rescued them, about fifty replied, "Yashka." This was communicated to the Commander, who recommended me for an Order of the 4th degree, "for distinguished valor shown in the saving of many lives under fire." [. . .]

There is great satisfaction in aiding an agonized human being. There is great reward in the gratitude of some pain-convulsed boy that one wins. It gave me immense joy to sustain life in benumbed human bodies. As I was kneeling over one such wounded, who had suffered a great loss of blood, and was about to lift him, a sniper's bullet hit me between the thumb and forefinger and passed on and through the flesh of my left forearm. Fortunately I realized quickly the nature of the wounds, bandaged them, and, in spite of his objections, carried the bleeding man out of danger.

I continued my work all night, and was recommended "for bravery in defensive and offensive fighting and for rendering, while wounded, first aid on the field of battle," to receive the Cross of St. George. But I never received it. Instead, I was awarded a medal of the 4th degree and was informed that a woman could not obtain the Cross of St. George.

I was disappointed and chagrined. Hadn't I heard of the Cross being given to some Red Cross nurses? I protested to the Commander. He fully sympathized with me and expressed his belief that I certainly deserved the Cross.

"But," he added, disdainfully, shrugging his shoulders, "it is *natchalstvo*."[2] [. . .]

Every twelve days we were relieved and sent to the rear for a six days' recuperation. There the baths of the Union of Zemstvos, which had already extended its activities in 1915 throughout the front, awaited us. Every Divisional bath was in the charge of a physician and a hundred volunteer workers. Every bath-house was also a laundry, and the men, upon entering it, left their dirty underwear there, receiving in exchange clean linen. When a company was about to leave the trenches for the rear, word was sent to the bath-house of its coming. There was nothing that the soldiers welcomed so much as the bath-house, so vermin-ridden were the trenches, and so great was their suffering on this account.

More than anybody else did I suffer from the vermin. I could not think at first of going to the bath-house with the men. My skin was eaten through and through, and scabs began to form all over my body. I went to the Commander to inquire how I could get a bath, telling him of my condition. The Commander sympathized.

"But what can I do, Yashka?" he remarked, "I can't keep the whole Com-

2. *Natchalstvo*: officialdom.

pany out to let you alone make use of the bath-house. Go with the men. They respect you so much that I am sure they won't molest you."

I could not quite make up my mind for a while. But the vermin gave me no rest, and I was nearing the point of desperation. When we were relieved next and the boys were getting ready to march to the bath-house I plucked up courage and went up to my sergeant, declaring:

"I'll go to the bath-house, too. I can't endure it any longer."

He approved of my decision, and I followed the Company, arousing general merriment. "Oh, Yashka is going with us to the bath-house!" the boys joked, goodnaturedly. Once inside, I hastened to occupy a corner for myself and demanded that the men stay away from there. They did, although they kept laughing and teasing. I was awfully embarrassed the first time, and as soon as I got through I hurried into my new underwear, dressed quickly and ran out of the building. But the bath did me so much good that I made it a habit to attend it with the Company every two weeks. In time, the soldiers got so accustomed to it that they paid no attention to me, and were even quick to silence the fun-making of any new member of the Company.

"Introduced to No Man's Land," in *Yashka, My Life as Peasant, Officer, and Exile,* trans. Isaac Don Levine (New York: Stokes, 1919), 86–102.

✝ Attack

The order from General Valuyev, Commander of the Tenth Army, was for our whole Corps to go over the top at 3 A.M., July the 8th [1917]. [. . .]

The Colonel, the Company Commanders and some of the braver soldiers tried to persuade the regiment to go over the top. Meanwhile, day was breaking. Time did not wait. The other regiments of the corps were also vacillating. The men, raised to a high pitch of courage by Kerensky's oratory, lost heart when the advance became imminent. My Battalion[3] was kept in the trench by the pusillanimous conduct of the men on both flanks. It was an intolerable situation, unthinkable, grotesque.

The sun crept out in the east, only to cast its rays on the extraordinary spectacle of an entire corps debating their Commander's order to advance. It was four. The debate still raged. The sun rose higher. The morning mist had almost vanished. The artillery fire was slackening. The debate continued. It was five. The Germans were wondering what in the world those Russians were going to do with their offensive. All the spirit accumulated in the Battalion during the night was waning, giving

3. The Women's Battalion of Death.

way to the physical strain under which we labored. And the soldiers were still discussing the advisability of attacking!

Every second was precious. "If they would only decide in the affirmative, even now it might not be too late to strike," I thought. But minutes rolled into hours, and there was no sign of a decision. It struck six, and then seven. The day was surely lost. Perhaps all was lost. One's blood boiled with indignation at the absurdity, the futility of the procedure. The weak-kneed hypocrites! They feigned interest in the prudence of starting an offensive on general principles, as if they hadn't talked for weeks about it to their hearts' content. They were plain cowards, concealing their fear in bushels of idle talk.

Orders were given to the artillery to continue the bombardment. All day the cannon boomed while the men debated. The shame, the humiliation of it! These very men had given their words of honor to attack! Now the fear for the safety of their hides had overwhelmed their minds and souls. The hour of noon still found them in the midst of the debate! There were meetings and speeches in the immediate rear. Nothing more stupid, more empty of meaning could be imagined than the arguments of the men. They were repeating in halting tones those old, vague phrases that had been proven false again and again, to the complete satisfaction of their own minds. And yet they lingered, drawn by their faint souls towards doubt and vacillation.

The day declined. The men had arrived at no final resolution. Then, about seventy-five officers, led by Lieutenant-Colonel Ivanov, came to me to ask permission to enter the ranks of the Battalion for a joint advance. They were followed by about three hundred of the most intelligent and gallant soldiers in the regiment. Altogether, the Battalion's ranks had swollen to about a thousand. I offered the command to Lieutenant-Colonel Ivanov as to a superior, but he declined.

Every officer was provided with a rifle. The line was so arranged that men and women alternated, a girl being flanked by two men. The officers, now numbering about a hundred, were stationed at equal distances throughout the line.

We decided to advance in order to shame the men, having arrived at the conclusion that they would not let us perish in No Man's Land. We all felt the gravity of the decision. We had nothing to guide us in the belief that the boys would not abandon us to our fate, except a feeling that such a monstrosity could not happen. Besides, something had to be done. An offensive had to be launched soon. The front was rapidly deteriorating to a state of impotence.

Colonel Ivanov communicated to the Commander by telephone the decision of the Battalion. It was a desperate gamble, and every one of us realized the grimness of the moment. The men on our flanks were joking and deriding us.

"Ha, ha! Women and officers will fight!" they railed.

"They are faking. Who ever saw officers go over the top like soldiers, with rifles in hand?"

"Just watch those women run!" joked a fellow, to the merriment of a chorus of voices.

We gritted our teeth in fury but did not reply. Our hope was still in these men. We stuck to the belief that they would follow us and, therefore, avoided alienating them.

At last the signal was given. We crossed ourselves and, hugging our rifles, leaped out of the trenches, every one of our lives dedicated to "the country and freedom." We moved forward against a withering fire of machine guns and artillery, my brave girls, encouraged by the presence of men on their sides, marching steadily against the hail of bullets.

Every particle of time carried death with it. There was but one thought in every mind: "Will they follow?" Each fleeting instant seemed like an age that lurid morning. Already several of us were struck down, and yet no one came after us. We turned our heads every now and then, piercing the darkness in vain for support. Many heads were sticking out from the trenches in our rear. The laggards were wondering if we were in earnest. No, it was all a ruse to them. How could a bare thousand of women and officers attack after a two days' bombardment on a front of several versts? It seemed incredible, impossible.

But, dauntless of heart and firm of step, we moved forward. Our losses were increasing, but our line was unbroken. As we advanced more and more into No Man's Land, the shadows finally swallowing us completely, with only the fire of explosions revealing our figures at times to the eyes of our boys in the back, their hearts moved.

Through the din and crash of the bombardment we suddenly caught the sound of a great commotion in the rear. Was it a feeling of shame that stirred them from their lethargy? Or was it the sight of this handful of intrepid souls that aroused their spirit? Anyhow, they were awake at last. Bounding forward with shouts, numberless bodies climbed over the top, and in a few moments the front to the right and left of us became a swaying mass of soldiers. First our regiment poured out and then, on both sides, the contagion spread and unit after unit joined in the advance, so that almost the entire Corps was on the move.

We swept forward and overwhelmed the first German line, and then the second. Our regiment alone captured two thousand prisoners. But there was poison awaiting us in that second line of trenches. Vodka and beer were in abundance. Half of our force got drunk right there, throwing themselves ravenously on the alcohol. My girls did splendid work here, destroying the stores of liquor at my orders. If not for that, the whole regiment would have been drunk. I rushed about appealing to the men to stop drinking.

"Are you going insane?" I pleaded. "We must take the third line yet, and then the Ninth Corps will come to relieve us and keep up the drive."

I realized that the opportunity was too precious. "We must take the third line and rip their defenses open," I thought, "so as to turn this blow into a general offensive."

But the men were succumbing one by one to the bitter scourge. And there were the wounded to be taken care of. Some of my girls were killed outright, many were wounded. The latter almost all behaved like Stoics. I can see, even now, the face of Klipatskaya, one of my soldiers, lying in a pool of blood. I ran up to her and sought to aid her, but it was too late. She had twelve wounds, from bullets and shrapnel. Smiling faintly her last smile, she said:

"Milaya, nitchevo!"[4]

"Attack," in *Yashka, My Life as Peasant, Officer, and Exile,* trans. Isaac Don Levine (New York: Stokes, 1919), 209–13.

4. *Milaya, nitchevo!:* My dear, it's nothing.

✝ Zabel Bournazian
Turkish Armenian

In an account written after the war, Zabel Bournazian describes her Armenian community's armed resistance to the Ottoman repression at Chabine-Karahissar. The rebels held out for twenty-one days, until food and water were exhausted. After the fall of the fortress to which they had retreated, Bournazian survived the deportation and massacre of Armenians by bribing a policeman and finding shelter with a Greek family for her mother-in-law, her baby, some relatives, and herself.

✝ The Heroic Combat of Chabine-Karahissar

In early March, 1915, the commander of a detachment of 400 Turkish volunteers (*tchetas*) spoke to the priest of the village of Pourk, with 200 habitants, near Endiress, demanding that he resupply and house his men for three days.

The Armenian villagers fed them not three days but two weeks. But when supplies were exhausted, the *mukhtar*[1] and priest were forced to announce that they were no longer able to feed the Turks. Then the commander of the *tchetas* had them whipped until they bled. Indignant, the young men of the village intervened. The volunteers took up arms and an Armenian was killed; this incident provoked a melee between Armenians and Turks. It lasted twenty-four hours and was stopped only by the intervention of the *kaimakam*[2] of Endiress. The arms of the Armenians were confiscated and their owners imprisoned.

All sorts of tortures were invented to force the young prisoners to confess

---

1. *Mukhtar:* town elder, elected mayor.
2. *Kaimakam:* deputy governor, part of the Ottoman administration.

the source of the arms. Unable to stand the torture, a young man named Chahnazar denounced the members of the Tachnak[3] committee of Karahissar: H. Karagozian, Vahan Hussussian, and brother Lukas. Warned, they were forced to go into hiding. However, in the absence of his son, the Turks arrested the father of Hussussian and other personalities, who after several days in prison were turned over to the bloody *vali*[4] of Sivas, Mouammer.

The old Hussussian was hung and the others shot. In the meantime, after a mendacious telegram calling Father Vaghinak to the patriarchate of Constantinople, the unfortunate prelate was imprisoned in Endiress and killed amid horrible tortures.

After several days of calm the Turks surrounded the Tach-han of Karahissar and 200 Armenian notables were arrested. They were kept in jail ten days, then under the pretext of sending them into exile, the Turks assassinated them. Some of these prisoners were shot on the banks of the river Kaïl and the others cast into the water. Among the prisoners, a young man named Karnig Beylerian wrenched away the weapon of a policeman and killed him instantly; while his brother Sénékérion made futile attempts at self-defence with nothing better than a pocket knife. Unhappily surrounded on all sides, these half-attempts at defence had no impact. Ardachès Bournazian, Setrak Hussussian and others were the only ones able to flee and take refuge in the fortress. The news of this cruelty spreading in the town, the committees of the Tachnakists and the reform Henchakists[5] held a meeting at which they decided to take refuge in the fortress and then go on the defensive.

Immediately circulars were sent to all the members of these parties and the retreat of the Armenians of Karahissar, 1000 families, took place that night. No one hesitated to obey this order, although the climb to the fortress was quite difficult for the women, children, and old men. Armenian sentinels stood guard along the way. Each Armenian had the password, *trutzik*,[6] which was whispered at each encounter with the sentinels.

With my seven-month-old baby tied on my back I followed the column with great difficulty. Since I was weak, I didn't think I was capable of finishing this march, but our brave youth were stationed everywhere and while watching they helped us as much as possible. We arrived finally at an Armenian church at the foot of the fortress, where we rested. Then came the order to continue the climb in order to arrive at the fortress before day break.

In the morning the Turks were quite surprised to find the Armenian quarters evacuated!

When the Turks learned of our withdrawal, they immediately began to attack. The combat between our courageous defenders and the enemy was unequal but each armed man was convinced that it was better to die than to abandon his post.

The situation was desperate. No one had any illusions, but everyone,

3. *Tachnak:* Armenian Revolution Federation Party.
4. *Vali:* governor of a *vilayet,* an Ottoman administrative unit.
5. *Henchakists:* a nationalist party with socialist leanings.
6. *Trutzik:* kite.

man and woman alike, had decided to die rather than fall into the hands
of an unworthy enemy.

We learned that the *vali* of Sivas had ordered that the houses of Armenians be burned and that any Muslim who refused to execute this order
be hanged.

At the first fusillades we realized that the fortress was surrounded by
Turkish hordes come from all parts on the order of the *mutessarif.*[7] Balls
fell like rain on us. We were bewildered by the noise of the fusillade. Our
defenders posted at all the passageways successfully responded to the
enemy fire. The combat lasted fifteen days uninterrupted, until reinforcements arrived for the Turks. Six thousand regular soldiers came from
Erzerum with cannon of 7 to 7.5 caliber; Firidin Topal Ossman, the head of
the *tchetas,* came with 150 criminals released from prison to join the forces
of Erzerum; and also the commander of the garrison of Kirassunde with a
few hundred men. Thus reinforced the Turks began to attack again. Several times they tried to reach our heights by using grenades, but the heroic
defence by our men forced them to turn back with important losses.

How did we organize ourselves inside the fortress? In truth, we survivors
will never forget those days of anguish and heroism during which, with
tears of pride, we felt the spirit of resistance, of perseverance, and of sacrifice that never failed our defenders.

Those Armenians who had deserted from the Turkish army refusing to
serve the cause of the enemy were in the front lines and fought like lions
to defend the life and honor of their people. The members of all the parties meeting took new dispositions to face the situation. After examining
the tactical positions of the fortress, they decided they had to barricade
the passageways, and they called on everyone to help them execute their
plan of action. The women, girls, and even children passed from hand to
hand the stones and other materials necessary to construct walls; after that
men were chosen to stay on duty at these posts. [. . .]

All our force consisted of 800 armed persons. It was necessary to guard the
seven main passageways; since there was no phone, boys and girls 10 to 11
years old were charged with establishing communication from one position
to another. As soon as positions received word that the enemy had appeared
on one side, the men of the menaced position received munitions. The volley picked up and Turkish corpses rolled down the flanks of the hill.

Like the organisation of the defence, it was important to take care of
feeding the refugees. It was not easy for the children, women, and old men
to pass whole weeks out of doors. Everyone began to collect stones and
make shelters for their families. The spirit of fraternity was so complete that
people helped each other quite naturally. Everyone had confided their
food provisions to the leader, brother Lukas, and a regular and equal distribution was set up. For 24 days each received 100 grams of unleavened
bread, a portion of meat, sugar, and boiled wheat, and the distribution took
place with such discipline that no one had reason to complain.

7. *Mutessarif:* governor of local town.

Most difficult was the shortage of water. We discovered a cave named Sar-Sarnitch where we hoped to find water by digging. We immediately set to work, but the water we found deep underground was quite insufficient.

Sometimes at night we were forced to build a new barricade. People of every age at once took up the task and walled the threatened side with extraordinary rapidity. In the morning the enemy discovered the labor we had accomplished with astonishment and redoubled fury. During the day it became more and more impossible to move about; countless enemy shots menaced our communication routes, but nothing could discourage us any longer. We began to build narrow paths walled on both sides along which we could come and go without danger.

It was easy to prepare shot for our old rifles: a group of women and children was enrolled for this task, while other children carried to the ranks bombs that we called in our argot "apples." The service rendered by the children will remain unforgettable. Thus it was that with all means both possible and impossible, we continued the struggle.

On the seventeenth day, some Armenian women who had remained in a distant quarter of Karahissar were sent accompanied by a couple of police as delegates for negotiations. The Turks had these delegates say that by imperial *iradé*[8] the politics of persecution had ceased, and that we could come down without fear, we would be indemnified for our material losses, the life and honor of all Armenians would be assured, and that in any case we could expect a tranquil life. After these declarations the women delegates left. Our leaders met and decided that we needed definite information. A delegation composed of a priest and two civilians was sent to the Turks. On their return, it was not hard to establish that the promises of the Turks were mendacious. The delegation of the Turks returned for our response. To present our conditions, we held it necessary to send our delegates. We never saw them again. . . .

The bombardment began, the enemy fusillade was extended, our brave men made desperate efforts to push back every enemy attempt to reach closer to us. Finally, the Turks with their superior forces began to attack the entrance to the fortress under cover of bombardment. Then it was that the Armenian soldiers, forced to leave their posts, began hand to hand combat.

After four hours of pitiless and bloody combat, it was still the Turks who were forced to retire leaving many dead behind. During this combat we had lost Hemaïak Karagueuzian, Hagop Bournazian and several other *fédaïs*.[9] We owed our unexpected success as much to the superhuman effort of our combatants as to the abundance of our munitions.

We had reached the twenty-third day, our nourishment and munitions were becoming exhausted day by day, while the Turks were reinforcing the siege. What should be done? Again the leaders met and decided to make a sortie through the enemy ranks. Everyone accepted this desperate resolution. The eve of the execution of the plan all the leaders met at the gate

8. *Iradé:* Sultan's decree.
9. *Fédaïs:* resistance fighters.

of the fortress. We were there too and a feeling of solemn resignation presided at that fatal hour. Mothers had to part from sons, wives from husbands, sisters from brothers.

We embraced and our farewells rang on all sides. The first and fourth groups left the fortress in files, their firearms ready.

The Turks had guessed our intention. The battle began again frenetically, at the price of many Turkish victims. Our fifth, sixth, seventh, and eighth groups left the fortress in turn and came to the rescue of our men. The enemy forces were about to weaken, but unfortunately in the obscurity of the melee, one hundred Armenians fell in the explosion of a bomb. . . .

When our men drew away from the fortress a profound sadness followed the intense will that we had mobilized at the moment of separation.

The uncertain fate of those who had left and our own desperate situation sufficed to inspire us with terror. Our hearts beating and eyes dim with tears we waited in anguish. From daybreak the Turkish soldiers and hordes rushed upon us, entering the fortress with a rage for destruction and carnage. Bayonets in their fists, the soldiers surrounded us and brutally ordered "Men separate from the women!" In fact there were only little boys and old men. They led them to a neighboring hill and shot them. I shall never forget the patter of that sinister fusillade. We were shaken by horror. Then like ferocious beasts the Turks fell upon us taking money, jewels, and clothes with such fury that they tore as they came off. I do not want to speak of the horror of rapes committed under circumstances impossible to describe. I had closed my eyes; I did not want to see; I remembered suddenly that we had brought a bottle of violent poison. Women and girls drank it and died in serenity. When in turn I asked for the flask of freedom, it was empty.

After three hours of pillage and all sorts of torture, the Turks forced the survivors to come down from the fortress and threw a large number into the river Kaïl. The women from rich families were separated from the others and after reassembling us in the public garden, the Turks forced us under menace of death to reveal the hiding places of our treasures. They dragged us through our homes taking whatever we had that was precious.

We already foresaw the exodus toward a certain death after having suffered all the tortures of the road, stripped of everything, starved.

New order: the young and beautiful girls were sorted out now to be sent to harems.

Thanks to a policeman who stayed in our house, whom I had bribed with jewels and a large sum, I was able to escape to Kirassunde with my baby, my mother-in-law, and some near relatives. There a Greek family sheltered us, where we spent our sad life darkened by so many nightmares until the armistice.

"Les combats héroïques de Chabine-Karahissar," in *Témoignages inédits sur les atrocités turques commises en Arménie,* ed. Azkanever de Constantinople (Paris: Dubreuil, Frèrebeau, 1920), 59–75.

✝ Sophja Nowosiełska, née Lipowicz (b. 1900) *Polish*

Sophja Lipowicz was born January 22, a day she proudly recalled as the anniversary of the 1863 Polish insurrection, whose heroines such as Emily Plater and Henryka Pustowojt were the subject of her grandfather's reminiscences. "It became my indomitable desire to follow in the footsteps of these great women and show the boys it is not their exclusive privilege to fight for the freedom of their country." Although she was first in her class at convent school, she enjoyed the freedom of a tomboy on family estates in Romania and the Carpathians. Once, in an effort to punish her rambunctious behavior, her aristocratic parents "put pants on me. The effect was rather exciting, my greatest heart's desire being fulfilled. Now I could run around unhampered in the fields and woods with the village children, ride horseback, and be independent."

In 1914 the fourteen-year-old made an abortive attempt to run away and join the Polish Legions of Piłsudski, as her brother did. She was quickly discovered and returned to her family to care for her pregnant mother and five younger sisters in the absence of her father, who had been drafted into the Austrian Army. During the clashes between Cossacks, Hungarians, Austrians, and Germans, the family became refugees, caught in the crossfire; one sister and a newborn brother died. The Lipowiczes temporarily lost their ravaged home and much of their property. In 1917 Sophja began to serve the Polish Military Organization as a courier, smuggling letters, money, and arms. After her father's return in the summer of 1918, she dressed in men's clothing and enlisted in a volunteer Polish defense force. After suffering shrapnel wounds to the head and leg, she convalesced in captivity behind Russian lines, then escaped to the Polish side, where she joined the Polish Women's Voluntary Legion; her unit was decorated with the Order of the Eaglets for bravery at the front, and Lipowicz won a score of decorations, including two crosses for bravery and a silver Merit Cross.

Lipowicz continued to fight for five years after the 1918 armistice, attaining the rank of lieutenant. In 1920, during a lull in front-line service, she taught literacy to peasants in exchange for food and established two dozen libraries. When conditions permitted, she audited university classes as well. Ordered back into combat, she was captured briefly by a Bolshevik patrol, then escaped by seizing a Cossack horse to rejoin her regiment. At the end of the war she married Lieutenant Eugene Nowosielski, with whom she had a son, Bozydar, and became a teacher.

CS

♱ Lwów

It was terrible inside the City. Everywhere you could see Ukrainian shooters, and untractable peasantry roaming in bands and robbing. Their faces were dirty, abhorrent and inflamed with passion. With a wild delight the shooters were placing rifle barrels to the chests of the passersby, and firing into the air to demonstrate thus their strength. If somebody appeared in a window they were immediately aimed at.

At the winding of St. Lazarus Street, a band of Austrian heroes met a soldier.

"Are you Ukrainian?" they asked.

"No, I am a Pole."

They shot him instantly.

I cannot comprehend yet in what miraculous way I succeeded in passing behind the backs of the Ukrainian guards till I reached St. Elizabeth's Church, where a battle was already raging, fought solely by youngsters.

We had exchanged our coats for men's clothing in a Jewish store, and after putting them on joined the fighting ranks. Lieutenant Szram who had captured a magazine, became suddenly ill and we were put under the command of Lieutenant Feldstajn.

The first attack succeeded excellently. I already had a rifle and many cartridges. Sergeant Sikora asked me whether I knew how to shoot. I said that I did but turned red up to the ears. He probably did not believe me, as he watched me very closely, and when, after the first shot, I closed the hammer, he crept toward me and asked what happened.

"The trigger is jammed," I said. He looked at me and spat. "No, girl citizen, it is a safety rifle," he explained, and under the fire of the enemy bullets he gave me instructions in the use of a rifle. "Oh, that's nothing," he consoled me, "I had to teach the other kids yesterday in the same way."

I realized that if it were known I was a girl I would be subjected to a great deal of unpleasantness.

Therefore one of the boys gave me a Polish national cap "Maciejówka," under which I hid my long braids, folded so tightly around my head that it began to ache me. Besides, my skirt left under my men's clothes also caused me a great deal of uneasiness, so I got rid of it at the first opportune moment.

Next to me in line, a 15-year-old Johnny was shooting.

"Lady citizen, how long are you with us?" he inquired.

"Since this morning," I said.

"Gee, I am here since yesterday," he commented boastfully, and looked at me in a manner in which only an old veteran can gaze at a recruit.

Another neighbor, Tony, came to my defense and recited Johnny's argument with his mother, who wanted to take him away forcibly from the ranks. Johnny refused to go and scorned her by saying:

"Keep away from me, Mother. I am going, when I have to go, and you had better go before I lose my temper." And he remained.

None of us had uniforms and our caps were of different makes. But great joy overcame the young fighters as soon as the Lieutenant announced that we would all receive the same Polish eagles as emblems.

I was freezing in my percale blouse, so they gave me an Austrian uniform and a pair of very spacious boots, which caused blisters on my feet. It was in this disguise that a noncommissioned officer questioned me:

"What's your name?"

"George Krawczyk," I answered, without any hesitation. But why I had chosen that name I do not know till now. Tony was overjoyed that I had so promptly found a way out of this embarrassing situation, and poked me in my side with his fist. At the same moment Captain Tatar gave the command: "Attention! Look at your right! Report!" Then again the command: "Forward March!" We entered Polna Street, and there we met the first Ukrainian automobile. Without any command we had thrown ourselves on the enemy, covering them without interruption with rifle fire, till they finally disappeared in flight.

Our officers were cursing, and I myself was taken by the ear by some legionnaire and brought back to the ranks. The others were reproved in the same way by their superiors.

Finally we got out of the City, and were continually drilled and taught how to handle a rifle. One of the officers looked at me wonderingly, and I, being afraid that he would realize that I was a girl, pushed my cap deeper over my ears, and asked him for a cigarette.

It did not help me much. He guessed my sex, but he respected my secret. When we reached the railroad depot, an engine appeared. We were commanded to lay down and take shelter behind the shrubs. I was extremely fatigued, and completely exhausted from hunger. Then for two days we marched constantly, without rest or sleep, without a roof over our heads, in rain and in mud.

1920

"Lwów," in *In the Hurricane of War*. Published by Lieutenant Mrs. Sophie Nowosielski [1929?], 48–50.

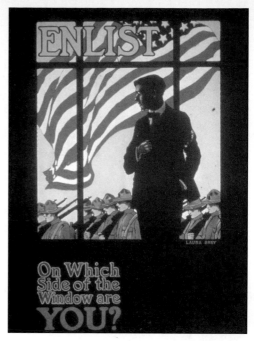

Lucy Kemp Welch. "Forward! Forward to Victory. Enlist Now." 1915, British. Poster. From the Bowman Gray Collection, University of North Carolina at Chapel Hill.

Laura Brey. "Enlist. On Which Side of the Window Are You?" 1917, American. Poster Collection, U.S. 2000, Hoover Institution Archives.

Lina von Schauroth. "Kaiser's and People's Offering of Thanks for the Army and Navy. Frankfurt Christmas Gift, 1917. Donations Accepted at Bureau 5, Theaterplatz 14." 1917, German. Poster. Imperial War Museum, Q80351 (7270).

Joyce Dennys, "Women's Royal Navy Service. Apply to the nearest employment exchange." c.1918, British. Poster. Imperial War Museum, Q80319 (2766).

Joyce Dennys, "V.A.D. Nursing members, cooks, kitchen-maids, clerks, house-maids, ward-maids, laundresses, motor-drivers, etc. are urgently needed." 1916–17, British. Poster. Imperial War Museum, Q80369.

Marthe Picard, "Eat Less Meat to Conserve Our Livestock." 1918, French. Poster. Private collection.

Helen Johns Kirtland, "Secrets of the Camouflage Artists." *Leslie's Magazine*, November 12, 1918.

Charlotte Schaller-Mouillot, "Fallen in action on the threshold of a little village church." 1914–18, French. *Histoire d'un brave petit soldat.* (Paris: Berger-Levrault).

Henriette Damart, "What a jig, children!" 1914–18, French. *Toinette et la guerre,* by Lucie Paul-Margueritte (Paris: Berger-Levrault).

LA PETITE SŒUR D'ADOPTION

Henriette Damart, "The little adopted sister." 1914–18, French. *Toinette et la guerre* by Lucie Paul–Margueritte (Paris: Berger-Levrault).

Ethel Rundquist, "This is that famous scene 'over there.' Arriving in a strange town, preferably late at night, and finding nary a 'Y' representative or an army man to meet us." 1921, American. *Entertaining the American Army: The American Stage and Lyceum in the World War.* By permission of the Y.M.C.A., U.S.A.

Mairi Chisholm, "Shellburst at Pervyse." 1914, British. Photograph. Imperial War Museum, Q105858.

Mairi Chisholm, "Wooden duckboards leading to the Belgian Advanced Position on the Yser." 1914, British. Photograph. Imperial War Museum, Q106043.

Mairi Chisholm, "The Third Poste as we found it." 1918, British. Photograph. Imperial War Museum, Q105900.

Mairi Chisholm, "Our room as we made it." 1915, British. Photograph. Imperial War Museum, Q105899.

Florence Farmborough, "The unknown soldier lies on the battlefield." 1916, British. Photograph. Imperial War Museum, Q98431.

Florence Farmborough, "Launching of a new Russian 'aerostat.'" 1916, British. Photograph. Imperial War Museum, Q98423.

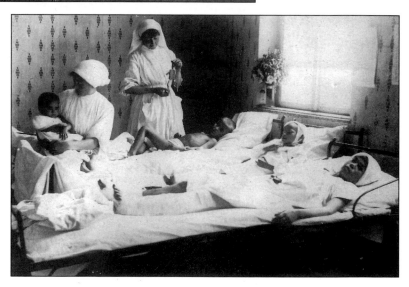

Florence Farmborough, "Children wounded during German bombardment. Roumania." 1917, British. Photograph. Imperial War Museum, Q98421.

Olive Edis, "Wrecked tank by the Menin Road." 1919. Private collection. Photograph courtesy of the National Portrait Gallery, RN48540.

Marie Curie, "X ray of a hand. A large shell fragment is visible whose presence was revealed by the X ray. Fracture of two bones of the metacarpus and carpus." X ray undated, French. *La Radiologie et la guerre.* (Paris: Alcan, 1921), facing 66.

Olive Edis, "F.A.N.Y. convoy car, Calais." 1919, British. Photograph. Imperial War Museum, Q7950.

Anna Airy, *Shop for Machining 15-Inch Shells*
1918–19, British. Oil. Imperial War Museum,
2271 (Pic 2090).

B. A. Laurenson, "Wren Telephonist."
1917, British. Pen and ink. Imperial
War Museum, G4955.

Olive Mudie-Cooke, "The V.A.D. in Theory, in Popular Fiction, in Real Life." 1920,
British. Lithograph. Imperial War Museum, 4062 (Pic 2197).

Olive Mudie-Cooke, "Péronne: Old Gateway." 1920, British.
Lithograph. Private collection.

Olive Mudie-Cooke, "Etaples Military Cemetery." 1917, British. Lithograph.
Private collection.

Nathalia Goncharova, "Condemned City." From *Misticheskie Obrazy Vojni* [Mystical Images of War]. 1914, Russian. Lithograph. Cabinet des estampes du Musée d'art et d'histoire, Geneva.

Nathalia Goncharova, "Angels and Airplanes." From *Misticheskie Obrazy Vojni* [Mystical Images of War]. 1914, Russian. Lithograph. Cabinet des estampes du Musée d'art et d'histoire, Geneva.

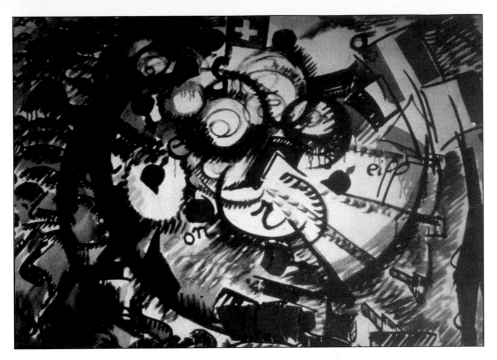

Alice Bailly, *The Battle*. c.1917, Swiss. Oil and collage on paper. Private collection.
Photograph courtesy of Paul-André Jaccard.

Olga Vladimirovna
Rozanova, "Airplanes over
the City." From *Vojna* [War].
1916, Russian. Collage.
Cabinet des estampes du
Musée d'art et d'histoire,
Geneva.

Olga Vladimirovna Rozanova, "Battle in Three Spheres." 1916, From *Vojna* [War]. Russian. Wood engraving. Cabinet des estampes du Musée d'art et d'histoire, Geneva.

Käthe Kollwitz, "The Mothers." From *Krieg* [War]. 1922–23, German. Wood engraving. William Benton Museum of Art, University of Connecticut.

Käthe Kollwitz, "The Volunteers." From *Krieg* [War]. 1922–23, German. Wood engraving. William Benton Museum of Art, University of Connecticut.

Olga Vladimirovna Rozanova, "Destruction of the City." From *Vojna* [War]. 1916, Russian. Wood engraving. Cabinet des estampes du Musée d'art et d'histoire, Geneva.

Kathleen Scott Kennet, *The Thinking Soldier.* 1923, British. Bronze. Huntingdon Market Square, England. Photograph courtesy of Nick Crumpsty.

Gertrude Vanderbilt Whitney, *Cast for Saint-Nazaire Memorial, France.* 1926, American. Bronze. By permission of the Preservation Society of Newport County, Collection of the Breakers.

Louise Lantz Lyon, "Pendant encasing shrapnel that wounded her husband." French. Private collection.

Phyllis Bone, *The Tunnelers' Friends.* 1927, British. Stone. Scottish War Memorial, Edinburgh.

Émilie Rolez, *Cursed Be War. To the children of Équeurdreville who died during the war, 1914–1918.* 1931, French. Marble. Équeurdreville, France.

Margaret Winser, *Pilot.* 1922, British. Bronze panel. Hastings, England. Photograph courtesy of Hastings Borough Council.

Lady Feodora Gleichen, *Memorial to the 37th Division.* 1921, British. Bronze. Monchy-le-Preux, France.

Deborah Bright, "Beaumont Hamel: Battle of the Somme (France) 1 July 1916. Duration: half an hour." From *Battlefield Panoramas*. American. View of heavily shelled no-man's-land from the trenches of the Newfoundland Regiment (*foreground*) looking towards German dugouts 600 yards distant. The Newfoundland Regiment's 87th and 88th brigades were annihilated as they marched in parade formation into the machine-gun fire of the German lines. Of the regiment's 801 troops who went into battle that day, only 68 stood to answer roll call the next morning. Barbed wire supports still riddle the area. Halfway down the slope (near the herd of sheep) an isolated tree marks the area where German shrapnel was particularly deadly. The Newfoundlanders called it "the danger tree" and its twisted skeleton has been preserved as a memorial. Photographed July 1981.

✝ A Real War

Lieutenant Niedzielski was in command of the advancing column. The boys reported that we already had our own artillery, which was wrested by the legionnaires, with the encampment of the 31st Regiment. I was so weakened that I had no strength to rejoice over this great news. I was marching mechanically, with my last effort; there was a ringing in my ears, and my only desire was for some sleep and rest.

Finally quarters. I was assigned to a small corner in a peasant's hut. Oh, how well a hot brew and potato soup tasted.

One of the legionnaires asked:

"Why, citizen, do you not take off your cap in the house?"

But how could I take it off, when under its cover my long braids were concealed. I went outside, but a soldier who knew what was embarrassing me followed me and, without any ceremony, cut off my long hair, which, when spread out covered my uniform like an overcoat. This soldier is now a fireman in Lublin, where I met him one day recently, and greeted him very sincerely.

I was generally taken for a 15-year-old boy, though I was already 18. My young guardian, a simple boy of humble descent, was very proud that such a young girl of refinement was fraternizing with him, so he provided me with foot wraps when we had captured a new magazine, and had to return with our booty,—consisting of cannons,—to Lwów.

Our slogan, as defined by Captain Maczynski and Lieutenant Walerian Sikorski, expressed itself in the following rule: "With sticks against rifles, with rifles against cannons," and we took it verbally, and directed ourselves accordingly.

In the meantime the battle was already raging in many sectors. Country boys were joining the ranks of the Polish Military Organization, and some of the suburbs were defending themselves very furiously. We were divided into smaller detachments and assigned to duty in different parts of the City.

November the 6th the Polish Artillery began to roar.

Kenarski's school and the detachment near the Post Office fought most desperately. The battle for the possession of this building had been in progress for several days. At last a truce was formed which was stealthily broken by the Ukrainians.

On November the 9th we advanced to support the fighting units near the Post Office. Lieutenant Wozny blew up the portal from Sykstuska Street. First, the sixteen-year-old boys rushed inside, followed by some of the women.

The building was partially burned up and full of holes like a sieve, but we had to drive out the enemy, conquering every single stair and every corner. I forgot then that I was a woman. I knew only that I had to fight, and to fight hard to avenge the Polish losses. I did not feel the pain, though

my right cheek was swollen and blood was flowing from my hands and
forehead.

And then for the following three days we barraged the citadel. The Jewish Militia, notwithstanding their declared neutrality, had steadily supported the Ukrainians, an action which enraged the Poles of Jewish
religion, who fought obstinately and with great sacrifice in our ranks.

The women had very laudably distinguished themselves on this occasion. Mrs. Zagorska had formed a voluntary legion of women, who took
under their care the safety and guard service at the front. The services of
this peculiar formation were of immense value to the Polish cause.

Even the deaf and dumb had offered themselves as volunteers as well as
the old and the crippled. The Polish City of Lwów had raised its head and
shown its claws. Mothers would enlist in the same ranks with their sons and
daughters. The boys were unwilling to disclose their age and nearly every
one added some years to appear older. In fact, many of them who passed
for 14 years of age were scarcely 13 years old.

When some of these lads were taken to the hospital and had to lie in
bed they would play with toys there, like every other child, but as soon as
they were discharged they at once became old soldiers.

One of the lads, a thirteen-year-old schoolboy, brought with him as initiation proof, four rifles he had captured from the enemy. How could you
refuse admittance to this kind of a fellow? Another little chap simply
grabbed a rifle from a Ukrainian who was on guard duty and ran away with
his booty to our ranks.

Near me a young boy had placed a little pillow beneath his coat to lean
the butt end of his rifle on, as his gun kicked frightfully when shooting. It
had been doing the same to me for a long time. Many lost their lives but
none were lost in vain. Once seven legionnaires wrested, with bare hands,
10 rifles and 6 revolvers, and another time, sixty of us, mostly children,
had repulsed an attack of 700 Ukrainians.

On the sector of Kleparow and Zamarstynow, Lieutenant Walerian
Sikorski had been fighting with great daring. He not only had repulsed an
attack of a three times stronger enemy, but also drove him away in the
direction of Zamarstynow. I had been twice in touch with his company,
when I had to force my way through to deliver orders. The commander
praised him very highly for the great valor he displayed in action in a special day's order, which eulogized his merits in a good cause.

The Ukrainians were mercilessly destroying the City. In the places that
had been in their possession you could not find a whole window, the doors
were forcibly pulled out, people were hiding in the basements and cellars,
as they were murdering without reason everyone who was in their way. No
wonder that you could find among the fighting women an older lady who
joined the ranks to thus avenge her two boys who were previously killed.

The smallest children were also taking to arms and it was not unusual
to observe, in many instances, that the rifle was bigger than the fighter.
These little ones understood well that it was impossible to leave the
beloved City in the hands of the unrestrained barbarians who had vowed

to reduce Lwów to nothing.

Before these children many elders had to blush with shame. Instead of fighting, these cowards were hiding in cellars when children, girls and women were dying, and as soon as the danger was over they crept from their holes, and posed as heroes, stretching out their greedy hands for the decoration of the Eaglets, awarded only to the valiant defenders of the City.

At last, after so much bloodshed, the hard-won victory came. The Ukrainian flag disappeared from the City Hall. Hurrah! The boys were laughing, but from my eyes tears were falling as I could not behave as they did, though outwardly I resembled them, like one poppy seed does another.

I looked like all of these little bums, soiled with mud, blackened with smoke. My hands, have mercy, Oh, Lord! My fingers in a frightful shape, swollen, my hands unproportionately big and livid, and my voice changed. I am sure my mother would not have recognized me at that moment.

1920

"A Real War," in *In the Hurricane of War.* Published by Lieutenant Mrs. Sophie Nowosiel-ski [1929?], 52–56.

✠ Marina Yurlova
(b. 1900) *Russian/American*

A Cossack child adopted by a regiment when she was fourteen, Marina Yurlova served as hostler, chauffeur, ambulance driver, and soldier. Following a tradition of women soldiers inspired by Nadezhda Durova, a Cossack fighter during the Napoleonic Wars, Yurlova was wounded three times and decorated. During the retreat to Erivan and the Araks River, she lost her mentor and protector among the troops. She retreated across Siberia with the Czech army; she sailed to Japan in 1919, en route to the United States, where she became a dancer.

✠ Scheherezade

I found that our army was still slowly retreating; sometimes we would stay for days on end in the same place; and never once did we know where we were going or why. There were a few minor engagements—little better than skirmishes—to enliven this somewhat lethargic progress of ours. That summer of 1915 was an inglorious one. Most of our casualties, and there were many of them, were due to sickness; most of our deaths were due to Kurds.

About three weeks after Stepan was killed (I have already told of that) our regiment was moved up towards the top of a small mountain range, and my Hundred had been sent off to a little plateau; like a last outpost of the Russian Empire, we gazed down upon mile after mile of enemy territory. It was a land of the silent; nothing but a row of lifeless brown hills, falling gradually away towards an empty horizon. Nothing stirred; not a distant flock of sheep, not a mountain goat, not even a bird in the breathless sky.

Nothing but one thing. . . . Below us a river wound through the gash of a shallow canyon; and the cool, discreet noise of water running over stones mocked us where we lay about, crouched in the scarce shade of a few sun-baked rocks. We could not make use of that river; Kurny told us that he had been warned about it in advance—it was known to be carefully guarded. As soon as the sun went down, he said, ten of us could go there for water; until then we must wait.

As twilight fell, ten of us—myself amongst them—crept down the canyon side and moved cautiously towards the river; we carried two buckets apiece, and our only weapons were daggers. A detachment was to follow us as far as the river side in case we should need assistance.

Just below our plateau, however, the rocks ran too steeply into the water for us to fill our buckets there; and we wandered off round the corner, out of sight of our comrades, still looking for a convenient place: perhaps we had gone half a mile before we found one.

It was quite light yet; the canyon was still and peaceful; the cool blue shadows breathed with a little evening wind. There was no sound but the canvas buckets splashing into water.

I looked up. A large rock, just a little way beyond, had stirred in the most unaccountable manner. I looked at it again, more closely; nothing. I began to fill my second bucket.

And then the rock came to life . . . quite silently. A large band of men rose up from behind it, ragged brown men with hooked noses and round, sunken, fierce black eyes, who pointed their guns at us and motioned us to surrender. It was at once terrifying and unreal—that wordless capture, in the cool of evening, in the deep peace of our little canyon.

There was nothing to do. One shout for help and we should have been killed on the spot. We stood there, petrified, while one of them came over and took our daggers from their sheaths; because I had no dagger one of them spoke to me in Turkish, and I stared at him, my teeth chattering and little beads of cold sweat on my forehead.

As we moved off, I whispered to the man nearest me:

"Who are they?"

"Kurds!"

Kurds. I remembered Stepan's body, roped across the back of a sweating horse, and the stories of unspeakable tortures they had practiced on other captives; there was nothing but evil and agony to be expected from these people—these mongrel gypsies, part Turkish, part Persian, part Satan himself.

Was there any hope for us at all? We rounded another twist in the canyon, and their leader called a halt, and looked us over. When his eyes fell on me, he started, stared more intently, and began to smile to himself; then he entered into a loud conversation with the Kurd in charge of us.

"You talk Turkish, Ivan," said one of the Cossacks. "For God's sake, what are they jawing about? Go over and speak to them."

"What shall I tell them?" asked Ivan.

"Idiot, tell them you speak Turkish."

Ivan slouched over, and began to talk with the leader; at last: "He wants to know if she's really a girl," he flung at us over his shoulder. "He says she's to take her jacket off."

I hesitated. "Do as he tells you, *malyi*,"[1] someone whispered fiercely, "otherwise they will cut our throats just for the fun of it."

I stripped off my jacket, and the Kurdish leader sauntered over to me. He looked like a walking rag heap, for it was quite impossible to tell where one garment ended and another began. Through his filthy tatters I caught a glimpse of even filthier skin. As he looked me over his round brown eyes were very like an animal's eyes. He licked his lips incessantly. He broke into a wide, almost toothless smile, and laughed queerly down in his throat. Then he touched my face. I shivered and closed my eyes, but made no attempt to resist him. He smelled vilely, with a smell that I hope never to encounter again. His hand wandered through my hair, over the back of my neck, round under my chin: downward over my breast and up again. And he laughed so strangely that I could stand it no longer. I jumped back, picked up my jacket, and thrust it on.

The Kurd said something to Ivan.

"He wants to know what you are doing here."

"Tell the old——that she's a wounded Cavalier of St. George," said Gritsko, with desperation in his voice. "Spin him a yarn, Ivan, can't you?"

Ivan did his best; just as he seemed on the point of giving out, I found my voice. "Ask him if I can go to the river and wet my bandage," I said; and, consent being given, I sat down, pulled off my boot, and started to unwrap the bandages. The Kurd commander examined my wound intently, and made no attempt to stop me when I walked off to the river. Bending down to dip my bandages into the river, I suddenly realized that we had been moving downstream all this while, for there, caught in the rocks below me, was a canvas bucket which I had dropped in my fright a good half mile back. At the foot of the canyon, then, about a mile upstream, the small detachment that had been sent to guard us was still waiting.

Ivan called me back.

"He wants to see your Cross. I told him you blew up a bridge across the Araks, and he wants to know how you did it."

While the commander fingered my Cross, Ivan added:

"Tell 'em any story you like, *malyi*, and I'll interpret it. Stick it on. A Kurd will give anything for a good story. If they like it, they'll take us back to their officer. Otherwise it's all up with us."

And so I began my story.

I shall never tell another one like that, in so strange a setting to so hideous an audience. It was growing very dark, and though the sky above us was still blue, one could detect the beginning stars here and there. The river whispered and muttered. The wind was growing colder, setting up an empty moan under the canyon walls.

1. *Malyi:* little one.

I need not repeat my story in detail. Fear made me decorate that tale with the most extravagant fancies; Ivan's voice trembled with emotion as he passed it on to the listening Kurds. Then I noticed that they were quite genuinely fascinated by what I was saying.

I began to walk upstream. . . .

Terror was my guide, and nothing more than terror. I could not have stopped talking then, even if I had been told to. I could not have stopped walking upstream, even if they had realized where I was leading them. But they didn't. Limping—partly from nervous exhaustion, partly from the ache in my leg—I leaned on the arm of Ivan on one side . . . and of the Kurd commander on the other. I was telling them how two men burned the two wooden bridges, single-handed. . . . We had rounded the first curve of the canyon and were mid-way to the second; I took one look at Ivan, and the whites were showing all around his eyes. . . . How, under cover of the flames and the smoke, a charge was laid beneath the concrete bridge. Fear lent me a romantic skill which surprises me even today. The more exciting my story became, the more dramatic became Ivan's inter-pretation of it, and the more it intrigued the Kurd on whose arm I was leaning, and the Kurds who were following. We were almost at the second curve now.

We were rounding it.

"And then," I said, "there was an explosion like the end of the world—"

"Halt! Give up your arms!" It was Kurny's voice.

The Kurd dropped my arm. His followers, so intent upon the story that they had lost all sense of danger or direction, were too amazed to make any resistance. They just stood there, with their mouths open.

I limped over to our men.

"Here are some Kurds for you," I said—but my voice was only a hoarse croak.

I sat on the ground, nursing my leg which was really paining me very badly. As I sat there I heard one of our *sotnia*[2] say: "That girl brought in forty Kurds, single-handed!"

"What a fool!" I thought. "If only you knew how frightened I was." But I was too tired and too confused to argue with him; or with the *sotnik*[3] when he patted me on the shoulder and said: "I'm proud to have you in the Company. You used your head, *synok.*[4] You deserve the Cross"; or with Kurny when he called me "a real hero."

The next day we moved off the plateau, and I was summoned to head-quarters, where the *sotnik* brought me before our general once more, who told me that it would be his great pleasure to recommend me for a second soldier's Cross of St. George. There was no arguing with the general, so I saluted and got out of the room just as quickly as I could.

2. *Sotnia:* squadron of cavalry.
3. *Sotnik:* commander.
4. *Synok:* my little son.

It was not long before the story came back to me, with all the embroidery of a hundred re-tellings. . . . I had crept out into the canyon, alone
and armed with nothing more than a dagger, and had captured a hundred
Kurds!

And so, for all I know, it may still be told.

"Scheherezade," in *Cossack Girl* (New York: Macaulay, 1934), 110–16.

✠ The Hut

Our soldiers ran true to form in the building of their quarters—little rude
huts, with ten men assigned to each. And they could easily have made
them five times as large, with a whole army on hand to build them.

And now a new problem arose. It was one thing to sleep near my "brothers," wrapped in a blanket under the open sky; it was quite another to
share these cramped quarters with them.

My first night will serve as an example for the rest. It had been raining
all day, but we had gone through our drills just the same, and had come
back to Kosel's hut, and hung our uniform coats up to dry.

Supper was over. The windows were tightly shut. The air was foul with
the fumes of *mahorka*—a crude peasant tobacco—and the stench of
unwashed bodies. I lay curled up in my bunk, watching the men with an
entirely new feeling: modesty. That is what four walls can do to you.

The oil lamps were lit, and a stove was burning. Kosel had found a pack
of cards, so greased and dirty that the figures on them were barely visible,
and the men were playing for matches instead of money. You don't have
anything to spare out of a few cents a month; but the disputes were just as
loud and the play just as intense as if a million rubles hung in the balance.

After that they took to singing songs and telling stories. They were very
good to me, those men; for though—since Kosel and the commander had
made no objections to me—they had come to take me for granted, they
were very careful to whisper any story that wasn't fit for me to hear. The
two noisiest there were the huge Gritsko and Fedka, a red-haired good-for-
nothing about half his size, and all they argued about was the amount of
liquor each could swallow without feeling it.

But this is the scene that I remember still with a sort of horror. My nine
companions had decided at last to hunt for cooties, and there they all
were, crouched around the stove, which was burning fiercely in the center
of the hut. First they took off their blouses and singed the seams, then they
pulled off their shirts. . . .

The lamplight threw grotesque, great shadows on the walls, and
gleamed on their white skins and hairy chests. I'd never seen a half-naked
man before and lay in my bunk, staring at them with horrified fascination.
Their conversation was brief and monotonous; they were so intent on

their task that they had forgotten all about me. Outside a dog howled miserably, and a thin, drizzling rain pattered on the roof.

The stove threw a red glow on Kosel's matted chest.

Nothing makes you so lonely as shame. I was suddenly conscious, as I lay there, of the predicament I was in; of my girl's body—for the first time in my life, I think; of the strangeness of my surroundings—that I, a colonel's daughter, should be here, in this place that smelled so horribly of bad air and bad tobacco, of singeing shirts, of damp foot wrappings hanging up to dry, of unwashed bodies and feet.

Somebody—it was the great Gritsko, I think—rose slowly to his feet, muttering to himself, stretching his arms. He was quite naked.

I pushed my fist into my mouth and bit on it until it bled. Then I crawled from my bunk and stumbled to the door—out into the night, into the rain and mud.

When I came back at last, chilled and miserable, they had all gone to sleep. There was still a glow from the stove, and I thought I could safely take my own clothes off now to dry them, and to hunt for cooties as the men had done. But my shirt was only half off my head when somebody snored loudly and twisted over in his sleep, and I scrambled into my shirt again, and went and curled up, shivering, in my bunk.

When at last I fell asleep, I had a dream of Kosel.

He had the body of a goat, four legs, and a great shaggy coat of fur.

A naked Gritsko was driving him round and round the hut. . . .

"The Hut," in *Cossack Girl* (New York: Macaulay, 1934), 52–54.

MEDICINE

✝ Lidiia Zakharova
Russian

When news of the war broke, Lidiia Zakharova's family was at the beach. After her husband left for the front, she joined a nursing corps and placed her two children in the care of her mother. She first saw severely wounded men during her train trip to the front, at the stations she passed. This new life "swallowed up" the nurses and carried them forward on its mighty stream. She writes, "My consciousness has been altered: from this moment I am not the same woman who lived, suffered, and rejoiced up to this minute. . . . I am not called by my former name, I am the 'sister,' a new human being with totally different interests, sorrows, and joys." At the front she reports going into no man's land to pick up the wounded, where she encounters male nurses from the other side recovering their own. Among the hardships of work at the front was the exposure to naked bodies covered with grime, pus, and blood. Exhausted, she fell ill and was sent home, where she published her memoir in 1915.

✝ Diary of a Red Cross Sister in the Front-Lines

That evening I saw the German trenches for the first time. I can't deny it—our enemies were rather comfortably ensconced. Their trenches were one great labyrinth, an entire complex system of underground corridors, nooks, dugouts, and blind alleys.

In the officers' dugouts the ground was covered with boards, some floors even laid with rugs. Everywhere there were camp beds and collapsible furniture stolen from those very estates that burned so quickly and furiously, illuminating the land all around with a purple glow. On the table—wine bottles, china, and crystal beside crude soldiers' mugs. There were greasy plates with some scraps of food, corks, and cigarette butts.

In one of the dugouts my attention was drawn to a discarded, toppled child's high chair. The presence of this mute witness to the bloody episode that had just been played out was as disturbing as the presence of the chair's little master would have been, and it made even more horrifying and monstrous the sight of trenches overflowing with masses of dead bodies.

It was a gruesome spectacle. A city of the dead, its inhabitants frozen in the most unlikely positions, as if a raging, deadly hurricane had just swept past. Some were lying on their backs, others face down. They were all intertwined, so you could not tell whose arms and legs were whose. Many were sitting in poses that made them seem alive, leaning on the parapet or the back wall of the trench. But most terrible were those who had not fallen, but stood shoulder to shoulder, still holding their rifles, eyes open and glazed with the tranquillity of non-existence, as if they were listening to the ominous cries of the crows flying overhead.

There is a limit, by the way, beyond which the human mind can perceive no more horrors, as a saturated sponge can soak up no more water. This thought was not original with me, but I remember I realized its full meaning only at that time in the dugouts of the German trenches, and I was astounded at how the person who pronounced it had truly understood the capricious and multifaceted nature of human beings.

We simply went on with our work, neatly and efficiently, only rarely exchanging a few necessary words.

"A stretcher."

"Help me, nurse, hold his head. . . ."

"Come here, please. . . ."

And again, "A stretcher . . ."

In one place we came across a strange group. A Russian and a German soldier caught in hand-to-hand combat had been killed on the spot by a shell exploding nearby. So they lay in each other's arms, recent enemies reconciled by the majesty of death. Evening fell. Low gray clouds crept over the field, once plowed up—now blown up by shells. It was raining, destroying any hope for the return of warm days.

The orderlies carried electric lanterns whose yellow lights appeared in the fog to be dim little dots. Some of our group had already started back to the field station.

"We should go now, nurse, it's getting awfully dark. It's pitch black—" called out from behind the orderly who was accompanying me.

And suddenly it seemed horrible to leave in the dark, cold, and damp of a nasty autumn night any of these unfortunates who had been deceived into seeing our safety lanterns as a flicker of hope.

"Please, please, let's look a little more," I begged, and not waiting for a reply, I stepped quickly to the side.

Suddenly and unexpectedly close to me voices rang out, an unfamiliar language.

—Germans—flashed clearly and briefly through my mind.

In fact it was German orderlies who had been picking up their wounded. Immediately I recalled all the stories I had heard about the savagery of the "cultured Teutons." But it was too late to retreat and, overcoming my uneasiness, I boldly entered into negotiations with a German orderly.

In all fairness, I must admit that the Germans treated me quite gallantly: we even exchanged a few prisoners and parted amicably, with mutual bows.

Nonetheless, this incident with the Germans had very unexpected and unpleasant consequences for me. Stupidly I became separated from my people and became lost at night—in a field strewn with dead bodies.

B-rrr . . . it was one of the most terrifying impressions I received during that difficult time!

Dark. Rain. Cold. Underfoot was some kind of mush, God knows what; all around me a mute population of dead men, whose presence I could nonetheless feel with every nerve; it was impossible to orient myself in these unfamiliar surroundings. My first impulse was to cry for help, but I was afraid even to call out and disturb with the sound of a human voice what was concealed in the dark and silence.

I began to wander aimlessly and would have done so for a long time, if the moon had not finally come out and lit up with its pale radiance a sinuous line of dark, forbidding trenches. By following their curves and looking for familiar markers, totally exhausted, cold, and frightened, I at last reached our field station, my promised land. [. . .]

We finally made it. We delivered the sick. We fed the exhausted horses, let them catch their breath, and we ourselves rested.

Beneath the windows of the hospital on the streets of the little town, life, peaceful and mundane, streamed by. People were passing by, hurrying about their business, dirty, ragged kids were running around, goods for sale were set out in colorful window displays.

And it was strange and terrible to think that a few versts away the bloody tragedy of war was in full swing, that the quiet, provincial life I was observing was streaming along a crater more treacherous and uncertain than the crater of a volcano.

Time was flying, however, and I had to hurry to reach before dusk the village to which the doctor had directed me.

I quickly said good-bye to the nurses who had warmed me and nurtured me like one of their own, and not without regret, I scrambled up onto the cart.

Passing one of the stores, I took the opportunity to make a purchase whose necessity I had come to realize in practice. I bought a heavy flannel-lined leather jacket and wrapped myself up in it right there.

With God's help my transformation succeeded—there remained in me less and less of the feminine, and I didn't know whether to be sorry or glad.

Translated by Cynthia Simmons

Dnevnik Sestry miloserdiia na peredovykh positsiiakh (St. Petersburg: Izdatel'stvo Biblioteka "Velikoi Voiny," 1915), 50–54, 72–73.

✝ Katherine Hodges North
(1888–1982) *British*

Daughter of an actor and playwright, Katherine Hodges trained as a dancer. In her unpublished memoir, she describes her enthusiastic enlistment in August 1916 as an ambulance driver with the Scottish Women's Hospitals headed by Dr. Elsie Inglis, whose Transport Unit was run by the Honorable Evelina Haverfield. Hodges immediately cut her hair (to her mother's dismay), purchased her kit, and was off to Serbia—she thought—in ten days. Their boat steamed to the Arctic circle to avoid submarines; it docked at Archangel, where "gigantic Russian soldiers" lifted their Fords out as if they were perambulators. Traveling at ten miles an hour, a wood-stoked train took them south via Moscow to Odessa, forty miles from the fighting in Romania. En route she taught herself a "smattering" of Russian and Serbian, and eventually learned a bit of Romanian, all supplemented by schoolgirl German and French.

In the driving rains of September they joined the First Serbian Division in Romania, but by the end of October were forced to retreat to Braila on the banks of the Danube, a town whose inhabitants seemed insensible to "the shattering horrors from which we had just emerged." There she and two doctors, separated from the rest of the Inglis unit, joined a military hospital to try to deal with the flood of casualties generated in the retreat. Shunting between constantly shifting troops and hospitals, Hodges had to cope not only with mud and shell holes on drives across open fields, but even with runaway horses that dragged a gun carriage over her loaded ambulance.

At the end of 1916, she quit the Scottish Women's unit and traveled to Russia, where she visited Lady Muriel Paget's hospital at Petrograd. Proceeding to the Galician front, she went to work nursing in hospitals at Zabeschiki and later Podgayzce, five miles behind the lines (where Florence Farmborough also served); for her service she was awarded the Medal of St. George and the Order of St. Stanislas. By spring 1917 the impact of the February revolution was already felt in a breakdown of hospital discipline: orderlies refused their tasks, and Hodges decided to return to England that summer.

In London she drove for the YMCA until October 1917, then was posted as a driver with the all-female Hackett-Lowther unit to "Inspection Permanent, Section Armée Est" at Creil in January 1918, and later to the "Second Army Corps, Third French Ambulance" at Compiègne. As a *poilu* she was paid two sous a day—on paper. Their seventeen cars, she estimated, carried more than ten thousand wounded in four months. When gassed she was awarded the Croix de Guerre; the unit won five Croix de Guerre. On Armistice day, she wrote, "I don't remember feeling any emotion at all except a feeling of relief at the thought that one would perhaps now get a rest."

At the end of the war she married Captain E. S. ("Peter") North, who had fought on the Western Front, and who became a society photographer; they had no surviving children. During the Blitz in the Second World War she drove ambulances in London; she continued to work for the Red Cross until 1968. In 1934 she typed up an account of her experiences, "A Driver at the Front," into which she inserted letters she had written home to her mother from 1916 to 1918, some of them censored.

✝ Diary: A Driver at the Front

October 6th, 1916
Roumania

Darlings,

I haven't had any time to write since my last letter. Interesting things have really begun to happen now. I am sitting in a barn waiting for wounded as I write, only a few miles from the firing line. The guns are booming away all the time and have been for the last few days, a very big battle raging, thousands of wounded and not nearly enough hospitals for them.

Well, I'll go back to where I left off writing last time. We got to a place where we left the train at last with the cars, loaded them on to barges, went on with them, and for two days went down a river till we reached the next place where we unloaded again. We slept in the cars on the barges, got on shore about 4 P.M. We had some dinner, then tuned up the cars and went to sleep in the cars again on the road, and four people had to be sentries for two hours each. My turn was at 4 A.M., and it was pouring in torrents, tropical rain. It was quite a whisht feeling, wandering in and out of the cars in the dark by oneself, and nothing in the way of a weapon if anyone did try any monkey tricks. Then at 6 A.M. everyone got up and we filled up with petrol etc., and in still tropical rain started off to the place where we were to be. I've never dreamed of such roads! One was in a cold sweat all the way. Mud two foot deep and enormous holes, large enough to hold the car, huge ditches full of water up to your wheel hubs right across the road, and worst of all, the road often on a slant with a big drop off it, and with the skiddiness it was a hairbreadth chance all the time whether you could keep on the road or not. There were hundreds of carts with soldiers etc., and frightfully restive horses which pranced out at you, long lines of them. All very trying and most dangerous.

Well, we got to our destination saturated, of course. Next day we started off on our real work. We went about twenty miles over roads you cannot imagine in England. Nothing but tracks straight across fields, wheat fields, ploughed fields, any fields, and shell holes everywhere, and mud beyond words. All the time on the horizon little puffs of grey smoke and the incessant booming of the guns, eventually we—two poor soldiers have just gone by dead on stretchers with priests saying the burial service, they don't cover them up at all—To continue—we got to a little village on the top of a hill with tents, a field dressing station, and there we loaded the ambulances. We had a very bad abdominal case and a head case in ours, and then we had this twenty miles back over dreadful bumps with these poor devils inside, every bad bump they screamed and one could do nothing but drive slowly and hope for the best. I had to get out and shove the back wheels heaps of times and twice the ambulance only just missed going over. One's heart was in one's mouth all the time.

October 21st [1916]

Since I last wrote we have had a very exciting time and are having still. On the 19th about 8 A.M. we had a very bad air raid, about six aeroplanes, and dozens of bombs dropped. Some right in our camp. One girl's coat sleeve was torn and her arm bruised by a splinter, but nothing worse, though in the village about two hundred yards from where I was, four bombs dropped and twelve men were killed and several badly wounded. I never heard such a noise as the four bombs made bursting at once. I *was* frightened! Then the guns began very much nearer and wounded from the front started pouring in. We were all day taking them to and from hospitals and stations. Oh, I forgot, after the air raid at ten o'clock the Serbian general came and ordered our camp down at once, so we had to pack up, take down our tents and all migrated to a very small schoolroom in the village. We went on driving the wounded all day and at 7 P.M.—

October 28th

I was interrupted then by orders for the car and ever since we have been through the retreat from the front, *hell*, nothing else describes it. We are now in Braille [Braila]. I will go back to where I left off if I can remember, and try to tell you all that has happened.

At 7 P.M. on October 21st we were told not to go to bed but to hold ourselves in readiness to clear out at any minute. As a matter of fact we were out evacuating wounded till 4 A.M., when we lay down on the floor and tried to sleep. At eight o'clock orders came to move at once to a village about ten miles further back, which we did. All our cars were huddled into a little rickyard and we shoved up one tent. We were carrying wounded all day and at night again were told to prepare to move at any moment. All the time streams of troops were coming *back, back*. It was tiresome driving through them. The guns sounded louder and louder. The next day we again carried wounded and at 9 P.M. suddenly were told to go at once. From 7 P.M. till 9 P.M. I was alone in the rickyard in charge of the stores there and I shall never forget it. All the other ambulances had gone up to the front for wounded, C. too. It was dark, pouring rain, the guns like incessant thunder all the time, the sky a red flare from horizon to horizon, and in the direction of the village where the cars had gone, flames. They were ages away and it was awful wondering if they were all right. Well, they were, thank God, though half an hour after they had left the village the enemy had shelled it to pieces.

We all started off at ten o'clock in pitch darkness along dreadful roads, went about ten miles, then the road was so hopeless, enormous cavities and river to ford, etc., that we all struck and said "Blast the enemy, we'll camp the night on the road in the cars," which we did, and at 4 A.M. we started off again across country, making for a place where we were to meet the first Serbian division and get further orders. All the time we were going we heard guns nearer and nearer, as we were going to another part of the front near Constansa. Well, we eventually found the General in a field in a valley with crowds of soldiers and guns etc. We waited there an hour and all the time just over the hill the shells were bursting and flames from the burning town and oil wells could be seen. Two or three shells burst over us while we waited. Then the order was given to get on, *retreat*, and all the soldiers had to go first. We were the very last of all and when we'd got about a quarter of a mile our [blasted] car stopped and wouldn't budge, so with great calmness! with shells coming nearer and nearer, we cleaned the plugs, oiled various bits and eventually after half an hour's playing about, she started, and we raced after the others. We then went about ten miles on, all this mind you, across *fields,* no road at all. Then we halted again while the military authorities burbled to each other. It was getting towards sunset, there was a scarlet sky, a vast undulating plain ahead, behind us the crash of ever nearing guns and the long lines of soldiers coming wearily back. Again orders to move, and again we were kept to the last and it began to pour. Off we went, and I shall always see that sinister plain and the rain and the grey ghostlike figures of the soldiers and guns retreating. Well, we had gone for about two hours when we discovered that one of our big lorries had stuck. We waited and waited while they tried to get it going and the shells got closer and closer. At last we had to abandon it after smashing the engine with a hammer, removing the magneto[1] etc. Then we went on until about 10 P.M., when we came to a village

1. *Magneto:* generator.

and we slept in the cars there, as we were all done and couldn't see an inch, and besides no one knew where to go, as the charming army had jolly well cleared off without waiting for us, after keeping us to the last. That village was pandemonium all night, guns, guns, guns crashing and Roumanian, Russian, and Serbian troops all mixed up in hopeless confusion in the retreat, not knowing where to go or what to do. At 4 A.M. we started off again, and from then until we got here it was *Hell*. Imagine to yourself an enormous stretch of country like the back of the Downs, only gigantic, and through the centre of it one not very wide or good main road, running to the River Danube and the frontier, and from *every* direction on this plain as far as you could see, behind and before and all around, streams and streams of carts and horses and women, men, children, herds of cattle and sheep, soldiers, guns, bullock wagons, every conceivable thing, and *all* converging on to this one road! A Nation in Retreat and only *one* road. The wretched peasants in rough carts made of a few planks roped together, and on them all their worldly goods, furniture, pigs, geese and children all huddled together. Old women and young with babies in their arms trudging along beside them. There were five or six carts deep across the road, we had awful difficulty in moving at all and every yard we were beseeched to take people. We couldn't, we had wounded with us in most cars and the others were full up with stores, petrol etc. Every hundred yards or so you would see a tragic group of wailing women over one of these wretched carts which had broken, and there were all the things they possessed fallen in the mud and ditch, and being trampled over by the passing crowds. It was dreadful. And then about 10 A.M. a rumour spread that Bulgarian cavalry were coming over the hills at our back, and then panic seized the poor wretches. The soldiers and their wagons whipped up their horses and drove furiously on over everything and every one. All the people began to *scream* and *scream* and run for their lives. They tried to jump on the cars and one man with a little baby in his arms ran in front of one of the cars, threw the baby on the ground and jumped on to the step. We jolly well chucked him off and gave the baby to a woman. Never can I forget the terror on the faces of those people.

[Braille, 1934 memoir]

When I look back on those days in Braille they seem quite fantastic. It was incredible that any place so near to the fighting zone, in which such a terrible and utter collapse was taking place should appear so completely ignorant and, to the outward eye, indifferent to the state of things then existent. Their hospital preparations were ridiculously inadequate, there was only one surgical hospital in the town and one civilian hospital. The medical supplies were practically non-existent. We ourselves had got separated from most of our hospital unit and stores during the retreat and had only two of our doctors as far as I remember, Dr. Inglis being one of them, and a few nurses with us, a tiny amount of hospital equipment also, but very very little. For some days we did not know where the rest of our Unit and supplies were. They eventually turned up at Galatz, some miles up the river from Braille. Our doctors and nurses offered their services to the military hospital at once, and as wounded were beginning to pour in in thousands they were most thankfully accepted.

I have never seen anything so awful as that hospital, because in a day or two's time beds were all full, patients were lying on the floor, all along the corridors, down the stairs, in the hallways, anywhere that there was enough room to lie them down. The pressure of work was so enormous that half the time they couldn't stop to clear up. I went into the Theatre one day. There were four operating tables going, instruments were being thrown across from one table to another, some operations were being done without anaesthetics as the supply had begun to give out, amputated limbs, bits of flesh, pails and pools of blood were all over the floor. The whole place looked like a shambles. How the doctors stuck it I don't know. They were working night and day in a vain endeavour to keep up with the ever increasing numbers.

M. who was quite untrained was working all hours giving Tetanus injections.

In the meantime we used to drive to the station, which had a huge open space in front of it, and as cattle truck after cattle truck of wounded arrived, they were taken from the train and laid on the ground in rows. We used to get our stretchers out, load up the ambulances, then drive around the town till we could find access to an empty house, get the wounded out and into the house where we unloaded them onto the floors, then go back to the station and fetch more till the house was full, then go off to the main hospital to see who could be sent to take charge. As a rule a nurse or a V.A.D. would be dispatched to do the best they could until such time as a doctor could get along.

I remember one house with a pretty little Roumanian V.A.D. in charge, doing her level best, poor child. The house had a winding staircase, and D. and I had a very big heavy man on a stretcher. How we ever got him up those corkscrew stairs I don't know, but we did. When we got the stretcher down we put our hands and arms underneath him and lifted him gently on to the floor. When we withdrew our hands they were scarlet, and our sleeves were saturated with blood. I lifted my hands and asked the little Roumanian girl for a towel. She cast a horror-stricken look at us and covering her face with her hands, burst into tears.

Then we took such small amount of medical dressings as we had with us and put up a notice to the effect that in a schoolroom near the station we would dress anybody's wounds who could manage to get to us. Poor things, there were hundreds of them. We worked all day and all night till at about three in the morning we hadn't an inch of bandage or anything else left, and so reluctantly had to close down and turn the patiently waiting, pathetic crowds away.

I forgot to say that we were told, with how much truth I do not know, that both in Russia and Roumania a great percentage of the nursing staffs were recruited from the demi-monde classes. We certainly had instructions in Petrograd to remove our Red Cross armlets as otherwise we should be taken for ladies of the streets. All honour to them for the fine work they did.

[1917, in Galicia, 1934 memoir]

The Russian methods were very drastic, they never soaked dressings off, simply stripped them. In amputations they cut straight across the limb, then cut away inside the skin, leaving the skin and about three inches of bare bone in the centre, packed round the bone with very tightly rammed gauze then bandaged. This was left for some considerable time, then they unbandaged and ripped the tightly packed gauze out. It must have been hellish for the patients.

I had never fainted in my life, but I came nearest to it one morning in the dressing room. I was working with E. on a patient and at the other end of the room a man who had a dreadful head wound was being dressed. The top of his head was split open and his brain was bulging out, suddenly he began to scream, a scream that I soon began to know only too well. I hope I may never have to hear it again. His voice went up into a high thin piercing shrill note, it was inhuman, it was frightful. One realised that it was the sound produced from a human being in a state of agony, which eliminated reason. It was so appallingly dreadful that for a minute or two the room was black and swaying in front of me. I shoved my head down and prayed for control, and thank goodness in a few moments was all right, but I was dripping with perspiration from head to foot.

[near Noyon, France]
August 21, 1918

We have been frightfully busy these last days as we have been attacking in our Sector with success. It has been most interesting as each day the Poste has been further forward and we have followed up with it. It is extraordinary going to places the day after the Boche has left them. Terrible devastation everywhere, and the *smells!* Unburied dead lying in every wood. Horrible! The roads, of course, are unspeakable. Shell holes full of water, large enough to take two or three cars, all over the place. It's pretty harassing driving over a road of that description that you've never been on before, in the pitch dark. I did an hundred and eighty miles the other day, never got off the car except for loading in the cases. Most of it at night and a dark night too, lots of gas about. We have to wear our masks often. One thing is you are so occupied and worried with getting the car over the awful roads that you don't notice the shells unless one bursts frightfully near. All the cross roads have been blown up by the Boche on their retreat and it's a chatty job getting over them I can tell you. We now do twenty-four hours on, twenty-four hours off, forty-eight hours on, twenty-four hours off. Pretty strenuous.

I had a most interesting time the other day. The Poste was at the foot of a hill two and a half miles long, like Harting Hill only much steeper and wooded on both sides. I was stationed on the road about a quarter of a mile from the top. The trenches were just over the top and the cases were brought down by hand to me and I took them down to [the] Poste. I did this for sixteen hours, up and down and up and down. In the darkest time of the night I was sent down to work back, as the hill road was considered impassable at night for a car. It was thrilling as all the batteries were all round me. We put up a heavy barrage for four hours. I had the pleasure of being taken up to a 75 gun by the captain of the battery and watched them for some time, and then he asked me if I would like to fire it, so I did. It's fun to say I fired a 75 in one of the biggest attacks, isn't it? It was pretty tricky work that day as they were shelling the batteries a lot and also shelling the Poste with gas shells. However, I find I don't care a damn in the daytime, but the strain at night makes one's nerve a bit jumpy. One is jolly glad of the arrival of the relief cars when one's duty time finishes. We very often have to drive in front of our own guns and you have to be careful not to buzz round a corner fast in case you come slap in front of a battery firing. There's one battery of "210" guns which we pass and if you get in front of one of them, good bye-ee. They are enormous terrifying looking things.

We all stay at one place to start with in the morning and the cars are sent to the various Postes from there. Our waiting place is on the side of the main road between a mortuary shed and an enormous open grave where they bury twenty at a time. Once again the smell! However you get used to everything and now one sits and munches bread and cheese, while watching the grave diggers putting chloride of lime on the bodies. Two stretcher bearers passed me the other day carrying the remains of a poor devil whose legs were in pulp and his head half off, smothered in blood and lime, and as they passed they cheerily called "Bon appetit, mademoiselle." Awful to get so callous, but it's the only way if you want to preserve your reason. One man died as I lifted him out of the car the other day and yesterday my cushions, my food basket, my coat were all drenched and saturated with blood, as I'd left them in the well under the stretcher and the poor fellow had a hemorrhage. You sleep any old where, the other night in a dug-out with about fifty soldiers, such a fug, and half-way through the door opened and a voice yelled "Look out. Gas!" so we all sat and sweltered in our gas masks for about four hours, perfectly awful.

[1934 memoir]

When I first started driving up and down the precipitous hill described in my letter I very nearly met my end. I took over the Ford from the girl who'd been on duty driving at the bottom of the hill and with no time to overhaul it started up. At the place on the roadside where I had to wait for cases I began to turn the car, so that I should be ready to go down. The road was on a severe cant down towards a very steep drop. I backed the car towards the hill side of the road and then went forward intending to stop and back again. When I put the brakes on to my horror nothing happened. I slid forward helplessly and yelled. The French orderlies around leapt forward and caught my back wheels as the front ones were just going over the edge. It was a very nasty moment. I drove the car, when loaded, down in first gear, and swapped it with one of the other drivers who was only working on a level piece of road. When I started up with the second car I found she was overheating terribly. I had a look and discovered that the ball and socket joint controlling the spark had worn and that the ball was out of the socket, so that when I retarded or advanced the spark lever nothing happened. However, necessity being the mother of invention, I found an ordinary pin and edged the ball into the socket with it, and thus drove quite comfortably for the remaining twenty-four hours of my duty. On one of my ascents in that twenty-four hours as I turned one of the winding corners, crawling up on first gear, I thought what a funny smell of burning metal. Then it flashed on me "Gas." I slapped my mask on as quickly as possible, but even that brief sniff left me with a streaming nose, running eyes and a burning sore throat for about three days afterwards.

Department of Documents, the Imperial War Museum, 92/22/1.

✟ Tatiana Ivanova Alexinsky
(1886–1968) *Russian*

Born in Moscow, Tatiana trained as a doctor. In 1907 she married Grigori Alexinsky, who had belonged to the second *Duma,* or parliament, in 1906; he declared, "The woman question will be resolved only with the final victory of the proletariat." They emigrated from Russia to France in 1908, splitting with Lenin to form the "Forward" group. After the war broke out, Alexinsky returned to Russia with her small son, as she explains in her diary, in a spirit of socialist patriotism. She worked on a hospital train shuttling between the front and hospitals at the rear; she was occasionally able to see her son, who stayed with her family in Moscow. She kept a record of her work, *With the Russian Wounded,* for her husband, which he arranged to have translated into French and English in 1916. A year later, she published an account in Russian, *Zhenshchina v voinie i revoliutsii* (Women and war in revolution, 1917). With the advent of the revolution, she returned to Paris and her allegiances shifted to the right.

✟ A Hospital Train

Our hospital train is like a town on wheels—a little provincial town, with all its petty business, petty concerns, petty interests.

In the middle of the train there is a first-class car for the staff; next to it is a third-class car, half of which is used as a dining-room and the other as a bandaging-room. Then there are the kitchen, the refrigerator, the linen-press, and the dirty-linen compartment. Another car is set apart as a dormitory for the hospital workers—that is, the orderlies, stretcher-bearers, etc. Except for these men the staff is "civilian," and is composed exclusively of women. Ours is a feminist train, and I am proud of it.

*   *   *

The administrative and staff cars of our train are linked between cars fitted out for the wounded, a second-class car for officers, fourteen goodswaggons for the men, fitted out with stretchers, and called *tieploushki*, and supplemented with eight fourth-class cars. These are set apart for slightly wounded men, while the fourteen waggons are reserved for the seriously wounded. Some of them are provided with eight movable beds with spring mattresses, on which the stretchers bearing the wounded are laid.

Our train is constantly on the move. It was made up at Moscow, and left there at the beginning of the war in an embryonic condition, fully equipped with medical requirements and staff, but without its proper complement of rolling-stock. This was completed at one of the big towns near the front, where the train attained its present constitution—that is, a long hospital train of three dozen cars.

When I first made the acquaintance of my colleagues I was, I own it, not a little surprised, on hearing the names of our staff, to discover that all their names had a German ring—there was not a Russian among them. Many of our orderlies had the typical appearance of the Germans: blue eyes, fair or red hair, soft features, slow deliberate movements. And this was no illusion: they are, in fact, Germans. They are Menonites, members of an evangelical sect which came to Russia in the time of Catherine the Great, who loved French philosophers and German immigrants. They took refuge with us from the religious persecution inflicted on them at first in the United Provinces and subsequently in Prussia.

Russia is indeed a country of boundless possibilities. Its Government, which was engaged in the persecution of sects among its own subjects, welcomed these men who had been denied liberty of conscience abroad. It gave them fertile land in South Russia, exempted them from taxation, and respected their religion, which forbade them to kill and to make war, excused them from armed military service, and used them for the auxiliary and hospital services.

As orderlies, these Russian Germans are perfect: very gentle with the wounded, very punctual, and very intelligent. It was plain to all of us that we could trust them entirely.

In each *tieploushka* there is room for a dozen wounded men. A *tieploushka* is a goods-waggon with a stove in the middle; beds on the floor, or fixed to the sides in three tiers. The full complement of cars for the wounded on our train is thirty-two. A lady doctor, assisted by a Sister, has charge of ten cars of "slightly wounded" or of six "seriously wounded." I have charge of six "seriously wounded" cars.

Before the train leaves the base we have to question each wounded man to find out when his wounds were last dressed and how he is.

You have to climb up into the *tieploushki* by movable steps, which are taken away when the train starts. You have to hurry to examine all the casualties before the train moves, or you run the risk of being left in the *tieploushka* until the next stop, because there is no communication between the cars, and there is no means of moving from one to the other without getting out. And there is no knowing when the next stop will be, as there is no fixed time-table in war-time. Sometimes the train jogs along for hours at a stretch, and sometimes it stops every ten minutes.

Once, as the train started, I had gone to the pharmacy, which was in a third-class carriage.

I had to wait until I could get back to the *tieploushka*.

I readjust the dressings when necessary, and sit on one of the beds and draw the men into conversation. They all tell me how they were wounded and taken away, and give me their impressions.

"Sister," said one of the men, "they are taking us to N——, and my people live at V——. Our train will go through V——. Let me get out there. I will see my relations, and come on after you to N——."

I told him I had no right to let him leave the station, and even the chief surgeon could not do it, as it rested with the military authorities.

"Then I can only stop at V—— without leave?" said the soldier half-questioningly.

"I can't give you permission, but I can't keep you by force in the train," said I. "Anyhow, don't forget that you are bound for N——, and, if you stay a few days at V—— with your people, come on to N—— and report yourself to the commandant."

Two other men also expressed a desire to stay at V—— to see their people. I laughed, and told them that a whole car-load of wounded men could not stop at V—— without attracting attention.

The train stopped. I went to another *tieploushka,* and here, too, dressed the men's wounds and talked. At the next stop I went to a third, and so to all six in turn. Night fell. Worn out, I came to the end of my work and went to the dining-car. My colleagues were waiting for me, and we sat down at table—dinner-time.

"A Hospital Train," in *With the Russian Wounded,* trans. Gilbert Cannan (London: T. Fisher Unwin, 1916), 1–7.

☦ Types of Nurses

The medical staff of our train consists of thirteen people, of whom eleven are women. It is truly a feminist train.

The chief surgeon is a lady-doctor of forty. Her energy is equal to that of any man. Her hospitality is that of a great hostess: she makes every guest welcome. She treats her subordinates well, but she has her little caprices, or rather her peculiarities. She keeps a keen eye on the sentimental propensities of the girls working in her train, and intervenes, sometimes very roughly, whenever she suspects a romance in the making. Every now and then she gives them an address, in which she violently attacks what she calls somewhat contemptuously "the sexual instinct" and revolts against the "weakness" of women.

Her androphobia may perhaps be explained on personal grounds. She divorced her husband ten years ago. Before the war she was living an independent life as a physician, under a provincial zemstvo.[1] She has a son at school. When war was declared she left her ordinary work, her patients, her son, and went to the front.

The other women working in our train are mostly Russian intellectuals who can find no satisfaction in their ordinary life in the provincial corners of our immense Russia, and are seeking an outlet for their moral energy and their social aspirations. The war has the same attraction for them as the struggles and sufferings of the people used to have.

One of my colleagues came in the hope of finding oblivion and relief from her sorrow; she had lost her son, whom she loved passionately, and her husband, who was not only the man she loved, but a real friend and comrade.

Another, quite a young woman, had spent ten years in the country as a school-mistress. She had tilled the soil of popular education under very disadvantageous conditions, among coarse and illiterate people, and hidebound by the oppressive authority of the bureaucracy and the police. She is hard and embittered, and does not at first make a good impression. But when she is tending the wounded, the real depths of her soul are revealed, and through her usual tone of deliberate rudeness comes the glint of a kindly word, or a tender smile, with which she puts heart into the suffering men.

"There's nothing to groan about, is there? Patience! Just a minute! Does the dressing hurt you? It will cure you for all that. Of course it will!"

And she looks through her spectacles as though she were begging the man's pardon. . . .

Another sister is also a school-mistress. She has known poverty and toil. Her old father used to live in a village ten versts away. She loved him dearly, and wanted to see him as often as possible, but as she had no money to hire a carriage, she used to go and see him several times a week on foot, like a dutiful daughter, through all the mud and the bitter weather.

"I put on my big moujik's boots, and go and see my father. I am used to long walks," she would say apologetically, when she confided her secret dream of joining the army as a volunteer for active service.

She had only joined our train to be nearer the fighting line, and to join a fighting regiment at the first opportunity, to become a soldier, and to share the lot of the others. She had spent half her life among the peasants,

---

1. *Zemstvo:* local district council

teaching their children, and now that they had become soldiers, she wanted to stay with them and to be among them.

Fortunately, her desire will soon be consummated.

"Types of Nurses," in *With the Russian Wounded,* trans. Gilbert Cannan (London, T. Fisher Unwin, 1916), 10–13.

✝ More Wounded Than Beds

The journey from Kiev to Ir—— took a whole day, and we did not arrive until evening. We loaded the train all night, for we had to hurry.

There were more casualties than beds, and there were eleven men left, whom I could not accommodate.

I tried to convince them:

"There is nothing to be done but to wait for the next train. Be patient, my men."

They agreed to go back to the clearing-station, and I was just going with them, when a gentleman who had overheard the conversation said:

"No, Sister. You mustn't take them back to the clearing-station. If you have no room in your train, put them in P——tsh's train, which is just behind yours."

The gentleman, who was wearing a rain-proof coat with an officer's epaulettes, and a chauffeur's goggles on his nose, saw that I was doubtful, and added:

"They will be well looked after in the train."

"Come," I said to the men. . . . "But what am I to tell them on the train?" I asked the gentleman as he moved away. "I must give the name of my authority for taking them."

What? This was P——tsh himself! This was the fierce reactionary and instigator of pogroms, and I am a "sister" to him! Only the war could produce such results. The German social-democrats are my "enemies," and I, a Russian Socialist, have become a "sister" to P——tsh! . . .

We are awaiting our orders at F——. We have been waiting for more than a day. The hours creep by horribly slowly. News comes in, more and more alarming: the Austrians are still advancing, and are near Mel——. And Mel—— is not far from F——. We are told that there are many casualties at Mel——. We begged the Chief to send us with a few *tieploushki* to collect the wounded. The Chief would not consent:

"I have no instructions."

Another day crept by as we waited for our instructions. A telegram came during the night: our train is to go to Mel—— at once. And we got there in the morning.

There were two trains in the station. One was laden with rails and munitions: the other was carrying a "revictualling detachment."

The wounded were lying on the platform and the track. There were numbers of them. Those who could walk got up and went to the fourth-class cars, and rapidly filled the three tiers of beds, and thronged the corridors. All the available space was occupied. Those who could not walk were taken—even the dying, and those *in extremis*. The movable beds in the *tieploushki* were pulled out, the wounded were placed in them, and carried into the cars.

While we were arranging our men an Austrian aeroplane appeared. The staff were too much occupied to notice the danger, but the wounded outside moved about anxiously on their stretchers.

"Take us away from here! Take us away! It is straight above us!"

"We have escaped from one death to meet another!"

"Start the train!"

Suddenly—boom! The bomb fell from the aeroplane. It burst not far from the train and wounded a soldier. He was hurried into a *tieploushka*.

Our guns began to fire on the aeroplane. Our gunnery seemed to be effective, for the machine sped away and disappeared from view.

The seriously wounded were still being brought in. All the beds were full already. Where could we put the newcomers? I sought out our Chief. She was talking to the doctor attached to the revictualling train.

"We must take all the wounded away as soon as possible," she said, with great emotion. "They are going to couple seven goods-waggons on to our train. We will put the slightly wounded in them. If we still want room we will put the men on the floors of the *tieploushki*."

"All the beds are filled with the seriously wounded," said I. "We can't put the seriously wounded on the floor."

A Sister from the revictualling train came up to me, and said in a low voice:

"Everything is ready for the retreat. As soon as your train starts ours will follow, and then they are going to blow up the station. We can't leave the wounded to the Austrians. We must take them all, even the dying. Your train has room for four hundred and fifty cases. Even if ten, fifteen, or twenty-five die on the road, you will save the lives of six hundred others by taking them away from here."

"We must make haste," said the Chief.

I ran back to my trucks.

"There is a man dying in my car," said one of the orderlies, as soon as I arrived.

I went into the *tieploushka*. The man leaped up from his bed. The orderly held him down. The blood was oozing through the bandages round his stomach.

"Pass me a compress," I said to my assistant. "Quick!"

I took the man's hand; his pulse was weak and irregular; his eyes were staring into space.

I injected camphor. The man groaned, glared at me, and murmured:

"They are going to take us back to our own province, aren't they?"

He slipped back into unconsciousness. An hour later he was dead.

My assistant and I visited all the beds, readjusting badly-tied bandages, and giving injections of camphor and morphia. . . . We were urged to hurry up, but we had to fill the seven goods-waggons which had been added on to our train for the wounded. At last the train was full up. All the wounded had been removed, and we started.

I sat with my assistant in one of our *tieploushki,* looking with a feeling of utter helplessness at the heap of humanity contained in it. All of them were in a serious condition; their dressings were saturated; and some of them were spitting blood. Where was I to begin? Evening was falling; it was difficult to work by the light of a candle. But I had to do what I could. And we set to work. . . .

When everybody had been attended to we went to the doorway. An enormous column of red light stood out against the sky; sparks were flying.

"I suppose that is Mel—— burned down," I said. "That means that our men have already withdrawn from there."

"More Wounded than Beds," in *With the Russian Wounded,* trans. Gilbert Cannan (London: T. Fisher Unwin, 1916), 148–55.

✝ Countess Nora Kinsky
(1888–1923) *Hungarian*

Born in Vienna, the precocious sixth child of Count Zdenko Kinsky and of Countess Festetics de Tolna, Nora grew up in a chateau at Chlumec in Bohemia. Bored at the conclusion of school, she took over the care of her three younger siblings, while continuing her own study of music and foreign languages. To absorb her overflowing energies, her father put his ten-year-old daughter in charge of his stables, and a few years later made her his secretary.

When war broke out, she set up a hospital with 110 beds in the stables (now emptied of their horses) at Chlumec, and in 1916 she was selected by the Austro-Hungarian imperial ministry of war to inspect Russian camps for prisoners of war, from Nikolsk, near Vladivostok, to the Caspian. This mission, on which she was always accompanied by a neutral Danish Red Cross delegate as well as a Russian escort, required her to register complaints by prisoners, check conditions for violations of The Hague conventions, draw up lists of those buried in Russian cemeteries, and seek for those missing in action. She persuaded authorities to let soldiers set up workshops for cobblers and bakers inside the camps; she protested harsh punishments. She struggled against snowstorms, drunk camp commanders, lackadaisical American liaisons, and the "goose-gabble" of silly female volunteers. In her negotiations, her mastery of English, French, Italian, Czech, Polish, Croat, and Romanian as well as German and Hungarian was indispensable, and she taught herself Russian and Turkish during her travels. One of her Russian escorts spent evenings reading aloud to her from Tolstoy, Gogol, Pushkin, and Turgenev. After accomplishing with great difficulty her mission in Eastern Siberia, she returned to Petrograd in February 1917. There, while she waited to hear if she would receive permission to stay in Russia near her younger brother Zdenko, the revolution broke out.

Regardless of what her family thought, she was determined to stay in Russia, where she could relish her independence and where it was "in any case more interesting than in Chlumec." After a struggle with a shifting and unstable bureaucracy, she received papers allowing her to remain as a nurse and set off to choose a hospital; she eventually settled in Astrakhan at Hospital 121, where she worked beside Dr. Balogh, a Hungarian prisoner, with tubercular prisoners, many of them Turkish allies of the Austrians. She also arranged to have her brother Zdenko and his friend Ferdinand Wilczek moved to a nearby camp. In August 1917, she was awarded the Hungarian Queen Elisabeth medal for her humanitarian service. By year's end the Russian civil war had made her position precarious and heightened her suffering from hunger, cold, and malaria. When she attempted to return to Petrograd, her trip was thwarted by damaged rail lines, harsh weather, and the constant movement of troops, which sent her on a zigzag route to the Black Sea before she finally returned to Vienna. Her shattered health delayed her marriage to Dr. Ferdinand Wilczek until 1921; she had one daughter—Gina, who became Princess of Liechtenstein—before she died in 1923. The diary she kept in Russia from 1916 to 1918 was published in German, with her negative comments on Germans censored; this translation of selected entries is based on a transcript of the French original.

✝ Russian Diary, 1916–1918

September 19, 1916   Nikolsk

Here I am back from my first trip to the camp. Commander Jegorov, a very unpleasant man, then Colonel Bodisko, who is rather agreeable, and Captain Wallicki, who will accompany us everywhere, to Blagowjeschensk, received us. Tomorrow we shall visit the hospital and the cemetery and then we will hear the report of the soldiers representing the camp. As there will undoubtedly be many complaints, this will be very painful. I found five disabled men who had not been freed, three of them blind. There were only three men imprisoned, whom Bodisko freed in my honor, which was nice of him. There is a shortage of shoes and uniforms and there have been thefts of the goods distributed by the Swedish Red Cross. Very few blankets for the beds and the food is bad. As for bread, the ration is large compared to ours at home, 2 ½ pounds per person and per day, but the soldiers won't eat it. The prisoners sleep on planks without pillows or mattresses, only their coats; most don't look well, but I found them gay, especially the Hungarians. I found here the servant of Toni Sigray, Jozsef Kolloman, who is very likeable and knows everyone. He asked me for news about Laszlo Cz. and it was very odd to be talking about it at several thousand kilometers from home!

I don't know what impression I made on the prisoners, but I hope they noted my good will. The doctors are all Hungarian except for one Pole; they are good and seem to like their patients, which is the essential thing.

The non-commissioned officers are not all irreproachable and our soldiers don't like being under the command of Prussians, which is understandable. I must also find a more practical way of pursuing the question
of the missing. In general I think it will be a while before we can do this
job quickly and well. Here I found by accident two German officers (the
camp is only for soldiers) on their way to Chabarowsk. There was an
unpleasant altercation between them and the commander. It's true that
the "Boches" are very arrogant, even in captivity. Tomorrow they will let
me take a batch of letters from the prisoners as well as lists organized by
regiment. I am very happy because it is a concession on the part of the
commander who is not obligated to do this. Unhappily they won't let us
work after six in the evening, as the Russians want to go home and we can't
begin either before nine in the morning. They have promised me to
assemble the prisoners working outside the camp in the neighborhood, so
that I can see and speak to them. There have been lots of complaints
about "confiscation" of money by the Russians. Tomorrow I must examine
the books, the postal money orders. All in all, the camp itself has not made
a bad impression; the barracks are large and high-ceilinged, and there is
so very much bread! You see it lying about in corners. The non-
commissioned officers look too affluent and satisfied by comparison with
the soldiers; the contrast is not pleasing. I hope it's an accident and that it
won't be true in the other camps. It's very painful to hear soldiers com-
plaining about their superiors.

September 22, 1916

Spent the day at Skotowo with the officers. A lack of order and discipline
that is heartrending. The camp is not far from the sea, with a very beautiful
view, but the barracks are too little, there is too little room for the number
of prisoners, which doesn't contribute to their good humor. We ate with the
Russian officers, as we were not permitted to dine with our compatriots, and
they gave us meat from animals with mad-cow disease. The soldiers here are
well and the noncoms quite likeable, which pleased me. This hospital made
a good impression; the head doctor, Dr. Möstl, a good Viennese, whom the
sick seemed to like. I found the morale of the officers worse than that of
soldiers. It's natural, since they suffer more from captivity. The lack of occupation is terrible for them. I was touched by their pleasure at our arrival and
the gratitude the prisoners showed for the least effort on their behalf. They
seemed completely to forget that it is simply my duty.

The officers who accompany us, the commander of the camp Sokolov
and Colonel Markosov, are bland and repellent.

January 25, 1918   Astrakhan

This morning I was awakened by cannon fire that shook our quarters.
The cossacks fire ceaselessly and their target is the tower of the fortress
almost opposite us. When they will have broken all our windows, it will be

quite cool. We evacuated immediately the sick from the fourth floor to the third, because people think that during the day or tomorrow they will start to throw hand grenades or bombs, I'm not quite sure what they call the projectiles that destroy buildings. They want to make me leave my room, which overlooks the street and is on the ground floor, which could become dangerous if there is streetfighting. For the moment I don't dream of leaving it, I am staying there. All the sisters are in tears and cry out at every discharge. They will soon lose their voices if the cossacks have enough ammunition.

This morning after the first cannon fire (at four in the morning I was still in bed) Blecha came to my door to tell me that I should get up to be safe, but I sent him away telling him I would naturally get up as usual, unless a patient needed me. Then several sisters came to squawl behind my door and I sharply begged them to let me sleep, since I have neither the habit nor the opportunity to do so during the day. I heard them tell old Vladimir Nikolaevic, who was going around in slippers, that I have no nerves and want to sleep. He said "haraso tak"[1] and laughed. What stupid geese! The only thing that would be unpleasant would be if we had no more water or light.

They have just brought our first wounded, I must go down. I have several empty beds, so I am sure they will put them with me. E.L.[2] is too nervous, the only normal person is Dr. Balogh. What noise these cannon make, even though they are not of a large caliber, according to our soldiers. The men are very amused and happy that I am not afraid.

January 26, 1918

We spent a bad night. We are effectively the target of the cannon and I wonder if we will not be destroyed if this continues, or at least burnt down. The bolsheviki have already taken the position at the corner of our short narrow street and set fire to the houses opposite us, the high school and town pharmacy! They blew up the latter with barrels of benzine that had been stored there. We are suffocating here in the heat and smoke of the houses burning around us. Everyone is worried and Balogh says it will be a miracle if we escape the flames, because the fire is too close. We wouldn't know what to do if our house catches on fire because you can't go into the street. They fire on anyone who shows himself out there.

Last night we all thought the house was on fire, the flames seemed so close. I could see from my window how the scoundrels were dousing the walls with gasoline, which they lit. It seemed like the cinema and you forget the danger when it's just inert mass, not men, being destroyed. They are talking of evacuation, *djeduška*[3] and the others have lost their heads. I wonder where they could send us. All our neighborhood is a theater of

1. *Haraso tak:* that's good.
2. *E.L.:* Eugenia Leonidowna Korsakowa, a Red Cross nurse.
3. *Djeduška:* "grandfather," an older orderly.

murderous operations. They constantly bring us wounded. The wounds are terrible—enormous. Heaven knows what these people are shooting with! The sisters are quite hysterical, won't touch anything, and spend their time groaning in the officers' hall. E.L. is "on the verge of a break-down" and must be managed. I am quite anxious about the *bratja*.[4] I wonder if they have been able to stay at their place. War is such a dirty thing! And soldiers say it's worse than at the front! At any rate it's worse than last year in Petrograd.

By permission of Prince Hans-Adam II of Liechtenstein.

4. *Bratja:* brothers, Kinsky's nickname for her brother Zdenko and his friend Ferdi-nand.

✝ Olive "Jo" King
(1885–1958) *Australian*

When Olive King was fifteen, her mother died, leaving her and her elder sister Sunny to be raised by their father, a businessman who remained a loving influence in Olive's life. Educated partly at home outside Sydney by a governess, and partly at a grammar school run by the Church of England, she was then sent off to finishing school in Dresden with her sister. Upon her return home, King felt restless and constrained by the rigid social life of the British Empire in the early twentieth century; her romantic flings gave her a reputation as "harum-scarum." She spent the prewar years traveling (with a watchful chaperone) in Asia, Europe, and America. In 1910 she became the third woman to climb Mount Popocatépetl in Mexico, leaving her chaperone exhausted at the bottom.

When the war broke out in August 1914, King was in England, where she immediately volunteered to work with the Allies Field Ambulance Corps in Belgium, supplying her own large ambulance ("Ella"), which seated sixteen patients. She and two other women drivers were briefly arrested upon suspicion of being spies, and just managed to escape the invading German army and return safely to England. In May 1915 she joined the Scottish Women's Hospitals (many of whose members were suffragettes), with whom she went to Troyes, France, where they were attached to the French army. Shocked by the "brutal gas-shells" of the "Bosches," she was nonetheless optimistic that the British, with whom as an Australian she identified, would quickly win the war. Five months later her unit embarked for the Balkans, serving several weeks at the Serbian border before the Bulgarian advance forced them to retreat to Salonika, Greece.

King's letters to her father and sister (who was also driving an ambulance) record some of the hardships she had to endure in the field, such as the struggle to keep tents standing in blustering storms, but they also show a cheerful determination to spare her loved ones any worries. She writes to her father soon after arriving in Salonika: "I don't suppose this interests you a bit, Daddy darling, and you probably think it's very disgusting! I'm sorry!" Like the Serb military who felt cooped up in the Greek port city, she lamented her distance from battle: "There doesn't seem to be much chance of my dream of being in the thick of things coming true." In July 1916 King joined the Serbian army as a driver, still driving "Ella" as well as a smaller vehicle, "Bridget." She fell in love with a Serbian liaison officer for the British army, Captain Yovitchitch, but they drifted apart when he was assigned elsewhere; she firmly refused other offers. By the next year, when Salonika burned on August 17, 1917, she was the only female driver left with her unit, and drove for twenty-four hours to rescue the inhabitants of the city. In October she received a Silver Medal for her bravery.

As the war drew to a close in 1918, King recognized that the Serbian soldiers and refugees were on the brink of starvation and proposed a nonprofit canteen selling foodstuffs, for which she enlisted her father's aid raising funds in Australia and England. In the midst of her preparations she wrote that "now it seems Fate means me to work for Serbia for a time . . . I always knew there was some purpose that sent me out here." She believed that "a free united Serbia is absolutely vital to the life of the British Empire." She helped feed the refugees for two more years, until 1920, when she split the remaining proceeds between the University of Belgrade and a hospital for tubercular children.

After closing the canteen in 1920, King returned to Sydney and to the placid domestic life that she had never previously enjoyed. She remained friends with her beloved Captain Yovitchitch, but never married. King was active in local municipal government in the 1920s, and in 1935 and 1937 she was given the King George V Silver Jubilee Medal and the King George VI Coronation Medal for her work during the war. She wrote poems and short stories, but was not confident enough to publish her work. Nearly thirty years after her death, her wartime letters were gathered into a narrative of her experiences in the Balkans.

CW

✝ Letter to Her Father, August 31, 1917

I haven't told you anything about the fire, I'm sending you one of the souvenir copies of the Balkan News, the first published after. It gives a very good account so I'll just briefly tell you of my own small part. I was ordered out to Mikra at 4 that Saturday afternoon. On the way back at 6.30 I tried by all possible means to persuade the officers I was driving to let me take them into town, but couldn't get further than the White Tower. Of course I could see there was a thumping big fire on, could see it all afternoon, &

was naturally longing to get in & have a look at it. There were some books
I was very anxious to buy too. I thought I'd manage it when they said they
wanted to go to the White Tower, but just as I was nipping away one
wretched old fat fellow clambered back & said he wanted to go to the
garage. Cursing internally (I'd have cursed more if I'd known that those
precious books would be ashes before midnight!) the unfortunate chauffeur could do nothing but take the old blighter back. We got to the garage
just on 7, & I was going over to give Sondi an English lesson when a breathless orderly tore up with an order for three cars to go & evacuate from the
Serb Intendance. I don't know what that is in English, unless perhaps it's
Ordnance. Bridget & I hopped about breathlessly, hoping to get the order,
but three other cars were ordered, & I never would have gone only Lukar
ran up to the Narednik [Master-Sergeant] just as they were off & said
"Please Sir, Gospajitza's screaming to go". So he said "Want to go?" I said
"Rather!" so he laughed & said "All right, ide". You may be sure I "Idee-d"
for all I was worth, with 3 passengers, all keen to see the wonderful sight,
who crowded in a [sic] & hid till we'd got past the Captain. We went down
Ignatia St. to be as near as possible (the old Via Ignatia built by the
Romans, from Rome to Constantinople). From Venizelos Street to the
place christened by the A.S.C. & now universally known as Piccadilly Circus, about 2 kms. all the Turkish quarters on the right of Ignatia were one
roaring blaze. It's impossible to describe the scenes of pandemonium in
the streets, the jammed mass of panic-stricken people getting their goods
away in bullock carts, on their own backs, in little open fiacres, or in those
long narrow falling-to-pieces little Greek carts that make driving here so
difficult. There was a continuous roar of the flames, every moment came
a great crash & millions of sparks as some buildings, [sic] a Vardar hot-
wind gale was blowing & showers of sparks & burning fragments poured
over us all the time. It was not yet dark, but everything was lit by the weird
golden glow, like a wonderfully brilliant sunset. The Intendance was to the
left, one block down. I got my load, & was ordered to No. 1 Wireless. As
my way was past the garage I called in for my lamps which were on Ella.
The Captain said the Slagalishta (our medical H.Q. stores) were nervous,
& I was to go back there & report. I left my load, got a wonderful view from
the hill where the Wireless is, & dashed down to the Stores. They had 2
cars waiting, the chauffeurs asleep in them, & didn't want me yet. They
only wanted cars in case the fire spread dangerously, & told me to go back
to the Intendance. There I met Captain Peshitch (you remember him, we
used to give him English lessons) who begged me to go to his house, in
the burning Turkish quarter, as all the Intendance was then saved. I got as
near as I could, he & his orderly & Major Koppitch rushed off to pack, saying they'd be about ½ an hour. The most brilliant journalist couldn't
describe the scenes in that little street where I waited, the fire roaring not
ten yards away, me dancing all over Bridget beating out the falling sparks.
Some tommies came along with the trunks of some American Mission people, & asked me to get them away. When I came back I changed a tyre in
the intervals of putting out sparks, & was just pumping when two Serb offi-

cers & their families came along & implored me to move their stuff. I said I couldn't till Peshitch came, but they said they were going only ten minutes away, one of the women began to have hysterics because her dress caught from a bit of flying wood, so finally I left one of the officers to wait for Peshitch, & set off, Bridget fairly staggering with the load, the calmest of the women to show me the way. She was so excited she lost her head, & what was worse, lost the way four times, but finally we got there & dumped the stuff. I came back to find the officer mounting guard over P's things. He said P. had come, said I was to finish their job, & P. had gone back for more of his own things. Bridget went off with another load more fit for a camion [truck or lorry] than for her poor little self. When we got back, P. was beating out the sparks on his stuff, waiting for his orderly who had gone for more, & sent me to save a Serb family. We got the last kid into the car, & hadn't gone two yards when the house fell in with a deafening roar. Finally it was poor patient Peshitch's turn. We went out to Zeitenlik to Major Koppitch's hospital. From the hill there the sight was so awful it seemed absolutely incredible. In fact all night I was saying to myself "This is too dreadful, it *can't* be true, it's too frightful to be really happening." [. . .]

As we came down the hill it seemed as if every building in the town were burning. From Piccadilly to the White Tower was just one leaping flame & the awful hot wind & dust never stopped. They wanted me to go to the rescue of some of their friends, but I insisted on going first to the Stores. Passing the end of Ignatia St, & looking up thru a wall of fire, with the frenzied pushing people & the crash of falling buildings, was something Dante might have described but certainly I couldn't. We got to the Stores at 12:45 A.M., found them working like demons. Captain Millitch said I must stay there, so P & K. departed. We took the stores to a piece of waste ground not more than 200 yds. away but having no buildings near they thought they'd be safe. I'd only done 3 runs when Bridget stopped dead. Winding & grinding only made empty noises, & I realised the awful truth—no petrol. I tore frantically about, & at last struck a lorry with a spare can. They kindly gave me enough to get to a French ambulance station I knew of a mile away, where I knocked them up. They were most kind and charming, & filled me up. It was they who first told me it was burning right down to the sea, & that we were cut off from the garage by four miles of fire. [. . .]

Every moment there was a fresh glare in the sky. They were expecting an air-raid, so at the Dump every man, sleepy and grumbling, was cursing at his post. But Mr Bulgar missed the chance of his life, & no aeroplanes arrived until next morning, when one wandered over to gloat over the damage. I shall never forget that dawn, gradually breaking thru the smoke & glare & flame. And the sun, that even by midday Sunday, shone feebly thru the dirty haze, like a London sun on a foggy day. Every run the fire was nearer, the houses behind the stores went up in a sheet of flame, & for hours the officers & N.C.Os. (we couldn't spare any men) stood on the roofs with fire extinguishers & hand grenades. We had a little hand-pumped hose, used by the wine firm beside us to fill their barrels, & this was playing for hours on the roofs, wherever sparks fell. That big empty court-yard for the wine-barrels was, I think, what saved us, for in the end our precious stores were saved. Always that dreadful hot wind, & for one terrible ½ hour the wind changed & the sparks fell all over the stores we had saved. The officer in charge there sent me dashing back for old tents soaked in water which we pulled over those stores. I drove like a fiend that Sunday morning, smoking 'cos I was so hungry, Bridget screaming her siren all the way, thru the mass of people, not caring a cuss if she went over them or not. She began to scream as she left the yard, shrieked all the way, & kept it up all the way back from the dump. By this time the people were in a sort of dumb apathy, but luckily Bridget has very strong lungs, & her piercing yell galvanised them into sufficient life to leap away from her reckless little feet. Soon after dawn the wine-barrels burst, the street beside the stores ran with wine, six or eight inches deep in the gutters, & overflowing in a trickle all over the street, like blood. Dagoes & the soldiers of two of our Allies threw themselves down, & lying full-length in the gutters, drank & drank. A few hours later they could be seen lying everywhere, a horrid mess beside them, sleeping it off. [. . .]

Looting & shooting were rife, but I'm proud to say not one Tommy looted a thing. The people knew it & trusted them with anything. It gives you a glow sometimes to realize you belong to the only nation that's trusted & respected wherever it goes. [. . .]

It's a responsibility to be British, but by gum! it's worth while. By ¼ past 12 the danger for the stores was over, the dreadful wind had dropped, & the chauffeurs & men, worn-out, went to sleep. I took a walk round town to see the damage, & the tales I heard and the looting I saw—& other things—wouldn't pass the censor! At 3, being the only chauffeur awake, Millitch asked me if I would try to get thru & make a bolt for home, & send him out four fresh cars, or at any rate four fresh drivers. So I went off, was warned by the guard I went at my own risk, but got along the quay somehow. You never saw such a sight as the quay presented that first day. All the best buildings had been there, everything gutted, the tram wires hanging loose in the middle of the road the remains of a motor-car, the buildings all smouldering, some still blazing (today is fourteen days but everywhere the ruins are smouldering, & late this evening I saw another new line of hose being run out) people, most soldiers, rooting in the ruins for loot, others lying about dead-drunk—you couldn't believe it was real. I stared at the Cinemas, & couldn't believe that when I want to go to a cinema there'll be none to go to, & at the Splendid I couldn't believe that I'll never have another meal in their much-advertised, horrid new restaurant. The two best hotels, with their fine outsides & their bugs inside, the Sister Club, the beautiful new Red Cross rooms, the shops, the bars, the restaurants, the "Palais de Varieties"—gone, all gone. I saw it happening, & all day long I'm driving among the ruins, & yet I can't realize it, so how in the world can I make you? I was jolly proud of my little Bridget, from 4 o'clock when she started for Mikra, until ¼ past 12 Sunday she never stopped running, over 20 hours, except the ½ hour at Zeitenlik at midnight, & an occasional two or three minutes when there were other lorries loading up ahead. She only had one puncture & up till the last two hours went like a bird. The last two hours she went poisonously, but I wasn't surprised when I filled her up at midday, & found the radiator was less than half full. I got home at 4, to find the floor of my "salon" (otherwise hall) covered with refugees, a woman & 9 children. I plumped straight down on my bed & went to sleep, got up at 6, had a bath, made tea for the refugees, & went round to Yovi. We were dining with Captain Shapovitch. I was so hungry, so it was rather a blow to be met with "I hope you're not hungry, I can't get any food anywhere". It was, alas, only too true. We had a tin of sardines & a very small tinned tongue for dinner. The next day I carted refugees from 7 A.M. till 10 P.M. & the following day started at 5 A.M. I didn't get any loot, at the time I was too busy, & besides it never occurred to me until two days later, when I heard what others had got & then it was too late. This is an enormous letter, poor Daddy, it will take you a week to read it. I meant to write a very brief concise account, but got so excited I couldn't stop. However I promise to now!

From *One Woman at War: Letters of Olive King, 1915–1920,* ed. Hazel King (Melbourne: Melbourne University Press, 1986), 58–61. By permission of Hazel King.

✞ Maria Luisa Perduca
(1896–1966) *Italian*

Born in Pavia, Maria Luisa Perduca lived a life dedicated to the service of others. Fluent in several languages, she was a teacher of French by profession. From 1915 to 1918 she volunteered as a nurse in base and field hospitals in the war zone, an experience she described in *Un anno d'ospedale* (A hospital year, 1917). For her service she was awarded the silver Medal of Merit of the Red Cross (1917), and the Medal of Public Welfare (1922). In 1914 she addressed an article to "the province of Pavia," urging women to assume patriotic tasks. Other wartime pieces included a set of lectures on art and war, "Il gran cimento" (The great trial, 1916). Perduca also edited the letters left by a friend, nurse Maria Cozzi, who died in France a few days following the Armistice.

After the war Perduca gave time to pacifist religious organizations. The savory dialect and spontaneous spirit of her beloved Pavia, where she founded a Red Cross division, were the subject of another book. Mobilized again in World War II, she worked especially with soldiers suffering from tuberculosis or from mutilations; for this service she was given a field medal and the Red Cross bronze Medal of Merit (1950). At the end of the war she worked with the resistance. She won numerous other medals, including the Red Cross gold Medal of Merit (1953).

✞ The Vigil

And I remain alone, to keep vigil.

The first vigil in the milky half-light of the silent wards, of the very white rooms, is somehow mysterious and sacred, it frightens me.

It is the first time that I leave my mother, my home, that I live one night so alone with my duty and with my youth.

The veiled lamps let slope a poor light, the small Christ nailed on the black cross casts a shadow on the immaculate wall. There is a great calm on all things, lethargy.

The military guard, tired, now and again falls asleep on the bench; the entire hospital is silent, immobile.

I feel as though I have been immersed in the limpidness of an Alpine lake of pure vein and now leave it to walk alone, all white, on great layers of intact snow, where my steps leave no trace. . . .

From the atrium I can hear the echo of the large antique clock: a dream, a mystery, something invisible and unattainable, the quiver of all the remote and very faraway hours that it has marked.

A bouquet of violet fuschias dies at the bottom of a cup, slowly; Luigi, the small gunner, calls me, wants milk, I bring it to him, he drinks, falls asleep again.

I go back to my post, under the veiled lamp; again a great silence. . . .

Outside in the night, strange voices waver, indistinct ones, like fleeting gasps, the breathing of leaves, the fluttering of wings; the whimpering of a dog, the screeching of wheels.

Inside, the thinned faces, the sunken eyes eroded by pain become youthfully sweet during sleep.

The untiring pioneers sleep, those who loaded the cannon, who cut the barbed wire, who moved cautiously up the cliff to attack, who pushed the tanks along the mined bridges of the roaring Isonzo, who made firm the new paths of Italy on the granite of the Alps.

They sleep, their unwearying arms flaunt the peace of their hardworking muscles, their skin raised by large veins, and from their chests seems to spring the vast breath of the Italic race = ΙΤΑΛΟΣ.

In the infinite quiet of the great starry night, I hear the vast and equal breathing, like the puffing of the sea, and the pulsating of the stars.

And it seems to me that in this vigil, something of my soul dies, and something is resurrected, purer; perhaps faith, or an infinite desire for good . . . something that I did not know.

Outside, in the garden, the leaves of the trees shiver vaguely; the sky curves splendid, immense, mysterious, like infinity, in which all of our miserable human thought sinks, fascinated and conquered.

It is the great calm, in which every brutality dies, sensitivity is refined. . . .

A weak lament, an uncertain hand stretched out, as if searching, as if asking; it is Davide the Martyr, his body covered with sores from sternum to malleoli.

—Davide . . .

—Sister, stay here, nearby, the pain seems to go away.

And I remain.

I have no other remedy, only my pity, my hands outstretched, and words that I again utter poorly:

—It will end, Davide, you will see. . . . I am here with you, I suffer with you for your suffering.

His eyes filled with savage grief, almost nostalgia, eyes that remind one of an imprisoned wild beast, thank me, suddenly very sweet.

In the garden throats of invisible insects seem to cast the night blinking with stars an unending anguished question, one that has no answer.

July 1915

Translated by Sylvia Notini

"La Veglia," in *Un anno d'ospedale (giugno 1915–novembre 1916): Note di un' infermiera* (Milan: Fratelli Treves, 1917), 9–12

✝ An Amputation

This too; after all the horrors that have torn our souls, that have sunken us in a mute, sour anguish, one that stupefies us.

Angelo, brother, poor foot-soldier from the Marche region, your face thin, your eyes sad as though you could foresee the end; these words are for you, they are like the flowers that I send to your tomb.

He had come here from another hospital, accompanied by his father, who had always taken care of him after he was wounded; not for love, but so that the military mess would remember to nourish him.

His knee had been shattered by a grenade; was it a knee or was it a shapeless mass of bleeding ground flesh, from which greenish pus ran? No one could look at it for long.

Every attempt was made to save him from amputation; but all failed. One evening the surgeon asked us to make a decision.

Nothing could be more difficult or more painful than this, to persuade a creature of twenty to either die or be deformed for the rest of his life.

None of us had the courage, none of us knew how to find the proper words; but the matron and chaplain gradually convinced him.

He let them speak looking at us sadly, as though thinking:

—Yes, go ahead, I'm going to die anyway.

The next morning, before the operation, we found him calmly chatting with his family; two obtuse laborers who seemed not to understand, not to hear, confused by their bestial daily existence.

The operating room was ready.

Around the glazed iron bed stirred the white garments of the surgeon, his assistant and the matron all busily occupied with sterilizing.

On the tables the scalpels, the gouges, the tubes, the scissors, the needles for stitching, the bobbins of silk and rubber all gleamed; the corporal nurse had sharpened the knives and the saws.

Two soldiers carried him away from his room; he glanced at his mother once more, touched her hand, then sank on their powerful shoulders.

They placed him on the bed, he trembled like a leaf calling us softly:
—Stay near me, stay near me.
He desperately grabbed at my arms.
—Yes, dear, yes, I'm here, Angelo.

The assistant put the mask in place and let a few drops of chloroform fall.
His hollow torso rose and fell quickly; they held his wrist, his arteries pulsed dizzily.
He breathed with difficulty, his pupils began to shrink.
He fell asleep.
Only the very center of his brain continued to work; the man vegetated, lived mechanically, insensitive; it was nearly death.
In his narcotic sleep he seemed to complain gasping incomprehensibly; every now and then I would look at the orb of his inert eyes.

The surgeon examined the horrible knee, pierced here and there by tubes. He removed them one by one; he asked that a tourniquet be applied to the thigh, washed his hands once again, picked up the amputating knife, and began to mark a circle in the nude flesh as far as the femur.
The blood gushed from the cut vessels; he dried; he stopped again, put down the amputating knife; the matron handed him the saw, he grasped it ordering that I inject the patient with morphine. He placed the tool between the torn limbs and began to saw.
A long creak, a blunt blow, it was over.
That instant penetrated us, our brains, our nerves, our flesh, our spirits, and did not abandon us for many days.
The leg fell by sheer force into the basin placed below, like an object that was dead, finished.
A soldier wrapped it in a wax sheet and took it away; and by a strange contrast, we felt as though something alive were being taken away, a person.

The stump resembled the trunk of a tree that had been sawn, within which we could see the nerves and the white circle of the marrow. The flaps of the skin were stretched to cover the red of the flesh and the white of the bone; the matron handed over the curved and threaded needles, the surgeon stitched.

Angelo continued to sleep, unconscious.
The assistant removed the mask. His pupils enlarged gradually; as soon

as he was in his warm bed, surrounded by the affectionate eyes of his companions, he woke up, looked at us and smiled. He could not remember.

—I'm fine—he said.

We had to look the other way to hide our faces.

February 1916

Translated by Sylvia Notini

"Un'amputazione," in *Un anno d'ospedale (giugno 1915–novembre 1916): Note di un' infermiera* (Milan: Fratelli Treves, 1917), 54–57.

✝ Margarete Kühnhold
German

As a nursing sister with the German Women's Red Cross for the Colonies, Grete Kühnhold worked before the war in Tanga and Dar es Salaam in East Africa during two outbreaks of malaria. In late 1913 she went to up-country Cameroon to combat sleeping sickness. Her memoir, *In Friedens- und Kriegszeiten in Kamerun* (In peace and wartime in Cameroon, 1917), depicts the Douala and other tribal groups she encountered as treacherous, resistant to hygienic resettlement programs, and even cannibalistic. When war broke out she left Kumbe in the highlands, where nearly half the population were ill, and moved her clinic to a series of new locations: Carnot, Yaoundé, and Eseka, a settlement beside the railroad halfway between Yaoundé and Edéa. In the end, she was obliged to leave with a group of sick and pregnant white women for Ebolowa in the south; they crossed the Spanish border to Bata and eventually sailed to Germany. Through the lens of her own expectations and needs, she depicts a devastated land whose inhabitants have few provisions to spare for the passing Europeans and who melt into the forest to escape forced labor as carriers.

✝ Work in a War Hospital

In early January 1915, I was suddenly sent to the Eseka military hospital beside the midland railroad. During an attack on Edéa, on the Sanaga river, strongly defended by the French, our troops had suffered severe losses, and the European and colored wounded had all been brought to this hospital.

 After two hours in the Governor's car I reached Ngoumou, which would have been one and a half to two days' march southwest from Yaoundé. On the highway to the coastal town of Kribi, a gigantic tree trunk fallen across the road sufficed to create a half hour stop. The inhabitants of the next village when called upon zealously rushed to remove the obstacle that had lain there for fourteen days. Country place: disgrace. Such obstacles to traffic did not bother the locals in the least.

Besides my cot, a trunk, and my houseboy I could not take anything in the car; with just a few carriers, an hour later I set off on a forced march, always following the rail lines through empty bush and extensive farms of plants, cassava and maccoboy. Toward evening I reached a so-called telephone post, whose inhabitant welcomed me in his bush hut and gave me a room to sleep in. The next morning he accompanied me a stretch, since my people were unfamiliar with this deserted region. And he did well: in the afternoon as luck would have it they went astray, and only after a long search back and forth, uphill and down, along narrow paths in thick bush without any view did I catch sight below me of the railway and a few Europeans. Through their friendliness I soon found an empty house in which I could have my bed set up. The next morning I could happily continue my trip with a train ordered by phone and arrived after a six-hour journey through the romantic mountains at Njok, my goal. I traveled in an open goods car, which had the advantage of allowing an unimpeded view, at times deep into the valley, at times up to heights covered with thick primeval forest, but which offered no protection from sunburn or the wind.

In the middle of the forest, halfway between Edéa and Yaoundé, lay the hospital, set up for war. A "bamboo" house with walls of palm-ribs was hung with wool blankets to ward off the continuous drafts. The wounded and invalids lay in primitive field beds. A small open room was the isolation ward, in which lay a serious typhus case, a young sailor who had been on a delta steamer at Lagos when war broke out. After England declared war the steamer with others had taken refuge in Douala and later was sunk there. Like many other sailors, this man had salvaged only what he wore on his back.

A small path led from this room to our more than primitive shelter. Corrugated sheet iron surrounded a small square, roofed with mats weak from age and black with smoke, which had once covered the workers' huts. A corner of the small walkway, called a veranda, was our dining room, but was useful only on days free of tornadoes. The whole rested on shaky posts, with an equally shaky step.

The less sick were housed in bush huts and tents erected on both sides of the main building. The compound was surrounded by thick jungle, from which rang a concert of every kind of animal cry at night. Lovely by bright sunshine, all the gloomier on rainy days when a heavy damp settled over everything, and thick dripping fog hung in the trees, erased every outline and painted everything gray on gray. Charming in the bright moonshine or in the dark evening, when countless glowworms lit up in the thicket of leaves.

Sighing, Sister Maria, who had been here since the end of October, recounted the great difficulties caused by the care of the invalids, whose numbers had grown so suddenly. Nothing could be had in this empty region. There were no fresh fruits, no vegetables, neither eggs nor chicken nor meat. Always rice and tinned meat? For the sick, to boot?— Could that not be changed?—Thank God, it could be changed. Fourteen days later the first caravan of supplies arrived from Yaoundé, followed each week by another. So we regularly received eggs, chickens, fresh fruit, a few goats and sheep, as well as potatoes, maccoboy or cassava, secured by friendly Sister Luise for us with great expense of time and patience in Yaoundé and the surrounding area; naturally, commissioned by the government.—And even a few bottles of wine came for the severely ill and to celebrate the Kaiser's birthday, saved for such occasions. The Europeans slowly recovered from their wounds; many of the colored soldiers suffered from them longer. The others patiently bore their fate; only all were troubled that the attack on Edéa had been unsuccessful.

In February suddenly a rumor arose that German war boats lay before Douala. Some said they had heard heavy artillery fire, a thousand speculations circulated. Unfortunately the rumor did not prove true. How could help come from outside?—From Bata in Spanish Río Muni war news occasionally arrived giving the British side—but it usually did not correspond to the truth. They could not shake our faith.

After relatively calm weeks in March battles broke out again along the Yaoundé-Edéa road. The enemy had received reinforcements and advanced with these fresh troops to the railway line at kilometer 120 by So Dibanga, and also to the so-called new Yaoundé road. After weeks of battles our hospital received in mid-April the order to break camp and retreat to Yaoundé. We packed with heavy hearts: in spite of all difficulties and discomforts, our work site had become dear to us. We were downcast that we had to leave our farms carefully established in preparation for protracted war. On the morning of April 17 a train stood ready, whose open goods cars accommodated as well as possible the sick with all their possessions, the scanty hospital inventory, and ourselves. Already the day before almost everything in Eseka had been transported, including the command and commissary.

Around ten o'clock our train was ready to leave. Above on the loaded railcars sat and lay the sick colored men, our orderlies, and house boys. Up to kilometer 198 we managed without any incident, if slowly, in about three and a half hours. Here the first surprise awaited us. The crates with the food prepared for our sick were apparently in the bottom of the railcars, impossible to reach them. We were in a pinch. Everyone was hungry and thirsty as well. In this stretch of land however there was nothing, not even a few papaya or bananas. Finally a few tins of meat and vegetables that should have been kept as iron rations for yet harder times turned up, were warmed over three stones with a quick fire, and divided evenly among the Europeans. At six we should arrive at the day's goal, Mangele.

With fresh strength the journey continued at three o'clock. After five minutes the first stop—a few natives jumped off, quickly gathered some wood lying around, jumped back on, and it continued—for a minute. Then again a stop, search for wood, and after a short stretch the same theater. In response to outraged cries, the locomotive engineer explained he had forgotten to bring coal and the wood was not worth much. What should we do? Even the sick were full of humor in this plight; as soon as the train stopped they called on all sides, "Firewood!" and the natives sprang off to gather firewood. In the evening at eight, after five hours of vexation we finally reached kilometer 207, having made a trip of nine kilometers in no less than five hours.

And now our somewhat original engineer suddenly left with the locomotive, calmly leaving the train standing on an open stretch. Luckily it wasn't raining; it had been dark since six. Now even the patient staff doctor felt that it was too dumb. A few of the less sick offered to go to Mangele for another locomotive, which then luckily arrived around midnight and in another two hours of nocturnal journey through the jungle brought us to our goal. About three o'clock finally all the hungry stomachs were satisfied and the sick brought into a spacious supply room, so far as possible. We two sisters had our tent beds set up in an open goods wagon, in the hope that Jupiter Pluvius would spare us. For two hours we slept in our clothes, wonderfully. Shortly thereafter the trip began again to the railhead and from there another few kilometers on foot, up the mountain to the railway hospital at kilometer 218. In the evening we learned that the radio tower we had seen the day before high above us had been blown up by our side. The young official who had worked there was brought to the hospital with a bad case of malaria.

For our sick there was a day of rest, much needed after the adventurous railway travel, then the journey through the bush began.

The almost endless caravan moved slowly forward; besides the Europeans there were more than forty colored invalids in hammock-slings. Those who were convalescent or slightly sick went on foot. In the villages where we rested, first the severely ill were housed in the cleanest of the native huts, tents were put up, beds set up, the kitchen too in a hut, water and firewood brought by the carriers and coffee quickly made, that is, war-coffee made of burnt maize or soybean grounds. By the second day bread could no longer be baked since there was no flour. The regular caravan of provision from Yaoundé arrived the first day of our march, just in time to banish the worst concerns about food.

Since we traveled with so-called construction porters, there were many unaccustomed difficulties, difficulties that I had not encountered on my previous journeys with carriers provided by the government. Just to set up a tent cost unsuspected trouble and happened only with strictest supervision, for better or worse under one's own eyes. The same was true of fetching wood and water. If unexpectedly a tornado blew up, then little was to be done. You were in the soup. As usual, from time to time a carrier took off, leaving us the problem of transporting the burden further.

On the second day we met "Schlosser" Company, which had been sent a few weeks earlier to reinforce an endangered point in the Southeast, but while en route had been ordered back to the Yaoundé-Edéa road, where the enemy was making a major effort to reach Yaoundé.

On the sixth day of our trip through the bush Yaoundé lay before us, and we reached the city around midday. Some of our invalids found shelter in the infirmary, some in town; the colored men went to the hospital for natives. I returned to my earlier cubbyhole, since our military hospital was dissolved; Sister Maria went to an even more primitive one. But the peace would not last long.

"Arbeit in einem Kriegslazarett," in *In Friedens- und Kriegszeiten in Kamerun* (Berlin: August Scherl, 1917), 24–29.

✠ Käthe Russner
(b. 1892) *German*

Born in Chemnitz, Germany, Käthe Russner trained as a surgical sister with the Red Cross and served on the western front. She combined her letters to her father with diary entries in a memoir, *Schwesterndienst im Weltkriege: Feldpostbriefe und Tagebuchblätter* (Nursing in the Great War: Field letters and diary pages, 1936). Faced with a room packed with wounded, dying "like animals," she lamented: "But think of all the youth, the blooming youth and powerful manliness that lies here destroyed. Father, Father, can this truly be the will of God?"

✠ Diary Pages and a Field Letter

October 9, 1918

Today, Germany allegedly made a peace offer; it will surrender Belgium and Alsace-Lorraine. The Alsatian nurse who is now sharing a room with me and nurse J.G. wept bitterly at the thought of becoming French. J. and I ran to the railway station in hope of hearing some new reports. This uncertainty about the way things are brewing is almost unbearable. There were no new telegrams but we arrived just as a hospital train was being unloaded. A stretcher with a corpse was also laid on the platform. It lay there a long, long while before anyone had time to see to it. The living have priority! On the way back we picked up a few men with minor injuries who were walking around, searching for their assigned hospital. We showed them the way and took their heavy luggage from them. They looked pale and exhausted. When a railway official on the other side of the street saw our little troop, he came over and took the rest of their baggage.

In the meantime the first admissions have arrived at our hospital. The room intended for the Reception is far too small. The great entrance hall of the industrial school is already full: stretcher after stretcher crammed side by side. They wait to be deloused, bathed, and transferred to beds. Pale, haggard faces with hollow, feverish eyes. When they spot us, there are beseeching cries from all sides: "A drink, nurse, a drink!" We can barely fill the beakers and pass along the rows fast enough, so parched are their burning lips. And lots and lots of grateful looks and many a "thousand, thousand thanks" repay a little drop of water.

October 10, 1918

Ten o'clock and I'm dog tired! I have such a headache, I think my skull will explode; but I must stay awake. My two roommates, who have been ill for a few days now, are both lying in hot packs and I still have to change them. Just so long as I do not have to take to my bed—so many nurses are seriously ill with influenza at present. I am sure I have only a touch of tonsillitis with fever. With plenty of aspirin and Pyramidon I should be able to stay on my feet, albeit with difficulty.

Since the sixth, perpetual transports, all seriously or fatally wounded. The worst, mainly head wounds, are brought to the smaller rooms on the second floor, the others to the large hall where we have about ten nurses. We take charge of them here, after they have been deloused and their wounds redressed in the treatment room. Five to six hundred in one hall in which there is of course never a moment's peace. And yet they are still so patient and grateful.

Oh God! What misery, what wretchedness we witness here.

Sister J. came along, very distraught. She received a telegram; her sister has suddenly died of influenza, so she travels home tonight.

God, my God. How I am seized by fear for my loved ones!

October 11, 1918

My dear Father,

I must write you a few lines, even though we have our hands completely full and I could drop with weariness. But I'd like to thank you for writing to me so regularly. Longingly I await your Sunday letters and would be bitterly disappointed if one did not arrive.

I can understand only too well how strongly you feel about the fate of our fatherland. It weighs on us too, like a ton. Only our charges, in their awful agony and in recollection of those horrors they left behind, which probably none of us can imagine, yearn for just one thing, peace, peace at home. Why, then, the sacrifice of all these lives? Thinking about it could drive one insane. Will posterity find an answer?

Posterity? I believe it will be completely unable to gauge the unspeakable suffering this war has brought. It will lead its own life, it will pass by without noticing those who became cripples in their prime, it will pass by without noticing those thousands of women whose lives from now on are filled with loneliness. World history will roll on.

And yet one thing we may not and must not forget: Germany is not yet a heap of rubble; German men and women must not yet work for the enemy. What that means we see here with our own eyes; or rather we can only suspect but cannot fathom it in all its harshness and tragedy. And that it has not yet come that far for us, we thank those who, in pain and agony, groan here that it is deplorable. Yesterday a parcel for our charges arrived from schoolgirls in Dresden, arranged through one of our nurses on leave. Little bags with five cigarettes or candies or the like, and most important, a charming little letter for each. For example, one wrote at the end, "You must not address me formally as 'Sie' when you write to me, because I am only eleven years old." You have no idea what joy this parcel brought. Not everyone by any means could receive something— every tenth man at best—but the little letters were passed around and faces brightened for a few hours. Indeed, it is truly startling how grateful the people are for the slightest relief from their lot, so grateful that one is ashamed. For what is it that we can do for them? Give them a little light and love and sunshine. What is that in comparison to what they have done for us, what they have surrendered in youth, strength, and future in order to protect us against the enemy? That we can never, never repay.

Is it not so, Father? And is it not terrible that there are so many now who have completely forgotten or else never fully grasped its magnitude? The poor fellows are immeasurably embittered by this. An N.C.O. from Baden, one of my charges, a profound and tender soul, tells me that people sometimes avoid soldiers on leave at home, or even mock them for "shirking their duties," etc. It is painful to hear and there are no words of comfort. I could only give him my hand—with tears in my eyes, I assure you—and say, "D., there are still those who know they have much to thank you for."

And now I have to ask you a huge favor. Recruit some friends and relatives for a collection of alms. If each contributes just a small trifle and a kind word—a little can amount to a great deal! Tell them how bitterness gnaws at them all; how it makes them incapable of further sacrifice. Tell them how, even in feverish dreams, the thought of "Germany, home" pursues them; how responsive they are to an encouraging line from home. Tell them that, were it not for these fine, brave men, we would have a pile of rubble for a homeland and would have to serve the enemy.

Oh, if you were to see them here in their hundreds and thousands, young, once sturdy, merry fellows who now lie there as helpless as little children, who for weeks and months are unable to move one centimeter by themselves, for whom day after day, endless sleepless nights, week after week passes with grim and wretched thoughts about their future and that of their family. If you were to see them in their agony, if you heard the groans and lamentations that do not cease day or night, you would find the words to soften the coldest and most stubborn heart and to stir the indifferent.

October 12, 1918

When I walked into the hall this morning and was about to begin the daily chores, I heard somewhere above me a cry of despair, "Nurse! Nurse!" And again, penetrating the marrow, "Sister! Sister!" I rushed to the second floor but it did not come from there. So on to the third floor, which had been unoccupied until now. I flung open a door from behind which the cries seemed to be coming and stood rooted to the spot. A large room full of severely injured men—shot in the head, in the stomach, in the thigh, or suffering from pneumonia. Not one of them could move, many were unconscious. They had arrived during the night and had been brought up there because there was no way the Reception could hold so many new admissions, and no one on day duty knew about it. They had not been given drinks or any other assistance. It was a heartbreaking scene, and they cried, no, they bawled at me, "We cannot die here like animals."

But think of all the youth, the blooming youth and powerful manliness that lies here destroyed. Father, Father, can this truly be the will of God?

1918

Translated by Trudi Nicholas

From *Schwesterndienst im Weltkriege: Feldpostbriefe und Tagebuchblätter* (Leipzig; Breitkopf & Härtel, 1936), 98–102. Copyright © 1936 by Breitkopf & Härtel, Wiesbaden.

✝ Madeleine Clemenceau Jacquemaire
(1870–1949) *French*

D aughter of Georges Clemenceau, the doctor turned politician, the tall and svelte Madeleine was considered a brilliant catch when in 1889 she married a rich lawyer twenty years older, Numa Jacquemaire. Her husband died in 1902, rumored to have committed suicide after discovering her in bed with a lover. She moved in political circles and entertained literary figures like Marcel Proust in her salon.

Jacquemaire recorded her work with the Red Cross during the war in *Hommes de bonne volonté* (1919). After the war she published biographies of Mme Roland (1926) and Louis XIV (1946). Her articles appeared in *Figaro* and *L'Illustration*. Her sketches about French culture, *French Country Life*, were translated in 1928. She also wrote several novels, including *Monime* (1935), a roman à clef.

✝ Returns

As soon as night falls on a sky studded with stars, the projectors light up on all sides like an aurora borealis, bluish cones, luminous bundles. All types of flares shoot up from the lines with a slow grace until they shatter in a rain of stars and the flashing "finishers" spread out along the soil their crafty gleams.

On the right in the distance a conflagration blazes.

In the nurses' barrack all is silent. Madame Berton, head nurse, stands guard tonight with Madame Jallin, Mademoiselle Mignet and Mademoiselle Larrouy. Spread out on their cots, they await the arrival of the first ambulances. They are tired, aching all over, with burning feet. The field hospital had to be set up in mid battle. They haven't rested by day or by night. Some have not had leave for seven months, and tonight more than one overworked brain has the blues. They think:

"Always the same terrible thing, the arrival of the severely wounded! They come in quivering in the middle of buckets of hot water, uniforms drenched in blood that have to be cut off the body, shoes full of mud, while the mugs, the helmets full of holes and camouflaged in mire, drag on the ground with the disemboweled haversacks. . . . Ah! when will it be over, can the victory be fine enough to console us for what we shall have seen?"

It is very cold. The month of April has been glacial. Rats carry on a hollow din under the beds and eat the underside of the flooring. The sick bitch Nikè gives a plaintive bark occasionally. The record player, joy of the wounded, broke today. The flowers are frozen, the potatoes undercooked. Few letters arrive, no packages at all. Impossible to get clean clothes. The orderly Sauvage left to join the divisional stretcher bearers, and his replacement, Barbier, has a stupid air, in spite of a ravishing lock of hair curled in three waves (three times around itself!) in the middle of his forehead. It is 9 o'clock. The wind whistles between the barracks. Military cars pass in the distance. The cannon makes everything tremble. Someone knocks on the window pane. It is the mobilised washerwoman who has come to give unintelligible explanations for the delay in delivering the laundry. The truth is that she washes clothes for the Americans in secret and no longer has time to do her work for us. She talks about coal, the weather, "Monsieur the Officer," and the laundryman who apparently said to her,

—If you want to amuse yourself with me, my wife won't know about it.

—Then I gave a good answer, she said in a great burst of indignation. Imagine, a man forty-one years old!

But a brusque hand knocks outside on the door and opens it immediately. A voice vibrates in the night and announces in an oddly questioning tone:

—The returns[1] are here.

—The returns are here, repeat voices echoing each other. In a second the four women are up, together on the threshold and adjusting their capes.

—Don't forget your flashlights, recommends Madame Berton, and the little group hastily moves off, avoiding the puddles to paddle in mud, since the duckboards built for the men's large feet are impractical for them, especially at night. All have pulled themselves together and go briskly to the work that waits, the good work, the saving work.

"Rentrants," *L'Illustration*, March 29, 1919, 350–53.

---

1. (*Rentrants*) No one knows why this terrible French grammar has become commonplace in field hospitals, but so it is. [M.C.J.]

✛ Maria Naepflin
(b. 1894) *Swiss*

A Swiss nurse who volunteered with the Austro-Hungarian forces during the war, Maria Naepflin served in hospital trains and in field stations in Poland, Serbia, and Romania in 1914–15. For her work as a volunteer in a cholera unit, she was given a Red Cross silver Medal of Merit. When she fell ill and became depressed in early 1916, she sought relief in morphine, to which she became addicted. Her memoir *Fortgerungen, durchgedrungen bis zum Kleinod hin* (Wrenched forth, pierced to the core, 1922) recounts that she was assigned not only to hospitals in Bulgaria, Turkey, Croatia, Trieste, and Vienna, but also to trains on which she chaperoned prostitutes on their rotation from a Viennese military brothel to one in the Tirol. The number of the wounded was so great, she writes, that hospitals were staffed with volunteers, while professional nurses like herself shuttled in converted freight trains between field hospitals and the rear: "These transports proved how worthless a spent human life is to Moloch Militarism." Upon being wounded herself, she had a nervous breakdown; she was also drawn into a spy affair and put on trial. After the war she married an Austrian; they had a daughter who died young. In the 1930s, when she and her husband became Fascists, they were driven from Austria. Her 1922 memoir was at first popular in Germany, but then banned by Goebbels as "pacifist," and she was imprisoned in Dachau before her escape to Switzerland. Her second memoir, *Heimatlos, staatenlos* (Homeless, stateless, 1946), describes these crises, in particular her efforts to regain Swiss citizenship, as she was pushed across frontiers as a stateless person by the Austrians, Germans, Swiss, and French.

✝ Hospital Train

Peace and quiet were at an end. For internal hospital service, voluntary attendants were brought in beside qualified theater nurses, while professional nurses were assigned to transporting the wounded. Some nurses saw to the transport of convalescents to the hinterland. I was assigned to the frontline of Bielitz-Cracow-Tarnow, a position of trust, for the transfer of seriously wounded from field hospitals at the front to the nearest permanent hospital was a great responsibility, a task fraught with difficulty.

The wounded were at the most painful stage: after a provisional operation and bandaging at the field hospital, racked with fever, lying between life and death with nothing to relieve the pain, no peace—oh, the painful cries of these poor men cut to the quick! It took strong nerves, cold blood, and yet real compassion to care for these poor creatures and make their lot a little easier.

These transports proved how worthless a spent human life is to Moloch Militarism. Trains for the wounded were for the most part composed of freight cars in which the wounded were placed on stretchers or else laid down on straw. Hospital trains were already a rarity. In the hierarchy of transportation our trains were ranked lowest. Wait! wait! we were told at every station. The tracks must be clear for trains carrying troops or munitions; that was the most common refrain. We used the many waiting periods to replace blood-sodden dressings, to feed the wounded, and to unload the dead, who would be buried by the railway crew of that particular town. Thus the three-hour stretch from Cracow to Bielitz often became an eight- or ten-hour journey. Arriving dog tired in Bielitz simply meant travelling on the next train back to Cracow to take over a new transport there. [. . .]

"Sanitätszug," from *Fortgerungen, durchgedrungen bis zum Kleinod hin* (Meiningen: Loeptien, 1922), 73–74, 99–102.

✝ Morphine

Already in Serbia I had realized that several doctors were morphine addicts, and even one of the most competent had that reputation. Since the poison relieves pain through sedation, I was surprised that doctors turned to it; a stimulant would be more desirable for their exhausting work. I could never convince myself to try it; basically it was a vice, so I left it alone.

When I came back to Vienna from Serbia ill, crushed, and broken, I recovered physically during the month's leave, but my mental depression remained. The best remedy was work. So I became a ward nurse under Nurse Superior Rosa. I could not have wished for anything better! I wanted to prove myself reliable and competent, a model nurse, so joyfully I put all my energy into my service. But my strength could no longer hold out; I had already drained it, and after many a hectic day I collapsed exhausted in the evening. Then I was overcome by the desire to try morphine, and now I was at the source; I had limited charge of a pharmacy, where there was morphine in powder and liquid forms. If only there were no supervision. Nurses had a somewhat freer hand with morphine powder; the substantial consumption would permit a small theft to go unnoticed, so I tried three to four powders a day. After a brief period of use, I was satisfied with my progress and especially with my improved state of mind. My heavy thoughts seemed blown away. But now I could not stop and I soothed my conscience with the thought that I too as a sick person had a right to treatment. Whether a conscientious doctor would have prescribed just this cure I leave for you to decide. So I helped myself, not aware that the effect of this poison diminishes when the body becomes accustomed to the dosage, so that an ever greater amount is necessary for it to take effect. I had to maintain alertness; otherwise I would have fallen back into a greater predicament, which could not be permitted. Therefore I took the only way out, doubling the dose. It worked wonders. My energy and desire to work revived. To myself I seemed younger, which wasn't a delusion or self-deception, since the doctor confirmed it. Sister Rosa admitted openly how glad she was that I had regained the courage to face life and that my performance was very satisfactory, so that even the chief doctor, very grudging with his praise, had expressed his appreciation to her. With that, my morphine addiction was sealed. There was no going back. [. . .]

The nursing profession requires much strength and inner security to cope with everything. While professional responsibilities were not easy, it was even harder to remain a respectable nurse. In my experience, most professional nurses were truly imbued with an honorable sense of duty and led an irreproachable life. Undeniably many a romantic attachment was also formed between nurses and officers or doctors, but most led to marriage, facilitated by the so-called "war wedding." But the female assistants, often a random assortment, were man-crazy adventuresses who degraded our profession with their shameful behavior and provided rich material for slander. One of the saddest developments in later war years was the continuous increase of these "pretties," breeding another enemy within our country. For the spread of venereal diseases accelerated at a horrifying rate and a considerable number of soldiers were disabled by this inner enemy. Already in Serbia I had observed that this promiscuity was due not only to silent tolerance by the military authorities but even to their protection. Recognized pleasure houses were a fixture at every stop along the rail lines, often with high attendance. These guesthouses and their inhabitants enjoyed plentiful care and most sufficient rations.

Invalids from these railstops already filled the hospitals and the destruction of manpower progressed inexorably. [. . .]

"Morphium," in *Fortgerungen, durchgedrungen bis zum Kleinod hin* (Meiningen: Loeptien, 1922), 113–15, 121–22.

☦ Fiasco

According to my instructions I was to travel from Vienna to Innsbruck with a transport train; I was not a little surprised when I was appointed escort to police over one hundred fallen girls. I was disgusted by these sick women, who strutted in their elegant dresses, believing that fur and silk could conceal their sick bodies from public eyes. Not ten girls among this vicious pack seriously repented or even regretted their moral fall. The others held lewd conversations and displayed a wantonness that betrayed their moral depravity. It was the oddest transport I accompanied during the course of the war. The front cars, naturally first class, sheltered the sinful goods confided to my care. The other twenty cars carried the saddest victims of war, invalids sent back as disabled to hospitals at home— Salzburg, the Tirol, and Vorarlberg. During the trip I spent time with these soldiers, whose cares and stories interested me more than the smutty conversation of the hussies . . . "To make us forget our hunger and filth, the military authorities offer us the dubious pleasure of squandering our remaining health with infected 'field mattresses.' "

Translated by Trudi Nicholas

"Fiasko," in *Fortgerungen, durchgedrungen bis zum Kleinod hin* (Meiningen: Loeptien, 1922), 192–95.

✝ Mary Britnieva
(b. 1894) *Russian*

Born to an aristocratic family in St. Petersburg and English on her mother's side, Mary Britnieva volunteered as a nurse on the southern Russian front during the war and received the medal of the Order of St. George. She married Dr. Alexander Britnieva, whom she met in her mobile medical unit; they had two children. After the revolution, she took her children to England, then returned to Russia to find her husband, only to learn after months of vain searching that the Bolsheviks had imprisoned and executed him. Rejoining her children, Britnieva became a teacher of languages in London.

✝ Sister Vera's Story

It was in 1916 that the Russian Red Cross applied for permission from the German authorities to send a mission consisting of a small medical staff to visit the prisoners of war camps in Germany and Austria. Sister Vera M., one of the outstanding nurses of our sisterhood, was chosen to accompany the Mission.

They could not have made a better choice: Sister Vera was not only one of our best nurses—she had a wonderful personality which made itself felt the moment one saw her. Tall and stately, she had a beautiful and typically Russian face which seemed to radiate kindness and sympathy, her manner was charming and simple, and she had a special way of speaking to the soldiers which at once endeared her to them—it was so obvious that she knew, understood and loved them with all her great heart. To me she always seemed to personify Russia itself—her looks, her manner, her speech were so typical of our country.

The consent of the German authorities having been obtained, the

members of the Mission left via Sweden and Denmark and were away for
several months.

When I next saw Sister Vera she had many interesting and moving stories to tell me, but one especially remained in my memory as an example
of quite outstanding idealism and devotion. I will try to write it down as I
heard it from her.

It happened in Galicia, in one of the small concentration camps visited
by the Mission. The prisoners—about fifty of them—were working in the
fields, and Sister Vera went out to them. There was a fallen tree lying by
the side of the field, and here they all collected around her, eager to see
and hear the "Sestritza" who had brought them tidings from their far-away
homes. First she said a few words to them, words of comfort and hope, and
then they asked her individual questions and handed her letters or asked
her to carry out various commissions. Afterwards, they sang Russian folk-
songs and finally they all prayed aloud and chanted parts of the beautiful
Orthodox Church service. It was evening, the sun was setting and its glowing rays bathed the quiet field, adding to the sense of peace and of beauty
that prayers and singing had evoked in the hearts of these poor outcasts.
The time came for Vera to return to headquarters and, one by one, the
men filed past to shake hands and to wish her godspeed. One of the men
stretched out a hand that was terribly mutilated—all the fingers were missing and only part of the thumb remained. "How did that happen," asked
Vera horrified, "was it a shell?" The man flushed and drew back shyly, hiding his hand behind his back. "No, it didn't happen at the front," he muttered and turned away. But Vera's interest was aroused and she repeated
her question. The man hung his head and stood silent—but here his companions broke in ". . . go on, tell the Sister, Petruha, there's nothing to be
ashamed of, tell her how it happened."

Vera had a good look at him. What she saw was a simple, homely and
good-natured peasant face with a reddish beard and kind, child-like grey
eyes. She drew him gently towards her, and sitting down on the tree trunk,
said encouragingly:

"Sit down next to me, Petruha, and tell me how it happened—I want
you to tell me yourself." Petruha smiled shyly and began his tale:

"You see, Sestritza, I was taken prisoner in East Prussia with several others and we were all put to work in a factory. I was made a stoker. All day
long I shovelled coal into a furnace with never a thought in my head: I was
unaccustomed to the work and my back and arms ached, but after a few
days, when I had got more used to things, my mind began to work again,
and suddenly I realized that I was doing wrong: 'Oh, God'—I thought in
terror—'here am I actually helping to make shells and bullets for the
enemy!—Shells and bullets destined to kill my own brothers, to kill our
brave allies whom we have promised to help. No, I must not do it. I must
not! I cannot be a traitor to them all—let them punish me, let them do
what they like to me, but I cannot lose my very soul.' And this thought,
constantly in mind, I had no peace that night, and the next morning,
when we were led down to the factory, I refused to work. I was led away and

they suspended me from a beam by my wrists, my toes just touching the ground. I hung like that for twelve hours and it was terribly painful. When they took me down, they put me in hospital, and I remained there for three weeks. At the end of that time I was pronounced well enough to resume work and they sent me back to the same factory. Once again they put me down to stoke the boilers and again I refused to work, it was the only way in which I could save myself from being a foul traitor, for now I realized more clearly than ever that every shovelful of coal put on by me helped to make that which meant death, yes, Sestritza, *death,* to my brothers. And I couldn't kill my own blood and flesh. They led me away and suspended me as before, but this time I hung for twenty-four hours. The blood rushed through my head, my ears felt as if they would burst and I bled by the nose—it was painful agony. . . . They took me to hospital again and I lay there for three months. But I recovered and I was taken back to the same factory. As I was being marched along the road, my soul was full of anguish and I prayed and prayed to the Lord to give me strength so that I should not give in, for I knew that if I did, my soul would perish—I would have sold it to the devil. But as we neared the gate, a terrible fear came over me—I knew too well what would happen when I refused to work: again they would hang me up by my wrists and probably add other punishments this time and I feared that I might not be able to bear it all, so I prayed to the Lord for help and that He might in His mercy show me some way out.

"When we entered the gate and were being marched across the yard, I suddenly saw something that shone brightly lying on a tree-stump that stood in the middle of the yard; after a few paces I saw that it was an axe, a beautiful new axe. There it lay reflecting the sunshine almost as a mirror would and, as this thought occurred to me, I suddenly seemed to feel that a voice inside of me had spoken to me pointing out the way. It was the answer to my prayer. God had had that axe put there to help me. I broke away from the line of prisoners and ran swiftly to the tree-stump, I made the sign of the cross and saying to myself: 'For Faith, Tsar and Country,' I seized the axe in one hand, and placing the other on the stump, with one blow I chopped off my fingers."

"Sister Vera's Story," in *One Woman's Story* (London: A. Barker, 1934), 45–48.

✠ Mercedes Astuto
Italian

The work of Mercedes Astuto, a writer of fiction for adults and children, is deeply marked by her Catholicism and nationalism. She published a "romance" and collections of novellas in the thirties and forties, including *La lettera a Mussolini* (The letter to Mussolini, 1938). *I vivi, diario di guerra* (The living, war diary, 1935), her diary about World War I, was printed by the Italian Ministry of War. A voluntary nurse with the Red Cross, she had served with two other women from her family in the surgical ambulance at Armata, an advance post that was exposed to enemy bombardment. All three women were awarded medals of honor. As the preface to her book states, she was decorated "with the blue of a Medal for Military Valor." In 1938 she wrote a spiritual guide for nurses, *L'infermiera cattolica nelle vie della carità. Appunti di formazione spirituale professionale* (The Catholic nurse in paths of charity).

✠ Hospital Train

November 1, ordered to leave. At midnight we are at the station of Portonaccio; the train, Red Cross XIV, is just passing through, coming from Naples. It is empty, moving back north to pick up the wounded.

We exchange consignments with our colleagues getting off and, right away, we deal with where we will stay, as we have nothing else to think about for now: two cabins with two beds each, one above and one below, like those on a ship. We prepare the beds; how difficult it is with these blankets that are too large and too heavy—they hang out everywhere! We get undressed and go to bed. Tu-tum, tu-tum, the train moves slowly, towards the war.

*   *   *

The first embarkation of the wounded. We move north with no destination. Between Florence and Bologna we make the beds with fresh-laundered linen. Each half-wagon has twelve stretchers supported by shelves, making just as many sleeping berths; halfway along the wagon, two washbasins; at the head and at the back, closets with linens and dishes for twenty-four; at the head of the wagon-wards the medication-wagon and pharmacy. I have two and a half wagons: sixty beds.

At night we move in the dark with the curtains drawn; in the morning we are up early. The "war zone" has a physiognomy all its own; we anxiously look for its typical aspects. We embark in Udine; crowded gray-green station, brilliant sun and heat of autumn that seems to make summer longer. The loading site is marked and we begin to work. There is some confusion at first, shouting from the Major and the Captain, inevitable events in the circumstances of life. . . . But then everything moves into place: one by one the beds are filled, the sacks prepared; each one ready on the corresponding bed, we help to undress the wounded and put their clothing in the sacks; then the sentinels take the sacks to the warehouse-wagon.

In the meantime the train has taken off again; barely glimpsed, the margin of the war is already out of sight! Temperatures are taken, diets are noted down, names are collected for the Information Office that carefully follows from afar the movements of the wounded.

Mealtime: each one has a cup, a spoon, and a glass; how difficult it is to distribute wine, milk, and soup as the train moves! Later, once again, temperatures, distribution of medicine, rations; then little by little they all fall asleep, tired, rocked by the train and by the tenuous light of the turquoise lamps, they sleep contentedly because the train moves south, towards the houses, away from the theater of war where their suffering began. . . . Even for those who cannot sleep for the pain, this night insomnia is comforted by the thought.

In Ferrara we unload a soldier who is too ill to continue the journey.

Food, temperatures, some medications, dressings, the soldiers, correspondence; there is always something to be done when we move southward. In Naples we let the wounded off. Each of us keeps records of the patients in her ward. The soldiers are all ready to sit on their beds, and those who move with uncertainty immediately get down; we unload the stretchers that hold the seriously ill. The train is again empty; the beds are unmade, the used linens collected and recorded for each ward. Then we are free until the evening.

Prisoners. In our last trip—our shift is about to end—we go to Cividale to load the train. Winter can be felt and the entire curtain of mountains is beautiful—names that the war has consecrated—dark violet and snow white on an even gray sky. We must load the prisoners, soldiers and six officers; the latter will be in my ward. One of these, a Hungarian, immediately tells me that during peacetime he had wanted to travel to Italy, and that the war is fulfilling this wish. . . .

An act of charity must be carried out, as soon as the train starts moving:

to put a father and son together, both of them wounded, badly, on the Sabotino river, not on the same day—they found each other in the hospital. The son is a volunteer, fifteen years old, a pleasant boy, open, lively, blond, who looks as if he should still be playing at war. We immediately become friends and he wants to show me a photograph, taken at home before leaving, his mother, father, and five children of which he is the oldest, dressed in a sailor suit with shorts. There is also another boy with a wounded foot, but he is really a child, a plump red peasant-child, the blond explains: "not soldier, work, work trench." No, this is certainly not a soldier. . . .

There is one who is very ill, his entire body broken, a leg, an arm, and he trembles like a leaf because of a fever that keeps rising. Why must he leave in these conditions? The shaking of the train must make him suffer atrociously and I can do nothing for him. He is a Romanian from Transylvania and he talks and talks, but no one can explain what he is saying; if he asks for something, I am certainly the last person on this earth who can help him. One of the six officers, the Hungarian, could perhaps help me and I ask permission of the lieutenant who commands the armed escort, to allow him to come next to the bed of the dying soldier. He explains that the soldier would like a boiled egg to eat and some wine. "But," he adds, "we need not take the whims of these people seriously. . . ." The soldier is given an egg and wine; how could I not answer such a modest request! And he continues to talk, he takes my hand, and throws off the blankets. In the same wagon, but at the other end, I find a Hungarian soldier with an amputated thigh, who can understand him a little. He is delirious; the infection poisons his blood and his brain: he wants to leave; where is the carriage and the horse? He wants to leave because they are expecting him at home. . . . The train stops at Cassino to unload him; it is inhumane to make him suffer any longer and not allow some tranquility to his agony. . . .

From Cividale to Salerno, three days of traveling. The armed escort changes four times; in one of the shifts, there are heavy artillery soldiers, territorial ones, huge soldiers with moustaches like Napoleonic *grognards*[1]; when I walk next to them—they do sentry duty at the head and at the back of every wagon with a Wetterly rifle and a bayonet set—I feel like a thin straw used to sip drinks. . . .

And even this long and difficult trip ends. It is raining in Salerno, when the column of wounded prisoners starts moving on foot under the rain. . . . Yesterday enemies: today brothers, together in their suffering.

Translated by Sylvia Notini

"Treno ospedale," in *I vivi, diario di guerra* (Rome: Ministero della Guerra, 1935), 15–18.

1. *Grognards:* footsoldiers.

✝ Louise Weiss
(1893–1983) *French*

A journalist, pacifist, and suffragist, Louise Weiss was the child of a conservative engineer and an anticlerical Dreyfusard mother. They moved to Paris in 1899, where Weiss enrolled at the Lycée Molière, an elite public school for girls. Under the influence of her mother and maternal grandfather, she developed a commitment to pacifism and leftist ideals—fighting in the schoolyard for her political views. Her father's disapproval of her studies, compounded by her university examiners' comment that she did not look like a woman teacher, made her insecure about her "feminine inadequacy." An excellent student, in July 1914 she was first in the national examination for the *aggrégation,* the qualifying certificate for teachers in secondary schools. When the war interrupted her education, she set up a convalescent home for wounded soldiers in Brittany.

With her father, Weiss began to coauthor a series of articles for an opposition paper, the *Radical,* which criticized governmental incompetence. "Inebriated" by journalism, she continued to write on her own, submitting propaganda pieces to the *Revue de Paris* about deportations of civilian populations in the occupied northern zone and about bestial conditions in soldiers' quarters. For *La vie féminine* she wrote the first report on the Italian experience of the war, and under the pseudonym Louis Le Franc produced a daily column, "C'est la guerre" (That's war), for the *Radical.* Briefly she wrote reports for a senator in the French legislature, until he was attacked by the right for relying on a woman for his information.

Politicized by her reporting, Weiss collaborated in procuring visas for Italian revolutionaries escaping to France; her relationship with a Czech nationalist inspired a series of impassioned articles on the war in Czechoslovakia. With the publicist Hyacinthe Philouze in 1917 she founded *L'Europe nouvelle,* a weekly review dedicated to democracy and self-determination. The review urged authorities "to improve the lot of indigenous peoples in the colonies; to accord women political status; to reevaluate in

terms other than of military betrayal the events tearing apart Russia; to
support democratic streams of thought in Germany; to understand the
nature of the upheavals in China; and finally, to organize a league of
nations." The issue dedicated to the Armistice called for a common market, an international monetary system, higher standards of living, and
greater international cultural exchange. The journal's sympathy for avant-
garde artists garnered the support of Picasso, Apollinaire, Jean Cocteau,
Matisse, and Dufy, among others.

In the interwar years Weiss continued as a journalist, writing not only
for her own review but also for other papers such as the *Manchester
Guardian*. A trip to Moscow in 1921 led to a series of articles based on
interviews with leaders such as Trotsky. An advocate of international arbitration, she conceived of a "science of peace," modeled from 1930 to 1936
by an "Ecole de la Paix" at the Sorbonne, a forum where European elites
could meet weekly for discussions across nationalist and party lines. Discouraged by the polarizing effects of the Depression and the rise of Hitler,
she sought comfort in a brief marriage to an architect. Weiss also turned
to the cause of women's rights, leading a feminist group, La Femme Nouvelle. Frenchwomen failed to win the vote in 1937, and the following year
were denied the right to do noncombatant military service. Offered a min-
isterial position in Léon Blum's Popular Front government, Weiss
declined, declaring, "I have struggled not for the sake of being nominated, but for the right to be elected."

During the last months of peace, while Weiss organized aid for refugees
from Eastern Europe, she fell in love with a man who was later killed at an
artillery post outside Paris in 1941. The German Occupation curtailed her
medical relief work and forced her into hiding. The failure of the League
of Nations embittered her, turning her toward a militant Western chau-
vinism; she supported French colonialism during the Algerian war. Finally,
in the 1960s, she embraced a Gaullist view of a unified Europe to contest
totalitarian ideologies, nationalism, and racialism. Elected to the first
European parliament in 1979, she devoted her final years to forging a
"European people." At her death she was honored as "the grandmother of
Europe."

JS

‡ The First Autumn

At nightfall on a rainy day, the station master at the little junction sent me
a message: "The wounded have arrived without warning. I'm waiting for
you. Hurry."

Just time to notify Madame Heurtel, some cousins, and Dr. Latty. I
arrived on the quai of the local. What a spectacle! Two dozen soldiers
flopped in the little hall, seated or lying down, with bristling cheeks, dull

eyes, their capes stained with blood and mud, bandages indistinguishable from their woollen clothing and their lumpy knapsacks. Among them some tattooed Moroccans and huge scarred Sénégalais. All were dead tired, either come straight from the trenches, or put on between Paris and Saint Brieuc after first aid, to clear out the flooded emergency posts. No N.C.O. No doctor. No nurses. Even less medicine.

Madame Heurtel exclaimed, "What a shame! Get in, my little boys. I'll lift you!"

With her herculean arms, she seized these warriors at once stiff and floppy as dolls stuffed with bran. Other cars suddenly appeared from farms that had somehow been warned and offered help. We transported all these men to La Vallée. The infantry, the Queen of Battles, seemed to me the Empress of Mud. In any case, I had no means to nurse Her. I was dismayed.

"Let's give them some café au lait," said one of my cousins.

"What if they have stomach wounds?"

"Let's ask."

Their fatigue was such they could not answer.

"And how shall we divide them?" asked another cousin.

"By wound or by fever," I suggested.

But this distinction turned out to be impossible.

"By color," said Delange, the mess cook. "You will see, it works fine."

The idea of gathering like unto like seemed wise. In a flash, Negroes and Moroccans were more or less undressed, more or less washed, more or less sated with warm milk and put to bed on the ground floor. When their temperatures had been taken, they plunged into a sleep against which finally they no longer needed to struggle. Then we took our other pensioners to the second story. Most could go up without help. One, however, could not climb the stairs. One of the local women took him by the armpits. I took his feet. He groaned. At the landing, I missed my footing. The chap slipped on to me. His pants split open and his penis, thwack! was crushed against my face.

"So you got your wounded men," mocked one of my brothers when I took my place at the family table.

Several hours supervising the railways in the company of the territorials had not stemmed his thirst for glory.

"Shut up," I told him. "Tomorrow morning you will come to the pharmacy with me to help carry the medicines we need."

When mobilised, the pharmacist of Portrieux had shut his shop. At dawn I hung on the bell of the good woman to whom he had left his keys. The old woman turned them over to me without any other formality. My younger brother raised the iron shutters. The electricity had been cut. We found ourselves in a pale world of pots, drawers, and bottles.

"Write," I told my brother. "I will dictate to you the list of what I'm taking."

Sniffing, feeling, weighing, deciphering, I filled our two wheelbarrows with bands, cotton, alcohol, ether, syrups, oxygenated water, aspirin, castor oil, camphor, assorted balms, vaseline, syringes, test tubes. These articles were not prepared as they are today, when pharmacists disdain prescriptions and sell ready-made drugs. I also confiscated an important quantity of iodine pills and even pastilles of licorice and jujubes. Then we pushed our wheelbarrows under the red eye of a dull sun striped by the branches of the apple trees. At the top of the first hill my load lost its balance. My liters of oxygenated water rolled on the pavement and broke into foam.

"Le premier automne" in *Mémoires d'une Européenne, 1893–1919* (Paris: Payot, 1968), 187–88.

HOME FRONT, WAR WORK

✛ Isabelle Rimbaud
(1860–1917) *French*

Isabelle and her sick husband, Pierre, were forced to leave their home at Roche near the Belgian frontier during the first weeks of the war. Before they left, she bade farewell to her "precious relics"—books in leather bindings, silver, and papers—hoping that if she left keys in their locks, less would be stolen or broken. They could take very little with them because of the swift German advance, but she was careful to preserve a portrait of her brother Arthur Rimbaud. As the French army retreated, the couple set out on roads choked by carts piled with heterogeneous articles, amid cows, soldiers, and other refugees on foot. The Rimbauds sought refuge in Rheims, but when they arrived, that city was already under siege. As she recorded in her diary, *Dans les remous de la bataille* (1917; *In the Whirlpool of War*, 1918), she witnessed the bombardment and was present during the notorious shelling by Germans of the city's historic churches after its defenders had already surrendered, perhaps as a result of broken communications.

✛ Diary Entry

Wednesday, September 16, [1914]

We go downstairs at about eight o'clock, heads aching and cheeks drawn. During breakfast we again discuss the subject of the forts holding out. Our good hostess persists, on the strength of some rumours, that a British naval gun will try conclusions with them to-day. As a matter of fact, nobody knows anything. Food is becoming scarcer and scarcer, and the farms on the southern outskirts of the town which the Germans did not pillage are now our only source of supplies.

The shells have not waited for eight o'clock to begin falling on the city. With clock-like regularity they burst more or less close to us every ten minutes. Now come four terrifying explosions, shorter intervals apart. Pierre, who was somewhere near at hand, returns and orders Nelly and me to get ready quickly to seek shelter in the fields beyond reach of the guns, as other people are doing.

While we dress Hélène we are told that the shells which just made such a din fell in the Square of Saint-Pierre, in the Rue Chabaud, and in other adjacent streets, killing and wounding many people. The inhabitants of the centre of the town pass in crowds, carrying provisions with them, and looking like people who have spent the night on their feet. Clad in wraps and handkerchiefs, they steer southwards; and we follow them.

After passing through the Paris gate and the avenue of the same name, I stop not far from the Muire bridge, hypnotised by reading the direction plate referring to the two roads to Paris—that *via* Soissons on the right, that *via* Dormans on the left. We may not take the Soissons road to-day, as it is guarded by the military, so we take the other. Here below us is a burnt farm, with only a barn and some blackened walls left. In front of us and on both sides of the gently-rising road is open country and a peaceful stretch of fields, vineyards, and woods.

We visit with interest the trenches in which the Germans defended themselves last Saturday. They are like ditches a yard wide and almost two yards deep, almost entirely covered by boards, doors, shutters, even furniture, on the top of which were piled tufts of grass and beetroots—the better to hide them. In the mud and water at the bottom of these trenches lay a quantity of heterogeneous objects—chairs and, most common of all, empty bottles. When we were but a few feet from these military works we recognised that their positions had been selected skillfully; the French soldiers advancing on Reims could not see them until they were right on the top of them. People point out to us on the horizon Forts Montbré and Pompelle, recaptured from the Germans. To our left is the village of Meneux, whence Reims was bombarded on September 4. [. . .]

Far behind us shells are bursting pitilessly; thick clouds rise here and there, and the wind, which has risen a little, wafts the smell of fires to our noses. We reach the edge of a huge basin-like stubble-field, opposite which is a vineyard, and pass along a hedge at the side of the steep-banked railway from Epernay. This is where we will stop. "From this elevation," says Remy, "you can see the forts; and we shall be able to watch the fighting."

From the bank on the edge of the vineyard one commands the whole of Reims and an extremely extensive view beyond it. The splendid nave of the Cathedral and its towers, all rosy-red in the autumn sun, dominate the city, rise far above it, hover over it. Right and left of the pile and behind it fires are blazing; the glorious edifice, standing out against a background of variously coloured smoke, appears invulnerable. The conflagration to the right of it is so furious that at every instant mighty sheaves of flames pierce the smoke, writhe, tower upwards, and bend over as if they wish to devour the whole town. Shells are still raining on the city. You can see quite clearly the flash as they leave the gun, their flight through the air, and where they strike and raise a dirty black cloud of smoke. The noise of the burst does not reach us till some time afterwards, mingled with that of falling houses. At every shot one asks oneself sadly: "Did that kill anybody? How many homes has it wrecked? How many people has it made desolate?" You can conjure up the cries of the wounded, the trickling blood, the horribly mutilated bodies. . . . Remy names in turn the places from which these accursed engines of destruction are fired. Below, on the left, is Brimont fort, and next to it from left to right those of Fresnes, Vitry and Nogent. The villages seen near the fort bear the same names respectively. That of Brimont is ablaze; so are the others. On the slopes between Vitry and Nogent-l'Abbesse are the Cernay and Bearru woods, from which at short intervals rise the transient puffs of smoke from batteries in action.

What we can see is really the battle, the artillery battle. We do not see armies advancing, firing, charging, and engaging in straight lines, as engravings represent them; nor the famous squares, nor generals' waving plumes. The field of action is an absolute desert. Here and there, and especially in places where there is a fold in the ground, puffs of white or grey smoke rise and disperse; and one hears the now familiar roar of the guns—but that is all. Yet, thanks to this apparent nothingness, hundreds of our kin—and others—are being cut to pieces by steel. And something is happening in the sky as well. A swarm of aeroplanes is manœuvring to the roar of engines, gliding, swooping, cruising at a moderate height. Their varied hummings coalesce into a harmony like that of concerted organs and distant bells. From where we stand they seem to be just above the stubble, yet they cannot be so, and in truth are reconnoitring the positions of the armies. Continuously, differently coloured fires and smokes surround the planes. Are they signals or shrapnel? Sometimes one of the great birds swoops slowly round right overhead, and we feel ourselves under observation. The children then indulge in the game of running to hide themselves in the briers of the tall hedge that fences off the railway. We elders note the black iron crosses on the underside of the wings and fish-like tail of the monster, while we instinctively get away from a point exactly below its flight. It hovers a minute or so and then makes off.

The bombardment seems to die down at six o'clock. The dew has fallen, and it is cold. To reach the town by a short cut we go down into the hollow stubble-field, and when we reach the bottom of it terrifying shell explosions send us back post-haste to our original positions. Dusk is on us; night is closing in. More fires blaze up, while, yonder, the artillery duel continues. Amid the red, yellow and violet flashes on the horizon the Brimont furnace stands out like the maw of hell itself.

It is quite dark when we thread again the lanes of the Faubourg Sainte-Anne, in rear of the crowd. Citizens standing at their doors tell the passersby, in whispers, of houses gutted during the day; of people killed and wounded. As we pass through the row of poplars along the canal we see some engineers climbing among the branches of the trees, with rolls of wire round their bodies. Are they engaged on putting them up, or on preparations for departure? We ask them, but they return no answer.

From *In the Whirlpool of War,* trans. Archibald Williams (London: T. Fisher Unwin, 1918), 201–9.

✝ Zofia Nałkowska
(1884–1954) *Polish*

Daughter of a prominent Warsaw scholar and publicist, Wacław Nałkowski, Zofia Nałkowska was raised in the rarefied environment of the avant-garde and in her youth belonged to the Young Poland movement. She married Leon Rygier and later Jan Gorzechowski. Nałkowska began her literary career by publishing poetry in the modernist journal *Chimera*. The novel *Kobiety* (1906; *Women*, 1920) explored an intellectual woman's awakening; it was praised as "very unusual" but also criticized by Czesław Miłosz for its unrealistic aestheticism and "oversophistication." During the war, which she said taught her about human suffering, Nałkowska wrote short stories, *Tajemnica krwi* (The secret of blood, 1917). *Hrabia Emil* (Count Emil, 1920) showed war as "a terrible evil, regardless of what it is waged for."

During the interwar period, she was an active member of the Polish PEN club. She crafted a simple, lucid style in her later novels, including *Ściany świata* (Walls of the world, 1931). Her finest novel, *Granica* (The border, 1935), explores boundaries one cannot transgress without ceasing to be oneself. Named in 1937 as the first female member of the Polish Academy of Literature, Nałkowska reigned as patron of a popular literary salon and was responsible for the publication of Bruno Schulz's short stories. Her literary development can be viewed as an attempt to come to terms with political and historical upheavals in the first half of the twentieth century, with ever greater economy in representing "written reality."

At the end of the Second World War, she became a member of parliament and served on the International Commission for the Investigation of War Crimes. *Medaliony* (Medallions, 1946), a collection of short stories about the Holocaust, drew on eyewitness testimony with laconic power.

✝ Wartime Diaries

The Mountains, Górki, 2 ix 1914

Tales from Warsaw: thousands and thousands wounded. Yesterday, for the first time, official news of a significant defeat sustained here on the Kingdom's terrain. Now those who left for there not long ago are returning in droves. Now they are sick, exhausted to death by the transport, stripped naked, filthy, stinking, covered with lice, thirsty, even starving. Despite the mass mobilization of aid organizations, there aren't enough hands to dress the wounds, to operate (*sans* chloroform), to wash and to nurse. There is neither bedding nor linen.

I envy all those who can be there to help alleviate, at least in small measure, that uncontained, boundless evil. I stand before it with such stupid Suttner-pacifist thoughts,[1] an idiotic shiver of tearful, heart-rending empathy raking through me. Inconsolable is that useless toil of suffering, that senseless effort to go on, experience, and bear it all. Such collective suffering seems to me precisely an effort, an enormous labor, taken up for no purpose. How many people now cry or stop themselves from crying out, force themselves to endure the quick, painful medical care. How many, in the fog of fever, are caught off guard by approaching death. How many despair, grow angry. How many agonize. But then war is not qualitatively different from life. It is only a condensation of it, an acceleration of its evil, or even, just barely, the hint of a visual manifestation. I think that mines are like cemeteries, and factories like hell, that the dumb sorrow of peasants and the hospitals and insane asylums scattered over the earth belong to the same order, akin. War takes unto itself that which already lay in wait: savagery, misery, suffering, and death.[2]

The Germans are now throwing all their force from behind the Franco-Belgian border to the East—and thus we are lost. They are strong, fit, organized, perfectly suited to battle, full of hatred, meaning precisely that they have a warrior spirit. One wounded prisoner of war ordered a nurse who was caring for him, "Weg da, polnische Schwein!"[3] I think this is just how it should be when it's war. From the farther climes of the psychological partition of Poland: Włodzimierz Tetmajer, who organized the Austrian detachment of marksmen, took his own life at Jędrzejowy.[4] Eight hundred Poles from Austria reached France where they are to volunteer and form

---

1. Baroness Bertha von Suttner (1843–1914), née Kinsky, was an Austrian writer who won the Nobel Peace Prize in 1905 for her pacifism, including the widely read *Waffen nieder!* (1889). [D.K.]

2. This paragraph is reproduced in the story "Gloves," in *The Secret of Blood* (Warsaw, 1917 [1916]). [D.K.]

3. "Get away, Polish swine!" [D.K.]

4. Tetmajer did not commit suicide. [D.K.]

a new Polish legion.[5] Three prisoners in marksmen's uniforms were led through Warsaw streets yesterday amid the chicanery of the army, which was being hailed with flowers.

The Mountains, Górki, 7 ix 1914

The wondrous spring days, so crisp and sunny, are passing. Only that collective scream, reaching even this place from the passing trains, reminds us that a war is being fought. That scream and the newspapers which report just how close the siege of Paris is, that Halicz and Lwów have been captured by the Russian army, that Kalisz has been left barely standing. We are trying to figure out a way of getting to Warsaw. Because of the over-burdened transportation system, our stay here and ability to earn a living are fast proving impossible. In Warsaw, perhaps tutoring or some other work would allow us to get by. This last month, we have been managing without any help, and our first priority is to feed the dogs, chickens, ducks, and hogs. A girl, specially hired for the task, lugs the water. And of course all these tasks are discharged in scrupulously clean clothing and with the most aesthetic of gestures. If there is no change, after a couple of weeks of such frugality and self-denial, either hunger will come knocking on our door or we will be reduced to begging at the appropriate institution. I like such women's housework, though it tires me so physically, and I must watch as mother accomplishes so much more.

I like working and lounging in the hammock and reading and pondering things equally good and horrible. I like being alive. I am convinced that if I were not ill, I would be able to say to myself that I am truly happy. Watching the world from my hammock, the balcony, from various vantage points in the forest. Thinking, thinking, thinking—from morning, when I am so worn out and sleepy that it seems as though there had been no night at all, until evening, when looking at myself in the mirror I see that I am no longer a young woman. Sad, yes, but not terribly vital, since my curiosity about the world is still very much alive—my impatient, burning curiosity. Numerous writing projects are swimming in my head, and the unsolvable riddles of the relation of technique to theme, the intricacy of laws according to which everything is either good or evil, disturb my quiet, though without my feeling any writer's guilt.

I wonder, is it possible to write the truth about, for example, war. War is an anachronistic thing, not only from the humanitarian point of view, but also from the perspective of contemporary cultural psychology. From the beginning war elaborated for itself its own aesthetic categories. And these categories are prescribed, almost obligatory. [. . .] I am rather perturbed that for me war will always be more important as a phenomenon than as a

5. The Bayonne Legion, the first Polish volunteer military unit formed in France at the beginning of the war, and later incorporated into the first regiment of the Foreign Legion. It fought from the fall of 1914 until spring 1915 on the front in Champagne; in June 1915, after heavy losses, the legion was disbanded. [D.K.]

theme. The psychology of war, not that for which one fights. [. . .] Those who are in the right should prevail, but very often they lose. So what can one surmise about this theme? One can only shed more tears. War is not so that something can happen, so that something can be defined or result from it. War must take place, and this is the whole of its meaning.

Poland. I have already considered it—in vain. Which is why it will never become material for my writing. Which is why it is aesthetically inaccessible to me. [. . .] If a new Poland were to emerge from the present war (as is projected in the articles published today in "Temps" and "Times") it would be a fantastical accident practically irreconcilable with contemporary human imagination. How is it possible to intuit such an event, to foresee that a country could be reborn precisely when the three parts of its population are shooting at one another so conscientiously, not only as members of enemy armies, but as their allies as well. Another matter altogether is that this Poland will be national-democratic and antisemitic. I wouldn't be able to write even two sentences about this final enigma. Besides, it isn't all that important to me. . . .

Warsaw, 23 ii 1915

Today, like every other day, the army continues to file down the streets. The soldiers with their yellowed and blackened faces are emaciated and exhausted. Whenever they must halt because of the traffic, they collapse for a moment on the cobblestones, mired in mud, despite the protests of their superior officers. Like animals, they greedily and mournfully inhale the buns the pedestrians give them. A little spaniel, held on a leash by an elegant gentleman, began to nudge the elbow of one soldier sitting on the ground. The soldier petted it automatically but, absorbed in his temporary respite, immediately stopped paying attention to its joyful barking.

Warsaw, 24 viii 1915

Whole cavalcades of workers departed with the refugees to the East, chasing after phantom factories. At this time, the unemployed are eager to emigrate to the West. And so a new defeat is manufactured—decreased ethnography, towns emptied to welcome the flood of foreigners. After the arrival of a few legionnaires[6] for a brief stay, a new wind of romanticism began to blow in the better Warsaw circles. At meetings, the warriors tell their stories. This was all new to me. Here I witnessed an unbelievable transformation taking place in usually sober and rational people under the influence of these legionnaires. Through the smoke, blood, and improbability, the ghost of an independent Poland beckons. Old dreams of the past hundred years, tragic and bloody wonders. [. . .] And yet, the truth is that, in essence, the sacrificial battle—the heroic gesture of

---

6. *Legionnaires:* Polish battalions fighting on foreign soil for Polish independence. [D.K.]

despair—is only for show. "What matters is not with whom. What matters is for what." This is precisely how the Polish right to life is documented. It seems to me both defeat and drama even when the shadow of hope becomes hope, and improbability, probability. It represents, regardless, the squeezing of a whole intellectual and creative life into one historico-heroic sphere, the overwhelming of thought under the impetus of a nationalistic instinct. Europe has become savage this past year. We are in a better position here in that the drama involves the very root of our national feeling. It is from this that we get our hamletism, our tendency to meditation, our bitterness. And the saddest thought of all is that the best people are in these legions. Our defeat happened long before anyone else's. We lost them first, before the bullets claimed their lives. Of the best only a few were able to resist.

Translated by Diana Kuprel

From *Dzienniki czasu wojny: 1909–1917* (Warsaw: Czytelnik, 1976), 247–49, 249–51, 374, 393–94. By permission of the copyright holders.

✟ Muriel Dayrell-Browning, née Green-Armytage (1879–1935) *British*

The eldest of six children, Muriel Green-Armytage grew up in Clifton, England. Her mother was a novelist, philanthropist, and local historian. Two of her brothers pursued careers as army officers in India. Clever and gifted at learning languages, Muriel went to a German finishing school at Neuwied am Rhein. To escape from what she considered a provincial life, she married a gold-mining engineer who took her to Rhodesia; after a failed attempt to grow tobacco, the family returned to England. She left her husband, taking her eight-year-old daughter and leaving her young son with a nanny in Liverpool. By 1914 she was forced to provide for herself and her two children. Notwithstanding all difficulties, she was by her daughter Vivien's account high-spirited, intrepid, and curious about topics ranging from Egyptian antiquities to cookery. A suffragist, she made Vivien wear a purple sash and distribute leaflets for the cause. During the war, Dayrell-Browning, who had learned African languages in Rhodesia, used her linguistic skills for the War Office. She also wrote subversive propaganda leaflets to be dropped over Hanover and Schleswig-Holstein.

⸸ Letters to Her Mother

Strathmore Hotel, 15 Tavistock Square, W.C.
Sept 4. 14

Dearest Mums,

I will now tell you about the Raid last night—the Sight of my Life!

It was the second night of London's lighting or rather no-lighting orders. At 2:30 I was wakened by a terrific explosion and was at the window in one bound when another deafening one shook the home. Nearly above us sailed a cigar of bright silver in the full glare of about 20 magnificent search lights. A few lights roamed round trying to pick up her companion. Our guns made a deafening row and shells burst all around her. For some extraordinary reason she was dropping no bombs. The night was absolutely still with a few splendid stars. It was a magnificent sight and the whole of London was looking on holding its breath. She was only a little way to the East of me and I had a topping view as there's a stone balcony outside my window. I yelled for field glasses to Captain Hernani but he was escorting the whole houseful to the cellars (cook was howling—she's Irish) so sat on the window ledge in my dressing gown. The Zepp[1] headed slowly north amid a rain of shells and crashing artillery fire from all quarters. She was pretty high up but was enormous 600 ft long I shd say. Capt. H came up and joined me and we watched for another 5 minutes when suddenly her nose dropped and I yelled "Getroffen."[2] But she righted again and went into a cloud (uh—possibly she made herself!). Then the searchlights scientifically examined that cloud to help the airmen but she didn't appear and we thought the fun was over as the guns stopped. Then from the direction of Barnet[3] and very high a brilliant red light appeared (we thought it was an English fire balloon for a minute!). Then we saw it was the Zepp diving head first. *That* was a sight. She dived slowly at first as only the foremost ballonet was on fire. Then the second burst and the flames tore up into the sky and then the third and cheers thundered all round us from every direction. The glare lit up all London and was rose red. Those deaths must be the most dramatic in the world's history. They fell—a cone of blazing wreckage thousands of feet—watched by 8 millions of their enemies.

It was magnificent the most thrilling scene imaginable.

[This afternoon I went out to Barnet (and so did 3/4 of London!). The wreck covers only 30 ft of ground and the dead are under a tarpaulin. The

---

1. *Zepp:* Zeppelin, German dirigible used to bomb London and other allied sites.
2. *Getroffen:* hit (German).
3. *Barnet:* suburb of London.

engineer was gripping the steering wheel and one man was headless. I hope they will be buried with full military honors. They were brave men. R.I.P. They say the airman who bombed them was only 18. His name won't be given as they will try for revenge as in the case of Warneford. The engine is at the W/O.[4] The Zepp fell close to Cuffley Church and telescoped when she hit the ground.]

International Club, 74 Prince's Square, Kensington Gardens
[1915]

Dearest Mums,

I am very nearly brilliant! What do you think of me at the War Office saving the Empire. Yes *really*. I went there on Sat. to pass my tests on French German Dutch Flemish and being very full of swank I put "Matabele" and "Zulu" on my paper.[5] (Simply for doggo as I never thought it would be of *any* use to me again!)

But hist—

The German agents in Hamburg and Tembu-land are writing to each other in Kaffir re 1) assassination of Native Commissioners on receipt of smuggled arms and 2) the details of the gun-running scheme were given—dates and all! Other important matters too re shipping thereof.

Now you see, there are Englishmen in plenty who speak and even write in Kaffir but for instance "guzaza qwambilinje" means absolutely nothing to them as not knowing German they fail to perceive that it would be the German way of spelling "Kusasai kuempili" and no one could find the former in any dictionary and thought it *obscure dialect* and gave it up. But MDB the Sleuth hound with the aid of Kropf's German-Zulu dic got the whole message down to *dot* and you would have blushed to hear the things said to your daughter. They said I ought to be on the W. African censor job and would get it if I applied. So I have.

Guy Eden said to me that "You have a great claim on the Govt even if you had not passed the other language tests and I shall want you in my Dept!"

There was not a soul in the WO who could do it and all squeaked in the test room when they saw "Zulu" on my paper. I gave Mr. Howell as one ref: as he's a JP and no relation and knows I love him. You might show him this letter as then he will see the use of the job.

It really is a snip and I may have saved hundreds of white lives and prevented the landing of thousands of guns ammunition and Assegai heads[6] in Tembuland and district. Tally ho. One to me!

[P.S.] You must keep this W. African business *dark*. Don't want them to stop writing. See? Hamburg does not know we can use it.

Department of Documents, the Imperial War Museum 92/49/1.

---

4. *W/O:* War Office.
5. *Matabele, Zulu:* South African languages ("Kaffir").
6. *Assegai:* iron-tipped wooden spear.

✟ Mireille Dupouey
French

Married to naval Lieutenant Pierre Dominique Dupouey in May 1911, Mireille Dupouey lost her husband five months after the war broke out. In her notebook, she continued to compose letters to him as an intercessor, beseeching him to help her accept the pain accorded her by God; the letters merge into prayers that fuse her human passion with spiritual devotion. With her husband, she had sought to dedicate herself to a Christian mysticism inspired by Teilhard de Chardin, who found in the war moments of "exaltation and initiation." Together they had read literature in English, including Edgar Allan Poe's "Annabel Lee," about "a love that was more than love," and that could not be severed by death. After the death of Pierre, who was treated as a patriotic martyr by the right-wing Action Française, she rededicated herself. "Lord Jesus, I asked for the Cross in order to receive love—now you bring me to Calvary, thank you. May my sufferings adore you—and if you tear apart my heart, may my torn heart adore you." Mireille refused attentions from another man, writing to Pierre, "You are not dead and I am not a widow." Her dark, deep, and immutable mourning was "infinitely dear" to her as the image of her fidelity. She almost never refers to her son, "this sweet treasure who is you and whom I shall love for you," but she promises to bring him up to be "valiant."

After the Armistice, she traveled to Pypegaal, Belgium, where she found the grave of a friend in a naval cemetery, but not that of her husband.

✝ Notebook Entries

Le Rody, 30 July 1915

My dear Pierre, my heart,

I love you—keep me—receive all my love as it mounts up—ceaselessly until the blessed day when I shall find you again. Oh! I know well that you now possess God entirely and that you need nothing—but I have your promise, we have each other's promise to cherish each other eternally. Let me not forget anything of you—I beg the most atrocious martyrdom of my heart, rather than forgetfulness.

Oh! when will these long months come to an end, when everything drags me outwards, when I must speak, laugh, listen to banalities, and never even have time to think of you—of you my love, my delight, my heavenly friend—my blessed Pierre—Oh! yes, I want to be abandoned to Jesus and to find him in everything, since each morning he is mine—but see, my love, this cowardice, this scorn for his call, this rejection of his grace. To let the rest pass before him! what misery! and how should I ask him after such poor days to return to my soul tomorrow. Pierre, pray, my dearest—conjure, supplicate, intercede. Remember our love at the same time last year. The 29th, Jean V dined with us, with what enthusiasm for war. The 30th, we scarcely saw each other, you were on duty. Friday the 31st, we prayed together for our dear marriage. And now, I ask if these four years were not a dream, if I have not just closed the book after a splendid poem like "Annabel Lee." You are the one who has entered the kingdom and I who cherished you, I remain separated from you by this great sea, all my life. Pray, because I am nothing: you see now, my dear, my dearest love. Draw me to the place to which you have departed; support me as you knew so sweetly how to do—one day I will see you again, say it to me in my soul—pray, pray, pray—until then, until that hour tomorrow when the terrible sweet Jesus will return in his full glory.

I offer him your praise and your adoration through all this night to compensate for this neglect and for this refusal.

Sing to the Virgin Mary the psalms of my office and beg her to forgive me. Pray also for all my loved ones—how dark the future of this house is, and yet I had hoped to be crushed to spare them. . . . But I was not worthy of such suffering.

Saturday, 19 [July 1919]

Pilgrimage to Pypegaal in search of the tomb of F.

Departure from Furnes by tramway to Woesten. There are no ruins, we are west of the front where the cantonments of December 1914 were. This is the soft Flemish land, the peace of lazy canals under the great light of summer, scattered trees and distant horizons.

Oost-Vleteren! O Pierre dearest, the tender little words on the small calendar of 1915 engraved for ever in my heart the name of this village where you wrote them. I would like to embrace the soul of this countryside, more than the kiss of veneration by my eyes—and to carry it away, to keep it with me everywhere, not as a dead and rigid frame for the life and last action of Pierre—but as the living memory of a living earth which participated in the final, finest gestures of his life.

At Woesten I take the map and start on a burning road, a desert where for kilometers there is no inhabitant. Walking in a straight line toward the Steenstraat front where the sailors fought so hard in December 1914—but then later it was only the line of defense, no longer of desperate combat. The vegetation perhaps understood. One might say it does not dare to grow back elsewhere and brings all the delicacy of symbols, closing red flowers beside the graves. Here it allows the insouciant wild oats right up to the edges of shelters—and the hideous corrugated tin of the English will soon succumb at the edge of the paths.

Crossroads of Pypegaal—allee of poplars before the cemetery. The little Flemish girl with blue eyes whom I met on the tram is my guide: she was the fiancée of a first mate, killed in 1917. She comes from La Panne to see his tomb.

In vain we search for that of M.F. in the poor abandoned cemetery. The weeds have overgrown some crosses and several plaques have fallen. I sob at the thought of having to tell my poor friend . . . but no, we must look further—and first pray. I kneel on the tomb of Rioualan, the first mate, the "Pierre" of the little Flemish girl—but she stands and I feel she is occupied with him alone, not God—with the grave, not paradise.

The only clue to find the grave of M.F. is a ruined mill, which luckily the girl knows. To get there we cross the ruins (already a bit restored) of a large farm that served as rescue post for the sailors. There doubtless little Simon, whom Pierre loved, was carried. There Pierre slept under an open sky. The few nights of rest they were allowed during that hard year's end of 1914. From there, on Christmas Day, he wrote, "Man's purpose is to give his life for that which goes beyond life and to testify to this light that makes life blossom." O my love, for whom the invisible light never died no matter what wind tried to shake it. My heart suddenly imagines the winter landscape, the snow in the great courtyard, a damped fire in the farm room, a black sky, the thought of the friends just fallen, the preparation for the next assault. O my Lord, how right he was, how "Christmas in this farm without mass faintly echoes that at our dear Lorient." No church song, no visit from Jesus, no sweet exchange of kisses after the communion, on our return to our little living room.

It was a very inward Christmas—and for you who loved, it was not a Christmas without joy,—for you wrote that day: "May the Lord be blessed who permitted us to be one flesh and one heart, you and I, and that I find repose from so far away in your faithful and fervent prayers and love."

Close to the first cemetery a great ruined building that was part of the farm served as chapel for the sailors. Blessed site, holy land where I would like to stay, having so much to thank God for the grace granted to Pierre and to his men in this same place.

Opposite the fine ruined mill, another little cemetery (they are every-where at Pypegaal—it's the only field harvest this year, the harvest of the eternal barns of our father). In this one almost all are sailors from 1914–1915. F. sleeps there in the shadow of a great black cross that domi-nates the grains grown almost tall as trees.

From *Cahiers* (Paris: Le Cerf, 1944), 1:29–31; 2:48–52.

✠ Countess Laura Godzawa de Turczynowicz, née Blackwell
American/Polish

M arried to a Polish aristocrat, the American-born Countess Laura Godzawa de Turczynowicz found herself in a corner of Poland repeatedly overrun by military forces. As she records in her 1916 memoir, during six months in 1915 she attempted to run a local hospital, sharing equipment with Russian nurses, but her equipment was eventually confiscated by occupying German troops. Parted by the war from her husband, who worked with the Red Cross, she and her children suffered virtual imprisonment in their country house, where she housed General von Hindenburg and other officers, as armies of different nationalities swept through and despoiled the village. The children survived the typhus epidemic, hunger, and the violence to which civilian populations are subject. Turczynowicz records the rape of a woman who had just given birth, when passing troops discovered her in bed in a cottage by the roadside; she tells us that she failed to rescue her teenaged maid from forcible prostitution, even though the girl was sick with typhus. After Turczynowicz's return to the United States in 1917, she recruited five hundred Polish women trained by the YWCA to work as Gray Samaritans, or nurse's aides, with the Polish army and in the postwar period of emergency relief under Herbert Hoover. The YWCA records her name as Countess "Laura de Grozdawa Tarcyznourcz."

✠ A Crippled Lazarette

On the 28th day of August—my birthday—a Russian Sister came to me to see if we could help their hospital—a field lazarette, with about one hundred and fifty beds. They had been turned back from the front and could not get supplies. There were three doctors, four nurses, and various order-lies—quartered in one of the barracks—with almost seven hundred wounded! Of course the staff were exhausted, and no supplies! What could four nurses do with such a mass of humanity? I went there with some of my people to see what could be done to help out. The memory of that place will always remain, for there, for the first time, I came face to face with awful suffering. At the very door one heard the low murmur of mis-ery; one room after another packed with men, who could not be helped. There were no medicines—no disinfectants—no linen. In one corner were some prisoners. The sister (nurse) on duty asked me to go to them because I spoke German. One poor fellow, turning restlessly from side to side—calling ceaselessly for water—was quieted when I spoke to him, ask-ing what he wanted. He begged for a drink, and that I should write to his wife, as he felt death upon him. While I was doing what was possible to help him, the poor fellow began to talk. He told me that he had been a bookkeeper, that he was twenty-six years old, and had a wife and children, a little house of his own, had never harmed any one in his life, took no interest in anything outside of his work and family, until with three hours' notice he was ordered to join his regiment, and leave it all.

"The great lords have quarrelled and we must pay for it with our blood, our wives, and children." This man was transported that same day, and died on the way to the station.

So hopeless it was trying to help until there was something to help with, that I drove back to the city to see different people, and in a short time had gathered more than a thousand roubles with which to replenish the lazarette—bandages, cotton-wool, sublimate, plaster, asperine, iodine, etc., and a great share of our spiritus. It was pitiful to see how the sisters rejoiced to get the things!

In my own hospital there was great dissatisfaction because so much was given to someone else. I had a battle royal over the linen I insisted on giv-ing, but my husband was on my side and we gave all that was absolutely necessary to the lazarette, and afterwards regretted that it was not more, for the Germans got all that linen and our supplies! I remember the gen-tlemen still played cards then—and to my fund for the lazarette went all the money won.

In that lazarette for the first and only time I had to give up and go away for a moment to keep from fainting—for on a cot I saw what appeared to be a ball of cotton and bandages—with three black holes, just as if a child had drawn mouth and nose and eyes—and the flies! . . . It was a shock to hear a voice with a cultured accent coming from such an object—a Polish voice begging whoever it was not to go away, but to give him water; his hands were burned to a crisp, he could not move, and the flies! . . . The odour from the gangrene was so awful that I was overpowered for a time—but, afterwards, sent my maid home for netting, as much as she could find; and then helped the sister in charge to rebandage and veil that remnant of a man. He had been near a bursting shell—and lain four days in the field after he was wounded. He asked if his eyes were burned away.

"Yes—quite gone." If he would live or die?—

"Die."

"God has not forgotten me—but please, then, let me drink—drink."

"A Crippled Lazarette," in *When the Prussians Came to Poland* (New York: Putnam's, 1916), 22–26.

✠ Typhus!

When the cook came at five o'clock to sit with the children while I rested, she found me for the first time in all those days not dressed in my uniform, but wearing a thin kimono, and saying how warm it was. She was frightened. It was so difficult for me to speak. My tongue would not obey me, but I made her understand that Wladek was better—saved—and that for Staś the crisis would likely come that night. The poor creature began to cry, saying, "Oh, my lady, you also are ill with the fever!"

That I could not agree to. There was no time for me to be ill. We spoke of the need of fuel. A Jew had some wood and wanted fifty roubles for it. Another had a few potatoes. These things were sorely needed. But no milk! For Wladek it was so absolutely necessary. There was still a ten-pound package of sugar. Wladek was conscious, too weak to speak, pitiful beyond measure. I tried to force myself to have energy enough to dress his hand,—succeeding after a terrible effort. Staś was calling out, talking wildly as usual. For my little daughter the problem of food faced me. What to give her! She was always difficult to please with food—and now would hardly touch our fare.

The day wore away. Late in the afternoon the doctor came. I had quite forgotten about Manya.

"You have also the typhus!"

In a voice that seemed to belong to some one else, I told him, "No—I have no time for the typhus, the children would die if I gave up," and refused to go to bed.

That night the fever laid its hand heavily upon me, and I went to bed. My cook told me afterwards how I sang what she called "church music" till she thought the end was near—that already the angels were there!

Seemingly a hundred years after, in reality a few hours, it was borne in upon my consciousness by a pure mother instinct undoubtedly, that some one was crying. I opened my eyes to see the cook bending over Staś, crying, "if my lady would only wake up, and tell me what to do!"

I forced my voice back from the far-away country, telling her to put Staś beside me, compresses also, that I could attend him, and, with God's help, I did; after awhile getting to my feet, keeping always a tight hold of my senses, lest they wander. The very overpowering anxiety for my children cast the fever off!

Staś lived through the crisis that night, just as Wladek had done. I sat in the big chair between the little cribs, telling the cook what to do.

For two days it was difficult to drag about. It was as if I had never rested or sat down in my life.

The second day when the doctor came, there suddenly flashed across my mind the story of Manya, and I asked him where she was. He told me it was "not my affair." Wladek's second finger had to have an operation, but knowing the tender methods of the doctor, I bathed it in ether myself.

Wladek was hungry,—like a wolf. I gave him the juice of my strawberry preserves. The hunger of the boys grew so alarmingly, and I had only the tea, toast, and preserves, not a diet for typhus patients. The Jew had sold his potatoes to some one else.

Four days after Manya's disappearance, news was brought to me that she was in the house of an old Jewess, a cigarette maker. Leaving the cook with the children, and hardly able to drag myself along, I went with Jacob to find his daughter. How strange it was in the streets, the soldiers were everywhere, staring curiously at us. Impossibly dirty, it bore no resemblance to the town I had known; bits of furniture were standing about, all sorts of things spilled over the streets.

After many difficulties, we finally found the place, and paying no attention to the soldiers about, pushed our way into the room where Manya was, . . . what *had been* Manya. When she, poor creature, saw us, she threw herself on the floor, sobbing; springing up when I knelt beside her. An officer came in to ask our business with the girl.

"She is my maid—stolen! This is her father. I have come to take her home."

"I am very sorry, but you are not allowed to take her, she belongs to the soldiers."

"Don't you see *Herr Offizier,* the girl is dying?"

"Ill she is, and shall have the best of care. We have a doctor to attend just such cases," and *I had to leave her!* Jacob's face was without expression, he seemed to have lost the power to think or feel,—his little girl—[. . .]

I complained about Manya, and was promised that the case should be taken up, "made an example of." So it was! The old Jewess, though quite innocent in the matter, was arrested, kept five days on bread and water (what the rest of the town lived on, too!) and made to pay a fine of three hundred marks! How the case was made out was difficult to imagine. When I told them the old Jewess had done nothing, that she was simply turned out of her own home, I was told that the doctor could not be even questioned, he belonged to the military, but that a Jew *could always be punished!*

"Typhus!" in *When the Prussians Came to Poland* (New York: Putnam's, 1916), 135–41.

✠ Louise E.
French

Louise E., whose father was a soldier in the French army, was living in Lille when the German government undertook the surprise deportation of about 20,000 women and young boys from occupied towns in the region. The hostages were rounded up over two weeks, beginning at 3 A.M. Easter Saturday, 1916. Loaded into cattle cars, they were transported to agricultural regions that were farther behind the front lines, in order to perform agricultural labor and, in some cases, work related to the German military effort, such as filling sandbags, shoring up trenches, and repairing roads. Women were forced to submit to gynecological examinations in front of soldiers. The French government accused the Germans of violating the 1907 Hague conventions, and feminist journalists took up the cause of women who said they had been forced into prostitution. In 1918 a thousand prominent men and women were taken hostage in the northern cities and sent to prisons in Germany and Poland.

✠ Letter to Monsieur E.

May 9, 1916

Dear Papa,

On Thursday, 20th April, placards were put up in the evening—"The attitude of England makes the provisioning of the population more and more difficult. In order to lessen the misery, the population will be deported. By Order."

The following night the military began their brutal work in [the district of] Fives. At 3 o'clock in the morning there was a knocking at the doors, an officer came in and chose the people who were to go. A soldier was on sentry duty, with fixed bayonet, at the door. A few minutes were given for packing. Machine guns were placed at intervals; the streets were full of patrols and blocked by soldiers; fixed bayonets everywhere. They collected the people in the church of the district, and they were all sent off promiscuously in cattle trucks. What morals, what hygiene!

Mothers with young children alone got exemption. As we all three came under the conditions, we packed our luggage in great depression.

Monseigneur and the Mayor courageously had several conversations with the General; as Monseigneur was energetically standing up for the population, he was answered with these courteous words: "You, Bishop, be quiet and go!"

The Germans operated by police districts; Rue I., our old street, was dealt with on the night of Easter Sunday to Monday. People were sleeping peacefully, for the night before they had been told that a despatch from neutrals had put an end to this disgraceful state of affairs. The Mlles J., who had been carried off with their brother and their maid, have been released. Madame L.'s maid has been taken, and generally speaking, all servants; as our street is in a different district, it was only dealt with on the night of Wednesday to Thursday. Fortunately, before reaching us the Germans had made enormous raids at Wazemmes, and they were less unpleasant. Mother stayed in bed, saying she was ill. A. and I received the officer, who authorised us to stay. I think the picture of father in uniform, which we have had in the dining room since the separation, saved me. I said I was the daughter of an officer of whom we had had no news since the battle of the Marne. It was pretty terrifying, this military visit. We thank God every day for leading your steps to Naerd. You would certainly have been carried off, both of you.

"Annexe 23," *The Deportation of Women and Girls from Lille* (New York: Doran, 1916), 27–28.

✝ Mayy Ziyadah, pseudonym: Isis Copia (1886–1941) *Palestinian*

The writer and critic Ziyadah was christened Mary by her Palestinian mother and her Lebanese father, a journalist, but later assumed what she considered a more poetic name; she attended the 'Aintourah Institute for Girls. When her family moved to Egypt in 1908, her father became an editor at a newspaper, for which she also worked and wrote articles. Immersed in the literary and intellectual culture of Cairo, she began writing in French, publishing *Fleurs de rêve* (Dream flowers, 1911). Most of her work was in Arabic, but Ziyadah also learned English, German, and Italian, traveling to Europe between 1932 and 1934.

An ardent feminist, Ziyadah met Huda Sha'rawi at the Egyptian National University and wrote a book on the feminist Malak Hifni Nasif (pseudonym Bahithat al-Badiyya). As she wrote to Kahlil Gibran, she believed "in the basic premise of freedom for women" to choose their husbands, but rejected adultery as unnatural for women. Begun in 1912, her platonic correspondence with Gibran (who called her "a divine voice") was interrupted by the war. After the war she published *Sawanih Fatah* (Thoughts of a young girl, 1922) and *Zulumat wa Ashi'ah* (Darkness and sunlight, 1923), in addition to two biographies, poetry, translations, and criticism. In her forties, when the shock of successively losing several people dear to her caused a severe depression and a suicide attempt, her family committed her to an asylum for several years. She returned to public life briefly before her death.

✝ Letter to Amin al-Rihani[1]

Egypt, February 1916

What are you doing now . . . ? How happy you are to live in that new and distant country so rich in meanings. As one of the greatest American thinkers, Emerson, said, "travelling is a fool's paradise."[2] If I were a man I would set aside at least four months a year for traveling. But since I am a woman I have to content myself with traveling between the shores of Egypt and Syria. True, travel now is not an amusement of either stupid or intelligent people, but an idiotic, possibly fatal, venture. But since death is inevitable, it is better to die in the arms of the waves. There in the immortal depth is the eternal repose where the voices of the cruel living and their footsteps would not disturb or hurt the dead.

You ask how we are these days. What do you think is the condition of small nations? What could be the seal set upon them in present circumstances, but humiliation and more humiliation? I know very little about politics and I admit that I would be imposing if I were to tackle the history of nations and their fate. But the little I know from what I have studied tells me that sincerity between nations is scarce and that honesty in people's souls is a poetic illusion with which leaders seek to influence the minds and affections of others, in order to make them pay with their blood and their lives. Why? For economic gain. That is all! Particularly during a war, to someone with a critical eye, "freedom" seems a rhetorical wine to intoxicate the people's hearts. Freedom has beautiful and precious meaning, but everything sweet and dear is impossible. Had the people tasted real freedom even for a second, they would have been gods. Indeed divinity is absolute freedom.

Don't make fun of me as a sophist, O poet philosopher. It cannot be hard for you to understand how the war has destroyed in our glowing souls beliefs we thought eternal and how it has injured whatever hopes we had, the greatest and most splendid hopes. Tell me: if we despair of progress, we who have dedicated to it all our thoughts and spiritual energy, what can we hope for? And where can we search for a base on which to build the palaces of hope?

The attitude of the Egyptians towards the British is what the servants of the government supporting the British can afford; not because they believe that the British presence will revive Egyptian prosperity, but because they think of their own private interest. The British have been here for almost 25 years, yet only ten percent of Egyptians can read. This might have been all right in the past, but scarcely in the present. Then why

---

1. Amin al-Rihani (1876–1940) was a Lebanese writer who migrated to New York in 1888. During the war he was in the United States.
2. Ralph W. Emerson, *Self-Reliance.*

should we expect the British to improve our status? If they were to do that they would stupidly work against their own interests.

Meanwhile our exalted Sultan generously throws many dinner parties for foreigners and locals alike, and busily awards titles and privileges to notables and learned men, distributing many medals and offering great gifts. He is lowly and humble of heart, as the Christians say of Jesus. He visits the commander of the occupation army and sips tea at the viceroy's home and dines at the tables of the ambassadors of France and Britain. A nice man in every sense of the word. 'Abdeen Palace has become a suitable royal palace. They have fixed it in and out, out in particular. There is a nice iron railing, proper lighting, triumphant soldiers, drums and wind instruments, and lots of posh, such as sharp swords, and shining buttons on the chests of the officers and white shoes, etc. Passing by 'Abdeen Square now makes you happy, as some of our local ladies say.

Do you really expect that the glory of the Abbasids will be resurrected in any Arab country? I wish this might be realized, but do you think it is possible?

I like to talk about politics and everything that comes from you. Don't hesitate to send me your news and articles, even the political ones. Where is your poetical article on the love of country? Perhaps you've sent me the magazine as you promised, but the censor didn't find it appropriate to send it to me because they open most of the letters which come in and some that go out. If they open this letter they will learn from it that I love France and England not with a political love, because I don't know anything about politics, but an esthetic one: I love their literatures, poetry, and some individuals.

I really like subtle ideas and communication with refined people who take you beyond daily chores and small sad events.

From *Bouquets de Jardin du Mai,* ed. Farouk Saad (Beirut: Dar Al-Hidal, 1973), 112–13.

✝ Joséphine Barthélemy
(b. 1896) *French*

The child of a rural laborer, Joséphine Barthélemy became a maid in a village hotel. When German troops occupied the area, she was forced to work in their military hospital, where she was raped one evening by a German soldier. Because she could not identify her attacker, the German commandant could not help her and repatriated her in early 1916. She returned to her sister's home in a suburb of Paris, where she concealed her pregnancy, then by her own account let the infant die. (Abortion, of course, was illegal.)

When interrogated about the infanticide in September 1916, she told the court that as a virgin and practicing Catholic, she had been too ashamed to tell anyone about her rape. In response to the judge's question whether she had premeditated infanticide, she answered, "I didn't think about it . . . I didn't want the child of a Boche." The prosecution contested her claim that she was raped, since she had not confessed to her sister. The defense responded that a Frenchwoman had the right to refuse maternity imposed by the enemy. When Barthélemy was acquitted in 1917, newspaper articles and letters from readers were divided between sympathy and protests that Barthélemy should have given her child to public assistance. The court records were destroyed later in a fire; an excerpt of her testimony from the trial dossier survives in a contemporary study by Georges Docquois.

✝ Testimony in Court: Defense Against Charge of Infanticide

September 9, 1916

My father is a woodcutter in Ville-sur-Yron, near Mars-la-Tour. We are five children, four daughters and one son, who was killed at Verdun. In 1912, I was placed at Mars-la-Tour as a maid in a café. After six months I was placed at Chambly as a maid in the hotel of Mme Rolot. Then the Germans came to Chambly and I had to work for them.

They had created a hospital in a church; I washed the dishes of the wounded and the orderlies.

At first I had refused to work for the Germans. The commander made me come to him and for three months they forced me to wash the linens and the dishes for the hospital in the church. In the middle of December 1915, without my being able to be more precise about the date, four German soldiers from the Red Cross entered the little room at the side of the church, a little sacristy, where I was working. They spoke to me in German but I did not understand. They laid me on the ground holding my arms and legs, and one of them took me by force. He hurt me. I swear that I had never had relations with a man. I cried out but no one came.

The next day I went to complain to the commander who asked me if I knew my aggressors. I answered that I didn't. The commander said he couldn't find the one who attacked me among all the soldiers, and fifteen days later I was evacuated with fifty other people.

We left January 5 for Mars-la-Tour and we reached Annemasse in four days through Switzerland. I spent two months as a refugee at Toulette (Drôme), then three months in the Côte d'Or and finally, my sister, married to a factory worker, had me come and found me a job at the café-hotel Delorme, 11 ave de Pont de Saint Ouen, where I remained until my arrest.

My periods stopped December 20.

On arriving at Gennevilliers I didn't want to say anything to my sister. During the last months she saw I was getting big. She questioned me but I didn't want to tell her anything.

During the night of the 14th or 15th of August I felt cramps and I gave birth in my room in the middle of the night, sitting up on my chamberpot, into which the infant fell. I remained seated until the next morning on a chair. I swear that the child did not cry.

From Georges Docquois, *La chaire innocente: l'enfant du viol boche* (Paris: Albin Michel, 1917), 173–75.

✟ Angèle ("Gegèle") Fournier
French

T he wife of a soldier in the infantry, Angèle ("Gegèle") Fournier
worked in a factory in Paris. Her announcement of a general strike
in Paris led the censor to confiscate her ungrammatical letter, which
was deposited in the French military archives at Vincennes. The spring of
1917, when the disastrous Nivelle offensive was mounted, witnessed growing unrest because of home front shortages and high battlefront losses.
Other women's letters that were caught in the net of the censors also
report on strikes, ask about soldiers' mutinies, or mention coal shortages
that caused growing unemployment and led to worker revolts.

✟ Letter to Her Husband

To: Charles Auguste Fournier
36e Infie 5 Cie 1 section

Paris 28/5/17

My beloved Charles,

Yesterday Sunday I was at Meaux and staid at the station all day without
budging, hoping always to see you arrive: disappointed hope. I was forced
to go away, it was bad luck that you were not able to come.

I was with a woman who was also waiting for her husband who belongs
to the 36th; she lives at Sèvres near St Cloud. They asked what area you
were in they told us you were at Nogent d'Artois is that true in this case
why not tell us the exact place in that locale it would have been more
certain.

Well, tell me clearly where you are and if I can go there, I wold rather do that than to Meaux since it must be too far from you, think how vexed I was.

Write me right away since if you can have permission for Sunday I'll risk it again, in any case if you haven't changed unless you don't want to; but I hope that it's not bad will.

In short, I'm waiting for a response right away to know if yes or no for Sunday or before if it's feasible.

I had taken the Paris train at 6:02 in the morning and was at Meaux at ten of 8 you see how I cooled my heels and I staid the whole time in the station.

Quick an answer and in the hope that I I hope wont be disappointed to see you soon I give you a big hug since I love you.

Things are hopping in Paris.

The women are rebelling. Lets hope that will do some good and above all bring the end. I am not working everyone's on strike.

Your little Gegèle for life but who is quite vex at not having seen you

        Well see you soon, keep it up, patience, it will come

Another big smack
Gegèle

By permission of Service Historique de l'Armée de Terre, Château de Vincennes (16N 1552).

✝ Mata Hari (Margaretha Geertruida MacLeod, née Zelle) (1876–1917) *Dutch*

Born in a small Dutch town, Margaretha Zelle at age fifteen went to a training school, where she was seduced by the headmaster. Responding to an advertisement in 1895, she married Captain MacLeod, a colonial officer who took her to Java; they had a son and daughter before returning to Holland. They quarreled over sex and money, however, and separated in 1902 after the death of their son.

By 1904 she was living as an exotic dancer and demimondaine, traveling throughout Europe. Appropriately enough for a woman later charged with espionage, her stage name Hari means "eye of day" in Javanese. Colette, whose own dancing in the nude helped displace Mata Hari from popular favor, reports that "she scarcely danced but knew how to undress gradually and move her long lustrous, slender, proud body." She took wealthy lovers to support her extravagant habits.

War made her travels more difficult and led to the blocking of her bank account in Berlin as well as the confiscation of her belongings for unpaid debts. She was recruited as an agent by the French in the summer of 1916, and she passed information to a French attaché at Madrid about German use of secret inks for correspondence. Arrested in February 1917 in France on suspicion of serving as a double agent for the Germans, she was condemned and executed in October 1917, despite inconclusive evidence. The morning of her death she selected her finest dress and refused to be blindfolded. The doctor who accompanied her recalled he had met her in 1914 on an inspection of a Paris bordello. Regardless of her actual guilt or innocence, Mata Hari became a symbolic figure who crystallized fears of the enemy alien and the wayward woman.

JS

✝ Letter to Captain Bouchardon

5 June [1917]

To the Captain Reporter of the 3rd Council of War
Dear Captain,

There is yet another matter that I beg you kindly to consider. It is this: Mata-Hari and Mme Zelle MacLeod are two totally different women. Today the war and my passport have forced me to live and sign as Zelle, but that woman is unknown to the world.

Yet I consider myself to be *Mata Hari*. For twelve years I lived under this name. I am known in every country and I have relations everywhere. What Mata Hari the dancer is allowed, Madame Zelle MacLeod is certainly not allowed. Events that happen to Mata Hari do not happen to Mme Zelle. The people who address the one do not address the other. And the actions and life style of Mata Hari and of Mme Zelle cannot be the same.

With regard to this, Captain, do not be surprised at what has happened. It is very simple and natural. I see many other cases, I assure you. Mata Hari is really obliged to defend herself. I learned this through losses. Everywhere I dance, I am celebrated, I arrive with jewels, furs—but as I am a stranger everywhere, belonging to a little country that has no public opinion, nowhere am I defended by anyone but myself.

Everywhere I am the coveted prey of the tradesmen who serve theaters. There are many trials, seizures are immediate, and to avoid these, either I or a lover "pays"—or I must abandon in the hands of these people my coveted objects. I know there is nothing to be done. It's the life of a woman—of all women of the theater. These are "things" one does not say.

But you remake yourself when the occasion presents itself. And that is what happened with my furs in Berlin when the war broke out. I assure you, Captain, that at 8 in the morning, the Berlin police inspected all the hotels knocking at every door to see who was living there, the morning of the declaration of war. . . . The Bank had seized the deposits and valuables of foreigners. All the tradesmen presented their bills and because almost no one among the foreigners could pay, they seized the trunks, the stored furs. And what happened to me happened to others and because they claimed that I had lived more than ten years in France, and that I had lost my Dutch nationality, I was treated with extreme severity.

I have told you that our minister and the Dutch courts arranged for the Bank to return my money and my jewels but the furs remained there.

Well, Mata Hari had an opportunity to compensate herself a little and she did so.

All this letter is to tell you again that everything that happened, happened to Mata Hari and not to Mme Zelle. It is Mata Hari who was *forced* to go to Paris to protect her interests. Mme Zelle had nothing to do with it.

I beg you, Captain, take all this into consideration and do not be too harsh with me. Remember that all my life as a woman, I have lived as Mata Hari, that I think and act as such, that I have lost all notion of travel, distances, dangers, nothing exists for me. Even the differences among the races. Everywhere in society I have met trash and fine people. I lose—I win—I defend myself when someone attacks me—I take when someone has taken from me.

But I beg you to believe that I have never worked as a spy against France. Never. Never.

And I beg you, captain, I have suffered enough. Let me leave St. Lazare. It is not fair to keep me imprisoned. I have not done espionage.

Respectfully,
Mata Hari

By permission of Service Historique de l'Armée de Terre, Château de Vincennes.

✠ Virginia Woolf, née Stephen (1882–1941) *British*

As novelist, essayist, critic, and diarist, Virginia Woolf articulated the feminist and modernist ideals that so many writers in the twentieth century have emulated. She had a privileged childhood, meeting artists and philosophers through her father, Leslie Stephen, editor of the *Dictionary of National Biography*. The death of her mother, Julia Duckworth Stephen, when she was thirteen, compounded by that of her favorite sister, precipitated a bout of mental illness. Her stepbrothers abused her sexually; one half-sister was mentally retarded. At her father's death in 1904 Virginia had another mental breakdown.

With her sister Vanessa, a painter, she moved to Bloomsbury, where the two sisters and their brothers formed a circle of friends that included the economist J. M. Keynes, the art critic Roger Fry, the novelist E. M. Forster, and the political theorist Leonard Woolf, an intelligent, moody man who became her husband in 1912. Together they started Hogarth Press, which published Sigmund Freud and other important contemporaries such as Katherine Mansfield and T. S. Eliot.

Woolf's first novels, *The Voyage Out* (1915) and *Night and Day* (1919), were realistic in treatment, but in the twenties she moved toward increasingly radical formal experiment. Through "stream of consciousness" narrative, Woolf explored questions of perspective and the connection between inner states and outer realities in *Jacob's Room* (1922), *Mrs. Dalloway* (1925), and *To the Lighthouse* (1927). Major examples of her modernist technique, these novels turn on the experience of the war, also invoked in the later works *The Years* (1937) and *Between the Acts* (1941). These texts foreground the domestic as a counterpoint to masculine war, which was, for Woolf, a male enterprise that ignored the civilians and women it affected. After reading *The Times* in January 1916, Woolf questioned "how this preposterous masculine fiction keeps going a day longer." Taking mind and memory for her artistic subject matter, her works inevitably bear the scar of the conflict in their action and in the characters' thoughts. Several of her short stories, collected after her death in *A Haunted House* (1943) and *Moments of Being* (1976), indirectly invoke the war and its haunting impact.

In 1925 Woolf began a relationship with Vita Sackville-West, a bisexual novelist, which influenced *Orlando* (1928), the story of a soul who switches genders through the generations.

In her essays Woolf took up the subject of women as professional writers; her *Room of One's Own* (1929) has become a canonical text for feminists. *Three Guineas* (1938) attacks fascist and patriarchal institutions that deprive women of the political and economic power to influence the course of history. Her literary criticism, assembled in *The Common Reader* (1925) and *The Second Common Reader* (1932), has been praised as some of the most brilliant stylistic analyses of this century.

A pacifist worried about the outbreak of another world war, Woolf wrote in 1939, "I should, if it weren't for the war—glide my way up & up into that exciting layer so rarely lived in: where my mind works so quick it seems asleep; like the aeroplane propellers." Faced with the likelihood of another mental breakdown, Woolf drowned herself in 1941.

KCS

✝ Diary Entry

Saturday 19 July [1919]

One ought to say something about Peace day, I suppose, though whether its worth taking a new nib for that purpose I dont know.[1] I'm sitting wedged into the window, & so catch almost on my head the steady drip of rain which is pattering on the leaves. In ten minutes or so the Richmond procession begins. I fear there will be few people to applaud the town councillors dressed up to look dignified & march through the streets. I've a sense of holland covers on the chairs; of being left behind when everyone's in the country. I'm desolate, dusty, & disillusioned. Of course we did not see the procession. We have only marked the rim of refuse on the outskirts. Rain held off till some half hour ago. The servants had a triumphant morning. They stood on Vauxhall Bridge & saw everything. Generals & soldiers & tanks & nurses & bands took 2 hours in passing. It was they said the most splendid sight of their lives. Together with the Zeppelin raid it will play a great part in the history of the Boxall family. But I don't know—it seems to me a servants festival; some thing got up to pacify & placate 'the people'—& now the rain's spoiling it; & perhaps some extra treat will have

1. On 19 July 1919 official peace celebrations were held throughout Britain, with processions, massed choirs, firework displays and so forth. The proceedings were marred by almost continuous rain all day. [A.O.B.]

to be devised for them. Thats the reason of my disillusionment I think. There's something calculated & politic & insincere about these peace rejoicings. Moreover they are carried out with no beauty, & not much spontaneity. Flags are intermittent; we have what the servants, out of snobbishness, I think, insisted upon buying, to surprise us. Yesterday in London the usual sticky stodgy conglomerations of people, sleepy & torpid as a cluster of drenched bees, were crawling over Trafalgar Square, & rocking about the pavements in the neighbourhood. The one pleasant sight I saw was due rather to the little breath of wind than to decorative skill; some long tongue shaped streamers attached to the top of the Nelson column licked the air, furled & unfurled, like the gigantic tongues of dragons, with a slow, rather serpentine beauty. Otherwise theatres & music halls were studded with stout glass pincushions which, rather prematurely, were all radiant within—but surely light might have shone to better advantage.[2] However night was sultry & magnificent so far as that went, & we were kept awake some time after getting into bed by the explosion of rockets which for a second made our room bright. (And now, in the rain, under a grey brown sky, the bells of Richmond [are] ringing—but church bells only recall weddings & Christian services.) I can't deny that I feel a little mean at writing so lugubriously; since we're all supposed to keep up the belief that we're glad & enjoying ourselves. So on a birthday, when for some reason things have gone wrong, it was a point of honour in the nursery to pretend. Years later one could confess what a horrid fraud it seemed; & if, years later, these docile herds will own up that they too saw through it, & will have no more of it—well—should I be more cheerful?

2. The decoration of London's streets and buildings was a feature of the celebrations. VW's image of pincushions was perhaps prompted by the resemblance between the clusters of coloured electric bulbs and glass-headed pins. [A.O.B.]

✝ Gadarinée Dadourian
Armenian

Gadarinée Dadourian was a mother with five children living in Gurün when the deportation of Armenians from eastern Anatolia began; her husband was in America. On the way to Der el Zor she lost three of her five children. The last two were killed at an extermination site; she herself survived the blows that knocked her unconscious and was saved by Arab women in the neighborhood. They healed her and kept her as a servant for the rest of the war.

✝ A Mother's Deportation

The deportation of Armenians from Gurün happened under the same conditions as everywhere else.

The road we took to Der el Zor presented to view an enormous hecatomb. Luckily, my husband was already in America. I went into exile with my five children, three of whom died along the way, the two others at Der el Zor. At first they left us alone, but when the *mutessarif*[1] was dismissed, the monster Zeki followed and the massacres of 1916 began.

Since it was not easy to assassinate 50,000 Armenians at once, the more so that two women from Zeitun had killed four *tchetas*[2] in self-defence, the Turks put the Armenians into separate groups in order to prevent any new attempt.

Once a week, groups of three to four thousand Armenians, under pretext of transporting them elsewhere, were taken away and exterminated. The river Murad was choked with corpses; an escort of military laborers

1. *Mutessarif:* governor of the local town.
2. *Tchetas:* members of the militia.

was called to the spot to free the blocked waters of the river. The children of these martyrs were assembled in an orphanage; there were at least 6,000. Town criers warned that any Arab who sheltered Armenians in his house would be hung. They were authorized to keep only women, without children, as servants.

I was in the last caravan to leave the city; we knew they were leading us to our deaths. After two hours' march, we were halted at the foot of a hill. The Turks led the women in groups higher up. We did not know what was going on there. My turn came too; holding my two children by hand, I climbed the calvary. Horror! There was a well wide open where the executioners immediately threw the women they were stabbing. I received a sword blow on my head, another on my neck; my eyes were veiled at the moment I was thrown into the well with my children. I was on a pile of cadavers wet with blood. My head wound bled and my face was bloody.

I scarcely had the strength to drag myself toward a cavity in the well, where I lost consciousness. When I regained my senses I was in an Arab house. After the departure of the Turks, Arab women had come to search among the corpses in hope of finding some survivors. That is how they found me and seeing I was alive, they saved me. From then on I lived in this family as a servant.

I was anxious about the fate of my children, and the Arabs told me they had been taken in by other Arabs; I sought them but did not find them. Since orphans were carried to Constantinople, I went there in the hope of finding them. They must have died, because on the feast day of Bairam, the Turks took the thousands of children of Der el Zor outside the city, where they were burned alive. Only a few children survived by throwing themselves in the Euphrates, then gaining the further shore.

"Récit," in *Témoignages inédits sur les atrocités turques commises en Arménie,* ed. Azkanever de Constantinople (Paris: Dubreuil, Frèrebeau, 1920), 55–58.

✝ Addie D. Waite Hunton
(1875–1943) American
Kathryn M. Johnson
(1878–1955) American

The daughter of a businessman who founded the Negro Elks and was prominent in the AME church, Addie Waite lost her mother early and was reared by an aunt in Boston. After teaching in a vocational college, in 1893 she married William A. Hunton, a Canadian descendant of African Americans who had emigrated at the time of the Revolution; Hunton had come to the United States as a YMCA administrator. They had four children, of whom two survived; after several moves, the family settled in Brooklyn. Hunton traveled in Europe and studied at the University of Strasbourg. In 1907 the YMCA asked her to work with students; she also assisted her husband until his death in 1916.

In 1918 she volunteered to go to Europe as a canteen hostess for the black troops with the American forces. *Two Colored Women with the American Expeditionary Forces* (1920), the book she wrote with Kathryn Johnson, records the "passing strange" sight of "our own men" guarding German prisoners—a "refreshing" change from the United States, "where it seemed everybody's business to guard them." Nonetheless, she reminds us that Bordeaux and other ports had particularly large concentrations of "colored soldiers" as well as colonial troops and laborers. There she taught literacy and organized entertainment. She was the first international secretary of the YMCA for colored men. After the war, she served on the Council on Colored Work of the YWCA, was vice president of the NAACP, and visited Haiti for the Women's International League for Peace and Freedom in 1926.

*   *   *

Raised in Ohio, Kathryn Johnson studied at Wilberforce University and the University of North Dakota to become a schoolteacher. She taught in Ohio, Indiana, North Carolina, and Arkansas, where she became the first field worker for the NAACP, establishing branches and soliciting member-ships, at first on commission and later on salary. Perhaps because of her commitment to an all-black organization, she was dismissed from the NAACP in 1916. She joined Hunton as a YMCA worker in France in 1919. Their purpose, according to Emmett Scott's *Official History of the American Negro in the World War,* was to be a "refining influence" and to "render eas-ier the disciplinary work of the army." They fed, entertained, and educated soldiers in "hostess houses." In the postwar period Johnson worked for the Association for the Study of Negro Life and History.

✢ The Y.M.C.A. and Other Welfare Organizations

It was our privilege to go overseas as welfare workers under the auspices of the Y.M.C.A., and from the time we entered active duty until we finished our work at Camp Pontanèzen, we can conscientiously say that we had the greatest opportunity for service that we have ever known; service that was constructive, and prolific with wonderful and satisfying results.

The contact with a hundred thousand men, many of whom it was our privilege to help in a hundred different ways; men who were groping and discouraged; others who were crying loudly for help, that they might acquire just the rudiments of an education, and so establish connection with the anxious hearts whom they had left behind; and still others who had a depth of understanding and a breadth of vision that was at once a help and an inspiration. [. . .]

But to help to mar the beauty and joy of this service was ever-present war, with its awful toll of death and suffering; and then the service of the colored welfare workers was more or less clouded at all times with that bit-ing and stinging thing which is ever shadowing us in our own country, and which marked our pathway through all our joyous privilege of giving the best that was within us of labor and devotion.

Upon our arrival in Paris we met Mr. Matthew Bullock and his staff of four secretaries, including the first colored woman, who had been ordered home as *persona non grata* to the army; this was done on recom-mendation of army officials in Bordeaux, who had brought from our southland their full measure of sectional prejudice.

This incident resulted in the detention of many secretaries, both men and women, from sailing for quite a period of time, and no more women came for nearly ten months, thus leaving three colored women to spread their influence as best they could among 150,000 men.

An incident, in some respects similar, occurred in connection with the work in the city of Brest. During the days when it became the greatest embarkation port in France, at times there were as many as forty thousand men of color, at Camp Pontanèzen, waiting for transportation home, and up until about the 18th of June, 1919, there was only one colored Y man there and no women. This, too, at a time when Paris had as many as forty colored men and women, who had returned from their posts of duty, and were willing and anxious for reassignment. This spectacle would no doubt have continued until the close of the work, had not the writers remained in Paris for a period of ten days, requesting continuously that they be permitted to go to Brest. They were finally admitted through the intercession of Mr. W. S. Wallace, who had become the head of the personnel department. When they arrived they were told by the secretary at the head of the woman's work for that region, that she had tried repeatedly to get colored women, but for some reason the Paris office had refused to send them. But the Paris office had said each time, upon being questioned with regard to the matter, that the office at Brest did not desire colored women secretaries. This misunderstanding came about, no doubt, when, one year previous, the first colored woman sent there had been returned to Paris. With the necessary tact and investigation on the part of the proper authorities, the matter could no doubt have been very easily adjusted, when the original men in authority at Brest had been replaced by others who were more reasonable, and who had more sympathy for the colored men; in that case we would not have been confronted with the spectacle of numbers of colored workers idle in Paris for a period of from four to six weeks, just one night's ride from thousands of colored soldiers, who were necessarily centered at the great home-going port. Had they been there they could have been of wonderful service, at a time when waiting was a task that tried men's souls.

Commendable things were accomplished, however, through the limited number of colored secretaries, the sum total of whom finally became seventy-eight men and nineteen women, the rank and file of whom were splendid, giving excellent service in whatever portion of the A. E. F. to which they happened to be assigned. [. . .]

While welfare organizations other than the Y.M.C.A. did not employ colored workers, still, we had the opportunity of observing the attitude they assumed toward the colored troops. It was a part of the multiplicity of the duties of colored Y women to visit the hospitals; here they found colored soldiers placed indiscriminately in wards with white soldiers, while officers were accorded the same treatment as were their white comrades. However, we learned that in some places, colored officers would be placed in wards with private soldiers, instead of being given private rooms, as was their military right; and one soldier tells how, after being twice wounded in the Argonne drive, he was taken to Base Hospital No. 56; here he, and others, waited three days before they could secure the attention of either a doctor or a nurse; but when these attendants finally came, the colored soldiers were taken from the hospital beds and placed on cots which were shoved into one end of the room where there was no heat; they then received medical attention, always after the others had been well attended, and were given the food that remained after the others had been served.

There was one notable incident of discrimination on the part of the Knights of Columbus. It occurred at Camp Romagne, where there were about 9,000 colored soldiers engaged in the heartbreaking task of reburying the dead. The white soldiers here were acting as clerks, and doing the less arduous tasks. The Knights of Columbus erected a tent here and placed thereon a sign to keep colored soldiers away. The colored soldiers, heartsore because they, of all the soldiers, German prisoners, etc., that there were in France, should alone be forced to do this terrible task of moving the dead from where they had been temporarily buried to a permanent resting place, immediately resented the outrage and razed the tent to the ground. The officers became frightened lest there should be mutiny, mounted a machine gun to keep order, and commanded the four colored women who were doing service there to proceed at once to Paris. [. . .]

The largest Y.M.C.A. hut in France was one built at Camp Lusitania, St. Nazaire, for the use of colored soldiers. . . .

To this hut one of us was assigned, and served there for nearly nine months. The work was pleasant and profitable to all concerned, and no woman could have received better treatment anywhere than was received at the hands of these 9,000 who helped to fight the battle of St. Nazaire by unloading the great ships that came into the harbor. Among the duties found there were to assist in religious work; to equip a library with books, chairs, tables, decorations, etc., and establish a system of lending books; to write letters for the soldiers; to report allotments that had not been paid; to establish a money order system; to search for lost relatives at home; to do shopping for the boys whose time was too limited to do it themselves; to teach illiterates to read and write; to spend a social hour with those who wanted to tell her their stories of joy or sorrow.

All of this kept one woman so busy that she found no time to think of anything else, not even to take the ten days' vacation which was allowed her every four months. In a hut of similar size among white soldiers, there would have been at least six women, and perhaps eight men. Here the only woman had from two to five male associates. Colored workers everywhere were so limited that one person found it necessary to do the work of three or four. [. . .]

The last, and perhaps the most difficult piece of constructive work done by the colored workers, was at Camp Pontanèzen, Brest. It has been told in another chapter how one of the writers received Brest as her first appointment, and how she was immediately informed upon her arrival that because of the roughness of the colored men, she would not be allowed to serve them. That woman went away with the determination to return to Brest, and serve the colored men there, if there was any way to make an opening; so after finishing her work in the Leave Area, she and her co-worker, who had been relieved from duty at Camp Romagne, were finally permitted to go there, as has been previously explained.

Upon their arrival, they were told that they would be assigned to Camp President Lincoln, where there were about 12,000 S. O. S. troops. Here there were several secretaries and chaplains, and the need was greater at Camp Pontanèzen, where there were 40,000 men, and only one colored secretary. The writers requested that they be located there. The appointment was held up for one day, and finally they became located at Soldiers' Rest Hut, in the desired camp.

They were told that they must retain a room in the city, as the woman's dormitory at Camp Pontanèzen was filled to its capacity. But they contended that to do so would take them away from the soldiers at a time in the evening when they could be of the greatest service. Finally, it was arranged for them to stay in the hut, much to the dissatisfaction of the white secretary in charge.

The next morning before they left their room, a message was received, telling them that transportation would be at the door at any moment they desired, to take them back to Brest; that Major Roberts, the Camp Welfare Officer, had said that they must not stay in the hut. Upon investigation by Mr. B. F. Lee, Jr., the lone colored secretary at this tremendous camp, it was learned that Major Roberts had been told that the women were uncomfortable, and did not wish to stay.

Mr. Lee explained that such was not true. The Welfare Officer then visited the hut, talked with the women, recognized the situation, gave his consent to their staying, and assured them that he was willing and ready to do anything in his power to make them comfortable, and assist in equipping the hut. The white secretary, seeing that the women were going to stay, acquiesced in the situation, instead of moving out, and did everything he could to assist.

After this there was no difficulty experienced at Camp Pontanèzen.

"The Y.M.C.A. and Other Welfare Organizations," in *Two Colored Women with the American Expeditionary Forces* (New York: Brooklyn Eagle Press, 1920; reprint, AMS, 1971), 22, 23–25, 30–31, 32–34, 35–37.

✝ Halidé Edib Adivar
(1884–1964) *Turkish*

Born into the family of a palace official, Halidé Edib was educated at the American College for Girls in Istanbul, becoming its first Muslim Turkish graduate. When she obtained her doctorate in 1901, she was named inspector of lycées, the high schools left behind by French missionaries. Participating actively in public life, Edib campaigned for the education of women, and tried to free women from the veil. Official opposition to articles she wrote for the liberal paper *Tanine* on female emancipation forced her to flee Turkey briefly. She was elected to Ojak, a nationalist club, but she understood that "nationalism used to political purposes is an ideal turned into a monstrosity." In 1910 she divorced the mathematician Salih Zeki Bey (by whom she had two sons) when he took a second wife.

During the war Edib condemned the massacres of the Armenians but later was convinced that Armenian attacks on the Turks had justified their repression. Sent by Djemal Pasha to Syria and Lebanon after his repression of the Arab pro-French movement, she established schools in Damascus, Beirut, and elsewhere to replace French lycées and religious schools. She organized workshops to shape a new community within an orphanage at Aintoura where twelve hundred children of Armenians, Kurds, and Arabs had been thrown together, each of whom "had had its parents massacred by the parents of the other children." She foresaw cooperation replacing Turkish rule over Arabs, and sympathetically noted the defections of Arab conscripts. Her memoirs comment that "the entire war was a folly from every point of view." With a sharp eye for character, landscape, and social conditions, they describe the "heat, the dust, and the sadness of the lonely women" of Konia, forced in the absence of men to cultivate barren fields, to supply food for Turkey and its army; a "scene of misery" at the train station presents the "hopeless and entirely expressionless" faces of survivors of the Armenian massacres.

In 1917, Edib married in absentia the activist Dr. Abdülhak Adnan Adivar, who was translator for Mustafa Kemal Pasha's nationalist forces. Between 1919 and 1922, Halidé fought in the army of Mustafa Kemal (who later took the title Atatürk), winning the rank of staff sergeant. As his first minister of education, she continued to advocate freedom of speech and the equality of women. After a break with Atatürk, she and her husband went into exile in England and the United States from 1923 to 1938. More than thirty novels appeared in Turkish during the course of her career. In 1939 Edib returned to Turkey to become professor of English at Istanbul University, where she had taught previously in 1918–1919. From 1950 to 1954 she served as a deputy in the National Assembly.

✝ Drifting into War

I am against war in general, and so I cannot defend our going into it on any side, but if one disentangles the mass of knotted political arguments of the day and tries to see clearly the psychology of the Young Turk leaders who entered the war, one sees these causes: First, the desire for complete independence; that is, the abolition of the capitulations. The Young Turks tried hard, but in vain, to enlist the sympathies of the Allies. But the Allies wanted their neutrality without paying anything in return. Secondly, the inherited and justified fear of Russian imperialism. Whether Constantinople was promised in 1914 or in 1916 to Russia, the Young Turk leaders believed that England must use Turkey as a bait to catch Russia, to whom she was a traditional and political enemy. Thirdly, the deplorable financial position of Turkey. Even to insure neutrality she needed financial aid, and she could not procure it from the Allies. A well known statesman of to-day told me once that after the refusal of England to pay for the war-ships she had confiscated, the government was strongly carried away by the pro-war element. If this is not the whole of the truth it is at least a significant part of it, and it shows the sore need of Turkey for financial aid. Fourthly, the decided and openly prejudiced pro-Christian attitude of the Allies, who always helped the Christian minorities to gain economic, even political predominance against the interests of the Moslem and Turkish majorities. Fifthly, the psychological insight of Germany into the weak spots of the Turkish situation, and her cleverness in seizing the right moment.

The Young Turk leaders used all the available arguments to justify their entry into the war and to turn the Turkish people against the Allies, who were still very popular in Turkey. It is queer to observe that public opinion turned against the Allies and began to feel the arguments of the Young Turks justifiable only after the Young Turks had passed out of power. The Greek occupation and atrocities under British patronage, and the Armenian atrocities against Adana under the patronage of the French, were talked of as the symptoms of the allied justice and rule in Turkey foreseen by the Unionists before the war.

In 1914 not only the masses but most of the intellectual and leading forces of the Unionists were against the war. Only Enver Pasha and a certain convinced military group, along with the profiteers, were in favor of war. Somehow the war seemed an impossibility, although a great many people feared it and felt uneasy, knowing the strength of military dictatorship in Turkey.

I received two different visits and had two memorable conversations during the first days of October. First came Djemal Pasha, the minister of marine, who took tea in my house with Madame Djemal Pasha.

"I am afraid our government is drifting into war," I said point-blank.

He laughed as if I had said something absurd and childish. I remember the determined expression of his face as he said these very words:

"No, Halidé Hanum, we will not go into war."

"How will you manage that?"

"I have power enough to persuade them not to. If I fail I resign. It would be extreme folly."

Three days later Djavid Bey called. He had an air of despondency and looked seriously troubled.

I asked him the same question.

"If they go into war, I resign," he said. "It will be our ruin even if we win. There are others who will resign as well, but we hope to prevent it. Talaat is against it at the moment."

On the eighteenth of the same month Turkey entered the war.

Djavid Bey with some of his colleagues resigned. Djemal Pasha did not resign.

He called soon after to take leave. He was appointed commander of the third army; that is, on the Russian front. He seemed in good spirits and tried to explain his change of opinion. His chief argument was the Russian one. He already believed that Constantinople would pass to Russia if the allied forces won, and as the Allies did not give sufficient guarantee in return for our neutrality, the supreme duty of the Turkish army was to help the side opposing Russia; and in the event of German and Turkish victory, in which he firmly believed, he thought that the Turks would be free as they have never been before, and that the capitulations and foreign interference generally would cease.

It is very sad to think to-day that if the Allies had consented to the abolition of the capitulations and given some assurance about Constantinople the military party could not have driven Turkey into war.

Djavid Bey was in disgrace and was keenly watched. He did not leave his house for some time. He was sharply attacked and even called a traitor by the extreme Unionists.

Djemal Pasha's destination was changed to Syria as the commander of the fourth army. He was to attack Egypt and try to keep the English busy and make them concentrate great forces on the Syrian front.

The terrific defense of Gallipoli was the first great event of the World War in Turkey. I will not speak of its almost superhuman heroism and sacrifice. For me, all the honor is due to the common Turkish soldier whose name no one knows and who cannot appear in moving pictures as the hero of the day. Mr. Masefield's book, "Gallipoli," makes one realize the great human and great war material which such a nation as the British has lost, and it makes one realize at the same time the fighting value of the Turkish army which could successfully defend Gallipoli against the allied forces and fleets. There was a keen sense in the men of defending the gates to the main Turkish lands; there was a more than keen sense of fighting against the Russian hallucination projected in their brains by the allied forces.

With the allied attack on the Dardanelles, many families once more left Constantinople, and I had to send my children away to Broussa.

It was about the time of the great battle of March 5 that Youssouf Akehura invited the nationalist writers to gather in the offices of "Turk Yourdu" and seriously discuss their future plans if the Allies should force the straits and enter Constantinople. They were to decide in case of such disaster whether they were to stay on in Constantinople and go on keeping the ideals of nationalism in the hearts of the people or pass on and work in safer and more favorable lands.

There was a series of lengthy gatherings and long discussions, which in the end took a somewhat melodramatic turn. But they never lost their hot and passionate character. Dr. Adnan was asked to preside as the most cool-headed person present.

First every one was to define his nationalistic creed. The younger writers, Kuprulu Fuad and Omer Seifeddine, declared that nationalism was the search and the discovery of a nation's ego, and the teaching of it to the individuals of the nation. As to the fundamental elements of the national ego, they were vague. Omer, who became my friend in later years, confessed to me in his humorous way that Keuk-Alp Zia, their master, who was not in Constantinople then, was always changing the fundamental elements of the national ego; they could never be definite for fear they might be called on to formulate something quite different on the same subject.

Aga Oglou Ahmed, as an old nationalist, declared that nationalism was a common mentality composed of four different elements; namely, language, religion, origin, and common customs. And around these four elements and the order of their importance the discussion raged. As political tendencies in Turkish nationalism depended very much on the order of their importance, it made the discussions instructive and illuminating. Hussein Zade Ali, a venerable old unionist and nationalist, declared that religion and language were the foremost elements, and origin came next. "A Moslem negro who speaks Turkish and calls himself a Turk is nearer to me than the originally Turkish Magyar," he said. Thus he stuck to Pan-Islamism in a mild way, while the younger generation insisted more on origin and language, regarding religion as the least important, and thus stuck to Pan-Turanistic tendencies.

Finally the meeting tried to decide with rather melodramatic speeches whether or not the writers who symbolize Turkish nationalism should stay on in Constantinople or go elsewhere. It was then that Mehemmed Ali Tewfik, a young journalist, made a most emphatic speech full of rhetorical effect enthusiastically suggesting that these writers should not only stay but should even find some way of being martyred, and thus seal the sacred cause of nationalism with their blood. Although in those days it was easy enough to get oneself killed, still the writers thus complimented as being worthy of death looked a little queer. Mehemmed Emin, whose name was the first, sat with his hands folded, contemplating, and my humble self, who was also among the chosen, wondered what sort of death Mehemmed Emin contemplated. There were twinkles in many friendly eyes. And I really think that it was the supreme joke in those tragic days.

From *Memoirs of Halidé Edib* (New York: Century, 1926), 379–85.

✝ Manya Wilbushevitz Shohat
(1879–1961) *Russian/Israeli*

Manya Wilbushevitz grew up on an estate near Grodno, Lithuania (Belorussia), the eighth of ten children in a wealthy Jewish family, pulled in different directions by her strict, religious father, her secular mother, and her politically engaged and highly talented older siblings. Three of her brothers founded the earliest chemical, food, and machine industries in Palestine. Several siblings committed suicide.

Manya's early observation of the hardships of the peasants on her father's estate and the workers in one brother's factories shaped her future as a political activist. Her biographer, Shlomo Shva, reported that she said, "I remember myself among the workers, all of them non-Jews. The exploitation was severe and they worked up to sixteen hours a day. . . . Sometimes there were accidents—a hand torn off, fingers cut off. This shocked me and left its mark for many years."

Disguised as a boy, Wilbushevitz at age fifteen became an apprentice carpenter in a brother's factory in Minsk, where she organized educational circles among Jewish workers and became involved in revolutionary activities. At eighteen she joined a group carrying out emergency health services in Kazan, where she observed collective child care and shared housing in a village commune. On her return to Minsk she formed an urban collective with her friends.

Imprisoned in 1899 during the repression of Bundist sympathizers, Wilbushevitz adopted a new czarist policy of economic reform coupled with political quiescence. Upon her release from prison, in concert with Zubatov, the chief of the Moscow secret police, she helped found the Jewish Independent Labor Party (JILP). During the brief reign of the JILP, workers gained many freedoms, including the right to organize. Manya even secured permission from the authorities to hold a Zionist Conference in Russia. In 1903, after the infamous Kishinev pogroms convinced Manya that Jews must take up arms in self-defense, she joined a group plotting to assassinate Minister of the Interior von Plehve, assuming the task of raising funds to purchase arms; while she was abroad her fellow conspirators were killed.

In 1904 Wilbushevitz traveled to Palestine, where she devised a plan to create collective agricultural settlements to absorb fleeing Russian Jews. With the help of Israel Shohat, who had formed the secret self-defense group named Bar-Giora, and of Eliyahu Krause, who ran a farm to train agricultural workers, Manya created Sejera, the first collective settlement in Palestine.

At the end of the year, Manya and Israel married; they founded Hashomer (the Watchman), a pioneering group dedicated to collective farming and employed as armed guards to defend other settlements against marauders.

During World War I the Ottomans ordered Jewish settlers to turn in their arms. Arrested in 1914 on suspicion of harboring weapons, Manya became the first wartime Jewish prisoner. Brought to Jaffa for interrogation by the much-feared governor Baha al Din, she lectured him on Zionism. After her trial in Damascus she was exiled with her husband and other Zionist leaders to Anatolia, where her daughter, Anna, was born.

In 1917 Britain signed the Balfour Declaration acknowledging the claims of the Jewish people to Palestine. On Shohat's return with her family, she helped form kibbutz Kfar Giladi on the northern border, where immigrants and arms could be smuggled. She traveled frequently to the United States and Europe to raise funds.

Shohat consistently advocated the equality of women and men, Jewish self-defense, collective entrepreneurship, and friendship between Arabs and Jews. She cofounded the League for Arab-Jewish Friendship and was active in every major social movement and institutional undertaking in the emerging State of Israel.

✝ My Meeting with Baha al Din

When I was arrested in November 1914, I was imprisoned in Jaffa in the French monastery, which the Turks had turned into an army barracks. Underneath my cell was a cellar in which Jewish and Arab prisoners were tortured at night with inhuman cruelty by order of the *Kimkem* of Jaffa, Baha al Din. And usually for trivial deeds. The screams and the sobs of the tortured pierced my cell through the thick floor and walls every night and drove me crazy.

A hatred for Baha al Din burned in me and I felt compelled to seek revenge against him. About two weeks after my arrest I was brought to his office for interrogation. He interrogated me about the Zionist movement. At first he spoke politely and then he suddenly leapt from his seat and erupted furiously in shouts and curses about the Jewish settlement using different terms, such as "liars," "traitors," "dogs," and the like.

My hatred for him reached a peak, my reason stopped functioning, and all I wanted was to kill him. On his desk was a very sharp *shabaria* or dagger with a pretty handle, made by an artisan. During the interrogation I picked it up and held it several times aimlessly, and each time he would take it back from me and put it in its place. Suddenly I was seized with the desire to stab him. I grasped the *shabaria* and with all my strength I swung it at his neck. He managed to duck behind the table. There he had an alarm bell. The guards came in and he ordered that I be returned to my cell.

After this "friendly" conversation he reported that I was a very dangerous woman and demanded that I be given the death penalty.

Translated by Alma Hadar

Shulamit Reinharz located this document in the Hashomer Archives in Kibbutz Kfar Giladi, Israel, and revised the headnote by Alma Hadar. Jerusalem-based Yad Izhak Ben-Zvi (Institute for Research on Eretz-Israel, Its People and Cultures) prepared the Hebrew text.

✠ Anna Eisenmenger
Austrian

Anna Eisenmenger, who dedicated her book, *Blockade: The Diary of an Austrian Middle-Class Woman, 1914–1924,* "to all the women in the world," wished to entreat her readers "without distinction of race or creed, of nationality or of party" to set themselves against war. No medals, monuments, or pensions, she said, could compensate for the suffering on the battlefield and in the home. A belated pacifist, she was an enthusiastic defender of the war for its duration; passing comments reveal her anti-semitism and imperialism. Throughout she condemns the "cruel and exorbitant" terms of the Armistice, which imposed payments and confiscated agricultural machinery and railway stock in compensation for war damages. Above all she condemns the "offensive" against German and Austrian civilians by the continuation of the blockade, compounded by the loss of food and coal from the newly independent regions of the former Austrian Empire.

Eisenmenger's husband, doctor to Archduke Franz Ferdinand, was among the first to learn of the assassination; opposed to the war, he worked incessantly in his Viennese hospital until he died of a heart attack. Her three sons, aged nineteen, seventeen, and fifteen when the war broke out, were drafted; the oldest was reported missing on the Russian front in 1915.

The autobiography skips the "interminable war years with their inhumanly destructive conflicts," beginning with diary entries from October 25, 1918. At first, she says, housewives were willing to skimp and make do with inadequate rations, in the belief that their sacrifices were bringing peace nearer; when she learned in 1918 of soldiers' rotted shoes and chronic hunger, however, she rebelled and bought food on the black market. In spite of her efforts, by November 1918 her aunt and grandson had rickets, her daughter tuberculosis. In the war her son-in-law, Rudi, lost both legs; Erni, the youngest son, returned blinded; and Karl, shell-shocked, became dedicated to the violent overthrow of the Kaiser and of the bourgeoisie. He betrays his mother to a militia group when she illegally hoards food and coal (twenty-eight hundred pounds instead of the legal fifty), in order to care for the disabled and sick members of her extended family.

Although presented as a factual diary, both the retrospective narrative form and the hyperbolic conjunction of romantic events such as suicide, murder, and heroic self-sacrifice suggest that this memoir was fictionalized.

✝ Diary

November 20th, 1918

MOMENTOUS DECREES: HEATING OF ROOMS SUSPENDED. ONLY ½ CWT. COAL PER WEEK AND KITCHEN. ONLY ONE ROOM PER HEAD ALLOWED.

Our flat consists of six rooms, with kitchen, maids' room and bathroom. As eight persons live in these rooms, we have nothing to fear from the Government Control Commissions, which are rigorously commandeering unused rooms. Erni and Wolfi are sleeping in my bedroom. Karl has his own room. Aunt Bertha is in the writing-room. Liesbeth and Rudi I have put in what used to be our dining-room, since, in view of the difficulty of heating, we make do with one room as sitting-room and dining-room. This is the large room which used to be the drawing-room, looking on to the garden and containing the piano. Up to now I have been able to keep this room at a tolerable temperature of 12–14 degrees Réaumur by means of a small iron stove. The room has two windows and a double glass door leading on to the verandah. As we get all the winter sunshine on this side, we have even now heat and light. I have furnished this room as best I could, and have taken pains to reserve a special place for every member of the family. Under the large glass chandelier stands the dining table. At every window I have set a writing table. The large gentleman's writing table with its many drawers has been appropriated by Karl. My own writing table is used alternately by Liesbeth and myself. Poor Rudi, who is still lying in hospital and is visited daily by Liesbeth, is to have his wheel chair placed before the glass doors, which, with Kathi's help, I have sealed against draughts expressly for this purpose. The wheel chair has two handles by means of which the invalid is able to propel himself. Liesbeth, who is still suffering from the discomforts of her pregnancy and was quite crushed by Rudi's misfortune, has roused herself a little in response to my entreaties. She looks after Erni and has studied the alphabet for the blind with him, so that now they can read together. Erni, however, thinks that this is all quite superfluous, as he is convinced that he will very soon have recovered his sight. He submits to this instruction for the blind mainly because he enjoys Liesbeth's company and it helps to pass the time.

Wolfi has become Erni's best and most faithful friend. He takes him for walks; he tells him about everything he sees and never leaves him without asking whether there is anything he wants and assuring him that he will very soon be back again. Wolfi also visits poor Aunt Bertha, who can now hardly walk at all and only moves from her bed to her armchair and back again. Yet she is always cheerful and good tempered, with a genius for diffusing consolation all around her. As she has the room next to the sitting-room, I was able, by opening the door, to maintain a tolerable temperature in her room too. The bedrooms were only heated very little and according to the outside temperature. Not until the temperature sank to freezing point did Kathi heat the bedrooms a little after she had tidied them. As in other years, I had during the summer saved up a little stock of coal in the cellar. When the decree was issued that no one must possess or consume more than ½ cwt. of coal per week and that it must be used exclusively for cooking purposes, I ought to have notified to the authorities my little supply of coal, which amounted to about 1½ tons. Probably it would be requisitioned; possibly I should be fined. During the War there had been no Government restrictions in regard to wood and coal. The prices were very high compared with peace prices, but it was possible to secure considerable quantities from a coal-merchant if one had been a regular customer. Now the difficulty of supplying coal for household needs has suddenly become very painfully aggravated, for the Czechs have completely stopped the export of coal to Austria and Germany, while the German coal-mining districts are occupied by the French or the Poles, who likewise refuse to supply any coal to the vanquished nations. My simple woman's brain tries in vain to understand why the victors have adopted these measures. The temperature has fallen considerably during the last weeks. Heating of the living rooms has been forbidden by the authorities. A new struggle, which we were spared during the War, is being imposed upon us housewives: the struggle against the winter cold in our homes.

Since I, like most other housewives, had already infringed the law by resorting to complicated and forbidden methods of procuring the most necessary articles of food, I resolved to run the further risk of keeping my little stock of coal and, in consequence, of coming into conflict with the new authorities. As the cellars were to be searched by the Volkswehr for supplies of wood and coal, I had to act at once. I came to an understanding with our good-natured house-porter, promising him 2 cwt. of coal if he would quietly transfer on to the verandah the stock of coal in my cellar. The other people living in the house must not see it, for how often it had happened that an envious and less fortunate neighbour had secretly given information to the authorities! At eleven o'clock at night, when everyone else was asleep, I began, aided by Kathi and the house-porter, to transport to our verandah the supply of coal in the kitchen. The porter used the Viennese "Holzbutte," a large wooden pail carried on the back. Kathi and I together carried the washing-basket. As we live on the third floor, we had to go up and down four storeys each time, for there is no lift in our house. By two o'clock in the morning Kathi was so exhausted that I had to send her to bed. At four o'clock we had almost all the coal on the verandah. But both I and the porter were utterly worn out. I hastily gave the old man a glass of plum brandy, washed myself clean of the coal-dust, and crept quietly into bed, so as not to disturb Wolfi and Erni.

That I should one day, in order to escape freezing in my own home, carry up my coal and thereby constitute myself a criminal, was something that no one had prophesied at my cradle. But this is war, the war of the housewives against that lack of primary physical necessities which is evidently not to cease even after the cessation of the Great War in the trenches.

From *Blockade: The Diary of an Austrian Middle-Class Woman, 1914–1924* (London: Constable, 1932), 75–79. Reprinted by permission of Constable Publishers.

✝ Louise Thuliez
(1882–1966) *French*

A schoolmistress from Lille, Louise Thuliez was caught behind German lines while she was on vacation near Mons, Belgium, in August 1914. She had lost her mother when she was ten, and her father just before the war broke out. She quickly became part of a network of resistance that concealed Allied soldiers and local men of draft age, eventually conducting hundreds of them to safety at the Dutch border. Rationing made long-term concealment of men difficult; when hidden men were discovered, villages were subjected to punitive taxes and suspected collaborators were imprisoned and several were executed. By the end of September 1914, Thuliez had met Reginald and Marie de Croÿ, who described her as a mere girl; she persuaded them to use their chateau to hide men whose condition did not permit the harsh and unsettled underground life of forest hideouts. In 1915, under different pseudonyms, she regularly "passed" men to Brussels. Her task was somewhat thankless: the young soldiers she helped threatened her, for fear she would betray them, and villagers held her responsible for German raids. When arrested on July 31, 1915, she was carrying false identity papers, an encoded address book, letters from soldiers, and patriotic pamphlets. During her trial for high treason with thirty-five codefendants, she explained her motive under cross-examination: "because I am French." Her lawyer had not been allowed to speak to her or to consult the judicial dossier.

The leaders of the network, Philippe Baucq and Edith Cavell, were sentenced to death (plus "one year and one month" of imprisonment) and executed immediately in spite of pleas for clemency from the American consul, the pope, and Alfonso XIII of Spain. Thuliez and six others were also condemned, but their sentences were commuted, and she spent the rest of the war in German prisons. After the war she returned to teaching. In World War II she worked for the resistance again organizing escapes. When she died, she was the most decorated woman in France.
  JS

✝ In Open Country

Strangely, our protégés did not seem to realize the dangers they ran and made us run.

For our last departure from Englefontaine, four men were brought to us, three of them drunk. We had to cross the whole forest, the roads were soaked with recent rains, and we wondered with anguish what would happen to us if we met patrols, the usual reaction in this case being to disappear in the brush or to fall flat on the ground. Luckily, after an hour's walk, by dint of the great cold and rain, the men recovered a normal state and we crossed the forest without any incident.

The forest was not an absolutely certain refuge. The paths were traveled by Germans hunting or strolling. One day, Mademoiselle Mariamé left me in thick woods with seven men, while she scouted the villages we were to cross that evening. We were talking in low voices when one of the men, his finger on his lips, beckoned us to throw ourselves on the ground. We did so instantly, and since the thicket was not very leafy, we saw passing at ten meters two Germans bearing rifles, who were calmly chatting without any suspicion of our presence or the fear they had caused us.

At night after the curfew we left the forest. The roads were deserted. Everyone stayed at home carefully concealing light to avoid inopportune visits of German soldiers quartered in the region. Travel continued to be dangerous, because we had to go alongside a main road at points.

The stretch that separated us from Bellignies, our new resting place, which normally could be covered in four hours on foot, required six or seven because of the detours and false alarms. Since our men did not know the countryside, we had to allow for the possibility of becoming dispersed. One of us went before the group by thirty meters or so, and if she met Germans, was to drop a white handkerchief.

When the routes were unknown to us, we used smugglers as guides, and it must be said that they were among our best assistants. But these men, accustomed to danger, sometimes lacked prudence: the only time we dared confide to one of them a night expedition with ten men, he forgot the rule of silence and got himself arrested. The troop dispersed and the passage had to be undertaken a second time.

On our trips we had noted sunken paths where the men were allowed to smoke and refresh themselves with the fresh water of a stream. For these nocturnal trips the men wore rope espadrilles to deaden the noise of their steps and advanced slowly in columns, ready at the first warning to throw themselves into the ditch beside the road. We feared cars, foot patrols, German bicyclists, supply convoys that immobilized us for long periods hidden in the meadows or lying in the fields, and we cursed the dogs whose barking awoke sleeping villages.

One evening, forced to undertake by myself the passage of fourteen men coming from Maroilles, I had as usual spent the day in the forest which I left towards nine at night. I had split the men into three groups and led the first to show the way, while I had confided to the second group the supervision of the third. At the edge of the forest, there was a choice among three roads: two led to occupied villages, the third, the one we should follow, allowed us to take paths sheltered from unwanted encounters. We went along at a good pace and we had just met a couple of peasants to whom in passing we mumbled our usual unintelligible "good evening," when a soldier of the second group caught up with us to warn me that since the last bend the others were no longer following. That worried me, because they could stray a good distance in the opposite direction or get very far along on the wrong road. I left the first and second groups in a meadow bordered by hedges, urging the men not to move and to wait patiently for my return. I retraced my steps and crossed the woman I had met before, who said to me brusquely, "You are looking for the Englishmen, but rest assured, they took the road to Gommegnies and my husband will bring them back to you."

"I don't know what you mean," I answered in an indifferent tone, "and I don't know if there are Englishmen in this area." "No," replied this woman, "I just passed you, and you were with some Englishmen." Since she seemed sincere, I thought it was simpler to tell her the truth and a few minutes later her husband rejoined us, bringing the four stray soldiers.

I got back to the meadow, where the others were waiting. To my great surprise, I found on the roadside a series of luminous points: my protégés, having found that time hung on their hands, had scattered along the road and lit up cigarettes without a thought for the patrols who might pass by there.

From *Condamnée à mort* (Paris: Flammarion, 1933), 68–74.

✟ Marthe Richer, née Betenfeld, pseudonym: Marthe Richard (1889–1982) *French*

Born in 1889 to working-class parents, Marthe Betenfeld was the third of four children, her twin sister having died within hours of birth. Although her parents were firmly secular, when she entered school, the French had not yet nationalized girls' education, so she attended a Catholic primary school. While young she was haunted by feelings of inadequacy due to her family's chronic poverty; at twelve she became housekeeper for a German professor, from whom she learned the fluent German so useful later in her life. One year later she was forced to leave school and become apprenticed to a seamstress, a time she remembered as "enslavement" that nearly drove her to suicide. At age seventeen she ran away to Paris, where she was caught by the police, who confined her in a jail with prostitutes, then in a clinic, from which she soon escaped. Thus began a life at the edge of authority.

After a brief affair with an Italian, Marthe met the wealthy Henri Richer in 1906, whom she resisted marrying, as she feared constraints upon her independence; they lived together in luxury, both learning to fly in 1912 after meeting the Wright brothers. Just before Henri went off to war they finally married. During his absence, Marthe organized a group of female pilots to carry army supplies and messages, but the services of her group were rejected by the French authorities, who would not hear of women in the military. In 1916 Henri was killed, and Marthe decided to "fight for my country as my husband had done."

Introduced to Captain Georges Ladoux of the counterespionage office, Richer offered him her expertise as a flyer and linguist. After an initial venture to Sweden that ended in failure, she reluctantly became the mistress of the chief of German espionage in Spain, Captain Hans von Krohn. When von Krohn discovered in late 1917 that she had been feeding him false information, she escaped to France, only to discover that Captain

Ladoux meanwhile had been arrested on a charge of conspiring with the Germans. At a hospital where she had begun to work, she met her second husband, Thomas Compton, an Englishman who died in 1928. In 1932 a highly embroidered account of her espionage was published by Captain Ladoux, and she was awarded the Legion of Honor in 1933.

World War II once again saw her fighting the Germans: she evaded the Gestapo, who sought retribution for her work in the previous war, and with her brother helped Alsatian Jews escape from France to safety. In 1944 she was elected to the municipal council of Paris; in this office she initiated the Marthe Richard Law, which ordered the closing of Parisian brothels, and gained a reputation as a specialist in prostitution and women's social conditions. The three books she wrote about her experiences as a spy—*Ma vie d'espionne, au service de la France* (I spied for France, 1935), *Espions de guerre et de paix* (Spies in war and peace, 1938), and *Mon destin de femme* (My destiny as a woman, 1974)—as well as her biographies all testify to her cool, courageous determination and to the irrepressible mythologizing that springs up around the life of a female spy.

CW

✝ Preface

My life as a spy. I write these words proudly. To be a spy in wartime does not mean, as is sometimes imagined, to throw oneself into a novelistic adventure in which danger sharpens the pleasure; it is not to play the role of femme fatale, to turn heads, to capture secrets that you deliver in exchange for piles of gold.

To be a spy means, first of all, to serve. A "secret service" where everything happens in the shadows and whose soldiers fall silently, as if into a trap. It is to serve leaders whose role and virtual duty is to distrust you. Terrible profession! Mistrust confines you on all sides. Your mission is to make the enemy believe that you betray your country. But the enemy hesitates. . . . She who betrays may be a spy, a double agent. . . . And those who have sent you doubt. . . . Thus the secret agent who serves her country as a double agent is subject to one of the most cruel tortures imaginable; she is caught between two fires—and those fires may sometimes become salvoes.

I have known this suffering; perhaps I would have refused the missions given me by the Fifth Bureau if I had known what price I would pay, not for the failures, but for the successes themselves. I wanted to fight. My husband had been killed at the front. Before the war I was a pilot. I had planned to join our heroes, the aviators, and I had founded the Patriotic Union of French Women Flyers.

I knocked at every door. Having learned that the British accepted women flyers, I proposed they accept Frenchwomen. Alas, no one wanted women among the combatants. One front remained: the secret service. I went.

The Fifth Bureau was poor. It was with my own money that I paid my way on my first missions. The money the Germans gave me for my pseudo-betrayals I handed over to my chiefs to feed the budget for counter espionage.

If I write these memoirs fifteen years after the war, when I would have preferred never to speak of myself and to enjoy a restored peace, it is solely to show the wretched life of those who fought and fell without glory in the service of France.

January 23, 1933, the government named me Chevalier of the Legion of Honor. May those who then responded with sarcasm to the praise this distinction brought me read this *truthful* report of my life as a spy, and then say if this glorious reward seems to them unmerited.

From *Ma vie d'espionne, au service de la France* (Paris: Éditions de France, 1935), i–ii.

✝ Antipyrine and Collargolium

"Why that's magnificent," cried Captain Ladoux when I had evoked before him the silhouette of the man, the leader, who had engaged me. "You have caught the one you were to find in Spain: it's the Baron von Krohn, the German naval attaché in Madrid, the nephew of Marshal von Ludendorff, general of the German army."

I modestly accepted this triumph. But I confess it pleased me, a first revenge for my past failures. The interview at the rue Jacob with "M. Delorme" this time was to my advantage.

"You again, after less than a month?" he had said when I arrived.

"I came back because I have succeeded. I think I am bringing you something interesting and important." Proud of my trophies, I placed before my chief the secret procedure for spy writing, unknown in France up to then and indecipherable.

Captain Ladoux examined my evidence not without emotion: grains of collargolium and the pen with it.

Since the beginning of the war, German spies had been corresponding with their leaders without our having been able to discover their invisible ink, and thus intercept their correspondence.

This time, Captain Ladoux did not hustle me. He seemed even careful with me. He must have felt some pride in my success, since he had discovered me. "Thanks to you many lives will be saved, Martha. It's excellent. I am happy."

Shall I confess it? At that moment I regretted nothing. Neither the refusal by the air force, nor the misadventures I had had in Sweden. I was a spy, true, but a spy in wartime and in those days no one thought about ethics. My role had only one meaning: danger. I served my country, I was useful.

I was happy, happy, as only women know how to be when their sacrifice is not in vain. I told Captain Ladoux in detail about my first Spanish encounters: Walter . . . Stephan . . .

"Your Baron," I added, "was oddly troubled; I think I don't displease him. I had to call him to order. I'm willing to be a spy, but that's all. This gentleman seems to want to unite the useful with the pleasurable."

"He is waiting for you?" asked the captain.

"He can wait forever. I don't want to see him again. He is too ugly."

For the rest of my life I shall not forget the following scene: the captain jumped up and began to pace the room. His face traced in successive traits the disorderly movement of his thought. He drew nervous puffs of smoke and crushed off the ashes that fell on his vest. After a few moments of vehement reflection, he approached and declared, "You came of your free will to the service. You have begun. It is impossible to go backwards. Your duty is to return, to continue your mission. You are a woman; you will act as you see fit."

Brusquely my joy faded. "I am a woman, yes, but if I stay in Spain one day I will no longer be able to avoid . . ."

Simulating sang-froid, the captain leaned on a table and continued: "It's indispensable, you must return. . . . Martha, think of the sacrifice of the men in the trenches, the country that may be invaded. You are French, you have the chance to serve your country better than any other. It is an opportunity. Don't refuse."

From *Ma vie d'espionne, au service de la France* (Paris: Éditions de France, 1935).

✝ Isak Dinesen, pseudonym of Karen Christence Blixen (1885–1962) *Danish*

The five children in Karen Blixen's aristocratic Danish family were educated at home; the girls learned primarily domestic skills, languages, and decorative arts. Her father—who had served in parliament, lived among North American Indians, and fought in more than four military campaigns—committed suicide when she was ten, deeply altering the family structure. Karen turned to writing, producing a play for her family, poems, and stories influenced by Danish folktales, sagas, and myths.

Like her father, Blixen relished travel, studying first in Switzerland in 1898: "I was constantly in flight, an exile somewhere." Both a talented painter and a writer, she enrolled in drawing school, entering the Danish Royal Academy as a student in 1902, and in 1904 she spent a year perfecting her English at Oxford. Under the pseudonym Osceola, she published stories that received encouraging responses from publishers and critics; in the same years she studied art in Paris and Rome.

At twenty-seven Blixen became engaged to her cousin, Baron Bror Blixen-Finecke, who with help from her family purchased farmlands in British East Africa (Kenya). They married in 1914. The farm was unprofitable, as the land was too elevated to grow coffee; the marriage also failed after Bror infected her with syphilis so severe that she was forced to return to Denmark in 1915 for treatment. They separated in 1921 and divorced in 1925. Despite her ill health, Blixen ran the farm alone, forming ties both to the settlers and to the native Kikuyu and Masai. There she fell in love with the English pilot Denys Finch Hatton, who inspired her to begin writing again. After he died in a 1931 crash, she returned to Denmark. With financial help from her brother she published her first success, *Seven Gothic Tales* (1934), under the pseudonym Isak Dinesen ("Isak" means laughter in Hebrew).

Blixen's *Out of Africa* (1937) secured her literary reputation through its vivid landscapes, sharply realized characters, and sense of drama. She published *Winter's Tales* (1942) and *Angelic Avengers* (1944), collections of stories notable for their subtle prose and their blend of the fantastic with the simple. In the postwar era the "Baroness" gathered a circle of younger intellectuals and literary figures around her; she became famous for a series of radio talks. When she died she left her house to the Danish Literary Academy and the family parklands of Rungstedlund were preserved as a bird sanctuary.

TP

✝ A War-time Safari

When the war broke out, my husband and the two Swedish assistants on the farm volunteered and went down to the German border, where a provisional Intelligence Service was being organized by Lord Delamere. I was then alone on the farm. But shortly afterwards there began to be talk of a Concentration Camp for the white women of the country; they were believed to be exposed to danger from the Natives. I was thoroughly frightened then, and thought: If I am to go into a ladies' Concentration Camp in this country for months,—and who knows how long the war is going to last?—I shall die. A few days later I got the chance to go, with a young Swedish farmer, a neighbour of ours, to Kijabe, a station higher up the railway line, and there to be in charge of a camp to which the runners from the border brought in their news, which had then to be telegraphed on to Headquarters in Nairobi.

At Kijabe I had my tent near the station, amongst stacks of firewood for the railway engines. As the runners came in at all hours of the day or night, I came to work much together with the Goan Stationmaster. He was a small, wild man, with a burning thirst for knowledge, unaffected by the war around him. He asked me many questions of my country, and made me teach him a little Danish, which he thought would at some time come in highly useful to him. He had a small boy of ten, named Victor; one day as I walked up to the station, through the trellis-work of the Verandah, I heard him going on teaching Victor his grandson: "Victor, what is a pronoun?—what is a pronoun, Victor?—You do not know?—Five hundred times have I told you!"

The people down by the border kept on demanding provisions and ammunition to be sent to them; my husband wrote and instructed me to load up four ox-waggons and to send them down as soon as possible. But I must not, he wrote, let them go without a white man in charge of them. For nobody knew where the Germans were, and the Masai were in a state of high excitement at the idea of war, and on the move all over the Reserve. In those days the Germans were supposed to be everywhere, and we kept sentinels by the great railway bridge of Kijabe to prevent them blowing it up.

I engaged a young South African by the name of Klapprott, to go with the waggons, but when they were all loaded up, on the evening before the expedition was to start off, he was arrested as a German. He was not a German, and could prove it, so that only a short time afterwards he got out of the arrest and changed his name. But at that hour I saw in his arrestation, the finger of God, for now there was nobody but me to take the waggons through the country. And in the early morning, while the old constellations of the stars were still out, we set off down the long endless Kijabe Hill, with the great plains of the Masai Reserve,—iron-grey in the faint light of the dawn,—spread at our feet, with lamps tied under the waggons, swinging, and with much shouting and cracking of whips. I had four waggons, with a full team of sixteen oxen to each, and five spare oxen, and with me twenty-one young Kikuyus and three Somalis: Farah, Ismail, the gun-bearer, and an old cook also named Ismail, a very noble old man. My dog Dusk walked by my side.

It was a pity that the Police when arresting Klapprott, had at the same time arrested his mule. I had not been able to recover it in all Kijabe, so that for the first few days I had to walk in the dust beside the waggons. But later I bought a mule and saddle from a man whom I met in the Reserve, and again some time after a mule for Farah.

I was out then for three months. When we came down to our place of destination, we were sent off again to collect the stores of a big American shooting Safari that had been camping near the border, and had left in a hurry at the news of the war. From there the waggons had to go to new places. I learned to know the fords and water-holes of the Masai Reserve, and to speak a little Masai. The roads everywhere were unbelievably bad, deep with dust, and barred with blocks of stone taller than the waggons; later we travelled mostly across the plains. The air of the African highlands went to my head like wine, I was all the time slightly drunk with it, and the joy of these months was indescribable. I had been out on a shooting Safari before, but I had not till now been out alone with Africans.

The Somali and I, who felt responsible for the Government's property, lived in constant fear of losing the oxen from lions. The lions were on the road, following after the big transports of supplies of sheep and provisions, which now continually were travelling along it to the border. In the early mornings, as we drove on, we could see, for a long way, the fresh spoor of the lions in the dust, upon the waggon-tracks of the road. At night, when the oxen were outspanned, there was always a risk of lions round the camp frightening them, and making them stampede and spread all over the country, where we would never find them again. So we built tall circular fences of thorn-trees round our outspanning and camping places, and sat up with rifles by the campfires. Here both Farah and Ismail, and old Ismail himself, felt at such a safe distance from civilization that their tongues were loosened, and they would narrate strange happenings of Somaliland, or tales out of the Koran, and the Arabian Nights.

Both Farah and Ismail had been to sea, for the Somali are a seafaring nation, and were, I believe, in old days, great pirates of the Red Sea. They explained to me how every live creature on the earth has got its replica at the bottom of the sea: horses, lions, women and giraffe all live down there, and from time to time have been observed by sailors. They also recounted tales of horses which live at the bottom of the rivers of Somaliland, and at full-moon nights come up to the grass-land to copulate with the Somali mares grazing there, and breed foals of wonderful beauty and swiftness. The vault of the nocturnal sky swung back over our heads as we sat on, new constellations of stars came up from the East. The smoke from the fire in the cold air carried long sparks with it, the fresh firewood smelt sour. From time to time the oxen suddenly all at once stirred, stamped and squeezed together, sniffing up in the air, so that old Ismail would climb on to the top of the loaded waggon, and there swing his lamp, to observe and to frighten off anything that might be about outside the fence.

We had many great adventures with lions: "Beware of Siawa," said the Native leader of a transport going North, whom we met on the road. "Do not camp here. There are two hundred lions at Siawa." So we tried to get past Siawa before nightfall, and hurried on, and as haste makes waste on a Safari more than anywhere else, about sunset a wheel of the last waggon stuck on a big stone, and it could go no farther. While I was now holding the lamp to the people working to lift it off, a lion took one of our spare oxen not three yards from me. By shouting and cracking the whips, for my rifles were with the Safari, we managed to frighten off the lion, and the ox, that had run away with the lion on his back, came back to us, but it had been badly mauled, and died a couple of days later.

Many other strange things happened to us. At one time an ox drank up all our supply of paraffin, died on us, and left us without light of any kind until we got to an Indian dhuka in the Reserve, deserted by the owner, where strangely some of the goods were still untouched.

We were for a week camped close to a big camp of the Masai Morani, and the young warriors, in war-paint, with spears and long shields, and head-dresses of lion-skin, were round my tent day and night, to get news of the war and of the Germans. My own people of the Safari liked this camp, because here they bought milk from the Morani's herd of cattle that trekked about with them and was herded by the young Masai boys, the Laioni, who as yet are too young to become warriors. The juvenile Masai soldier-girls, very lively and pretty, came into my tent to call on me. They would always ask for the loan of my hand-mirror, and, when they held it up to one another, they bared their two rows of shining teeth to the mirror, like angry young carnivora.

All news of the movements of the enemy had to pass through Lord Delamere's camp. But Lord Delamere was moving all over the Reserve in such incredibly swift marches, that nobody ever knew where his camp was to be found. I had nothing to do with Intelligence Work, but I wondered how the system worked for the people employed in it. Once my way took me within a couple of miles of Lord Delamere's camp, and I rode over with Farah and had tea with him. The place, although he was to break camp next day, was like a city, swarming with Masai. For he was always very friendly with them, and in his camp they were so well regaled that it had become like the lion's den of the fable: all footsteps turning in and none out. A Masai runner, sent with a letter to Lord Delamere's camp, would never show himself again with an answer. Lord Delamere, in the centre of the stir, small, and exceedingly polite and courteous as ever, his white hair down on his shoulders, seemed eminently at ease here, told me everything about the war, and offered me tea with smoked milk in it, after the Masai fashion.

My people showed great forbearance with my ignorance of oxen, harness and Safari ways; they were indeed as keen to cover it up as I was myself. They worked well for me all through the Safari, and never grumbled, although in my inexperience I asked more of everyone, both men and oxen, than could really be expected of them. They carried bathwater for me on their heads a long way across the plain, and when we outspanned at noon, they constructed a canopy against the sun, made out of spears and blankets, for me to rest under. They were a little scared of the wild Masai, and much disturbed by the idea of the Germans, of whom strange rumours went about. Under the circumstances I was to the expedition, I believe, a kind of guardian Angel, or mascot.

Six months before the outbreak of the war, I had first come out to Africa on the same boat as General von Lettow Vorbeck, who was now the highest in command of the German forces in East Africa. I did not know then that he was going to be a hero, and we had made friends on the journey. When we dined together in Mombasa before he went farther on to Tanganyika and I went up-country, he gave me a photograph of himself in uniform and on horseback, and wrote on it:

Das Paradies auf Erde
Ist auf dem Rücken der Pferde,
Und die Gesundheit des Leibes
Am Busen des Weibes.[1]

Farah, who had come to meet me in Aden, and who had seen the General and been aware that he was my friend, had taken the photograph with him on the Safari and kept it with the money and the keys of the expedition to show to the German soldiers if we were made prisoners, and he attached great value to it.

How beautiful were the evenings of the Masai Reserve when after sunset we arrived at the river or the water-hole where we were to outspan, travelling in a long file. The plains with the thorntrees on them were already

1. Paradise on earth
   is on a horse's back,
   and a body's health
   on a woman's breast. (ed.)

quite dark, but the air was filled with clarity,—and over our heads, to the West, a single star which was to grow big and radiant in the course of the night was now just visible, like a silver point in the sky of citrine topaz. The air was cold to the lungs, the long grass dripping wet, and the herbs on it gave out their spiced astringent scent. In a little while on all sides the Cicada would begin to sing. The grass was me, and the air, the distant invisible mountains were me, the tired oxen were me. I breathed with the slight night-wind in the thorntrees.

After three months I was suddenly ordered home. As things began to be systematically organized and regular troops came out from Europe, my expedition, I believe, was found to be somewhat irregular. We went back, passing our old camping-places with heavy hearts.

This Safari lived for a long time in the memory of the farm. Later on I had many other Safaris, but for some reason,—either because we had at the time been in the service of the Government, a sort of Official ourselves or because of the war-like atmosphere about it,—this particular expedition was dear to the hearts of the people who had been on it. Those who had been with me then came to look upon themselves as a Safari-aristocracy.

Many years afterwards they would come up to the house and talk about the Safari, just to freshen up their memory of it, and to go through one or another of our adventures then.

✝ Alexandra Piłsudska, née Szczerbińska
(1885–1963) *Polish*

One of twelve children, Alexandra, or "Ola," was orphaned when she was ten; she was raised by her grandmother in Suvałki, a Polish town under Russian rule and strictly segregated along ethnic lines. The grandmother, who had participated in the insurrection of 1863, admonished Ola, "When one is born a Pole one must of necessity be born a patriot." As a child Ola was secretly educated by a Polish schoolteacher, then hastily learned Russian in order to complete school at the local Russian Gymnase. She studied law and economics at a Warsaw business college that accepted women. Upon graduation in 1904 she took a job as a clerk in a factory in order to mobilize workers for the Polish Socialist Party.

In 1905, while supporting herself as a private tutor, she joined a militant socialist group (Organizacja Bojowa, renamed Frakcja Revolucyjna), for which she managed the central arms depot in Warsaw, smuggling and storing weaponry. By limiting knowledge to a few links in any chain of transmission, she protected her network from betrayals, but was arrested briefly in 1907. In 1912 she formed the women's intelligence section of the Riflemen's Association, a military force set up by Jozef Piłsudski under Austrian command. In 1914 as a courier with the Polish Legions she passed between Russian and Austrian Poland with military information, propaganda, and supplies. In 1915 she was arrested and held in a prisoner-of-war camp, first at Szczypiorno, then at Lauban for a year. In July 1917 Piłsudski too was captured. Released when the Germans granted Poland partial independence, she worked with the Liga Kobiet, which supplied provisions to the Polish Legions. Half a year after Piłsudski's arrest, she gave birth to their first daughter, Wanda; Jadwiga was born in 1920 and the couple married in 1921.

Jozef Piłsudski, who ruled as Polish head of state and commander of the armed forces from 1918 to 1922, died of cancer in 1935. Alexandra was active in organizations to serve children, the unemployed, and ex-combatants. When the Germans invaded Poland in 1939, Alexandra Piłsudska escaped with her daughters to England, where she composed her memoirs and did relief work.

✠ A Prisoner of War

During the year 1915 I was one of the women couriers in the Legion and travelled continually to and fro between the different local centres carrying propaganda and aiding recruiting. It was inevitable therefore that sooner or later I should come under the ban of the German police.

The attitude of the German authorities towards Pilsudski at that time was a compound of surface cordiality and suspicion. With their hidebound conception of military etiquette they looked upon his First Brigade as an irregular guerilla troop led by a revolutionary, and distrusted his political activities. But as allies of Austria they could not show open hostility to the Legions and were constrained to accept, or at least tolerate, the man who commanded them. On the other hand, they could, and did, use every effort to suppress the P.O.W.[1] on the ground that it was a secret military organization acting against the Government.

At the close of 1915 two-thirds of the country was under German occupation. In Warsaw the Prussian Governor-General, von Beseler, ruled with an iron hand. The Kaiser's secret police poked long inquisitive fingers into every crevice and corner of the city, searching for agitators, as those of the Czar had done before them; the gaols were occupied once again by a new batch of political prisoners. Thus it happened that one afternoon in November I arrived at the house where I was staying in the city to find two German police agents waiting to arrest me on a charge of "inciting citizens to join an illegal organization known as the P.O.W."

I was taken to the Paviak prison, now under German administration. It appeared to have changed little since I had last seen it eight years before, except that the jailers wore different uniforms and the corridors were slightly cleaner. I was put into a cell with two other women, both of whom were classified as criminals, although there was no evidence against them. They were, I discovered, victims of the iron system of German justice. Having the misfortune to be married to men charged with various crimes they had been automatically arrested with their husbands and would probably be detained in the prison for an indefinite period. For the first ten days I remained with them locked in a damp cell which was generally in semi-darkness, for the light filtered in through one small grille which took the

---

1. *P.O.W.:* Polska Organizacja Wojskowa, Polish military organization to which Piłsudska belonged.

place of a window. After nightfall we had not even a candle and we used to sit huddled together round the little stove which was our sole means of heating, telling stories to pass the time. Later I was removed to a separate cell which I occupied with one other woman, Madame Klempinska, a political prisoner like myself, and a member of the P.P.S.[2]

The conditions of the prison were much the same as they had been under the Russian regime; the food was little better. Breakfast consisted of a cup of weak tea and a slice of bread without butter; dinner was a plate of kascha; in the evening there was nothing but a cup of boiling water. After my trial, however, I was allowed to have a parcel of provisions sent in by my lawyer, Mr. Pazchalski, and I and my companion in misfortune lived on it for a couple of days. Never did food taste so delicious!

The German court found me guilty of political agitation and ordered me to be put in a detention camp. At the end of a further fortnight in the Paviak I was taken to Szczypiorno, near Kalisz, one of the biggest camps for prisoners of war in Poland.

My first impressions of Szczypiorno were discouraging to say the least.

Imagine a windswept, desolate field, knee-deep in mud in many places, crossed and re-crossed by lines of dug-outs in which some four thousand prisoners of war and a hundred civilians were herded together. That was the picture which greeted me when I arrived in the gloom of a bleak December afternoon with Madame Klempinska and four men, Polish civilians, who were also to be interned. Wooden-faced Bavarian soldiers received us from the police who had accompanied us from Warsaw; a young lieutenant ran his finger down a list setting forth our names, occupations and sentences, reeled off a perfunctory warning on the folly of trying to escape and then handed us over to the guards. The four men were marched off in one direction, Madame Klempinska and I in another.

The camp had been originally planned in the form of huts, but at the last moment timber had apparently run short, and there had been a compromise resulting in dug-outs, sunk deep into the earth and topped by a flimsy structure of wood about three feet in height and containing small windows. Seen from the front the effect was rather like rows of dolls-houses.

Madame Klempinska and I crossed the field in a thin drizzle of rain which our guard cheerfully informed us fell nearly every day during the winter months, and descended a flight of wooden steps into a sort of cave. It reminded us irresistibly of a vault and had the same musty, earthy smell. When our eyes grew accustomed to the dim light we saw that it was a comparatively large apartment, divided into two by a trench which was spanned by duckboards, a necessary measure for after days of heavy rain it became like a moat. This primitive accommodation was designed for eighty men but as we were the only women in the camp we had it to our-

2. *P.P.S.:* Polish Socialist Party.

selves until we were joined by a young servant girl. It was bitterly cold in those winter days for the one small stove in the centre only gave out heat within a limited radius and the icy winds of December curled through the doors and windows. In one corner were two heaps of sacks filled with sawdust and covered with army blankets. Our beds. There was no furniture of any description, not even a table. For the first few minutes we were too stunned even to give voice to our dismay, but when the guard returned with some papers which we were to sign I asked for an interview with the Commandant of the camp. At first he refused even to pass on the request, saying that it was against the regulations at that hour of the day, but I was so persistent that at length he departed, very reluctantly, to consult the officer on duty. Half an hour later he returned with the message that the Commandant would see me, after I had been disinfected. He stared at me in blank astonishment when I burst out laughing and then explained that the process of disinfection was part of the routine of arrival at the camp. A few minutes later Madame Klempinska and I were initiated into it.

We were taken into a room where a tall grim-looking German woman divested us of our clothes which she rolled up in bundles. Then she led us to two small bath tubs which she proceeded to fill with a very small quantity of water and a great deal of strong disinfectant. After telling us to get into them she departed carrying our clothes, and leaving the door open so that the wind whistled round our naked forms until I ran shivering to shut it. The process of bathing was the reverse of pleasant. The atmosphere in the room was almost glacial for there were no panes in the windows, and the water in the baths was almost boiling. Consequently we were alternately chilled and scalded, while the disinfectant stung our skins until we were the colour of lobsters. After we had endured about fifteen minutes of this the German woman returned bringing two wraps of coarse towelling in which we were bidden to clothe ourselves until our own garments were dry. In the meantime she washed our hair in a strong carbolic lotion which left it as hard and as brittle as straw and so sticky and unmanageable that it took weeks to recover.

The next process was a hasty examination by the German army doctor attached to the camp, who pronounced us in good health and gave us each a couple of injections for typhus. Evidently the theory of disinfection did not extend to this, for he plunged the hypodermic needle first into me and then into Madame Klempinska without even troubling to wipe it.

While we were undergoing all this our clothes were being disinfected in another room with Germanic thoroughness. Apparently they were dealt with even more drastically than we were for when they were returned to us my blue dress had turned green while poor Madame Klempinska's gloves had shrunk so much that she could not get them on.

The rite of purification having thus been accomplished I was taken to see the Commandant, an elderly man, a Prussian officer of the old school with charming manners. He received me courteously and listened sympathetically to my complaint regarding the quarters which had been allotted to me. The camp, he explained, had not been intended for the accommodation of women prisoners, and we were in fact the first whom he had received there. He had already sent in a request to headquarters for beds and mattresses for us and hoped that they would be forthcoming before long. In the meantime he suggested that I should go round with him next morning and see whether I could find among the unoccupied huts one better than our present one.

With this I was forced to be content, but the night that followed was one of the most unpleasant I have ever lived through. I lay awake hour after hour in the darkness listening to the rats scurrying up and down the planks. The trenches were infested with them, and they grew so bold that they used to run over us as we lay on our sacks. I still shudder at the remembrance of those wet, hairy bodies crawling over my arms and neck! After the first few nights I got into the habit of wrapping my blankets round me so tightly that not even my head was left uncovered. Although the Commandant kept his word and moved us to another hut which was slightly less damp and in time even secured camp beds for us the rats continued to be one of our worst trials.

The days passed slowly for us and we had no means of killing time and no contact with the outside world. In theory we were allowed to receive letters but for some reason or other they never seemed to reach us. During the greater part of a year I only heard once from Pilsudski, yet he wrote to me many times. The absence of news was one of the hardest things to bear. One tortured oneself wondering what was happening. Occasionally one of the guards brought in a German newspaper, which was passed round from hut to hut until it almost fell to pieces. We had only one book, the life of Julius Cæsar. We read it over and over again, from cover to cover.

The prisoners of war were divided into two camps, French and Russian. They had their separate cookhouses and were responsible for cooking their own meals. Although the food which was supplied to them was the same—exceedingly good and in enormous quantities—their manner of preparing it was entirely different, characteristic of the two races. The French, although there were no professional cooks among them, expended time and care on their meals and managed to achieve a very creditable example of the cuisine française. The Russians, fatalistic and indifferent, used to heap everything that was given to them—fish, meat, potatoes, cucumber, or anything else that happened to be going—into one stewpan, put it on the fire and then ladle it out in vast platefuls. Madame Klempinska and I and the little servant used to eat in our own hut but we had to fetch our food from the Russian canteen, and we were so disgusted at the unappetizing mess that was served out to us that we petitioned to be allowed to share the food of the French prisoners. However, official red tape would not stretch so far.

The last weeks of December were inexpressibly dreary. The rain poured down in torrents, filling the trenches and turning the field into a bog. Christmas Eve dawned in an atmosphere of gloom for guards and prisoners alike. Madame Klempinska and I sat crouched over the stove and talked of past Christmases, which is a foolish time for anyone, except the very happy, to do [*sic*]. And so my thoughts went back along the years to Suvalki, and I saw myself as a child again, standing at the window watching the snowflakes spreading a soft, glistening blanket over Grandmother's garden, and searching the sky for the first pale star; the Star of Bethlehem, Aunt Maria had said. Only after it had appeared could the Christmas feast begin, and I was hungry for I had fasted since the night before. In imagination I could hear the laughter and chatter in the kitchen where Anusia and Rosalia were putting the finishing touches to the dishes they had been preparing all day, the twelve symbolical dishes of fish and the sweet cakes filled with honey and spices and poppy seeds. My sisters and I had helped too, strewn fragrant herbs and grasses on the tablecloth in remembrance of the first Christmas that had dawned in a stable, and hung the Christmas tree with sweets and red apples from the garden.

"No, not apples" . . . said Madame Klempinska . . . "Paper dolls. I used to make them for a full month before Christmas, and we had cakes on our tree instead of sweets."

"Toys are the best" . . . said a deep bass voice from the doorway . . . "My father used to carve them out of wood for us in the winter evenings." . . .

It was the tall German sentry who could speak a little Polish and wanted to join in the conversation. So he told us stories of Christmas in his peasant home in Bavaria where he and his brothers had gone out into the forest and cut down a young fir tree to be brought and decorated by the mother with toys and gingerbread and little almond cakes made in the shape of crowns for the Kingdom of the Babe of Bethlehem.

Then we talked of the war and he asked me why the Polish Legions were in it . . . "We hear that they were not mobilized as we were, but that they volunteered of their own free will" . . . he said . . . "My comrades and I have often wondered why. Do you Poles love the Emperor Franz Josef so much then that you would shed your blood for him?"

I explained that we loved our freedom and were fighting for that.

"Ah, that is what the whole world would fight for if we knew how" . . . he answered . . . "The Socialists promised it to us, but I do not believe that we shall get it although I am a Socialist. . . ."

Of the war he seemed to know nothing except where it directly concerned him. For him it was narrowed down to his own officers, his own battalion, the strip of Front on which he had fought the Russians. Of the wider issues he had scarcely even heard. He said in his soft Bavarian German . . .

"Gnädige Frau, I see that you have had much more education than I or any of the men in my regiment, so perhaps you can answer for me a question I have often asked myself. Why precisely are we fighting this War?"

Remembering the Russian prisoners from whom I had so often heard the same words, I thought how heavy was the moral responsibility of the rulers who had sent out those vast masses of men, in blind obedience to destroy one another.

Madame Klempinska and I remained at Szczypiorno until the middle of February, and then we were sent for by the Commandant who told us that he had arranged for us to be transferred to another camp at Lauban, where he believed we should be much more comfortable. Then he said good-bye to us as courteously as though we had been his guests instead of his prisoners. I have nothing but pleasant recollections of this man who was the best type of German—cultured, kind and considerate.

Lauban was a pretty little town in Silesia, surrounded with woods which were carpeted with wild flowers later in the year. In February, however, it was intensely cold and we shivered as we walked between guards across the quadrangle to the women's quarters. It was a mixed camp, consisting of a number of enormous wooden huts holding thousands of prisoners of war and civilians, all separated from one another by wooden palisades. Civilians were in one section, French prisoners of war in another, Russians in a third and two Englishmen had one all to themselves in solitary state. A great many of the civilians were Lithuanians who had been evacuated from villages in the firing line. The women and children, who numbered several hundred, were next to us and to pass the time I gave lessons in Polish to many of them. Our hut housed a curious assortment of types and nationalities. Madame Klempinska and myself, a French governess who had been unable to escape from Warsaw before the German occupation of the city, a beautiful Polish girl, who had been the mistress of a well-known Russian spy and was suspected of being herself an international agent, and another woman who owned a large estate behind the firing line and was married to a Polish officer. [. . .]

In one hut were several women who were kept apart from the rest, classified, with true Germanic directness, as "prostitutes." Actually only one of them merited the name as a professional. The rest had been forced by starvation to sell themselves in the streets of Warsaw. Two of them had been teachers in private schools which had closed because of the war, another had been a saleswoman in an exclusive dressmaker's shop which had also put up its shutters, a fourth had been secretary to a rich foreign woman who had hurried back to her own country at the first threat of war. Behind each one was an individual tragedy.

Their lot at the camp was unspeakably wretched. They were subjected to countless humiliating restrictions, and were openly insulted by the guards when they went out for exercise. Yet at night the young soldiers used to climb over the palisade into their huts and force them to accede to them. One of them, a girl of seventeen who had been sent for detention with her mother, cried so bitterly when she told me of this nightly degradation that I protested to the German doctor attached to the camp. He seemed surprised at what he evidently thought a most unreasonable complaint, reminded me that the women were prisoners, and that it was wartime. He flatly refused to do anything in the matter. Eventually matters were brought to a head by an open scandal.

We were sitting in our hut one evening when a Lithuanian woman burst in screaming that all the women in Hut Number X were dying. "Number X" was what was officially known as "The Prostitutes' Quarters."

We hurried there and found some of the women writhing in agony while others sat on their mattresses crying. In the extremity of their misery they had broken up the contents of several packets of needles and swallowed them.

We sent one of the guards for the doctor but he came back with the report that he could not be found and that the dispensary was locked. The nearest hospital was miles away and time was precious. We had no medicine or any means of treating the poor women, and we could think of only one remedy. Fortunately the kascha for our evening meal had just been cooked. We fetched great bowls of it and forced it down their throats. It saved their lives for although some of them were very ill they recovered.

Their tragic attempt at suicide was reported to the Commandant of the camp and an inquiry was instituted. As a result the youngest of the girls was, at our request, allowed to come to our hut.

From *Memoirs of Madame Pilsudski* (London: Hurst & Blackett, 1940), 240–51.

✚ Gogo Dorothy Liwewe
Malawi

In the course of compiling a history of "the Karonga war," named for the northernmost government station in Nyasaland, which was threatened early in the war by attack from German East Africa, Melvin Page interviewed nine elderly Malawi women. Gogo Dorothy Liwewe, like several other women, reported that men were captured at night, assembled on the lakeshore next to the *boma,* or district station, then sent on a lake steamer to Tanganyika to work as porters or soldiers in the war against the Germans. The dearth of men made villages vulnerable to attack by animals or other tribes, and made agriculture more difficult. In some villages fugitives from conscription accused the chief of selling his men, and some women were held hostage until their men emerged from hiding in the forest. When the men returned, many died of illness or starvation; accustomed to live off the land, they "could come and take anything from you" (Abiti Maunde).

✚ Excerpts from Interview with Melvin Page, December 28, 1972

Chichewa language; Penama Village, Nkhotakota District, Malawi

I heard there was war at Tukuyu, and so white men were capturing people in upland districts. . . . They were taking people from there and here and kept them together. People said it was war, and men were being taken away. When they went to war they were made to serve as carriers. Men went, what would women do there? They did not want to go, but they were captured and tied up in chains of palm leaf rope. And then they were put on a steamer and taken to Tukuyu. There they were made carriers. Only crewmen were made soldiers.

The chiefs did not want their men to go, it was just because it was war, and young men were just caught and taken away. They were taking anyone here in Linga in Nkhotakota. They did not say each village should give so many men. There was no friendliness or courtesy in it. They were just capturing people, because they knew—what would the people do? They went by a steamer, HMS *Guendolen*. Some ran away. . . .

The way it was, there was no preparation so the men might take some things. When they were captured, they were given food there at the district office, beans and rice. They didn't say anything. They already knew they were going to war. They did not tell their parents anything, and that's what war is. They were just collecting people as they traveled, and left the men's relatives crying.

After men went to war most of the land was not inhabited. It was sparsely populated. There were very few people. There used to be many people here in Nkhotakota, but most of them had gone to war. Women were in trouble here in the villages. They were worried and said there were no men to dig in the fields for them. How were we to survive? . . .

I did not see whether the government paid money to a conscript's parents. We did not see any money, but many people who went to war died there, and so too from here. Most of them were very thin when they came back. They wore cloth made from sacks. They also had some sacks on their shoulders, probably those bags in which they were given maize flour. The few that came back on their way home took the old road to Ntchisi from here. If they found you digging out cassava, they would ask for a lot of cassava, and if you were too lenient, all the cassava would be gone. Even if the cassava was bitter, they would still chew it as they went their way. As they went through Nkugi, they died as they went along. . . .

What could the chiefs think? They just said the men were gone and whoever was lucky would come back alive. We did not ask that they should come with money. We just heard many people died there. They didn't write letters home. How could they, since the war was still being waged? There was just fighting between the Germans and the British. We heard many people had died at war. And in other villages—do you think they couldn't think of their relatives who were dying at war? . . .

Eh! When they came back, they came a few at a time. Each trip the steamer brought some of them home. When they were taken from Kumtunde, they slept in the open ground at Chanzi stream here. There was a huge crowd gathered as if President Banda were there. But when coming back from the war, two or three, four or five came back, but they would not all get home. According to God's will, that is if he wished, whoever was unlucky died on the way home, mostly in Nkugi. There were no cars, they walked, they were sort of prisoners. Yes, that is why most of them died on the way. There were no cars. Those who came back were thin, but were fed. But if God so wished, they died in their homes. They went to their own villages, where they met their relatives, and were treated as before, so they easily regained their health.

Their relatives were just happy that a man was back alive. They asked what war or fighting was like. And then he would explain that they faced hardships, they ate beans and corn porridge, and it used to cause loose bowels. They also carried baggage. We pitied them. They explained that it was like this and that many people lost their lives there. When a man came to a village, many people gathered showing happiness, and asking him how they traveled and about their experiences generally.

For those who died they held a funeral meeting, like any other death when their relatives had died at war. . . . Because of those who came back alive, we noticed that some of those who had gone to war did not come back. If others came back, where would your relatives then be? That's how they knew. Those who came back also said that many had died at war. There at Tukuyu, dead bodies lay by the hundreds in all types of awful positions. There was no real burial of those who died. . . .

After the war, there was no trouble with the white men. The land was once again at peace, just like before. No one gave white men trouble, they also stayed at peace. Do you think the people could fight white men? The people were afraid. . . . There were rules laid down by the government and the people feared the government. Could they then cause a war? . . . People just stayed because this land was under white rule. Otherwise a war would have arisen between white and black men.

Translated by Melvin E. Page, with Solomon Liwewe

✝ Abitisindo
Malawi

One of the women Melvin Page interviewed in 1973 had served as a courier during the war: Abitisindo accompanied her husband to Manda, where he fought with the King's African Rifles, and where she worked with other women who carried messages. When asked about the cause of the war, she responded that it was the affair of the British government, whose Superintendent of Native Affairs in Nyasaland, J. C. Casson, gave his orders to her. Recalling an individual incident early in the "Karonga" war, she described the capture of a German from German East Africa (Tanganyika) and the attempt by the British to indoctrinate the women.

During the war, white soldiers, by some reports, got women from within the villages: "Women were going for them for two reasons, one, to make money, and two, just to know what type of people they were; but mostly money. Why, it's money that mattered" (Manamu Abiti Mbali). Money was also clearly a motive for Abitisindo, whose husband earned "uncountable amounts," and who never paid the hut tax again after the war.

✝ Excerpts from Interview with Melvin Page, April 4, 1973

Yao language; Chindamba, Malawi

The war was declared by the governor at Zomba. What else: K.A.R. [King's African Rifles], first battalion, second regiment, was what the governor said, this is what [J. C.] Casson said.

Do you think I know why they fought? I went there to eat, that is all. This war was waged for Casson. Where is he? Why can't you go and ask him? . . .

A German wrote a letter, stating clearly the date he would come to fight the British. The British in response dug trenches, deep and long trenches into which they heaped in everything including food and water. This trench was surrounded by barbed wire. While this was happening the British had captured a German soldier. They had kept him.

At the same time the man blew a whistle calling all the women who were around. We rushed in, we were almost 30. We stood in a line and we were all given money. After this a corporal commanded us to run to Lilambi where the German prisoner of war was kept. We were asked not to bring any goods with us. The money that we received was for buying foods on our way. We ran all the way up to the place the German political prisoner was. There we were called by our names. We were told that the German was after the white man who was there taking care of the prisoner. We were further told that the German would take us and marry us to his African soldiers. But we were advised that if war came, we should not escape into our houses, but rather hide in the trenches.

The following morning we were running again all over the place. And you could hear the sound of the drums of the bullets in Songea. War was in progress. Our male soldiers investigated the source of the bullets we heard in Songea. They discovered that the army, the German army, had entered their area. It was going to Kondowe. There was only one person who died on the side of the British, and of course he wasn't Yao. Many perished on the side of the Germans.

We kept on running up to Manda, where we found so many white soldiers. Casson was there again. Casson didn't want to give us leave, he feared that we might tell about the military hardships we envisaged. He gave us a letter. From there we went to board a ship. There were many ships, HMS *Guendolen, Chauncy Maples* and so many others. These were going to Songea. At Songea, Germans ran away up to Maiwa, next to the Indian Ocean. From there they went to Mtamal. Here again Casson came.

Our husbands complained on our behalf to him, saying that we were being overworked. Whereupon Casson said that we warned you, it would be first battalion, second regiment of the K.A.R. So we remained there with our husbands, with Mr. Green. Mr. Green brought us back to Liwela. It is at this place that Manyowa was captured and that marked the end of the war. . . .

I have never seen women fighting war, except for your war. I was there because I was serving my husband. Our husbands were paid, not us. We only earned money in the absence of our husbands. We were paid and again given food. Our husbands were recruited here at Bala, where they were doing their marching. Our husbands earned uncountable amounts, unlike the poor war of the second. We were throwing away money in the first world war. . . .

Are you not fighting for us people and is it not for the tax moneys that you are fighting? Not for people . . .

Translated by Melvin E. Page, with Sigele Chilole

✝ Émilie Carles, née Allais
(1900–1979) *French*

Born into a peasant family in the Briançon region, Émilie Allais was four when her mother died; her dour, almost illiterate father supported his six children as a farmer and part-time sheep smuggler. Joseph Allais strapped Émilie to a mule at age five and introduced her to a peasant's harsh life of labor; when she fell two stories from a barn loft at the age of six, he fatalistically went off to work. After she received first place in the district's primary school exam, he allowed her to accept a state scholarship to secondary school.

Émilie's plan to become a teacher was interrupted by the war, which turned their peaceful rural existence upside down; in 1916 she had to turn down the next stage of study, because she was needed at home. Since her two brothers were fighting at the front, she and her older married sister, Catherine, helped her father on the farm. Catherine's death in childbirth was one in a series of tragedies from which Émilie would emerge as her family's only survivor. Her brother Joseph, who opened her eyes to the needless horrors of war on a trip home in 1916, died of hunger in a German prisoner-of-war camp on the day the Armistice was signed. She outlived all her siblings, including a brother who killed himself and Marie-Rose, a sister whose abusive husband had driven her into a psychiatric ward. She buried the father who had raised her without demonstrating affection or grief at their many losses; her six-year-old daughter, run over by an army truck in World War II; and her beloved husband. Despite these traumas, Carles preserved her energetic and generous spirit, throwing herself into raising her two surviving children and Marie-Rose's four children, whom she adopted.

Joseph's wartime disillusionment had planted in his sister the seeds of rebellion against the patriotic and patriarchal coalition of the French church and state. After the war, she sought to escape the oppressive life of a peasant by going to Paris to earn a teaching certificate in 1920, then a "license" in Italian. At the Sorbonne she became the friend of a libertarian draft evader who urged her to use her position as a teacher to "topple old customs" and to push her students to become freethinkers. Perceiving her to be a radical and "pagan," the mountain villages in which she taught were scandalized by her modernizing agenda. Jean Carles, the man she married at age twenty-seven, was an intellectual; together they supported the pacifist left and the Popular Front in the 1930s, joined worker strikes, and housed refugees from the Spanish civil war. Their pacifist radicalism made them targets for a local administrator's list of suspects during World War II. During the wars in Indochina and Algeria of the 1950s, they demonstrated against imperialism. After her husband died in 1957, Émilie Carles remained in the mountains that had always been home to her, teaching until her retirement in 1964. At the end of her life she won national recognition as founder of a peasant movement to protect the land against government proposals for highways and urban development. The notebooks of memories that she had compiled over many decades to "communicate my love of people and nature, and my revolt against injustice" were turned into a book two years before her death.

CW

✝ You Must Know the Truth

I was still far from rebelling. I could not imagine that other people had chosen to say no to war. No one I knew had questioned the rightness of the French cause against domineering, barbaric Germany. Every Sunday the priest inflamed the French to combat in his homily. He justified their patriotism and condemned the cruelty of their opponents. To hear him, you would have thought France was God's treasured child while Germany was the devil's own land. *Poilus* had no duty more sacred than tearing the guts out of the *Boches*. I am not exaggerating, that's the way it was.

In the middle of the winter of 1916, my brother Joseph materialized. There is no other way to describe it, he materialized out of nowhere, nobody was expecting him. He'd managed to wangle a leave and his visit was like a ray of sunshine for me.

He tapped on the pane and waited outside for me to open the window. His first words were:

"Émilie, don't come close and don't touch me, hand me some trousers, a shirt, socks, and a sweater, but don't you come out."

I got out what he asked for.

"Throw them here," he said, and through the window I watched him change. He put his army togs into the water of the *bachal*,[1] and only then did he come inside. He had more to say:

---

1. *Bachal:* the hollowed-out tree trunk into which spring water flows. [E.C.]

"Émilie, I don't want you to touch those things, I'll take care of them tomorrow, I don't want you picking up any lice."

That is what he did first thing the next day, cleaning his belongings with patience and care, examining every seam for nits, pulling them out and squashing them one by one.

I found Joseph changed. He'd been gone hardly a year, but he was more solemn than before, even more serious . . . with sorrow written in the depths of that seriousness. He told me the war was hounding him, that you couldn't forget it just by coming home on leave: life in the trenches was a vermin less easily routed than lice and fleas.

He was the person who opened my eyes. During his few days at home, he spoke mostly to me and of course he talked about the war. For us in Val-des-Prés, except for the men going off, there was something abstract about the war, whereas Joseph had seen it up close, living the life of the trenches on the front line, and he'd come back full of bitterness and resentment, desperate and sad.

"You see," he'd tell me, "all that stuff the teacher told us, about patriotism and glory—well, it's nothing but nonsense and lies. He had no right to have us sing 'Wave little flag.' What does it mean, anyway! Can you tell me?"

I did not know. I did not see.

"Émilie, if you do teach some day, you must tell children the truth, because it's very simple, the guy on the other side, the German, certainly has a plow or some work tool waiting for him back home. After the war, he and I, if we're not dead, if we haven't lost every shred of our human dignity, we'll have to get back on the job fixing up the ruins left by the war. But the war, well, neither he nor I will get anything out of it. When it's all over, the profits will be in the hands of the capitalists and the guys rolling in money from selling their weapons, the career soldiers will have the stripes and promotions they've won, but not us, we won't have anything to show for it, we won't have won anything. You understand?"

So many words, so much rebellion left me dumbstruck. I had never seen him like that, he'd been gentleness incarnate.

"You understand, Émilie? And when all is said and done, what's going to happen when they decide it's enough? We'll be the turkeys, us in the trenches, me and the man on the other side. No, war is *not* what they told us, it's monstrous, I'm against it, a thousand percent against it. I have not killed anyone and I am not going to kill, I won't have any part of it, and the only thing I ask is that they don't kill me either because I didn't do anything to them."

". . ."

"You understand?"

I think I understood why he was talking like that. He had suffered too much. His words expressed his revolt against the suffering and the injustice.

"You understand?"

I nodded my head. Deep inside I was afraid Joseph would use the same language in front of our father who would not have put up with it. His sense of duty, his respect for law—that was his whole life. Joseph knew it too and he told me so, he had no intention of discussing it with him. Telling me lightened his burden.

"Because you're young, you want to be a teacher, you must know the truth."

We went around the farm together. He realized the work it represented and tears came to his eyes. I had seventy-five sheep, eight cows, I made the butter in a hand churn, I took care of the hay and harvests, I was sixteen years old.

"What! You, the student, you with all that hard studying to be something more than a peasant, how can you do all this? Émilie, if I come back, I promise you'll go back to school. Money won't be a problem. I'll work, I'll manage, but I swear to you that you'll finish, and you won't just be a schoolteacher, you'll be a professor." . . .

Before he left, Joseph taught me to plow. The hardest part wasn't so much dealing with a mule or a yoke of cows as holding onto the handle. I was not tall. I remember we had an ordinary plow, the swing type, with a handle designed for a man. It was far too high for me. When I cut furrows with that contrivance, I got the handle in the chest or face every time I hit a stone. For me plowing was the road to Calvary. One day I was struck so hard that I let go and the animals bolted. I'd been knocked half senseless for the moment. My father, following in my wake, blazed into a fury and came at me with the thick handle of his wooden rake raised high, ready to strike.

"Off with you! Off! Catch them! Pick up that plow immediately!"

There was as much rage and despair as pain in the tears I shed, but I picked up the plow handle and straightened the furrow.

1977

Translated by Avriel Goldberger

From *A Life of Her Own: A Countrywoman in Twentieth-Century France,* by Émilie Carles, as told to Robert Destanque. Trans. Avriel H. Goldberger (New Brunswick: Rutgers University Press, 1991), 54–56, 60–61. © 1991 by Avriel H. Goldberger. Reprinted by permission of Rutgers University Press.

✝ Ambara Salam al-Khalidi
(1897–1986) *Lebanese*

Ambara Salam was the daughter of a Lebanese Arab nationalist, Selim Ali Salam, a member of the Ottoman parliament, who provided her with a liberal education by both Christian and Moslem tutors. At fourteen she began writing under a pseudonym articles on the rights of women, which she published in magazines and newspapers. She defended the right to equal education, equal inheritance, and rights in marriage; she opposed the veil. With her father's support, in her twenties, she gave a lecture unveiled—the first Arab woman to speak thus from a public podium. In spite of her soft-spoken gentility she showed great courage in fighting for her principles.

To resist conscription by the Turks, the eldest of her eight brothers, Ali, was hidden for the duration of the war in a space carved out between the ceiling of the first floor and a tiled divan on the second floor. The family adopted two orphaned Armenian girls. When Salam was nineteen, the young journalist with whom she was in love, Abdel Ghani Araissi, was hanged by Cemal Pasha for Arab nationalist sedition against the Ottoman Empire. The day of the execution, May 16, 1916, when over thirty equally distinguished young nationalists were hanged, is now celebrated as Martyrs' Day.

With friends, Salam set up a cultural club for the education of girls just before the war. As her memoirs testify, she was oppressed by the misery the war brought to the people of her country. Widespread famine, disease, and dislocation were the lot of both urban and rural Lebanese, whose men and draft animals had been forcibly conscripted, whose orchards and forests had been cut for the Turkish railways, and who were unable to pay punitive taxes levied after the execution of Arab nationalists. When Cemal Pasha convoked the ladies of Beirut to consider how to relieve the starvation of the Lebanese, she spoke to him with repressed rage about the desperate needs of her people; she helped to organize the welfare organizations that he proposed. They established shelters and workshops for middle-class women, who had been pushed to the edge of prostitution by their poverty; more than one thousand found employment weaving carpets under the direction of Armenian refugees.

There was a twenty-five-year span between Salam and Rasha, the sister whom she brought up as her own daughter until she moved to Jerusalem to marry at age thirty-two. She adopted the two children of her husband, Ahmed Samih al-Khalidi, and had five children of her own, including one who was stillborn and one who drowned young.

In later years she continued to be politically active on behalf of women's issues and Arab nationalism, making many speeches, radio talks, and television appearances. Her elegant style made her writings into textbook models. Among her publications are Arabic translations from English of the *Iliad*, the *Odyssey*, and *The Aeneid*, which are still read in Arab schools and universities.

✝ The Meeting with Cemal Pasha

The days of the war were prolonged, and so were the images of suffering. And the methods of violence and injustice were extended to all the Arab countries. It is enough to remember what my own eyes saw in Beirut of horrors, which my reader may not believe could ever happen to human beings.

Poverty began creeping slowly over the land as a result of the Turkish leaders' policy to impoverish the Arab countries, particularly Lebanon, including Beirut.[1] Death opened its jaws wide to devour the hungry who were thrown at either side of the road, screaming, "I am famished, I am famished." We used to rush to the windows and the balconies encouraging those who were able to walk to pick up the food we threw to them, or else we would send to those who could not walk whatever pittance of food or drink was enough to silence their hunger.

I remember whenever my mother left the house she used to carry with her a bit of bread or dry food to distribute instead of the little piasters that bought nothing.

I saw with my own eyes small children searching through the garbage for bits of food, I saw them fighting with dogs over the food. I remember once my heart bleeding as we were leaving one of the stores in the Bourg, or city center. The streets were almost totally empty, when a fruit vendor approached and we bought bananas from him. No sooner did we start to peel them than dozens of little children rushed up, fighting over the peels

1. The war brought poverty and starvation to many Arabs in Egypt, Palestine, Syria, and Lebanon. After the execution of Arab nationalists in 1915 and 1916, Cemal Pasha levied confiscatory taxes on land and personal property; he also blockaded the region of Mount Lebanon.

and eating them. This made us stop eating and we offered them whatever remained of the fruits. The very looks of human beings became distorted. We saw children with swollen bellies and hair standing on end, who resembled monkeys more than human beings.

How many women from respectable homes were now dressed in rags with dirty hands, attacked by lice and diseases. At first they would approach some of the more fortunate homes but shyness forbade them to ask for help. Only when their needs pressed and all other paths were foreclosed, did they stretch out their palms unconcerned about the shame of their demand. Some would shed their dignity in front of an arrogant Turkish officer and offer to him what was most precious, in order to feed children incapacitated by hunger. This was their last resort after the long absence of their breadwinners in the hell of the battlefields, without any signs of their being alive, and after they had sold their furniture piece by piece, then their houses, removing window frames and unhinging doors for prices too low to silence the hunger. Once the war was over, we saw many a house both in Beirut and the countryside standing silent, bare except for its ruined stones, lamenting the past and mourning its dead inhabitants. As we witnessed these disasters befalling our countrymen, hatred would swell inside us and our rage would grow. We reached the stage where we longed to emerge from this oppressive rule by any possible means. And though we had formerly rejected any foreign rule, we began hearing murmurs repeating: "Let the monkeys come and rule us, for they are better than this repressive regime."

At the beginning of 1917 while war was drawing to its end, something, I don't know what, prompted the Turkish rulers to begin welfare work and to design a project opening four shelters in Beirut to house hungry homeless street children and two workshops for women and girls in which they would learn handicrafts, in return for their food and a symbolic salary for the few who were skilled among them.

I don't know whose idea this was originally, but I know that Cemal Pasha asked the ladies of Beirut to meet at the home of Mr. Omar al Daouk to discuss these projects and to assign committees of ladies to work in this field. What I remember is that Ahmad Mukhtar Beyhum, whom we considered a brother to my father, came to our house one day and asked to talk to me personally, naturally from behind the veil. He surprised me with a request to prepare a speech to be delivered at this meeting, scheduled for that same afternoon. As for myself, how far I was from such an idea. Could I stand, an orator, in front of Cemal the Butcher? What was I to tell him? Was I to thank him and laud him for all the repression and the inequities which he imposed on my countrymen? I would prefer to send bullets through his heart, to rid the world of his evil. "No, no, Uncle Abu Amin, I am not the one who will address a speech to this unjust despot. In fact it's impossible for me even to be present at a meeting where he is to be found. I cannot, I cannot bear this, it's more than my nerves can bear." Only Ahmad Mukhtar Beyhum continued persuading me and talking to me, trying to convince me that this would in fact be a service to my coun-

trymen who were in need of this active help, and saying, leave your personal feelings aside and think of how this project will save hundreds of
children and women from death. And he said also that his request to me
to deliver the speech came in support of another request, sent by the wali
of Beirut, Azmi Bey, in which he reminded me that my gesture would be
in answer to a former gesture by the wali, when he had exerted his efforts
to save my father from the noose.[2] Perhaps, he continued, your words in
describing conditions in Beirut will be more potent than the bullets you
want to fire at him. I faced a dilemma, not knowing what to say, particularly when all my family were of the opinion that I should respond positively to this request. I accepted despite myself and sat down to write a
speech in which I am not sure what I said.

All I remember is that I carried it and went to the meeting to find the
wide inner salons of the house filled with Beiruti women from every level
of society, while the outside halls were crammed with a great number of
Beiruti men, as well as military and civilian rulers. Once everyone was present Cemal Pasha walked in. Severity and arrogance could be detected in
his stride. I felt that the earth was sinking under his steps. A shudder shook
my being at his entrance and I felt as if fire were being poured over my
head. Behind him entered all the men. As for him, he offered everybody
a military greeting as all the women stood up to receive him fully veiled.[3]
After everybody was seated, they signalled me, I stood up and delivered
the address I had written with a shaking hand. I delivered it with suppressed emotion but overflowing with frustration, and despite this, it was
received well by everyone, as I had poured into it all that my countrymen
were suffering from the horrors of everyday life and from malnutrition
that drove them to death in large numbers behind closed doors and in
open spaces. After that Cemal Pasha presented his project to the Beiruti
women, which included the establishment of two shelters and a workshop
in the eastern part of the city and the same in the western part. He said
that the government was ready to offer everything required to set up these
projects, as well as the concomitant necessities of housing, food, and
clothes, etc. He left to the ladies the task of electing the committees from
among themselves. At which point he left the meeting to an outer salon
and asked Mr. Omar al Daouk to call me to him. What was I to do now? I
had taken the first step. Was it possible for me to turn back? What was my
excuse now? How was I to run away from this painful situation? How was I
to meet this man while my heart was still bleeding? I felt like a bird caught
in the net of a hunter, who is beating its wings not knowing how to escape.
For the first time in my life I thanked God for the veil which kept him from
seeing my features full of hatred and painful memories. Yet I went while I
was shaking with indignation and confronted him as if I were confronting
an ogre. And true enough in his physique he was short and fat. In his

2. The father of Ambara was several times sent to prison and threatened with being
hanged for his nationalist activities; the wali, or governor of Beirut, had protected him.
3. Women would not usually stand in the presence of men.

shortness and fatness and his thick black beard and piercing eyes there was something ogre-like. He started by congratulating me on my speech. And then he asked me whether I knew Turkish. I answered in the negative. No. The translator was Sheikh Assad al Shukeri who was the mufti[4] of the fourth army. Cemal said, "There is a famous Turkish intellectual in Beirut these days called Halidé Edib, who has been assigned to direct the normal school" located in the monastery al Nassirah in Ashrafiah. "I suggest that you two meet and that she teach you Turkish, while you teach her Arabic. I wish you to swear to do this, and I will talk to Halidé Edib about the matter." I think that this particular scene was the most difficult in my life. I was confronted with this suggestion while still young and lacking in experience and courage in such conditions. Also I was afraid that my emotions would push me to fall into some grave error. I felt a pain that tore me with bitterness and frustration, and I said to myself, this is a new torment. Is this what is left for me to do—learning the language of the enemy? Where are those who put me in such a situation, and will they save me from it now? I was torn among the many possible answers, the purpose of which was to refuse the offer. How could I do that? I don't know how I was saved by my intuition, although I am not usually quick witted. I said, "Our prime duty in times of war is to work in the field of welfare. We have in fact stopped our studies in order to enlist in this field. When the war ends, God willing, we will resume talking about this issue." I believe he accepted this answer and it seemed to convince him. No sooner did the meeting end, than I went back home completely worn out, seeking only to be alone and to cry and wishing that it were possible for me to discharge this anger that filled my being. And all that I heard in congratulation regarding the success of my speech felt like stabs to my heart.

Translated by Randa al-Khalidi

From *Jawla fil-dhikrayat bayna Lubnan wa Filastin* (A journey through memories between Lebanon and Palestine) (Beirut: al-nahar, 1979; reprint 1997). Reprinted by permission of al-nahar.

4. *Mufti:* religious leader.

✝ Spirita Arneodo
(b. 1891) *Italian*

Spirita Arneodo was one of ten children in a family living in a mountain community; her father worked in France while her mother took care of the family and farm. By sixteen she was an apprentice in a dairy and did agricultural work with her parents. Married at twenty to Michele ("Miclin") Arneodo, she soon had her first child. After working in a dairy, the young couple moved to a small plot of land. With the arrival of war, Arneodo became responsible for all the field labor, as well as for defending her farm from marauders and herself from lechers.

✝ Interview with Margherita Bertolotti

My husband and I went to a *ciabot* [a small piece of property] of twelve acres, he and I alone. We already had a son aged two and a half, we paid rent. I was married in '11, on February 20, and my son was born November 17, 1912. In '14 my husband, the child, and I went to live there in the *ciabot* near the railroad tracks that go from Cuneo to Turin.

We had nothing in the house. We had a bench to sit at the table, with two chairs. When his father died, they had divided the things, and he had taken these. I borrowed money to buy salt, the first kilo of salt that I used to cook for the first time, I borrowed the money from my sister-in-law, she knows.

What happened to me? Much worse. We were happy to work, to eat, to raise this child. In the spring, May 27, 1915, he received the mobilization note, he left and I remained alone, with my twelve or so acres. So we yoked the animals and I worked the land all day. I learned to do everything and I had a twelve-year-old boy, a *vacherot*, a farmboy, to help me. With my son and the animals I went alone to till, I found no one to help me, I cut the wheat, I tied it. My life was a martyrdom, a martyrdom.

One year, two years went by, he was a soldier for a long time: he left May 25, 1915, he was discharged September 15, 1919, you can imagine. . . . In the meantime I remained alone, I ran the house as best I could. At night I would irrigate, fetch the water to water the fields, and in those days there were no waders. Then he came back, but there was also something I need not remind you of, the Spanish flu. In 1918 the Spanish flu struck, he had not come, at home my mother was bedridden, my sister was sick, the other one married, while I was in San Chiaffredo di Busca. They came to tell me: "Look here, Maddalena is dead." Alone, not even the boy who helped me was there, he had gone to his house because his father too was half dead. I was alone with the child, I left him with a neighbor, and ran and saw them once more, my sister and her daughter: dead. I went there Wednesday morning, I wrote my mother Friday. I went to market in Busca on foot, I got a notecard and wrote my husband who was in Mantebelluna: "Look, my sister Madlinin [little Maddalena] and her daughter are dead. My mother, my sister and all those at home are bedridden, sick, and I'm still on my feet." But I had a terrible headache. A few days later I was in bed too, with my six-year-old baby, and I caught the Spanish flu too. The doctor had 120 patients to visit and had only a small horse, no car.

One day the police sergeant comes; I was in bed, I told the neighbor to let him in. He wanted me to take some hay to the government. From my bed, I said, "Aren't you ashamed to ask for hay from me, me here in bed, while all the time my husband has been a soldier, young as he is, they have never given him an hour of leave? and I'm here in bed with nobody to help me, aren't you ashamed?"

Finally then they sent my husband a telegram and gave him ten days' leave. He arrived, I was just beginning to speak, but I couldn't understand what they said from the foot of the bed. It was the Spanish flu. One day, while I had the medicine on the night table, my uncle the priest arrived, looked at me, and asked, "But did you take this?" "Yes." "Dear me." When I went to pay the pharmacist he asked, "Did you take this? And you're here now?" I don't know what I had taken, we were trying everything. The doctor said then to my husband, "Out of one hundred like your wife who take this, I save one."

Once on a Sunday, when I was in the vegetable garden, my neighbor— he had a wife at home, a beautiful wife—began to talk about the wind and rain, and then he said, "Don't you suffer not having Miclin at home?" "I don't suffer, look for your self." At that time, I mean, I weighed more than 70 kilos, I was fat; when the doctor came to see me for the Spanish flu, he had said, "Oh, what a parcel of a spouse!" The neighbor says, "I will come one evening to see you." I laughed. Leave it to the devil, he came the next night. I was in the stable, I had the boy with me, my child was asleep already, we were keeping an eye on the stable. I said to the boy, "Battista, milk the cow, give some to the calf, and take the rest into the house." I didn't enter the house, because I thought that pig might follow me in. He milked the cow, gave the calf the milk, and then went into the house. At that moment the ignoramus said, "Are you ready?" "For what?" "For what I said up there." "Oh yes. The door is there." I was serious! He got up, said nothing more, and left. A few days went by, I met him at the railroad tracks, he said: "You made a fool of me the other night!" "I made a fool out of you? It will be the first and last time." He answered: "Not with me." "What? Not with you? Another word and you'll end up at the bottom of the canal; you're not too big for me." I had other things on my mind, and he had his wife there.

I swear that I never even thought about that kind of thing, because of my preoccupations, my husband a soldier, the child, the animals, the land, everything, and the debts to pay. That one never said anything to me again. When I met him, he would look down, but I never spoke to him, shameful brute!

At another time policemen were always passing near the railroad tracks, night and day, but I never spoke to anyone. There were two nice ones, they always bought eggs and paid for them. One day one came with a man I had never seen before, a giant of a policeman, who said, "Are these apples good?" "No, they are not ripe yet." "But are they good or not?" "For me, they're not good, but if you want to eat one, take it."

"Well, my wife is in Milano, and I'm here letting things go to ruin." I understood but pretended not to: "Nowadays, to let things go to ruin, with rationing, I wouldn't let anything go bad." He then got heated up, the rogue, fortunately the other policeman and the neighbor were there. "Do they have rooms here?" "Yes, beautiful furnished rooms upstairs," I said in jest. "Then come up to the room with me," he said. "O sure, it's a single." He was stupid! The other one was honest, he said, "Come on, the train is passing, they will fine us!" "I would prefer ten minutes with this spouse, and to blazes with the train, to blazes with everything!" It's a good thing that the other policeman and my honest neighbor were there; she was about seventy years old, and if she saw someone in the courtyard she wouldn't go home until they had left.

That policeman would go visit the woman whose husband had played a trick on me. The night he had come to me, I wanted to say to him, "I am not your wife, for sure!" But I was quiet, I thought, "Do what you want."

There were girls that were not serious, and nothing ever happened to them—no, one had a child with her boss. I know they said they did it, but as for us, when we got married, we were more ignorant than a newborn baby. We didn't know anything.

1981

Translated by Sylvia Notini

Interview with Margherita Bertolotti, *Problemi e aspetti della condizione femminile in una comunità rurale*, thesis, Turin, 1982.

✝ Berthe Cros
(b. 1910) *French*

Born at Villesèquelande, ten kilometers from Carcassonne, Berthe Cros was only four when the war broke out. Her recollection (in a 1981 interview with her granddaughter) differs from the war enthusiasm imputed to civilians; it foreshadows the hardships of daily life that rural communities would face.

✝ Mobilization

Although I was only four when war was declared, I remember well that day because it began something terrible. My parents were threshing with a roller on the ground and it was very hot. Suddenly the bells began to ring. The tocsin. Everyone cried out: "It's war!" People dropped everything and gathered at the town hall, the only place to get information, since there was neither radio nor television. Papa had to leave the same evening for Perpignan and everyone wept. My parents had only fifty francs in all, which Papa took, saying to Maman: "I cannot leave without money, but you will sell the oats." (Which they were just threshing.) That's what I remember. When he was gone, everyone wept. . . .

After seven or eight days he wrote that he was leaving for the front, that he would pass through Carcassonne at eight and that Maman should come to the station with my sister and me. An uncle brought us to Carcassonne in a horse-drawn wagon. We left early, because it took two hours to reach the city and we waited a long time at the station because the train was late. At midnight it had not yet passed through, and my uncle was talking about leaving, when Papa's train was announced. I was half asleep on Maman's shoulder. It was terrible, I can still see the soldiers at the doorways, with everyone screaming when the train arrived. We didn't see Papa until the train was starting off. Maman could not say anything to him, nor could she give him the packet she had prepared.

1981

From *Années cruelles, 1914–1918,* ed. Rémy Casals, Claude Marquié, and René Piniès (Villelongue: Atelier du Gué, 1983), 16–17. Copyright © Atelier du Gué.

☦ Ihssan Baiyat Al Droubi
Syrian

In her 1982 biography of her husband, Sami Al Droubi, Ihssan Baiyat Al Droubi retold a story about the time of suffering under Ottoman rule during World War I, when Syrian men were forcibly mobilized to fight or do auxiliary labor for the Ottoman troops. At home, their families were devastated by famine. In 1992, Ihssan Baiyat Al Droubi gave a copy of her book, embroidered by this story about how memories of war become inscribed in women's lives, to Nādiyah al-Ghazzī, a feminist lawyer and writer of fiction. Al-Ghazzī, in turn, repeats the story in the preface to her novel about the Great War, *Barhūm's Baggy Pants: Days of the Seferberlik* (1993), which is illustrated with harrowing photographs of the famine and is dedicated "to all who have died of hunger."

MC

☦ The Embroidered Pants

An old peasant woman once came and she presented Mr. Shafiq al-Imam, at that time the chief administrator of the ancient Azm Palace, with a pair of brightly colored, embroidered baggy pants. She had sewn and embroidered these pants during the days of the *seferberlik,* or the forced mobilization during World War I.

She said: "I was a bride when they took my husband of a month to the military. . . . I was hoping that when he came home and all the loved ones would come to greet him he would be wearing a beautiful pair of baggy pants. So I bought the material and went to the fountain where I would sit and contemplate the colors of the flowers. Then I would embroider them on the baggy pants. Then the war ended. . . . And I waited. . . . I waited. . . . My groom did not return. . . . So I put these pants into a box. Whenever I missed him I would open the box and take the pants out and then return them just as they were. . . . This went on for forty years. . . . But now I'm sick and I need medicine and treatment, and the most precious thing I own is this pair of baggy pants. . . . Will you buy them for a gold lira and a half? That's the price of the material and thread. I'm not asking anything for the embroidery work."

Translated by Miriam Cooke

From *Sami Al Droubi* (Damascus: Dar al Karmil, 1982), 116.

✠ IV ✠

SHORT
FICTION

Fiction, even if it is realistic, implies a distance from the literal imposed by the concern for the crafting of language and narrative, and that distance has had special importance for women. The very fact of World War I has nonetheless affected twentieth-century literature, so much so that current novels about the war continue to win coveted prizes. Much of our canonized Modernist literature was colored by the experience of the war, which exploded old beliefs about the social order and led writers to break with received forms. The question has arisen whether women did or even could participate in this Modernist rupture, since their experience of the war was so different from that of men. Because women as a rule were more distant from combat, their war fiction has been thought to be doubly distant from the facts—the point from which Edith Wharton's "Writing a War Story" starts. Wharton goes on to hint at the problems that crop up in the *reading* of a war story by a woman. On the premise that women did not suffer as men had suffered, critics have accused women's war writing of failures in both fact and irony—the artistic value most prized in war stories.

Yet irony itself is a way to find a telling distance from local experience, and as these works of fiction demonstrate, women have deployed irony to express a lively sense of the illogicality and "backwash" of war, understood as a systemic phenomenon. Nurses' sketches expose the cognitive dissonance of attempting to heal men who want to die—or whom military commanders will simply send back out to their deaths. A colonial writer notes the paradox of an empire mobilizing its colonies on behalf of the "mother nation." A socialist points to the eruption of a second "front" within a nation like Germany, when a government allied with industrialists assaults workers who strike for bread and peace.

Certainly, direct experience did feed many women's creative war writing. Some of their most powerful fiction was written by women who had served in medical units, such as Ellen LaMotte, Mary Borden, and Hortensia

Papadat-Bengescu. Their "fragments" and "sketches" from the front lines reveal the images burned in their memories of death, disease, and despair. Other writers, including Edith Wharton, drew their verbal energy and ironies from brief visits to the front and from relief work with refugees from the war zone. Even those women like Elizabeth Bowen who remained on the home front could, by assessing their everyday encounters, achieve insight into the contradictions and corruption of wartime society. Their vision of the ongoing processes of a society at war can broaden our understanding of what it means to write fiction about "war." The language they invented, like that of the male Modernists, was transformed by the war: we find sexual terminology that would have been taboo before, narrative structures that resist artificial order or unity, and descriptions stripped of sentiment and conventional pathos.

Readers may question whether the "authenticity" of eyewitness testimony can or should be distinguished from that of semiautobiographical fiction. A memoir composed long after the fact may lack the searing immediacy of a fictionalized sketch that is sharply observed. But it cannot be assumed that distance in time, place, or form means emotional or tonal remoteness. A nurse may prefer to cast her perception of the war as a narrative, rather than as a public report or factual diary. Fiction allows a control that may enable the emotional mastery of a traumatic experience, and it affords narrative tools for the representation of war that are not always at hand in more documentary writing. While diaries and letters often overflow under the pressure of events, fiction can breathe, shape a rhythm, and give point to a paradox. It frees us from a mechanical measure of time to help us grasp how the ghosts of war return to haunt us.

MEDICINE

✝ Ellen Newbold LaMotte
(1873–1961) *American*

orn in Kentucky, Ellen LaMotte graduated in 1902 from the nursing
school of Johns Hopkins Hospital. She worked in Baltimore as a visiting nurse and helped organize nurses. Her first book, *The Tuberculosis Nurse* (1915), records her experiences between 1910 and 1913 as
superintendent of the tuberculosis division of the Baltimore Health
Department. In later years she lived in Washington, D.C., maintaining a
country home at Stone Ridge, New York, and keeping up memberships in
the Johns Hopkins alumni association, the Huguenot Society, and the
Society of Women Geographers.

While LaMotte was working as a nurse at the Johns Hopkins Medical
School, she met Gertrude Stein; Stein may have written the four-line poem
"Separated" (1921) about her, after they saw each other again in Paris.
According to Stein's gossipy *Autobiography of Alice B. Toklas,* LaMotte, who
"was very heroic but gun shy"—collected memorabilia from the trenches
for her cousin Du Pont De Nemours. With her friend Emily Chadbourne,
LaMotte planned to go to Serbia, where many British nurses and doctors
were volunteering. Instead, Stein introduced them to Mary Borden
Turner, under whom they worked in a mobile field hospital at the front in
Belgium from 1915 to 1916; a number of LaMotte's sketches reveal themes
parallel to those of Borden.

LaMotte's first impressions of France at war appeared in the *Atlantic
Monthly* in 1915; she published articles in *Harper's* and the *Nation.* She then
collected a searing group of portraits and reflections in *The Backwash of
War* (1916). Her sketch on "women and wives" echoes a statement by a
French general that "the tart and the prostitute are a necessary distraction,
whereas the wife who represents the hearth weakens the soldier's heart."
The book went into a second printing, then was repressed; a second edi-

tion appeared, with a preface about her experience of censorship, in 1934. A socialist coloration can be detected in her sketches about the war, as well as in essays she wrote for *The Masses*.

In 1917 LaMotte and Chadbourne went to the Orient, where they combated the opium trade. Six more books came out of her experiences in China: *Tales of the Orient* (1919) and *Snuffs and Butters* (1925), a collection of sketches; a memoir in the form of letters, *Peking Dust* (1919); and three works of medical observation and polemic, *The Opium Monopoly* (1920), *The Ethics of Opium* (1924), and *Opium at Geneva, or How the Opium Problem Is Handled by the League of Nations* (1929), a collection of articles for the *Nation*. She was sharply critical of the Western powers' responsibility for the opium trade. She was awarded the Lin Tse Hu Memorial Medal in 1930 by China for her work, as well as a special order of merit from the Japanese Red Cross.

✝ Heroes

When he could stand it no longer, he fired a revolver up through the roof of his mouth, but he made a mess of it. The ball tore out his left eye, and then lodged somewhere under his skull, so they bundled him into an ambulance and carried him, cursing and screaming, to the nearest field hospital. The journey was made in double-quick time, over rough Belgian roads. To save his life, he must reach the hospital without delay, and if he was bounced to death jolting along at breakneck speed, it did not matter. That was understood. He was a deserter, and discipline must be maintained. Since he had failed in the job, his life must be saved, he must be nursed back to health, until he was well enough to be stood up against a wall and shot. This is War. Things like this also happen in peace time, but not so obviously.

At the hospital, he behaved abominably. The ambulance men declared that he had tried to throw himself out of the back of the ambulance, that he had yelled and hurled himself about, and spat blood all over the floor and blankets—in short, he was very disagreeable. Upon the operating table, he was no more reasonable. He shouted and screamed and threw himself from side to side, and it took a dozen leather straps and four or five orderlies to hold him in position, so that the surgeon could examine him. During this commotion, his left eye rolled about loosely upon his cheek, and from his bleeding mouth he shot great clots of stagnant blood, caring not where they fell. One fell upon the immaculate white uniform of the Directrice, and stained her, from breast to shoes. It was disgusting. They told him it was *La Directrice,* and that he must be careful. For an instant he stopped his raving, and regarded her fixedly with his remaining eye, then took aim afresh, and again covered her with his coward blood.

Truly it was disgusting.

To the *Médecin Major*[1] it was incomprehensible, and he said so. To attempt to kill oneself, when, in these days, it was so easy to die with honor upon the battlefield, was something he could not understand. So the *Médecin Major* stood patiently aside, his arms crossed, his supple fingers pulling the long black hairs on his bare arms, waiting. He had long to wait, for it was difficult to get the man under the anesthetic. Many cans of ether were used, which went to prove that the patient was a drinking man. Whether he had acquired the habit of hard drink before or since the war could not be ascertained; the war had lasted a year now, and in that time many habits may be formed. As the *Médecin Major* stood there, patiently fingering the hairs on his hairy arms, he calculated the amount of ether that was expended—five cans of ether, at so many francs a can—however, the ether was a donation from America, so it did not matter. Even so, it was wasteful.

At last they said he was ready. He was quiet. During his struggles, they had broken out two big teeth with the mouth gag, and that added a little more blood to the blood already choking him. Then the *Médecin Major* did a very skillful operation. He trephined the skull, extracted the bullet that had lodged beneath it, and bound back in place that erratic eye. After which the man was sent over to the ward, while the surgeon returned hungrily to his dinner, long overdue.

In the ward, the man was a bad patient. He insisted upon tearing off his bandages, although they told him that this meant bleeding to death. His mind seemed fixed on death. He seemed to want to die, and was thoroughly unreasonable, although quite conscious. All of which meant that he required constant watching and was a perfect nuisance. He was so different from the other patients, who wanted to live. It was a joy to nurse them. This was the *Salle* of the *Grands Blessés,*[2] those most seriously wounded. By expert surgery, by expert nursing, some of these were to be returned to their homes again, *réformés,*[3] mutilated for life, a burden to themselves and to society; others were to be nursed back to health, to a point at which they could again shoulder eighty pounds of marching kit, and be torn to pieces again on the firing line. It was a pleasure to nurse such as these. It called forth all one's skill, all one's humanity. But to nurse back to health a man who was to be court-martialed and shot, truly that seemed a dead-end occupation.

They dressed his wounds every day. Very many yards of gauze were required, with gauze at so many francs a bolt. Very much ether, very much iodoform, very many bandages—it was an expensive business, considering. All this waste for a man who was to be shot, as soon as he was well enough.

---

1. *Médecin Major:* surgeon in command.
2. *Salle of the Grands Blessés:* ward for the severely wounded.
3. *Réformés:* discharged.

How much better to expend this upon the hopeless cripples, or those who were to face death again in the trenches.

The night nurse was given to reflection. One night, about midnight, she took her candle and went down the ward, reflecting. Ten beds on the right hand side, ten beds on the left hand side, all full. How pitiful they were, these little soldiers, asleep. How irritating they were, these little soldiers, awake. Yet how sternly they contrasted with the man who had attempted suicide. Yet did they contrast, after all? Were they finer, nobler, than he? The night nurse, given to reflection, continued her rounds.

In bed number two, on the right, lay Alexandre, asleep. He had received the *Médaille Militaire*[4] for bravery. He was better now, and that day had asked the *Médecin Major* for permission to smoke. The *Médecin Major* had refused, saying that it would disturb the other patients. Yet after the doctor had gone, Alexandre had produced a cigarette and lighted it, defying them all from behind his *Médaille Militaire*. The patient in the next bed had become violently nauseated in consequence, yet Alexandre had smoked on, secure in his *Médaille Militaire*. How much honor lay in that?

Here lay Félix, asleep. Poor, querulous, feeble-minded Félix, with a foul fistula, which filled the whole ward with its odor. In one sleeping hand lay his little round mirror, in the other, he clutched his comb. With daylight, he would trim and comb his mustache, his poor, little drooping mustache, and twirl the ends of it.

Beyond lay Alphonse, drugged with morphia, after an intolerable day. That morning he had received a package from home, a dozen pears. He had eaten them all, one after the other, though his companions in the beds adjacent looked on with hungry, longing eyes. He offered not one, to either side of him. After his gorge, he had become violently ill, and demanded the basin in which to unload his surcharged stomach.

Here lay Hippolyte, who for eight months had jerked on the bar of a captive balloon, until appendicitis had sent him into hospital. He was not ill, and his dirty jokes filled the ward, provoking laughter, even from dying Marius. How filthy had been his jokes—how they had been matched and beaten by the jokes of others. How filthy they all were, when they talked with each other, shouting down the length of the ward.

Wherein lay the difference? Was it not all a dead-end occupation, nursing back to health men to be patched up and returned to the trenches, or a man to be patched up, court-martialed and shot? The difference lay in the Ideal.

One had no ideals. The others had ideals, and fought for them. Yet had they? Poor selfish Alexandre, poor vain Félix, poor gluttonous Alphonse, poor filthy Hippolyte—was it possible that each cherished ideals, hidden beneath? Courageous dreams of freedom and patriotism? Yet if so, how could such beliefs fail to influence their daily lives? Could one cherish

4. *Médaille militaire:* military medal of honor.

standards so noble, yet be himself so ignoble, so petty, so commonplace?

At this point her candle burned out, so the night nurse took another one, and passed from bed to bed. It was very incomprehensible. Poor, whining Félix, poor whining Alphonse, poor whining Hippolyte, poor whining Alexandre—all fighting for *La Patrie.*[5] And against them the man who had tried to desert *La Patrie.*

So the night nurse continued her rounds, up and down the ward, reflecting. And suddenly she saw that these ideals were imposed from without—that they were compulsory. That left to themselves, Félix, and Hippolyte, and Alexandre, and Alphonse would have had no ideals. Somewhere, higher up, a handful of men had been able to impose upon Alphonse, and Hippolyte, and Félix, and Alexandre, and thousands like them, a state of mind which was not in them, of themselves. Base metal, gilded. And they were all harnessed to a great car, a Juggernaut, ponderous and crushing, upon which was enthroned Mammon, or the Goddess of Liberty, or Reason, as you like. Nothing further was demanded of them than their collective physical strength—just to tug the car forward, to cut a wide swath, to leave behind a broad path along which could follow, at some later date, the hordes of Progress and Civilization. Individual nobility was superfluous. All the Idealists demanded was physical endurance from the mass.

Dawn filtered in through the little square windows of the ward. Two of the patients rolled on their sides, that they might talk to one another. In the silence of early morning their voices rang clear.

"Dost thou know, *mon ami,*[6] that when we captured that German battery a few days ago, we found the gunners chained to their guns?"

1915

"Heroes," in *The Backwash of War* (1916; reprint, New York: Putnam, 1934), 15–24 (page citations are to reprint edition).

✝ Women and Wives

A bitter wind swept in from the North Sea. It swept in over many miles of Flanders plains, driving gusts of rain before it. It was a biting gale by the time it reached the little cluster of wooden huts composing the field hospital, and rain and wind together dashed against the huts, blew under them, blew through them, crashed to pieces a swinging window down at the laundry, and loosened the roof of *Salle I* at the other end of the enclosure. It was just ordinary winter weather, such as had lasted for months on

5. *La Patrie:* the fatherland.
6. *Mon ami:* my friend.

end, and which the Belgians spoke of as vile weather, while the French called it vile Belgian weather. The drenching rain soaked into the long, green winter grass, and the sweeping wind was bitter cold, and the howling of the wind was louder than the guns, so that it was only when the wind paused for a moment, between blasts, that the rolling of the guns could be heard.

In *Salle I* the stove had gone out. It was a good little stove, but somehow was unequal to struggling with the wind which blew down the long, rocking stove pipe, and blew the fire out. So the little stove grew cold, and the hot water jug on the stove grew cold, and all the patients at that end of the ward likewise grew cold, and demanded hot water bottles, and there wasn't any hot water with which to fill them. So the patients complained and shivered, and in the pauses of the wind, one heard the guns.

Then the roof of the ward lifted about an inch, and more wind beat down, and as it beat down, so the roof lifted. The orderly remarked that if this Belgian weather continued, by tomorrow the roof would be clean off—blown off into the German lines. So all laughed as Fouquet said this, and wondered how they could lie abed with the roof of *Salle I*, the *Salle* of the *grands blessés*, blown over into the German lines. The ward did not present a neat appearance, for all the beds were pushed about at queer angles, in from the wall, out from the wall, some touching each other, some very far apart, and all to avoid the little leaks of rain which streamed or dropped down from little holes in the roof. This weary, weary war! These long days of boredom in the hospital, these days of incessant wind and rain and cold.

Armand, the chief orderly, ordered Fouquet to rebuild the fire, and Fouquet slipped on his *sabots* and clogged down the ward, away outdoors in the wind, and returned finally with a box of coal on his shoulders, which he dumped heavily on the floor. He was clumsy and sullen, and the coal was wet and mostly slate, and the patients laughed at his efforts to rebuild the fire. Finally, however, it was alight again, and radiated out a faint warmth, which served to bring out the smell of iodoform, and of draining wounds, and other smells which loaded the cold, close air. Then, no one knows who began it, one of the patients showed the nurse a photograph of his wife and child, and in a moment every man in the twenty beds was fishing back of his bed, in his *musette*,[7] under his pillow for photographs of his wife. They all had wives, it seems, for remember, these were the old troops, who had replaced the young Zouaves who had guarded this part of the Front all summer. One by one they came out, these photographs, from weather-beaten sacks, from shabby boxes, from under pillows, and the nurse must see them all. Pathetic little pictures they were, of common, working-class women, some fat and work-worn, some thin and work-worn, some with stodgy little children grouped about them, some without, but all were practically the same. They were the wives of these men in the beds

7. *Musette:* haversack.

here, the working-class wives of working-class men—the soldiers of the trenches. Ah yes, France is democratic. It is the Nation's war, and all the men of the Nation, regardless of rank, are serving. But some serve in better places than others. The trenches are mostly reserved for men of the working class, which is reasonable, as there are more of them.

The rain beat down, and the little stove glowed, and the afternoon drew to a close, and the photographs of the wives continued to pass from hand to hand. There was much talk of home, and much of it was longing, and much of it was pathetic, and much of it was resigned. And always the little, ugly wives, the stupid, ordinary wives, represented home. And the words home and wife were interchangeable and stood for the same thing. And the glories and heroisms of war seemed of less interest, as a factor in life, than these stupid little wives.

Then Armand, the chief orderly, showed them all the photograph of his wife. No one knew that he was married, but he said yes, and that he received a letter from her every day—sometimes it was a postcard. Also that he wrote to her every day. We all knew how nervous he used to get, about letter time, when the *vaguemestre*[8] made his rounds, every morning, distributing letters to all the wards. We all knew how impatient he used to get, when the *vaguemestre* laid his letter upon the table, and there it lay, on the table, while he was forced to make rounds with the surgeon, and could not claim it until long afterwards. So it was from his wife, that daily letter, so anxiously, so nervously awaited!

Simon had a wife too. Simon, the young surgeon, German-looking in appearance, six feet of blond brute. But not blond brute really. Whatever his appearance, there was in him something finer, something tenderer, something nobler, to distinguish him from the brute. About three times a week he walked into the ward with his fountain pen between his teeth— he did not smoke, but he chewed his fountain pen—and when the dressings were over, he would tell the nurse, shyly, accidentally, as it were, some little news about his home. Some little incident concerning his wife, some affectionate anecdote about his three young children. Once when one of the staff went over to London on vacation, Simon asked her to buy for his wife a leather coat, such as English women wear, for motoring. Always he thought of his wife, spoke of his wife, planned some thoughtful little surprise or gift for her.

You know, they won't let wives come to the Front. Women can come into the War Zone, on various pretexts, but wives cannot. Wives, it appears, are bad for the morale of the Army. They come with their troubles, to talk of how business is failing, of how things are going to the bad at home, because of the war; of how great the struggle, how bitter the trials and the poverty and hardship. They establish the connecting link between the soldier and his life at home, his life that he is compelled to resign. Letters can be censored and all disturbing items cut out, but if a wife is permitted to

8. *Vaguemestre:* military postman.

come to the War Zone, to see her husband, there is no censoring the things she may tell him. The disquieting, disturbing things. So she herself must be censored, not permitted to come. So for long weary months men must remain at the Front, on active inactivity, and their wives cannot come to see them. Only other people's wives may come. It is not the woman but the wife that is objected to. There is a difference. In war, it is very great.

There are many women at the Front. How do they get there, to the Zone of the Armies? On various pretexts—to see sick relatives, in such and such hospitals, or to see other relatives, brothers, uncles, cousins, other people's husbands—oh, there are many reasons which make it possible for them to come. And always there are the Belgian women, who live in the War Zone, for at present there is a little strip of Belgium left, and all the civilians have not been evacuated from the Army Zone. So there are plenty of women, first and last. Better ones for the officers, naturally, just as the officers' mess is of better quality than that of the common soldiers. But always there are plenty of women. Never wives, who mean responsibility, but just women, who only mean distraction and amusement, just as food and wine. So wives are forbidden, because lowering to the morale, but women are winked at, because they cheer and refresh the troops. After the war, it is hoped that all unmarried soldiers will marry, but doubtless they will not marry these women who have served and cheered them in the War Zone. That, again, would be depressing to the country's morale. It is rather paradoxical, but there are those who can explain it perfectly.

No, no, I don't understand. It's because everything has two sides. You would be surprised to pick up a franc, and find Liberty, Equality, and Fraternity on one side, and on the other, the image of the Sower smoothed out. A rose is a fine rose because of the manure you put at its roots. You don't get a medal for sustained nobility. You get it for the impetuous action of the moment, an action quite out of keeping with the trend of one's daily life. You speak of the young aviator who was decorated for destroying a Zeppelin single-handed, and in the next breath you add, and he killed himself, a few days later, by attempting to fly when he was drunk. So it goes. There is a dirty sediment at the bottom of most souls. War, superb as it is, is not necessarily a filtering process, by which men and nations may be purified. Well, there are many people to write you of the noble side, the heroic side, the exalted side of war. I must write you of what I have seen, the other side, the backwash. They are both true. In Spain, they bang their silver coins upon a marble slab, accepting the stamp upon both sides, and then decide whether as a whole they ring true.

Every now and then, Armand, the orderly, goes to the village to get a bath. He comes back with very clean hands and nails, and says that it has greatly solaced him, the warm water. Then later, that same evening, he gets permission to be absent from the hospital, and he goes to our village to a girl. But he is always as eager, as nervous for his wife's letter as ever. It is the same with Simon, the young surgeon. Only Simon keeps himself pretty clean at all times, as he has an orderly to bring him pitchers of hot water every morning, as many as he wants. But Simon has a girl in the village, to whom he goes every week. Only, why does he talk so incessantly about his wife, and show her pictures to me, to every one about the place? Why should we all be bored with tales of Simon's stupid wife, when that's all she means to him? Only perhaps she means more. I told you I did not understand.

Then the *Gestionnaire*, the little fat man in khaki, who is purveyor to the hospital. Every night he commandeers an ambulance, and drives back into the country, to a village twelve miles away, to sleep with a woman. And the old doctor—he is sixty-four and has grandchildren—he goes down to our village for a little girl of fourteen. He was decorated with the Legion of Honor the other day. It seems incongruous.

Oh yes, of course these were decent girls at the start, at the beginning of the war. But you know women, how they run after men, especially when the men wear uniforms, all gilt buttons and braid. It's not the men's fault that most of the women in the War Zone are ruined. Have you ever watched the village girls when a regiment comes through, or stops for a night or two, *en repos*, on its way to the Front? Have you seen the girls make fools of themselves over the men? Well, that's why there are so many accessible for the troops. Of course the professional prostitutes from Paris aren't admitted to the War Zone, but the Belgian girls made such fools of themselves, the others weren't needed.

Across the lines, back of the German lines, in the invaded districts, it is different. The conquering armies just ruined all the women they could get hold of. Any one will tell you that. *Ces sales Bosches!*[9] For it is inconceivable how any decent girl, even a Belgian, could give herself up voluntarily to a Hun! They used force, those brutes! That is the difference. It's all the difference in the world. No, the women over there didn't make fools of themselves over those men—how could they! No, no. Over there, in the invaded districts, the Germans forced those girls. Here, on this side, the girls cajoled the men till they gave in. Can't you see? You must be pro-German! Anyway, they are all ruined and not fit for any decent man to mate with, after the war.

They are pretty dangerous, too, some of these women. No, I don't mean in that way. But they act as spies for the Germans and get a lot of information out of the men, and send it back, somehow, into the German lines. The Germans stop at nothing, nothing is too dastardly, too low, for them to attempt. There were two Belgian girls once who lived together in a room, in a little village back of our lines. They were natives, and had always lived there, so of course they were not turned out, and when the village was shelled from time to time, they did not seem to mind and altogether they made a lot of money. They only received officers. The common soldiers were just dirt to them, and they refused to see them. Certain women get known in a place, as those who receive soldiers and those who receive officers. These girls were intelligent, too, and always asked a lot of intelli-

9. *Ces sales Bosches!:* Those filthy Germans!

gent, interested questions, and you know a man when he is excited will answer unsuspectingly any question put to him. The Germans took advantage of that. It is easy to be a spy. Just know what questions you must ask, and it is surprising how much information you can get. The thing is, to know upon what point information is wanted. These girls knew that, it seems, and so they asked a lot of intelligent questions, and as they received only officers, they got a good lot of valuable information, for as I say, when a man is excited he will answer many questions. Besides, who could have suspected at first that these two girls were spies? But they were, as they found out finally, after several months. Their rooms were one day searched, and a mass of incriminating papers were discovered. It seems the Germans had taken these girls from their families—held their families as hostages—and had sent them across into the English lines, with threats of vile reprisals upon their families if they did not produce information of value. Wasn't it beastly! Making these girls prostitutes and spies, upon pain of reprisals upon their families. The Germans knew they were so attractive that they would receive only officers. That they would receive many clients, of high rank, of much information, who would readily fall victims to their wiles. They are very vile themselves, these Germans. The curious thing is, how well they understand how to bait a trap for their enemies. In spite of having nothing in common with them, how well they understand the nature of those who are fighting in the name of Justice, of Liberty and Civilization.

1916

"Women and Wives," in *The Backwash of War* (1916; reprint, New York: Putnam, 1934), 103–18 (page citations are to reprint edition).

✝ Hortensia Papadat-Bengescu
(1876–1955) *Romanian*

R aised in Moldavia by a protective family, Hortensia Papadat-Bengescu was educated at a French boarding school. Partly to escape familial repression, she married a judge, living first in the provinces and later in Bucharest, Romania. Encouraged by her friend Constanta Marino-Moscu, she began to write articles and poems in French; she was part of the circle around Eugène Lovinescu's *Sburatorul* (The sylph), to which she dedicated several volumes. Her first books were Proustian collections of short stories about the inner life of women. She wrote drama and novels noted for the psychological dissection of bourgeois relations. She is particularly admired for the symbolist texture of her prose in novels such as *Fecioarele despletite* (Disheveled maidens, 1926), *Concert din muzica de Bach* (Bach concerto, 1927), *Drumul ascuns* (The hidden path, 1932), and *Radacini* (Roots, 1938). These novels present a society incapable of dealing with the consequences of the war, a sick world which has exhausted its energy in endless futile attempts to adapt to a new style of life. Five volumes of her collected works, *Opere* (1972–1975), as well as many reprints testify to her continuing popularity. In 1946 she received the Romanian National Award for prose.

Papadat-Bengescu's fourth book, *Balaurul* (Dragon, 1923), a "document novel," from which a chapter is translated here, arose from her direct observations as a Red Cross nurse during the war. In July 1916 she wrote, "I await and wish for the brutality of war as a remedy for my suffering, since I am preparing myself to become a nurse who can transcend the fatigue of facing physical suffering." She wanted to record the minutiae of what she had seen during the war at Focsani: the stages of suffering, the impotence of doctors faced with the agony of the wounded, the inner strength that springs from suffering. At first her novel was not well received, because of her idiosyncratic diction, rife with neologisms; more recently, however, it has been praised for its cold, exact presentation of hospital experience, and for what Lovinescu believed to be "the confes-

sion of perhaps the first European conscience to reflect on the tragedy of
the war from a feminine perspective."

‡ The Man Whose Heart They Could See

Not in the eyes, not on the lips, nor on the hands. Not in the loyal look
which offers the naked soul, nor in the honest word and clear voice. Not
in the hand reaching out.

Nor down the slippery slope of forgetfulness; in words behind your
back; in deceiving hands.

Not in the heart of the good, nor in that of the evil. That which can
hardly ever be seen, which can sometimes be seen. The mysterious heart
which urges man against the current, though reason steers the boat. No,
not that heart!

At the crossroads, twenty feet from the hospital gate, Laura saw a lively
group of people. They were the best nurses of the modern Red Cross. Tall
and voluptuous Milly, who had a special gift for surgery and who, when
chaos was still running the place, was consulted by the internists left
behind for no reason, for the exclusive practice of surgery, for the war
butchery. The internists confessed their ignorance and worked the saw
over a man's finger for more than an hour. As in many places, these were
the effects of a poor division of labor, results of a first impulse, to say
the least, without looking for evil motives. Dudu was there too, loyal, sensu-
ous, nimble, the precious asset of the infirmary. The head nurse and many
others.

Laura, who was on her way to the other side of the city, where the lonely
and modest charity of her station infirmary was waiting for her; who had
started walking alone, her thoughts isolated and distant; who condemned
by her own sufferings but also passionate about them had surrendered to
the collective misery, but had chosen a different path—Laura wondered
how to avoid them.

They had seen her and their growing restlessness now confronted her
directly. There was no way out. She came closer but did not even have time
to ask.

"Have you seen? Did you find out? Do you know?" the voices grew
closer, aroused by curiosity and alarm.

"The one brought in last night. . . . It's horrible. . . . A unique case!"

Laura went through all the misery that had passed before their eyes and
through their hands in the last month with supreme resignation. The hor-
rific ingenuity with which people were mocked by endless hacking: hands
and legs torn off their bodies; broken skulls, burnt eyes, ground flesh, the
open hearth of the wounds; the whimsical, burlesque, and cruel fantasy of
blind destruction.

She prepared herself for the daily apprenticeship of pity and pain which consumed her with every new patient, barely protected against them all by her own suffering. She was surprised, however, that her colleagues, more useful than sensitive, more industrious than impressionable, seemed so deeply moved.

"Have you seen? You have to see! . . . Such horror!"

The man whose heart they could see . . .

The words fell unexpectedly. Fantasy is but a humble apprentice compared to the huge genius of evil.

The words seemed to fall out of the sky, squeezed and pressed against each other, too small for the capacity of compassion. They simply fell—and Laura opened her eyes wide, as wide as she could, to see the beating heart of a living man.

. . . He was from the Arges squad, a peasant . . . Handsome, young, with such distinguished features . . . He had been carrying that wound for three days . . . and was still living . . . Even the doctors were wondering. A unique case . . . Upstairs, in D hall.

Laura said nothing. She would go later, of course, to see . . . the man's heart.

Rather calm, she kept walking with no storm of feeling. It was as if her feelings were walled in, just as Manole had once walled in his wife, and from inside her feeble voice was only now calling for mercy. It wasn't mercy, though, nor fear, nor tenderness. It was as if the words were hammered into her brain. Yes! Truly horrible! . . . the man whose heart they could see.

Even this was not a clear notion in her mind. She couldn't imagine it. It seemed somehow noble . . . like an altar unveiling itself . . . The body opening to show the sacred organ of life to anyone! . . . She imagined a scene without blood. Immaculate . . . intact . . . and? . . . she could see the heart. Here her vision stopped, reduced to words. She did not search further in her imagination. . . . There, in the tight circle of her daily duties, she told everybody: a man whose heart they could see had come to their hospital.

Like her, the others shook their heads and bit their lips in wonder, arrested by that unusual gathering of words. Today she lectured the clients of the infirmary, those dirty and forgotten passersby who in their miserable wanderings stopped to ease the rash under their bandages. They should suffer! Be patient! There were larger pains in the world! And she reproached them severely. After all, nobody could see their hearts.

In the evening she went straight upstairs to the D ward where the officers were. The nurse pointed with terrified respect toward a bed at the end of the row.

Among the white sheets in a white nightgown, lying on his back, tall, fair, the handsome oval of his face white, white, almost lacking pallor—the man lay motionless, his clear blue eyes open. A quick, light breath passed through his rested lips.

He was as she had imagined him, only—she couldn't see his heart.

Before bending forward to give him the slow psalm of words of kind-

ness, she listened to a strange and disquieting whistling noise inside the
ward. She looked around. She knew all the patients. . . . She met their look
shadowed by a fearful worry.

"Have you seen it?" one of them asked sadly. Laura kept listening.

"It is him!" Then she looked at the man again. That sharp whistling
noise came from under the sheets that he kept throwing aside, furiously.
His closed lips were barely breathing.

She spoke no words. There were no words for this "psalm." She was
trapped inside her own fright, wholly bricked in.

"Ah! Ah!" she said to the other patient after a while, "he is making that
noise."

The man did not move his body or his eyes. He was lying on his back,
white, his face exhibiting unusually distinctive features.

"Is he a soldier?" she asked, though she had been told before.

"Is he Romanian?" It was a unanimous, distinct impression. He had the
foreign air of Northern lands. He had a noble appearance, the refinement
of a skillful portrait. He almost seemed disguised.

"He's a peasant from Arges. . . . He has a wife and kids."

"Does he talk?" she whispered while she felt an unrestrained frustration
growing inside, triggered by that strange whistling which could not be
stopped. But she did not speak to him.

She studied again his white, well proportioned face, his blond hair, his
mouth harmoniously drawn under the gold shadow of a moustache, his
wide, smooth forehead, and his intense blue eyes.

She thought of the natural gentility of her people.

But there was still something about him that outlined from the depth
of his being the best features . . . something that idealized him . . . His pallor? His immobility? . . . or the fact that his organic functions, which con-
fuse the circulation of our blood and alter the purity of our image, seemed
somehow ecstatically suspended in him because of the enormous trouble
with his heart?

Laura left amid the quiet whispers of the ward.

In the corridors, inside the wards, the same mysterious rumor . . . "How
beautiful he was? . . . What a misfortune? . . . Terrible? . . . He could not
be a peasant!"

A legend would have been born, had it not been for the strict regulations. There was indeed in that patient something of an untamed noble-
ness which called for curiosity and secrecy, and that something was his
martyrdom.

The next morning she came again to see him.

The doctor was there. They exchanged a startled, desperate look.

"Have you seen it?" he asked. "No," she answered with her eyes.

Then he threw the sheets aside.

"I'm just changing his bandage."

Laura watched fearfully the wounded man's face. His head was
propped up by the pillows, pushed back as usual; his wide open eyes, blue,
diamond like, were staring at the ceiling with their motionless gleam.

Then she knew. He . . . he was afraid . . . afraid to move, to blink even, over the frozen pupil . . . afraid? And he kept his head like that, pushed back, not to see . . . To see what? . . . Maybe he had already seen . . .

Afraid the *man* might see . . . his own *heart*.

Laura turned her head from this terrible fear and looked at the doctor. He held the gauze in his hands.

"Look!" he said.

Unwillingly she turned away from the doctor and glanced toward the abyss of the open wound . . . there, to the left, where there lay the naked heart of a man. She cast a desperate look; she looked again and saw nothing but grey . . . like the opening of a pit. . . . After a while she turned to the doctor.

"It's horrible!" she said so that he wouldn't make her look again. "How did it happen?" she asked to find out what she had not seen.

"Shrapnel ripped through his chest and left his heart untouched, but bare. Because of the heart we cannot treat the wound, and because of the wound the heart cannot function properly."

"So, it was like that . . . of course . . . Well, you never know where the steel breaks, do you?"

From all the hidden hollows death carved into life's tissue, this was by far its most lacerated piece of artistry, worked into the poor human body.

The next day she listened again to the hissing storm growing inside the stiff body. The gust which raised the sheets just over the terrible wound was stronger.

The entire hospital was under the pressure of a meditative silence, a melancholy gravity. The noisy ant hill seemed trapped inside this embarrassing monotony. Respect and depression surrounded the strange tragic case.

The fourth day Laura found the bed occupied by a corporal.

She asked. He upset the other patients. It made a bad impression. Nobody could sleep. Besides, he had become agitated. They had taken him to a ward downstairs.

She found him again downstairs in ward no. 7. He didn't look mysterious anymore in the rough linen. His face seemed less serene. He pushed his head back, stubbornly.

"He won't listen, miss," the nurse complained. "He keeps taking off the bandage."

The man argued. It wasn't true . . . Nobody took care of him . . . Nobody changed his bandage. He threw off the covers and through the rumpled gauze Laura saw—but she couldn't tell what she saw. She covered him, trembling, and scolded him.

He didn't do anything. . . . How could he? . . . The doctor refused to take care of him.

"The doctor just left. He changed his bandages once."

"Let him change them again."

She went to see the intern herself.

"What? Again?"

"Come!"

The doctor followed her. He scolded the patient asking him to rest, but mildly, without ill feeling. He was a good man, diligent.

"He's in a different stage now. He has these attacks."

Laura remained by his bedside. From the heights of martyrdom his suffering had descended to human turmoil. Her silent, her sacred fear gently dissolved and crept down to the feet of mercy.

Once his wound was tended to he seemed calmer, his whistle dimmed by the smoothness of the fresh bandage. Laura walked to other beds where troubled patients were casting angry looks.

The nurse's voice called her back, as if struggling with somebody.

With his head bent down toward the odious wound, the man was greedily tearing with both hands at the bandages which, fastened tight, would not come off. His face was convulsed and he struggled to breathe. The nurse restrained him with all her strength.

They made him lie on his back. He begged in a sorry voice for a bandage. . . . How could he stay *like that* . . . How could they leave him *like that?*

Laura couldn't. She had seen all the horrors, but there . . . no . . . no, no. She couldn't.

She went to look for the intern.

This was his usual state now. Overcome by rage, unaware, he would tear off everything, tormented by pains unknown to science, by turmoils whose superhuman restlessness could not be imagined, for nothing like that had worked the human heart before.

One evening they tied his hands to the edge of his bed. Laura covered her face. The tortures to which people subjected the dying in an attempt to fulfill their duties to life! Why wasn't he dying? His body was apparently a machine of perfect resistance.

The man turned to her with a desperate look: "See how they tie me!" he said painfully. The pain was digging deep lines into his face tortured by spasms.

"Untie him!"

"We can't ma'am, we can't. It's orders from the boss. He scratched the wound with his nails, they were all bloody."

A look of madness came from the patient's blue eyes as he looked at his hands with their long thin fingers. It was true: the sapphire light of the eyes found on the pale nails a sparkling red impurity.

"Wash his hands," Laura whispered, "wash his hands quickly!"

The nurse obeyed morosely.

Out of the legend and mystery that surrounded him, out of the sacred terror of the superman, the martyr was falling. He struggled with the petty selfishness of the body within which life and death engaged in a terrible battle.

"He stuck his hands into . . .?" Laura didn't finish her thought. Not into the heart, really! He couldn't have survived!

Possessed by the madness that threw him like a beast against the "enemy" inside his chest, with the rage of his blood convulsed by a terrible revolution, with all that blind dementia which bent his head with staring eyes toward the red boiling brute, guided by a supreme instinct, he must have clutched not his heart, but feeling its way around the "monster," his uncontrollable spasm must have grasped the tissue close to the bloody tearing of the raw altar . . . But what if . . .? Laura buried her soul in brick and stone to hear no more the calling of a compassion which was barely enough for itself. A tiny rivulet of blood from the immaterial wound of pity ran down the side . . . And thus the noble martyr, intact as a sublime effigy of pain, his chest bearing the scores of a primitive icon, a fabulous laceration which left his heart bare, stooped with every passing hour to the humiliating pettiness of his degrading flesh. The agitated hum of the hospital now swallowed him too. In that turmoil where energies struggled to prolong lives, in contrast and in accord with the energies of war which asked for the sacrifice, the man whose heart they could see was one of the "casualties," an irreversible loss. How could he still be alive? He had been there for six days. On the evening of the sixth day she did not find him downstairs in ward no. 7.

"They took him away," the other patients blurted out in joy. "He's in intensive care." The chamber of agonies! The absurd resistance of that organism was broken. He was finally dying? . . . Inside the general feeling of indifference; within the realm of natural negligence that rejected everything no longer useful; inside a place where forces were grouped around profit, not loss; inside the old-fashioned aura of all decadent urges, after a short supernatural shining of suffering, like a melancholy and sarcastic *sic transit gloria* . . .

Inside that hive a different order of things, independent of any systematic distribution of work, made all of them use their instincts. Laura went about her business taking care of those patients as she would of any other, coming and going, as her work as a nurse required. But her daily routine brought along the secret of another kind of ritual, the litany of a different religion. She was the soul of a poor priestess of hopeless pain, her voice a comfort for those of lesser fortune. It was in her eyes and on her lips that the eyes of the dying were looking for the changing shapes of a last mirage.

She had incense to burn and prayers to say on the ruins of all deserted temples. She devoted herself to everything thrown there as not useful to the immediate purposes of existence, but it could be that she was also serving as the mysterious connection between the limited, conscious life and the infinite one.

After taking care of a few things, before leaving, she went to the intensive care unit. The task there was beyond her powers and she performed it horrified, but with an enigmatic serenity that comforted those who needed and to whom, after all, she owed the deception.

That day she found everybody there. At least she would not feel lonely.

The contact of those wounds with organic "matter," the penetration of organisms by shrapnel of varied texture inside those bodies, permitted live, morbid putrefaction. In tandem with the standard rational treatments there simmered and burst out unexpectedly new and strange epidemics: typical gangrenes independent of the progress of the cure; infectious pustules linking disparate cases. A flora specific to modern wars.

This morbidity was also caused by the multiple complications that had brought together nations, climates, and organisms by the numberless formulae the human brain had found for destruction: newly named gases, original metallurgical conglomerates, all those procedures which industrious and honest scientists were still offering with innocence and praise to the vampire of war.

The stinking pit of those amalgamated causes had now given birth to a microbe which grew on the patients' mouths devouring the tissue.

The little room in back held a dead body, and five patients were dying in the hallway.

Close to the door on a stretcher with another dying man, face to face, chests touching, his miserable remains almost impossible to recognize, lay the Man whose heart they could see. The other man's mouth was devoured by worms and the infested blood called for his end.

Cursed agony! They were too much alive and conscious. Crammed in there, thrown away, inert like filthy patches, when Laura approached them they spoke. The one with that Mouth and the Man with a voice that seemed to come out of the chaos of an infernal factory . . . and their voice there . . . like that . . . drove you down on your knees.

They complained about the treatment; they argued; they invoked their rights.

"They put me right next to this filthy one, with his worms! How can I get better?"

A twisted hope still tied to treacherous life the Man who in his magnanimity had shown them the miracle of his live naked heart.

"Me, close to this filth! How can I get better when I'm afraid . . . I'm afraid to *hear* and *see* his heart!"

. . . and their indignation was at once solemn, ridiculous, and terrifying.

Unable to move lest they should roll off the stretcher, they lay there glued to each other; one with his glazed blue eyes fixed on the wormy mouth; the other fascinated by the hideous opening inside which the heart was choking.

Still alive . . . too much alive! . . . as good as dead . . .

Laura's duty resembled the somber sermon of another hell.

Even the doctor was saying that his had been indeed a unique case in the museum of war surgery—a liminal form of the huge ingeniousness with which destruction humiliated and dismembered worn out bodies.

1923

Translated by Dayana Stetco

"Omul căruia i se vedea inima," in *Balaurul* (1923). Reprinted in *Opere*, ed. Eugenia Tudor-Anton (Bucharest: Minerva, 1975), 2:75–84.

✞ Mary Borden,
pseudonym: Bridget MacLagan
(1886–1968) *American/British*

Born in Chicago, Mary Borden graduated from Vassar in 1908. She had three daughters with her first husband, George Douglas Turner. With *Collision* (1913), she began to publish fiction in England under the pseudonym Bridget MacLagan.

From 1914 to 1918 Borden nursed in France, first under the French Red Cross, then directly under the French General Headquarters. Her 1946 memoir, *Journey Down a Blind Alley*, vividly recalls her starting work at Malo-les-Bains in a former casino converted to a typhoid hospital with no nursing equipment, then moving to a frontline unit flooded with overwhelming numbers of wounded coming directly from the battle lines; she became "a sleepwalker, an automaton" in her exhaustion. With permission from General Joffre, commander in chief of the allied armies, Borden—at her own expense—equipped and ran a mobile surgical hospital that followed the lines of battle between Belgium and the Jura Mountains along the Franco-Swiss border. Her Anglo-French unit had a French military commanding officer, surgeons, chemists, and orderlies; the nurses selected by Borden were British, Anzac, American, and French.

In Paris, Borden met Gertrude Stein, who relished dinners with the Chicago "millionaire" (Borden had heat, while Stein did not). Stein gave Borden copies of her work (perhaps *Three Lives* and *Tender Buttons*) that Borden reportedly took "to and from the front." Stein also introduced Borden to Ellen LaMotte, who worked in her hospital; there are striking parallels between the war sketches by Borden and by LaMotte from this period. Some of Borden's searing poetry and sketches about her observations as a nurse appeared under the name Borden Turner during the war in *The English Review* (1917); these were collected along with new prose in *The Forbidden Zone* (1929). For her service to France Borden was awarded

British war medals and the Croix de Guerre; she was also named a member of the Legion of Honor.

In the freezing muck of the battlefield and amid "unparalleled slaughter," Borden met Captain Edward Spears when she was nursing at Bray-sur-Somme. Married in 1918, they stayed in Paris during the peace conference, entertaining such luminaries as British Prime Minister David Lloyd George, Edvard Beneš of Czechoslovakia, King Faisal, poet and philosopher Paul Valéry, poet Anna de Noailles, writer and artist Jean Cocteau, and painter Marie Laurencin. Spears resigned from the army in 1921; he then became a member of Parliament. Michael, their only son, predeceased them. Over the next thirty years Borden published twenty novels, including *Sarah Gay* (1931), a collection of short stories, and a nonfiction book, *The Technique of Marriage* (1933).

In 1940 she again established a mobile hospital unit in France (the Hadfield-Spears unit); "this was the same war," she thought, "and I was the same person carrying on with my hospital." In fact, it was what the French call the "funny war," in which little combat took place and no wounded needed to be cared for. One year later the unit went to the Middle East; Borden served in Syria, Libya, Egypt, and elsewhere. Spears was made major general in 1940; he left his mark through his negotiations with the prickly General de Gaulle.

☦ Blind

The door at the end of the baraque kept opening and shutting to let in the stretcher bearers. As soon as it opened a crack the wind scurried in and came hopping toward me across the bodies of the men that covered the floor, nosing under the blankets, lifting the flaps of heavy coats, and burrowing among the loose heaps of clothing and soiled bandages. Then the grizzled head of a stretcher bearer would appear, butting its way in, and he would emerge out of the black storm into the bright fog that seemed to fill the place, dragging the stretcher after him, and then the old one at the other end of the load would follow, and they would come slowly down the centre of the hut looking for a clear place on the floor.

The men were laid out in three rows on either side of the central alley way. It was a big hut, and there were about sixty stretchers in each row. There was space between the heads of one row and the feet of another row, but no space to pass between the stretchers in the same row; they touched. The old territorials who worked with me passed up and down between the heads and feet. I had a squad of thirty of these old orderlies and two sergeants and two priests, who were expert dressers. Wooden screens screened off the end of the hut opposite the entrance. Behind these were the two dressing tables where the priests dressed the wounds of the new arrivals and got them ready for the surgeons, after the old men had undressed them and washed their feet. In one corner was my kitchen where I kept all my syringes and hypodermic needles and stimulants.

It was just before midnight when the stretcher bearers brought in the blind man and there was no space on the floor anywhere; so they stood waiting, not knowing what to do with him.

I said from the floor in the second row: "Just a minute, old ones. You can put him here in a minute." So they waited with the blind man suspended in the bright, hot, misty air between them, like a pair of old horses in shafts with their heads down, while the little boy who had been crying for his mother died with his head on my breast. Perhaps he thought the arms holding him when he jerked back and died belonged to some woman I had never seen, some woman waiting somewhere for news of him in some village, somewhere in France. How many women, I wondered, were waiting out there in the distance for news of these men who were lying on the floor? But I stopped thinking about this the minute the boy was dead. It didn't do to think. I didn't as a rule, but the boy's very young voice had startled me. It had come through to me as a real voice will sound sometimes through a dream, almost waking you, but now it had stopped, and the dream was thick round me again, and I laid him down, covered his face with the brown blanket, and called two other old ones.

"Put this one in the corridor to make more room here," I said; and I saw them lift him up. When they had taken him away, the stretcher bearers who had been waiting brought the blind one and put him down in the cleared space. They had to come round to the end of the front row and down between the row of feet and row of heads; they had to be very careful where they stepped; they had to lower the stretcher cautiously so as not to jostle the men on either side (there was just room), but these paid no attention. None of the men lying packed together on the floor noticed each other in this curious dream-place.

I had watched this out of the corner of my eye, busy with something that was not very like a man. The limbs seemed to be held together only by the strong stuff of the uniform. The head was unrecognisable. It was a monstrous thing, and a dreadful rattling sound came from it. I looked up and saw the chief surgeon standing over me. I don't know how he got there. His small shrunken face was wet and white; his eyes were brilliant and feverish; his incredible hands that saved so many men so exquisitely, so quickly, were in the pockets of his white coat.

"Give him morphine," he said, "a double dose. As much as you like." He pulled a cigarette out of his pocket. "In cases like this, if I am not about, give morphine; enough, you understand." Then he vanished like a ghost. He went back to his operating room, a small white figure with round shoulders, a magician, who performed miracles with knives. He went away through the dream.

I gave the morphine, then crawled over and looked at the blind man's ticket. I did not know, of course, that he was blind until I read his ticket. A large round white helmet covered the top half of his head and face; only his nostrils and mouth and chin were uncovered. The surgeon in the dressing station behind the trenches had written on his ticket, "Shot through the eyes. Blind."

Did he know? I asked myself. No, he couldn't know yet. He would still be wondering, waiting, hoping, down there in that deep, dark silence of his, in his own dark personal world. He didn't know he was blind; no one would have told him. I felt his pulse. It was strong and steady. He was a long, thin man, but his body was not very cold and the pale lower half of his clear-cut face was not very pale. There was something beautiful about him. In his case there was no hurry, no necessity to rush him through to the operating room. There was plenty of time. He would always be blind.

One of the orderlies was going up and down with hot tea in a bucket. I beckoned to him.

I said to the blind one: "Here is a drink." He didn't hear me, so I said it more loudly against the bandage, and helped him lift his head, and held the tin cup to his mouth below the thick edge of the bandage. I did not think then of what was hidden under the bandage. I think of it now. Another head case across the hut had thrown off his blanket and risen from his stretcher. He was standing stark naked except for his head bandage, in the middle of the hut, and was haranguing the crowd in a loud voice with the gestures of a political orator. But the crowd, lying on the floor, paid no attention to him. They did not notice him. I called to Gustave and Pierre to go to him.

The blind man said to me: "Thank you, sister, you are very kind. That is good. I thank you." He had a beautiful voice. I noticed the great courtesy of his speech. But they were all courteous. Their courtesy when they died, their reluctance to cause me any trouble by dying or suffering, was one of the things it didn't do to think about.

Then I left him, and presently forgot that he was there waiting in the second row of stretchers on the left side of the long crowded floor.

Gustave and Pierre had got the naked orator back on to his stretcher and were wrapping him up again in his blankets. I let them deal with him and went back to my kitchen at the other end of the hut, where my syringes and hypodermic needles were boiling in saucepans. I had received by post that same morning a dozen beautiful new platinum needles. I was very pleased with them. I said to one of the dressers as I fixed a needle on my syringe and held it up, squirting the liquid through it: "Look. I've some lovely new needles." He said: "Come and help me a moment. Just cut this bandage, please." I went over to his dressing-table. He darted off to a voice that was shrieking somewhere. There was a man stretched on the table. His brain came off in my hands when I lifted the bandage from his head.

When the dresser came back I said: "His brain came off on the bandage."

"Where have you put it?"

"I put it in the pail under the table."

"It's only one half of his brain," he said, looking into the man's skull. "The rest is here."

I left him to finish the dressing and went about my own business. I had much to do.

It was my business to sort out the wounded as they were brought in from the ambulances and to keep them from dying before they got to the operating rooms: it was my business to sort out the nearly dying from the dying. I was there to sort them out and tell how fast life was ebbing from them. Life was leaking away from all of them; but with some there was no hurry, with others it was a case of minutes. It was my business to create a counter-wave of life, to create the flow against the ebb. It was like a tug of war with the tide. The ebb of life was cold. When life was ebbing the man was cold; when it began to flow back, he grew warm. It was all, you see, like a dream. The dying men on the floor were drowned men cast up on the beach, and there was the ebb of life pouring away over them, sucking them away, an invisible tide; and my old orderlies, like old sea-salts out of a lifeboat, were working to save them. I had to watch, to see if they were slipping, being dragged away. If a man were slipping quickly, being sucked down rapidly, I sent runners to the operating rooms. There were six operating rooms on either side of my hut. Medical students in white coats hurried back and forth along the covered corridors between us. It was my business to know which of the wounded could wait and which could not. I had to decide for myself. There was no one to tell me. If I made any mistakes, some would die on their stretchers on the floor under my eyes who need not have died. I didn't worry. I didn't think. I was too busy, too absorbed in what I was doing. I had to judge from what was written on their tickets and from the way they looked and the way they felt to my hand. My hand could tell of itself one kind of cold from another. They were all half-frozen when they arrived, but the chill of their icy flesh wasn't the same as the cold inside them when life was almost ebbed away. My hands could instantly tell the difference between the cold of the harsh bitter night and the stealthy cold of death. Then there was another thing, a small fluttering thing. I didn't think about it or count it. My fingers felt it. I was in a dream, led this way and that by my acute eyes and hands that did many things, and seemed to know what to do.

Sometimes there was no time to read the ticket or touch the pulse. The door kept opening and shutting to let in the stretcher-bearers whatever I was doing. I could not watch when I was giving piqûres[1]; but, standing by my table filling a syringe, I could look down over the rough forms that covered the floor and pick out at a distance this one and that one. I had been doing this for two years, and had learned to read the signs. I could tell from the way they twitched, from the peculiar shade of a pallid face, from the look of tight pinched-in nostrils, and in other ways which I could not have explained, that this or that one was slipping over the edge of the beach of life. Then I would go quickly with my long saline needles, or short thick camphor oil needles, and send one of the

1. *Piqûres:* injections.

old ones hurrying along the corridor to the operating rooms. But sometimes there was no need to hurry; sometimes I was too late; with some
there was no longer any question of the ebb and flow of life and death;
there was nothing to do.

The hospital throbbed and hummed that night like a dynamo. The
operating rooms were ablaze; twelve surgical équipes[2] were at work; boilers steamed and whistled; nurses hurried in and out of the sterilizing
rooms carrying big shining metal boxes and enamelled trays; feet were
running, slower feet shuffling. The hospital was going full steam ahead. I
had a sense of great power, exhilaration and excitement. A loud wind was
howling. It was throwing itself like a pack of wolves against the flimsy
wooden walls, and the guns were growling. Their voices were dying away.
I thought of them as a pack of beaten dogs, slinking away across the dark
waste where the dead were lying and the wounded who had not yet been
picked up, their only cover the windy blanket of the bitter November
night.

And I was happy. It seemed to me that the crazy crowded bright hot
shelter was a beautiful place. I thought, "This is the second battlefield. The
battle now is going on over the helpless bodies of these men. It is we who
are doing the fighting now, with their real enemies." And I thought of the
chief surgeon, the wizard working like lightning through the night, and all
the others wielding their flashing knives against the invisible enemy. The
wounded had begun to arrive at noon. It was now past midnight, and the door
kept opening and shutting to let in the stretcher-bearers, and the ambulances kept lurching in at the gate. Lanterns were moving through the
windy dark, from shed to shed. The nurses were out there in the scattered
huts, putting the men to bed when they came over the dark ground,
asleep, from the operating rooms. They would wake up in clean warm
beds—those who did wake up.

"We will send you the dying, the desperate, the moribund," the Inspector-
General had said. "You must expect a thirty per cent mortality." So we had
got ready for it; we had organised to dispute that figure.

We had built brick ovens, four of them, down the centre of the hut, and
on top of these, galvanised iron cauldrons of boiling water were steaming.
We had driven nails all the way down the wooden posts that held up the
roof and festooned the posts with red rubber hot-water bottles. In the corner near to my kitchen we had partitioned off a cubicle, where we built a
light bed, a rough wooden frame lined with electric light bulbs, where a
man could be cooked back to life again. My own kitchen was an arrangement of shelves for saucepans and syringes and needles of different sizes,
and cardboard boxes full of ampoules of camphor oil and strychnine and
caffeine and morphine, and large ampoules of sterilized salt and water,
and dozens of beautiful sharp shining needles were always on the boil.

It wasn't much to look at, this reception hut. It was about as attractive

2. *Équipe:* team.

as a goods yard in a railway station, but we were very proud of it, my old ones and I. We had got it ready, and it was good enough for us. We could revive the cold dead there; snatch back the men who were slipping over the edge; hoist them out of the dark abyss into life again. And because our mortality at the end of three months was only nineteen per cent, not thirty, well it was the most beautiful place in the world to me and my old grizzled Pépères,[3] Gaston and Pierre and Leroux and the others were to me like shining archangels. But I didn't think about this. I think of it now. I only knew it then, and was happy. Yes, I was happy there.

Looking back, I do not understand that woman—myself—standing in that confused goods yard filled with bundles of broken human flesh. The place by one o'clock in the morning was a shambles. The air was thick with steaming sweat, with the effluvia of mud, dirt, blood. The men lay in their stiff uniforms that were caked with mud and dried blood, their great boots on their feet; stained bandages showing where a trouser leg or a sleeve had been cut away. Their faces gleamed faintly, with a faint phosphorescence. Some who could not breathe lying down were propped up on their stretchers against the wall, but most were prone on their backs, staring at the steep iron roof.

The old orderlies moved from one stretcher to another, carefully, among the piles of clothing, boots and blood-soaked bandages—careful not to step on a hand or a sprawling twisted foot. They carried zinc pails of hot water and slabs of yellow soap and scrubbing brushes. They gathered up the heaps of clothing, and made little bundles of the small things out of pockets, or knelt humbly, washing the big yellow stinking feet that protruded from under the brown blankets. It was the business of these old ones to undress the wounded, wash them, wrap them in blankets, and put hot-water bottles at their feet and sides. It was a difficult business peeling the stiff uniform from a man whose hip or shoulder was fractured, but the old ones were careful. Their big peasant hands were gentle—very, very gentle and careful. They handled the wounded men as if they were children. Now, looking back, I see their rough powerful visages, their shaggy eyebrows, their big clumsy, gentle hands. I see them go down on their stiff knees; I hear their shuffling feet and their soft gruff voices answering the voices of the wounded, who are calling to them for drinks, or to God for mercy.

The old ones had orders from the commandant not to cut the good cloth of the uniforms if they could help it, but they had orders from me not to hurt the men, and they obeyed me. They slit up the heavy trousers and slashed across the stiff tunics with long scissors, and pulled very slowly, very carefully at the heavy boots, and the wounded men did not groan or cry out very much. They were mostly very quiet. When they did cry out they usually apologised for the annoyance of their agony. Only now and then a wind of pain would sweep over the floor, tossing the legs and arms, then subside again.

---

3. *Pépères:* old fellows.

I think that woman, myself, must have been in a trance, or under some horrid spell. Her feet are lumps of fire, her face is clammy, her apron is splashed with blood; but she moves ceaselessly about with bright burning eyes and handles the dreadful wreckage of men as if in a dream. She does not seem to notice the wounds or the blood. Her eyes seem to be watching something that comes and goes and darts in and out among the prone bodies. Her eyes and her hands and her ears are alert, intent on the unseen thing that scurries and hides and jumps out of the corner on to the face of a man when she's not looking. But quick, something makes her turn. Quick, she is over there, on her knees fighting the thing off, driving it away, and now it's got another victim. It's like a dreadful game of hide and seek among the wounded. All her faculties are intent on it. The other things that are going on, she deals with automatically.

There is a constant coming and going. Medical students run in and out.

"What have you got ready?"

"I've got three knees, two spines, five abdomens, twelve heads. Here's a lung case—hæmorrhage. He can't wait." She is binding the man's chest; she doesn't look up.

"Send him along."

"Pierre! Gaston! Call the stretcher-bearers to take the lung to Monsieur D——." She fastens the tight bandage, tucks the blanket quickly round the thin shoulders. The old men lift him. She hurries back to her saucepans to get a new needle.

A surgeon appears.

"Where's that knee of mine? I left it in the saucepan on the window ledge. I had boiled it up for an experiment."

"One of the orderlies must have taken it," she says, putting her old needle on to boil.

"Good God! Did he mistake it?"

"Jean, did you take a saucepan you found on the windowsill?"

"Yes, sister, I took it. I thought it was for the casse-croûte[4] it looked like a ragout of mouton. I have it here."

"Well, it was lucky he didn't eat it. It was a knee I had cut out, you know."

It is time for the old ones' casse-croûte. It is after one o'clock. At one o'clock the orderlies have cups of coffee and chunks of bread and meat. They eat their supper gathered round the stoves where the iron cauldrons are boiling. The surgeons and the sisters attached to the operating rooms are drinking coffee too in the sterilizing rooms. I do not want any supper. I am not hungry. I am not tired. I am busy. My eyes are busy and my fingers. I am conscious of nothing about myself but my eyes, hands and feet. My feet are a nuisance, they are swollen, hurting lumps, but my fingers are perfectly satisfactory. They are expert in the handling of frail glass ampoules and syringes and needles. I go from one man to another jabbing the sharp needles into their sides, rubbing their skins with iodine, and

4. *Casse-croûte:* snack.

each time I pick my way back across their bodies to fetch a fresh needle I scan the surface of the floor where the men are spread like a carpet, for signs, for my special secret signals of death.

"Aha! I'll catch you out again." Quick, to that one. That jerking! That sudden livid hue spreading over his form. "Quick, Emile! Pierre!" I have lifted the blanket. The blood is pouring out on the floor under the stretcher. "Get the tourniquet. Hold his leg up. Now then, tight—tighter. Now call the stretcher-bearers."

Someone near is having a fit. Is it epilepsy? I don't know. His mouth is frothy. His eyes are rolling. He tries to fling himself on the floor. He falls with a thud across his neighbour, who does not notice. The man just beyond propped up against the wall, watches as if from a great distance. He has a gentle patient face; this spectacle does not concern him.

The door keeps opening and shutting to let in the stretcher-bearers. The wounded are carried in at the end door and are carried out to the operating rooms at either side. The sergeant is counting the treasures out of a dead man's pockets. He is tying his little things, his letters and briquet,[5] etc., up in a handkerchief. Some of the old ones are munching their bread and meat in the centre of the hut under the electric light. The others are busy with their pails and scissors. They shuffle about, kneeling, scrubbing, filling hot-water bottles. I see it all through a mist. It is misty but eternal. It is a scene in eternity, in some strange dream-hell where I am glad to be employed, where I belong, where I am happy. How crowded together we are here. How close we are in this nightmare. The wounded are packed into this place like sardines, and we are so close to them, my old ones and I. I've never been so close before to human beings. We are locked together, the old ones and I, and the wounded men; we are bound together. We all feel it. We all know it. The same thing is throbbing in us, the single thing, the one life. We are one body, suffering and bleeding. It is a kind of bliss to me to feel this. I am a little delirious, but my head is cool enough, it seems to me.

"No, not that one. He can wait. Take the next one to Monsieur D——, and this one to Monsieur Guy, and this one to Monsieur Robert. We will put this one on the electric-light bed; he has no pulse. More hot-water bottles here, Gaston.

"Do you feel cold, mon vieux?"[6]

"Yes, I think so, but pray do not trouble."

I go with him into the little cubicle, turn on the light bulbs, leave him to cook there; and as I come out again to face the strange heaving dream, I suddenly hear a voice calling me, a new far-away hollow voice.

"Sister! My sister! Where are you?"

I am startled. It sounds so far away, so hollow and so sweet. It sounds like a bell high up in the mountains. I do not know where it comes from. I look down over the rows of men lying on their backs, one close to the other,

5. *Briquet:* cigarette lighter.
6. *Mon vieux:* old chap.

packed together on the floor, and I cannot tell where the voice comes from. Then I hear it again.

"Sister! Oh, my sister, where are you?"

A lost voice. The voice of a lost man, wandering in the mountains, in the night. It is the blind man calling. I had forgotten him. I had forgotten that he was there. He could wait. The others could not wait. So I had left him and forgotten him.

Something in his voice made me run, made my heart miss a beat. I ran down the centre alley way, round and up again, between the two rows, quickly, carefully stepping across to him over the stretchers that separated us. He was in the second row. I could just squeeze through to him.

"I am coming," I called to him. "I am coming."

I knelt beside him. "I am here," I said; but he lay quite still on his back; he didn't move at all; he hadn't heard me. So I took his hand and put my mouth close to his bandaged head and called to him with desperate entreaty.

"I am here. What is it? What is the matter?"

He didn't move even then, but he gave a long shuddering sigh of relief.

"I thought I had been abandoned here, all alone," he said softly in his far-away voice.

I seemed to awake then. I looked round me and began to tremble, as one would tremble if one awoke with one's head over the edge of a precipice. I saw the wounded packed round us, hemming us in. I saw his comrades, thick round him, and the old ones shuffling about, working and munching their hunks of bread, and the door opening to let in the stretcher-bearers. The light poured down on the rows of faces. They gleamed faintly. Four hundred faces were staring up at the roof, side by side. The blind man didn't know. He thought he was alone, out in the dark. That was the precipice, that reality.

"You are not alone," I lied. "There are many of your comrades here, and I am here, and there are doctors and nurses. You are with friends here, not alone."

"I thought," he murmured in that far-away voice, "that you had gone away and forgotten me, and that I was abandoned here alone."

My body rattled and jerked like a machine out of order. I was awake now, and I seemed to be breaking to pieces.

"No," I managed to lie again. "I had not forgotten you, nor left you alone." And I looked down again at the visible half of his face and saw that his lips were smiling.

At that I fled from him. I ran down the long, dreadful hut and hid behind my screen and cowered, sobbing, in a corner, hiding my face.

The old ones were very troubled. They didn't know what to do. Presently I heard them whispering:

"She is tired," one said.

"Yes, she is tired."

"She should go off to bed," another said.

"We will manage somehow without her," they said.

Then one of them timidly stuck a grizzled head round the corner of the screen. He held his tin cup in his hands. It was full of hot coffee. He held it out, offering it to me. He didn't know of anything else that he could do for me.

"Blind," in *The Forbidden Zone* (London: Heinemann, 1929; New York: Doubleday, 1930), 144–68 (page citations are from the 1930 edition). Copyright © 1930 by Doubleday, a division of Bantam Doubleday Dell Publishing Group. Used by permission of Doubleday, a division of Bantam Doubleday Dell Publishing Group, Inc.

✝ Moonlight

The moonlight is a pool of silver on the linoleum floor. It glints on the enamel washbasin and slop pail. I can almost see the moon reflected in the slop pail. Everything in my cubicle is luminous. My clothes hanging on pegs, my white aprons and rubber boots, my typewriter and tin box of biscuits, the big sharp scissors on the table—all these familiar things are touched with magic and make me uneasy. Through the open door of the hut comes the sweet sickish scent of new-mown hay, mingling with the smell of disinfectants, of Eau de Javel and iodoform, and wet mud and blood. There is wet mud on my boots and blood on my apron. I don't mind. It is the scent of new-mown hay that makes me uneasy. The little whimpering voice of a man who is going to die in an hour or two comes across the whispering grass from the hut next door. That little sound I understand. It is like the mew of a wounded cat. Soon it will stop. It will stop soon after midnight. I know. I can tell. I go on duty at midnight, and he will die and go to Heaven soon after, lulled to sleep by the lullaby of the guns.

Far beyond him, out in the deep amorous night, I can hear the war going on. I hear the motor convoys rumbling down the road and the tramp of feet marching. I can tell the ambulances from the lorries and distinguish the wagons that carry provisions. Reinforcements are coming up along the road through the moonlit fields. The three-inch guns are pounding. All along the horizon they are pounding, pounding. But there will be no attack. The section is quiet. I know. I can tell. The cannonade is my lullaby. It soothes me. I am used to it. Every night it lulls me to sleep. If it stopped I could not sleep. I would wake with a start. The thin wooden walls of my cubicle tremble and the windows rattle a little. That, too, is natural. It is the whispering of the grass and the scent of new-mown hay that makes me nervous.

The war is the world, and this cardboard house, eight by nine, behind the trenches, with a roof that leaks and windows that rattle, and an iron stove in the corner, is my home in it. I have lived here ever since I can remember. It had no beginning, it will have no end. War, the Alpha and the Omega, world without end—I don't mind it. I am used to it. I fit into it. It provides me with everything that I need, an occupation, a shelter, companions, a jug and a basin. When winter comes my stove is red hot, and I sit with my feet on it. When it rains I sleep under a mackintosh sheet with an umbrella over my pillow and a basin on my feet. Sometimes in a storm the roof blows off. Then I wait under the blankets for the old men to come and put it back again. Sometimes the Germans shell the cross roads beyond us or the town behind us, and the big shells pass over the hospital screaming. Then the surgeons in the operating hut turn up the collars of their white jackets, and we lift our shoulders round our ears. I don't mind—it is part of the routine. For companions there are, of course, the surgeons and the nurses and the old grizzled orderlies, but I have other companions more intimate than these. Three in particular, a lascivious monster, a sick bad-tempered animal, and an angel; Pain, Life and Death. The first two are quarrelsome. They fight over the wounded like dogs over a bone. They snarl and growl and worry the pieces of men that we have here; but Pain is the stronger. She is the greater. She is insatiable, greedy, vilely amorous, lustful, obscene—she lusts for the broken bodies we have here. Wherever I go I find her possessing the men in their beds, lying in bed with them; and Life, the sick animal, mews and whimpers, snarls and barks at her, till Death comes—the Angel, the peace-maker, the healer, whom we wait for, pray for—comes silently, drives Pain away, and horrid, snarling Life, and leaves the man in peace.

Lying in my bed, I listen to the great, familiar, muttering voice of the war and to the feeble, mewing, whimpering voice of Life, the sick bad-tempered animal, and to the loud triumphant guttural shouts of Pain plying her traffic in the hut next to me, where the broken bodies of men are laid out in rows with patches of moonlight on their coverlets. At midnight I will get up and put on a clean apron and go across the grass to the sterilizing room and get a cup of cocoa. At midnight we always have cocoa in there next to the operating room, because there is a big table and boiling water. We push back the drums of clean dressings and the litter of soiled bandages, and drink our cocoa standing round the table. Sometimes there isn't much room. Sometimes legs and arms wrapped in cloths have to be pushed out of the way. We throw them on the floor—they belong to no one and are of no interest to anyone—and drink our cocoa. The cocoa tastes very good. It is part of the routine.

But the moonlight is like a pool of silver water on the floor, and the air is soft and the moon is floating, floating through the sky. In a dream I see her, in a crazy hurting dream. Lovely night, lovely lunatic moon, lovely scented love-sick earth—you are not true; you are not a part of the routine. You are a dream, an intolerable nightmare, and you recall a world that I once knew in a dream.

The mewing voice of the wounded cat dying in the shed next door to me is true. He is my brother, that wounded cat. This also is true. His voice goes on and on. He tells the truth to me. He tells me what I know to be true. But soon—quite soon—I hope and think that his voice will stop. Now the monstrous mistress that he has taken to his bed has got him, but soon he will escape. He will go to sleep in her arms lulled by the lullaby of the pounding guns that he and I are used to, and then in his sleep the Angel will come and his soul will slip away. It will run lightly over the whispering grasses and murmuring trees. It will leap through the velvety dark that is tufted with the soft concussion of distant shells bursting from the mouths of cannon. It will fly up through the showery flares and shooting rockets past the moon into Heaven. I know this is true. I know it must be true.

How strange the moon is with its smooth cheeks. How I fear the whispering of the grasses and murmuring of the trees. What are they saying? I want to go to sleep to the old soothing lullaby of the cannon that rocks me—rocks me in my cradle—but they keep me awake with their awful whispering. I am drowsy and drugged with heavy narcotics, with ether and iodoform and other strong odours. I could sleep. I could sleep with the familiar damp smell of blood on my apron, but the terrible scent of the new-mown hay disturbs me. Crazy peasants came and cut it while the battle was going on just beyond the canal. Women and children came with pitch-forks and tossed it in the sun. Now it lies over the road in the moonlight, wafting its distressing perfume into my window, bringing me waking dreams—unbearable, sickening, intolerable dreams—that interrupt the routine.

Ah! The great gun down by the river is roaring, is shouting. What a relief! That I understand—that giant's voice. He is a friend—another familiar, monstrous friend. I know him. I listen every night for his roar. I long to hear it. But it is dying away now. The echo goes growling down the valley, and again the trees and the grasses begin that murmuring and whispering. They are lying. It is a lie that they are saying. There are no lovely forgotten things. The other world was a dream. Beyond the gauze curtains of the tender night there is War, and nothing else but War. Hounds of war, growling, howling; bulls of war, bellowing, snorting; war eagles, shrieking and screaming; war fiends banging at the gates of Heaven, howling at the open gates of hell. There is War on the earth—nothing but War, War let loose in the world, War—nothing left in the whole world but War—War, world without end, amen.

I must change my apron now and go out into the moonlight. The sick man is still mewing. I must go to him. I am afraid to go to him. I cannot bear to go across the whispering grass and find him in the arms of his monstrous paramour. It is a night made for love, for love, for love. That is not true. That is a lie.

The peaked roofs of the huts stand out against the lovely sky. The moon is just above the abdominal ward. Next to it is the hut given up to gas gangrene, and next to that are the Heads. The Knees are on the other side, and the Elbows and the fractured Thighs. A nurse comes along carrying a lantern. Her white figure moves silently across the ground. Her lantern glows red in the moonlight. She goes into the gangrene hut that smells of swamp gas. She won't mind. She is used to it, just as I am. Pain is lying in there waiting for her. It is holding the damp greenish bodies of the gangrene cases in her arms. The nurse will try to get her out of those beds, but the loathsome creature will be too much for her. What can the nurse do against this she-devil, this Elemental, this Diva? She can straighten a pillow, pour drops out of a bottle, pierce a shrunken side with a needle. She can hold to lips a cup of cold water. Will that land her, too, in Heaven one day? I wonder; I doubt it. She is no longer a woman. She is dead already, just as I am—really dead, past resurrection. Her heart is dead. She killed it. She couldn't bear to feel it jumping in her side when Life, the sick animal, choked and rattled in her arms. Her ears are deaf; she deafened them. She could not bear to hear Life crying and mewing. She is blind so that she cannot see the torn parts of men she must handle. Blind, deaf, dead—she is strong, efficient, fit to consort with gods and demons—a machine inhabited by the ghost of a woman—soulless, past redeeming, just as I am—just as I will be.

There are no men here, so why should I be a woman? There are heads and knees and mangled testicles. There are chests—with holes as big as your fist, and pulpy thighs, shapeless; and stumps where legs once were fastened. There are eyes—eyes of sick dogs, sick cats, blind eyes, eyes of delirium; and mouths that cannot articulate; and parts of faces—the nose gone, or the jaw. There are these things, but no men; so how could I be a woman here and not die of it? Sometimes, suddenly, all in an instant, a man looks up at me from the shambles, a man's eyes signal or a voice calls "Sister! Sister!" Sometimes suddenly a smile flickers on a pillow, white, blinding, burning, and I die of it. I feel myself dying again. It is impossible to be a woman here. One must be dead.

Certainly they were men once. But now they are no longer men.

There has been a harvest. Crops of men were cut down in the fields of France where they were growing. They were mown down with a scythe, were gathered into bundles, tossed about with pitchforks, pitchforked into wagons and transported great distances and flung into ditches and scattered by storms and gathered up again and at last brought here—what was left of them.

Once they were real, splendid, ordinary, normal men. Now they mew like kittens. Once they were fathers and husbands and sons and the lovers of women. Now they scarcely remember. Sometimes they call to me "Sister, Sister!" in the faint voices of far-away men, but when I go near them and bend over them, I am a ghost woman leaning over a thing that is mewing; and it turns away its face and flings itself back into the arms of Pain, its monster bedfellow. Each one lies in the arms of this creature. Pain is the mistress of each one of them.

Not one can escape her. Neither the very old ones nor the young slender ones. Their weariness does not protect them, nor their loathing, nor their struggling, nor their cursing. Their hideous wounds are no protection, nor the blood that leaks from their wounds on to the bedclothes, nor the foul odour of their festering flesh. Pain is attracted by these things. She is a harlot in the pay of War, and she amuses herself with the wreckage of men. She consorts with decay, is addicted to blood, cohabits with mutilations, and her delight is the refuse of suffering bodies.

You can watch her plying her trade here any day. She is shameless. She lies in their beds all day. She lies with the Heads and the Knees and the festering Abdomens. She never leaves them. Even when she has exhausted them, even when at last worn out with her frenzy they drop into a doze, she lies beside them, to tease them with her excruciating caresses, her pinches and twinges that make them moan and twist in sleep. At any hour of the day or night you can watch her deadly amours, and watch her victims struggling. The wards are full of these writhings and tossings, they are agitated as if by a storm with her obscene antics. But if you come at midnight—if you come with me now—you will see the wounded, helpless, go fast asleep in her arms. You will see them abandon themselves to deep sleep with her beside them in their beds. They hope to escape her in sleep and find their way back to the fields where they were growing, strong lusty men, before they were cut down.

She lies there to spoil their dreams. When they dream of their women and little children, of their mothers and sweethearts; when they dream that they are again clean, normal, real men, filled with a tender and lovely love for women, then she wakes them. In the dark she wakes them and tightens her arms round their shrivelled bodies. She strangles their cries. She pours her poisoned breath into their panting mouths. She squeezes their throbbing hearts in their sides. In the dark, in the dark she takes them; she takes them to herself and keeps them until Death comes, the gentle angel. This is true. I know. I have seen.

Listen. Do you hear him? He is still mewing like a cat, but very faintly, and the trees are still murmuring and the grasses whispering. I hear the sound of many large creatures moving behind the hedge. They are panting and snorting. A procession of motor lorries and ambulances is going heavily down the road. They pass slowly, lumbering along with their heavy loads, and through the huge laborious sound of their grinding wheels threads the whirr of a swift touring car. You can hear it coming in the distance. It rushes nearer. It dashes past with a scratching shriek of its Klaxon. It plunges down the road and is gone. Some officer hurrying on some terrible business, some officer with gold leaves on his hat and a sword on his hip, in a limousine, leaning back on his cushions, calculating the number of men needed to repair yesterday's damage, and the number of sandbags required to repair their ditches. He does not see the lovely night and the lovely moon, and the unseemly love affair that is going on between the earth and the moon. He does not notice that he has passed the gate of a hospital, or know that behind the hedge men are lying in the dark with patches of blood and patches of moonlight on their coverlets. He is blind, deaf, dead, as I am—another machine just as I am.

It is twelve o'clock. The nurse has disappeared. She has left her lantern outside my door. There is no one to be seen. Nothing moves in the moonlight. But the earth is trembling, and the throbbing of the guns is the throbbing of the pulse of the War; world without end.

Listen! The whimpering mew of the wounded cat has stopped. There's not a sound except the whisper of the wind in the grass. Quick! Be quick!

In a moment a man's spirit will escape, will be flying through the night past the pale, beautiful, sentimental face of the moon.

✝ Conspiracy

It is all carefully arranged. Everything is arranged. It is arranged that men should be broken and that they should be mended. Just as you send your clothes to the laundry and mend them when they come back, so we send our men to the trenches and mend them when they come back again. You send your socks and your shirts again and again to the laundry, and you sew up the tears and clip the ravelled edges again and again just as many times as they will stand it. And then you throw them away. And we send our men to the war again and again, just as long as they will stand it; just until they are dead, and then we throw them into the ground.

It is all arranged. Ten kilometres from here along the road is the place where men are wounded. This is the place where they are mended. We have all the things here for mending, the tables and the needles, and the thread and the knives and the scissors, and many curious things that you never use for your clothes.

We bring our men up along the dusty road where the bushes grow on either side and the green trees. They come by in the mornings in companies, marching with strong legs, with firm steps. They carry their knapsacks easily. Their knapsacks and their guns and their greatcoats are not heavy for them. They wear their caps jauntily, tilted to one side. Their faces are ruddy and their eyes bright. They smile and call out with strong voices. They throw kisses to the girls in the fields.

We send our men up the broken road between bushes of barbed wire and they come back to us, one by one, two by two in ambulances, lying on stretchers. They lie on their backs on the stretchers and are pulled out of the ambulances as loaves of bread are pulled out of the oven. The stretchers slide out of the mouths of the ambulances with the men on them. The men cannot move. They are carried into a shed, unclean bundles, very heavy, covered with brown blankets.

We receive these bundles. We pull off a blanket. We observe that this is a man. He makes feeble whining sounds like an animal. He lies still; he smells bad; he smells like a corpse; he can only move his tongue; he tries to moisten his lips with his tongue.

This is the place where he is to be mended. We lift him on to a table. We peel off his clothes, his coat and his shirt and his trousers and his boots. We handle his clothes that are stiff with blood. We cut off his shirt with large scissors. We stare at the obscene sight of his innocent wounds. He allows us to do this. He is helpless to stop us. We wash off the dry blood round the edges of his wounds. He suffers us to do as we like with him. He says no word except that he is thirsty and we do not give him to drink.

We confer together over his body and he hears us. We discuss his different parts in terms that he does not understand, but he listens while we make calculations with his heart beats and the pumping breath of his lungs.

We conspire against his right to die. We experiment with his bones, his muscles, his sinews, his blood. We dig into the yawning mouths of his wounds. Helpless openings, they let us into the secret places of his body. We plunge deep into his body. We make discoveries within his body. To the shame of the havoc of his limbs we add the insult of our curiosity and the curse of our purpose, the purpose to remake him. We lay odds on his chances of escape, and we combat with Death, his saviour.

It is our business to do this. He knows and he allows us to do it. He finds himself in the operating room. He lays himself out. He bares himself to our knives. His mind is annihilated. He pours out his blood, unconscious. His red blood is spilled and pours over the table on to the floor while he sleeps.

After this, while he is still asleep, we carry him into another place and put him to bed. He awakes bewildered as children do, expecting, perhaps, to find himself at home with his mother leaning over him, and he moans a little and then lies still again. He is helpless, so we do for him what he cannot do for himself, and he is grateful. He accepts his helplessness. He is obedient. We feed him, and he eats. We fatten him up, and he allows himself to be fattened. Day after day he lies there and we watch him. All day and all night he is watched. Every day his wounds are uncovered and cleaned, scraped and washed and bound up again. His body does not belong to him. It belongs to us for the moment, not for long. He knows why we tend it so carefully. He knows what we are fattening and cleaning it up for; and while we handle it he smiles.

He is only one among thousands. They are all the same. They all let us do with them what we like. They all smile as if they were grateful. When we hurt them they try not to cry out, not wishing to hurt our feelings. And often they apologise for dying. They would not die and disappoint us if they could help it. Indeed, in their helplessness they do the best they can to help us get them ready to go back again.

It is only ten kilometres up the road, the place where they go to be torn again and mangled. Listen; you can hear how well it works. There is the sound of cannon and the sound of the ambulances bringing the wounded, and the sound of the tramp of strong men going along the road to fill the empty places.

Do you hear? Do you understand? It is all arranged just as it should be.

"Conspiracy," in *The Forbidden Zone* (London: Heinemann, 1929; New York: Doubleday, 1930), 124–29 (page citations are from the 1930 edition). Copyright © 1930 by Doubleday, a division of Bantam Doubleday Dell Publishing Group. Used by permission of Doubleday, a division of Bantam Doubleday Dell Publishing Group, Inc.

HOME FRONT, WAR WORK

✝ Helen Gansevoort Edwards Mackay
(1876–1966) *American*

After attending public schools in upstate New York, Helen Edwards married Archibald Mackay when she was twenty. She moved to France, where she lived most of her life. For her four years of service during World War I at the Hôpital St. Louis in Paris, she was awarded the medal of Reconnaissance française. As the titles of her books suggest, her preferred literary form was a brief narrative sketch of a few pages that caught a particular irony in people's lives, or a characteristic cultural trait. Her many sketches of French life include *Houses of Glass* (1909), *Accidentals* (1915), *Journal of Small Things* (1917), and *Chill Hours* (1919). A book of poetry about England and the war, *London One November* (1916), also engages in scene-painting; other sketches appear in *Stories for Pictures, The Cobweb Cloak* (1931), and *Half Loaves*. Mackay was sufficiently fluent to write poetry in French, gathered in *Ma tour et le vent* (My tower and the wind, 1958), as well as a novel, *Il était trois petits enfants* (There were three children, 1936), and two patriotic books about France during World War II, one with a preface by Antoine de Saint-Exupéry.

✝ London, September

The night Ian went out was pretty bad.

There were several other officers with him, and their wives and mothers and sisters and children all came to see them off.

Every one knew quite well what it meant, and every one pretended not to know.

I had come to feel, like the rest of them, that one has simply got to pretend.

We all pretended as hard as we could that it was splendid.

There was a woman on the platform who must have been crazy, I think.

She did not belong to any one going out. She was one of those dreadful things you see in London, with a big hat heaped with feathers, and draggled tails of hair. I think she had a red dress.

She came up to us under the windows of the train, and stood nodding her dreadful feathers and waving her dreadful hands and calling things out.

She called out, "Oh, it's all very fine now, you laugh now—but you won't laugh long. You won't laugh out there. And who of you'll come back and laugh, my pretty boys, my gay boys!"

Nobody dared take notice of her. If any one of us had taken notice of her, nobody could have borne it. There seemed to be no guard about to stop her, and not one of us dared admit that she was there.

"My pretty boys, my gay boys," she kept calling out, "you laugh now, my poor boys, but you won't laugh long."

There were some little Frenchmen, cooks, I think, or waiters, from some smart hotel, going to join the colours. They were in a third-class carriage next the carriage of the British officers.

They heard the woman calling out like that. They were little pasty-faced cooks or waiters.

But they began to sing. They began to sing the *Marseillaise* to drown the woman's voice out.

They did it just for us, our men going out, there on the platform.

Our men began to whistle it and hum it and stamp it. And we tried to.

The crazy woman called out those terrible things, that were so true.

And our men and the little Frenchmen sang and whistled and stamped. And so did we.

And the train went out like that.

"London, September," in *Journal of Small Things* (New York: Duffield and Company, 1917), 31–32.

✝ Americans

He did not seem so very ill. He had not that look of being made of wax. And he talked all the time. Most of them die so silently.

He lay in the bright ward and talked all of the time.

He had enlisted in the Foreign Legion and fought since the beginning, and was wounded last week in the Argonne.

He wanted me to sit beside him and listen. I hated the things he said.

He said he was a fool, they all were fools, and they all knew it now. He said there was no glory. They had thought that war was glorious. And it was hideous; sardine tins and broken bottles, mud or dust, never a green thing left to live. There was no enemy. Just guns. When a man fell, nobody had hit him, only a gun. If he was dead, lucky for him. When they were wounded they made noises like animals. It killed you to pick them up. He said they "went sorter every which way" in your hands. If they fell between the trenches you couldn't get to them. It seemed as if they'd never die. Sometimes they made noises like wolves and sometimes like cats. That was the worst, the noises like cats. You never knew if it weren't cruel to throw them bread. If you threw them bread, they lived and lived. The trenches were full of rats. The rats came and ate your boots and straps and things while you slept. The smells were "something fierce." "Gee, what fools we were," he said.

He picked at the bedclothes and grinned at me and said, "Say, kid, ain't you homesick for back over across the Duck Pond?"

I said, "Oh, no, no."

I looked out of the window to the sky of France that never has failed me of dreams, and I said, "No, no, no."

Oh, why did I? Why didn't I pretend for him that I was homesick too?

"Americans," in *Journal of Small Things* (New York: Duffield and Company, 1917), 48–49.

✝ Svarnakumari Devi
(1856–1932) *Indian*

A member of a distinguished Bengali family, Svarnakumari was the tenth child of Debendranath Tagore, born on the eve of the First Indian War of Independence, known as the Sepoy Rebellion, or Mutiny, of 1857. Educated at home in Calcutta, Svarnakumari had lessons in Sanskrit and English; she was immersed in a cultivated environment where aesthetics held a place next to political and social issues. At the age of thirteen she married Janakiram Ghosal, and one year later published anonymously a novel that met with acclaim for its artistry. Her later novels and fiction range in subject matter from personal relations, especially love, to history. *Virodha* (Revolt, 1890) depicts tribal revolts, and two of the stories collected in 1919 draw on responses to World War I. Svarnakumari also published an opera, farces, and poetry including *gatha* (long philosophical poems). In 1878 she founded the journal *Bharati*, a literary magazine, which she edited for thirty years. Addressed to women who could not read English, the journal covered cultural and scientific topics; it published the work of prominent writers and also offered Svarnakumari a political platform. Active on behalf of women, she helped form Sakhi Samiti, a relief organization, and attended the meetings of the Indian National Congress. She was cast under a shadow by her younger brother Rabindranath Tagore, who treated her with condescension as someone with "just enough talent to keep her alive for a short period." The revival of interest in her work, however, has led critics to reconsider her possible influence on Tagore.

✝ Mutiny (A True Story)

We—my son and I—were staying by the sea at Alibag, in the Bombay Presidency, and dining at the house of Mrs. A, when this true story was related by our hostess. The gentlemen lingered, in English fashion over their wine, while we ladies chatted on the verandah of the bungalow.

It was a beautiful night. Silvery moon-beams danced on the dark sea that stretched in front of us. The mighty water, swelling and heaving with the rising tide, seemed to be unable to contain its deep emotions and to strive, passionately, to flood the whole world. After washing the Fort of Kolaba near by, and overflowing the far-reaching expanse of white sand, the sea ran up to a mass of black rock near the bungalow, just in front of which stood two pillars, dedicated to two *Satis*. Here, at the foot of the pillars, the foaming, heaving water for a moment seemed to come to a sudden stand still. It was as though at the sacred touch of the pillars, its boldness vanished, and it sank back in wonder and awe, after paying its repeated homage to the Satis, and singing them a hundred hymns of praise.

Far away, in the west, the dark forms of the two island Forts of Andhari and Kandari were dimly discernible in the moon-light. Not so very long ago, only in the eighteenth century, the famous pirate chieftain Kanhoji Angray is said to have kept his captives imprisoned on one of these islands. The reader will remember that this notorious Mahratta was in his time the terror by land and sea of English, Portuguese and Moguls alike. Europeans called him "pirate," and such in truth he was; but in the days when might was right, what chief, or ruler, or founder of a dynasty was not a robber or a pirate? With success, piracy only receives another name. Angray had many noble qualities, and his soldiers worshipped him like a Napoleon. His power extended far and wide, and Balaji, the Maharatta ruler of that time, was obliged to make him the Raja of the provinces that he had brought under his control. Angray's descendants, though bereft of most of their ancestral possessions, still hold the title of Raja. The two forts stand out proudly towards the sea, and tell their own story of the glory of the past. The incessant washing of the waves has not broken away one stone. None could subdue the indomitable spirit of Angray but Death. And the Island Forts—his monuments—still stand erect and strong defying the waves of the ocean. Andari is now a complete desert, and Kandari has been converted into a light-house. And a light-house keeper, with one servant for a companion, tends the revolving light on the Kandari Fort which flashed before our eyes as we sat on the verandah and talked, then gradually grew dim and for a moment disappeared altogether, like the intermittent glow of a firefly.

With such a scene in front of us, we talked about the great war that is now convulsing the world.

Conversation turned on the topic of national courage, and our hostess proudly declared that one French man is equal to five Germans, and one Englishman the equal of three Frenchmen.

Proud words these, and true, perhaps! I, too, felt a glow of pride, as at the praise of a dear friend; for are not the English the most intimately related to us? And have we not cast in our lot with them, as the sharers of their destiny? Do we not pray for the victory of the English as fervently as they do themselves and feel proud to sacrifice our men and money to save the honour of England?

In this connection, I, too, could have remarked with pride that our sepoys are in no degree inferior to the soldiers of other nations,—that, led by good officers, they show exceptional courage and bravery on the battle field; and that they are the first to march forward fearlessly into the jaws of death. But if I dressed my views would they be appreciated? Most probably not. Now is a time of misunderstanding and is not mere suspicion positive proof against lifelong loyalty? Then who knows what next— indictment, or internment? So one has to think twice even before giving utterance to the simplest truth.

Moreover, however proud we may feel at the bravery of our sepoys, can we call it a national pride? Alas! have we not lost the privilege of calling ourselves a nation? What nation do we belong to? Our Rulers are of the West and we are not a bit less loyal for it—possibly more. For it is the English who have made modern India, for which we are supremely grateful. But still the shoe pinches some where. Our King is not one but many. The merest boy even if he be a half caste, thinks himself a King in India, demands our allegiance and arrogates to himself privileges which are denied to us. Of these thousands of Kings we must be the lawful and loyal subjects. But even the simple rights which loyal citizens expect do not belong to us. We are not treated as equals, nor do we receive the affection that according to our own national ideas, rulers should show to their subjects. If one among so many millions of us shows a disloyal spirit, then we are all considered to be deserving of the gallows. And lest one or two should go wrong we are deprived of the privilege of carrying fire-arms with which to defend ourselves even from wild beasts!

Of what nation are we then? Certainly we are not one with our rulers. We have not the rights of children of the soil that belong to us. Surely our fore-fathers, asleep in heaven, would be disturbed by the very idea, and curse us for our degeneracy! Was it not in this ancient land that science, literature and the arts flourished at the dawn of time? Our very posterity, also, will rise up in anger against so preposterous a nation, since at this very moment are we not renowned among the nations, in the things of the mind. We are, then, in the position of our mythological hero Harischandra's father Trisangu who could find no place either in heaven or on earth, and remained suspended in vacant space. So it is natural that occidentals should look upon our courage as reflected glory, and our loyalty and self-sacrifice as cringing, dog-like virtues!

And I kept silence.

Never before had I been made to feel my racial inequality in my intercourse with English people. I had always been treated as one of themselves. But this deference and friendliness had been paid to me individually, as being due to my social position. To-day, these expressions of a woman belonging to a free nation, made me feel myself an utter stranger among English people. Humbled and mortified, I called to mind our past Aryan glory, and with a suppressed sigh, I asked rather abruptly:—

"Are not those Sati pillars yonder in memory of Raja Angray's wives?"

Mrs. B——, another guest, replied: "So they say. What a terrible custom!"

"What terrible courage!" said I.

Mrs. B—— was silent, but her curling lip seemed to say:

"Courage indeed! To allow oneself to be burnt alive and not to have the power to utter a word! That is your courage! To be trodden under the heel of subjugation and feel it to be the happiness of virtue. This is indeed natural for a brave people like you."

If she had really spoken these words, what could I have said in reply? Could ever faith, love and devotion stand the test of argument? They are part and parcel of the divinity and a thing apart from human logic. Fortunately, I was not put to such a test. Said Mrs. A——: "Are not those two islands, Raja Angray's prisons? How daring he must have been!"

"And how horrid!" exclaimed Mrs. B——. "For he was only a pirate."

(True enough! What is bravery in a victorious nation, is contemptible courage and barbarism in the conquered.)

Miss C——, who was staying with Mrs. A—— and who had just come out from England, thought we were talking about the Mutiny, and exclaimed:—

"Oh! How dreadful! Were you here during the Mutiny?"

"No, I was not," laughed Mrs. A—— "and for the good reason that I was not born at the time. But my father was in India then."

Scotch people are said by their English neighbours to be wanting in humour, so we all looked at Miss C—— while she asked, quite simply, "Had your father any experiences of the Mutiny?"

"No," replied Mrs. A——, "he was not a soldier, but I went through a Mutiny once."

"How awful!" exclaimed Miss C——.

"Really?" said Mrs. B——. "But was there ever a mutiny in this part of India?"

We were all eager to hear the story and begged Mrs. A—— to tell it to us. And when it was finished, I did not know whether to laugh or to cry.

MRS. A——'S STORY

I had just come out to India after my marriage. Years before, when I was quite a child, I had once been in Bengal—but I was too young at that time to remember anything, and this was, in fact, my first experience of this country and the people in it. My husband was an Assistant Collector in Sukkar, and we settled down in our new home quite comfortably. When my husband went "on tour" I always accompanied him, and after knocking about for a few days in Camp, we were always glad to return to our cosy little bungalow and thoroughly enjoyed the rest and quiet of home-life. Only once I stayed at home alone. My husband had to go to a small village for two or three days, and I decided not to go with him. The house was full of servants and sepoys, so I felt that I should be quite safe during my husband's absence. But my friends in the Station thought differently. They were filled with anxiety on my account, and the Superintendent of Police offered to let me have a guard of his own sepoys. I thanked him for his kindness, but refused, saying it would show want of confidence in our own men. Before coming to India, I had had the impression that the servants of this country are cruel and treacherous. Horrible accounts of the mutiny had given me this idea, but my actual experience after coming to India had proved quite different, and I had found the servants and the sepoys docile, and very faithful and intelligent. I trusted our own sepoys and felt that I should be quite safe in their care, and I thought the Police Sahib's proposal quite unnecessary and even ventured to tell him so. My husband laughed at my enthusiasm; but the Police Sahib seemed annoyed and tried to make me change my mind. But I declined to do so, and I thought the matter had ended there.

My husband had gone away, and I had retired for the night, feeling quite safe and happy. Little did I think that I was to pay so heavily and so soon for my independence! My Ayah was the sole attendant in my room, and when I fell asleep, she was lying on the floor beside my bed. At about midnight, I awoke, hearing a noise outside the house. I was startled and only half conscious, and I heard cries and the sound of fire arms. A horrible feeling of fear overcame me. The thought of the Mutiny of 1857 came to my mind and I remembered that rumour of a disturbance in the interior had reached us. That this was another mutiny I felt certain.

"Oh! God, save me," I cried.

Like a drowning man who clutches at a straw, I called out "Ayah, Ayah!"

But she was not in the room. Had she, too, joined the mutineers? Ah! why had I been so sanguine, why had I not listened to those who knew the people of the land?

Stricken with utter terror, I lay in bed, motionless, in a halfconscious state and inwardly praying. Just then the Ayah returned.

"Madam Sahib!" she said; and her voice was respectful and natural as usual.

Thus reassured and finding a friend near me, I recovered from my state of stupor, and confidence in our own men returned. But still I thought that the sepoys of the Sukkar Fort had rebelled, and an attack had been made on the bungalow and that our few men had been fighting to save me.

All this flashed through my mind, and I asked in a trembling voice:—

"What is this noise, ayah? What has happened? Where are our men?"

The ayah in reply said many things, but I had not learnt the language well enough to understand more than that "Police" "Sepoy" "Fighting." So I was right. I had heard that there were a great many soldiers kept in secret in the Fort of Sukkar. A mutiny must have broken out among them. (I did not know then the difference between a court sepoy and a soldier sepoy.) I cried out wildly. "Fighting! Mutiny! Are they going to kill me? Oh! help, help, help!"

The ayah, although she did not understand English, could see that I was very much frightened, and she said "No, no, Madam Sahib, no, no." But I thought there was no help for me. The noise of arms and the cries seemed to come nearer and to grow louder. Frantic with terror, I tried to rise, but unable to do so, fell back unconscious. Oh! what a dreadful night!

Mrs. A——paused, and Miss C——gave vent to her feelings.

"Dreadful is not the word for it," she said. "But go on. What happened then?"

"I was not killed, that's certain," said Mrs. A——laughing, "for I have lived to tell you the tale."

"But what was the end. Was it really a mutiny?"

"No, I am afraid it was not. It was only a storm in a tea pot. On returning to consciousness, I found that it was morning and the ayah was standing beside me. All was quiet outside. It could not have been a dream, a nightmare, so I asked my ayah:—

"I think I heard a noise outside during the night. Has anything happened?"

"No, Madam Sahib," she said. "Go, sleep."

But I could not sleep then, for the sun was up, and I asked again:—

"Ayah, I thought I heard a noise outside last night. What was it?"

She began to talk volubly, but I could not understand what she said. So I sent her for a Sepoy who could speak a little English and he told me the whole truth. The Police Sahib had been at the bottom of it all. In spite of my declining to have his Sepoys, he had sent a guard to the bungalow at night. My men had been angry and had told them to go away and at last, it had come to blows. The Police Sahib, however, as I learnt later on, had not been solely to blame. The God of Love had had something to do with it. Since my ayah was sought in marriage by one of our Sepoys, and a young Sepoy of the Police force was also in love with her, the two rivals had found it a good opportunity to fight out their quarrel; and the noise of their fighting, in the silence of the night, had been exaggerated a hundredfold by my wild imagination and fears. I felt very angry at the Police Sahib's well-meant interference, which had terrified me out of my senses and nearly killed me with alarm. But when my husband returned, I said very little about it, for I think I was a little ashamed of myself.

At this juncture the gentlemen came into the verandah, and one of them said to us:—

"A cable had just arrived saying that Indian troops have been safely landed in Europe, and the French people have covered them with flowers."

"And England feels proud to have them!" exclaimed our host, "Brave warriors of an ancient civilization, to fight side by side with English soldiers against the common enemy."

Since then, "les Hindous" as the Indian troops are called by the French, have gone to the Front, have thrown themselves into the thick of the fight and have saved the "Izzat" of their mother-land and earned the highest praises of their King and commanders by their whole-hearted camaraderie and brilliant achievements. The bravery of the Indian troops is on every tongue in England; and the English soldiers desire that they should share with them the Victoria Cross and other coveted military honours. And the Government? It too, has been touched by this enthusiastic self-sacrifice, and it is believed that after the war is over, India will receive her just demands.

All honour to our brave country-men, and to the foreigners who appreciate their gallant efforts.

"Mutiny," in *Short Stories* (Madras: Ganesh, 1919), 226–39.

✝ Edith Newbold Jones Wharton
(1862–1937) American

Edith Newbold Jones was born into one of New York's elite families, for whom class stratification and patrician mores were unquestionable values. Barred by her mother from reading any recent fiction, she instead retreated to her father's library, where she found Milton, Plutarch, and the British Romantics. When she was sixteen, the family published her first volume of poetry, *Verses* (1878); Henry Wadsworth Longfellow published one of her poems in *The Atlantic Monthly*.

She entered an unhappy, childless marriage in 1885 with a sportsman, Edward Wharton, which cost her a nervous breakdown in 1894. She then turned to writing, producing at first short stories that attracted the public: *The Greater Inclination* (1899), *The Descent of Man and Other Stories* (1904), *Madame de Treymes* (1907), and *Tales of Men and Ghosts* (1910). She also collaborated on *The Decoration of Houses,* which reflected her relish for European domestic culture. In 1905 Wharton published her extremely popular *House of Mirth,* a tragedy about a woman's navigation through the contradictions of New York society. Living in France, Wharton fell in love with a friend of Henry James, Morton Fullerton. In 1913 she divorced Teddy, who had been embezzling her money and supporting a mistress. Many of her best novels written during this period—*Ethan Frome* (1911), *The Reef* (1912), *The Custom of the Country* (1913), and *Summer* (1917)—represent characters trapped in confining unions.

As an expatriate during World War I, Wharton energetically devoted herself to relief work. Based in Paris and at her country estate in St. Brice, she organized volunteer programs for refugees from Belgium and northern France, established institutions for soldiers with tuberculosis, funded mobile hospital units, and established "American Convalescent Homes" for ill and dispossessed children and civilians. She wrote about her travels to the front in *Scribner's,* essays that were collected in the propaganda book *Fighting France: From Dunkerque to Belfort* (1915). In 1916, a year in which she edited *The Book of the Homeless,* a collection of poetry, artwork, and prose by many famous hands to benefit war charities, her volunteer work earned her the Cross of the Legion of Honour. In 1918 she published a patriotic novel, *The Marne*, considered at the time "the most poignant story of the war," and began work on *A Son at the Front*, which did not go to press until 1923. By then the public had ceased to take interest in the war, she felt. In her autobiography, *A Backward Glance* (1934), she recalled, "I saw the years of the war, as I had lived them in Paris, with a new intensity of vision, in all their fantastic heights and depths of self-devotion and ardour, of pessimism, triviality, and selfishness."

After the war Wharton's literary successes continued, with a Pulitzer Prize for *The Age of Innocence* (1920). *Glimpses of the Moon* (1922) was a best-seller, for which F. Scott Fitzgerald wrote a screenplay. She continued to write prolifically until her death.

KCS

✠ Writing a War Story

Miss Ivy Spang of Cornwall-on-Hudson had published a little volume of verse before the war.

It was called "Vibrations," and was preceded by a Foreword in which the author stated that she had yielded to the urgent request of friends in exposing her first-born to the public gaze. The public had not gazed very hard or very long, but the Cornwall-on-Hudson *News-Dispatch* had a flattering notice by the wife of the Rector of St. Dunstan's (signed "Asterisk"), in which, while the somewhat unconventional sentiment of the poems was gently deprecated, a graceful and ladylike tribute was paid to the "brilliant daughter of one of our most prominent and influential citizens, who has voluntarily abandoned *the primrose way of pleasure* to scale *the rugged heights of Parnassus.*"

Also, after sitting one evening next to him at a bohemian dinner in New York, Miss Spang was honored by an article by the editor of *Zigzag*, the new "Weekly Journal of Defiance," in which that gentleman hinted that there was more than she knew in Ivy Spang's poems, and that their esoteric significance showed that she was a *vers-librist* in thought as well as in technique. He added that they would "gain incommensurably in meaning" when she abandoned the superannuated habit of beginning each line with a capital letter.

The editor sent a heavily-marked copy to Miss Spang, who was immensely flattered, and felt that at last she had been understood. But nobody she knew read *Zigzag*, and nobody who read *Zigzag* seemed to care to know her. So nothing in particular resulted from this tribute to her genius.

Then the war came, and she forgot all about writing poetry.

*   *   *

The war was two years old, and she had been pouring tea once a week for a whole winter in a big Anglo-American hospital in Paris, when one day, as she was passing through the flower-edged court on her way to her ward, she heard one of the doctors say to a pale gentleman in civilian clothes and spectacles, "But I believe that pretty Miss Spang writes. If you want an American contributor, why not ask her?" And the next moment the pale gentleman had been introduced and, beaming anxiously at her through his spectacles, was urging her to contribute a rattling war story to *The Man-at-Arms,* a monthly publication that was to bring joy to the wounded and disabled in British hospitals.

"A good rousing story, Miss Spang; a dash of sentiment, of course, but nothing to depress or discourage. I'm sure you catch my meaning? A tragedy with a happy ending—that's about the idea. But I leave it to you; with your large experience of hospital work of course you know just what hits the poor fellows' taste. Do you think you could have it ready for our first number? And have you a portrait—if possible in nurse's dress—to publish with it? The Queen of Norromania has promised us a poem, with a picture of herself giving the baby Crown Prince his morning tub. We want the first number to be an 'actuality,' as the French say; all the articles written by people who've done the thing themselves, or seen it done. You've been at the front, I suppose? As far as Rheims, once? That's capital! Give us a good stirring trench story, with a Coming-Home scene to close with . . . a Christmas scene, if you can manage it, as we hope to be out in November. Yes—that's the very thing; and I'll try to get Sargent to do us the wounded V. C. coming back to the old home on Christmas Eve—snow effect."

It was lucky that Ivy Spang's leave was due about that time, for, devoted though she was to her patients, the tea she poured for them might have suffered from her absorption in her new task.

Was it any wonder that she took it seriously?

She, Ivy Spang, of Cornwall-on-Hudson, had been asked to write a war story for the opening number of *The Man-at-Arms,* to which Queens and Archbishops and Field Marshals were to contribute poetry and photographs and patriotic sentiment in autograph! And her full-length photograph in nurse's dress was to precede her prose; in the table of contents she was to figure as "Ivy Spang, author of *Vibrations: A Book of Verse.*"

She was dizzy with triumph, and went off to hide her exultation in a quiet corner of Brittany, where she happened to have an old governess, who took her in and promised to defend at all costs the sacredness of her mornings—for Ivy knew that the morning hours of great authors were always "sacred."

She shut herself up in her room with a ream of mauve paper and began to think.

At first the process was less exhilarating than she had expected. She knew so much about the war that she hardly knew where to begin; she found herself suffering from a plethora of impressions.

Moreover, the more she thought of the matter, the less she seemed to understand how a war story—or any story, for that matter—was written. Why did stories ever begin, and why did they ever leave off? Life didn't—it just went on and on.

This unforeseen problem troubled her exceedingly, and on the second morning she stealthily broke from her seclusion and slipped out for a walk on the beach. She had been ashamed to make known her projected escapade, and went alone, leaving her faithful governess to mount guard on her threshold while she sneaked out by a back way.

There were plenty of people on the beach, and among them some whom she knew; but she dared not join them lest they should frighten away her Inspiration. She knew that Inspirations were fussy and contrarious, and she felt rather as if she were dragging along a reluctant dog on a string.

"If you wanted to stay indoors, why didn't you say so?" she grumbled to it. But the Inspiration continued to sulk.

She wandered about under the cliff till she came to an empty bench, where she sat down and gazed at the sea. After a while her eyes were dazzled by the light, and she turned them toward the bench and saw lying on it a battered magazine—the midsummer "All Story" number of *Fact and Fiction*. Ivy pounced upon it.

She had heard a good deal about not allowing one's self to be "influenced," about jealously guarding one's originality, and so forth; the editor of *Zigzag* had been particularly strong on that theme. But her story had to be written, and she didn't know how to begin it, so she decided just to glance casually at a few beginnings.

The first tale in the magazine was signed by a name great in fiction, one of the most famous names of the past generation of novelists. The opening sentence ran: "In the month of October, 1914—" and Ivy turned the page impatiently. She may not have known much about story writing, but she did know that *that* kind of a beginning was played out. She turned to the next.

" 'My God!' roared the engineer, tightening his grasp on the lever, while the white, sneering face under the red lamp . . ."

No; that was beginning to be out of date, too.

"They sat there and stared at it in silence. Neither spoke; but the woman's heart ticked like a watch."

That was better but best of all she liked, "Lee Lorimer leaned to him across the flowers. She had always known that this was coming . . ." Ivy could imagine tying a story on to *that*.

But she had promised to write a war story: and in a war story the flowers must be at the end and not at the beginning.

At any rate, there was one clear conclusion to be drawn from the successive study of all these opening paragraphs; and that was that you must begin in the middle, and take for granted that your reader knew what you were talking about.

Yes; but where was the middle, and how could your reader know what you were talking about when you didn't know yourself?

After some reflection, and more furtive scrutiny of *Fact and Fiction*, the puzzled authoress decided that perhaps, if you pretended hard enough that you knew what your story was about, you might end by finding out toward the last page. "After all, if the reader can pretend, the author ought to be able to," she reflected. And she decided (after a cautious glance over her shoulder) to steal the magazine and take it home with her for private dissection.

On the threshold she met her governess, who beamed on her tenderly.

"Chérie, I saw you slip off, but I didn't follow. I knew you wanted to be alone with your Inspiration." Mademoiselle lowered her voice to add: "Have you found your plot?"

Ivy tapped her gently on the wrinkled cheek. "Dear old Madsy! People don't bother with plots nowadays."

"Oh, don't they, darling? Then it must be very much easier," said Mademoiselle. But Ivy was not so sure—

After a day's brooding over *Fact and Fiction*, she decided to begin on the empiric system. ("It's sure to come to me as I go along," she thought.) So she sat down before the mauve paper and wrote "A shot rang out—"

But just as she was appealing to her Inspiration to suggest the next phrase a horrible doubt assailed her, and she got up and turned to *Fact and Fiction*. Yes, it was just as she had feared, the last story in *Fact and Fiction* began: "A shot rang out—"

Its place on the list showed what the editor and his public thought of that kind of an opening, and her contempt for it was increased by reading the author's name. The story was signed "Edda Clubber Hump." Poor thing!

Ivy sat down and gazed at the page which she had polluted with that silly sentence.

And now (as they often said in *Fact and Fiction*) a strange thing happened. The sentence was there—she had written it—it was the first sentence on the first page of her story, it *was* the first sentence of her story. It was there, it had gone out of her, got away from her, and she seemed to have no further control of it. She could imagine no other way of beginning, now that she had made the effort of beginning in that way.

She supposed that was what authors meant when they talked about being "mastered by their Inspiration." She began to hate her Inspiration.

On the fifth day an abased and dejected Ivy confided to her old governess that she didn't believe she knew how to write a short story.

"If they'd only asked me for poetry!" she wailed.

She wrote to the editor of *The Man-at-Arms*, begging for permission to substitute a sonnet; but he replied firmly, if flatteringly, that they counted on a story, and had measured their space accordingly—adding that they already had rather more poetry than the first number could hold. He concluded by reminding her that he counted on receiving her contribution not later than September first; and it was now the tenth of August.

"It's all so sudden," she murmured to Mademoiselle, as if she were announcing her engagement.

"Of course, dearest—of course! I quite understand. How could the editor expect you to be tied to a date? But so few people know what the artistic temperament is; they seem to think one can dash off a story as easily as one makes an omelet."

Ivy smiled in spite of herself. "Dear Madsy, what an unlucky simile! So few people make good omelets."

"Not in France," said Mademoiselle firmly.

Her former pupil reflected. "In France a good many people have written good short stories, too—but I'm sure they were given more than three weeks to learn how. Oh, what shall I do?" she groaned.

The two pondered long and anxiously; and at last the governess modestly suggested: "Supposing you were to begin by thinking of a subject?"

"Oh, my dear, the subject's nothing!" exclaimed Ivy, remembering some contemptuous statement to that effect by the editor of *Zigzag*.

"Still—in writing a story, one has to have a subject. Of course I know it's only the treatment that really matters; but the treatment, naturally, would be yours, quite yours. . . ."

The authoress lifted a troubled gaze upon her Mentor. "What are you driving at, Madsy?"

"Only that during my year's work in the hospital here I picked up a good many stories—pathetic, thrilling, moving stories of our poor poilus; and in the evening, sometimes, I used to jot them down, just as the soldiers told them to me—oh, without any art at all . . . simply for myself, you understand. . . ."

Ivy was on her feet in an instant. Since even Mademoiselle admitted that "only the treatment really mattered," why should she not seize on one of these artless tales and transform it into Literature? The more she considered the idea, the more it appealed to her; she remembered Shakespeare and Molière, and said gayly to her governess: "You darling Madsy! Do lend me your book to look over—and we'll be collaborators!"

"Oh—collaborators!" blushed the governess, overcome. But she finally yielded to her charge's affectionate insistence and brought out her shabby copybook, which began with lecture notes on Mr. Bergson's course at the Sorbonne in 1913, and suddenly switched off to "Military Hospital No. 13. November, 1914. Long talk with the Chasseur Alpin Emile Durand, wounded through the knee and the left lung at the Hautes Chaumes. I have decided to write down his story. . . ."

Ivy carried the little book off to bed with her, inwardly smiling at the fact that the narrative, written in a close, tremulous hand, covered each side of the page, and poured on and on without a paragraph—a good deal like life. Decidedly, poor Mademoiselle did not even know the rudiments of literature!

The story, not without effort, gradually built itself up about the adventures of Emile Durand. Notwithstanding her protests, Mademoiselle, after a day or two, found herself called upon in an advisory capacity and finally as a collaborator. She gave the tale a certain consecutiveness, and kept Ivy to the main point when her pupil showed a tendency to wander; but she carefully revised and polished the rustic speech in which she had originally transcribed the tale, so that it finally issued forth in the language that a young lady writing a composition on the Battle of Hastings would have used in Mademoiselle's school days.

Ivy decided to add a touch of sentiment to the anecdote, which was purely military, both because she knew the reader was entitled to a certain proportion of "heart interest," and because she wished to make the subject her own by this original addition. The revisions and transpositions which these changes necessitated made the work one of uncommon difficulty; and one day, in a fit of discouragement, Ivy privately decided to notify the editor of *The Man-at-Arms* that she was ill and could not fulfill her engagement.

But that very afternoon the "artistic" photographer to whom she had posed for her portrait sent home the proofs; and she saw herself, exceedingly long, narrow and sinuous, robed in white and monastically veiled, holding out a refreshing beverage to an invisible sufferer with a gesture halfway between Mélisande lowering her braid over the balcony and Florence Nightingale advancing with the lamp.

The photograph was really too charming to be wasted and Ivy, feeling herself forced onward by an inexorable fate, sat down again to battle with the art of fiction. Her perseverance was rewarded, and after a while the fellow authors (though Mademoiselle disclaimed any right to the honors of literary partnership) arrived at what seemed to both a satisfactory result.

"You've written a very beautiful story, my dear," Mademoiselle sighed with moist eyes; and Ivy modestly agreed that she had.

The task was finished on the last day of her leave; and the next morning she traveled back to Paris, clutching the manuscript to her bosom, and forgetting to keep an eye on the bag that contained her passport and money, in her terror lest the precious pages should be stolen.

As soon as the tale was typed she did it up in a heavily-sealed envelope (she knew that only silly girls used blue ribbon for the purpose), and dispatched it to the pale gentleman in spectacles, accompanied by the Mélisande-Nightingale photograph. The receipt of both was acknowledged by a courteous note (she had secretly hoped for more enthusiasm), and thereafter life became a desert waste of suspense. The very globe seemed to cease to turn on its axis while she waited for *The Man-at-Arms* to appear.

Finally one day a thick packet bearing an English publisher's name was brought to her. She undid it with trembling fingers, and there, beautifully printed on the large rough pages, her story stood out before her.

At first, in that heavy text, on those heavy pages, it seemed to her a pitifully small thing, hopelessly insignificant and yet pitilessly conspicuous. It was as though words meant to be murmured to sympathetic friends were being megaphoned into the ear of a heedless universe.

Then she began to turn the pages of the review; she analyzed the poems, she read the Queen of Norromania's domestic confidences, and she looked at the portraits of the authors. The latter experience was peculiarly comforting. The Queen was rather good-looking—for a Queen—but her hair was drawn back from the temples as if it were wound round a windlass, and struck out over her forehead in the good old-fashioned Royal Highness fuzz; and her prose was oddly built out of London drawing-room phrases grafted onto German genitives and datives. It was evident that neither Ivy's portrait nor her story would suffer by comparison with the royal contribution.

But most of all was she comforted by the poems. They were nearly all written on Kipling rhythms that broke down after two or three wheezy attempts to "carry on" and their knowing mixture of slang and pathos seemed oddly old-fashioned to the author of "Vibrations." Altogether, it struck her that *The Man-at-Arms* was made up in equal parts of tired compositions by people who knew how to write, and artless prattle by people who didn't. Against such a background, "His Letter Home" began to loom up rather large.

At any rate, it took such a place in her consciousness for the next day or two that it was bewildering to find that no one about her seemed to have heard of it. *The Man-at-Arms* was conspicuously shown in the windows of the principal English and American bookshops but she failed to see it lying on her friends' tables and finally, when her tea-pouring day came round, she bought a dozen copies and took them up to the English ward of her hospital, which happened to be full at the time.

It was not long before Christmas and the men and officers were rather busy with home correspondence and the undoing and doing-up of seasonable parcels but they all received *The Man-at-Arms* with an appreciative smile, and were most awfully pleased to know that Miss Spang had written something in it. After the distribution of her tale, Miss Spang became suddenly hot and shy, and slipped away before they had begun to read her.

The intervening week seemed long; and it was marked only by the appearance of a review of *The Man-at-Arms* in the *Times*—a long and laudatory article—in which, by some odd accident, "His Letter Home" and its author were not so much as mentioned. Abridged versions of this notice appeared in the English and American newspapers published in Paris; and one anecdotic and intimate article in a French journal celebrated the maternal graces and literary art of the Queen of Norromania. It was signed "Fleur-de-Lys," and described a banquet at the Court of Norromania at which the writer hinted that she had assisted.

The following week, Ivy re-entered her ward with a beating heart. On the threshold one of the nurses detained her with a smile.

"Do be a dear and make yourself specially nice to the new officer in Number 5; he's only been here two days and he's rather down on his luck. Oh, by the way—he's the novelist, Harold Harbard; you know, the man who wrote the book they made such a fuss about."

Harold Harbard—the book they made such a fuss about! What a poor fool the woman was—not even to remember the title of *Broken Wings*! Ivy's heart stood still with the shock of the discovery. She remembered that she had left a copy of *The Man-at-Arms* in Number 5, and the blood coursed through her veins and flooded her to the forehead at the idea that Harold Harbard might at that very moment be reading "His Letter Home."

To collect herself, she decided to remain a while in the ward, serving tea to the soldiers and N.C.O.'s, before venturing into Number 5, which the previous week had been occupied only by a polo player drowsy with chloroform and uninterested in anything but his specialty. Think of Harold Harbard lying in the bed next to that man!

Ivy passed into the ward, and as she glanced down the long line of beds she saw several copies of *The Man-at-Arms* lying on them, and one special favorite of hers, a young lance-corporal, deep in its pages.

She walked down the ward, distributing tea and greetings; and she saw that her patients were all very glad to see her. They always were; but this time there was a certain unmistakable emphasis in their gladness; and she fancied they wanted her to notice it.

"Why," she cried gayly, "how uncommonly cheerful you all look!"

She was handing his tea to the young lance-corporal, who was usually the spokesman of the ward on momentous occasions. He lifted his eyes from the absorbed perusal of *The Man-at-Arms,* and as he did so she saw that it was open at the first page of her story.

"I say, you know," he said, "it's simply topping—and we're so awfully obliged to you for letting us see it."

She laughed, but would not affect incomprehension.

"That?" She laid a light finger on the review. "Oh, I'm glad—I'm awfully pleased, of course—you *do* really like it?" she stammered.

"Rather—all of us—most tremendously—!" came a chorus from the long line of beds.

Ivy tasted her highest moment of triumph. She drew a deep breath and shone on them with glowing cheeks.

"There couldn't be higher praise . . . there couldn't be better judges. . . . You think it's really like, do you?"

"Really like? Rather! It's just topping," rang out the unanimous response.

She choked with emotion. "Coming from you—from all of you—it makes me most awfully glad."

They all laughed together shyly, and then the lance-corporal spoke up.

"We admire it so much that we're going to ask you a most tremendous favor—"

"Oh, yes," came from the other beds.

"A favor—?"

"Yes; if it's not too much." The lance-corporal became eloquent. "To remember you by, and all your kindness; we want to know if you won't give one to each of us—"

("Why, of course, of course," Ivy glowed.)

"—to frame and take away with us," the lance-corporal continued sentimentally. "There's a chap here who makes rather jolly frames out of Vichy corks."

"Oh—" said Ivy, with a protracted gasp.

"You see, in your nurse's dress, it'll always be such a jolly reminder," said the lance-corporal, concluding his lesson.

"I never saw a jollier photo," spoke up a bold spirit.

"Oh, do say yes, nurse," the shyest of the patients softly whispered; and Ivy, bewildered between tears and laughter, said, "Yes."

It was evident that not one of them had read her story.

She stopped on the threshold of Number 5, her heart beating uncomfortably.

She had already recovered from her passing mortification; it was absurd to have imagined that the inmates of the ward, dear, gallant young fellows, would feel the subtle meaning of a story like "His Letter Home." But with Harold Harbard it was different. Now, indeed, she was to be face to face with a critic.

She stopped on the threshold, and as she did so she heard a burst of hearty, healthy laughter from within. It was not the voice of the polo player; could it be that of the novelist?

She opened the door resolutely and walked in with her tray. The polo player's bed was empty, and the face on the pillow of the adjoining cot was the brown, ugly, tumultuous-locked head of Harold Harbard, well-known to her from frequent photographs in the literary weeklies. He looked up as she came in, and said in a voice that seemed to continue his laugh: "Tea? Come, that's something like!" And he began to laugh again.

It was evident that he was still carrying on the thread of his joke, and as she approached with the tea she saw that a copy of *The Man-at-Arms* lay on the bed at his side, and that he had his hand between the open pages.

Her heart gave an apprehensive twitch, but she determined to carry off the situation with a high hand.

"How do you do, Captain Harbard? I suppose you're laughing at the way the Queen of Norromania's hair is done."

He met her glance with a humorous look, and shook his head, while the laughter still rippled the muscles of his throat.

"No—no; I've finished laughing at that. It was the next thing; what's it called? 'His Letter Home,' by—" The review dropped abruptly from his hands, his brown cheek paled, and he fixed her with a stricken stare.

"Good lord," he stammered out, "but it's *you!*"

She blushed all colors, and dropped into a seat at his side. "After all," she faltered, half laughing too, "at least you read the story instead of looking at my photograph."

He continued to scrutinize her with a reviving eye. "Why—do you mean that everybody else—"

"All the ward over there," she assented, nodding in the direction of the door.

"They all forgot to read the story for gazing at its author?"

"Apparently." There was a painful pause. The review dropped from his lax hand.

"Your tea—?" she suggested, stiffly.

"Oh, yes; to be sure. . . . Thanks."

There was another silence, during which the act of pouring out the milk, and the dropping of the sugar into the cup, seemed to assume enormous magnitude, and make an echoing noise. At length Ivy said, with an effort at lightness, "Since I know who you are, Mr. Harbard—would you mind telling me what you were laughing at in my story?"

He leaned back against the pillows and wrinkled his forehead anxiously.

"My dear Miss Spang, not in the least—if I *could*."

"If you could?"

"Yes; I mean in any understandable way."

"In other words, you think it so silly that you don't dare to tell me anything more?"

He shook his head. "No; but it's queer—it's puzzling. You've got hold of a wonderfully good subject; and that's the main thing, of course—"

Ivy interrupted him eagerly. "The subject is the main thing?"

"Why, naturally; it's only the people without invention who tell you it isn't."

"Oh," she gasped, trying to readjust her carefully acquired theory of aesthetics.

"You've got hold of an awfully good subject," Harbard continued; "but you've rather mauled it, haven't you?"

She sat before him with her head drooping and the blood running back from her pale cheeks. Two tears had gathered on her lashes.

"There!" the novelist cried out irritably, "I knew that as soon as I was frank you'd resent it! What was the earthly use of asking me?"

She made no answer, and he added, lowering his voice a little, "Are you very angry with me, really?"

"No, of course not," she declared with a stony gaiety.

"I'm so glad you're not; because I do want most awfully to ask you for one of these photographs," he concluded.

She rose abruptly from her seat. To save her life she could not conceal her disappointment. But she picked up the tray with feverish animation.

"A photograph? Of course—with pleasure. And now, if you've quite finished, I'm afraid I must run back to my teapot."

Harold Harbard lay on the bed and looked at her. As she reached the door he said, "Miss Spang!"

"Yes?" she rejoined, pausing reluctantly.

"You were angry just now because I didn't admire your story; and now you're angrier still because I do admire your photograph. Do you wonder that we novelists find such an inexhaustible field in Woman?"

"Writing a War Story," in *Woman's Home Companion* 46, September 1919. Reprinted in *The Collected Short Stories* (New York: Scribner, 1968), 359–70 (page citations are to the reprint edition).

✝ Berta Lask
(1878–1967) *German*

Born into a Galician commercial family, Berta Lask was barred from professional study by her mother. In 1901 she married Doctor Louis Jacobsohn, with whom she had a daughter and three sons. Influenced by the misery she saw as the wife of a Berlin doctor, by the Russian Revolution of 1905, and by the world war, she joined the worker movement. The expressionist poetry she published after the war, *Stimmen* (Voices, 1919) and *Rufe aus dem Dunkel* (Cries from the dark, 1921), is marked by her pacifist feminism. She published proletarian books for children, wrote for communist newspapers, and in 1923 joined the Communist Party. In the 1920s she produced several revolutionary "mass" plays (*Leuna, Thomas Münzer*) that combined agitprop, worker choruses, and documentary film clips; in book form they were immediately censored. She wrote politically inflected fairy tales for the young that vividly describe social conditions. In 1933 Lask was briefly imprisoned and one of her sons was murdered by Nazis; she emigrated from Germany to the Soviet Union, returning to East Berlin after the war, where she wrote an autobiographical novel, *Stille and Sturm* (Calm and storm, 1955). She won several national medals, including the Clara Zetkin Medal in 1957.

✝ Women in Battle: A Story from the World War

A dull circle of light cast by the gas lamp brought out the thin face of Anna Moller, a young wife of a dockworker. Her stiff dry skin drew taut over her pinched cheekbones. Under her knitted brows lay eyes as blue-green as cut glass. With quick, hard movements she drew her patched coat over her cotton dress, tied a cloth over her head, and picked up her hard leather boots with wooden soles in her hand, in order not to make too much noise. Hastily she gulped down a few sips of a cold brownish liquid, took a bite from a slice of brown bread spongy and sodden with turnip-flour additive, then, bread in hand, put out the light and slipped outside.

The steps creaked. Door latches dropped. From the corridor of the tenement house six workers' wives stepped into the cold gray of morning. Wet snow fell softly on their faces and dispersed the heaviness of sleep. Alert and sharp their eyes searched through the poorly lit streets.

From a side alley came another troop of women. The quiet eyes of Anna Moller suddenly flashed; they are coming, they are keeping their word. A quiet call, a short greeting. For a moment the dark swarm hangs together. Scattered into small groups the women go on. The closer they get to the harbor, the thicker the groups grow. A bitter wind springs up, drives the ballooning dark sails with women's heads through the dusky streets to the harbor.

Anna Moller stretches her head out, holds her hand over her eyes against a light that isn't there. The dark mass back there: yes, there they are. A sharp call runs zig-zag through the sails as they shoot forward. Already the clenched dock group is happily waving. The wives of the striking dockworkers are all in place.

Even old Schulten is there with her single tooth stump in her empty lower jaw. Her skin is like a much folded cloth, and almost the same fawn color as her eyes. She has lost three sons in the war. The fourth is a dockworker and is one of the strikers. Anna stretches her hand out to her. Then she notices she has something in the hand. It is the piece of bread, completely wet with snow. Hungrily she puts it to her mouth. Suddenly the hunger tears at her empty stomach. Old Schulten looks with small, pinched eyes at the slice. Anna gives her half. The two women, old and young, stand next to each other, chew, and wait. All wait, without talking much; they whisper quietly.

"Behind there." "No." "Yes, one is coming." The dark silhouette comes closer, an old man with a small backpack on his back. Three others follow wearily shuffling. Then, a loud provocative step announces the large column of strikebreakers brought in from outside.

The women stand in chains, hand in hand, four chains one behind the other. No one says a word. The old Schulten merely turns her head once back and looks at the women. Her eyes shine from the folded skin as if newly set on fire.

The column of strikebreakers hesitates. One makes a joke. It works like a firing signal. A bullet-shower of insults rattles against the column: "Strikebreaker—scoundrel—ragamuffin traitor!" "You won't make it alive to the dock."

"Be reasonable, women. We must discharge the cargo."

"You turniptops, you jamshitters, we'll teach you to discharge." "They are on strike everywhere. The war must stop. The men must come back. We want to have bread."

The old men shuffle quietly in the side streets and don't look around anymore. Others stand indecisively. Gradually gaps open in the column. A couple of bold fellows unexpectedly attack the women and try to break through the front chain. The chain holds. The house facades resound with the women's scornful laughter.

The column of strikebreakers ebbs back, no longer closed, no longer striding with loud provocation. They tap hesitantly through the snowy slime.

The street is empty again. Only a few curious people gather nearby. The women look around. On the hungry faces red spots dance. Eyes flare feverishly. A broad, round woman rams her hands in her sides, shrilly laughs: "Jamshitters! We should have clobbered their heads into jelly."

"Keep together! Who knows what will come next." Like a commander, Anna Moller stands before the women.

Before long a closed rank flashes toward them. Helmet points, sabers, a tall lieutenant out front.

"Move apart!"

The chain stands mute.

"Move apart!"

"No strikebreaker will get through here," resounds the answer.

"The strikers want to break the Front out there," snarls the lieutenant.

"Our Front will not break." Anna Moller stands erect. A storm threatens in her sea-green eyes.

"Do you want to let the enemy into the land?"

"We already have them in the land. There they stand." Old Schulten has called out and stretches her thin arm toward the police.

A shouted command, sabers flash and ring. Anna sinks slowly into a soft, dark depth. After a year or a second she climbs back up. A flashing and ringing. She pulls all her strength together. Not yet die, first win the strike.

"Strike," cries the bleeding mouth. Then darkness again. It took a long time before the police were through with the women.

"Frauen im Kampf. Eine Erzählung aus dem Weltkrieg," in *Frauen kämpft für den Frieden* (Berlin: Paul Merker, 1929), 7–10.

POSTWAR CONVALESCENCE, MOURNING

✞ Claire Studer Goll
(1891–1977) German[1]

✞ The Wax Hand

The passengers spewed out of the train. A great many soldiers. A young officer was one of the first off. His eyes searched the platform. His young wife stood nearby, also looking anxiously around. As their eyes met she gave a start. Her glance fell from his eyes to his hand and remained rooted there. Rather uneasily he moved it about. Like some white beast, this hand crawled out from under his sleeve, ghostly pale. It was an artificial hand, made of wax. Like a poisonous flower it opened out. The woman trembled as she thought of it accidentally touching her. He approached her slowly, as though he wanted to give her time to get over the hand. The woman pulled herself together and hid behind a smile which she tried to make warm. Then they embraced. Hastily, words befitting a joyful reunion came tumbling out. But it was as though an invisible resistance lay between them, not a year of separation.

She stood at the window, gazing absentmindedly at the street below. Abstractedly she picked up a small black object and took it back into the room. She felt tired, shattered. Why now? Now, when she no longer had to wait for the tolls of death which could come by each and every post. Now, when there were no more lonely nights, black ships with the flapping sails of fear, cutting through the red sea of the war. Now, when the room no longer became the darkened stage of despair upon which her agitated imagination saw the man dancing like a puppet against the backdrop of

1. See page 88.

the battles. Now, when there were no more ties to link her to murder. What? Had not a black cloud of grief just now carried two young girls past her window? No ties? Pain would always bind them, the numb·ones, who heard every sound of every night because they could only lie awake, trembling mothers who had already lost everything and waited for the last of their sons, those standing between childhood and youth, to be demanded from them. Children cheated by a childhood that for three years had been without celebration, without laughter, surrounded by shadows. Brides, whose futures with their beloved ones had been stolen, their lives destroyed.

How she despised it, secretly, this senseless martyrdom, this dishonorable heroism which consisted of hurling people into misfortune, people like herself. The blind mass subjugation under the patriotic call whose senselessness many, including herself, recognized. Yet no one had the courage to speak. Man's undignified devotion to a uniform demanded of them by a cynical bunch, hiding behind a wall of corpses. To die for words and catchphrases handed down through time, unquestioned by those who grew up with them. Here she stood, understanding this. There stood Marc with his inherited enthusiasm. How was she supposed to get over this precipice, to find her way back to the carefree happiness of the first years of their marriage. Now her feelings towards him were too dull, almost hostile.

As ordinary and straightforward as he was, she had never amazed him or horrified him with her true self. She had always closed the door behind herself and when she drew near him, the real Ines, of whom he knew nothing, stayed outside. She had always restrained herself, so that he hardly knew her. She felt a black foreboding that they would not be reconciled upon the bridge of words. But could she mislead him again with silence, deny herself for the other woman he demanded her to be? If she remained silent today, the first day, she would remain silent all the days to come, and they would always pass by each other like strangers.

When he walked into the room she knew that she would have to speak. The artificial hand stood out against the dark civilian suit he had put on. For her this hand was a symbol of how many corpses stood between them. Taking a deep breath, she put her decision into action. Carefully, trembling, she pressed herself to him.

"You know, Marc, I suffer from our victories as much as from our defeats. While our flags flap in the sky, I see the enemy sprawled on the ground in his pain." He could not believe what he heard and said seriously, reprovingly, "Ines, while the starvation that they cause creeps through our towns, while we die, you betray us with compassion for them?"

"Starvation for women and children, or death by fire or drowning. We are all buried deep in the earth as long as we continue to hate. I am neither for them nor for us. I am against murder. I experience every victory as defeat, since each one proves that we are the better murderers." Uncomprehendingly, he raised his voice. "Those are shameless pacifist ideas that I will not tolerate."

"Tolerate? I had to put up with much more the year I spent alone," she retorted harshly. His face hardened. He played his trump card.

"Is that the thanks a man gets when he sacrifices his hand for you all upon the altar of the fatherland?" She fell silent. How often would he play his hand and his heroism against her?

"We are the excuse for such sacrifices. Why protect us with your bodies and not your minds? Why must people protect themselves from others with murder? As though true heroism were to be found in brutal strength and superiority of numbers and not in love alone." She pressed on, she shook him, she felt that her marriage was at stake. He took her seriously now. His heroism insulted, he admonished her even more harshly.

"We are men. We don't fight with our hearts, we fight with weapons. We kill in defence of ourselves and others. We protect you and the fatherland. That is sacred. It is an honor, and it is not for nothing that we are rewarded." He pointed proudly to his Iron Cross.

She despised it. For her, it became an iron wall between them. In her eyes he saw a strangeness, a harshness which provoked him. A poisonous feeling rose up inside him. First the falseness of their reunion and now this kind of talk. He was deeply hurt that she completely overlooked his martyrdom. He wanted to punish her, to stab her through the heart. With a cruel grin he began.

"It's a good thing that you do not get sent out. You would have spared the French fools, pathetic dreamers. Probably you would have performed vows of friendship with them during the battle." He waited. Slowly came the reply from her corner. "Why?" He sought to find the most tender words with which to torment her.

"In my last battle, in the middle of the thundering chaos of the assault, I found myself in a clearing, an island of calm against which Death was surging. Before me stood a man, a bayonet in his hand. Stiff, unmoving, like an apparition. A dreamy face with large heavenly eyes stared at me. Behind his lips, which almost formed a smile, there were pleading words. His gaze bore into me, questioningly, almost tenderly. Something inexplicable happened between us. For a moment I forgot he was the enemy. I saw the ring on his finger, saw his wife and for a few seconds, no longer, I softened. Then I heard my people pushing from behind. Around me groans and cries. I came to my senses. 'Traitor!' I yelled at myself. Emotion overwhelmed me. Automatically, I reached for my revolver. I expected him to defend himself but he did not move. 'Coward!' I shouted and fired. His bayonet fell. In immense pain, he stared at me unbelievingly and with outstretched arms, grotesquely, almost in a gesture of brotherhood, he fell against my breast. Before I could free myself from him, there was an explosion and black rain fell from the heavens. It was a grenade. My hand was crushed."

Startled, he fell silent. His story seemed to have had an unexpected effect. With his words he had wanted to beat Ines for her defection, but seemed to have done the opposite. She stood before him, her face white and contorted.

"You, you, you are a . . . Through the ring on his finger you could see his wife, waiting for him every night, believing in his survival, in his life, and yet you could kill. You saw the children praying for him every evening with folded hands, and yet you could kill. You are a murderer." She threw the words at him like stones. "You are a murderer."

With this sentence she broke through the protective wall of phrases which he, along with millions of other men, had built around his deeds in order to muffle the cries of his own heart.

"A person emerged from the concept of enemy, presented himself to you, and you sensed that he was your brother. You did not destroy a uniform, but a life and then a second life, his wife's, the woman who will be struck down by your heroism. You murderer. You double murderer."

Out of sheer bewilderment he had let her speak for so long. Frozen in his chair, he felt his anger surge to the surface. He rushed towards her, his right hand raised, accustomed to dealing with her. "The hand!" she screamed. At the last moment he drew back and ran from the room. The door slammed. The door leading to him. She knew it. The door to her marriage.

Her face was a stone mask. The hand had deadened it. An immense shock brought her to her senses, shook her to the core. Why had she said all that now, why not before? Why had she not shown him earlier that there were wives and mothers? Was he guilty of his deeds? Why had she let him go? Why had all women not thrown themselves in front of the trains? Why had they cheered the men and stuck flowers in their guns? They, the women, they knew that there were mothers over there. Why had they, the mothers of humanity, not united in resistance?

Did they not carry the greater guilt for the collapse of time? For they lived for tolerance, weakness, passiveness. They, who were called to the service of love, had not once understood how to balance, how to build bridges over men's violence and the raging flood of their warlike nature which divided lands.

Instead of bringing up their sons to be brothers, they had allowed them to be divided into friend and foe. Her thoughts raced from one condemnation to the next. "Men were the brains of the world, women the heart. Yet we were silent. Those born of us were made victims by others who were called heroes. But we remained silent. We were denied the dubious honor of serving in the war. But not once did we make use of the much greater honor of serving against the war. We remained silent. The greater part of the responsibility is ours."

Realization hit her straight to the heart. In the background, a hand floated towards her. The accusation of the dead. Her guilt. She collapsed into unrestrained tears.

Nighttime. She awoke, her widened pupils passed over her husband sleeping deeply, exhausted. She was no longer the same woman she was yesterday. The murdered man was in her heart, which lay in her like a rock in a sea of fear. With every beat he hammered against her conscience. He lived. He drifted in wide circles far beyond his death. Her gaze found him everywhere. The walls closed in around his image and threatened to suffocate her. The room was a tomb. Every room was now a tomb in which a woman slept with a shadow, whose life she had taken with her silence. The town was one big cemetery.

Her heart danced crazily through the black room in which she was all alone with her conscience. She groaned, she tossed and turned, and her hand hit something soft and smooth on the bedside table. The hand, the wax hand! He must have secretly taken it off and laid it there. By chance it was bent at the wrist so that the fingers pointed upwards. It pointed at her. Next to every woman lay such a hand, a hand of death, separating her from her husband, threatening, growing vaster than the night. It was the sign under which they all slept.

She writhed with fear. The hand filled the whole room. Every finger pointed to her and accused "you!" Her fear took on enormous dimensions. The hand crept nearer and nearer. Soon it would lie upon her all night long, every night. Every night she would have to sleep next to it, her whole life through. A cry rose up inside her. Her fear stretched out like a tightrope across her life, upon which she danced for the dead man. There was only one door out of her guilt, the door to death.

She tiptoed into the adjoining room, opened up a little box and carefully removed a little ball from a black paper bag upon which a white skull grinned at her. It was sugary pink like candy. She dropped it into a glass of water and took it to the next room, so that no scream would be heard. Slowly, her face becoming calmer, she drank it up.

1917

Translated by Trudi Nicholas

"Die Wachshand," in *Der gläserne Garten, Prosa 1917–1939*, ed. Barbara Glauert-Hesse for Fondation Yvan et Claire Goll, Saint-Dié-des-Vosges (Berlin: Argon, 1987), 3:151–58. © 1987 Argon Verlag GmbH, Berlin.

✠ Françoise Vitry, pseudonym of Odette Elisabeth Marie Baudie, Madame Le Dreux
French

✠ A War Widow's Diary

25 September

From this day on I ceased weeping.

I had *my* letter.

I had answered very quickly, the same day, enthusiastically. I was happy for the first time. I put on the rose-colored dress that he loved, as if he could see me.

For days I did not ask for any other news. I rarely went into the village. I was no longer afraid, I flouted destiny: I had my letter.

And as days passed, on the heels of other days, as my great joy diminished little by little, and as the hours of suffering came back, I took up my letter, I reread it as if I had never read it, and it seemed to me that I had just received its news.

When I had run through it, I was courageous for the whole day, and yet it was already so old!

Later, much later, one day in November, they brought me a poor képi covered with mud and blood: It was over.

I would never see Him again.

20 November

There are hours when my nerves are so on edge that the slightest impression of some external thing has the impact of a deep wound. There are two souls in me:

The one that loved movement and life is dead. She has gone to live over there, next to a tomb in Lorraine. Sometimes she tries to revive: she makes prodigious efforts; like a little child she tries to laugh, to sing, to love; she no longer can. She succumbs to the violence of the effort, sinks, and leaves the other soul alone.

That is the dreamer soul, who often returns from distant and unknown countries, and keeps something like nostalgia for them. How sad and tired she is! Whatever she sees, she sees too well. Before her eyes, the closest friend, the best thing, drops its mask and exposes an empty carcass.

Then my will is like boiling water that drop by drop falls back upon itself.

I hunger, I thirst for something that no one in the world can give me. And I'm cold, oh so cold!

I'm like a bird in a cage: it has a terrible desire to escape, to fly off out there, high up, into the unknown, with the hope that so far away one will no longer suffer. It leaps! and brusquely it meets the bars of the cage.

It's impossible, it cannot do it, and it falls back, more wounded than before.

I was the echo of René's thoughts. When I bend over a flower to inhale, I seek Him to share with Him this pleasure.

When the sun appears on the horizon and opens its great golden fan, I seek beloved eyes in which the sun is reflected. . . . And whenever a voice or a stringed instrument sings, sobs well up in my throat.

How long it is to be without Him so long! How alone I am! The tenderness of others annoys me, I respond to them with great chilliness. . . . And then, suddenly I begin to weep because it seems as if no one took pity on my solitude.

To be implacably alone—is that the destiny of those who have given everything of themselves, for ever?

Henriette there listens to me; she doesn't understand. Lord, how simple she is! . . . She is twenty. Her Marcel was killed too. She had one year, only one year of happiness, that's all . . . Well, it's as if she scarcely appeared to suffer. She has a nice little air, calm, resigned. She has big insignificant eyes that she lowers from time to time on her left hand, where on the fourth finger a large pearl swells—her engagement ring.— What is she thinking to remain so calm? To smile as she smiles? . . . If I question her, she answers, "I am still happy with the happiness of the old days, and I shall see Him again. . . . Above."

"Above"? . . . What does she imagine? . . . Her eyes seem empty. She has the air of a good little thing; all her life she will sit there as she now does, tranquil, calm, with empty eyes, bent over her engagement ring . . .

How I envy her! Who put this fire in me that devours me, this brutal desire to live, and yet at the same time this deep disgust at everything? Why do I want to see beyond the clouds, beyond the tomb?

Why is my soul a living thirst, that only His love could quench?

From *Journal d'une veuve de la guerre* (Paris: Maison française d'art et d'édition, 1919), 72–78.

✟ Katherine Mansfield, née Kathleen Mansfield Beauchamp (1888–1923) New Zealander

Daughter of the chairman of the Bank of New Zealand, Kathleen Mansfield Beauchamp was educated at the country's best secondary schools, where she began to write fiction; sent to London in 1903, she matriculated at Queen's College. After her parents brought her back home, Mansfield worked for a New Zealand journal. She was enthusiastic in temperament and critical of New Zealanders' lack of "intellectual society," arguing that "all the firm fat framework of their brains must be demolished before they can begin to learn."

In 1908 Mansfield returned to London, where she oscillated between romantic attachments to men and to women. Pregnant by a violinist who refused to marry her, she precipitously married, then abandoned, the singer George Bowden; she suffered a miscarriage on a trip to Bavaria. In Germany she had an affair with a Polish critic, Floryan Sobieniowski, who may have infected her with gonorrhea. On her return to London, she met John Middleton Murry, an editor and critic; they lived together for six years before marrying in 1918. Their union was unequal; Murry, a withdrawn and passive personality, explained, "I knew I was her inferior in many ways. . . . She had an immediate contact with life which was completely denied to me."

Mansfield's first collection of stories, *In a German Pension* (1911), explored female sexuality with "decided originality and liveliness," according to a reviewer in the *Athenaeum*. Virginia Woolf disapproved of Mansfield's sexual freedom, commenting that she "dressed like a tart and behaved like a bitch." Yet Woolf also found her "so intelligent and inscrutable that she repays friendship," and Mansfield felt they were both "after so very nearly the same thing."

The death of her brother Leslie Beauchamp, "blown to bits" while on training in France, caused her to hallucinate and rediscover their childhood in several stories. She visited the war zone in 1915, where she had a brief affair. Much of her writing reworks her relationship with her brother. "The Fly," written in 1922, not only satirizes the macabre grief of a father who has lost his son, but may also project her own suffering under experimental X-ray treatment for tuberculosis.

After years of publishing her stylistic experiments in small magazines, she brought out "Prelude" in 1918 with Virginia and Leonard Woolf's Hogarth Press. Depicting family life in New Zealand, she explores the inner lives of two enigmatic women; later stories such as "The Doll's House" and "The Garden Party" treat the same family in symbolic and suggestive prose. She published two collections of stories, *Bliss* (1920) and *The Garden Party* (1922), before she died of tuberculosis; two more appeared posthumously: *The Doves' Nest and Other Stories* (1923) and *Something Childish* (1924). Murry edited her diary after her death.

KCS

✝ The Fly

"Y'are very snug in here," piped old Mr. Woodifield, and he peered out of the great, green-leather armchair by his friend the boss's desk as a baby peers out of its pram. His talk was over; it was time for him to be off. But he did not want to go. Since he had retired, since his . . . stroke, the wife and the girls kept him boxed up in the house every day of the week except Tuesday. On Tuesday he was dressed and brushed and allowed to cut back to the City for the day. Though what he did there the wife and girls couldn't imagine. Made a nuisance of himself to his friends, they supposed. . . . Well, perhaps so. All the same, we cling to our last pleasures as the tree clings to its last leaves. So there sat old Woodifield, smoking a cigar and staring almost greedily at the boss, who rolled in his office chair, stout, rosy, five years older than he, and still going strong, still at the helm. It did one good to see him.

Wistfully, admiringly, the old voice added, "It's snug in here, upon my word!"

"Yes, it's comfortable enough," agreed the boss, and he flipped the *Financial Times* with a paper-knife. As a matter of fact he was proud of his room; he liked to have it admired, especially by old Woodifield. It gave him a feeling of deep, solid satisfaction to be planted there in the midst of it in full view of that frail old figure in the muffler.

"I've had it done up lately," he explained, as he had explained for the past—how many?—weeks. "New carpet," and he pointed to the bright red carpet with a pattern of large white rings. "New furniture," and he nodded towards the massive bookcase and the table with legs like twisted treacle. "Electric heating!" He waved almost exultantly towards the five transparent, pearly sausages glowing so softly in the tilted copper pan.

But he did not draw old Woodifield's attention to the photograph over the table of a grave-looking boy in uniform standing in one of those spectral photographers' parks with photographers' storm-clouds behind him. It was not new. It had been there for over six years.

"There was something I wanted to tell you," said old Woodifield, and his eyes grew dim remembering. "Now what was it? I had it in my mind when I started out this morning." His hands began to tremble, and patches of red showed above his beard.

Poor old chap, he's on his last pins, thought the boss. And, feeling kindly, he winked at the old man, and said jokingly, "I tell you what. I've got a little drop of something here that'll do you good before you go out into the cold again. It's beautiful stuff. It wouldn't hurt a child." He took a key off his watch-chain, unlocked a cupboard below his desk, and drew forth a dark, squat bottle. "That's the medicine," said he. "And the man from whom I got it told me on the strict Q.T. it came from the cellars at Windsor Castle."

Old Woodifield's mouth fell open at the sight. He couldn't have looked more surprised if the boss had produced a rabbit.

"It's whisky, ain't it?" he piped feebly.

The boss turned the bottle and lovingly showed him the label. Whisky it was.

"D'you know," said he, peering up at the boss wonderingly, "they won't let me touch it at home." And he looked as though he was going to cry.

"Ah, that's where we know a bit more than the ladies," cried the boss, swooping across for two tumblers that stood on the table with the water-bottle, and pouring a generous finger into each. "Drink it down. It'll do you good. And don't put any water with it. It's sacrilege to tamper with stuff like this. Ah!" He tossed off his, pulled out his handkerchief, hastily wiped his moustaches, and cocked an eye at old Woodifield, who was rolling his in his chaps.

The old man swallowed, was silent a moment, and then said faintly, "It's nutty!"

But it warmed him; it crept into his chill old brain—he remembered.

"That was it," he said, heaving himself out of his chair. "I thought you'd like to know. The girls were in Belgium last week having a look at poor Reggie's grave, and they happened to come across your boy's. They're quite near each other, it seems."

Old Woodifield paused, but the boss made no reply. Only a quiver in his eyelids showed that he heard.

"The girls were delighted with the way the place is kept," piped the old voice. "Beautifully looked after. Couldn't be better if they were at home. You've not been across, have yer?"

"No, no!" For various reasons the boss had not been across.

"There's miles of it," quavered old Woodifield, "and it's all as neat as a garden. Flowers growing on all the graves. Nice broad paths." It was plain from his voice how much he liked a nice broad path.

The pause came again. Then the old man brightened wonderfully.

"D'you know what the hotel made the girls pay for a pot of jam?" he piped. "Ten francs! Robbery, I call it. It was a little pot, so Gertrude says, no bigger than a half-crown. And she hadn't taken more than a spoonful when they charged her ten francs. Gertrude brought the pot away with her to teach 'em a lesson. Quite right, too; it's trading on our feelings. They think because we're over there having a look round we're ready to pay any-thing. That's what it is." And he turned towards the door.

"Quite right, quite right!" cried the boss, though what was quite right he hadn't the least idea. He came round by his desk, followed the shuffling footsteps to the door, and saw the old fellow out. Woodifield was gone.

For a long moment the boss stayed, staring at nothing, while the grey-haired office messenger, watching him, dodged in and out of his cubby-hole like a dog that expects to be taken for a run. Then: "I'll see nobody for half an hour, Macey," said the boss. "Understand? Nobody at all."

"Very good, sir."

The door shut, the firm heavy steps recrossed the bright carpet, the fat body, plumped down in the spring chair, and leaning forward, the boss covered his face with his hands. He wanted, he intended, he had arranged to weep. . . .

It had been a terrible shock to him when old Woodifield sprang that remark upon him about the boy's grave. It was exactly as though the earth had opened and he had seen the boy lying there with Woodifield's girls staring down at him. For it was strange. Although over six years had passed away, the boss never thought of the boy except as lying unchanged, unblemished in his uniform, asleep for ever. "My son!" groaned the boss. But no tears came yet. In the past, in the first months and even years after the boy's death, he had only to say those words to be overcome by such grief that nothing short of a violent fit of weeping could relieve him. Time, he had declared then, he had told everybody, could make no difference. Other men perhaps might recover, might live their loss down, but not he. How was it possible? His boy was an only son. Ever since his birth the boss had worked at building up this business for him; it had no other meaning if it was not for the boy. Life itself had come to have no other meaning. How on earth could he have slaved, denied himself, kept going all those years without the promise for ever before him of the boy's stepping into his shoes and carrying on where he left off?

And that promise had been so near being fulfilled. The boy had been in the office learning the ropes for a year before the war. Every morning they had started off together; they had come back by the same train. And what congratulations he had received as the boy's father! No wonder; he had taken to it marvellously. As to his popularity with the staff, every man jack of them down to old Macey couldn't make enough of the boy. And he wasn't in the least spoilt. No, he was just his bright natural self, with the right word for everybody, with that boyish look and his habit of saying, "Simply splendid!"

But all that was over and done with as though it never had been. The day had come when Macey had handed him the telegram that brought the whole place crashing about his head. "Deeply regret to inform you . . ." And he had left the office a broken man, with his life in ruins.

Six years ago, six years. . . . How quickly time passed! It might have happened yesterday. The boss took his hands from his face; he was puzzled. Something seemed to be wrong with him. He wasn't feeling as he wanted to feel. He decided to get up and have a look at the boy's photograph. But it wasn't a favourite photograph of his; the expression was unnatural. It was cold, even stern-looking. The boy had never looked like that.

At that moment the boss noticed that a fly had fallen into his broad inkpot, and was trying feebly but desperately to clamber out again. Help! help! said those struggling legs. But the sides of the inkpot were wet and slippery; it fell back again and began to swim. The boss took up a pen, picked the fly out of the ink, and shook it on to a piece of blotting-paper. For a fraction of a second it lay still on the dark patch that oozed round it. Then the front legs waved, took hold, and, pulling its small, sodden body up, it began the immense task of cleaning the ink from its wings. Over and under, over and under, went a leg along a wing as the stone goes over and under the scythe. Then there was a pause, while the fly, seeming to stand on the tips of its toes, tried to expand first one wing and then the other. It succeeded at last, and, sitting down, it began, like a minute cat, to clean its face. Now one could imagine that the little front legs rubbed against each other lightly, joyfully. The horrible danger was over; it had escaped; it was ready for life again.

But just then the boss had an idea. He plunged his pen back into the ink, leaned his thick wrist on the blotting-paper, and as the fly tried its wings down came a great heavy blot. What would it make of that? What indeed! The little beggar seemed absolutely cowed, stunned, and afraid to move because of what would happen next. But then, as if painfully, it dragged itself forward. The front legs waved, caught hold, and, more slowly this time, the task began from the beginning.

He's a plucky little devil, thought the boss, and he felt a real admiration for the fly's courage. That was the way to tackle things; that was the right spirit. Never say die; it was only a question of . . . But the fly had again finished its laborious task, and the boss had just time to refill his pen, to shake fair and square on the new-cleaned body yet another dark drop. What about it this time? A painful moment of suspense followed. But behold, the front legs were again waving; the boss felt a rush of relief. He leaned over the fly and said to it tenderly, "You artful little b . . ." And he actually had the brilliant notion of breathing on it to help the drying process. All the same, there was something timid and weak about its efforts now, and the boss decided that this time should be the last, as he dipped the pen deep into the inkpot.

It was. The last blot fell on the soaked blotting-paper, and the draggled fly lay in it and did not stir. The back legs were stuck to the body; the front legs were not to be seen.

"Come on," said the boss. "Look sharp!" And he stirred it with his pen— in vain. Nothing happened or was likely to happen. The fly was dead.

The boss lifted the corpse on the end of the paper-knife and flung it into the waste-paper basket. But such a grinding feeling of wretchedness seized him that he felt positively frightened. He started forward and pressed the bell for Macey.

"Bring me some fresh blotting-paper," he said sternly, "and look sharp about it." And while the old dog padded away he fell to wondering what it was he had been thinking about before. What was it? It was . . . He took out his handkerchief and passed it inside his collar. For the life of him he could not remember.

Century 104 (1922), 743–46.

Published in *The Doves' Nest and Other Stories* (London: Constable, 1923), 45–54.

✠ Marguerite Radclyffe Hall
(1880–1943) *British*

The lesbian poet and novelist Marguerite Radclyffe Hall was born to a troubled family; her promiscuous father, Radclyffe, and her often abusive mother, Marie, divorced when she was a child. At eighteen Hall was left a large legacy by her dying father, which enabled her to study at King's College and to travel in Germany and the United States. She called herself John, dressed like a man, and smoked. While living with her grandmother in 1906, Hall published the first of five books of poetry, *'Twixt Earth and Stars,* including a number of lyrics devoted to the pain and mutability of love. A year later she began an extended affair with Mabel Veronica Batten ("Ladye"), a woman many years her senior, who tolerated infidelities with Phoebe Hoare and then Una Taylor, Lady Troubridge. Hall converted to Roman Catholicism. Her next volume of poetry, *A Sheaf of Verses* (1908), made public her interest in lesbian themes and images, framed in traditional ballad or romance forms.

Hall responded with fervor to the war, but felt she could not leave Ladye, who was in ill health; instead, she wrote recruitment leaflets and tried to rally enlistment. After Ladye's death in 1916, Hall lived with Una Taylor, and turned from Catholicism to spiritualism.

Hall admired Colette's frank writings, finding the Frenchwoman "as hard as the sun-baked soil yet so able to perceive and to immortalize the pathos of life in all its forms." At first Hall's own frankness gave her difficulty in placing her short stories and her first novel, *The Unlit Lamp* (1924), took several years to find a publisher. Well received by reviewers, it explores the emotional, sexual, and intellectual control of a mother over her daughter, which frustrates the daughter's desire to leave home with a female friend. Hall satirized marriage in *The Forge* (1924) and *A Saturday Life* (1925) with "light-handed delicious rightness" (*Sunday Times* review). She won acclaim with *Adam's Breed* (1926), a story tracing an Italian orphan's desire to triumph on the battlefield and his failure to make it to the front; this portrait of spiritual despair and eventual enlightenment won the James Tait Black Memorial Prize and the Prix Femina.

In 1920 Hall met Barbara ("Toupie") Lowther, who with Miss "Desmond" Hackett in 1917 had founded the Hackett-Lowther ambulance unit, which operated beside the French army along the battlefront near Compiègne. Lowther became the inspiration for two of Hall's best-known works: "Miss Ogilvy Finds Herself," the title story of a collection published in 1934, and her most famous novel, *The Well of Loneliness* (1928). Right after completing the short story in 1926, Hall began *The Well of Loneliness,* which presents an ambulance driver's love for one of her colleagues. This candid study of youthful sexual confusion, initiation, fulfillment, and renunciation, which compares the suffering of a lesbian writer to that of Christ, was prosecuted for obscenity and defended by eminent writers such as Vera Brittain and Virginia Woolf. Hall said to Arnold Bennett, "I do not *want* the support of anyone who will not vouch for the decency of my book." Her next novel, *The Master of the House* (1932), focuses on the safer topic of a male soldier's sufferings.

Hall's last decade was marred by a painful relationship with a nurse, Evguenia Souline, which disintegrated in 1942, the year before her death. Her companion Una Taylor described her on her deathbed in terms of the conflict about which Hall had so often written: "It seemed a young airman or soldier who perhaps had died of wounds after much suffering. . . . Not a trace of femininity; no one in their senses could have suspected that anything but a young man had died."

KCS

✝ Miss Ogilvy Finds Herself

Miss Ogilvy stood on the quay at Calais and surveyed the disbanding of her Unit, the Unit that together with the coming of war had completely altered the complexion of her life, at all events for three years.

Miss Ogilvy's thin, pale lips were set sternly and her forehead was puckered in an effort of attention, in an effort to memorise every small detail of every old war-weary battered motor on whose side still appeared the merciful emblem that had set Miss Ogilvy free.

Miss Ogilvy's mind was jerking a little, trying to regain its accustomed balance, trying to readjust itself quickly to this sudden and paralysing change. Her tall, awkward body with its queer look of strength, its broad, flat bosom and thick legs and ankles, as though in response to her jerking mind, moved uneasily, rocking backwards and forwards. She had this trick of rocking on her feet in moments of controlled agitation. As usual, her hands were thrust deep into her pockets, they seldom seemed to come out of her pockets unless it were to light a cigarette, and as though she were still standing firm under fire while the wounded were placed in her ambulances, she suddenly straddled her legs very slightly and lifted her head and listened. She was standing firm under fire at that moment, the fire of a desperate regret.

Some girls came towards her, young, tired-looking creatures whose eyes were too bright from long strain and excitement. They had all been members of that glorious Unit, and they still wore the queer little forage-caps and the short, clumsy tunics of the French Militaire. They still slouched in walking and smoked Caporals in emulation of the Poilus.[1] Like their founder and leader these girls were all English, but like her they had chosen to serve England's ally, fearlessly thrusting right up to the trenches in search of the wounded and dying. They had seen some fine things in the course of three years, not the least fine of which was the cold, hard-faced woman who, commanding, domineering, even hectoring at times, had yet been possessed of so dauntless a courage and of so insistent a vitality that it vitalised the whole Unit.

"It's rotten!" Miss Ogilvy heard someone saying. "It's rotten, this breaking up of our Unit!" And the high, rather childish voice of the speaker sounded perilously near to tears.

Miss Ogilvy looked at the girl almost gently, and it seemed, for a moment, as though some deep feeling were about to find expression in words. But Miss Ogilvy's feelings had been held in abeyance so long that they seldom dared become vocal, so she merely said "Oh?" on a rising inflection—her method of checking emotion.

They were swinging the ambulance cars in midair, those of them that were destined to go back to England, swinging them up like sacks of potatoes, then lowering them with much clanging of chains to the deck of the waiting steamer. The porters were shoving and shouting and quarrelling, pausing now and again to make meaningless gestures; while a pompous official was becoming quite angry as he pointed at Miss Ogilvy's own special car—it annoyed him, it was bulky and difficult to move.

"Bon Dieu! Mais dépêchez-vous donc!"[2] he bawled, as though he were bullying the motor.

Then Miss Ogilvy's heart gave a sudden, thick thud to see this undignified, pitiful ending; and she turned and patted the gallant old car as though she were patting a well-beloved horse, as though she would say: "Yes, I know how it feels—never mind, we'll go down together."

2

Miss Ogilvy sat in the railway carriage on her way from Dover to London. The soft English landscape sped smoothly past: small homesteads, small churches, small pastures, small lanes with small hedges; all small like England itself, all small like Miss Ogilvy's future. And sitting there still arrayed in her tunic, with her forage-cap resting on her knees, she was

1. *Poilus:* French GIs.
2. *Bon Dieu! Mais dépêchez-vous donc!:* Heavens! Hurry up now!

conscious of a sense of complete frustration; thinking less of those glorious years at the Front and of all that had gone to the making of her, than of all that had gone to the marring of her from the days of her earliest childhood.

She saw herself as a queer little girl, aggressive and awkward because of her shyness; a queer little girl who loathed sisters and dolls, preferring the stable-boys as companions, preferring to play with footballs and tops, and occasional catapults. She saw herself climbing the tallest beech trees, arrayed in old breeches illicitly come by. She remembered insisting with tears and some temper that her real name was William and not Wilhelmina. All these childish pretences and illusions she remembered, and the bitterness that came after. For Miss Ogilvy had found as her life went on that in this world it is better to be one with the herd, that the world has no wish to understand those who cannot conform to its stereotyped pattern. True enough, in her youth she had gloried in her strength, lifting weights, swinging clubs and developing muscles, but presently this had grown irksome to her; it had seemed to lead nowhere, she being a woman, and then as her mother had often protested: muscles looked so appalling in evening dress—a young girl ought not to have muscles.

Miss Ogilvy's relation to the opposite sex was unusual and at that time added much to her worries, for no less than three men had wished to propose, to the genuine amazement of the world and her mother. Miss Ogilvy's instinct made her like and trust men, for whom she had a pronounced fellow-feeling; she would always have chosen them as her friends and companions in preference to girls or women; she would dearly have loved to share in their sports, their business, their ideas and their wide-flung interests. But men had not wanted her, except the three who had found in her strangeness a definite attraction, and those would-be suitors she had actually feared, regarding them with aversion. Towards young girls and women she was shy and respectful, apologetic and sometimes admiring. But their fads and their foibles, none of which she could share, while amusing her very often in secret, set her outside the sphere of their intimate lives, so that in the end she must blaze a lone trail through the difficulties of her nature.

"I can't understand you," her mother had said, "you're a very odd creature—now when I was your age . . ."

And her daughter had nodded, feeling sympathetic. There were two younger girls who also gave trouble, though in their case the trouble was fighting for husbands who were scarce enough even in those days. It was finally decided, at Miss Ogilvy's request, to allow her to leave the field clear for her sisters. She would remain in the country with her father when the others went up for the Season.

Followed long, uneventful years spent in sport, while Sarah and Fanny toiled, sweated and gambled in the matrimonial market. Neither ever succeeded in netting a husband, and when the Squire died leaving very little money, Miss Ogilvy found to her great surprise that they looked upon her as a brother. They had so often jibed at her in the past, that at first she could scarcely believe her senses, but before very long it became all too real: she it was who must straighten out endless muddles, who must make the dreary arrangements for the move, who must find a cheap but genteel house in London and, once there, who must cope with the family accounts which she only, it seemed, could balance.

It would be: "You might see to that, Wilhelmina; you write, you've got such a good head for business." Or: "I wish you'd go down and explain to that man that we really can't pay his account till next quarter." Or: "This money for the grocer is five shillings short. Do run over my sum, Wilhelmina."

Her mother, grown feeble, discovered in this daughter a staff upon which she could lean with safety. Miss Ogilvy genuinely loved her mother, and was therefore quite prepared to be leaned on; but when Sarah and Fanny began to lean too with the full weight of endless neurotic symptoms incubated in resentful virginity, Miss Ogilvy found herself staggering a little. For Sarah and Fanny were grown hard to bear, with their mania for telling their symptoms to doctors, with their unstable nerves and their acrid tongues and the secret dislike they now felt for their mother. Indeed, when old Mrs. Ogilvy died, she was unmourned except by her eldest daughter who actually felt a void in her life—the unforeseen void that the ailing and weak will not infrequently leave behind them.

At about this time an aunt also died, bequeathing her fortune to her niece Wilhelmina who, however, was too weary to gird up her loins and set forth in search of exciting adventure—all she did was to move her protesting sisters to a little estate she had purchased in Surrey. This experiment was only a partial success, for Miss Ogilvy failed to make friends of her neighbours; thus at fifty-five she had grown rather dour, as is often the way with shy, lonely people.

When the war came she had just begun settling down—people do settle down in their fifty-sixth year—she was feeling quite glad that her hair was grey, that the garden took up so much of her time, that, in fact, the beat of her blood was slowing. But all this was changed when war was declared; on that day Miss Ogilvy's pulses throbbed wildly.

"My God! If only I were a man!" she burst out, as she glared at Sarah and Fanny, "if only I had been born a man!" Something in her was feeling deeply defrauded.

Sarah and Fanny were soon knitting socks and mittens and mufflers and Jaeger trench-helmets.[3] Other ladies were busily working at depots, making swabs at the Squire's, or splints at the Parson's; but Miss Ogilvy scowled and did none of these things—she was not at all like other ladies.

For nearly twelve months she worried officials with a view to getting a job out in France—not in their way but in hers, and that was the trouble. She wished to go up to the front-line trenches, she wished to be actually under fire, she informed the harassed officials.

3. *Jaeger trench-helmets:* knit caps.

To all her enquiries she received the same answer: "We regret that we cannot accept your offer." But once thoroughly roused she was hard to subdue, for her shyness had left her as though by magic.

Sarah and Fanny shrugged angular shoulders: "There's plenty of work here at home," they remarked, "though of course it's not quite so melodramatic!"

"Oh . . . ?" queried their sister on a rising note of impatience—and she promptly cut off her hair: "That'll jar them!" she thought with satisfaction.

Then she went up to London, formed her admirable unit and finally got it accepted by the French, despite renewed opposition.

In London she had found herself quite at her ease, for many another of her kind was in London doing excellent work for the nation. It was really surprising how many cropped heads had suddenly appeared as it were out of space; how many Miss Ogilvies, losing their shyness, had come forward asserting their right to serve, asserting their claim to attention.

There followed those turbulent years at the front, full of courage and hardship and high endeavour; and during those years Miss Ogilvy forgot the bad joke that Nature seemed to have played her. She was given the rank of a French lieutenant and she lived in a kind of blissful illusion; appalling reality lay on all sides and yet she managed to live in illusion. She was competent, fearless, devoted and untiring. What then? Could any man hope to do better? She was nearly fifty-eight, yet she walked with a stride, and at times she even swaggered a little.

Poor Miss Ogilvy sitting so glumly in the train with her manly trench-boots and her forage-cap! Poor all the Miss Ogilvies back from the war with their tunics, their trench-boots, and their childish illusions! Wars come and wars go but the world does not change: it will always forget an indebtedness which it thinks it expedient not to remember.

3

When Miss Ogilvy returned to her home in Surrey it was only to find that her sisters were ailing from the usual imaginary causes, and this to a woman who had seen the real thing was intolerable, so that she looked with distaste at Sarah and then at Fanny. Fanny was certainly not prepossessing, she was suffering from a spurious attack of hay fever.

"Stop sneezing!" commanded Miss Ogilvy, in the voice that had so much impressed the Unit. But as Fanny was not in the least impressed, she naturally went on sneezing.

Miss Ogilvy's desk was piled mountain-high with endless tiresome letters and papers: circulars, bills, months-old correspondence, the gardener's accounts, an agent's report on some fields that required land-draining. She seated herself before this collection; then she sighed, it all seemed so absurdly trivial.

"Will you let your hair grow again?" Fanny enquired . . . she and Sarah had followed her into the study. "I'm certain the Vicar would be glad if you did."

"Oh?" murmured Miss Ogilvy, rather too blandly.

"Wilhelmina!"

"Yes?"

"You will do it, won't you?"

"Do what?"

"Let your hair grow; we all wish you would."

"Why should I?"

"Oh, well, it will look less odd, especially now that the war is over—in a small place like this people notice such things."

"I entirely agree with Fanny," announced Sarah.

Sarah had become very self-assertive, no doubt through having mismanaged the estate during the years of her sister's absence. They had quite a heated dispute one morning over the south herbaceous border.

"Whose garden is this?" Miss Ogilvy asked sharply. "I insist on auricula-eyed sweet Williams! I even took the trouble to write from France, but it seems that my letter has been ignored."

"Don't shout," rebuked Sarah, "you're not in France now!"

Miss Ogilvy could gladly have boxed her ears: "I only wish to God I were," she muttered.

Another dispute followed close on its heels, and this time it happened to be over the dinner. Sarah and Fanny were living on weeds—at least that was the way Miss Ogilvy put it.

"We've become vegetarians," Sarah said grandly.

"You've become two damn tiresome cranks!" snapped their sister.

Now it never had been Miss Ogilvy's way to indulge in acid recriminations, but somehow, these days, she forgot to say: "Oh?" quite so often as expediency demanded. It may have been Fanny's perpetual sneezing that had got on her nerves; or it may have been Sarah, or the gardener, or the Vicar, or even the canary; though it really did not matter very much what it was just so long as she found a convenient peg upon which to hang her growing irritation.

"This won't do at all," Miss Ogilvy thought sternly, "life's not worth so much fuss, I must pull myself together." But it seemed this was easier said than done; not a day passed without her losing her temper and that over some trifle: "No, this won't do at all—it just mustn't be," she thought sternly.

Everyone pitied Sarah and Fanny: "Such a dreadful, violent old thing," said the neighbours.

But Sarah and Fanny had their revenge: "Poor darling, it's shell shock, you know," they murmured.

Thus Miss Ogilvy's prowess was whittled away until she herself was beginning to doubt it. Had she ever been that courageous person who had faced death in France with such perfect composure? Had she ever stood tranquilly under fire, without turning a hair, while she issued her orders? Had she ever been treated with marked respect? She herself was beginning to doubt it.

Sometimes she would see an old member of the Unit, a girl who, more faithful to her than the others, would take the trouble to run down to Surrey. These visits, however, were seldom enlivening.

"Oh, well . . . here we are . . ." Miss Ogilvy would mutter.

But one day the girl smiled and shook her blond head: "I'm not—I'm going to be married."

Strange thoughts had come to Miss Ogilvy, unbidden, thoughts that had stayed for many an hour after the girl's departure. Alone in her study she had suddenly shivered, feeling a sense of complete desolation. With cold hands she had lighted a cigarette.

"I must be ill or something," she had mused, as she stared at her trembling fingers.

After this she would sometimes cry out in her sleep, living over in dreams God knows what emotions; returning, maybe to the battlefield of France. Her hair turned snow-white; it was not unbecoming yet she fretted about it.

"I'm growing very old," she would sigh as she brushed her thick mop before the glass; and then she would peer at her wrinkles.

For now that it had happened she hated being old; it no longer appeared such an easy solution of those difficulties that had always beset her. And this she resented most bitterly, so that she became the prey of self-pity, and of other undesirable states in which the body will torment the mind, and the mind, in its turn, the body. Then Miss Ogilvy straightened her ageing back, in spite of the fact that of late it had ached with muscular rheumatism, and she faced herself squarely and came to a resolve.

"I'm off!" she announced abruptly one day; and that evening she packed her kit-bag.

4

Near the south coast of Devon there exists a small island that is still very little known to the world, but which nevertheless can boast an hotel, the only building upon it. Miss Ogilvy had chosen this place quite at random, it was marked on her map by scarcely more than a dot, but somehow she had liked the look of that dot and had set forth alone to explore it.

She found herself standing on the mainland one morning looking at a vague blur of green through the mist, a vague blur of green that rose out of the Channel like a tidal wave suddenly suspended. Miss Ogilvy was filled with a sense of adventure; she had not felt like this since the ending of war.

"I was right to come here, very right indeed. I'm going to shake off all my troubles," she decided.

A fisherman's boat was parting the mist, and before it was properly beached, in she bundled.

"I hope they're expecting me?" she said gaily.

"They du be expecting you," the man answered.

The sea, which is generally rough off that coast, was indulging itself in an oily ground-swell; the broad, glossy swells struck the side of the boat, then broke and sprayed over Miss Ogilvy's ankles.

The fisherman grinned: "Feeling all right?" he queried. "It du be tire-some most times about these parts." But the mist had suddenly drifted away and Miss Ogilvy was staring wide-eyed at the island.

She saw a long shoal of jagged black rocks, and between them the curve of a small sloping beach, and above that the lift of the island itself, and above that again, blue heaven. Near the beach stood the little two-storied hotel which was thatched, and built entirely of timber; for the rest she could make out no signs of life apart from a host of white seagulls.

Then Miss Ogilvy said a curious thing. She said: "On the south-west side of that place there was once a cave—a very large cave. I remember that it was some way from the sea."

"There du be a cave still," the fisherman told her, "but it's just above highwater level."

"A-ah," murmured Miss Ogilvy thoughtfully, as though to herself; then she looked embarrassed.

The little hotel proved both comfortable and clean, the hostess both pleasant and comely. Miss Ogilvy started unpacking her bag, changed her mind and went for a stroll round the island. The island was covered with turf and thistles and traversed by narrow green paths thick with daisies. It had four rock-bound coves of which the south-western was by far the most difficult of access. For just here the island descended abruptly as though it were hurtling down to the water; and just here the shale was most treach-erous and the tide-swept rocks most aggressively pointed. Here it was that the seagulls, grown fearless of man by reason of his absurd limitations, built their nests on the ledges and reared countless young who multiplied, in their turn, every season. Yes, and here it was that Miss Ogilvy, greatly marvelling, stood and stared across at a cave; much too near the crum-bling edge for her safety, but by now completely indifferent to caution.

"I remember . . . I remember . . ." she kept repeating. Then: "That's all very well, but what do I remember?"

She was conscious of somehow remembering all wrong, of her memory being distorted and coloured—perhaps by the endless things she had seen since her eyes had last rested upon that cave. This worried her sorely, far more than the fact that she should be remembering the cave at all, she who had never set foot on the island before that actual morning. Indeed, except for the sense of wrongness when she struggled to piece her mem-ories together, she was steeped in a very profound contentment which surged over her spirit, wave upon wave.

"It's extremely odd," pondered Miss Ogilvy. Then she laughed, so pleased did she feel with its oddness.

5

That night after supper she talked to her hostess who was only too glad, it seemed, to be questioned. She owned the whole island and was proud of the fact, as she very well might be, decided her boarder. Some curious things had been found on the island, according to comely Mrs.

Nanceskivel: bronze arrow-heads, pieces of ancient stone celts;[4] and once they had dug up a man's skull and thigh-bone—this had happened while they were sinking a well. Would Miss Ogilvy care to have a look at the bones? They were kept in a cupboard in the scullery.

Miss Ogilvy nodded.

"Then I'll fetch him this moment," said Mrs. Nanceskivel, briskly.

In less than two minutes she was back with the box that contained those poor remnants of a man, and Miss Ogilvy, who had risen from her chair, was gazing down at those remnants. As she did so her mouth was sternly compressed, but her face and her neck flushed darkly.

Mrs. Nanceskivel was pointing to the skull: "Look, miss, he was killed," she remarked rather proudly, "and they tell me that the axe that killed him was bronze. He's thousands and thousands of years old, they tell me. Our local doctor knows a lot about such things and he wants me to send these bones to an expert; they ought to belong to the Nation, he says. But I know what would happen, they'd come digging up my island, and I won't have people digging up my island, I've got enough worry with the rabbits as it is." But Miss Ogilvy could no longer hear the words for the pounding of the blood in her temples.

She was filled with a sudden, inexplicable fury against the innocent Mrs. Nanceskivel: "You . . . *you* . . ." she began, then checked herself, fearful of what she might say to the woman.

For her sense of outrage was overwhelming as she stared at those bones that were kept in the scullery; moreover, she knew how such men had been buried, which made the outrage seem all the more shameful. They had buried such men in deep, well-dug pits surmounted by four stout stones at their corners—four stout stones there had been and a covering stone. And all this Miss Ogilvy knew as by instinct, having no concrete knowledge on which to draw. But she knew it right down in the depths of her soul, and she hated Mrs. Nanceskivel.

And now she was swept by another emotion that was even more strange and more devastating: such a grief as she had not conceived could exist; a terrible unassuageable grief, without hope, without respite, without palliation, so that with something akin to despair she touched the long gash in the skull. Then her eyes, that had never wept since her childhood, filled slowly with large, hot, difficult tears. She must blink very hard, then close her eyelids, turn away from the lamp and say rather loudly:

"Thanks, Mrs. Nanceskivel. It's past eleven—I think I'll be going upstairs."

---

4. *Celts:* prehistoric axe heads.

6

Miss Ogilvy closed the door of her bedroom, after which she stood quite still to consider: "Is it shell shock?" she muttered incredulously. "I wonder, can it be shell shock?"

She began to pace slowly about the room, smoking a Caporal. As usual her hands were deep in her pockets; she could feel small, familiar things in those pockets and she gripped them, glad of their presence. Then all of a sudden she was terribly tired, so tired that she flung herself down on the bed, unable to stand any longer.

She thought that she lay there struggling to reason, that her eyes were closed in the painful effort, and that as she closed them she continued to puff the inevitable cigarette. At least that was what she thought at one moment—the next, she was out in a sunset evening, and a large red sun was sinking slowly to the rim of a distant sea.

Miss Ogilvy knew that she was herself, that is to say she was conscious of her being, and yet she was not Miss Ogilvy at all, nor had she a memory of her. All that she now saw was very familiar, all that she now did was what she should do, and all that she now was seemed perfectly natural. Indeed, she did not think of these things; there seemed no reason for thinking about them.

She was walking with bare feet on turf that felt springy and was greatly enjoying the sensation; she had always enjoyed it, ever since as an infant she had learned to crawl on this turf. On either hand stretched rolling green uplands, while at her back she knew that there were forests; but in front, far away, lay the gleam of the sea towards which the big sun was sinking. The air was cool and intensely still, with never so much as a ripple or bird song. It was wonderfully pure—one might almost say young—but Miss Ogilvy thought of it merely as air. Having always breathed it she took it for granted, as she took the soft turf and the uplands.

She pictured herself as immensely tall; she was feeling immensely tall at the moment. As a matter of fact she was five feet eight which, however, was quite a considerable height when compared to that of her fellow tribes-men. She was wearing a single garment of pelts which came to her knees and left her arms sleeveless. Her arms and her legs, which were closely tat-tooed with blue zig-zag lines, were extremely hairy. From a leathern thong twisted about her waist there hung a clumsily made stone weapon, a celt, which in spite of its clumsiness was strongly hafted and useful for killing.

Miss Ogilvy wanted to shout aloud from a glorious sense of physical well-being, but instead she picked up a heavy, round stone which she hurled with great force at some distant rocks.

"Good! Strong!" she exclaimed. "See how far it goes!"

"Yes, strong. There is no one so strong as you. You are surely the strongest man in our tribe," replied her little companion.

Miss Ogilvy glanced at this little companion and rejoiced that they two were all alone together. The girl at her side had a smooth brownish skin, oblique black eyes and short, sturdy limbs. Miss Ogilvy marvelled because of her beauty. She also was wearing a single garment of pelts, new pelts, she had made it that morning. She had stitched at it diligently for hours with short lengths of gut and her best bone needle. A strand of black hair hung over her bosom, and this she was constantly stroking and fondling; then she lifted the strand and examined her hair.

"Pretty," she remarked with childish complacence.

"Pretty," echoed the young man at her side.

"For you," she told him, "all of me is for you and none other. For you this body has ripened."

He shook back his own coarse hair from his eyes; he had sad brown eyes like those of a monkey. For the rest he was lean and steel-strong of loin, broad of chest, and with features not too uncomely. His prominent cheekbones were set rather high, his nose was blunt, his jaw somewhat bestial; but his mouth, though full-lipped, contradicted his jaw, being very gentle and sweet in expression. And now he smiled, showing big, square, white teeth.

"You . . . woman," he murmured contentedly, and the sound seemed to come from the depths of his being.

His speech was slow and lacking in words when it came to expressing a vital emotion, so one word must suffice and this he now spoke, and the word that he spoke had a number of meanings. It meant: "Little spring of exceedingly pure water." It meant: "Hut of peace for a man after battle." It meant: "Ripe red berry sweet to the taste." It meant: "Happy small home of future generations." All these things he must try to express by a word, and because of their loving she understood him.

They paused, and lifting her up he kissed her. Then he rubbed his large shaggy head on her shoulder; and when he released her she knelt at his feet.

"My master; blood of my body," she whispered. For with her it was different, love had taught her love's speech, so that she might turn her heart into sounds that her primitive tongue could utter.

After she had pressed her lips to his hands, and her cheek to his hairy and powerful forearm, she stood up and they gazed at the setting sun, but with bowed heads, gazing under their lids, because this was very sacred.

A couple of mating bears padded toward them from a thicket, and the female rose to her haunches. But the man drew his celt and menaced the beast, so that she dropped down noiselessly and fled, and her mate also fled, for here was the power that few dared to withstand by day or by night, on the uplands or in the forests. And now from across to the left where a river would presently lose itself in the marshes, came a rhythmical thudding, as a herd of red deer with wide nostrils and starting eyes thundered past, disturbed in their drinking by the bears.

After this the evening returned to its silence, and the spell of its silence descended on the lovers, so that each felt very much alone, yet withal more closely united to the other. But the man became restless under that spell, and he suddenly laughed; then grasping the woman he tossed her above his head and caught her. This he did many times for his own amusement and because he knew that his strength gave her joy. In this manner they played together for a while, he with his strength and she with her weakness. And they cried out, and made many guttural sounds which were meaningless save only to themselves. And the tunic of pelts slipped down from her breasts, and her two little breasts were pear-shaped.

Presently, he grew tired of their playing, and he pointed toward a cluster of huts and earthworks that lay to the eastward. The smoke from these huts rose in thick straight lines, bending neither to right nor left in its rising, and the thought of sweet burning rushes and brushwood touched his consciousness, making him feel sentimental.

"Smoke," he said.

And she answered: "Blue smoke."

He nodded: "Yes, blue smoke—home."

Then she said: "I have ground much corn since the full moon. My stones are too smooth. You make me new stones."

"All you have need of, I make," he told her.

She stole closer to him, taking his hand: "My father is still a black cloud full of thunder. He thinks that you wish to be head of our tribe in his place, because he is now very old. He must not hear of these meetings of ours, if he did I think he would beat me!"

So he asked her: "Are you unhappy, small berry?"

But at this she smiled: "What is being unhappy? I do not know what that means any more."

"I do not either," he answered.

Then as though some invisible force had drawn him, his body swung around and he stared at the forests where they lay and darkened, fold upon fold; and his eyes dilated with wonder and terror, and he moved his head quickly from side to side as a wild thing will do that is held between bars and whose mind is pitifully bewildered.

"Water!" he cried hoarsely, "great water—look, look! Over there. This land is surrounded by water!"

"What water?" she questioned.

He answered: "The sea." And he covered his face with his hands.

"Not so," she consoled, "big forests, good hunting. Big forests in which you hunt boar and aurochs.[5] No sea over there but only the trees."

He took his trembling hands from his face: "You are right . . . only trees," he said dully.

But now his face had grown heavy and brooding and he started to speak of a thing that oppressed him: "The Roundheaded-ones, they are devils," he growled, while his bushy black brows met over his eyes, and when this happened it changed his expression which became a little sub-human.

"No matter," she protested, for she saw that he forgot her and she wished him to think and talk only of love. "No matter. My father laughs at your fears. Are we not friends with the Roundheaded-ones? We are friends, so why should we fear them?"

_____

5. *Aurochs:* extinct bison.

"Our forts, very old, very weak," he went on, "and the Roundheaded-ones have terrible weapons. Their weapons are not made of good stone like ours but of some dark, devilish substance."

"What of that?" she said lightly. "They would fight on our side, so why need we trouble about their weapons?"

But he looked away, not appearing to hear her. "We must barter all, all for their celts and arrows and spears, and then we must learn their secret. They lust after our women, they lust after our lands. We must barter all, all for their sly brown celts."

"Me . . . bartered?" she queried, very sure of his answer, otherwise she had not dared to say this.

"The Roundheaded-ones may destroy my tribe and yet I will not part with you," he told her. Then he spoke very gravely: "But I think they desire to slay us and me they will try to slay first because they well know how much I mistrust them—they have seen my eyes fixed many times on their camps."

She cried: "I will bite out the throats of these people if they so much as scratch your skin!"

And at this his mood changed and he roared with amusement: "You . . . woman!" he roared. "Little foolish white teeth. Your teeth were made for nibbling wild cherries, not for tearing the throats of the Roundheaded-ones!"

"Thoughts of war always make me afraid," she whimpered, still wishing him to talk about love.

He turned his sorrowful eyes upon her, the eyes that were sad even when he was merry, and although his mind was often obtuse, yet he clearly perceived how it was with her then. And his blood caught fire from the flame in her blood, so that he strained her against his body.

"You . . . mine . . ." he stammered.

"Love," she said, trembling, "this is love."

And he answered: "Love."

Then their faces grew melancholy for a moment, because dimly, very dimly in their dawning souls, they were conscious of a longing for something more vast than their earthly passion could compass.

Presently, he lifted her like a child and carried her quickly southward and westward till they came to a place where a gentle descent led down to a marshy valley. Far away, at the line where the marshes ended, they discerned the misty line of the sea; but the sea and the marshes were become as one substance, merging, blending, folding together; and since they were lovers they also would be one, even as the sea and the marshes.

And now they reached the mouth of a cave that was set in the quiet hillside. There was bright green verdure beside the cave, and a number of small, pink, thick-stemmed flowers that when they were crushed smelt of spices. And within the cave there was bracken newly gathered and heaped together for a bed; while beyond, from some rocks, came a low liquid sound as a spring dripped out through a crevice. Abruptly, he set the girl on her feet, and she knew that the days of her innocence were over. And she thought of the anxious virgin soil that was rent and sown to bring forth fruit in season, and she gave a quick little gasp of fear:

"No . . . no . . ." she gasped. For, divining his need, she was weak with the longing to be possessed, yet the terror of love lay heavy upon her. "No . . . no . . ." she gasped.

But he caught her wrist and she felt the great strength of his rough, gnarled fingers, the great strength of the urge that leapt in his loins, and again she must give the quick gasp of fear, the while she clung close to him lest he should spare her.

The twilight was engulfed and possessed by darkness, which in turn was transfigured by the moonrise, which in turn was fulfilled and consumed by dawn. A mighty eagle soared up from his eyrie, cleaving the air with his masterful wings, and beneath him from the rushes that harboured their nests, rose other great birds, crying loudly. Then the heavy-horned elks appeared on the uplands, bending their burdened heads to the sod; while beyond in the forests the fierce wild aurochs stamped as they bellowed their love songs.

But within the dim cave the lord of these creatures had put by his weapon and his instinct for slaying. And he lay there defenceless with tenderness, thinking no longer of death but of life as he murmured the word that had so many meanings. That meant: "Little spring of exceedingly pure water." That meant: "Hut of peace for a man after battle." That meant: "Ripe red berry sweet to the taste." That meant: "Happy small home of future generations."

7

They found Miss Ogilvy the next morning; the fisherman saw her and climbed to the ledge. She was sitting at the mouth of the cave. She was dead, with her hands thrust deep into her pockets.

1926

"Miss Ogilvy Finds Herself," in *Miss Ogilvy Finds Herself* (London: Heinemann, 1934), 3–35. Copyright © The Estate of Radclyffe Hall.

✝ Elin Wägner
(1882–1949) *Swedish*

orn in Lund in southern Sweden, Elin Wägner, an only child, was
orphaned at three and sent to live with her grandparents, who put
her in a boarding school for seven years. She went into journalism,
writing for the journal *Idun* for a decade, and became an activist engaged
in the fight for women's suffrage. In 1910 she married literary critic John
Landquist, from whom she was divorced in 1922. When she published her
first novel, *Pennskraft* (The penholder, 1910), its insights into female eroticism aroused controversy and it sold well. She established a radical
women's weekly, *Tidevarvet* (The epoch), and founded the Women's Citizens' College at Fogelstad.

After 1914 Wägner, a pacifist, published articles protesting the war. She
also published a novel, *Släkten Jernploogs framgang* (Success of the family
Ironplough, 1916). *Hanna from Ridge Farm* (1918), considered her best
novel, led critics to label her a "new woman" writer, using her powerful
prose to promote women's rights. She was awarded a major literary prize,
the Samfundet De Nio, in 1923 and was named to the Swedish Academy
for her biography of Selma Lagerlöf. She continued to pursue issues of
women's power and powerlessness in her novels of the next decades, *Sil-
verforsen* (The silver stream, 1924), *Vandkorset* (The turnstile, 1935), and
Vinden vande bladen (The wind turned the leaves over, 1947), and a collection of stories, *Gammalrödja: skildring av en bygd som ömsar skinn* (1931).
Wägner attained fame in her fiction for probing psychological portraits,
while in her journalism she was a respected critic of cultural and women's
history.

TP

✝ The Cheesemaking

A large, impressive-looking lady drove her shiny Chevrolet with casual skill along the main road that ran through Gammalrödja village. Sitting inside the car, she might have been indoors, hatless as she was, and dressed only in a thin, pale-gray summer frock. The breeze ruffled her gray curls, and she looked every inch the sophisticated foreigner, but her eyes were gleaming Gammalrödja blue with childlike anticipation as she negotiated Guardsman Skott's new road, which led to Bridge End Farm. For this was indeed none other than Hilma Skott's sister, who had gone off to America many years before, leaving behind only the lasting memory of her dazzling good looks. It must be clear from this introduction that things had turned out very nicely for her. She had married well, had three children, doubled her weight, and got herself a car, some gold fillings, and various other things to be revealed in due course.

The idea of arriving to visit her sister unannounced had appealed to her. Gammalrödja people are always in, so there was no risk in making it a surprise visit. In her mind she could still picture the gloomy, out of the way old cottage, and she almost believed she might be able to jump across the footbridges as lightly as she used to. She kept herself fit, so she ought to be able to manage it. But finding that Hilma now had a proper road, and land that had been cleared of rocks and stones, she had to admit that things were changing even in old Gammalrödja. And yet, when she stepped into the familiar old kitchen and found four women, with ages ranging from six to sixty, busily scrubbing out copper pans and wicker-work cheese molds, and discussing the pros and cons of home-produced rennet, and the newfangled sort they made you buy nowadays, then she knew she was home.

"Well I'm blessed, Hilma," she said loudly, lapsing into her native dialect. "Fancy you having a cheesemaking here today!"

Hilma turned round and stared.

Agda and the little girls stared too. There was a long pause.

"How old and ugly she's grown," thought Emerentia, regarding the handsome Hilma.

"Heavens, how fine and grand she is," thought Hilma enviously at the sight of her flabby sister.

"Yes, it's today they're all bringing their milk to make the cheese," she said at last, and went to the cupboard for an extra cup and saucer for Emerentia.

Before the sisters had a chance to start exchanging all their news, Agda's eldest girl piped up, "I can hear them coming."

Soon, the grown-ups too could hear the cheerful buzz of conversation from down by the gate. The guests were in high spirits, for the women of Gammalrödja were still just as fond as in the old days of putting on their

best clothes on a fine summer's afternoon and going along to a cheesemaking.

They didn't care if their menfolk jeered at them in a good-natured way
because they still went to each other's houses with milk for making cheese,
when there was a new dairy that bought the milk and sold them cheese at
a good price.

"It must be the coffee you go for," the menfolk would say.

But it wasn't the coffee at all; they could indulge their taste for that just
as well at home. No, the secret fascination of going to a cheesemaking was
that it was an old custom dating back to the days when everyone helped
everyone else with the really big jobs on the farm. When they came
together to make cheese, they were transported back for a while to that
time of mutual friendship and support, and it made them feel comfortable.
The menfolk just didn't feel the same about it, for although many years had
gone by since the common land had been parcelled out, the idea of being
their own bosses and looking after their own affairs hadn't lost its fascination for them, and if anyone came up with a new idea for some collective
venture, their mutual distrust soon put an end to the scheme. They continued to thrive, like plants, on their own reserves of food, trying not to
think about what the future might have in store for them.

Emerentia posted herself eagerly at the window. What a bit of luck that
the cheesemaking happened to be today, almost as if it had been laid on
specially for her. Now she would be able to see all her old acquaintances,
and show off to them a little.

Here came the churchwarden's wife from Foxes Farm. You could tell it
was her from her cotton dress: the stripes were just the same blue and
black as they had been in the old days. Otherwise though, she'd certainly
changed, grown old and wizened.

"Trust her to have brought such a small jug," said Hilma, who was still
nursing a grudge. She hadn't forgotten that Foxes Farm had tried to send
her to the workhouse because she couldn't pay the rent, before she had
come into money and been able to live decently.

"Oh look, here comes my old friend Märta from our confirmation class.
She used to pass the time of day with the lad from Ravens Farm, even
before I left, and now she looks very hoity-toity."

"Well, she married into the family at Ravens Farm, and her husband's a
magistrate now," Hilma said.

And here comes a young woman who's the very image of Sara of
Scriveners Farm, except that her hair is shingled and waved, and she's
wearing . . .

"Bless my soul, then that'll be Berta, her daughter," said Hilma in surprise, leaving the coffeepot on the stove to come and look. "Where did you
say you saw her? Well, fancy her turning up! And don't you recognize Sara
herself, now?"

"What, the old woman with her? But who's that man coming along carrying two jugs, and who are those women he's got with him?"

Hilma had to come and look again. Oh yes, that was Verner of West

Southacres Farm with his mother Fia, and the other one, in the black
checked dress that didn't look home-woven, was Viktoria from the East
Farm, whose clothes were still in mourning for her husband, though they
do say she did away with him herself.

Verner said his goodbyes out by the front porch, but even from indoors
they could hear him saying that he'd call back when he'd finished at the
peat bog and ask whether anyone wanted a lift home. The ladies were in
such high spirits that they even went so far as to joke about how it just happened that Verner had to go to the peat bog the same day Fia and Viktoria were going cheesemaking at Hilma's. But Viktoria pursed her lips and
blushed. Someone else, from outside the parish, was courting her now,
and anyway she had thought it was a secret.

Mrs. Emerentia Nelson was so convinced that she hadn't really changed
very much in twenty-five years, that she attributed the sudden silence when
they saw her to her rings and crepe de chine. But although the guests had
spotted the car, and Emerentia's name had sprung to mind, they remembered her as the prettiest girl in seven parishes, and it took them a
moment to find her blue eyes and delicate features in among all the layers of fat. Once they were certain, they greeted her without any fuss; it
took more than silk and rings and even the most well-endowed pair of hips
to surprise the ladies of Gammalrödja. And they had no fears about their
own appearances, because their cotton frocks were all made along the
same lines as Berta's, cut in one piece with a sash round the hips. Berta
had given the dressmaker strict instructions not to copy her pattern,
because it wouldn't suit the village wives half as well as their usual skirts
and bodices, you know. But they didn't care about that, and nor did the
dressmaker, because why should Berta be the only one wearing the latest
fashion? So it was only Sara, Berta's poor old mother, who was in a full skirt
and traditional jacket.

While the guests were emptying their jugs into the big copper vat,
Emerentia condescended to help carry out the things they would need for
the coffee to the pretty group of garden seats with its leafy canopy. That's
where they were all sitting now, all except Agda, who was in the kitchen
waiting for the magic moment when the milk curdled.

The sisters from Bridge End Farm hadn't been in touch with one
another for years.

"You didn't write and let us know your boy had been killed," Emerentia
said, "but anyway here's a stone I took from his grave when I was there!"
She took a little white stone from out of her bag, and said, with her mouth
full of cake, "I found it just by the cross on Ernst's grave."

No one was interested in the stone, which was just an ordinary stone,
but the news was a different matter. How come Emerentia had been in
France? What was the name of the place where Ernst was buried? Notre
Dame de la Lorette! How strange it sounded! How on earth had she found
her way there?

Berta, though, bent forward and picked up the little stone in her hand,
because it had lain near his cross. Her heart jumped, as it did at every

reminder of her obstinate, wayward, good-looking boy. Elegant Miss Berta Skrivare, who worked in the food hall of Stockholm's smartest store and sat on the committee of the new shop assistants' union, and was so busy, always took the long way round to avoid passing a plaque which bore Ernst's name, until even the detour pained her.

Now she carefully drew back out of the circle with the stone in her hand; she had decided that she wasn't going to give it back. You want to forget, but if a memento comes to hand, you steal it. . . . She didn't stop dreaming until Emerentia dropped her bombshell.

"You want to know how I came to be in France, Märta? Well then, I'll tell you. I sacrificed my eldest boy too, just like Hilma. I've got a grave as well, not far from hers. I went with a group of two hundred mourning mothers from Minnesota to visit our graves in France."

So saying, she produced from her bag something far more remarkable than the stone. It was a star-shaped medal, rather like the one Reverend Springer, the dean, wore for weddings, only bigger and showier. Its owner fastened it on in the same place, so to speak, as the Reverend wore his.

"We were all wearing these when we went to France," she said, and, lapsing into American speech, "You bet we made a sensation."

Hilma felt a sort of pang inside.

"Your husband must be well off," she said.

"You don't think he gave me the star, do you? You fool, it's a decoration awarded by the American authorities to all the mothers who've sacrificed a son. We all belong to an association called the Mothers of the Star. This is the Star, see, and I'm the Mother."

"What did you have to do to get it then?"

"What did I have to do? Well first I had the boy. You must know how you do that. And then I let him go off to war."

"You let him?"

"Yes, me. I sacrificed the dearest thing I had, because we were fighting for 'a high ideal,' as we say over there. Then he was killed in action, poor boy."

"But I think those who were killed should have had the stars themselves," said Berta.

Emerentia looked the young girl slowly up and down.

"You needn't worry yourself. The authorities took care of all that. But over there, they think that a mother who's given the best thing she had for her country ought to get some recognition too. But of course, you can't understand that over here in old Sweden. You're so used to doing yourselves down."

"Well we haven't had a war, thank God, and surely there won't be one now?" said Viktoria in alarm.

"Yes, may God protect our sons . . ."

"Why do you want Him to, when you could get a star on your breast like her, and a soldier's mother's pension," Berta said, in a voice which somehow spoiled the pleasant coffeetime atmosphere. She was a bundle of nerves these days, and this self-satisfied, star-decorated mother had infuriated her. Ernst was hers, wasn't he, and she'd sacrificed him, but what was she left with? A stone. A sting.

Her mother, alarmed, stopped her from going on by saying, "Why don't you go in, dear, and take over from Agda with the cheese, so she can come out for her coffee?"

Emerentia started fishing about in her bag again.

"If Berta's going in, she can take these with her to show Agda. They're her cousins."

But when the others heard this, they wouldn't let Berta go until they had seen Emerentia's children too. There they were: the eldest son who was dead and the daughter who was still alive, both in uniform. They were just as good-looking as their mother had been, but the son, hero though he was, paled into insignificance beside Mary H. Nelson—H for Hilma. It wasn't particularly remarkable that she should be slim and elegant, with curls and a smile; what caught their eye was the fact that she was wearing a jacket and trousers and a braid-trimmed cap. Hanging from her shoulders she had a broad, becoming military greatcoat, but even that wasn't as incredible as—the sword. Yes, a sword! She was like something in a painting, standing there to present arms to a very distinguished and very smug-looking gentleman with lots of stripes on his sleeve.

"Oh," said Berta, "she's in films."

"Films indeed!" snorted Emerentia. "It's plain you can't understand English, Berta, or you'd have seen it says here at the bottom, 'Colonel Mary H. Nelson.' 'Colonel' is an American military rank, and a colonel is what she is, not a film star."

"Heavens, aren't there any men left over there?" Hilma asked, thinking, "Then how will they be able to carry on paying my pension?"

"Are you mad, you fool," Emerentia retorted, "Mary's the colonel of a proper regiment with proper men. This is the whole corps of trainee reserve officers here, see. They were standing behind her when it was taken. And the one she's facing, that's General Field, who'd come to inspect the regiment. You just can't imagine what a sight they made. Even my Nelson cried, and as for little John, our youngest, I could hardly control him. And me, I clean forgot about my Charles in his grave."

"Mercy me, whatever next!"

"Did you ever see the like of it? What's that newspaper you've got there?"

"Well, wouldn't you like to hear what they wrote about her in the Minnesota Star?" Emerentia opened the newspaper and translated rapidly, as though she knew most of it by heart. "It's grand being a soldier, when the officers are as sweet as Mary H. Nelson, Newfield, Minn. Dressed in full uniform, and making even a sword look graceful, the little colonel leads parades, troop reviews and exercises. But when it's time for the regimental ball, she exchanges her uniform for something more feminine, and takes her place as the belle of the ball. If war breaks out, she says, she intends to go to the front and lead her boys into battle herself."

The women exchanged glances. They had learned to accept milking machines and airplanes, and some of the younger ones had even been to the cinema, but this they just *could not believe*. Any minute they expected Emerentia to start laughing at them.

"Good Lord, the things they think of!" they said cautiously. That could be taken to mean Emerentia herself, or the American government.

But Berta could understand a bit of English, and she could see that Emerentia had given a faithful translation. It was ridiculous and absurd, but none the less true for that.

"You know what, Hilma," she said to her hostess, "I think the authorities up in Stockholm have been downright unfair to you. You didn't get a star in exchange for Ernst, and Agda didn't get a sword, either."

Viktoria tittered. "I can just see Agda with a sword," she said.

Hilma had just been wondering whether perhaps she was far more special and deserving of much more recognition than she'd imagined.

"I've been too modest," thought the woman who believed that God had started the World War in response to her prayers. So she said, a trifle sourly, "What me, a poor old woman from a little province like Småland?"

Emerentia was disappointed in her old friends; they were too stupid to be properly knocked flat by what she had shown them. The vague stirrings of envy in Hilma were something, at least, and now she would play her trump card.

"Do you want to see me, when I was with the Royal Family in England?" she asked.

"You never were?"

The tone was one of mistrust, but even the doubters had to admit defeat, because there before their eyes, on the front page of an illustrated magazine, stood none other than Mrs. Emerentia Nelson with a crowd of other blissfully smiling Mothers of the Star, and who was that fine young gentleman in their midst but the heir to the British throne? Berta couldn't deny that she recognized him.

"Did he shake hands with you?"

"Yes, to greet us and when he said good-bye."

"I expect you could feel it right through you?"

"You just have to have been there; you can't describe it."

"Who's that he's talking to?"

"That's a lady who lost two sons. She was the leader of our group."

Poor Hilma, nothing like that would ever happen to her, even though Ernst had undoubtedly shot just as many idle Frenchmen and was just as dead as Charles.

"Come on, Hilma dear, you try on the Star and we'll take your photograph," said Emerentia generously.

They all watched while Hilma was decorated.

"Those two from Bridge End Farm, they always have to go one better," thought the magistrate's wife from Ravens Farm. "Even when we were girls, they were better-looking than the rest of us, and now they've got medals and pensions and shake hands with royalty."

"Of course, you think we're just cat's dirt here in Gammalrödja," she said. Emerentia protested lamely. "But all the same, Father and I are going into town on Saturday to visit our boy, who's in military service. We parents have got printed cards inviting us to see round the barracks, and stay to dinner afterwards. The card's got *Regimental Commander* at the bottom."

The others had already heard this remarkable bit of news, and they knew too what a stir it had caused in every household to think that the *wives* were being invited along to see the barracks and even being offered a meal there. Only Mia from Foxes Farm, who couldn't always follow what was happening, was taken by surprise. It was almost too much for her, after she'd had six sons do military service, and not got so much as a cup of coffee for it. She wasn't interested in the food, and fortunately for her she could manage without a pension or a star, but it was a blow that it should be Märta, wife of her enemy at Ravens Farm, sitting there boasting.

"Well, I must be getting back," she said, and got up.

They could all see that the fun was over for old Mia the churchwarden's wife. When she was killed, a week later, by her son Anton, they felt pangs of conscience, but just now they really didn't care.

"There, there, mother Mia," said Emerentia, pushing her back down into her seat. "Stay and have another cup of coffee, and then I'll give you a lift home in my car. Aren't you glad to hear that they're starting to appreciate the mothers in this country too? I certainly am. I would never have thought. . . . One of these days it'll be your turn too. You've got six boys, haven't you? It's people like you the authorities need to stay well in with."

"How strange," said Berta. "It's a topsy-turvy world."

Her mother looked at her in alarm. She knew what it meant when Berta's eyes narrowed and she bit her top lip.

But Emerentia didn't recognize the danger signs, and she asked provocatively, "In what way?"

"Well, I've heard from Father that they used to bribe the authorities when they came to inspect the roads and collect the taxes, and things weren't quite up to scratch. But it's something new when *those at the top* bribe the women. The Swedish authorities just couldn't . . . no, I don't understand all this."

"There's no need to start on about bribery, Berta," said Vendla from North Farm. "No one had to bribe me to send my lads to learn to defend their country. I come from the Five Lakes, where the Danes overran us like hordes of Turks, so I know very well that ours need to learn. Don't you laugh, Berta; it says in the history books that my family home was burnt down in 1643, and it's been called the Derelict Farm ever since."

"I'm not laughing at you, but I was just thinking that your lads haven't much to fear from the Danes these days."

"You never can tell," declared the magistrate's wife firmly. "Just when you think there's peace, along comes a war."

If the chairman of the district council, the magistrate, and the churchwarden could have seen their wives now, they would undoubtedly have been more astonished by them than by Emerentia and Mary H. Nelson with her sword. The womenfolk might talk as much as they liked about household chores, the weather, the neighbors, childbirth, and deathbeds, but it was customary and proper that they should stay silent or keep away when the men got onto politics and tried to work out who had started the war.

No one thought of asking them whether they had any views on the matter, and old Mia hadn't had a chance to put forward her idea that the whole cause of the war had been silk stockings.

What would the men have said, if they had heard Emerentia explaining that in other countries, the men didn't dare get into a war without buttering up the womenfolk first. They might just about have explained it away by saying that they have some funny ways in these foreign parts. But if they had seen Ebba, Sara, and Mia taking the regimental commander's invitation as a sign that things were the same in Sweden, they would have thought matters were getting quite absurdly out of hand. Was old Sweden so far gone that the king and his subjects couldn't manage to cope with defending the country without enlisting the women's support?

"I've never thought about it before, but I'm sure Emerentia's right," said Märta the magistrate's wife suddenly, reaching the end of her train of thought. "After all, how far would the authorities get without our lads?"

"What do you think would happen if we all said we weren't going to let our lads go?" said old Mia in the most scornful tone she could muster.

"I'll tell you what would happen," said Emerentia. "There wouldn't be a war."

"Is that so?" said Berta, furious with rage, and glaring at the fat lady who had got a star for her son. "Well then, I think you ought to get on and do it."

"I think you're all getting carried away," said mild-mannered old Sara, patting her daughter soothingly on the shoulder, which merely made her wilder. "We women don't run things, after all."

"Nor do the men," old Mia put in.

"You never know what God might be trying to do with a war," said Hilma, thinking of her own experience.

"Don't blame God!" cried Berta, beside herself. "It's not God!"

"Oh, so God's not in charge of the world any longer?"

"You watch out, talking about God like that! Jesus told us to love our enemies, didn't he? The men are the ones who've decided to kill each other. And if you mothers can stop it, but don't, and go prancing about wearing stars instead, like those poor Negro women who give away their poor little children in exchange for glass beads, then just you watch out, their blood will be on your hands."

She burst into tears and left the garden.

They all sat very quiet, feeling embarrassed. Were they powerless? Were they powerful? They didn't know. No, it couldn't be their fault. None of them wanted blood on their hands. They pulled themselves together. Poor Berta, Stockholm had been too much for her. The blood had always been on the hands of the Danes or the Russians or some other good-for-nothing lot of foreigners before.

Poor Viktoria was feeling, as she often did, that life was getting harder to live every day. It was hard enough for a widow to run a farm, when prices kept on falling, and now they said you were to blame for the war as well.

It was as though Berta's mother had guessed what everyone was thinking. "It's not easy when you've got a broken heart," she said softly. "Once it's broken, nothing can help."

"Time heals," said Märta from Ravens Farm.

"No, not even time," said old Sara.

A sigh came from old Mia, another from Vendla. This human suffering for something so hopeless brought home to them an echo of what war was really like. A young man was dead. The girl who had cared for him had grieved until she had made herself ill. For one short moment, they all understood what that meant, even Hilma with her pension and the star-bedecked Emerentia who had shaken hands with the Prince of Wales.

At that moment, Agda came bursting out of the house, crying out in a voice that shook with fear and desperation.

"It won't curdle!"

"Jesus, girl, have you heated it up properly?"

"Three times! But there must be some bad milk in it, sure as I've ever made cheese before."

"Well! So it's our fault is it? The Foxes Farm milk, I suppose?"

"Or North Farm's?"

"Give me back my jug!"

"I can tell you this is the last time I'll be coming here to make cheese!"

"It's that bought rennet, of course. Anyone can see that."

They forgot all about the war.

"The Cheesemaking," trans. Sarah Death, in *Longman Anthology of World Literature by Women, 1875–1975*, ed. Marian Arkin and Barbara Shollar (New York: Longman, 1989). Translated from "Yste med Köpelöpe," in *Gammalrödja: skildring av en bygd som ömsar skinn* (1931). Reprinted by permission of Devy Wägner and Maria Wägner and Sarah Death.

✝ Elizabeth Bowen
(1899–1973) *British*

Born into an Anglo-Irish family, Elizabeth Bowen spent her youth on the family estate in Cork, but family debt and her father's mental instability forced her and her mother to move to England, where she was educated. After her mother's death when she was thirteen, Bowen toured Europe and studied art, a background that she felt influenced her aesthetic strategies: "Much (and perhaps the best) of my writing is verbal painting." Following her graduation from school in 1916, she returned to Dublin to work with victims of shell shock. In 1923 Bowen married Major Alan Cameron, who suffered from his war wounds the remainder of his life. They had no children.

The year of her marriage, she published *Encounters,* her first collection of short stories. A steady flow of other collections followed: *Joining Charles* (1929), *The Cat Jumps and Other Stories* (1934), *Look at All Those Roses* (1941), and *The Demon Lover* (1945). Acerbic wit and enjoyment of the grotesque distinguish her style; she wrote that she found the supernatural "inseparable" from her sense of life. Among her novels, *The Death of the Heart* (1938), an allusive and intricate exploration of a young woman's maturation, and *The Heat of the Day* (1949), a suggestive narrative of a post-war affair, are celebrated as Bowen's masterpieces. Bowen's war fiction reveals her sensitivity to the psychological effects of war; in introducing stories about the German blitz attack on London, she explains: "Through the particular, in wartime, I felt the high-voltage current of the general flow." She describes her "discontinuous" writing as "disjected snapshots—snapshots taken from close up, too close up, in the mêlée of a battle." During World War II she also wrote for the Ministry of Information and worked as an air-raid warden.

Major Cameron had eye trouble resulting from trench poisoning in World War I, which led the couple to spend more time at Bowen Court after 1945. While in her forties, Bowen examined her family's Irish history in the autobiography *Bowen's Court* (1942), where she concedes that the power of Anglo-Irish landowners sprang from "a situation that shows an inherent wrong." A friend of Virginia Woolf, Edith Sitwell, and Iris Murdoch, Bowen was appointed a Commander of the British Empire (1948) and granted honorary degrees at Trinity College (1949) and Oxford (1957). She died of cancer.

KCS

✝ The Demon Lover

Towards the end of her day in London Mrs. Drover went round to her shut-up house to look for several things she wanted to take away. Some belonged to herself, some to her family, who were by now used to their country life. It was late August; it had been a steamy, showery day: at the moment the trees down the pavement glittered in an escape of humid yellow afternoon sun. Against the next batch of clouds, already piling up ink-dark, broken chimneys and parapets stood out. In her once familiar street, as in any unused channel, an unfamiliar queerness had silted up; a cat wove itself in and out of railings, but no human eye watched Mrs. Drover's return. Shifting some parcels under her arm, she slowly forced round her latchkey in an unwilling lock, then gave the door, which had warped, a push with her knee. Dead air came out to meet her as she went in.

The staircase window having been boarded up, no light came down into the hall. But one door, she could just see, stood ajar, so she went quickly through into the room and unshuttered the big window in there. Now the prosaic woman, looking about her, was more perplexed than she knew by everything that she saw, by traces of her long former habit of life—the yellow smoke-stain up the white marble mantelpiece, the ring left by a vase on the top of the escritoire,[1] the bruise in the wallpaper where, on the door being thrown open widely, the china handle had always hit the wall. The piano, having gone away to be stored, had left what looked like claw-marks on its part of the parquet. Though not much dust had seeped in, each object wore a film of another kind; and, the only ventilation being the chimney, the whole drawing room smelled of the cold hearth. Mrs. Drover put down her parcels on the escritoire and left the room to proceed upstairs; the things she wanted were in the bedroom chest.

She had been anxious to see how the house was—the part-time caretaker she shared with some neighbors was away this week on his holiday, known to be not yet back. At the best of times he did not look in often, and she was never sure that she trusted him. There were some cracks in the structure, left by the last bombing, on which she was anxious to keep an eye. Not that one could do anything—

1. *Escritoire:* writing desk.

A shaft of refracted daylight now lay across the hall. She stopped dead and stared at the hall table—on this lay a letter addressed to her.

She thought first—then the caretaker *must* be back. All the same, who, seeing the house shuttered, would have dropped a letter in at the box? It was not a circular, it was not a bill. And the post office redirected, to the address in the country, everything for her that came through the post. The caretaker (even if he *were* back) did not know she was due in London today—her call here had been planned to be a surprise—so his negligence in the matter of this letter, leaving it to wait in the dusk and dust, annoyed her. Annoyed, she picked up the letter, which bore no stamp. But it cannot be important, or they would know. . . . She took the letter rapidly upstairs with her, without a stop to look at the writing till she reached what had been her bedroom, where she let in light. The room looked over the garden and other gardens: the sun had gone in; as the clouds sharpened and lowered, the trees and rank lawns seemed already to smoke with dark. Her reluctance to look again at the letter came from the fact that she felt intruded upon—and by someone contemptuous of her ways. However, in the tenseness preceding the fall of rain she read it: it was a few lines.

Dear Kathleen,

You will not have forgotten that today is our anniversary, and the day we said. The years have gone by at once slowly and fast. In view of the fact that nothing has changed, I shall rely upon you to keep your promise. I was sorry to see you leave London, but was satisfied that you would be back in time. You may expect me, therefore, at the hour arranged.

Until then . . .

K.

Mrs. Drover looked for the date: it was today's. She dropped the letter on to the bedsprings, then picked it up to see the writing again—her lips, beneath the remains of lipstick, beginning to go white. She felt so much the change in her own face that she went to the mirror, polished a clear patch in it and looked at once urgently and stealthily in. She was confronted by a woman of forty-four, with eyes staring out under a hat brim that had been rather carelessly pulled down. She had not put on any more powder since she left the shop where she ate her solitary tea. The pearls her husband had given her on their marriage hung loose round her now rather thinner throat, slipping into the V of the pink wool jumper her sister knitted last autumn as they sat round the fire. Mrs. Drover's most normal expression was one of controlled worry, but of assent. Since the birth of the third of her little boys, attended by a quite serious illness, she had had an intermittent muscular flicker to the left of her mouth, but in spite of this she could always sustain a manner that was at once energetic and calm.

Turning from her own face as precipitately as she had gone to meet it, she went to the chest where the things were, unlocked it, threw up the lid and knelt to search. But as the rain began to come crashing down she could not keep from looking over her shoulder at the stripped bed on which the letter lay. Behind the blanket of rain the clock of the church that still stood struck six—with rapidly heightening apprehension she counted each of the slow strokes. "The hour arranged. . . . My God," she said, "*what* hour? How should I . . .? After twenty-five years . . ."

The young girl talking to the soldier in the garden had not ever completely seen his face. It was dark; they were saying goodbye under a tree. Now and then—for it felt, from not seeing him at this intense moment, as though she had never seen him at all—she verified his presence for these few moments longer by putting out a hand, which he each time pressed, without very much kindness, and painfully, on to one of the breast buttons of his uniform. That cut of the button on the palm of her hand was, principally, what she was to carry away. This was so near the end of a leave from France that she could only wish him already gone. It was August 1916. Being not kissed, being drawn away from and looked at intimidated Kathleen till she imagined spectral glitters in the place of his eyes. Turning away and looking back up the lawn she saw, through branches of trees, the drawing room window alight: she caught a breath for the moment when she could go running back there into the safe arms of her mother and sister, and cry: "What shall I do, what shall I do? He has gone."

Hearing her catch her breath, her fiancé said, without feeling: "Cold?"

"You're going away such a long way."

"Not so far as you think."

"I don't understand?"

"You don't have to," he said. "You will. You know what we said."

"But that was—suppose you—I mean, suppose."

"I shall be with you," he said, "sooner or later. You won't forget that. You need do nothing but wait."

Only a little more than a minute later she was free to run up the silent lawn. Looking in through the window at her mother and sister, who did not for the moment perceive her, she already felt that unnatural promise drive down between her and the rest of all human kind. No other way of having given herself could have made her feel so apart, lost and forsworn. She could not have plighted a more sinister troth.

Kathleen behaved well when, some months later, her fiancé was reported missing, presumed killed. Her family not only supported her but were able to praise her courage without stint because they could not regret, as a husband for her, the man they knew almost nothing about. They hoped she would, in a year or two, console herself—and had it been only a question of consolation things might have gone much straighter ahead. But her trouble, behind just a little grief, was a complete dislocation from everything. She did not reject other lovers, for these failed to appear: for years she failed to attract men—and with the approach of her thirties she became natural enough to share her family's anxiousness on this score. She began to put herself out, to wonder; and at thirty-two she was very greatly relieved to find herself being courted by William Drover.

She married him, and the two of them settled down in this quiet, arboreal part of Kensington: in this house the years piled up, her children were born and they all lived till they were driven out by the bombs of the next war. Her movements as Mrs. Drover were circumscribed, and she dismissed any idea that they were still watched.

As things were—dead or living the letter-writer sent her only a threat. Unable, for some minutes, to go on kneeling with her back exposed to the empty room, Mrs. Drover rose from the chest to sit on an upright chair whose back was firmly against the wall. The desuetude of her former bedroom, her married London home's whole air of being a cracked cup from which memory, with its reassuring power, had either evaporated or leaked away, made a crisis—and at just this crisis the letter-writer had, knowledgeably, struck. The hollowness of the house this evening cancelled years on years of voices, habits and steps. Through the shut windows she only heard rain fall on the roofs around. To rally herself, she said she was in a mood—and, for two or three seconds shutting her eyes, told herself that she had imagined the letter. But she opened them—there it lay on the bed.

On the supernatural side of the letter's entrance she was not permitting her mind to dwell. Who, in London, knew she meant to call at the house today? Evidently, however, this had been known. The caretaker, *had* he come back, had had no cause to expect her: he would have taken the letter in his pocket, to forward it, at his own time, through the post. There was no other sign that the caretaker had been in—but, if not? Letters dropped in at doors of deserted houses do not fly or walk to tables in halls. They do not sit on the dust of empty tables with the air of certainty that they will be found. There is needed some human hand—but nobody but the caretaker had a key. Under circumstances she did not care to consider, a house can be entered without a key. It was possible that she was not alone now. She might be being waited for, downstairs. Waited for—until when? Until "the hour arranged." At least that was not six o'clock: six had struck.

She rose from the chair and went over and locked the door.

The thing was, to get out. To fly? No, not that: she had to catch her train. As a woman whose utter dependability was the keystone of her family life she was not willing to return to the country, to her husband, her little boys and her sister, without the objects she had come up to fetch. Resuming work at the chest she set about making up a number of parcels in a rapid, fumbling-decisive way. These, with her shopping parcels, would be too much to carry; these meant a taxi—at the thought of the taxi her heart went up and her normal breathing resumed. I will ring up the taxi now; the taxi cannot come too soon: I shall hear the taxi out there running its engine, till I walk calmly down to it through the hall. I'll ring up— But no: the telephone is cut off . . . She tugged at a knot she had tied wrong.

The idea of flight . . . He was never kind to me, not really. I don't remember him kind at all. Mother said he never considered me. He was set on me, that was what it was—not love. Not love, not meaning a person well. What did he do, to make me promise like that? I can't remember.— But she found that she could.

She remembered with such dreadful acuteness that the twenty-five years since then dissolved like smoke and she instinctively looked for the weal left by the button on the palm of her hand. She remembered not only all that he said and did but the complete suspension of *her* existence during that August week. I was not myself—they all told me so at the time. She remembered—but with one white burning blank as where acid has dropped on a photograph: *under no conditions* could she remember his face.

So, wherever he may be waiting, I shall not know him. You have no time to run from a face you do not expect.

The thing was to get to the taxi before any clock struck what could be the hour. She would slip down the street and round the side of the square to where the square gave on the main road. She would return in the taxi, safe, to her own door, and bring the solid driver into the house with her to pick up the parcels from room to room. The idea of the taxi driver made her decisive, bold: she unlocked her door, went to the top of the staircase and listened down.

She heard nothing—but while she was hearing nothing the *passé*[2] air of the staircase was disturbed by a draught that travelled up to her face. It emanated from the basement: down there a door or window was being opened by someone who chose this moment to leave the house.

The rain had stopped; the pavements steamily shone as Mrs. Drover let herself out by inches from her own front door into the empty street. The unoccupied houses opposite continued to meet her look with their damaged stare. Making towards the thoroughfare and the taxi, she tried not to keep looking behind. Indeed, the silence was so intense—one of those creeks of London silence exaggerated this summer by the damage of war—that no tread could have gained on hers unheard. Where her street debouched on the square where people went on living she grew conscious of and checked her unnatural pace. Across the open end of the square two buses impassively passed each other; women, a perambulator, cyclists, a man wheeling a barrow signalized, once again, the ordinary flow of life. At the square's most populous corner should be—and was—the short taxi rank. This evening, only one taxi—but this, although it presented its blank rump, appeared already to be alertly waiting for her. Indeed, without looking round the driver started his engine as she panted up from behind and put her hand on the door. As she did so, the clock struck seven. The taxi faced the main road: to make the trip back to her house it would have to turn—she had settled back on the seat and the taxi *had* turned before she, surprised by its knowing movement, recollected that she had not "said where." She leaned forward to scratch at the glass panel that divided the driver's head from her own.

2. *Passé:* old, from the past.

The driver braked to what was almost a stop, turned round and slid the glass panel back: the jolt of this flung Mrs. Drover forward till her face was almost into the glass. Through the aperture driver and passenger, not six inches between them, remained for an eternity eye to eye. Mrs. Drover's mouth hung open for some seconds before she could issue her first scream. After that she continued to scream freely and to beat with her gloved hands on the glass all round as the taxi, accelerating without mercy, made off with her into the hinterland of deserted streets.

1945

✛ V ✛

POEMS

It used to be thought that women did not write poetry about the Great War—at least not any good poetry. The assumption that their "domestic" topics had nothing to do with war led readers to overlook women's contributions to the poetic representation of war experiences. Anthologists who included a few women's lyrics often singled out the most jingoistic or the most "feminine" productions—the kind of patriotic verse represented here by Isolde Kurz and Jessie Pope—with predictable results. The image of women as survivors of war lamenting the loss of their men in traditional elegies also contributed to the neglect of their poetry in an age dominated by the Modernist break away from older forms. This low assessment of women's accomplishment has now been substantially corrected by the work of feminist literary historians, especially by those who have made the range of women's poetic production more readily available.

Poetry might be considered a form of writing even more distant from actual experience than fiction: the hallmark of poetry has been its technical arrangement and its play with lyric conventions. Yet like the elegy and military march, war poetry is defined by theme. Some forms of war poetry, such as the "letter" to or from the front (exemplified here by the verse of Maria Benemann and Eleanor Farjeon), deliberately echo personal prose like the letter or the diary and thus inaugurate the confessional trend in twentieth-century poetry.

Even when verse converges on the emotion of loss or on a single image, such as the mud of the battlefield (as in a poem by Mary Borden), it resists interpretation solely in terms of theme. For the best war poetry is not solely about war. Voice is important. The play of ironic language (sometimes underestimated in prose forms such as propaganda and journalism) comes to the fore in this epochal moment.

The mastery of poetic forms implies an education, and many of the women represented here came from privileged circumstances, a factor that distinguishes them from the many soldier poets who were working-class. Perhaps because these women were trained in traditional modes and sought acceptance into the canon, fewer of them engaged in radical formal experiments. Nonetheless, their work possesses a growing power to shock and to provoke thought. Read in chronological sequence, women's poetry reveals a surprisingly early, bold resistance to the verbal clichés and heroic formulae of war verse, a resistance exemplified by Henriette Sauret-Arnyvelde, Anna Akhmatova, and Gertrud Fauth. It also reveals the continuing pertinence of the war to poetry in the decades that follow the Armistice.

The range of women's poetic production mirrors their talents and concerns. Some of the lyric voices here use familiar structures like the sonnet to convey loss; they may find the springs of irony in a taut grammatical turn or a resonantly ambiguous image. Others break down into a violent despair that rejects the comforts of form and faith. Modernists such as Henriette Charasson, Margit Kaffka, and Amy Lowell turn to free verse as a tool that will allow them to cast off old solutions, both ideological and formal. Innovators like Gertrud Kolmar and Danica Marković challenge conventional views of war, of masculinity, of the uses of empathy, and of the meaning of patriotism. The strongest of these poems all force us to repeat a question asked sixty years after the event in a song recited by a villager in Malawi: "Why did people die?"

✝ Isolde Kurz
(1853–1944) *German*

orn into the liberal family of the novelist and librarian Hermann
Kurz, Isolde Kurz was taught at home in Tübingen with her brothers
by her mother, a freethinking aristocrat. After the death of her
father, she went to Munich in 1876, where she met Paul Heyse and his circle, but was not caught up in the aestheticist movement. She lived over
three decades in Florence, caring for a sick brother and her mother and
moving in an artistic circle that included the painter Arnold Böcklin and
critic and sculptor Adolph Hildebrand. Her short fiction from this period
ranges from nostalgic regionalist recollections of Swabia to resonant figures of Renaissance men of power.

At the outbreak of war, she returned to Germany, where she lived in
Munich until the year of her death. Her work falls in the romantic tradition; her first collection of poems (1889) focuses on love, nature, and
death. She published novellas, delicate lyrics, and strictly formal stories.
Schwert aus der Scheide (Sword unsheathed, 1916) celebrated Germany's
engagement in the war. A first collection of her works appeared in 1925;
she went on to win the Goethe medal and an honorary doctorate from the
University of Tübingen in the thirties. Her autobiography, *Die Pilgerfahrt
nach dem Unerreichlichen* (Pilgrimage to the ineffable, 1938), runs from her
childhood in Swabia to the revolutionary days in Munich at the end of
World War I.

☦ Fatherland

Fatherland,
holy land,
which the world ablaze surrounds!

Your iron sons stand sentinel.
Take comfort: for the hand
of wrathful love will
wrest you from the jaws of hell.

Hatred and scorn reward
the heart that embraced the world!
You came to offer a feast
of light to other peoples,
while they whetted the murder-iron
to threaten your all-nourishing breast.

Fatherland,
holy land,
now danger makes us understand!
Who still nurses wishful delusions?
Pains that belong to him alone?
All our senses, our intentions,
turn, great mother, to you and home.

Keep comfort,
as the wave of hatred roars!
At the close of the iron game,
pure hands of saviors will award
the lot you won: the crown of fame.

"Vaterland," in *Zeit-Echo*, I.6 (1914), 80.

✝ Frida Schanz
(1859–1944) *German*

The daughter of poets, Frida Schanz was brought up in Dresden, where she taught and wrote for children. In 1885 she married Ludwig Soyaux, but kept her name for her publications. From 1895 to 1904 she coedited *Junge Mädchen* (Young girls), as well as the annual *Kinderlust* (Children's pleasure), until she took over the editorship of *Daheim* (Home) and *Velhagen und Klasings Monatshefte* in 1905. Besides poetry and stories for children she also composed aphorisms, ballads, and lyrics for adults collected in *Mein Weg* (My path, 1919). A memoir of her childhood appeared in 1920. *Die Tägliche Rundschau* printed her poem "Silence" on August 17, 1914.

✝ Silence

Silence, which unfolds to the most dreadful of beats.
Silence, for days now, for many days now.
A giant lifts the baton. The hall is locked.
Three orchestras perform the concert.
One spirit, one God, one will of primeval strength
Marks the beat in the hall of breathless silence.

1914

Translated by Trudi Nicholas

"Stille," in *1914, Der deutsche Krieg im deutschen Gedicht*, ed. Julius Bab (Berlin: Morawe, 1914–1919) 1:30.

✚ Henriette Charasson
(b. 1884) *French*

A poet of Catholic inspiration, Charasson wrote journalism for such middle-class papers as *La vie intellectuelle* (Intellectual life), *La vie féminine littéraire* (Women's literary life), and *La femme de France* (The woman of France). In 1915 she joined the conservative nationalist group Action Française, for whose journal she wrote. She nonetheless remained a friend of the feminist Dr. Suzanne Noël, whose soroptimist group in the interwar period brought together a mixed elite of liberals, antifeminist reformers, and feminists. Charasson gathered her wartime poetry in the collection *Attente, 1914–1917* (Waiting, 1919).

In 1920 Charasson married René Johannet, who wrote for the *Mercure de France,* as did she; they had three sons. Her subsequent prose is maternalist and conservative: *Les heures du foyer* (Hearth hours), *Grigri* (1923), *Le livre de la mère* (The mother's book), and the autobiographical *Trois petits hommes et leur mère* (Three little men and their mother, 1928). "Men do not understand," she wrote, "the meaning of a little being whom one has nourished for months with one's blood and breath . . . the meaning of this flesh that has been molded with one's own flesh." Her later works were *Sacrifice du soir* (Evening sacrifice, 1952) and a preface to Rose Casanove's *Sur ma route de clarté* (My path to illumination, 1962).

✝ Evening of 25 September 1914

To my brother Cam

O my God, if you exist in the far reaches of your heaven,
So distant in your dark heaven where tonight only a crescent of a pale
  moon descends,
Do you not hear the sad clamor that rises from your ravaged earth?
It is Rachel who weeps still in Rama day after day,
It is the eternal voice of mothers who for centuries you heard during scar-
  let wars,
Like an immense swell, like a lamentable tide, like a flow and ebb of
  pains . . .
The moon has hidden behind the hillside laced with trees,
The night, immense and black, overhangs the looming fields,
In the fixed silence even nature seems to hold her breath.
And during these peaceful and cold hours, my brothers fight and die,
My unknown brothers will shortly feel their souls torn violently from their
  bodies.
Is it true, my God, that for months we will have to bear witness to your
  wrath,
Is it true that you want these things and that we have merited them,
And that day after day the women who stayed at home must
Listen trembling to the ring of the postman's step on the threshold?
We all know well that there are sad things in our souls,
And that there have already been sad things in our lives,
Ah! we have not weeded the garden of our souls enough,
I know well that we have let weeds grow in the paths
And that we love with a strong weakness the flowers that we should not.
But, my God, we are not gods, we are only poor beings,
And you see well that we have already made the effort, some to risk their
  lives, and others to let those depart whom they love more than their
  own flesh,
And we cannot do more, and we cannot, in spite of the atrocity of the wish,
  not desire that it be *the others* who die . . .
Dost thou not hear, my God, the poor egoistical voice that, like a dryad,
  weeps deep in each human trunk,
And cries desperately to thee: *Not mine, O Lord, not mine!*
We have all suffered already, and we cry out to thee: leave me *this* happi-
  ness!
Leave me the bread of my love, as my teeth have already gnashed the ashes
  of other human joys.
My God, what am I, to pray to you,
I, who do not even use the phrases consecrated by centuries of prayer?
My God, you must exist, because I am there calling you,

Do you not also hear Rachel's eternal lament, that monotone I catch in
  the silent dark?
She cries like an abandoned dog through the long night.
Can it be that all our gestures toward you vanish in empty space like per-
  fume evaporating in air,
A dying sound, a rocket that blazes upward only to fall extinguished, back
  on earth?
I've placed my knees on the ground and I've joined my unaccustomed
  hands,
And then I ask you humbly: What do you want?
No, not the necessary test, no, no, not the necessary test!
Ah! why does my soul not want to give itself, wholly, in every part?
Will you punish me,
Is *that* necessary to make me come back to you?
Will you spatter my soul with the blood of the brother dear to me?
No, do not believe that I rebel, I pray to you only with humility and with
  all my soul's power,
I beg you only to take pity on my weakness
And to extend your helping hand over the one you know,
Our Father who art in Heaven, Our Father who art in Heaven!

  "Soir du 25 septembre 1914," in *Attente, 1914–1917, Poèmes* (Paris: Emile-Paul, 1919),
9–15.

✟ Margit Kaffka
(1880–1918) *Hungarian*[1]

✟ I Tried to Pray

I tried to pray in a particularly cruel hour, when thoughts like this had to be said.

God, so far from us now, and perhaps only there because strength and faith are needed to defend against doubt; God, if you glanced at your world from behind the clouds which hide you, would you now delight in it? Are you not ashamed of the species which imagined you and formed you into the God of Terror? Can you take pleasure in the music of your spheres, and can the songs of your angels cut out the cries and sounds of death, which shout towards you from this fevered earth?

How could you possibly weave your way among our prayers, sad spirit whose office embraces truth, goodness, love of our enemies? Nations appear before you, imploring with prayers and psalms, that you might grind their enemies to dust, but should be saying in their several tongues "We love you."

O God, look around—there are no happy people now on earth!

For a long time now your people have not been divided or driven to killing merely for offering their wine on different altars; surely you must have been pleased! Don't be pleased any more! Now your abundant streams, the chain of your beautiful wooded hills, separate people who prepare for slaughter.

How marvellously we all differed from each other, we millions and millions of individuals; in what myriad ways we mirrored your countenance! Your thoughts were above our thoughts and we painted with your boughs and flowers. In our hearts we made your music, dedicated ourselves to you and carved your invisible face in our own likeness. We knew our identities and differences. And now, along your endless and desolate paths they all march in the same garb to the same step, each obeying the same com-

1. See page 97.

mand to explode murderous clouds upon others of your young men. Does this please you, O Lord?

You who created them from dust, have you permitted them to turn their brethren beyond the hills and waters into dust?

Their fathers, who loved their mothers, did not hate each other. Those parents having raised children, peacefully permitted them in their turn to take over the management of their land. In that knowledge they died on the pillows of their beds. Do these young men differ from their fathers and are they dying a better death?

And look, O Lord, at the female half of your people—at those who are mourning: they bring down the blue of your heavens with their tears, their lives and hearts are broken from the root. Alive and in fear they guard the ruffled nests.

O Lord! No prison is more cruel than this time. And every moment is deathly vivid as they try to protect lives far away, knowing that to be ineffectual. Guilty, lying on the soft bed; food indigestible as it cannot be shared with the other.—How many millions of minutes and thousands of hours of your time does it take, the nurturing from woman's womb to maturity, the making of a person; one blind moment of male anger and your whole wondrous creation ceases. My Lord! I am a woman but believe me I would rather be a little wild creature dreaming peacefully in my winter burrow because precious ammunition is saved now from the hunters. . . .

I am a woman, O Lord, and have never even killed a caterpillar! Your heavenly butterflies flutter about to lay their eggs that young larvae in spring may find food—though the parent herself will never see the joy of it! What sense is there now in the fecundity of female animals?—Your menfolk have judged your sayings meaningless, but as a woman I involuntarily marvel at your eternal wisdom. Do you, God of Men, find meaning in the actions of your menfolk? O Gaea, more ancient female deity, hundred breasted and with rooted legs, why did your world pass?

O Hadur, terrible Lord of War, more dreadful than Janus, what offering could we make to appease you?

Look at my people, the Hungarians, and know that, innocent as the lamb, they did not want this. Without hate but in sorrow, they kill (O God, let me believe at least this!); to the fallen prisoner they hand fraternal bread, and when he is disarmed, speak kindly to him as their guest.

During this sad time our singers do not threaten with hatred. Sad and noble, serious and clean are their songs, still recognisably individual the plucking of the lute, the resonance of the string. Good and wise people are these, my Lord, full of promise for your future garden; you should take special care of their seed, cover them gently with the shadow of your cloak.

You will have need of them if you yet cherish the human race when it has so abused your Son.

O dread Lord of men, let the cruel times pass quickly.

So that all of us may begin life again or prepare for death—those whom it has pleased you to turn into suffering widows and orphans; let this terrible eternity pass over us! See how a thousand times in every moment we send our lives to those with whom we were united. We are so cut off we can hardly hear news of them, and can do nothing for them. Return to us their lives which are unrepeatably greater treasures than any of your ornate temples! They call you Merciful Father: brotherly teaching Son and Holy Spirit. Prove it! We are not yet decadent, proud, and wasteful intellectually as some older nations. Allow us to enjoy a good future.

The Messiah will come (you told us in the scriptures) when nations turn their swords into plowshares and everyone rests beneath his fig tree. If you could consider this land of the Hungarians your land, O Liege Lord, do not forget that we might yet do your purpose!

Behind the harsh face visible to us I sense another milder presence, the watchful smile of the Virgin Mother. And to that face of yours I beseechingly pray—O you, envisioned by man, born as man, sad and loving God.

Christmas, 1914

Translated by Charlotte Franklin

"Imádkozni próbáltam," in *A révnél* (Budapest, 1918), 234–38. Reprint in *Az Élet Utján* (Budapest: Szépirodalmi Könyvkiadó, 1971).

✝ A Cry Through the Storm (A Letter)

How many you are!
Millions of small soldiers tramping
Through blood-thick mist, frozen marshes, rutted filthy roads
(From far wild valleys cold winds start to blow);
Dreary the rhythm of marching, sombre their grey garb.
Superfluity of life, mass of individual dust specks,
In the dazed crowd none dares question where, or why.
Continuing, ignorant of what power drives them, the madness;
Forsaking home and work, the cares and familiar ways
To cross these ravaged villages through blood-thick mist, frozen marshes.
If the order came they would kill with horrendous explosion
Because neighbors of another tongue and place would behave thus.
Each advances to call the land his own,
Though land is forever theirs who work and live upon it.
No, they don't understand. Who wanted this? Whence came the terrible
    compulsion?
Of men hunting men, creeping like animals from trenches
(Lucky the animals now, ammunition would be wasted on them,
Sleeping their winter dreams, mates together in peace.)
They don't understand, resting, gazing at the fire, amused to be alike,
Mud-covered brothers, lice-infested, cold,

Though some recall their books and old familiar music.
A soldier imagines nightmare in the flames,
All can remember voices, warm hands of women, mothers,
And wonder how long this sick mad time can last.
Each would like to continue the life he knew from childhood
But now he can only obey, eyes downcast, advancing,
Yielding himself—it's the best way—relieved to be alive.
Compassion is kept from his heart with a single thought, "I live."
Dry-eyed he buries a comrade, "Poor fellow, his turn, not mine."
Alas, my love, in such massive misery your own must be invisible.

And how many are we.
Millions of little women
Crying at home for our partners, anguished we measure the time.
Write cheery letters as tears blot the ink.
Wait for the post: "Does he who wrote it live?"
At table one place is empty, hot food sticks in the throat,
Alone in bed we muse: "Where is the other resting?"
She prays and plans, how she will make his meals,
Spare him from worry, try always to please him,
Never make excuses, gently accept his words,
Tiptoe around him, heal his heart with quietness,
Forget mutually all the terrible sights,
"God, bring him back, him only! If he is ill I shall heal him,
If crippled cure him, I shall restore his life,
If disfigured he can look into the mirror of my heart,
If changed I shall return him to his real self,
Let my life be a small gift, dedicated to him!
How good we shall be after this: simple, peaceful, tolerant!
How can survivors from the avalanche lose their balance on a pebble?"
So say the women now, painfully measuring time
To preserve a little sanity, prostrate from alien work.
Dressing the wounds of strangers, might God notice us after all,
If he isn't hiding in shame under cover of his wide sky?
Alas, among all the sufferers, I shall never be noticed.

And yet . . . only you and I!
I call out to you on this grim night,
Nothing beyond us exists, we have only ourselves!
And if we go, with the shutting of our eyes the whole world ceases. . . .
Do you remember? This summer, above stones in the ancient forum
And tombs of ancient virgins we called out to each other,
And at the foot of beautiful hills you said, "Wars were fought here."
Did we feel any tremor then, in our wholly private world?
You, my companion, partner, first true love;
I, your companion, partner, and first true love;
Exploring our two hearts we exclaimed, "It is one!"

Amazed, with no embarrassment, we embraced.
Listen, my love! This catastrophe is not happening to us,
It's an accident without sense or cause from within us,
We only exist for one another: faith, life, dedication.
We have tried it and together can live anywhere on earth,
Somewhere we lit a candle, around us peace sang out.
Do you remember the balcony, overlooking that olive grove,
A pretty stone fountain below us cascading in the moonlight?
"Now I am happy!" there I said that, the first time I ever said that.
Gently you covered me, for suddenly a cold wind hissed,
And next morning news came you had to go. The world continued,
Avalanche started, storms raged, the world sank. . . .
Look, here is a secret, I'll tell you why it all happened:
Because for the first time ever I said, "Now I'm happy," I said it!
Though God is eternal in his jealousy you and I were one,
And God who wrought it cannot alter that.

You far away, I here,
We view the same moon, our hearts rest together.
Though no moment of our lives is similar, and news takes weeks to come,
Though you march through mud and blood, through winter fields,
And I write in tears by your sad and empty bed
What can happen to us?
Will they kill you? I will confound that weapon
Never pausing to let it discover your dear heart.
As of old we are one, our path continues as one.
Could time blur my image?
I need only say one word, you will recognise me,
Returning from anywhere to Solveig's evening song.
I am sealed within your heart, as a brand upon your arm;
Love is strong as death, hard as a coffin
Is true love.

Budapest, 1914

Translated by Charlotte Franklin

"Záporos folytonos levél," in *Az Élet Utján* (Budapest: Nyugat, 1918), 86–89.

✝ Henriette Sauret-Arnyvelde
(1890–1976) *French*

The daughter of the liberal general Henry-Sébastien Sauret, Henriette became a journalist and a member of the French Union for Female Suffrage. She married the journalist André Arnyvelde, who died in 1942. Besides journalism, she published short stories, poetry, and biographies; *Je respire* (I breathe) appeared just before the war. She moved in avant-garde circles, meeting feminist and pacifist leaders.

During the war Sauret did volunteer work, including accounting, sawing wood, and even pulling a cart of coal. From September 1914 she ran a soup kitchen at Pantin, a suburb of Paris. She wrote for *La voix des femmes* (Women's voice) from 1917, and when Hélène Brion was arrested for pacifist activities, Sauret was her active defender. Her volume of political poetry, *Les forces détournées 1914–1917* (Forces deflected, 1918), with a preface by the leading feminist Séverine, was censored, omitting the last six lines of "Old Age Asylum" and parts of other poems. A second volume on the war followed, *L'amour à la Géhenne* (Love in Gehenna, 1919). She denounced the debasement of language by war, and especially the lies told to women to encourage them to maintain order on the home front and become "baby-makers." Her poetry exploited women's assignment to the hearth to charge them with their obligation to protect their family by opposing the war. In it she drew on fairy-tale images to depict the war as an ogress.

Her radical politics aligned her with the republicans during the Spanish Civil War, when she adapted Sofia Blasco's *People of Spain, War Diary of the Madrecita* (1938); in the same year she dedicated a study to the French feminist Marie-Louise Bouglé, *Une apôtre sociale* (Social apostle, 1938).

✝ The Ladies' Peace

Marguerite of Austria and Louise of Savoy,
Seeing endless war destroy their states,
Went to Cambrai without guard or display,
For a feminine solution to these debates.

Not seeing each other as the foe,
But ranking parties and sterile hate
Beneath the sum of human woe,
These two women of one mind met.

No doubt together then they shed
Tears at so many killed in vain
And cursed the stubborn, fatal heads
Of those whose nature rancor changed.

With the calm faith of loyal hearts,
They talked over all of this,
Then worked out the points and parts
Of the charming Ladies' Peace.

I like this reasoned, gallant treaty.
Who might now show such wise address?
Who could renew the intelligent feat
You once performed, o deep princesses?

1914

"La paix des dames," in *La voix des femmes* (April 17, 1918).

✝ Old Age Asylum

Among the people in hurried waves who left
the train, they bobbed in a slow and somber wake.
One by one I studied them, astonished.
Were these faces—hidden in bonnets, beneath
black hats—these rags, these little heaps of grey,
these crumpled skins? How old these old ones were!
Could one be older? Not a thought in their eyes.
Mere scraps, debris, pulled from a box and hauled out
terrified. A few solicitous nuns
led forth the parade of all these fearful forms,
while the exhausted old ones clutched their arms.
The grimacing troop advanced step by step.

The crowd murmured, "It's Saint Christopher's.
It's people from the asylum.—They've escaped
catastrophe, poor people, by leaving in haste.
This little hunchback, who trembles—he is one hundred
years old. This one is blind and that one babbles,
The third's a deaf mute. . . . The aged woman they carry
is paralyzed. . . . And they have saved them all!
What coolness, what authority it required!
It's truly superb! These sisters are heroic!"
Each observer stresses in rapturous terms.
Then the Mother Superior with some pride
recounts the adventure and its various risks.
"I had ten bed-bound; of those, four quite sick.
The townsfolk had already fled.
Cannon fire shattered the dormitory panes.
We had less than an hour to leave.
I didn't waste time!"
She was headstrong, skillful, willful,
to steal from death these quaking wretches!
She's as black as they, black from collar to toe.
Yet her height marks her out,
beside these twisted spines, so very straight.
The hollow within her stiff headdress sets off
her face, an almost luminous mask of white,
in contrast to the old ones' somber traits.
But this cold guide who shields her pitiful suite,
sister to the old—is she herself alive?
leading in ritual pomp her infernal cortege
she says serenely, with meaning, to herself:
"They have reached harbor at last, by the grace of God. . . .
Thank you, my Lord!" Indeed it is cause for joy
to have sheltered these, my sister. They will extend
sterile minutes. Useless nuisances, they
will endure, they'll vegetate at ease.
                                        Meanwhile,
We throw beneath the shells our radiant children.

September 1914

"Asile de Vieïllards," in *La voix des femmes* (April 17, 1918).

✝ Anna Akhmatova, pseudonym of Anna Andreyevna Gorenko (1889–1966) *Russian*

Anna Akhmatova, one of the greatest poets of the twentieth century, was the fourth of six children born into the family of a naval officer in a suburb of Odessa. Her father was dismissed by the secretary of the navy for having been friends with a revolutionary. A notorious philanderer with many illegitimate children, he sent his family away in 1905. This breakup of her family devastated Anna, who tried to commit suicide by hanging herself, but failed when the nail popped from the wall. Tuberculosis ran through her family; her mother and her three sisters died of it. Akhmatova herself suffered chronically from tuberculosis and Graves' disease. Her early education was private or acquired on her own; she started writing poetry at age eleven. Although she studied law at Kiev, she left school to marry the poet Nikolai Gumilyov in 1910. Together they traveled to Africa and France, and she gave birth to a son in 1912. When their marriage failed, she had several passionate affairs.

With Osip Mandelstam and Nikolai Gumilyov, Akhmatova played a leading role in the literary movement of acmeism. She assumed the name of her great-grandmother for her first volume of poetry, *Vecher* (Evening, 1912). Influenced by symbolism and acmeism, her poetry evoked loneliness and passion with aphoristic lucidity. Her emotional distresses sought refuge and release in religion, nature, and poetry. The duality of her persona, both pure and passionate, became popular with the public as an image of the feminine and led critic Boris Eichenbaum to refer to her as "half nun, half harlot."

When war was declared on July 19, 1914, by the Russian calendar, Akhmatova prophetically remarked, "We aged a hundred years, and it all happened in an hour." Devotion to her country kept her from emigrating during the war and subsequent revolution, saying that it took greater courage to stay behind and accept what came. She recorded the gruesome destruction and tragedy: "All is sold, all is lost, all is plundered, Death's wing has flashed black on our sight, all's gnawed bare with sore, want, and sick longing." Although the period from 1914 to 1922 was one of her most productive, much of her writing was not published until later.

The advent of the Soviet Union brought repression and personal loss: her former husband Gumilyov was shot in 1921, and Stalin imprisoned their son in labor camps three times. Her second husband (who burned her manuscripts) died of tuberculosis a year after their marriage; her third husband, Nikolai Punin, perished in a labor camp a few weeks before Stalin's death. During World War II, she was evacuated to Tashkent, where her work vanished from view. Only in 1964 was she permitted to travel outside Russia to receive the Italian Etna Taormina Prize. In 1965 she received an honorary doctorate from Oxford University.

TP

☦ July 1914

1

There's a burning smell. Four weeks
the dry peat's been burning in the bogs.
Even the birds haven't sung today,
the aspen no longer shivers.

The sun's become disfavored by God,
since Easter no rain sprinkles the fields.
A one-legged passerby came through
and, alone in the courtyard, said:

"Horrible times are near. Soon
we'll be crowded with fresh graves.
Expect famine, tremors, death all around,
eclipsing of the heaven's lights.

Except the enemy won't divide
our land as easily as that:
the Mother of God will unfurl her white
folds over our great griefs."

2

A sweet fragrance of juniper
floats from the burning woods.
For their soldier boys the wives are wailing,
widows' moans ring through the fields.

Not in vain were the public prayers,
O how the earth yearned for rain!
With red liquid the trampled fields
were warmly watered.

Low, low the empty sky,
and a voice is softly praying:
"They wound Your holy body,
they gamble for Your robes."

July 29, 1914, Slepnyovo

Translated by John Henriksen

"Iyul' 1914," in *The Complete Poems of Anna Akhmatova,* ed. and with an introduction by Roberta Reeder (Somerville, MA: Zephyr, 1990), 1:426–428.

✝ Prayer

Give me bitter years, sick,
gasping, sleepless, fevered,
take away my child, my friend,
my secret gift of song—
that's what I pray at your liturgy
after so many days of torment,
to make the stormcloud over dark Russia
a white cloud in sunrays' glory.

May 1915. Day of the Holy Ghost. Petersburg

Translated by John Henriksen

"Molitva," in *The Complete Poems of Anna Akhmatova,* ed. and with an introduction by Roberta Reeder (Somerville, MA: Zephyr, 1990), 1:434.

✝ In Memoriam, July 19, 1914

We aged a hundred years, and it
all happened in an hour.
The short summer was already dying,
smoke rose from the plowed plains' body.

All of a sudden the quiet road grew colorful,
a lament took off flying, silverly ringing.
I covered my face and begged God
to kill me off before the battles began.

Like a load now unneeded, songs' and passions'
shadows have vanished from memory, which
the High One has ordered emptied, to become
a terrible book of calamities to come.

Summer 1916. Slepnyovo.

Translated by John Henriksen

"Pamyati, 19 iyulya 1914," in *The Complete Poems of Anna Akhmatova,* ed. and with an introduction by Roberta Reeder (Somerville, MA: Zephyr, 1990), 1:448, 450.

☦ When in the Sad Boredom of Suicide

When in the sad boredom of suicide
the people awaited its German guests,
and the spirit of severe Byzantium
flew from the Russian Church,
when the capital on the Neva,
forgetting its majesty,
didn't know, like a drunken
streetwalker, who would take her,
I heard a voice. Consolingly it called,
it said, "Come here,
leave your deaf and sinful home,
leave Russia for good.
I'll wash the blood off your hands,
pull the black shame from your heart,
I'll hide the pain of defeats and insults
under new names."
But with equanimity and calm
I stopped up my ears with my hands,
so my saddened spirit would not be stained
by that unworthy speech.

Autumn 1917

Translated by John Henriksen

"Korda v toske samouiystve," in *The Complete Poems of Anna Akhmatova,* ed. and with an introduction by Roberta Reeder (Somerville, MA: Zephyr, 1990), 1:528, 530.

✚ Zinaida Nikolaevna Gippius
(1869–1945) *Russian*

As a poet, dramatist, and prolific writer of short fiction, Zinaida Gippius helped initiate Russia's symbolist movement. Well known for her literary talent and her shocking rejection of social conventions, Gippius was a central figure in St. Petersburg's avant-garde circle from the 1890s until her emigration in 1917. Influenced by decadence and mysticism, her early works sought release through free verse, surprising diction, synesthesia, and popular narrative. Later, she adopted a more intellectual and abstract style that revealed uncertainty and conflict. Gippius achieved notoriety by attacking biological sexual difference. She adopted a masculine or androgynous persona and rejected stereotypical notions of women's roles, writing, for example, to the younger poet Nina Berberova, "Frankly, I feel no maternal feelings for you; in fact, in general I don't seem to be capable of such feelings." Though she was married to the poet and slavophile Dmitrii Sergeevich Merezhkovsky, she also became involved with other men and women. Her shifts between aggressive eroticism and sexual ambivalence aroused the resentment of several contemporary male intellectuals. Trotsky wrote of her, "I do not believe in witches in general, not counting the above-mentioned Zinaida Gippius, in whose reality I believe absolutely, though about the length of her tail I can say nothing definite."

Between 1910 and 1917, when her country was ravaged by war, Gippius wrote prolifically. She commented, "I reject wars, because each war which ends with the victory of one state over another carries the seed of a new war, because it gives birth to national resentment, and each war retards the achievement of our ideal, ecumenicity." Though she initially supported not only Aleksandr Kerensky but the Bolsheviks, Gippius later attacked the October revolution, commenting that "The Neva's ice is bloody and drunken. . . . O, Nicholas's noose was cleaner than these cold monkeys' fingers." After 1919 she and her husband lived in exile, eventually becoming the center of an avant-garde circle in Paris that counted among its members Nikolai Berdyaev and Vasilii Rozanov. She published in the French symbolist journal *Mercure de France*. She and her husband supported Jozef Piłsudski against the Bolsheviks and later Mussolini and Hitler against Stalin.

TP

✝ Adonai

Thy peoples wail: for how long?
Thy peoples from the north and south,
Art Thou still unquenched? Permit
The sons of earth to cease their murder of each other.

Was it not Thou who shattered the words on the tablets,
Preparing the earth for another sowing?
And here again, again Thou art Jehovah,
The bloody God of vengeance and wrath.

Thou hast poured smoke and flame along the seas,
Thou hast garbed the land with scarlet water.
Thou destroyeth the flesh . . . But, Lord,
Thy weapon penetrates the soul of mothers.

Was not She enough
Who stood then under the cross early in the morning?
No, not for us, but for Her sake, for Her alone,
Remove the iron from maternal wounds!

Oh, touch the smoking-crimson haze,
Not with ancient terror—but with Love.
Father! Father! Bend to Thy earth:
It is soaked with Filial blood.

St. Petersburg, 1914

Translated by Temira Pachmuss

"Adonai," from *Zinaida Hippius, an Intellectual Profile*, by Temira Pachmuss (Carbondale: Southern Illinois University Press, 1971), 185. Copyright © 1971 Southern Illinois University Press.

✝ Without Justification

No, I shall never be reconciled.
My curses are genuine.

I shall not forgive, I shall not fall
   Into iron clutches.

Like everyone living, I shall die, I shall kill,
   Like everyone, I shall destroy myself,
But I shall not stain my soul
   In justification.

At the final hour, in darkness, in fire,
   Let not my heart forget:
There is no justification for war
   And there never will be.

And if this is the command of God—
   A bloody path—
My spirit will go into battle even against Him,
   Will rise up even against God.

April 1916. St. Petersburg

Translated by Temira Pachmuss

"Bez opravdanya," from *Zinaida Hippius, an Intellectual Profile,* by Temira Pachmuss (Carbondale: Southern Illinois University Press, 1971), 183. Copyright © 1971 Southern Illinois University Press.

☦ Today on Earth

There is something so hard,
something so shameful.
Almost impossible—
something so hard:

This is to lift one's lashes
and look into the face of a mother
Whose son has been killed.

But don't talk about it.

September 20, 1916. St. Petersburg

Translated by John Henriksen

"Segodnya na zemle," in *Stikhi: dnevnik, 1911–1921* (Berlin: Slovo, 1922), 62. Reprinted in Z. N. Hippius, *Collected Poetical Works,* ed. Temira Pachmuss (Munich: Wilhelm Fink, 1972).

✝ Marina Ivanova Tsvetaeva
(1892–1941) *Russian*

Born into an intellectual, artistic family in Moscow, Marina Tsvetaeva was exposed to the creative community at an early age. Her mother gave her rigorous musical training, lessons reflected in the rhythmic novelty of her poetry. She was fluent in French and German, and could read Greek and Latin. An art professor at the University of Moscow, her father later became director of the Moscow Fine Arts Museum. Her mother died in 1906. In 1910 she published a collection of poetry privately. In 1912 she married the eighteen-year-old student Sergey Efron and gave birth to her first of three children. Separated by the war from Efron, who served as an orderly, she had several love affairs with both men and women; the importance of her lesbian experiences is revealed in *Letter to an Amazon* (1932).

Torn between Russia and Germany, and absorbed by her emotional conflicts, she responded to World War I by turning to folklore motifs. She repeatedly voiced her distance from violence and parades by soldiers "the color of ashes and sand." Yet strife was one of her themes: "I can be grasped only in terms of contrasts, of the simultaneous presence of everything. . . . I am many poets; how I've managed to harmonize all of them is my secret."

She suffered great hardship in the years following the 1917 October revolution; one daughter died of malnutrition in a government orphanage. After the revolution she wrote several plays and cycles of poems. "My poems are a diary," she confessed. Her work was acclaimed by Aleksandr Blok, Vladimir Mayakovsky, Osip Mandelstam, and Boris Pasternak. She emigrated in 1922, going to Prague with Efron, who had fought with the White Army against the Bolsheviks, then to Paris in 1925. Living among exiles, she formed alliances with Rainer Maria Rilke, Anna Akhmatova, and Marcel Proust.

In the 1930s she became estranged from Efron, who embraced Soviet politics and worked as a Russian spy. After he narrowly escaped arrest in

1939, Tsvetaeva found herself ostracized by fellow exiles and in financial straits. She moved back to Russia, where within months of her arrival Efron was executed and her daughter and sister were sent to labor camps. In 1941 she and her son were evacuated to the Tartar Autonomous Republic; she hanged herself and was buried in an unmarked mass grave. Her son joined the army and is presumed to have been killed in action.

TP

☦ The War, the War!

The war, the war!—censings by icon cases
and the rattle of spurs.
But I have no business with the Czar's accounts,
with national spats.

On the tightrope seemingly frayed
I'm a small dancer.
I'm a shadow of someone's shadow. I'm a sleep walker
Of two dark moons.

July 16, 1914, Moscow

Translated by John Henriksen

"Voina, voina!" in *Stikhotvoreniya i poemy*, ed. Alexandr Sumerkin and Viktoria Schweitzer (New York: Russica, 1980), 1:172.

☦ I Know the Truth!

I know the truth! All earlier truths—begone!
On earth people shouldn't fight people.
Look, it's evening. Look, soon it will be night.
Poets, lovers, regimental commanders—what *about*?

Now the wind is creeping up, the earth is in dew,
Soon the stars' blizzard will freeze in the sky,
Under the ground we will all fall asleep,
Those who did not put each other to sleep on earth.

October 3, 1915

Translated by John Henriksen

"Ya znayu pravdu! vse prezhnie pravdy proch!" in *Stikhotvoreniya i poemy*, ed. Alexandr Sumerkin and Viktoria Schweitzer (New York: Russica, 1980), 1:194.

✝ The White Sun and Low, Low Stormclouds

The white sun and low, low stormclouds,
beside the gardens—behind a white wall—a graveyard.
And on the sand a row of scarecrows made of straw,
under cross-beams, tall as humans.

And, leaning through the fence slats,
I see: roads, trees, soldiers scattered.
An old woman—by the gate she chews and chews
A hunk of thick black bread with salt.

How did those grey huts get you so enraged—
God!—and why sweep bullets over so many chests?
A train went by and howled, and the soldiers howled,
and the retreating path was dusty, dusty . . .

—No, dying! Never being born would be better
than that piteous, mournful, convicts' wail
about black-browed beauties.—Oh, they're singing
now, the soldiers. O thou my Lord God.

Translated by John Henriksen

"Beloe sol'ntse," in *Stikhotvoreniya i poemy*, ed. Alexandr Sumerkin and Viktoria Schweitzer (New York: Russica, 1980), 1:238.

✝ Jessie Pope
(1868–1941) *English*

B orn in Leicester, Jessie Pope attended North London College. She married Edward Babington Lenton. Her humorous verse and articles appeared in the fashionable journal *Punch,* as well as newspapers and other magazines. Pope published several volumes of light verse, carrying impertinent titles such as *Paper Pellets* and *Hits and Misses,* as well as three volumes of war poetry. She also produced light fiction, primarily for children, and derived part of her income from advertising.

✝ Socks

Shining pins that dart and click
   In the fireside's sheltered peace
Check the thoughts that cluster thick—
   20 plain and then decrease.

He was brave—well, so was I—
   Keen and merry, but his lip
Quivered when he said good-bye—
   Purl the seam-stitch, purl and slip.

Never used to living rough,
   Lots of things he'd got to learn;
Wonder if he's warm enough—
   Knit 2, catch 2, knit 1, turn.

Hark! The paper-boys again!
  Wish that shout could be suppressed;
Keeps one always on the strain—
  Knit off 9, and slip the rest.

Wonder if he's fighting now,
  What he's done an' where he's been;
He'll come out on top, somehow—
  Slip 1, knit 2, purl 14.

"Socks," in *War Poems* (London: Grant Richards, 1915).

✠ Sarojini Naidu
(1879–1949) *Indian*[1]

✠ The Gift of India

Is there aught you need that my hands withhold,
Rich gifts of raiment or grain or gold?
Lo! I have flung to the East and West
Priceless treasures torn from my breast,
And yielded the sons of my stricken womb
To the drum-beats of duty, the sabres of doom.

Gathered like pearls in their alien graves
Silent they sleep by the Persian waves,
Scattered like shells on Egyptian sands,
They lie with pale brows and brave, broken hands,
They are strewn like blossoms mown down by chance
On the blood-brown meadows of Flanders and France.

Can ye measure the grief of the tears I weep
Or compass the woe of the watch I keep?
Or the pride that thrills through my heart's despair
And the hope that comforts the anguish of prayer?
And the far sad glorious vision I see
Of the torn red banners of Victory?

When the terror and tumult of hate shall cease
And life be refashioned on anvils of peace,

1. See page 64.

And your love shall offer memorial thanks
To the comrades who fought in your dauntless ranks,
And you honour the deeds of the deathless ones
Remember the blood of thy martyred sons!

August 1915

"The Gift of India," in *The Broken Wing* (London: Heinemann, 1917), 55.

✝ Poliksena Sergeevna Soloviëva
(1867–1923) *Russian*

Poliksena Soloviëva was born into an illustrious family; her father was president of Moscow University and her older brother Vladimir a poet and philosopher. As a young woman she studied painting and voice; she published several poems in symbolist journals and illustrated her own poems. Soloviëva stopped writing for a decade, then began to write again after moving to St. Petersburg in 1895. She befriended other writers, including Zinaida Gippius. Her poem "Hoarfrost," praised by Aleksandr Blok, received the Pushkin Prize in 1908. She addressed her poetry in a male voice to a female figure; written in simple meter, her works tended to be introspective, centering on themes of nature, grief, and loneliness. Between 1906 and 1913, with her companion, N. I. Manaseina, she created a children's magazine to which leading writers contributed. Soloviëva dressed and acted a male role throughout her life; the war made her sexual preference acceptable. *Latest Poems* appeared the year of her death.
TP

✝ To the War

Harboring a secret, foreign will
I must humbly do my heroic deed:
With deadly iron on the field of war
I'm sent to plow a bloody rut.

Forgetting my house, friends, family
I go. With each step our ranks are thinned,
Bullets buzz and ring, forgetting . . .
Onward, always onward! No path back.

All that I lived and I breathed on the eve
Withdraws like a far, unfeasible dream,
And the thought that dissolves in the bloody breaker
Stands up still like a cross of iron.

And the heart, burning, loving, angered
Foresees the eternal light in pitch-black hell:
For the world to come I go into battle,
For the life to come I go to death.

Translated by John Henriksen

"Voine," in *Voina v russkoi lirike,* ed. Vladislav Khodasevich (Moscow: universal 'naia biblioteka, 1915), 109.

✠ Maria Dobler Benemann
(1887–1979?) *German*

One of the strongest influences on Maria Dobler's life and convictions was her pietist inheritance from the Herrnhuter grandparents on her father's side, who had been missionaries in Surinam. Her father, Johann Theodor Dobler, retained dual citizenship and devoted himself to an ethnographic museum of materials collected by missionaries; he conveyed to his daughter a revulsion at the noisy patriotism associated with Prussians and at the racism his parents had fought. Her mother's cultured Mennonite family was somewhat more worldly. Although accidentally set on fire as a child, Maria was not visibly scarred; her beauty was such that in later years many of her artist friends painted her portrait.

In 1906 Maria married Gerhard Benemann, a bookseller, with whom she had two children. They moved about, living in Oldenburg, Hamburg, and then Berlin, where they set up the Horen Press and a bookstore that became an exhibition space for the artists' colony at Worpswede that included figures such as Paula Modersohn Becker and Rainer Maria Rilke. On a visit there, the thatched cottage Benemann had rented burned down, destroying her manuscript of her first book for children, influenced by Lewis Carroll, which was just ready for the press. Her poetry appeared in Franz Pfemfert's radical journal *Die Aktion,* in *Die weissen Blätter* (which published Rainer Maria Rilke, Franz Werfel, and Else Lasker-Schüler), and in a wartime anthology edited by the Berlin dramatist Julius Bab. Already in 1913 she wrote in one of her poems, "Catastrophes stand on the horizon, stiff with weapons."

In 1913–1914 Benemann developed an intense liaison with the established writer Richard Dehmel, which was broken off when his wife intercepted their correspondence. Dehmel gave Benemann insight into the literary and artistic landscape of Hamburg, exchanging poems with her. After their rupture, the erasure of her name from his correspondence and biography embittered her.

Her husband fought on the western front, and his diary entry about the

German army burning villages provided material for the poem included here; the story of his playing a piano in a ruined house in the small Belgian town of Visé was recounted to his wife by friends while on leave. After his death in 1914, she ran a guesthouse for artists and intellectuals, Bassah Selim's House; her lack of resources forced her to place her son and daughter with two different families. During the war she published *Wandlungen* (Changes, 1915), a collection of poems; *Die Reise zum Meer* (Journey to the sea, 1915), a collection of fairy tales; and *Kleine Novellen* (1916), a collection of short stories.

On a wartime visit to the émigré poet Franz Werfel in Zurich, Benemann caught glimpses of Lenin, Trotsky, the French pacifist Romain Rolland, and Claire Studer (later Goll), whose poetry she praised for its beautiful lyric confessions. With Werfel, unlike Dehmel, she said that she found herself on an even intellectual level. Other friends in these years included the art historian Aby Warburg, the architect Walter Gropius, and painters Emil Nolde and Paul Klee. Returning to Blankenhain near Weimar to live with her two children, she gave herself to social work for impoverished outcasts and inmates of a madhouse, some of them victims of the war. Apolitical, she nonetheless stood publicly against the war in its final phases and was courted by communists and reviled by right-wing patriots, who tried to deny her access to ration cards. In the economic depression that followed the war, she writes of seeing soldiers whose unrestrained tears bore witness to unspeakable suffering.

Besides poetry, Benemann wrote scholarly prose and a requiem that was set to music. Her autobiography, *Leih mir noch einmal die leichte Sandale, Erinnerungen und Begegnungen* (Lend me once more the light sandals, 1978), was edited by her son, Joachim.

✝ Visé (After a Letter from the Field)

Smoke-black the air, the city in rubble,
buildings reduced to beams all charred
that strew the streets like barricades.
No roof shields the weary, just distant stars.

On paving stones troops take hard rest,
barely covered by a coat.
Around, fatigue-dulled men breathe deep,
while you alone lie awake so late.

Behind, a heap of ashes haunts you,
an elegant house that you transformed
when hunting for a sniper's nest.

One room still held an instrument,
above it a fearful Virgin hung:
the quiet greeting and silent respite
caught you in their sudden embrace.

As light waned you plucked some chords,
hollow echoes of the home's dead souls.
The Queen you salvaged in your coat
to bring her to me, when you make peace.

Then set fresh flames: you do your duty,
blow this house up like all the rest.
. . . Was that a cry? or just a broken string?
Music, music behind you has collapsed.

1915

"Visé," in *1914, Der deutsche Krieg im deutschen Gedicht,* ed. Julius Bab (Berlin: Morawe, 1914–1919), 2:23. Reprinted by permission of Hans Christians Druckerei.

✝ Esther Harlan
German

✝ In the Kitchen

I make up my fire, I wash my cabbage.
Then he trudges in, my little Ulan.
Already wears his enormous coat.
"Farewell, sister, farewell!"

"You, a boy of sixteen years!
Not yet six months have gone
Since you shot sparrows in the garden.
What has happened in your soul?"

"Whoever can hit a sparrow
May well hit an Englishman.
Farewell, my dear. And do not weep.
Quick, a kiss! Quick, another!"

He clattered off. Now upon the stove
the pots . . . miserably undisturbed.
I peel the potatoes . . .
Oh my boy, to be in your place!

1915–16

Translated by Trudi Nicholas

"In der Küche," in *1914, Der deutsche Krieg im deutschen Gedicht,* ed. Julius Bab (Berlin: Morawe, 1914–1919), 6:31.

✠ Růžena Jesenská
(1863–1940) *Czech*

B orn in Prague into a family of modest means with many children, Růžena Jesenská trained to become a teacher. Her choice dictated celibacy while confronting her with the problems of a woman in a world of men. In her autobiographical collection of poetry, *Mladi* (1926), she gives a bitter account of the moral confrontations and animosities that affected advancement in her career. She was a woman of great determination and effectiveness, who began her literary career by composing didactic literature for girls and young women, then expanded her range to include poems, fiction, and drama in an oeuvre of nineteen volumes.

Jesenská's art is disciplined, unconventional, and free from the sentimentalism that weakened much Czech women's writing of the 1880s. Her truncated images and syntax achieve startling symbolist effects. While drawing her inspiration from contemporary events and conditions, she at the same time writes against the current, as the critic Jan Opolsky has pointed out. Often pensive, she also wrote comic dramas toward the end of her career. Jesenská edited first a children's periodical, *Dětské Besedy Máje* (Children's Maytime chat), then a calendar for women and girls. In 1929 she was elected a member of the Czech Academy, where her unbiased work on commissions was valued. When Jesenská's niece Milena became the friend of Franz Kafka, however, she displaced her aunt as a significant figure in Czech literary history.

EJ

✠ Fate

On a long path, a long
bridge arches over the river,
and in the tempo of ticking clocks
a crowd like a cloud passes over,
on their sad foreheads one sign:
fathers of families, children of families.

The bells are just ringing over the city
to all the endless pains
and their dissolved hearts
run down in a rain of metallic tears . . .
Then don't stare in the darkness of your eyes:
Behind every shadow a child, a woman.

The clouds of people go and go
through the air of clear freedom . . .
"Where is the root of our fates,
O God?" asked one of them.
And the last one sighs like a child,
"I was created in your image."

A long bridge arches over the river
into the long, long path ahead.
And with burning *presto* the bells shriek:
Never will he return, never,
from the bloody swoonings of ballads,
of images of God's millions.

1915   Translated by Eva Jonas

"Osud," in *Poslání, Básně* (Prague: Král. Vinohrady, 1919), 19–20.

✝ To Our People

Please tell our people: you storms blowing
away our last words, imprint
the images of atrocities and death, you floating clouds,
upon all eyes at home, let the fire blossom for them
from the purple of our blood, so that hearts will beat firmly
and brave strength enter their soul.

Please tell our people: you unmarked stones,
we of their kin lie dead here,
as the natural law of holy love preached,
we had to die for the life and freedom
of our distant country: May our shield be their defence
and support—as we fall, let them rise!

1918   Translated by Eva Jonas

"Našim," in *Poslání, Básně* (Prague: Král. Vinohrady, 1919), 30.

☩ Gertrud E. Fauth
(b. 1886) *German*

A teacher and writer, Gertrud Fauth studied in Munich and Strassburg, where she received a doctorate in 1914 for her study of the novelist Jörg Wickram. Between 1920 and 1934 she produced classroom texts, such as imitations of Aeschylus and Daniel Defoe, compilations of modern poetry, and books on the Orient for girls. She wrote a Wagnerian novel and a few poems.

☩ The First One

It was on patrol that he shot the first one.
Who fell face down from his nag.
Did not move.
He crawled from his cover of ripened barley,
turned the body over.
Saw: the dilated pupils, the fingers curled,
cigarette in the convulsing lips.
He muttered (casually, with wagging finger),
spat the dull taste from his tongue:
"One of the careless sheep.
Pity—it was a Norman boy."
But in the evening
   He could not sleep.

1916–17

Translated by Trudi Nicholas

"Der Erste," in *1914, Der deutsche Krieg im deutschen Gedicht,* ed. Julius Bab (Berlin: Morawe, 1914–1919), 10:13.

✝ Countess Anna de Noailles, née de Brancovan (1876–1933) *French*

Born in Paris, Anna de Brancovan was the daughter of a Romanian prince and a Greek mother; both parents were patriotically devoted to France, their adopted country. The family embraced French republican tradition; Anna and her husband maintained this liberal tradition by their support for Alfred Dreyfus, the Jewish soldier falsely accused of treason, during his second trial in 1898–1899. Educated in a richly artistic environment first by her father, then by an uncle, Anna began to write verse (much of it melancholy or sentimental) at age ten, when her father died. In 1897 she married Mathieu, Comte de Noailles; their son was born in 1900. Heeding her mother's advice, she had not yet published her poetry, but she now brought out her first volume, *Le coeur innombrable* (Incalculable heart), in 1901. Their home in Paris soon became the center of a literary and aristocratic circle that included Colette, Marcel Proust, André Gide, Paul Valéry, and Edith Wharton. She had liaisons with Maurice Barrès and with his nephew, who committed suicide.

"I want to be 100 men!" was young Anna's response to a military parade. When war actually erupted, she offered advice to neighbors such as Georges Clemenceau. While her husband fought in Belgium she volunteered briefly as a nurse in a clinic. The wartime poetry gathered in *Les forces éternelles* (Eternal forces, 1921) strikes a somber, if elevated, note of admiration and grief.

Devoted to an art that was "useless but irreplaceable," Noailles cultivated a classical verse form, richly adjectival and orientalizing. As the title of her first volume suggests, she invested in sensual verse images of the passions, of suicide, of failed love. Colette praised her "wildness" and idiosyncracy. Called the "muse of the kitchen garden" by critics, she has been left out of mainstream literary history. Noailles herself claimed that her writing was shaped by the opposing forces of "the bacchante and the nun."

Elected a member of the Belgian Royal Academy for French Language
and Literature in 1922, she was also named commander in the Legion of
Honor.

JS

✠ Our Dead

Stars that behold our world upon its way,
Pure legions camped upon the plains of night,
Mute watchful hosts of heaven, what must you say
When men destroy each other in their might?

Upon their deadly race each runner starts,
Nor one but will his brothers all outrun!
Ah, see their blood jet upward to the sun
Like living fountains refluent on our hearts,

—O dead divinely for so great a faith,
Help us, whose agony is but begun,
For bitterly we yield you up to death,
We who had dreamed that life and love were one.

Translated by Edith Wharton

"Our Dead," in *The Book of the Homeless,* ed. Edith Wharton (New York: Scribner's,
1916), 21–22.

✠ Verdun

Silence cloaks this world-famous name:
A boundless morrow wraps Verdun.
There French men came, one by one,
Step by step, by days, by hours,
To prove their most proud, most stoic love.

In the stygian test they have fallen asleep.

Their trembling widow, immortal Verdun,
As if to implore their transcendent return
Raises the two arms of her two high towers.

Passerby, do not seek to praise the place
Sheltered by angels sprung from French soil.
Blood pours in such plenty that no human voice
May mingle its vain and febrile complaint
With the endless vapors of this earthly incense.
In the carved and scarred plain here see
The sainted, unsounded power of the land
Whose finest hearts lie at rest beneath.

In this place one cannot give death a name,
So truly did each consent to that gift.
By swallowing all, earth made itself man.

Passerby, measure your gesture and words.
Watch, adore, pray—do not speak what you feel.

1917

"Verdun," in *Les forces éternelles* (Paris: Fayard, 1920), 13–14.

✠ Dame Edith Sitwell
(1887–1964) *British*

Poet, trendsetter, and artistic innovator, Edith Sitwell was the firstborn of the affluent and genteel Sir George and Lady Ida Sitwell. With her brothers Osbert and Sacheverell she suffered from her parents' oppression; they insisted she wear clamps on her nose and back, "a sort of Bastille of steel." While her brothers were educated at Eton, she took lessons at home from a series of governesses who familiarized her with classic English and French poetry, as well as pre-Raphaelite and symbolist verse. At twenty-six she moved from home to London with a former governess as her companion, to devote herself to her poetry.

Sitwell's first wartime volume, *The Mother,* and a collaboration with Osbert, *Twentieth-Century Harlequinade,* both appeared in 1916, a year in which she and her brothers also launched the radical anthology *Wheels,* to contest Georgian aesthetics. Over the next years *Wheels* presented work by Nancy Cunard, Iris Tree, Aldous Huxley, and Wilfred Owen, in a group of poets the *Times Literary Supplement* found "far too much inclined to stand outside the scene of life, grumble and make faces, and roll big words in their mouths." Experimental rhyme, imagism, nonsense, and eccentricity mark these volumes and her first major works, *Clowns' Houses* (1918) and *The Wooden Pegasus* (1920).

After publishing seven poems by Wilfred Owen in *Wheels,* Sitwell was asked to edit his work after his death, but Siegfried Sassoon in the end took over the project. Sitwell was deeply moved by Owen's work, which hits "home so hard that one finds oneself crying." To Robert Nichols, a poet and soldier, she wrote that the armistice "has made one's nerve go all to pieces, this sudden relief from the intolerable pain." She celebrated Armistice Day with the Woolfs.

In her most experimental work, *Façade* (1923), influenced by modern dance, Sitwell performed to music by William Walton. Scorned by the press, her iconoclastic performance did not please the public either: her brother Osbert wrote that they went about London "feeling as if we had committed a murder." When restaged in 1926, however, *Façade* won praise from reviewers such as Rebecca West, who declared that Sitwell wrote poetry "as gay as a flower garden, its confused joyousness half heard through jazz music."

Sitwell considered Virginia Woolf, "one of the only people whom I *really* enjoy talking to." Through Gertrude Stein she met Pavel Tchelitchew, a homosexual artist to whom she became unhappily devoted. She continued to publish poetry throughout the twenties, shifting from energetic satire into more introspective themes in *The Sleeping Beauty* (1924), *Troy Park* (1925), and *Rustic Elegies* (1927). Starting with *Gold Coast Customs* (1929), like her friend T. S. Eliot, Sitwell emphasized the insincerity of modern life in rhythmic dissonant experiments. Yeats praised her metrical virtuosity and the way she "exaggerated metaphors into mythology."

World War II confronted her with "unceasing misery, wretchedness, and, in minor ways, the boredom." She fought to keep a skeleton of the arts alive, and worked to exempt conscientious objectors from prison. She criticized the dropping of the atomic bomb, turning in the late forties and fifties to religious and spiritual issues; she entered the Catholic Church with Evelyn Waugh as her godfather. Made a Dame Commander of the Order of the British Empire in 1954, she penned a caustic autobiography, *Taken Care Of,* which appeared posthumously in 1965.

KCS

✟ The Dancers

(During a Great Battle, 1916)

The floors are slippery with blood:
The world gyrates too. God is good
That while His wind blows out the light
For those who hourly die for us—
We still can dance, each night.

The music has grown numb with death—
But we will suck their dying breath,
The whispered name they breathed to chance,
To swell our music, make it loud
That we may dance,—may dance.

We are the dull blind carrion-fly
That dance and batten. Though God die
Mad from the horror of the light—
The light is mad, too, flecked with blood,—
We dance, we dance, each night.

"The Dancers," in *Clowns' Houses* (Oxford: Blackwell, 1918), 2. Reprinted by permission of David Higham Associates.

✝ Amy Lowell
(1874-1925) *American*

A pioneer in the American imagist movement, Amy Lowell was born into one of Boston's most eminent families. She spent her child-hood at the family estate, Sevenels, and was educated at private schools in Boston; she read in her father's library and traveled extensively. At thirteen, with the help of her mother, she published *Dream Drops, or Stories from Fairyland* under the pseudonym "Dreamer."

Lowell struggled with the demands of gentility, in a conflict whose symptoms were extreme overweight and occasional "nervous prostration." Eventually she renounced social expectations of conformity, dressed in men's clothing, smoked small cigars, and established a lifelong relation-ship with an older woman, the actress Ada Russell, for whom she wrote vividly erotic poems.

Lowell began writing poetry in 1902; her first collection, *A Dome of Many-Coloured Glass*, appeared in 1912. She soon abandoned romantic conventions, turning toward British modernists. On journeys to England in 1913 and 1914 Lowell met H. D. (Hilda Doolittle), Richard Aldington, and Ezra Pound; and in 1915–1917 she edited two imagist anthologies. She began experimenting with vers libre, abandoned rhyme, and focused on the imagist tenet that a poem should suggest a visual impression of an object or scene.

Her wartime volumes of poetry—*Sword Blades and Poppy Seeds* (1914), *Men, Women, and Ghosts* (1916), and *Can Grande's Castle* (1918)–embody her imagist innovations, particularly her attempts to develop unrhymed "polyphonic prose" and vers libre. In *The Egoist* (1915) Richard Aldington described her art as that of "a modern poet . . . a poet of personality, a poet recording moods, not maxims." Her hard-edged, unsentimental war poetry elicited praise for its sense of narrative, evocative rhythms, and piti-less exposure of "the gangrenes of our civilization." She felt "the world needs poetry more than it ever needed it. . . . Most people are lost in the maelstrom which the war brings." To remedy the "social illness" of war she

paid for nearly three dozen libraries of modern poetry for military training camps. John Gould Fletcher responded to her war poetry, "One would
almost say . . . such an arraignment of warfare could only have been written by a man."

Further echoes of the war reverberate in *Pictures of the Floating World*
(1919). Working with Florence Ayscough, Lowell translated Chinese
poetry in *Fir-Flower Tablets* (1921). *What's O'Clock* won the Pulitzer Prize
posthumously in 1926. She also published significant criticism, including
Six French Poets (1915), *Tendencies in Modern American Poetry* (1917), and a
biography of Keats.

KCS

‡ The Allies

August 14th, 1914

Into the brazen, burnished sky, the cry hurls itself. The zigzagging cry of
hoarse throats, it floats against the hard winds, and binds the head of the
serpent to its tail, the long snail-slow serpent of marching men. Men
weighed down with rifles and knapsacks, and parching with war. The cry
jars and splits against the brazen, burnished sky.

This is the war of wars, and the cause? Has this writhing worm of men
a cause?

Crackling against the polished sky is an eagle with a sword. The eagle is
red and its head is flame.

In the shoulder of the worm is a teacher.

His tongue laps the war-sucked air in drought, but he yells defiance at
the red-eyed eagle, and in his ears are the bells of new philosophies, and
their tinkling drowns the sputter of the burning sword. He shrieks, "God
damn you! When you are broken, the word will strike out new shoots."

His boots are tight, the sun is hot, and he may be shot, but he is in the
shoulder of the worm.

A dust speck in the worm's belly is a poet.

He laughs at the flaring eagle and makes a long nose with his fingers.
He will fight for smooth, white sheets of paper, and uncurdled ink. The
sputtering sword cannot make him blink, and his thoughts are wet and rip-
pling. They cool his heart.

He will tear the eagle out of the sky and give the earth tranquillity, and
loveliness printed on white paper.

The eye of the serpent is an owner of mills.

He looks at the glaring sword which has snapped his machinery and struck away his men.

But it will all come again, when the sword is broken to a million dying stars, and there are no more wars.

Bankers, butchers, shop-keepers, painters, farmers—men, sway and sweat. They will fight for the earth, for the increase of the slow, sure roots of peace, for the release of hidden forces. They jibe at the eagle and his scorching sword.

One! Two!—One! Two!—clump the heavy boots. The cry hurtles against the sky.

Each man pulls his belt a little tighter, and shifts his gun to make it lighter. Each man thinks of a woman, and slaps out a curse at the eagle. The sword jumps in the hot sky, and the worm crawls on to the battle, stubbornly.

This is the war of wars, from eye to tail the serpent has one cause:

PEACE!

"The Allies," in *Men, Women, and Ghosts* (New York: Macmillan, 1916), 225–27.

✝ Peace

Perched upon the muzzle of a cannon
A yellow butterfly is slowly opening and shutting its wings.

"Peace," in *Pictures of the Floating World* (New York: Macmillan, 1919), 16.

✟ Anonymous
Irish

✟ Salonika

My husband's in Salonika,
I wonder if he's dead.
I wonder if he knows he has
a kid with a foxy head.

And when the war is over
what will the slackers do?
They'll all be after the soldier boys
for the loan of a bob or two.

And when the war is over,
what will the soldiers do?
They'll hobble along on a leg and a half
but the slackers will have two.

They taxed the pound of butter,
they taxed the ha'penny bun,
but still with all their taxes
they can't beat the bloody Hun.

They taxed the Coliseum,
they taxed St. Mary's Hall.
Why don't they tax the Peelers[1]
with their backs against the wall?

---

1. *Peelers:* policemen.

And when the war is over,
what will the slackers do?
For every kid in America
in Cork there will be two.

They takes us out to Blarney,
they lays us in the grass,
they puts us in the family way
and leaves us on our ass.

There's lino in the parlour
and in the kitchen too,
there's a glass-backed chiffonier
we got from Dicky Glue.[2]

Now never marry a soldier,
a sailor, or a marine,
but keep your eye on the Sinn Féin boy
with his yellow, white, and green.

1916–18

Sung by Catherine Cusse. From Tomás ó Cannaín, *Songs of Cork* (Skerries: Dalton, 1978), 60–61.

2. *Dicky Glue:* loan shark the north side of Cork.

✝ Alice Christiana Gertrude Meynell, née Thompson
(1847–1922) *British*

Alice Thompson spent part of a bohemian childhood in Italy, where she was educated thoroughly in English literature by her father and also became fluent in Italian and French; she converted to Catholicism, following her mother, a pianist. In 1877 Alice married Wilfred Meynell, a Catholic journalist and literary critic, with whom she coedited several magazines; she bore eight children, seven of whom survived. Among her close male friends were Francis Thompson, Coventry Patmore, and George Meredith. Her open house on Sundays was visited by W. B. Yeats, Oscar Wilde, and Katharine Tynan.

Her creative and critical work for periodicals and newspapers helped support the family; collections of her essays (described as "limpid" by George Meredith) include *The Rhythm of Life* (1893), *The Colour of Life* (1896), and *The Spirit of Place* (1899). She wrote biographies of the pre-Raphaelite Holman Hunt and of John Ruskin; she edited the works of Jean Ingelow, Elizabeth Barrett Browning, Christina Rossetti, and Charlotte Yonge.

Meynell's poetry, taut and intense, mystical yet witty, appeared in a series of volumes with sober titles such as *Other Poems* (1896) and *Later Poems* (1902). The first, *Preludes* (1875), was illustrated by her older sister, Elizabeth Thompson Butler, who achieved fame as a painter of military subjects in the tradition of Napoleonic battle paintings. It was to this sister, "E. B.," that Alice addressed the title poem of her World War I volume, *A Father of Women and Other Poems* (1917). Lady Butler had written that war brought out both the basest and highest qualities, but that one should not focus on the evil close at hand. By contrast, her feminist and suffragist sister Meynell wrote in "Parentage," a poem of 1896, "Those who slay / Are fathers. Theirs are armies. Death is theirs." The "intellectual passion" with which she infused her lyrics won her highest praise from Ruskin, Virginia Woolf, and Vita Sackville-West.

✠ A Father of Women

AD SOROREM E.B.

'Thy father was transfused into thy blood.'
Dryden: *Ode to Mrs. Anne Killigrew.*

Our father works in us,
The daughters of his manhood. Not undone
Is he, not wasted, though transmuted thus,
And though he left no son.

Therefore on him I cry
To arm me: 'For my delicate mind a casque,
A breastplate for my heart, courage to die,
Of thee, captain, I ask.

'Nor strengthen only; press
A finger on this violent blood and pale,
Over this rash will let thy tenderness
A while pause, and prevail.

'And shepherd-father, thou
Whose staff folded my thoughts before my birth,
Control them now I am of earth, and now
Thou art no more of earth.

'O liberal, constant, dear,
Crush in my nature the ungenerous art
Of the inferior; set me high, and here,
Here garner up thy heart!'

Like to him now are they,
The million living fathers of the War—
Mourning the crippled world, the bitter day—
Whose striplings are no more.

The crippled world! Come then,
Fathers of women with your honour in trust,
Approve, accept, know them daughters of men,
Now that your sons are dust.

"A Father of Women," in *A Father of Women and Other Poems* (London: Burns & Oates, 1917), 7–8

‡ To Conscripts

Compel them to come in—St. Luke

You "made a virtue of necessity"
    By divine sanction; you, the loth, the grey,
The random, gentle, unconvinced; Oh, be
    The crowned!—you may, you may.

You, the compelled, be feasted! You, the caught,
    Be freemen of the gates that word unlocks!
Accept your victory from that unsought,
    That heavenly paradox.

"To Conscripts," in *Dublin Review* 164 (1919), 128.

✟ Ricarda Huch, pseudonym: Richard Hugo (1864–1947) German

Educated in a wealthy, literary family in Braunschweig, Ricarda Huch studied history at Zurich, where she received her doctorate in 1891. She taught in Zurich, Bremen, and Vienna, but by 1897 decided to devote herself to writing history, drama, novellas, and poetry. In 1898 she married Ermanno Ceconi and had one daughter, but divorced eight years later; her second marriage to her cousin (and brother-in-law), Richard Huch, broke up after three years in 1910. Her two-part study of romanticism (*Blütezeit*, 1899; *Ausbreitung und Verfall*, 1902) identified her with neoromanticism, while her stylized, musical language and resistance to naturalism linked her among contemporaries to art nouveau.

Like Käthe Kollwitz, who dedicated a cycle to the peasants' war in the years leading to World War I, Huch expressed her fear of German militarism and her pessimism about German cultural decay in a three-volume history of the Thirty Years War (*Der grosse Krieg in Deutschland*, 1912–1914). During the war, she lived in Switzerland (1916–1918); upon her return to Munich she published *Gedichte* (1919), including the poems translated here. The war turned her toward religious philosophy and studies of Luther and the Bible. Her historical and biographical studies of *Wallenstein* (1915), *Michael Bakunin und die Anarchie* (1923), and *1848* (1948) explored figures and moments that not only typify a period but reflect her own social philosophy. She was made an honorary senator of the University of Munich in 1924 and won literary prizes in 1931 and 1944. The first woman elected to the Prussian Academy of Arts, she withdrew in 1933 in political protest. In the last decade of her life she completed a three-volume history of Germany that voiced her opposition to Hitler, but her study of the White Rose student uprising in Munich appeared only posthumously (1953).

☩ The War Year

Now is the great fall, the festival of freedom.
The heavens flare, storms chase without restraint,
Pressed from heavy fruit the black wine drips,
The gathered sheaves grow high as golden towers.

Swarms of leaves now rustle a final song,
Drums beat a hollow march to woo recruits.
Wreath-crowned, a mighty host of men stands up
And goes to meet a sacrificial death.

Their wide-eyed gaze sees the mighty god
Beckon with a sternly loving face.
Glowing they throng to battle and to death—
Where life wells out, to drink and seal their youth.

1917

"Das Kriegsjahr," in *Gesammelte Werke*, Bd. 5 (Köln: Kiepenheuer & Witsch, 1971), 275.
Copyright © 1971 by Verlag Kiepenheuer & Witsch, Köln.

☩ Ceremony for the Dead, I

Smiling and proud, as heirs apparent
Sweep to the throne up satin steps,
our brother goes off to fight and die.

Steep springs the ravine, the sun's last life
dims on the dulled rock, it grows dark and cold.
Light steps' hollow quake echoes afar.

Then around the shuddering figure noosed
like a tiger's hard claws on a gazelle's neck,
the basalt walls grind and crush.

In the narrowed bed united swell
the sea and gale, he fights, coughs, sinks,
springs up, appalled at night grow light.

See how the tender flesh gleams by firelight,
it twists, it drips like fading roses;
see, how the chaste mouth drinks the flames,

As if it were love's spring-sweet caress!
Though he kneels now powerless, mute, and disarmed,
through the seething glow and hellish roar

the blind eye shines like a sword.

1917

"Totenfeier," in *Gesammelte Werke*, Bd. 5 (Köln: Kiepenheuer & Witsch, 1971), 276–77. Copyright © 1971 by Verlag Kiepenheuer & Witsch, Köln.

✟ Mary Borden
(1886–1968) American/British[1]

✟ The Song of the Mud

This is the song of the mud,
The pale yellow glistening mud that covers the hills like satin;
The grey gleaming silvery mud that is spread like enamel over the valleys;
The frothing, squirting, spurting, liquid mud that gurgles along the road
    beds;
The thick elastic mud that is kneaded and pounded and squeezed under
    the hoofs of the horses;
The invincible, inexhaustible mud of the war zone.

This is the song of the mud, the uniform of the *poilu*.
His coat is of mud, his great dragging flapping coat, that is too big for him
    and too heavy;
His coat that once was blue, and now is grey and stiff with the mud that
    cakes to it.
This is the mud that clothes him.
His trousers and boots are of mud,
And his skin is of mud;
And there is mud in his beard.
His head is crowned with a helmet of mud.
He wears it well.
He wears it as a king wears the ermine that bores him.
He has set a new style in clothing;
He has introduced the chic of mud.

1. See page 363.

This is the song of the mud that wriggles its way into battle.
The impertinent, the intrusive, the ubiquitous, the unwelcome,
The slimy inveterate nuisance,
That fills the trenches,
That mixes in with the food of the soldiers,
That spoils the working of motors and crawls into their secret parts.
That spreads itself over the guns,
That sucks the guns down and holds them fast in its slimy voluminous lips,
That has no respect for destruction and muzzles the bursting shells;
And slowly, softly, easily,
Soaks up the fire, the noise; soaks up the energy and the courage;
Soaks up the power of armies;
Soaks up the battle.
Just soaks it up and thus stops it.

This is the hymn of mud—the obscene, the filthy, the putrid,
The vast liquid grave of our armies.
It has drowned our men.
Its monstrous distended belly reeks with the undigested dead.
Our men have gone into it, sinking slowly, and struggling and slowly dis-
    appearing.
Our fine men, our brave, strong, young men;
Our glowing red, shouting, brawny men.
Slowly, inch by inch, they have gone down into it.
Into its darkness, its thickness, its silence.
Slowly, irresistibly, it drew them down, sucked them down,
And they were drowned in thick, bitter, heaving mud.
Now it hides them, Oh, so many of them!
Under its smooth glistening surface it is hiding them blandly.
There is not a trace of them.
There is no mark where they went down.
The mute enormous mouth of the mud has closed over them.

This is the song of the mud,
The beautiful glistening golden mud that covers the hills like satin;
The mysterious gleaming silvery mud that is spread like enamel over the
    valleys.
Mud, the disguise of the war zone;
Mud, the mantle of battles;
Mud, the smooth fluid grave of our soldiers:
This is the song of the mud.

1917

"The Song of the Mud," in *The Forbidden Zone* (London: Heinemann, 1929; New York: Doubleday, 1930), 189–92. Used by permission of Doubleday, a division of Bantam Doubleday Dell Publishing Group, Inc.

✝ Eleanor Farjeon
(1881–1965) *British*

The only daughter of the novelist and playwright Benjamin Farjeon and his wife Margaret, Eleanor Farjeon was not given formal schooling but nurtured a passion for reading. Although her father had been reared as an orthodox Jew, the family practiced no traditional religion. While in her thirties, Farjeon fell in love with the poet Edward Thomas, who was married. His death at the front in 1917 devastated her, and only in 1958 did she complete his biography. In 1921 Farjeon began a decades-long affair with another married man, the scholar George Earle.

Farjeon was a celebrated writer for children and author of eight books. In her children's texts, Farjeon drew on her childhood and her own protracted sense of innocence. As she states, "I was never aware of my own sex till I was nearly thirty years old, and it took at least ten years more for emotional crudeness to get abreast of mental ripeness." *The Old Nurse's Stocking Basket* (1931) employs the narrative persona of a faithful, intimate observer. *A Nursery in the Nineties* (1935) fictionalizes her family's role-playing and her father's shopping sprees. And her story *The Little Bookworm* (1955) won both the Hans Christian Andersen Award and the Carnegie Medal. Farjeon also wrote poems and tales of saints' lives, eventually converting to Catholicism at seventy. After her death, the Children's Book Circle established an annual award in her name.

KCS

✝ Easter Monday

(In Memoriam E.T.)

In the last letter that I had from France
You thanked me for the silver Easter egg
Which I had hidden in the box of apples
You liked to munch beyond all other fruit.
You found the egg the Monday before Easter,
And said, 'I will praise Easter Monday now—
It was such a lovely morning'. Then you spoke
Of the coming battle and said, 'This is the eve.
Good-bye. And may I have a letter soon.'

That Easter Monday was a day for praise,
It was such a lovely morning. In our garden
We sowed our earliest seeds, and in the orchard
The apple-bud was ripe. It was the eve.
There are three letters that you will not get.

April 9th, 1917

First and Second Love (Oxford: Oxford University Press, 1959). Reprinted by permission of David Higham Associates, LTD.

✝ Peace

I

I am as awful as my brother War,
I am the sudden silence after clamour.
I am the face that shows the seamy scar
When blood has lost its frenzy and its glamour.
Men in my pause shall know the cost at last
That is not to be paid in triumphs or tears,
Men will begin to judge the thing that's past
As men will judge it in a hundred years.

Nations! whose ravenous engines must be fed
Endlessly with the father and the son,
My naked light upon your darkness, dread!—
By which ye shall behold what ye have done:
Whereon, more like a vulture than a dove,
Ye set my seal in hatred, not in love.

II

Let no man call me good. I am not blest.
My single virtue is the end of crimes,
I only am the period of unrest,
The ceasing of the horrors of the times;
My good is but the negative of ill,
Such ill as bends the spirit with despair,
Such ill as makes the nations' soul stand still
And freeze to stone beneath its Gorgon glare.

Be blunt, and say that peace is but a state
Wherein the active soul is free to move,
And nations only show as mean or great
According to the spirit then they prove.—
O which of ye whose battle-cry is Hate
Will first in peace dare shout the name of Love?

Sonnets and Poems (Oxford: Blackwell, 1918), 48. Reprinted by permission of David Higham Associates LTD

✠ Beatrice ("Bobo") Mayor, née Meinertzhagen (1885–1947) *British*

O ne of the ten children of Georgiana and Daniel Meinertzhagen and a niece of Beatrice Webb, Beatrice Meinertzhagen was born in London and educated in Paris at a Catholic school for girls, Les Marroniers. In 1912 she married Robin Grote Mayor, fellow of King's College, Cambridge, an Apostle and philosopher who worked as a civil servant for the board of education. They had three children: two daughters and a son who was to translate Proust. A disguised portrait of Beatrice as "Kathy" appears in a novel by her sister-in-law Flora Mayor, *The Rector's Daughter,* which was published by the Woolfs at the Hogarth Press in 1924.

Beatrice Mayor's first volume of poetry appeared in 1919, inaugurating an active career as a writer. In 1922 two plays by Beatrice Mayor were performed by the Playwrights Theatre in London: *The Girl in the City* and *Thirty Minutes in a Street,* the latter produced by the daughter of Ellen Terry. Mayor published several other plays for adults and children in the twenties and thirties, as well as two novels, *The Stream* (1933) and *The Story without an End* (1940), followed by a final collection of verse, *Voices from the Crowd* (1943). There are several references to "Bobo" Mayor in the diaries and letters of Virginia Woolf, whose hair she cut short in February 1927. "Bobo Mayor is a great seducer in her way," Woolf wrote to her lover Vita Sackville-West. "She has gipsy blood in her: she's rather violent and highly coloured, sinuous too, with a boneless body, and thin hands; all the things I like. So . . . I let her do it."

SO

☦ Spring 1917

It is spring.
The buds break softly, silently.
This evening
The air is pink with the low sun,
And birds sing.

Do we believe
Men are now killing, dying—
This evening,
While the sky is pink with the low sun,
And birds sing?

No . . .
So they go on killing, dying,
This evening,
And through summer, autumn, winter,
And through spring.

"Spring 1917," in *Poems 1919* (London: Allen and Unwin, 1919).

✝ Anna Dmitrievna Radlova, née Darmalatova

(1891–1949) *Russian*

Born into landed gentry, Anna Darmalatova married Sergei Radlov, a theater director, while one sister married the brother of Osip Mandelstam and another, Sarra, a sculptor, married the artist Vladimir Lebedev. In the 1920s, when Radlov organized mass revolutionary spectacles in Petrograd, Anna's home became a principal gathering place for the "cream of all artists." Radlova's translations of Shakespeare were used by her husband for his productions over the next decade.

Her poetry, which appeared for the first time in *Apollo* in 1915, defies classification. She dedicated to Sergei her first collection of poetry, *Soty* (Honeycomb, 1917). This and two later volumes, *Ships* (1920), a lament about the revolution, and *The Winged Guest* (1922), contain acmeist elements, with traces of archaic diction, centered on powerful religious motifs. Out of favor with the Bolsheviks, Radlova turned to translation of classics, including Shakespeare, Christopher Marlowe, Guy de Maupassant, and André Gide. In World War II the Radlov theater was evacuated and fell into Nazi hands; the couple began a nightmarish journey from one occupied territory to another, performing in POW camps. Upon their return to Russia at the end of the war they were sentenced to nine years in a labor camp, where Anna Radlova died.

TP

✝ Stars Are Falling, People Falling

"Stars are falling, people falling,
All will tremble before him,
People will lose their way to loved ones,
To the dead and to the pale living.

Fall to the ground, repent, and pray,
And do not hide your faces."
The black earth hears the laments.
The street. Song of the blind.

His voice like a ringing whip,
I remember the words by heart.
The sharp call rolls through the world.
Cry, repentant Rus.

December 1917

Translated by John Henriksen

"Zvezdy padayut, lyudi padayut," in *Soty* (Petrograd: Izd-vo "Fiametta," 1918), 36.

✝ Vera Brittain
(1893–1970) *British*

E ven today the feminist and pacifist novels, poems, and journals of Vera Brittain retain an audience of enthusiastic admirers. Born to a wealthy paper manufacturing family, Brittain attended St. Monica's School before entering Somerville College, Oxford, in 1914. In 1915 her fiancé, Roland Leighton, was killed in action in France; Brittain then took leave from college to join the Voluntary Aid Detachment (V.A.D.) as a nurse. The war's profound effect upon her manifests itself in *Verses of a V.A.D.* (1918), dedicated to the memory of Leighton. Her first novel, *The Dark Tide* (1923), presents a bleak view of postwar Oxford, with its "lost generation" of women. Her memoir, *Testament of Youth* (1933), filmed as a BBC serial in 1979, draws on her nursing experiences and traces the loss of Leighton, her brother, and friends, which left what she called "scars upon my heart." She also published *Poems of the War and After* in 1934. Published posthumously as *Chronicle of Youth* (1981), her 1913–1918 diaries expose how her naive enthusiasm at the outset of the war gradually yielded to bitterness and antimilitarism.

Returning to Somerville in 1918, Brittain forged a strong friendship with a classmate, Winifred Holtby, who had served in the Women's Army Auxiliary Corps. Together they moved to London, where they became active in feminist and pacifist groups and proponents of the League of Nations. In 1925 Brittain married George Catlin, a political philosopher at Cornell University, with whom she had a son, John Edward, and a daughter, Shirley Williams. Denying rumors of a lesbian relationship with Holtby, who lived in their household, Brittain criticized those who "are roused by any record of affection between women to suspicions habitual among the over-sophisticated." Five years after Holtby died of kidney disease, Brittain published the second volume of her autobiography, *Testament of Friendship* (1940), which chronicles her intense and idealistic fellowship with Holtby. *Testament of Experience* (1957) records her work from 1925 to 1950 for women's rights and pacifism. During World War II she attacked the Allies for blanket bombing in *Seed of Chaos* (1944). She also wrote nonfiction, including a

history of accomplished women entitled *Lady into Woman* (1953), *The Woman at Oxford* (1960), and *Radclyffe Hall: A Case of Obscenity?* (1968).
    KCS

✝ August 1914

God said, "Men have forgotten Me;
    The souls that sleep shall wake again,
And blinded eyes must learn to see."

So since redemption comes through pain
    He smote the earth with chastening rod,
And brought Destruction's lurid reign;

But where His desolation trod
    The people in their agony
Despairing cried, "There is no God."

Somerville College, Oxford

"August 1914," in *Verses of a V.A.D.* (London: Erskine Macdonald, 1918), 15. Reprint, London: The Imperial War Museum, 1995. Reprinted by permission of Vera Brittain's literary executors.

✝ Sic Transit—

(V.R., DIED OF WOUNDS, 2ND LONDON GENERAL HOSPITAL,
CHELSEA, JUNE 9TH, 1917)

I am so tired.
    The dying sun incarnadines the West,
And every window with its gold is fired,
    And all I loved the best
Is gone, and every good that I desired
    Passes away, an idle hopeless quest;
Even the Highest whereto I aspired
    Has vanished with the rest.
I am so tired.

London, June 1917

"Sic Transit—," in *Verses of a V.A.D.* (London: Erskine Macdonald, 1918), 34. Reprint, London: The Imperial War Museum, 1995. Reprinted by permission of Vera Brittain's literary executors.

✝ Marianne Moore
(1887–1972) *American*

The eccentric modernist Marianne Moore was a consummate professional writer, steadily publishing her own poetry through her lifetime and editing that of others for *Dial* magazine. After the breakdown of her father the year she was born, Moore was raised by her mother, who was a teacher. Graduation from Bryn Mawr in 1909 with a degree in biology, she said, "gave me security in my determination to have what I want." She traveled to Europe with her mother, then began teaching at an Indian school in Pennsylvania. During her last year of teaching, her first poems appeared. Some opposed the war; thus "To the Soul of 'Progress,' " which appeared in *The Egoist* in 1915, criticizes the intellectualization of the human costs of war: "You use your mind / Like a mill stone to grind / Chaff." Yet to her brother Warner, a minister, she wrote in 1915 that she would leave antiwar sentiment behind, since war primarily affected material and corporeal life. She worked during this period for women's suffrage.

Never married, Moore moved with her mother and brother to New York in 1918, where she became acquainted with the modernist circle that included William Carlos Williams, Wallace Stevens, H.D. (Hilda Doolittle), and Winifred Bryher. H.D. and Bryher arranged in secret to publish *Poems* (1921); reviewing the book, Richard Aldington called her "a poet whose mixture of whimsicality, subtlety, cool intelligence with nimbleness of apprehension and old maidenly priggishness is something quite original." An expanded edition brought out in America (*Observations*, 1924) won the *Dial* award for its modernist precision and "contractility." As editor from 1925 to 1929 of that magazine, Moore passed judgment on Ezra Pound, T. S. Eliot, Paul Valéry, Hart Crane, and José Ortega y Gasset. "A thing must have 'intensity.' That seemed to be the criterion," she wrote.

Moore's experimental syllabic metrics continued to appear in *Selected Poems* (1935), *The Pangolin and Other Verse* (1936), *What Are Years* (1941), and *Nevertheless* (1944). Her reaction to World War II invested her poetry with questions of morality and virtue. In a review of Louise Bogan's *Poems and New Poems* (1941), she asserts, "We need not be told that life is never going to be free of trouble and that there are no substitutes for the dead; but it is a fact as well as a mystery that weakness is power, that handicap is proficiency, that the scar is a credential, that indignation is no adversary for gratitude, or heroism for joy." The holocaust unnerved her.

After her important *Collected Poems* (1951), Moore was awarded the Pulitzer Prize (1952), the National Book Award (1952), and the Bollingen Prize (1953). Her continued popularity in the 1950s and 1960s testifies to mainstream acceptance of modernism. Her early poems, with their close observation of the natural world, were widely anthologized, and her playful comparisons have won a broad audience. Moore became a celebrity whose visits to the zoo and Yankee Stadium were followed by the press. She continued to publish until her death, producing *O, To Be a Dragon* (1959), *Tell Me, Tell Me* (1966), and *The Complete Poems of Marianne Moore* (1967).

KCS

✝ Reinforcements

The vestibule to experience is not to
    Be exalted into epic grandeur. These men are going
To their work with this idea, advancing like a school of fish through

Still water—waiting to change the course or dismiss
    The idea of movement, till forced to. The words of the Greeks
Ring in our ears, but they are vain in comparison with a sight like this.

The pulse of intention does not move so that one
    Can see it, and moral machinery is not labelled, but
The future of time is determined by the power of volition.

"Reinforcements," in *The Egoist* 5.6 (1918), 83.

✝ Adrienne Blanc-Péridier, pseudonym of Adrienne Boglione (1884–1965) *French*

I mbued with religious and patriotic fervor, Adrienne Blanc-Péridier's collection of poems *Le cantique de la patrie, 1914–1917* (Canticle of the nation, 1914–1917, 1918), celebrates the suffering soldier and consoles the victims of war. After the war she worked for female suffrage with the Union Nationale pour le Vote des Femmes. She wrote a biography of a feminist who had supported the war effort, *Une princesse de la Troisième République, Juliette Adam* (A princess of the third republic, Juliette Adam, 1936), as well as two biographies of a leading Catholic thinker, *La route ascendante de Maurice Barrès* (The rising path of Maurice Barrès, 1925) and *Maurice Barrès* (1929).

From the twenties through the sixties she wrote fiction and a dozen plays, including religious musicals for children. Among her comedies are *L'école des gendres* (The school for sons-in-law, 1933) and *La marraine de Musset* (Musset's godmother, 1962); her tragedies include *Le second festin de Cléopâtre* (Cleopatra's second feast, 1935).

✝ Virtuti Ignotae

O combien d'actions, combien d'exploits célèbres
Sont demeurés sans gloire au milieu des ténèbres.[1]
Corneille, *Le Cid*

Perhaps our greatest dead are those
Whose supreme valor we do not know,
Whose proud sacrifice and glowing deeds
Done without witness, will have no rewards.

No one will tell us how they died;
In battle, their voice could not be heard . . .
None saw their exploits or caught their cry;
We don't know what victory they had earned

Nor what struggle, what last gesture made
Before their generous spirit yielded.
Their glory, buried with them in the grave,
Sleeps forever sealed in secret.

Only the earth, maternal,
Taking in their hearts' good blood,
Knew that they had died triumphant
And rocked them stretched out on her breast.

And France accepted their heroic farewell
When they entered death with serene soul
Weaned from all human glory,
Magnificent, beneath the eye of God, alone.

"Virtuti Ignotae," in *Le cantique de la patrie, 1914–1917* (Paris: Plon, 1918), 70–71.

1. Oh how many acts, how many famed exploits,
   Remain unsung among the shades.

✟ Edith Södergran
(1892–1923) *Swedish/Finnish*

Edith Södergran belonged to the Swedish minority of Finland, which was part of the Russian Empire; her family lived in St. Petersburg, where she was born. Educated at a German school, she first wrote in German. After she was diagnosed as tubercular at sixteen (two years after her father's death), she left school and began to write in Swedish. From 1914, she lived in Raivola, a Finnish village, in poverty and poor health until her death at thirty-one. The poets she read included Rimbaud, Heine, Whitman, Swinburne, Else Lasker Schüler, and Mayakovski. Her four volumes of modernist poetry—*Dikter* (1916), *Septemberlyran* (1918), *Rosenaltaret* (1919), and *Landet som icke är* (1925)—were mocked by most reviewers for their willful defiance of rules. She herself described her unrhymed, visionary, incantatory verse about sexual desire, the natural world, and death, as "careless sketches" that seek "complete freedom."

✟ Prayer

God almighty, have mercy on us!

Look into our well of worship—it shall deepen.
Seven days and seven nights
we draw water
from our well for you.
Seven months and three years
in the same place
we ask for mercy:
Give us ingress to the quiet chamber where you deliberate.

1918

Translated by Brita Stendahl

"Bon," in *Samlade Dikter*, ed. Gunnar Tideström (Stockholm: Wahlström of Widstrand, 1950), 176. Copyright © 1949, by Holger Schildts Förlagsaktiebolag.

☦ Storm

Again, the earth is shrouded in black. It's the storm
that rises from gulfs of the night and dances
alone its ghostlike dance over the earth.
Again, men are fighting—phantom to phantom.
What do they want, what do they know? They are driven
like cattle from dark corners,
they can't tear loose from the chain of events:
the great ideas are chasing their prey before them.
In vain ideas flail their conjuring arms in the storm,
he, the dancer, knows well that his reign is supreme on the earth.
The world has lost control. One thing shall fall
like a house in flames, like a rotten tree,
another remain intact, spared by unknown hands.
And the sun sees all this, and the stars sparkle in icy nights
and man steals away on his lonely path toward boundless joy.

1919

Translated by Stina Katchadourian

"Storm," in *Edith Södergran: Love and Solitude, Selected Poems, 1916–1923*, trans. Stina Katchadourian (Seattle: Fjord Press, 1985). Translation copyright © 1985, 1992 by Stina Katchadourian.

✟ Dame Rose Macaulay
(1881-1958) *British*

Author of twenty-three novels, Emilie Rose Macaulay spent many of her early years in Italy. In 1903 she graduated from Somerville College with a degree in modern history. Her first novel, *Abbots Verney* (1906), which criticized her Anglo-Catholic upbringing, was praised for a "sustained blaze of brilliant conversation." *The Lee Shore* (1913) won a thousand-pound prize from the publisher; as a reviewer noted, it succeeded "by its exceptionally sympathetic treatment of unsuccess." In London, she found a "sparklingly alive" literary circle that included John Middleton Murry, Rupert Brooke, Hugh Walpole, and Walter De La Mare. When Macaulay became involved with the married novelist Gerald O'Donovan, a relationship that lasted until his death in 1942, she was barred from communion in the Anglican church.

During World War I Macaulay worked as a Voluntary Aid Detachment nurse and as a "landgirl" doing heavy agricultural work. *Non-Combatants and Others* (1916) describes a heroine determined after her brother's suicide at the front to do "something *against* war . . . something to fight it and prevent it coming again." The heroine's mother (in an echo of the Women's Peace Conference at The Hague) proposes "a continuous conference of the neutral nations." Macaulay's second volume of poetry, *Three Days* (1919), deals primarily with the psychic toll of war, which treats men as "unreasoning, blind" sheep.

In 1917 she joined the War Office, where her work in the office of information provided satiric material for *What Not: A Prophetic Comedy* (1918) and *Potterism* (1920), which criticizes the popular press. *Dangerous Ages* (1921) won the Femina Vie Heureuse Prize. A friend of Virginia Woolf, Macaulay experimented with modernist narrative in *Told by an Idiot* (1923), which has been likened to Woolf's *Orlando*; its pages, according to a reviewer in *The Nation*, are "liberally sprinkled with exploding bombs of wit."

Several of her novels concern themselves with the threat of war. *They*

Were Defeated (1932) examines the experiences of seventeenth-century monarchists, such as Robert Herrick, when confronted with civil war. *And No Man's Wit* (1940) takes civil-war Spain as its setting, while *The World My Wilderness* (1950) describes life in postwar Britain as psychologically damaged. Her own London apartment, with manuscripts and notes, was destroyed in a May 1941 air raid. She drove her car for the local ambulance station, enjoying the camaraderie of men who called her "mate." For her final novel, *The Towers of Trebizond* (1956), based in part on her experiences with the Anglican church, she won the James Tait Black Memorial Prize. In 1958 she was made a Dame Commander of the British Empire.
  KCS

✝ Picnic, July 1917

We lay and ate sweet hurt-berries
  In the bracken of Hurt Wood.
Like a quire of singers singing low
  The dark pines stood.

Behind us climbed the Surrey hills,
  Wild, wild in greenery;
At our feet the downs of Sussex broke
  To an unseen sea.

And life was bound in a still ring,
  Drowsy, and quiet, and sweet . . .
When heavily up the south-east wind
  The great guns beat.

We did not wince, we did not weep,
  We did not curse or pray;
We drowsily heard, and someone said,
  'They sound clear today.'

We did not shake with pity and pain,
  Or sicken and blanch white.
We said, 'If the wind's from over there
  There'll be rain tonight.'

• • •

Once pity we knew, and rage we knew,
  And pain we knew, too well,
As we stared and peered dizzily
  Through the gates of hell.

But now hell's gates are an old tale;
  Remote the anguish seems;
The guns are muffled and far away,
  Dreams within dreams.

And far and far are Flanders mud,
  And the pain of Picardy;
And the blood that runs there runs beyond
  The wide waste sea.

We are shut about by guarding walls:
  (We have built them lest we run
Mad from dreaming of naked fear
  And of black things done.)

We are ringed all round by guarding walls,
  So high, they shut the view.
Not all the guns that shatter the world
  Can quite break through.

● ● ●

Oh, guns of France, oh, guns of France,
  Be still, you crash in vain. . . .
Heavily up the south wind throb
  Dull dreams of pain, . . .

Be still, be still, south wind, lest your
  Blowing should bring the rain. . . .
We'll lie very quiet on Hurt Hill,
  And sleep once again.

Oh, we'll lie quite still, nor listen nor look,
  While the earth's bounds reel and shake,
Lest, battered too long, our walls and we
  Should break . . . should break. . . .

"Picnic, July 1917," in *Three Days* (London: Constable, 1919), 11–13. Reprinted by permission of the Peters Fraser & Dunlop Group Ltd.

✠ The Shadow

There was a Shadow on the moon; I saw it poise and tilt, and go
Its lonely way, and so I know that the blue velvet night will soon
Blaze loud and bright, as if the stars were crashing right into the
    town,
And tumbling streets and houses down, and smashing people like
    wine-jars. . . .
                Fear wakes:
                What then?
       Strayed shadow of the Fear that breaks
           The world's young men.

Bright fingers point all round the sky, they point and grope and
    cannot find.
(God's hand, you'd think, and he gone blind.) . . . The queer
    white faces twist and cry.
Last time they came they messed our square, and left it a hot
    rubbish-heap,
With people sunk in it so deep, you could not even hear them
    swear.
                Fire blinds.
                What then?
       Pale shadow of the Pain that grinds
           The world's young men.

The weak blood running down the street, oh, does it run like
    fire, like wine?
Are the spilt brains so keen, so fine, crushed limbs so swift, dead
    dreams so sweet?
There is a Plain where limbs and dreams and brains to set the
    world a-fire
Lie tossed in sodden heaps of mire. . . . Crash! Tonight's show
    begins, it seems.
              Death . . . Well,
              What then?
       Rim of the shadow of the Hell
          Of the world's young men.

"The Shadow," in *Three Days* (London: Constable, 1919), 17–18. Reprinted by permission of the Peters Fraser & Dunlop Group Ltd.

✟ Svarnakumari Devi
(1856–1932) *Indian*[1]

✟ To the Brave

Soldier and hero, O my Countryman!
In admiration of thee stands the world,
And I, though little, become great in thee,
My brother, and in thy proud state, forget
Myself the sorrows of my servitude.

Even as stars of burning beauty seem
Merely to shoot and in the ethereal vast
To loose themselves, and none perceives the heat
Of dreadful fire intense that in their being

Through every particle and atom breathes:
Even so thy sacrifice, but more splendid still
This death espoused, not for thyself, nor even
For Country, but for duty's sake alone:

Thy selfless death-pyre, holy warrior!
So long as bursts not yet the flood of doom,
And sun and moon within their orbits run,
Over her vesture thy great deeds shall earth
Blazon, thy glory's hymn proudly proclaim.

How shall we praise when speech to praise thee fails?
Thee, hope of Gods in this tremendous war!
I know not with what offering, I shall greet
Thee, in whose name, O hero, thy own land
Glories, and foreign lands feel blest indeed.

"To the Brave," in *Short Stories* (Madras: Ganesh, 1919).

1. See page 383.

✝ Beti women
Cameroon

S ung during work or travel, this antiphonal response in a Bantu
dialect (Ewondo) chronicles the departure from Yaoundé,
Cameroon, of Beti soldiers and carriers with German troops.
Cameroon had become a German colony in 1884; the war in Cameroon
began in late September 1914, with the surrender of the important coastal
port of Douala to the invading British. After holding out another fifteen
months, the Germans and their African troops were forced to retreat in
early 1916, southward to Spanish Equatorial Guinea and eventually the
island of Fernando Poo. Charles Atangana (c.1880–1943), a skilled translator and administrator, through his contacts with the Germans had
become leader of perhaps five hundred thousand people by 1915; he led
the two-month retreat of several thousand Beti, with seventy-two village
chiefs.

The song not only conveys the Beti people's experience of World War I
but records their complex cultural attitudes. The women rhetorically
address Atangana as "son of Ndono Edoa" or "Mindili Ebulu" (an important person whose house had nine roof beams instead of two), warning
him to flee, since the battle has been lost. The women debate what to do
themselves: flee with the Germans to Spanish Guinea, or profit from the
confusion of goods left unprotected during the retreat of the Germans.
The war was more devastating to the Beti than a limited, traditional war
would have been, costing large numbers their lives and their land. Furthermore, their leaders went into exile: Atangana and other chiefs were
sent by the Germans to Spain in 1918, where they stayed for two years. The
Germans hoped to present them at the Versailles Peace Conference as
representatives of a model colony, but the opportunity never arose. After
the war the French, operating under a League of Nations mandate, forced
the population to serve in road gangs and public works. Frederick Quinn
collected this song in conjunction with his study of Cameroon history.

✦ The War Is Over

Atangana Ntsama, the war is over.
Hé, Atangana Ntsama, the war is over!

The cannon are broken,
Run quickly, why do you languish there?

All you Ewondo, come and run quickly,
Go tell it to Mindili Ebulu, the son of Ndono Edoa.

How is it that you would like me to leave so many goods behind?

Hé! They will surprise you in your greed!

Such riches, I should take some!

You others, move off, what are you doing there?

Friend, there are as many goods as in a market.

Friend, we have marched through all of that without taking anything.

Translated by Frederick Quinn

From Frederick Quinn, "The Beti of Cameroun," in *Africa and the First World War,* ed. Melvin Page (New York: St. Martin's Press, 1987), 176.

✟ Charlotte Mew
(1869–1928) *British*

Poet Charlotte Mew's life was marked by adversity. Born into a middle-class London family, Mew endured the deaths of three siblings and the institutionalization of two others for insanity, which imposed a financial burden on the distraught family. She and her sister Anne vowed never to pass on their family's tendency to mental illness by marrying or having children. Mew was educated at Lucy Harrison's School for Girls and attended lectures at University College. In 1898, when her father's death compromised the family's strained finances, Mew earned money by publishing poetry and prose in magazines like *The Egoist, Temple Bar, The Englishwoman, The Nation,* and *The Yellow Book.* In the late 1890s she fell in love with Ella D'Arcy, an assistant at *The Yellow Book,* who did not share her feelings. A decade later, she apparently offended her mentor May Sinclair by her unwanted attention.

Living with her invalid mother and Anne, Mew found support in the friendship of Alida Monro and her husband. Her important dramatic monologue, "The Farmer's Bride," which appeared in *The Nation* in 1914, led to her promotion as a poet by the Monros, who published a collection with that title in 1916. Rebecca West and H.D. (Hilda Doolittle) gave it favorable reviews, and Thomas Hardy called her "far and away the best living poet, who will be read when others are forgotten." Her naturalistic monologues examine the psychological effects of thwarted passion and isolation.

During the war, Mew worked with wives of enlisted men to secure benefits due to them. She endured Zeppelin raids with composure. After prolonged infirmity, her mother died in 1923, "a stupefying blow" that made her feel "like a weed dug up and thrown over a wall." That year she was awarded a Civil List pension through the efforts of Hardy and John Masefield. After her sister Anne died in 1927, she moved into a nursing home, where nine months later she killed herself by drinking Lysol.

KCS

✝ The Cenotaph

September 1919

Not yet will those measureless fields be green again
Where only yesterday the wild sweet blood of wonderful youth
    was shed;
There is a grave whose earth must hold too long, too deep a stain,
Though for ever over it we may speak as proudly as we may tread.
But here, where the watchers by lonely hearths from the thrust of
    an inward sword have more slowly bled,
We shall build the Cenotaph: Victory, winged, with Peace,
    winged too, at the column's head.
And over the stairway, at the foot—oh! here, leave desolate,
    passionate hands to spread
Violets, roses, and laurel, with the small, sweet, twinkling
    country things
Speaking so wistfully of other Springs,
From the little gardens of little places where son or sweetheart
    was born and bred.
In splendid sleep, with a thousand brothers
                    To lovers—to mothers
                    Here, too, lies he:
Under the purple, the green, the red,
It is all young life: it must break some women's hearts to see
Such a brave, gay coverlet to such a bed!
Only, when all is done and said,
God is not mocked and neither are the dead.
For this will stand in our Market-place—
                    Who'll sell, who'll buy
                    (Will you or I
Lie each to each with the better grace)?
While looking into every busy whore's and huckster's face
As they drive their bargains, is the Face
Of God: and some young, piteous, murdered face.

"The Cenotaph," in *Collected Poems* (1953). Reprinted by permission of Carcanet Press Limited.

✜ Berta Lask
(1878–1967) *German*[1]

✜ The Jewish Girls

*After their rape by invading Russians, the Jewish girls of a
small Polish settlement threw themselves into the water.*

Her face against the wall
little Hanna lies cramped in horror.
On the floor in the middle of the room Esther sits.
She no longer watches her little sister.
A cloth hangs at the window and a strip of blue sky
forces its way between cloth and frame.
Esther stares at it with dark, ripe eyes,
with questioning, large eyes.
Her hands fall apart in her lap.
Her gaze is caught in the strip.
She wonders, did she already see this bright blue
when she went out with her sisters,
a thousand years ago, or yesterday?
It's different, it's so new.
She sees it with shuddering, shy eyes.
The door opens. Wrapped in thick folds
two girls come, holding each other's hands.
They come up to Esther and look shyly down
and complain with silent gestures.
And Esther nods.—And other girls come in,
some with sobs and screams,
some in a foam of hatred and rage,

1. See page 401.

some stiffly lost in a dream.
A dark one with eyes bright as a bolt cries,
"We will creep after them. They are not far.
We will throw bombs on their rails,
lay mines in their quarters.
I will mix poison in their food.
I will see how their eyes break and turn stiff."
She throws herself down and pounds on the planks with her fists.
Esther bends down, to cool her forehead.
The others stand about waiting.
She sits on the floor, large, serious, and heavy.
With her face against the wall
little Hanna shakes, cramped in horror.
Esther looks at the strip of light
and says,
"Once we received a soul from God.
But they took it from us
as if we were a lifeless clod of earth,
through which an alien will tears a path,
a path on which to step and storm—
and which it then abandons.
No prayer can help now."
Esther's silence questions. But all are still.
All wait to hear what Esther wants.
Only one trembling voice says, "I am so hollow.
Esther, I no longer have a soul."
Esther smiles painfully with a bright face
and speaks:
"The soul from God we carry within
cannot be trampled and beaten.
But it wants to hide in shame
since its envelope has ugly spots.
I don't know why or how that happened.
But our soul hides itself in shame.
We do not want our souls to hide.
Our souls should raise themselves up in pride.
We don't want them to lie on the floor and cry.
Our souls should rejoice and soar.
Who will help release our souls from pain?
We must wash their hulls clean, out in the sea."
Esther takes the trembling child from her bench
and draws her gently close to herself.
She presses the little face to her cheek
but she cannot look at it.—
And as they came to the dark water
several paled and became yet more silent.
Esther looked little Hanna in the eyes.

It's as if something in her were breaking.
And Esther speaks:
"Father, we ask you to let our life
continue to hover here over the water.
I am so afraid that we will quite disappear,
and little Hanna never again see the woods or sun.
We are so young, we are reluctant to die.
And you are so high and so far away.
If you can, take us up into your bosom!
Make us light and bright!
See, we wash ourselves clean."

And then they went out into the water.
In their arms' embrace they held each other.

"Die jüdischen Mädchen," in *Die Silbergäule* (Hanover: Steegemann, 1919), 26–28.

✟ Alice Ruth Dunbar-Nelson, née Moore
(1875–1935) American

New Orleans, where she grew up, provides the backdrop to much of Alice Dunbar-Nelson's poetry, journalism, and fiction. As a child, she was accused of being a "half-white nigger," and passing became one of the themes that recurs in her poetry. Educated in public schools and at Straight College, then at the Universities of Pennsylvania, Cornell, and Columbia, she taught in New Orleans, Brooklyn, and Wilmington, Delaware. Her thesis appeared as an article about Milton's influence on Wordsworth. Her first book, *Violets and Other Tales* (1895), a collection of largely sentimental essays, poems, and stories, included an essay, "The Woman," which extols independent unmarried women. She attracted the renowned poet Paul Laurence Dunbar, who had read her book, and in 1898 they married and moved to Washington, D.C. They modeled their relationship on that of Robert Browning and Elizabeth Browning; reviewers saw them as "rivals" in the telling of short stories. The four-year marriage dissolved in 1902, after many arguments over his alcoholism, infidelities, and cruelty.

Her second book, *The Goodness of St. Rocque* (1899), which incorporates Creole dialect and depicts diverse ethnic groups, participates in the tradition of New Orleans regionalists like Grace King and Kate Chopin. Paul Dunbar encouraged her "to contest" G. W. Cable with her Creole stories, in which he admired "the force, the fire, and the artistic touch." Her poetry and prose appeared in national publications such as *The Crisis, Collier's,* and *The Messenger,* as well as local papers. Dunbar-Nelson became a celebrated lecturer, traveling to speak on African American history and culture; she published articles on black Louisianans in the *Journal of Negro History* in 1916–17. She edited a volume to commemorate the Emancipation Proclamation, *Masterpieces of Negro Eloquence* (1914), and an anthology for children, *The Dunbar Speaker and Entertainer* (1920); in both she included Creole as well as standard English texts. An important educator, she taught English at Howard High School in Wilmington for eighteen years.

During the world war, she organized support among African American club women for the U.S. Council of National Defense, leading a 6,000 strong Flag Day demonstration in 1918. She also worked on behalf of women's suffrage and helped build a domestic workers' labor union. The Philadelphia *Public Ledger* rejected her application to report from overseas. Her 1918 play, *Mine Eyes Have Seen,* exposes the contradictions in American politics between the drafting of Negro soldiers and the rejection of volunteers for Red Cross Service, as well as the tolerance of lynching. She wrote a chapter on "Negro Women in War Work" for Emmett J. Scott's *Official History of the American Negro in the World War* (1919). There she described women's desire to serve their native land but also noted that "the story of the colored woman and the Red Cross is not altogether a pleasant one. . . . Colored women since the inception of the war . . . felt keenly their exclusion from overseas service." In the postwar period she was active in the American Friends Interracial Peace Committee, serving as its executive secretary 1928–31, and the Women's International League for Peace and Freedom (WILPF), through which she knew Addie Hunton.

Her household was dominated by women, since she had been joined by her mother, her sister, and her sister's children. In 1910 she secretly married Arthur Callis, a fellow teacher; they quickly divorced. Her marriage in 1916 to Robert ("Bobo") Nelson seems to have been founded on mutual respect and collaboration, if slender funds. In the early 1920s they coedited and published the Wilmington *Advocate* and then the Washington *Eagle.* She continued to work for the NAACP and the Association for the Study of Afro-American Life and History. Between 1921 and 1931 she kept a diary, in which she clearly alludes to a passionate, triangular, lesbian relationship with Fay Jackson Robinson and Helene Ricks London. In 1929, she read Radclyffe Hall's *Well of Loneliness.* Dunbar-Nelson died of heart problems in 1935.

KCS

✝ I Sit and Sew

I sit and sew—a useless task it seems,
My hands grown tired, my head weighed down with dreams—
The panoply of war, the martial tread of men,
Grim-faced, stern-eyed, gazing beyond the ken
Of lesser souls, whose eyes have not seen Death
Nor learned to hold their lives but as a breath—
But—I must sit and sew.

I sit and sew—my heart aches with desire—
That pageant terrible, that fiercely pouring fire
On wasted fields, and writhing grotesque things
Once men. My soul in pity flings
Appealing cries, yearning only to go
There in that holocaust of hell, those fields of woe—
But—I must sit and sew.

The little useless seam, the idle patch;
Why dream I here beneath my homely thatch,
When there they lie in sodden mud and rain,
Pitifully calling me, the quick ones and the slain?
You need me, Christ! It is no roseate dream
That beckons me—this pretty futile seam,
It stifles me—God, must I sit and sew?

"I Sit and Sew," in *The Dunbar Speaker and Entertainer*, ed. Alice Dunbar-Nelson (Naperville, Ill.: Nichols, 1920), 145.

✝ Nancy Cunard
(1896–1965) *British*

Nancy Cunard is remembered for her unconventional life during the 1920s, a decade in which she socialized with the greatest literary and artistic minds of her time. Daughter of an American expatriate and a wealthy businessman, she was educated at home by governesses, then in London and on the continent at fashionable schools. As a young adult, she published her first poems in Edith Sitwell's *Wheels* (1916). Her marriage in 1916 to the athletic Sydney Fairbairn, who was wounded at Gallipoli, dissolved after twenty months, leaving her with the sense of a simple "caesura."

Janet Flanner, a nonfiction writer and friend of Cunard, described Cunard as one of "an inseparable trio of beauties—a kind of Mayfair troika of friendship, elegance, intelligence, and daring as leaders of the new generation of debutantes, who in evening clothes watched the Zeppelins from the roofs of the great town mansions." On a darker note, returning to England from France in 1919, Cunard commented to her diary in troubled anger, "my first impression of return—everyone dead." She could not rejoice at the signing of the Versailles treaty: "some being dead and others not . . . got very sad and hated the demonstrations."

Shortly after the war, Cunard rejected the aristocratic circle of her parents and joined the French and English avant-garde. Among her literary friendships during the twenties were those with Virginia Woolf, T. S. Eliot, Aldous Huxley, and Ezra Pound. In Paris, Cunard mingled with the great figures of the dadaist and surrealist movements.

Several collections of poetry emerged from this period: *Outlaws* (1921), praised for the "pulse of an original mind"; *Sublunary* (1923); and *Parallax* (1925), which the *Times Literary Supplement* thought had "a complexity and grasp of reality . . . so frequently lacking from women's poetry." In 1928 Cunard founded The Hours Press, which issued works by Laura Riding, Pound, Samuel Beckett, Robert Graves, and Louis Aragon. Hostility to Cunard's interracial relationship with black musician Henry Crowder prompted *Black Man and White Ladyship* (1931), a bitter attack on her mother that led to a permanent break between the two.

Cunard continued to politicize her art with the anthology *Negro* (1934), a vast collection of essays, illustrations, poetry, and music chronicling the diasporic African tradition, "the struggles and achievements, the persecutions and the revolts against them, of the Negro peoples." Although well received by luminaries of the Harlem Renaissance, the work was generally ignored or used as an occasion to attack Cunard's communist sympathies and sexual improprieties. Only when a condensed version appeared in 1970 was *Negro* recognized for its progressive insights.

As a journalist Cunard worked on behalf of the Scottsboro Boys and reported on the Spanish civil war for the *Associated Negro Press,* Sylvia Pankhurst's *New Times,* and the *Voice of Spain.* She prompted poetry in support of the Spanish republicans by Tristan Tzara, Langston Hughes, and W. H. Auden. Cunard's progressive activism on behalf of social, economic, and racial equality marked her as a leader in a period of crisis and conflict.

KCS

✚ Zeppelins

I saw the people climbing up the street
Maddened with war and strength and thought to kill;
And after followed Death, who held with skill
His torn rags royally, and stamped his feet.

The fires flamed up and burnt the serried town,
Most where the sadder, poorer houses were;
Death followed with proud feet and smiling stare,
And the mad crowds ran madly up and down.

And many died and hid in unfound places
In the black ruins of the frenzied night;
And Death still followed in his surplice, white
And streaked in imitation of their faces.

But in the morning men began again
To mock Death following in bitter pain.

"Zeppelins," in *Outlaws* (London: Elkin Mathews, 1921), 26. Reprinted by permission of A.R.A. Hobson.

✝ Danica Marković
(1879–1932) *Serb*

Born in Čačak, Serbia, Marković moved to Belgrade to complete her diploma at the Teacher's Academy but returned to village life as a schoolteacher. Married to a wealthy lawyer, she had six children, three of whom died young. She was divorced in 1926. During World War I, she participated in the local Serb uprising against Bulgarian occupation. Despite her poor health, she published short stories and essays in scattered periodicals. The second of her two volumes of expressionist poetry, *Trenuci i raspolozenja* (Moments and moods), appeared in 1928. Unrecognized as a poet and impoverished, she died of tuberculosis.

In her bitter poem "June 27," a parade of militarist men (priests, intellectuals, poets, authorities) and a legion of beggars gather at a monument to fallen war heroes. June 27 refers to the midsummer festival of St. John, when girls pick flowers in the Serb Orthodox tradition. It is the eve of Vidovdan (St. Vitus's Day), June 28, a state holiday celebrated by patriotic songs and epic poems about national heroes. June 28 marks the anniversary of the defeat at Kosovo in 1389 by Turkish armies, which led to five hundred years of Ottoman rule. Commemorations of that battle have come to carry collective memories and nationalist ideology. For example, the assassination on June 28, 1914, of Archduke Franz Ferdinand by the Serb patriot Gavrilo Princip triggered World War I, and the same date in 1921 was chosen to inaugurate the Kingdom of Serbs, Croats and Slovenes (Yugoslavia) in Belgrade. Marković wrote her poem at the beginning of the twenties.

☦ June 27

The first straw fell, threshed in harvest.
On a summer's day in the wane of June,
With a bunch of Saint John's flowers clasped,
By the clear strum of a brook's tune

I walked to a village where grateful men
Raised for their hero a monument.
And so to invoke the past and Saint Vid
They gathered, thronged in that settlement.

Students were there as well as teachers,
Portly priests—friars in black,
Men of the pen and music makers,
Assorted beggars in a pack.

The monument by the fountain they praised
With many words and speeches in droves;
Song accompanied pompous phrases
Of patriotism and brotherly love.

All this I was condemned to stand!
My thirst seared me, the sun beat,
The flowers wilted in my hand,
And the hard stone bounced back the heat.

The following torment was worse yet:
At a long table, with brimming glass—
Where envy often malice met—
Amid inanities they caroused.

Then after the feast, music and dance,
Boisterous song and toasts again,
The huge crowd's frantic clamor
And rancor—witless vanity reigned.

At last, weariness, boredom, fatigue—
The gifts, the legacy of the repast—
The hideous din, slowly subsiding,
And dry flowers in my clasp.

Translated by Ellen Elias-Bursac

"27-mi Juni," in *Trenuci i raspolozenja* (Belgrade: Mlada Srbija, 1928), 34–35.

✝ Gertrud Kolmar, pseudonym of Gertrud Chodziesner (1894–1943?) *German*

Born in Berlin to a cultivated Jewish family, Gertrud Kolmar was two years younger than her cousin Walter Benjamin, the Marxist critic. During World War I she studied French and English, then was employed as a censor of letters in the Döberitz camp for prisoners of war. Her first collection, *Gedichte* (Poems), appeared in 1917. She worked as a private teacher in Berlin then as a schoolteacher in Hamburg; in her last fifteen years she lived at home again, caring first for her sick mother and then working for her father as long as he was permitted to practice law.

Wort der Stummen (Word of the dumb, 1933), in which "November 9, 'Eighteen" appeared, includes other political poems on topics such as the Roman heroes the Gracchi, Robespierre, imprisonment, and Jewishness; a cycle on Robespierre appeared posthumously. An admirer of Georg Büchner, Georg Trakl, Rainer Maria Rilke, and Annette von Droste Hülshoff, Kolmar experimented with ballad forms and cubist transpositions of imagery "to give a meaning to the apparently meaningless." Her cousin Benjamin wrote that at the end of the war "men returned from the battlefield grown silent—not richer, but poorer in communicable experience."

In the last years of her life Kolmar studied Russian and Hebrew, but her Hebrew poems have been lost. Great elegiac power and self-awareness of her own historic situation define her final work, *Welten* (Worlds, 1947), with its powerful metaphorics and free rhythms. From 1941 she did forced labor in munitions factories. Her brother and sisters emigrated. Her father died at Theresienstadt; in the spring of 1943 she was deported to Auschwitz. The date and place of her death are unknown. Few of her lyric poems and stories appeared in her lifetime. *Eine jüdische Mutter* (A Jewish mother) appeared posthumously in 1965.

☦ November 9, 'Eighteen

Soldiers stood there, strange in familiar paths;
Their eyes wandering, dusty from bunkers and graves,
Smooth and yellow as earth in which they had lain,
They bore mud and peace on their encrusted hands.

Their bolt-bright badge had rusted to bits on them,
The colorful snippets on their bodies all blanched;
They had tasted the foaming fame, the bitter lees,
They had smeared their branny bread with newsprint grease.

Then their silent grip smashed the big words;
They lay hollow as drums, an exploded and empty din.
The braggart lie crawled off in a clump to the corner,
And Germany was not just good, and France was not just evil.

Summer's growth gave them juices and plump brown pips
And rolled unused, fruit fallen to rot from the trellis;
They passed through blooming snow in winter's night with stars
That march a thousand years in silence across blue fields.

They planted gardens full of crosses and sowed the fields full of shots,
But the rays of the sun shone on eternally over the slaughter,
And the mountains spoke "evermore," and the rivers sang "everywhere";
The enemy seemed wilted away and became almost human.

They trampled his land into pulp and knew not why they were there.
They lobbed their shells out and did not ask if they hit.
They seldom thought any more and only felt what they wished:
Soup on their own table and a woman and bed for sleep.

They plunged through eddying craters, buried by sudden grenades,
Listened at mealtime to deaths that feed on moldy corpses,
Observed the grin of madness that deranges grey brains,
And measured the depths. . . . They have forgotten it all.

They enter the lovely forest, where light banners strut,
The wind-blown forest with posts eaten through by worms;
They mirror themselves in shine that will tarnish the day they rearm,
And cry out to idols above, bedizened with rags and noise,

They rejoice at the hopping drumbeat of clattering bones,
At the speeches more meaningless than midday buzzing of flies.
They have thrown aside muteness; to it they will bow down
In war.

23 August 1933

"Der 9. November Achtzehn," in *Das Lyrische Werk* (München: Kösel-Verlag, 1960),
757–59.

✣ Edna St. Vincent Millay, pseudonym: Nancy Boyd (1892–1950) American

P oet, dramatist, and political writer, Edna St. Vincent Millay is remembered for her popular verses and unconventional lifestyle. Raised in Maine by her mother, a practical nurse, Millay was called Vincent by her family after her parents' divorce in 1900. A self-sufficient woman, her mother encouraged the three daughters' study of music and literature. Already a poet when she was a child, at twenty-five Millay published *Renascence and Other Poems*; she composed music and wrote plays as well. Upon graduating from Vassar College, she moved to New York, where the Provincetown Players produced the play *Aria da Capo* (1919), which was compared by a reviewer in 1922 to O'Neill's *Emperor Jones* as one of "the high accomplishments of the art theatre in America." In rebellious Greenwich Village Millay formed relationships with Edmund Wilson, Arthur Fricke, and Floyd Dell. Although she supported the communist ideal of class equality, she never sympathized with the political arm of the communist movement.

A Few Figs from Thistles (1920), her first important volume of poetry, won both literary and popular notice for its brazen nonchalance. Floyd Dell found in it the essence of the postwar generation: "The state of the young mind is individualistic, egocentric, passionately rebellious against authority . . . the newer mode of girlhood, that mood of freedom which is dramatized outwardly by bobbed hair." Her next major volume, *The Harp-Weaver and Other Poems* (1923), won the Pulitzer Prize for poetry, the first awarded to a woman. The sonnets in these volumes illustrate her talent for fashioning concrete images of abstract ideals.

In 1923 Millay married Eugen Jan Boissevain, a Dutch importer who moved with her to a farm and took charge of "quotidian matters," for, as he stated in 1934, "it is so obvious that Vincent is more important than I am." She published essays for *Vanity Fair* gathered in *Distressing Dialogues* (1924), stories under the pseudonym Nancy Boyd, and a libretto for the

New York Metropolitan Opera. She became the lover of George Dillon, with whom she translated Baudelaire's *Flowers of Evil* (1936), and to whom many of her love poems in *Fatal Interview* (1931) are addressed.

Active in defense of causes on the left, Millay was arrested for opposing the death sentence of Sacco and Vanzetti in 1927. In the 1930s she denounced fascism and her poetry became increasingly political. Her collections *Make Bright the Arrows* (1940) and *The Murder of Lidice* (1942) supported war against the Germans; they have not won critical favor. Her passionate involvement with her subject matter, however, anticipated the confessional poets whose work would revolutionize American poetry.

KCS

✝ Conscientious Objector

I shall die, but that is all that I shall do for Death.

I hear him leading his horse out of the stall; I hear the
    clatter on the barn-floor.
He is in haste; he has business in Cuba, business in the
    Balkans, many calls to make this morning.
But I will not hold the bridle while he cinches the girth.
And he may mount by himself: I will not give him a leg
    up.

Though he flick my shoulders with his whip, I will not
    tell him which way the fox ran.
With his hoof on my breast, I will not tell him where the
    black boy hides in the swamp.
I shall die, but that is all that I shall do for Death; I am
    not on his pay-roll.

I will not tell him the whereabouts of my friends nor of
    my enemies either.
Though he promise me much, I will not map him the
    route to any man's door.

Am I a spy in the land of the living, that I should deliver
    men to Death?
Brother, the password and the plans of our city are safe
    with me; never through me
Shall you be overcome.

✝ Sylvia Townsend Warner
(1893–1978) *British*

Author of some thirty volumes of poetry, novels, biography, and short stories, Sylvia Townsend Warner was educated at home by her father, a history master at Harrow School. In 1916, after her father's death, Warner moved to London, where she joined the editorial board of the Church Music Project and assisted in publication of the ten-volume critical study, *Tudor Church Music*. As a relief worker in a munitions factory, she made shell cases at six shillings a day; her article about her work for *Blackwoods Magazine* in 1916 exposed the inequities of wages and the use of women for "dilution" to avoid payment of overtime to regular factory workers.

Warner's acquaintance in London with figures such as Nancy Cunard facilitated her entry into the literary world. In 1923 she met T. F. Powys, an odd novelist who influenced the gothic tone of her early poetry, especially *The Espalier* (1925). He introduced Warner to the poet Valentine Ackland, who became her lifelong companion, sharing a home with her from 1932 until her death in 1969. Together they enlisted as Red Cross volunteers in Spain in 1930 and joined the Communist Party in 1935. She was a member of the Association of Writers for Intellectual Liberty. Warner was praised for her "half-modern, half-archaic blend of naivete and erudition"; she left at her death much unpublished satiric poetry.

Warner's most famous novel, *Lolly Willowes* (1926), a fanciful story of an old maid turned witch, was nominated for the Prix Femina. The six novels and ten volumes of short stories that followed retain Warner's sense of the eccentric, often coupling extraordinary events with unusual settings. She admired Colette for her immediacy, a quality she thought characterized the best female fiction, and declared that Colette's tales take place "under one's very nose." While her prose style was energetic and mercurial, her poetic voice was calmly meticulous, often ironic, and was likened to that of Thomas Hardy. Her third volume of poetry, *Opus 7* (1931), describes an old woman's poverty following World War I in compelling, grandiose, yet

comic verse. Many of her stories and several of her poems first appeared
in *The New Yorker.* She was surprised at the attention she received in her
"extreme old age."
  KCS

✝ Cottage Mantleshelf

On the mantleshelf love and beauty are housed together.
There are the two black vases painted with pink roses,
And the two dogs carrying baskets of flowers in their jaws.
There are the two fans stencilled with characters from Japan,
The ruby glass urns each holding a sprig of heather,
And the two black velvet cats with bead eyes, pink noses, and white cotton
    claws.

All these things on the mantleshelf are beautiful and are married:
The two black vases throb with their sympathetic pink roses,
The puss thinks only of her tom and the dog of his bitch.
On the one fan a girl is coquetting and on the other a man,
Out of the same vein of fancy the urns were quarried,
Even the sprigs of heather have been dried so long you can't tell 'tother
    from which.

But amid this love and beauty are two uncomely whose sorrows
Isled in several celibacy can never, never be mated,
One of them being but for use and the other useful no more.
With a stern voice rocking its way through time the alarm clock
Confronts with a pallid face the billowing to-morrows
And turns its back on the enlarged photograph of young Osbert who died
    at the war.

Against the crumpled cloth where the photographer's fancy
Has twined with roses the grand balustrade he poses,
His hands hang limp from the khaki sleeves and his legs are bent.
His enormous ears are pricked and tense as a startled hare's,
He smiles—and his beseeching swagger is that of a nancy,
And plain to see on the picture is death's indifferent rubber stamp of
    assent.

As though through gathering mist he stares out through the photo's
Discolouring, where the lamp throws its pink-shaded echo of roses
On the table laid for supper with cheese and pickles and tea.
The rose-light falls on his kin who sit there with a whole skin,
It illumines through England the cottage homes where just such ex-voto

Are preserved on their mantleshelves by the living in token that they are
 not as he.

Uncomely and unespoused amid the espousals of beauty.
The cats with their plighted noses, the vases pledging their roses,
The scapegoat of the mantleshelf he stands and may not even cleave
To the other unpaired heart that beats beside him and apart;
For the pale-faced clock has heard, as he did, the voice of duty
And disowns him whom time has disowned, whom age cannot succour nor
 the years reprieve.

1935

"Cottage Mantleshelf," in *Collected Poems,* ed. Claire Harman (Manchester: Carcanet Press, 1982), 21–22. By permission of Carcanet Press.

✟ Louise Bogan
(1897–1970) *American*

T he second child of lower-middle-class Irish parents, Louise Bogan
characterized herself as "the highly charged and neurotically
inclined product of an extraordinary childhood" that was overshadowed by her parents' unhappy marriage. After attending a Catholic elementary school, Louise enrolled for "five most fruitful years" at the Boston
Girls' Latin School. At fourteen, the precocious teenager began to compose poetry, which she later wrote became a "life-saving process" that
released her from her troubled family life.

In 1916, after one year at Boston University, she turned down a scholarship to Radcliffe and left school to marry Curt Alexander, a professional
soldier. By the time she and her husband left for his posting in Panama in
1917, Louise was four months pregnant, and gave birth to her daughter
Maisie while in Panama. The marriage was a failure; in 1919 she left her
husband, who died only a year later. Her widow's pension allowed her to
travel to Vienna to sort out her emotional turmoil.

While she was in Panama, her older brother Charles fought in France,
where he was killed in October 1918, a month before the Armistice.
Charles's death marked a point in Bogan's life when she resigned herself
to the "fading of her hopes." She entitled her first volume of poems *Body
of This Death* (1923). Living in New York with Maisie, she met and married
a minor poet named Raymond Holden. The 1920s were a time of prolific
creativity (*Dark Summer* appeared in 1929), but Bogan also drank heavily,
and in 1931 she suffered her first of two nervous breakdowns. After her
final separation from Holden in 1934, she began a relationship with the
poet Theodore Roethke, her lifelong partner. In her autobiographical
"Journey Around My Room," Bogan candidly wrote, "I have very few of the
usual warm friendships that normal people have." Indeed, in 1964 she
again was hospitalized for depression.

Bogan attained a national reputation as a poet, critic, and translator.
From 1931 until her retirement in 1969, she was the poetry critic for *The

New Yorker, reviewing a number of women, including Edna St. Vincent Millay, Colette, and Rebecca West. Too shy just ten years earlier to introduce herself to Marianne Moore in the New York Public Library, Bogan now criticized Katherine Mansfield for writing with superficial emotion and characterized the style of Virginia Woolf's *A Room of One's Own* as a tedious "point-to-point method." Bogan enjoyed many prizes and accolades: she was a Consultant in Poetry to the Library of Congress in 1945, and a visiting professor at Brandeis University and the University of Washington. In 1955 she won the Bollingen Prize and in 1958 an Academy of American Poets Award for her reticent, yet sensual verse, its "bare stricken lines suggestive of riches," as Mark van Doren wrote.

CW

✠ To My Brother

KILLED: HAUMONT WOOD: OCTOBER, 1918

O you so long dead,
You masked and obscure,
I can tell you, all things endure:
The wine and the bread;

The marble quarried for the arch;
The iron become steel;
The spoke broken from the wheel;
The sweat of the long march;

The hay-stacks cut through like loaves
And the hundred flowers from the seed;
All things indeed
Though struck by the hooves

Of disaster, of time due,
Of fell loss and gain,
All things remain,
I can tell you, this is true.

Though burned down to stone
Though lost from the eye,
I can tell you, and not lie,—
Save of peace alone.

"To My Brother," in *Poems & New Poems* (New York: Scribner's, 1941), 79. Originally published in *The New Yorker.* Reprinted with permission of Ruth Limmer, literary executor.

✝ Lily Novy
(1885–1958) *Slovenian/Yugoslavian*

Born in Graz to an Austrian nobleman and a Slovenian mother, Lily Novy had an excellent education in German and French in schools in Vienna and Ljubljana. Her first poetry and translations were in German. In 1911 she married a Czech-German officer. After World War I she continued to translate Slovenian and other Yugoslav poets into German, contributing *Blätter aus der slowenischen Lyrik* (Leaves from Slovenian lyrics, 1933) to a PEN congress at Dubrovnik and *Frauenlyrik in deutschen Übertragungen* (Women's poetry in German translation), an anthology of Yugoslav women's poetry for a women's congress in 1936. She wrote a number of children's plays and collected her poetry in 1941. A posthumous second volume, *Oboki* (1959), gathered wartime writing of resistance and postwar poetry. A bust in her honor ornaments the house where she lived.

✝ Preparation

Now we cannot speak of ourselves
nor of the fragile things we love,
bound like flowers in a bouquet
in the fair springtime days.

Now we dare not tend frail beauties
as if there were still time for all:
countless fires rage on the peaks,
a sign that slaughter threatens.

Prepare for departure the heavy weapons,
don what you need, your shoes, your clothes:
your calm face grows pale and more severe,
and your heart knows for all.

Just as sleep ends a brief rest,
what awaits us now is like sleep,
there are no paths back to sweet pleasures,
all roads lead out.

We are all like iron fused by fire
in these fateful, doom-laden days;
now we cannot speak of ourselves
nor of the things we love.

Translated by Ellen Elias-Bursac

"Sprememba," in *Gorece telo: isbrane pesmi* (Ljubljana: Mladinska Knjiga, 1985). Translated by permission of Avtorska agencija za Slovenija.

☦ Nightmare

A terrible pressure now bears down
all that breathes, groundward.
A merciless tread shakes
the foundation of the earth.

Winter's white hands
defended with passion
But stained in blood
now they falter.

Its own sigh reawakens
a doom-laden spring.
Everything blossomed in blood
In her, in dream, the orchard.

A merciless tread shakes
the foundation of the earth.
A terrible pressure now bears down
all that breathes, groundward.

Translated by Ellen Elias-Bursac

"Mora," in *Gorece telo: izbrane pesmi* (Ljubljana: Mladinska Knjiga, 1985). Translated by permission of Avtorska agencija za Slovenija.

✚ Vida Jeraj, pseudonym of Frančiška Jeraj, née Vovk (1875–1932) *Slovenian*

Poet and playwright Frančiška Vovk was born in Slovenian Austria and became a village schoolteacher in 1895. Upon her marriage in 1901 to a noted violinist, she moved to Vienna. Her first book of poetry was *Isbrano delo* (1908); a book of children's poetry appeared after the war in 1921, as well as plays for children. Her work is a mix of modernism and traditional sentimental themes. She died in Ljubljana.

✚ 1914

I

Black berries in a rose wreath,
each a dead man's skull,
each a drop of blood,
May God have mercy!

Pray, pray, O Slovene,
perhaps God remembers you!
He who does not pray, shall curse:
May Satan have mercy!

II

From dreams a mother rises into night:
memory knocking at the door,
knocking at thousands of cottages.
On the battlefields lies my son!

Where does that red trail lead in the snow?
Where does the wind bear the last sigh?
Lands, waters, nine mountains high—
my son, how can I get across?

Translated by Ellen Elias-Bursac

From *Izbrano delo* (Zagreb, 1935). Translated by permission of Avtorska agencija za Slovenija.

✝ Anonymous
(Olivia Tambala, singer) *Malawi*

When interviewed in her village, Olivia Tambala may have been in her seventies. In 1914 the village chief reported to his people that war had broken out; the British then "came to the houses, carrying the young men away to where they were slain at the war." At the same time, influenza ("that coughing disease") killed many at home: "We wondered whether we the people would survive." When the men died at Karonga, the villagers held a funeral ceremony, in which songs such as this one were sung.

✝ Song

At Karonga
People perished there, at Karonga.
Why did they perish?

At Karonga
People perished there, at Karonga.
Why did people perish
At Karonga?

Young men died there.
Why did people die?

Sung by Olivia Tambala, in Chimwendo Village, Ntchisi District, Malawi. Recorded and translated by Melvin E. Page, August 1, 1973.

ARTISTS' BIOGRAPHIES

Note: No biographical information has been found for Laura Brey.

Anna Airy (1882–1964) *British*

Airy was a student for four years at the Slade School of Art in London, where she won its prestigious Nettleship Prize three years in a row. She focused on urban lowlife, reporting later that she had escaped arrest on the occasion of a murder in a gambling den. In 1908, she married Geoffrey Pocock. Airy was a member of the Royal Society of Painters and Etchers, as well as the Royal Society of Oil Painters; she published books on *The Art of Pastel* (1930) and *Making a Start in Art* (1951).

The Imperial War Museum commissioned her to paint oils depicting scenes of munitions factories but turned out to be intent upon receiving "more uninteresting technical drawings." Having offered her £250, they reduced the amount to £150 (men were offered £100 minimum per canvas). She reported on the harsh conditions of work at the shell foundry: "I've never felt such heat! The floor got 'black hot.' I burnt a pair of shoes right off my feet! . . . You have to paint these red-hot shells so very fast because of the color changing; so glancing rapidly up and down from a glowing shell to my canvas, I would suddenly catch sight of a black object apparently fallen onto the shell . . . a kipper being cooked to provide an impromptu meal!"

Alice Bailly (1872–1938) *Swiss*

The daughter of a German teacher and a postman named Bally, Alice Bailly (who added the *i* to her signature in 1909) studied at the École des Beaux Arts in Geneva. Attracted by the avant-garde Fauve painters such as Raoul Dufy, she visited Paris in 1904; her move there in 1906 marked the end of a first period of realistic descriptive work. In Paris, contact with Dufy, as well as Albert Gleizes, Robert Delaunay, and Marie Laurencin, shifted her palette to pastels and led her to define planes through color. Bailly's work was controversial: two of her paintings on exhibit in Geneva in 1907—*Rose Garden* and *Three Women's Torsos*—incited a scandal. Her painting *Maternity* was the first by a female painter to be exhibited at the Salon d'Automne (1909). In the years just before the war, the chromatic facets of her geometrical landscapes caught the notice of the poet Apollinaire, who noted her modern technique and "freshness of sentiment." Her works sold at higher prices than those of Delaunay in 1913, when she painted her best-known oil, the Futurist *Equestrian Fantasy with a Pink Lady*, which established her as the "most modern" of Swiss artists. Her transparent, fresh colors and dynamic movement belong to "Orphic" cubism and announce her own version of Futurism.

When the war broke out, Bailly returned to Switzerland, where she suffered increasing financial difficulties. In spite of censorship of any art that was not strictly neutral, she painted a number of clearly francophile subjects, including *The Child and His War* (1916–18), *Homage to the Colors of France* (1917), *Heroic Crowns*, and *To the Triumph of the Allied Colors* (1918). In 1916 she met the Dadaist circle in Zurich, whose influence can be seen in *Battle* (1917–20), with its collage, scattered letters, and political code (a reference to "espion," or a spy-scandal). At one Dada soirée, she displayed a large Swiss flag to explain that Swiss neutrality was a way to defend the whole world; she was critical of Tristan Tzara's nihilist derision. Bailly began to create "wool-paintings" that evoke in a different register the striated lines of her Futurist work, as the woolen *Homage* echoes her *Tricolor Bouquet.* For her there was no difference in artistic value between the media, and she even fused techniques. She relied on numerous portraits of friends to make ends meet.

Although one of her close friends was the feminist journalist Suzanne Bonard, Bailly refused to join the Society of Swiss Women Painters, Sculptors, and Decorators. "Art," she insisted, "is not a matter of a skirt or pants." She refused to show with the Salon des Femmes. Her quickness in repartee and persiflage sometimes further strained her intense relationships with other artists. In the decade following the war, Bailly returned to Paris, although she also kept a studio in Lausanne. Her work became darker, more static, and descriptive. In 1932–33 she organized a retrospective exhibit of her own work. At her death she established a foundation to support young artists.

AF

Phyllis Bone (1896–1972) *English*

A sculptor primarily of animals, Bone was born in Lancashire. She studied at Edinburgh College of Art, then went to Paris to work with Havellier, who was known for his animal sculptures; she also spent some time in Italy. Upon settling in Edinburgh she became an active participant in exhibitions, showing at the Royal Scottish Academy, the Glasgow Institute of Fine Arts, the Walker Art Gallery in Liverpool, the Royal Academy of London, and the Salon de la Société des Artistes Français in Paris (1921). In 1944, she became the first woman member of the Royal Scottish Academy.

During World War I, Bone drove a car for the Women's Legion. She was one of several women artists who contributed to the Scottish War Memorial at Edinburgh, which opened in 1927. Among the others was Gertrude Alice Meredith-Williams, who also sculpted the monumental memorial at Paisley, Scotland. The first visitors to the Scottish War Memorial at Edinburgh were King George and Queen Mary.

Deborah Bright (b. 1950) *American*

A professor of photography and art history at the Rhode Island School of Design, Deborah Bright has exhibited her work at the National Museum of American Art, the Victoria and Albert Museum, the Vancouver Art Gallery, Boston's Institute of Contemporary Art, and the Canadian Museum of Contemporary Photography. She was a Bunting Fellow at Radcliffe College in 1995–96. Bright has edited a collection of essays on photography and sexuality, *The Passionate Camera,* and her critical writing on photography and cultural issues has appeared in *Afterimage,* the *Art Journal, exposure,* and *Views.*

After reading John Keegan's *The Face of Battle,* Bright began to make a large-scale series, *Battlefield Panoramas,* to show the sites where major battles took place as they look today. The overlapping composite photographs, which provide high resolution, remind us that this was a "terrain of trauma" in which a tree or rise marked the line between survival and death. Bright resists formalist esthetic criteria by attaching a text to her dated pictures in the voice of a journalist who records the place, the number of casualties, and the duration of the fighting. She thus inscribes her own position as a chronicler of sites that "are constantly in evolution." At Beaumont Hamel the front lines were very close: German tourists along the German trenches are visible from the allied trench line where the photographer stands. For such tourists, Bright comments, the much transformed landscape is often "pastoral and romantic in appearance." One of her aims is to recapture "a sense of the trauma of the event that took place."

Mairi Chisholm (b. 1896) *British*

Eighteen when she left her aristocratic Scottish family to volunteer for war work, Mairi Chisholm first rode dispatch on her motorcycle for the Women's Emergency Corps, then became a driver for the mobile ambulance corps raised in the fall of 1914 by Dr. Harold Munro to assist the Belgian Army. In November Chisholm and Elsie Knocker, a trained nurse, set up a frontline post at the ruined village of Pervyse. Their rapid delivery of first-aid and immediate treatment of shock reduced fatalities and won them international fame; in February 1915, they were awarded the Belgian Cross by the King of Belgium himself. Sometimes working within twenty-five yards of German trenches, Chisholm carried men on her back to the ambulance. "Some of the wounds were pathetic; men emasculated and things like that." Repeatedly forced by shelling to move their first-aid "poste" from one house or cellar to another, the two women were finally obliged to quit their work after being badly gassed in 1918. Both women took photographs, but the photographs printed here are from Chisholm's personal album.

Marie Curie, née Manya Sklodowska
(1867–1934) *Polish/French*

Marie's mother directed a boarding school for girls; her patriotic father, Wladyslaw, a professor at a secondary school in Warsaw, was fired for his opposition to Russian rule. Her sister Sophie died of typhus in 1876, her mother in 1878. She brilliantly completed her studies in 1883, then gave illegal lessons in Polish culture and history in a "flying" or underground school.

In 1891, Marie's sister Bronislawa invited her to Paris, where she studied mathematics, physics, and chemistry, earning a *licence* in 1893 in physics and another in mathematics in 1894. She married Pierre Curie in 1895 and joined him in his laboratory. In 1896, she passed the *aggrégation* examination, permitting her to teach at a normal school for young women. In the following years she measured the ionization of uranium X rays and discovered polonium and radium with her husband; her doctoral thesis was devoted to radioactive materials (1903). In 1903, she was awarded the Davy medal and shared the Nobel Prize in physics. Two daughters, Irène and Eve, were born in 1897 and 1904. Pierre died tragically in an accident in 1906; she edited his works in 1908 and published his biography in 1924. At the university she took Pierre's position teaching physics, winning tenure in 1909. The following year she published a treatise on radioactivity, and in 1911, she was awarded the Nobel Prize in chemistry; the French Academy rejected her by one vote, simply, it is said, because she was a woman.

The university and the Pasteur Institute created a Radium Institute, with a laboratory under her direction devoted to radioactivity as well as another laboratory devoted to X-ray therapy. Due to open just as the war broke out, the laboratory was disrupted by the shortage of technicians. She turned to the provision of X rays at frontline stations and in mobile ambulances. With the support of the Union des Femmes de France, she designed the first radiology van, carrying a roentgen apparatus and dynamo, and equipped twenty such "little Curies" in the course of the war with her own funds, one of which she drove herself in emergencies along the front. She also established 200 fixed radiology rooms and trained 150 women as radiologists, including her daughter Irène.

At the end of the war Marie Curie published a study demonstrating the importance of X-ray technology for military medicine, *La Radiologie et la guerre* (Radiology and war, 1921). In 1922, she was elected to the Academy of Medicine; she published two more books on isotopes and radioactivity.

Henriette Marguerite Blanche Damart
(b. 1895) *French*

A student of Odilon Redon, Déchenaud, and Robert-Fleury, between 1911 and 1937 Damart exhibited in Paris at the Salon d'Automne and the Salon de Tunis. In 1911 she became a member of the Société des Artistes

Français. In 1920, she won the Prix Gallimard-Jambet, and in 1924, a silver medal, the Order of Nicham Iftikar, for her work, principally portraits of children and marine subjects. Her illustrated books include the charming feminist war book for children *Toinette et la guerre* written by Lucie Paul-Margueritte (undated).

Joyce Dennys (b. 1895) *English*

Daughter of a military officer, Dennys was born in India, but her mother immediately moved with her four children to England, where they lived with an assortment of cousins whose parents in government service had returned to India. Her parents were content that she was a girl, they told her, "because we thought you would be cheaper." At Exeter Art School she studied with Burman Morell. A number of her brothers and cousins disappeared during the war: one died in Mesopotamia, another in India; of her cousin Dick Dennys, a poet who died after receiving a head wound, she wrote that "he couldn't bear the ugliness of war any more." Through "vicissitudes" that she does not describe, Dennys served as a V.A.D.; six years after she first fell in love with Thomas Evans, a doctor who emigrated to Australia, then fought with the Australians at Gallipoli and at the Somme, she married him in January 1918; they had one daughter and lived in later years in Devonshire.

A prolific comic illustrator and writer of light fiction and drama, Dennys devoted several jaunty books to women's war work. With visual wit, *Our Hospital A(nzac) B(ritish) C(anadian)* (1916), set to text by Hampden Gordon and M. C. Tindall, captures the strains between trained nursing sisters and V.A.D.s, between nurses and doctors, and between volunteers who are society women and those who are scullery maids. Dennys teasingly raises the question whether nurses are "the right sort of wenches." A second collaboration with Gordon was *Our Girls in War Time* (1917), and *Rhymes of the Red Triangle*, devoted to the YMCA, followed in 1918. In the 1940s, Dennys illustrated a series of children's books by Rodney Bennett concerned with the adventures of Puffin, Twink, and Waggle "at Home," "at the Fair," "at the Seaside," and "at the Zoo." Active into the 1960s, she also produced seventeen short plays, many of them for women to perform, as well as plays and pantomimes for children. Among her last pieces were *Henrietta's War* (1985) and *Henrietta Sees It Through* (1986), compiled from articles she published during World War II in the *Weekly Sketch*. Her autobiography, *And Then There Was One* (1983), illustrated with line drawings, recalls childish escapades with relish.

Olive Edis (1876–1955) *British*

Educated at King's College, London, Olive Edis was forced by the death of her father, a gynecologist, to earn a living. In 1905 she set up a photographic studio on the coast with her younger sister, Katherine, following in the footsteps of a great-uncle who made his own camera and recorded the architecture of India while serving as Surgeon General. She was one of the first woman photographers to make color autochromes, patenting her own viewer; she won a medal for color transparencies in 1913, the same year she became a fellow of the Royal Photographic Society. In her favorite genre, portraiture, she favored a rich brown platinotype, using natural light only; she also took some local-color subjects.

In 1918 the Imperial War Museum's Women's Work Committee commissioned her to record women's work with auxiliary services in Europe; her trip was delayed until 1919 by the confusion of troop movements at the time of the Armistice, but more seriously by the resistance of Colonel Lee, the officer in charge of coordinating such documentation, who saw no reason for a woman to duplicate the work of his own male photographers. Edis took with her to France two field cameras and a folding Kodak (after signing an agreement to take no cameras at all into military territory). She was the fifth official photographer sent by Britain and the only woman. She traveled 2000 kilometers to some of the most famous battlefields, to destroyed towns, and to major V.A.D. and W.A.A.C. stations. Unable to use natural light for many of her official subjects, she nevertheless captured the sense of women at work.

In 1920, Edis held an exhibit of her war photographs, portraits, and other autochromes. She also traveled to Canada to take publicity photographs of the Rockies. She preferred to photograph men, she said, because a man "usually likes himself the way he is and wants his photograph to look like him," whereas women "are so anxious about their effects—particularly about the effect of their dress." In 1928, Edis married Edwin Galsworthy.

Florence Farmborough (b. 1887) *English*

Florence Farmborough, who would follow her famous namesake, Florence Nightingale, in becoming a nurse, was born in Buckinghamshire in 1887. After being educated in England, she went to Russia in 1908 at the age of twenty-one to teach English to children, working first in Kiev, then in Moscow for a doctor's family. When Germany declared war on Russia in August 1914, Farmborough saw in her own situation an opportunity for action, and she threw herself into Russia's war effort. Alongside the Russian crowds on the streets of Moscow, Farmborough felt the thrill of seeing Czar Nicholas II rally his country on to war, and she wrote: "We are elated beyond words. We too, in our small way are to help the country's cause."

Farmborough immediately entered a training hospital run by Princess Golitsi, and after six months had passed the exams to be assigned as a nurse to the 10th Red Cross Field Division for a Russian "flying" unit that followed frontline troops. By 1915, she had been sent with her unit to the lower Carpathian mountains and would remain on active service in this area of the western Ukraine and eastern Austria-Hungary until 1917, with the exception of a brief period of enforced recovery from paratyphoid in the Crimea in 1916. After the February Revolution, Farmborough saw Kerensky, as leader of Russia's new provisional government, speak to the

Russian troops in May 1917 and heard the soldiers' cheers as they rallied to "Free Mother Russia." But less than a year later, when the army had disbanded in chaos, Farmborough went back to her Moscow friends, then traveled home to England by a circuitous route, taking a train to Vladivostok filled with refugees, including the most famous Russian woman soldier, Maria Botchkareva.

During her three years of duty Farmborough worked with unfailing energy and enthusiasm to heal the sick and wounded. Equally important, she wanted to record what she saw and experienced in the field for future generations to share. Thus she devoted what little spare time she had to writing detailed diary entries about her experiences and to taking photographs on glass slides of the soldiers, country peasants, and refugees she encountered. In the thick of battle, she kept her diary on odd scraps of paper, sometimes writing a single word on each piece—then later put her entries together into one volume for publication; evidence of this interrupted composition can be seen in the sometimes truncated narrative. Her graphic, beautifully composed, and sometimes violent photographs tell a story in themselves. In response to the over eight hundred letters of praise that Farmborough received upon the publication of her diary in 1974, she published a separate book, *Russian Album 1908–1918*, which provides a brief narrative but relies primarily on photographs to tell the story of her experiences.

CW

Lady Feodora Gleichen (1861–1922) *British*

The sculptor Feodora Gleichen was an aristocrat who had been rigorously trained at the Slade School of the Arts under Alphonse Legros, as well as with her sculptor father, Count Victor Gleichen, and in Rome. A relative of Queen Victoria, she lived in St. James's Palace, London. Her work hung at the Columbian Exposition in Chicago, 1893, and the Paris Exposition Universelle, where she won a bronze medal in 1900. Gleichen did portrait busts of English nobility and political leaders, including a life-size sculpture of Queen Victoria and a tombstone for King Edward VII. Her sister Helena, who nursed in the Balkans, was also an artist; Helena's oil painting *Troops Moving into Gorizia After the Battle of 8 August 1916* was commissioned by the Imperial War Museum. The commissioning committee indicated in its correspondence that it was particularly concerned about her ability to draw on her experience as a Red Cross X-ray operator in Italy from 1915 to 1917 in a mobile unit with the second and third Italian armies. Feodora made a model of her sister and Mrs. Holling taking a radiograph of a soldier's leg, which was acquired by the Imperial War Museum. Sister of the first Commander of the 37th Division, Gleichen designed a naturalistic memorial to the division erected at Moncy-le-Preux, near Arras, which shows three men at ease, back to back in an informal triangle that invokes solidarity and mutual defence. The Imperial War Museum rejected her offer to present her cast of the memorial.

Gleichen exhibited at the Glasgow Institute of Fine Arts, the Grosvenor

Gallery, the Royal Academy, the Society of Women Artists, and the Walker Art Gallery in Liverpool. She was posthumously named the first woman member of the Royal Society of British Sculpture. Her works are scattered around the world—in Cairo, Khartoum, Montreal, Sydney, and France, as well as England.

Nathalia Sergeyevna Goncharova (1881–1962) *Russian*

Goncharova was born in a village in central Russia to aristocratic parents; her paternal grandmother was the daughter of the poet of Pushkin, and one of her ancestors had been the architect of Peter the Great. Brought up in a highly cultured atmosphere, she went away to school in Moscow, entering the School of Painting, Sculpture and Architecture in 1898. There she met in 1900 Mikhail Larionov, who became her lifelong companion and collaborator; the two influenced each other's multifaceted experiments—in painting, scene and costume design, book illustration, even wallpaper design.

Upon graduation in 1902, Goncharova turned toward Russian popular art and icons to develop a primitivist style of painting. In 1906, she took her work to the Salon d'Automne in Paris, where Diaghilev organized a show of Russian artists. Around 1909, she began designing sets and costumes for the theater. She and Larionov moved quickly toward abstraction, participating in Futurist and Rayonnist shows that stressed mechanical movement, modernity, and the structure of perception as ways of transcending objective representation. Together they organized a series of avant-garde group exhibits: "Jack of Diamonds" (1910), "Donkey's Tail" (1911), "Target Group" (1913), and "No. 4" (1913). In 1913, she held in Moscow a show of her own work, comprising 761 paintings. Two thousand people visited her 1914 show in St. Petersburg; 12 of 249 paintings were seized by the police as blasphemous. In June 1914, she and Larionov exhibited work in Paris; the pictures were seized by German authorities on their way back to Russia, but were saved from destruction by Herwarth Walden, a Berlin leader of the movement Der Sturm.

Called up to fight, Larionov was quickly wounded by shrapnel and discharged with nephritis as an invalid. Goncharova met his train: "I no longer remember where . . . but I still remember the platform, the steps, and the large white bandages around his legs." By year's end she had produced a powerful set of fourteen lithographs without text entitled *Voina: misticheskie obrazy voini* (War: Mystical images of war, 1914), whose apocalyptic images of death and destruction echo primitive woodcuts (*lubki*).

In 1915, she left Russia via Sweden and Norway to join Diaghilev in Switzerland and, with Larionov, painted theatrical decors for the Ballets Russes, traveling to Spain and Italy, Rome and Paris. After 1918, she and Larionov lived primarily in Paris, acquiring French nationality in 1938; there she worked on Diaghilev's *Les Noces* (1923) and *Firebird* (1926). Her painterly style over the following decades alternated between naturalism and abstraction.

AF

Lady Kathleen Scott Kennet, née Bruce (1878–1947) *British*

The youngest of eleven children, Kathleen Bruce was orphaned early and sent to boarding school. She studied sculpture at the Slade School of Art, and in 1896 studied in Paris. She volunteered in 1903 for relief work in Greece but caught typhoid; in the next several years she spent time in Italy, Greece, and Paris. In 1908, she married the Antarctic explorer Robert Scott, with whom she had one son; Scott died in 1912.

During the war Lady Scott first served at a frontline hospital of the French Army. On her return in 1915 to London, she briefly worked at a bench of the Vickers armaments works. On a trip to Carrara in 1916, she reported that she had stopped by an incomplete tombstone of an Italian soldier, picked up the workmen's tools, and finished it by fading light. Lady Scott volunteered at a *crèche*, then in 1917 was asked to be an administrative secretary at the Ministry of Pensions. In July 1918, she became "supervisor of modelling and casting at the new Ellerman facial hospital for officers." In her diary for October 5 she recorded creating a facial model for the plastic surgeon of a man with no mouth: "rather bad. They asked me if I could stand it, and I replied confidently that I could, and I did, but I was very unwell when the tension was over." Another day she wrote that she felt "terribly like God, the creator."

Her view of women artists was "absolutely negative," and when asked about helping women sculptors, she replied, "I don't believe in them. I don't consider them helpable or worth helping." Yet she herself was intensely happy when sculpting, working until exhausted. In 1922, she married Hilton Young, later Lord Kennet; her son Wayland was born in July 1923, four months before her war memorial, the "Thinking Soldier," was unveiled at Huntingdon. She devoted herself primarily to memorials, statues, and busts, including one of King George V.

Helen Johns Kirtland (1890?–1979) *American*

Just married to Lucien Swift Kirtland, a *Leslie's Magazine* photographic reporter, Helen Johns Kirtland traveled as a photographer to France and Italy. She was "the first and only woman correspondent," *Leslie's* claimed, to be allowed at the Italian front along the Piave since the famous battle of Caparetto. She was assisted by the YMCA, which provided her a driver to visit recently shelled towns, the roads along which the Italians were advancing, and Austrian trenches captured a few hours earlier. In France she photographed French women sewing linen covering for rebuilt Liberty planes as well as the American camouflage factory at Dijon. "When I arrived with my camera," she explained, no one knew what to make of me." Her "outside lens" violated a "sacrosanct" line, and her film had to be censored before she could see the results. Other women working for *Leslie's* were Alice Rohe, who photographed memorial services in Italy, and Florence Harper, who witnessed the struggle between Bolsheviks and Germans in Finland.

Käthe Kollwitz, née Schmidt (1867–1945) *German*

Born in East Prussia, Käthe Schmidt was supported by her socialist family in pursuing her calling as an artist; she studied copper engraving and design in Berlin, Munich, Paris, Rome, and Florence. Her ideas were influenced by the writings of Goethe, the art of Goya, and the work of her contemporaries Max Klinger and Ernst Barlach. Injustice, she felt, is worse than disorder.

In 1891, in Berlin, she married Dr. Karl Kollwitz, with whom she had two sons. Her husband was physician for a worker's health insurance fund in a poor quarter of the city; her studio was next to his office, and this exposed her to suffering and despair.

She first won acclaim for her cycle of etchings *The Weavers' Revolt* (1898), inspired by Gerhart Hauptmann, animated by "the desire for 'an eye for an eye.' " Kaiser Wilhelm II withheld a gold medal. Her preferred topics were social, her style expressionist. She returned to the subject of popular rebellion against exploitation in the 1905–8 engravings of the German Peasant War, or *Bauernkrieg*.

From the outset of World War I she questioned the legitimacy of war. In September 1914, she wrote in her diary, "In such times it seems so stupid that the boys must go to war. The whole thing is so ghastly and insane. Occasionally there comes the foolish thought: how can they possibly take part in such madness? And at once the cold shower: They must, must! All is leveled by death; down with all the youth! Then one is ready to despair." Her son Peter was killed on October 22, 1914, in Flanders. In December she was already working on his memorial. Two years later she noted: "Now the war has been going on for two years and five million young men are dead and more than that number again are miserable, their lives wrecked. Is there anything at all that can justify it?" In October 1918, she wrote a public response to the writer Richard Dehmel's call for a battalion of death to save Germany's honor: "Enough have died. . . . Seed for planting must not be ground." Her antiwar work included prints, posters, and the memorial sculptures of the *Mourning Parents*. Only after decades of artistic struggle to give her grief expression did she complete this monument at Roggefeld, near Dixmude, in 1932.

In 1919, Kollwitz had become a member of the Prussian Academy of Art, but she was forced out in 1933 under Nazi pressure, forbidden to exhibit and dismissed from teaching. Her grandson Peter was killed in World War II.

AH

B. A. Laurenson, *British*

Laurenson served as a WREN (G. 4955) in communications at the Royal Naval Base at Lerwick, Scotland, the northernmost outpost of the Women's Royal Navy. Five of the women were killed in an explosion in April 1915, when an ammunition store went off. The women were recruited locally, with two officers and sixteen "ratings." The commemorative volume from which this sketch comes includes cartoons, fine marginal pen-and-ink drawings of the port, and a history of the base, contributed by largely anonymous men and women who had served there.

Louise Lantz Lyon (1885–1948) *French*

Born at Mulhouse in Alsace (annexed by Germany in 1871 after the Franco-Prussian War), Louise Lantz came from a family of industrialists who manufactured printed textiles. In 1909, she married Jacques Lyon, a Parisian lawyer who later turned to politics, following in the footsteps of his father, who had presided at the French Conseil d'État. Shortly before her husband was mobilized in September 1914, their daughter was born. Wounded in March 1915, Jacques received the Croix de guerre and was transferred to noncombat posts, serving in 1916 in a military mission attached to the British army and later helping prepare the peace negotiations. The shrapnel extracted from his wound was transformed by Louise into a piece of jewelry, a memento of his suffering and survival. As a volunteer nurse with the Union des Femmes Françaises, Louise Lyon served near the front lines. After the war she continued to do volunteer medical work at a school in a Paris suburb from 1919 to 1932. In 1921, a son was born. When Germans occupied Paris in World War II, she organized her son's escape to England, where he served under General de Gaulle with the Free French forces.

Olive Mudie-Cooke (1890–1925) *British*

Mudie-Cooke trained in art at St. John's Wood and at Goldsmith's College, then traveled to Venice for further study. Throughout the war she served with the Voluntary Aid Detachment as an ambulance driver in France and Italy: according to an obituary by her fellow artist George Clausen she also served the V.A.D. as an interpreter of French, German and Italian. While on duty she began to make watercolor sketches of the sites where she was working. When the Women's Work Commission of the Imperial War Museum was funded, it commissioned her to draw V.A.D. activities; she was still on duty in France at the time. She was persuaded to accept a mere 5 guineas a drawing, much lower than the rate for male artists. In 1920, she compiled a folio of lithographs based on her original watercolors, which was exhibited at Cambridge, "chiefly as a souvenir album for the V.A.D. ambulance drivers with whom I worked during the war." After traveling and spending a winter in Madrid, she went on in 1923 to South Africa, where she was fascinated by the stark landscapes; she exhibited in Cape Town and Ruban. On her death in France at the age of thirty-five, Clausen wrote that her work was "not in any way conciliatory" but had "the real thing."

Marthe Picard (b. 1898) *French*

When the French National Committee for Planning and Saving organized a competition among Parisian schoolchildren for poster designs, the sixteen-year-old Marthe Picard was one of the winners. Wartime propaganda was fully integrated with school instruction, and one of its privileged themes was the war to be won on the home front by the efforts of all, including children. In this realm girls could demonstrate their patriotism as well as boys. The goal, as the poster caption baldly stated, was "the moral and material expansion of France." The solidarity to which this poster appeals was critical in the difficult years of 1917–18, when the failures of military strategy, mutinies, and a harsh winter all pointed toward a crisis.

Émilie Rolez, née Vallerey (1895–1986) *French*

Professor at the École des Beaux-Arts in Cherbourg, Émilie Rolez had lost a brother during the war. Her sculpture, unveiled in 1932, commemorated the 225 dead "children" of Équeurdreville, the fallen soldiers who left bereft families behind. Most of the 40,000 war memorials in France exalt the sacrifice of the common soldier. Only three carry the inscription, "Cursed Be War," which the socialist mayor took from the refrain of a popular pacifist song.

Olga Vladimirovna Rozanova (1886–1918) *Russian*

A nonobjective painter, illustrator, and poet, Rozanova studied at the Bolshakov Art College and Stroganov Art School in Moscow between 1904 and 1910. She was active with the Constructivists and Futurists in Moscow, and in St. Petersburg came to know Mikhail Matyushin, Kasimir Malevich (for whose journal, *Supremus*, she was secretary), and the poet Vladimir Mayakovski. At the 1912–13 "Union of Youth" exhibit in St. Petersburg, she showed fauvist canvases, with flattened figures and abstracted outlines. She also contributed to the avant-garde shows "Tramway V," "0.10," and "Jack of Diamonds," adapting cubist and Futurist elements in a move closer to suprematism. In 1915, she turned to decorative arts, designing textiles, clothing, and accessories for production by rural workshops.

Married in 1916 to the painter-poet Alexander Kruchenykh, she illustrated two important Futurist booklets he published that year: *Voina* (War), with collages and linocuts, and *Veselenskaia voina* (Universal war), whose brilliant collages have been attributed to both of them. She worked on a journal project with Malevich, Matyushin, and Liubov Popova and helped elaborate audacious innovations in Suprematist book design. In aesthetic articles she described words as "sound and letter" and advocated "the decomposition of nature's ready-made images." She wed the formal elements of planar displacement, conflicts of color, and issues of equilibrium with the theme of urban dehumanization.

In 1918, she became a member of the People's Commissariat of Enlightenment (IZO Narkompros), and with Alexander Rodchenko she directed the industrial art section under Vladimir Tatlin. She also taught textiles at the Free Art Studio (SVOMAS) and was a member of Proletkult; she did a series of fashion and embroidery designs. After she died of diphtheria in November 1918, at thirty-two, Ivan Kliun published a posthumous catalog of her work.

Ethel Caroline Rundquist, *American*

A painter, illustrator, and engraver, Rundquist was born and lived in Minneapolis, and studied at the Art Institute of Chicago. She served with the YMCA "lyceum" group of touring entertainers in Europe during the war. Her cartoons about this experience were printed in an official history of the YMCA work, *Entertaining the American Army* by James W. Evans (New York: Association Press, 1921).

Charlotte Schaller-Mouillot (b. 1880) *Swiss/French*

Born in Berne, Switzerland, Schaller adopted French citizenship at marriage to Mr. Mouillot. Between 1910 and 1920 she showed at the Salon d'Automne, the Salon des Indépendants, and the Salon des Humoristes in Paris. Extremely patriotic, she wrote and illustrated militarist books for children in 1914–18. The child protagonist of *En guerre* (1914; tr. *At War,* 1917), for example, makes a bonfire of German toys and grammar books; the melodramatic actions of war are illustrated with boldly outlined and colored stencils. *Histoire d'un brave petit soldat* (Story of a courageous little soldier, 1915) likewise effectively stylizes figures and settings to depict its toy actors. Schaller also collaborated on an anti-German satiric review, *La Baïonnette.*

Lina von Schauroth, née Holzmann (1874–1970) *German*

From her early childhood in Frankfurt am Main, Lina Holzmann was fascinated by animals and dedicated to the graphic representation of their movement and expression. Her wealthy family fostered her interest in art and architecture, giving her private lessons and sending her to Paris for study. Disappointed by French esthetic debates, she returned to study in Frankfurt and Munich, becoming an accomplished graphic artist. An ardent horsewoman, she decided to wear a rider's tailored frockcoat and bowtie—a style of dress that she never abandoned. At twenty she married Lieutenant Hans von Schauroth, with whom she lived in various garrison towns before his early death in 1909 after a fall from a horse. Widowed at thirty-five, she turned to her art for support; she left her son behind with a nursemaid when she went to study further in Munich.

Von Schauroth's devotion to her husband's memory drew her into relief work in 1914: she gathered packages for soldiers and drove with them to the western front, where she was able to observe and draw the bat-

tle of the Marne. She also drove to the eastern front to bring back the
body of her nephew. Her graphic designs from the period 1914–18
include postcards on military themes, posters for war bonds, and book
illustrations. Their realism is sharply modified in favor of pure decorative
lines outlining flat planes of somber color. In the final year of the war she
worked briefly in a munitions factory. One of her war memorials, a thirty-
foot mosaic column, survives in the evangelical church at Oberursel.

Intensely nationalist, von Schauroth encouraged the failed Kapp putsch
(1920). In the 1920s she developed a new career creating stained-glass
windows for homes, churches, and public buildings; she also illustrated
poems and designed books. Von Schauroth was distinguished with numerous medals and awards: the Prussian service cross, the Hessian war medal,
the Hindenburg cross, and Red Cross medals. In 1944, her house in
Frankfurt was bombed, destroying her archive of designs and much of her
work. During the reconstruction of Frankfurt after World War II she
received important commissions for monumental mosaics, stained-glass
windows, and architectural decor.

Lucy Kemp Welch (1869–1958) *English*

Taught at home by their mother and father, Lucy Kemp Welch and her
younger sister, Edith, kept a menagerie for friends, and both became
artists at an early age. Their father took them on rambles in New Forest,
transmitting to them his own amateur love for entomology and anatomy.
Petite and energetic, Lucy was showing her work in local exhibitions by
the age of fourteen, and by age sixteen had sold her first picture. Her
teens were overshadowed by her beloved father's tuberculosis; he died
when she was nineteen. Her first formal training came in local studios,
and in 1891, she and her sister entered the Herkomer School of Art in
Bushey, but temporarily withdrew when their mother died in 1892. Lucy
was a dedicated disciple of Hubert Herkomer and directed the school
when his health began to fail, then bought it and ran it until 1926.

Welch specialized in large, dynamic paintings depicting animals that
were often larger than herself; her preference, however, was not for the ele-
gantly bred horses that had been so popular among the British gentry and
aristocracy in earlier centuries, but rather working horses, straining and
shaggy, or the heroic horse of the military. Both she and her sister composed posters to support the war effort. At the same time that she continued to paint, however, she tried to volunteer for service on the Continent,
taking first-aid classes and driving lessons so that she could join an ambulance corps. The Red Cross instead assigned her to do filing. Among her
memorial commissions, she designed an allegorical group to represent
women's war work, which was purchased by the Empress Club in 1922.

In the 1920s and 1930s Welch toured with Lord John Sanger's Circus,
living in a caravan and painting the rough-and-tumble life of the troupe.
Edith, who had been her closest companion, died at forty-one of cancer.
At Lucy's death a gallery of her works was created at Bushey.

Gertrude Vanderbilt Whitney
(1875–1942) *American*

Born into one of the richest families in America and married into another, to newspaper reporters Whitney complained that as a woman of wealth she had difficulty being taken seriously as an artist. "Not only did I have to learn how to make my fingers more facile, but I had to fight, fight all the time, to break down the walls of half-sympathetic and half- scornful criticism." People would not believe that a woman her size "could build up a statue of that height," or that her studio was a site for serious work. Her husband, an alcoholic and depressive, spent many months apart from her hunting and camping; by contrast, she relished the drama of multiple affairs and the buzz of society life, wearing avant-garde ball costumes she designed herself. Her three children came of age during the war.

Gertrude's sister Gladys, Countess Szechenyi, aided the wounded in Austria; Gertrude decided to set up a hospital in France with her own funds, bringing over in November 1914 four surgeons, fifteen nurses, and six interns on the *Lusitania*. According to her diary, she traveled with a painfully heavy belt full of gold, chocolates, medicines, "stockings that are *not* openwork," and a Kodak camera. The five months of hospital work at Juilly drove home to her the suffering and pain of war and changed the character of her work as a sculptor. By 1917, she was sketching on war themes, although she also invested much of her time in charity work to support artists, or organizing a society "Hero Land" bazaar to raise funds for European relief efforts. She did sets for a war drama, and she supported Marcel Duchamp. Drawing on her overseas sketches and newspaper photographs, she sculpted *Refugees, Honorably Discharged, Orders, Spirit of the Red Cross Nurse, Château-Thierry, The 102nd Engineers,* and *Private in the 15th.* She designed two relief panels for the temporary Victory Arch at Madison Square in New York City. On November 4, 1919, she exhibited her *Impressions of the War,* including these works and small intense action pieces: *His Last Charge, Gassed, Blinded,* and *On the Top.* For memorials commissioned in the 1920s she created statues of soldiers as shattered survivors.

As a patron of the arts, Whitney sponsored contemporary artists who became canonical, such as Thomas Eakins and Edward Hopper. In May 1920, two weeks after the indictment of Sacco and Vanzetti, she opened the Whitney Studio to an exhibition of Soviet posters. Whitney believed in art for art's sake and in "useless" memorials, but her ecumenical taste made her a leading figure in the New York art world.

Margaret Winser, *English*

When the sculptor Margaret Winser competed for the commission to design a monument for the town of Hastings, England, she presented testimonials from Auguste Rodin and other sculptors, as well as the actress Ellen Terry. She was allowed £2,000 of the £20,000 that had been raised by subscription for erecting the monument. Its obelisk carried on its sides two pictorial bronze plaques depicting a pilot and sappers, beneath which 1,200 names were inscribed. (The names of those dead in World War II were added later.) She probably cleared about £160 after all expenses.

INDEX OF NAMES

Artists' names set in **boldface**.